A SYSTEM OF THE LAW OF Marine Insurances.

WITH THREE CHAPTERS

ON BOTTOMRY;

ON INSURANCES ON LIVES;

AND

ON INSURANCES AGAINST FIRE.

BY *JAMES ALLAN PARK*,
OF LINCOLN'S INN, ESQ. BARRISTER AT LAW.

Lex (de quâ agimus) *est fons æquitatis.* CICERO.

SECOND AMERICAN, FROM THE LATEST ENGLISH, EDITION.

THE LAWBOOK EXCHANGE, LTD.
Clark, New Jersey
2005

ISBN 1-58477-518-1

The quality of this reprint is equivalent to the quality of the original work.
The irregular pagination is reproduced as it was found in the original work.

Printed in the United States of America on acid-free paper

THE LAWBOOK EXCHANGE, LTD.
33 Terminal Avenue
Clark, New Jersey 07066-1321

Please see our website for a selection of our other publications and fine facsimile reprints of classic works of legal history:
www.lawbookexchange.com

Library of Congress Cataloging-in-Publication Data

Park, James Allan, Sir, 1763-1838.
A system of the law of marine insurances, with three chapters on bottomry, on insurances on lives, and on insurances against fire / James Allan Park.
p. cm.
Originally printed: Boston : Thomas and Andrews, 1799.
Includes bibliographical references.
ISBN 1-58477-518-1 (alk. paper)
1. Insurance, Marine--Great Britain--Early works to 1800. 2. Bottomry and respondentia--Great Britain--Early works to 1800. 3. Insurance, Life--Great Britain--Early works to 1800. I. Title.
KD1845.P37 2005
346.41'08622--dc22 2005008347

A

SYSTEM OF THE LAW OF Marine Insurances.

WITH THREE CHAPTERS

ON BOTTOMRY;

ON INSURANCES ON LIVES;

AND

ON INSURANCES AGAINST FIRE.

BY *JAMES ALLAN PARK,*

OF LINCOLN'S INN, ESQ. BARRISTER AT LAW.

Lex (de quâ agimus) *est fons æquitatis.* CICERO.

SECOND AMERICAN, FROM THE LATEST ENGLISH, EDITION.

PRINTED AT *BOSTON,*

FOR THOMAS AND ANDREWS, No. 45, NEWBURY-STREET,

DAVID WEST, No. 56,

AND JOHN WEST, No. 75, CORNHILL.

Sold at their ſeveral BOOKSTORES.

AUG. 1799.

TO THE HONOURABLE

SIR FRANCIS BULLER, BART.

ONE OF THE JUDGES OF HIS MAJESTY'S COURT OF COMMON PLEAS.

&c. &c. &c.

S I R,

THE venerable and illuſtrious perſon, to whom the former impreſſions of this Work were dedicated, being now no more, I am deſirous of inſcribing this Edition to you, who, with the late Earl *Mansfield*, firſt patronized and encouraged me in the proſecution of this undertaking. Thoſe early proofs of your attention and regard can never be effaced from my memory: and I rejoice in this opportunity of publickly declaring my grateful ſenſe of your uniform and continued friendſhip. Neither can I omit to mention upon this occaſion the obligations I am under, for many valuable improvements of this work ſuggeſted by you, with that liberality and condeſcenſion, which are ever found to accompany extenſive knowledge and eminent talents; and which demand from me

every

every public and private teſtimony of unfeigned reſpect and gratitude.

It was my wiſh to have given a ſketch of the judicial life and character of Lord *Mansfield*, by way of preface to this edition of a book, the contents of which might be conſidered as ſo peculiarly his own: and I was the more anxious to have done ſo, becauſe no other perſon had undertaken to pay this ſort of tribute to his memory, and becauſe the idea was approved of by you. But when I came to reflect upon the ſubject, when I conſidered his extraordinary talents, his great penetration, his perſuaſive eloquence, and the greatneſs of his whole character, I found my powers very unequal to ſuch an undertaking. However great my veneration and affection for his memory, and however gratifying ſuch a Work might have been to my own feelings, I ſhrunk from attempting the portraiture of a man, who, for above thirty years, had ſo eminently diſtinguiſhed himſelf in the adminiſtration of juſtice, as to excite the general admiration of *Europe*; who fixed the principles of Commercial Juriſprudence on the immutable baſis of reaſon and natural juſtice; and who, as it was well expreſſed by you, Sir, explained and commented upon thoſe principles, till his hearers

were

were loſt in admiration at the ſtrength and extent of the human underſtanding.

A conſciouſneſs of my own inability, therefore, is the only cauſe for my declining a work, which I ſhould have thought it my honour and my happineſs to have accompliſhed. But when hereafter it ſhall be undertaken by ſome faithful hand adequate to the execution of it, Lord *Mansfield* will then appear to poſterity to have been, what you well knew him to be, one of the wiſeſt and beſt men of the age in which he lived.

I have the honour to be, with ſincere reſpect and gratitude,

SIR,

Your much obliged

and faithful humble ſervant,

J. A. PARK.

CAREY-STREET,
May 27, 1796.

ADVERTISEMENT

TO THE

THIRD AND LAST ENGLISH EDITION.

A NEW Edition of this Work being called for, it was my duty to render it as valuable as possible, by inserting the various important cases, which have been decided both in the Court of King's Bench, and Court of Common Pleas, since the former impression was published. I have, however, preserved the pages of the second edition; and when new matter has occurred at the bottom of a page, I have continued the old page with the addition of a letter, thus 240 *a.* 240 *b.*—If the new matter happen to be inserted in the middle of a page, I have been obliged to continue the old page beyond the usual length: but this I hope will be attended with no inconvenience, as the page is always numbered at the top, and the cases may easily be found, the names being visible in the margin, even though the same page be in one or two instances necessarily protracted.

MAY, 1796.

PREFACE

TO

THE FIRST EDITION.

WHEN a man presumes to solicit public notice for any work of a literary nature, the world have a right to know the motives, that induced him to write, and upon what foundation he builds his claim to their attention. Notwithstanding the number of cases, which have of late years been determined in the *English* courts of justice upon the law of insurance, and the uniformity of principle which pervades them all; yet the doctrine of insurances is not fully known and understood. This in some measure happens from the decisions upon the subject being scattered in the various books of reports, according to the order of time, in which they were determined; and the connexion of which, from the nature of those publications, cannot be preserved. As many persons cannot spare time, and few will take the trouble, to collect the cases into one point of view; and as all cases of insurance must necessarily be attended with a number of facts, it is not to be wondered at, if from a cursory, inattentive, and unconnected perusal of them in a chronological order, a great part of the world should remain unacquainted with the true principles of insurance law. No book that I have met with in the *English* language, has ever yet attempted to form this branch of jurisprudence into

into a ſyſtematic arrangement, or to reduce the caſes to any fixed or ſettled principles.

Convinced of the utility of ſuch a work, I thought I could not employ my time more advantageouſly to my profeſſion or myſelf; nor better expreſs that reſpect which I, in common with every lawyer, feel for the venerable magiſtrate, (*a*) to whom this work is inſcribed, and for the other learned judges, who have aſſiſted in erecting this fabric, than by extracting all the caſes upon this ſubject from the maſs of other learning, with which they lie buried in the reporters; and thereby endeavouring to prove to the world that the doctrine of inſurance now forms a ſyſtem as complete in every reſpect as any other branch of the *Engliſh* law. Could any other incitement have been requiſite, the opinion of Mr. Juſtice *Blackſtone* would have had conſiderable weight. "The learning relating to "marine inſurances," ſays that elegant commentator, (*b*) "has of late years been greatly "improved by a ſeries of judicial deciſions, "which have now eſtabliſhed the law in ſuch a "variety of caſes, that (if well and judiciouſ-"ly collected) they would form a very com-"plete title in a code of commercial juriſpru-"dence." Urged by theſe motives, I was induced to undertake this work, which is now preſented to the world.

No ſubject can be properly underſtood, unleſs the materials be methodically arranged; and therefore the firſt object I had in view was to fix upon certain heads, which would be ſufficient to comprehend all the law upon inſurances. For

(*a*) The late *William* Earl *Mansfield*, to whom the firſt and ſecond editions of this work were dedicated.

(*b*) 2 *Blackſ. Com.* 490.

For this part of the work I alone am accountable, the deſign being entirely my own. It may however, in ſome degree abate the ſeverity of cenſure to recollect, that in the arrangement of the ſubject I had no example to follow, no guide to direct me; and I was left entirely to the impulſe of my own judgment. But to enable the profeſſion to judge of the nature of my plan, I will ſtate the reaſons that influenced me in the mode I have adopted.

As the policy is the foundation, upon which the whole contract depends, I have begun with that, and endeavoured to ſhew its nature and its various kinds; and I have alſo pointed out the requiſites which a policy muſt contain, their reaſon and origin, as they are to be collected from decided caſes, or the uſage of merchants. When we have aſcertained the nature of a policy, the next object is to diſcover by what general rules courts of juſtice have guided themſelves in their conſtruction of this ſpecies of contract. It is then neceſſary to deſcend to a more particular view of the ſubject, and to fix with accuracy and preciſion thoſe accidents, which ſhall be deemed loſſes within certain words uſed in the policy. Thus loſſes by perils of the ſea, by capture, by detention, and by barratry, will be a material ground of conſideration. When a loſs happens, it muſt either be a partial, or a total loſs; and hence it becomes neceſſary to aſcertain in what inſtances a loſs ſhall only be deemed partial, in what caſes it ſhall be conſidered as total; and how the amount of a partial loſs is to be ſettled; Hence alſo ariſes the doctrine of average, ſalvage, and abandonment. Theſe points therefore will be the next object of attention.

Having

Having confidered the various inftances in which the underwriter will be liable upon his policy, either for a part, or for the whole amount, of his fubfcription; we feem to be naturally led to the confideration of thofe cafes in which the underwriter is releafed from his refponfibility. This may happen in feveral ways: For fometimes the policy is void from the beginning, on account of fraud; of the fhip not being fea-worthy; or of the voyage infured being prohibited. There are alfo cafes, in which the infurer is difcharged, becaufe the infured has failed in the performance of thofe conditions, which he had undertaken to fulfil; fuch as the non-compliance with warranties; and deviating from the voyage infured: Thefe and many other points of the fame nature occupy feveral chapters.

When the underwriter has never run any rifk, it would be unconfcionable that he fhould retain the premium: Therefore after confidering thofe inftances, in which this is the cafe, it is natural next to afcertain in what cafes the underwriter fhould retain, and in what cafes he fhould return the premium.

It would be in vain to tell a man, that he was entitled to the affiftance of the law, and that his cafe was equitable and right, without pointing out in what *forum*, and by what mode of proceeding he fhould feek a remedy. I have endeavoured to point out the proper tribunal, to which a perfon injured is to apply; the mode of proceeding, which he is to adopt; and the nature of the evidence he muft adduce to fubftantiate his claim, with refpect to this contract: After the difcuffion of marine infurances, I have added three chapters upon fubjects, which, though they do not form a part of the plan, are fo materially

terially connected with it in the rules and principles of decifion, that it feemed to me the work would be deficient without them: Thefe are, bottomry and refpondentia, infurances upon lives; and infurances againft fire.

When I planned this work, I intended to prefix an introduction, containing a fhort, hiftorical account of the rife and progrefs of infurances in this country only. But upon the fuggeftion of one, to whofe opinion I bow with deference, and whofe judgment will always command obedience; I was induced to enlarge my defign. The reader will now find a fhort account of fuch of the ancient maritime ftates, as have promulgated any fyftem of naval jurifprudence; and alfo, of the progrefs of marine law among the various ftates of *Europe*. I have endeavoured to trace the origin of infurance to its fource; to point out thofe countries in which it has flourifhed, and the progrefs and improvement of it in our own. Such is the arrangement, which I have adopted, and on the propriety of which, the world and the profeffion are to decide.

As to the mode of treating the fubject, it will be proper to obferve that, at the head of each chapter, I have ftated the principles upon which the cafes on that point depend; and then have quoted the cafes themfelves to fhew, that they are agreeable and confonant to the principles advanced. If there are any cafes, which feem to differ from the others, I endeavour to prove, either that they depend upon different principles, or that there are circumftances in them, which make them exceptions to the general rules. In quoting cafes, I have been careful minutely to ftate all the circumftances, and alfo the opinion of the court without any alteration,

alteration, or comments of my own; convinced that the utility of a work of this kind consists in the true and accurate account of what the law is, not in idle speculations of a private man, as to what the law ought to be. Besides, one main purpose of such a composition is, to save the professors of the law the trouble of turning over vast volumes of reports, by collecting into one book, all the cases upon a particular subject.

But unless the cases are fully and faithfully reported, recourse must still be had to the original reporters, and the end of such a compilation is defeated. At the same time it ought to be observed, that sometimes, though not very often, several different points arise in one cause; and then, in order to preserve the system complete, it is necessary to separate them, and to assign to each its proper place. But still the opinion of the court is given fully on each of the points; and a reference is made from one part of the case to the other.

I had it in contemplation to have had a distinct chapter for the consideration of the law relative to this species of contract in other countries of *Europe*. But upon reflecting that insurances are founded upon the great principles of natural justice, rather than upon any municipal regulations; and that consequently the law must be nearly the same in all countries, I relinquished the idea. Besides, I have throughout the work, which seemed to be a better plan, taken notice in what respects the positive institutions of other maritime states agree or disagree with those of our own: A plan, which serves to illustrate and confirm the *English* system.

It

It remains to ſpeak of the materials I have uſed. Conſcious that the value of a law book depends upon the purity and excellence of the ſources, from which its contents are taken, I have never advanced any poſition, without referring to the book in which it was found; unleſs it be upon ſome unſettled point, where I have ſtated the arguments that may be adduced on both ſides, and left it to the reader to form his own concluſions. In my reſearches upon this occaſion, I have conſulted every foreign author that I could poſſibly obtain; and have made as much uſe of their labours, as the nature of the plan would admit.

With reſpect to the deciſions of the *Engliſh* courts of juſtice, I believe I have not omitted a ſingle caſe, that ever has appeared in print upon the ſubject: Beſides which, this collection contains a great number of manuſcript caſes, of which ſome have been determined at *Niſi Prius* only, and many have been the ſubject of deliberation in court upon caſes reſerved, or upon motions for new trials. For the latter, I myſelf am chiefly reſponſible, and upon ſome future occaſion, I ſhall be happy to correct any errors, which they may contain; as moſt of them were taken while I was a ſtudent, merely for my private uſe, without any view to future publication. I have, however, by comparing them with ſuch notes as I could obtain, done every thing in my power to render them worthy of the attention of the profeſſion. As to the *Niſi Prius* notes, I am indebted for them to the very liberal and generous communications of my young profeſſional friends; and to ſome alſo of thoſe, who are in the firſt rank at the bar. Indeed, to name any one would be an injuſtice to the reſt; and therefore,

fore, I muſt beg they will accept my general acknowledgments. I ſhould, however, be undeſerving of that attention and aſſiſtance with which I have been honoured, were I to omit this opportunity of returning my ſincere and grateful thanks to Mr. *Juſtice Buller*, whoſe abilities are only equalled by his eaſineſs of acceſs, his ready and liberal communication of that knowledge, which is the natural reſult of ſuch talents, and ſuch unwearied application to ſtudy. The many valuable hints I have received from that learned judge, will no doubt contribute much to the utility of this work.

To thoſe who are much engaged in the labours of the profeſſion, a full and complete table of the principal matters is of the utmoſt conſequence. I have uſed my endeavours to render this part of the work as uſeful as poſſible, by ſtating each point under all the heads, that will naturally be reſorted to for the ſolution of any doubt.

Having thus explained the nature of my arrangement, the mode which I have adopted in the diſcuſſion of each chapter, and the ſources from which my information is derived, I preſent this volume to the public. The utility and neceſſity of ſuch a work are univerſally acknowledged; the attempt is therefore deſerving of ſome praiſe, and for the defects in the execution, I throw myſelf upon the candour of my profeſſion. The ſubject was noble, and required greater talents than mine, to treat it as it deſerved; but if I ſhall have at all done juſtice to the great abilities of thoſe diſtinguiſhed charac-

ters

ters whoſe names appear in every page, I ſhall in ſome meaſure have attained the object of my wiſhes, and ſhall have the pleaſure of reflecting, that the time I ſpent in the compoſition of this work, has been at leaſt productive of much perſonal ſatisfaction and improvement.

CONTENTS.

CONTENTS.

INDEX OF CASES CITED.

Each Case may be found by the name either of the Plaintiff, or of the Defendant. Those Cases in *Italics* were never before in print.

Black

Depeiſter

Halkeld

Mac

Richardſon

Vandam

INTRODUCTION.

WHEN we confider the wonderful effects which commerce has produced on the manners of men, when we obferve that it tends to wear off thofe prejudices which give birth to diffenfions and animofities, that it unites mankind by the ftrongeft of all ties, the defire of fupplying mutual wants; and that it difpofes them to peace and concord, by eftablifhing in every community an order of men, whofe intereft it is to preferve public tranquillity; we are led to think that the hiftory and progrefs of it would not only be amufing, but highly important and inftructive to the inhabitants of every civilized fociety. Such a work would be in fact the hiftory of the intercourfe and communication of mankind, and muft neceffarily abound in events the moft interefting to every focial being, but particularly fo to the people of this country, whofe great importance in the eyes of *Europe* originated in commerce, and will endure no longer than whilft the fame attention continues to be paid to her commercial interefts. In a differtation upon commerce, Infurances form a very diftinguifhed part, and therefore it cannot but be agreeable to the fcholar as well as to the lawyer, to trace this branch of commercial law to its fource, and to give fome account of thofe various nations, which have been rendered famous by the extent of their commerce, and by the excellency of their maritime regulations.

regulations. Indeed, in tracing the origin of Infurances, an account of the maritime ftates that have exifted in the world, neceffarily forms a part of the inquiry.

2 Blackft. Comm. 458.

Infurance then is a contract by which the infurer undertakes, in confideration of a premium equivalent to the hazard run, to indemnify the perfon infured againft certain perils or loffes, or againft fome particular event. When infurance is generally mentioned by profeffional men, it is underftood to fignify marine infurances. It is in this light we are at prefent to confider it; and from the preceding definition it appears to be a contract of indemnity againft thofe perils, to which fhips are expofed in the courfe of their voyage from one place to another. The utility of this fpecies of contract in a commercial country is obvious, and has been taken notice of by very diftinguifhed writers upon commercial affairs. Infurances give great fecurity to the fortunes of private people, and by dividing amongft many that lofs, which would ruin an individual, make it fall light and eafy upon the whole fociety. This fecurity tends greatly to the advancement of trade and navigation, becaufe the rifk of tranfporting and exporting being diminifhed, men will more eafily be induced to engage in an extenfive trade, to affift in important undertakings, and to join in hazardous enterprifes; fince a failure in the object will not be attended with thofe dreadful confequences to them and their families, which muft be the cafe in a country where infurances are unknown. But it is not individuals only that derive advantages from the increafe of commerce;

3 Smith's Wealth of Nations, p. 148, oct. ed.

1 Magens 2.

commerce; the general welfare of the public is alſo promoted. It is an obſervation juſtified by experience, that as ſoon as the commercial ſpirit begins to acquire vigour, and to gain the aſcendant in any ſociety, we immediately diſcover a new genius in its policy, its alliances, its wars and negociations. No nation, that cultivated foreign commerce, ever failed to make a diſtinguiſhed figure on the theatre of the world, as the hiſtory of the ancients ſufficiently proves; and in proportion as commerce made its way into the various ſtates of *Europe*, they turned their attention to thoſe objects, and aſſumed thoſe manners, which diſtinguiſh poliſhed nations, and which lead to political conſequence and eminence amongſt the neighbouring powers. (*a*)

The origin of inſurance, like that of many other cuſtoms, which depend rather upon traditional than written evidence, and for the honour of inventing and introducing which rival nations contend, has occaſioned much doubt among the writers upon mercantile law. Indeed it is involved in ſo much obſcurity that, after all the reſearches which have been made on the preſent occaſion, any very ſatisfactory ſolution of this doubt cannot be promiſed. One truth however is clear, that, wherever foreign commerce was introduced, inſurance muſt have ſoon followed as a neceſſary attendant, it being impoſſible to carry on any very extenſive trade without it, eſpecially in time of war. Some of theſe writers have aſcribed the origin of this contract to *Claudius Cæſar* the fifth *Roman* emperor, on account

Molloy, Malyne.

(*a*) Vide Robertſon's View of the Progreſs of Society in Europe.

2 Atkyns, 554. count of a paſſage to be found in *Suetonius*. Other reſpectable authorities have given the honour of it to the *Rhodians*, thus laying a foundation for the idea entertained by many, that the law of inſurance had obtained a place in moſt of the ancient codes of juriſprudence. As the conſideration of this queſtion will be attended with pleaſure, it will tend much to the complete inveſtigation of it, to conſider the ſtate of commerce amongſt the moſt diſtinguiſhed of the ancient nations, from whence it will appear, that inſurances were in thoſe days wholly unknown; or, if they were known that the ſmalleſt proofs of the exiſtence of ſuch a cuſtom have not come down to the preſent times.

Schomberg's Obſerv. on Rhodian laws.

The *Rhodians* claim the firſt place in this inquiry: for although there is undoubted teſtimony, that nations of much greater antiquity than the people of *Rhodes*, (*a*) cultivated commerce, and carried it on to a conſiderable extent, yet there does not appear to be the ſmalleſt ground for entertaining an opinion that any of theſe naval powers had eſtabliſhed amongſt themſelves, much leſs communicated to mankind in general, any code or ſyſtem of marine law. *Rhodes* obtained the ſovereignty of the ſea, about 916 years before the *Chriſtian Æra*, which was almoſt two hundred years before the building of *Rome*. The ſituation and fertility of this iſland were peculiarly favourable

(*a*) Euſebius, in his account of maritime ſtates, mentions three anterior to the Rhodians; namely, the Cretans, the Lydians, and the Thracians; the firſt of whom flouriſhed about five hundred years before the Rhodians, the next two hundred, and the laſt, about eighty years. Euſeb. Chronicon, lib. 2.

able for the purpofes of navigation, for it lies in the *Mediterranean* fea, a few leagues from the continent of *Leffer Afia;* and its wealth and fertility have always been celebrated by the poets and hiftorians of antiquity. From thefe circumftances, joined to the activity and induftry of the people, it long maintained that fuperiority which it had acquired; its inhabitants were rich, its alliance was courted, though, from principles of policy, it generally obferved a ftrict neutrality. Notwithftanding this pacific difpofition, which commerce naturally infpires, the *Rhodians* at laft became an object of jealoufy, and were moft furioufly attacked and befieged by various foreign powers. But in all their wars they difcovered their great ftrength and fuperiority at fea, and conducted their enterprifes with fo much activity and fkill, as to attract the admiration of their enemies, and the applaufe of thofe hiftorians who have given an account of the wars in which they were engaged. In the *Punick* wars, the *Romans* found the benefit of their alliance, by the very effential fervice which they performed, in attacking the naval armaments of the *Carthaginians*.

See Anderfon's Hift. of Commerce.

Polybius, lib. 16. Schomb. Obf.

Wealth naturally produces luxury, which gradually enervates the powers of a ftate. This was the cafe with the *Rhodians;* for after maintaining their political importance from the time already mentioned till the termination almoft of the *Roman* republic, they vifibly began to decline in wealth and power. *Cicero*, in his fpeech on the *Manilian* law, obferves, that they were a people, whofe naval power and difcipline remained even to the time of

Cicero pro lege Manilia, cap. 13.

of his memory; and *Cicero* expired with the republic.

From this ſhort hiſtory it appears, that the *Rhodians* were very famous for their naval power and ſtrength: but however reſpectable they might be on that account, they were much more illuſtrious, and obtained a much higher praiſe among the nations of antiquity, for being the firſt legiſlators of the ſea, and for promulgating a ſyſtem of marine juriſprudence, to which even the *Romans* themſelves paid the greateſt deference and reſpect, and which they adopted as the guide of their conduct in naval affairs. Theſe excellent laws not only ſerved as a rule of conduct to the ancient maritime ſtates; but, as will appear from an attentive compariſon of them, have been the baſis of all modern regulations reſpecting navigation and commerce. The time at which theſe laws were compiled is not preciſely aſcertained: but we may reaſonably ſuppoſe, it was about the period when the *Rhodians* firſt obtained the ſovereignty of the ſea, which was about 916 years before the æra of Chriſtianity. *Selden* ſays, that the *Rhodians* maintained the ſovereignty of the ſeas 23 years; and that their laws were compiled in the days of *Jehoſaphat*, king of *Judah*. This opinion agrees exactly with the preceding calculation; for this king began his reign about 914 years before the birth of *Chriſt*. Notwithſtanding this, it will always remain a doubtful point, when they were compiled; nor perhaps is it very material that it ſhould be accurately aſcertained. It is of more conſequence to know when they were adopted by the *Romans*; but

Selden's Mare clauſum, lib. 1. cap. 10. f. 5.

but that is alſo a fact involved in ſome obſcurity. We meet with no traces of them in the time of the republic; and from the manner in which *Cicero* mentions them in the ſpeech laſt alluded to, he treats of them as laws, which had gained the admiration of the world, rather than of ſuch as then made a part of the *Roman* code. *Selden* ſays, that they obtained a place in the *Roman* law in the reign of *Tiberius Claudius*, a conjecture in which he is ſupported by *Peckius*, one of the commentators on the laws of *Rhodes*, and by the well known character of *Tiberius* himſelf, who diſcovered the greateſt attention to maritime affairs, and gave many ſignal inſtances of his attachment to *Rhodes*. But although theſe iſlanders were thus famous for their laws we cannot diſcover from the fragments that have come down to our times, that they had the ſmalleſt idea of the contract of inſurance; nor is there any tradition to induce us to conjecture, that they ever were acquainted with that mode of ſecuring their property. It is true, that this is not a concluſive argument; becauſe, although no ſuch contract is mentioned in the fragments which we have, it by no means follows that it did not form a part of their whole ſyſtem, more eſpecially as *Emerigon*, a very celebrated *French* writer of the preſent day, is of opinion that the real laws of the *Rhodians* have never reached us; and that the fragments which we ſee, are certainly apocryphal. But as theſe laws were adopted by the *Romans*, it is fair to conjecture, that whether we have the real regulations of *Rhodes*, or not, we ſhould have the contract of inſurance, if

Schomberg Obſ. on Rhodian Laws.

Mare clauſum, lib. 1. cap. 10. ſ. 5.

Sueton. Vita Tiberii Claudii.

Emerigon traité des Aſſurances, preface, p. 3.

if it had been known to them, incorporated with the other naval laws in the Imperial code. This idea is countenanced by the contract of bottomry, which is to be found in the fragments of the laws of *Rhodes*, and with which the people of that island were certainly acquainted; and in every book of the civil law, the contract *de nautico fœnore, de usurâ maritimâ*, also forms a considerable part. It is not going too far then to presume, that, as the *Romans* adopted a contract so beneficial to commerce as that of bottomry, they would not have passed over a contract, of which the influence is still more extensively useful in the promotion of navigation and trade, if those, from whom they borrowed their naval laws, had themselves been acquainted either with its nature or advantages.

Leg. Rhod. f. 1. art. 21. f. 2. art. 16. Digest. lib. 22. tit. 2. Cod. lib. 4. tit. 33.

Having said thus much of *Rhodes* and its laws, let us turn our attention shortly to the commerce of the *Greeks*. It is certainly true, that commerce flourished very much in several of the States of *Greece*, particularly in *Corinth* and *Athens*. The former separated two seas, was the key of *Greece*, and a city of the utmost importance; its trade was extensive, having a port to receive the merchandizes of *Asia*, and another those of *Italy*; and there have been but few cities where the works of art were carried to so high a degree of perfection. *Athens*, indeed, was particularly famous for commercial knowledge; for their manufactures of all sorts were in high repute, and emulation was excited by the public rewards and honours which were bestowed upon those who attained to excellence

Montesq. Esprit des loix, liv. 21. ch. 7.

Taylor's Civil Law, p. 507.

lence in any of the ufeful arts. The attention of this people to maritime affairs, (for they aimed at the fovereignty of the fea and obtained it) contributed much to their fkill in navigation. The many laws which they left to pofterity, with regard to imports and exports, and the contract of bargain and fale; the many privileges granted to the mercantile part of the ftate; the appointment of magiftrates, who had the cognizance of controverfies that happened between merchants and mariners; the attention which they paid to their market, and the many officers concerned in that department, give us a very favourable idea of their judgment in the true principles of commerce. But notwithftanding this, the *Athenians*, being of a very ambitious difpofition, being more attentive to extend their maritime power than to enjoy it, and having a government of fuch a caft, that the public revenues were diftributed among the common people to be fquandered at their pleafure (*a*) did not carry on fo extenfive a trade as might naturally be expected from the number of their feamen, from the produce of their mines, from their influence over

Potter's Grecian Antiq. vol. i. p. 80. 83, 84. 167.

(*a*) From feveral of the orations of Demofthenes it appears, that the poor were entitled to receive from the public ftock as much money as would admit them to the diverfions of the theatre; and befides this, it was made a capital offence for any one to propofe the reftoration of the theatrical money to its original ufes. This cuftom was at length fo much abufed, that, under pretence of theatrical money, almoft all the public funds were diftributed among the people. Hence the Athenians contracted an averfion for war, and fpent their time and money upon public fhews. Of this enormity Demofthenes vehemently complains, and inveighs againft it with as much warmth as, from the nature of the law juft mentioned, he durft venture to do. See the firft and alfo the third Olynthian.

over the cities of *Greece*, and from thofe excellent laws and inftitutions, which have been juft enumerated. Their trade was almoft entirely confined to *Greece* and to the *Euxine* fea. From fuch of their laws as we have feen, and from fuch accounts as we have obtained of their naval hiftory, we have not the fmalleft reafon to fuppofe, that this celebrated people knew any thing of the contract of infurance.

Montefq. Efprit des loix, liv. 21. c. 7.

Some notice fhould have been taken before now of the *Phenicians*, an ancient commercial and opulent people. Indeed, the height of grandeur to which they attained is a fufficient proof of the vaft refources of a commercial nation. Many writers, both facred and profane, from their florid and magnificent defcriptions, give a vaft idea of their wealth and power. I forbore to fpeak of them till I fhould have occafion to mention one of their colonies, that of *Carthage*, which, in opulence and the extent of her commerce and naval power, equalled, if not furpaffed, the parent ftate herfelf. Whether either, or both, of thefe maritime powers ever promulgated any code of naval law cannot now be afcertained: for the former was entirely deftroyed by *Alexander the Great*; and that it might never be reftored, he removed its marine and commerce to *Alexandria*, in which removal, probably all its naval regulations might be loft. *Carthage*, on the other hand, having long difputed with *Rome* the empire of the world, was at laft obliged to yield to her victorious rival, who, even after fhe gained the victory, retained fuch an hatred to the *Carthaginians*, that fhe rooted out every

Beawes Lex Merc. red. 4th edit. Introd. p. 3.

Quint. Curtius, lib. 4. cap. 8, &c.

every veſtige of their former greatneſs. No time, however, nor the hatred of the *Romans*, can wholly obliterate the amazing accounts which have come down to us, of the enterprizing ſpirit, and hazardous voyages of the *Carthaginians*, almoſt exceeding the bounds of credibility. Thus much is certain, that they took ſuch diſtant voyages, and went ſo far even without the *Mediterranean*, both to the *South* and *North* of it, as induced many people to ſuppoſe, that they were acquainted with the uſe of the compaſs. It is evident, however, that they only followed the coaſts. Beſides the ancients might ſometimes have performed ſuch voyages, as would make one imagine they had the uſe of the compaſs: for if a pilot were far from land, and during his voyage had ſuch ſerene weather that in the night he could always ſee the polar ſtar, and in the day, the riſing and the ſetting ſun, he might regulate his courſe by them, nearly as we do now by the compaſs. This however muſt be a fortuitous caſe, and not a regular plan of navigation. (*a*)

Anderſon's Hiſt. of Commerce. Introd. p. 31, 32. fol. ed,

Monteſq. liv. 21. ch. 8.

From

(*a*) What I have ſaid in the text has been ſuppoſed by ſome not to do ſufficient juſtice to the commercial and enterpriſing ſpirit of the Phenecians, who are ſaid to have viſited Britain about 900 years before Chriſt.* I have already admitted the almoſt incredible voyages which they performed; but as it is alſo undoubtedly true, that they were unacquainted with the mariner's compaſs, the honour of diſcovering which was reſerved for later times, they muſt, in moſt caſes, have followed the coaſts. Nor does their viſiting Britain militate againſt this idea; for by attending to the ſituation of the two places, the voyage might have been performed, though no doubt very tediouſly, without once loſing ſight of land.

* See Borlaſe's Hiſt. of Cornwall, p. 27, and Henry's Hiſt. Great-Britain, book 1, chap. 6.

From a ſlight attention to the commercial and maritime hiſtory of the *Romans*, it will appear that they were as great ſtrangers to the contract of inſurance, as any of thoſe people, of whom much has been already ſaid. It ſeems to be univerſally agreed that the *Romans* were never very conſpicuous as a maritime power, conſidered either in a commercial or warlike point of view. In the latter caſe they relied chiefly on their land forces, who were diſciplined to ſtand always firm and undaunted; and till towards the latter age of the republic, when we read of ſome wonderful naval exertions, they do not ſeem to have poſſeſſed any thing of a marine eſtabliſhment. They never were diſtinguiſhed by a jealouſy for trade, and even when they attacked *Carthage*, they did it as a rival for empire, and not for commerce. It is recorded by hiſtorians, that till the firſt *Punick* war, upwards of 400 years after the building of the city, the *Romans* were ſo entirely ignorant of ſhip building, that they took for a model a *Carthaginian* galley, which had been accidentally ſtranded at *Meſſina*. *Carthage*, it muſt be obſerved, was at that time in her zenith of power and greatneſs; and yet from the model of one of her gallies, the *Romans* were able in ſixty days from the time the timber was cut down, to fit out and man for ſea, one hundred gallies, of five tiers, and twenty of three tiers of oars. Such were the ſhips of the famous *Carthage*. The ſpirit of the people of *Rome* was entirely averſe from commerce; and fully juſtifies what was ſaid by a celebrated *Roman* hiſtorian, "*ſeſe quiſque hoſtem ferire, murum adſcendere,* "*conſpici, dum tale facinus faceret, properabat; eas* "*divitias,*

Monteſq. liv. 21. ch. 9.

Ferguſon's Rom. Rep. vol. i. p. 100.

Salluſt. Catilina, cap. 7.

"*divitias, eam bonam famam, magnamque nobilitatem* "*putabant.*" These exploits were the only glory of a *Roman*: no employment was deemed honourable but the plough and the ſword, and every ſpecies of gain was deemed diſgraceful to thoſe of Patrician rank. But it was from the conſtitution of the government, that individuals were poſſeſſed of this warlike ſpirit, ſo contrary to that which leads to eminence in commercial purſuits. The caſt of their civil government was of a military nature; and for a conſiderable time, the civil and military officer was the ſame perſon; he diſtributed juſtice in *Rome*, and commanded their legions in the field, till the vaſt increaſe of their empire, and the multiplicity of civil buſineſs, occaſioned a ſeparation. The natural conſequence of this was, that no man who was not of the profeſſion of his country, was much eſteemed at *Rome*; and accordingly we find that traders and mechanics were incapable of ſucceeding to any public honours. Nay, ſo far was commerce from being encouraged at *Rome*, that it was deemed prejudicial to the State. The *Romans*, by humanity, terror, triumphs, tributes, and taxes, which they impoſed on the conquered countries, increaſed the riches of their city. Laws were paſſed to prevent the exportation of their gold; the reaſon of which ſeems to be, that it carried away their money and brought them nothing in return but luxury, the bane of virtue, and deſtruction of empire. Could it be expected, ſays Doctor *Taylor*, that a people of ſoldiers, whoſe trade was their ſword, and whoſe ſword ſupplied all the advantages of trade; who brought the treaſures of the world into their exchequer, without exporting

Livy, lib. 21. cap. 63.

Taylor's Civil Law, p. 502.

Taylor, 498.

Civil Law, 501.

exporting any thing but their own perſonal bravery; who raiſed the public revenues, not by the culture of *Italy*, but by the tributes of provinces; who had *Rome* for their manſion, and the world for their farm; ſhould have leiſure to ſet forward the articles of commerce, or be likely to pay any regard to the character of its profeſſors? The terms of defiance, upon which they lived with all mankind, in conſequence of this martial ſpirit, would have prevented all the good effects of commerce, had their diſpoſition allowed them to purſue it. That reſtleſs ſpirit, which kept their armies on foot, and their ſwords in their hands, for a ſucceſſion of centuries, was fatal to factories and correſpondence. The world was in arms, and inſurances and underwriting were but a dead letter. This is very nearly a true repreſentation of the caſe, for it is certain that not one law was made in favour of commerce, in the time of the commonwealth; on the contrary, it was greatly diſcouraged as introductory of luxury, which was ſuppoſed not to be compatible with the ſeverity of their manners. It is alſo no leſs true than ſingular, that a people who were ſo well acquainted with the true principles of natural reaſon and juſtice, who applied thoſe principles with ſo much propriety to the various wants and neceſſities of human ſociety, and who had the honour of eſtabliſhing a ſyſtem of law, which has been adopted as the rule of action by the greateſt part of *Europe*, and which continues to be ſo even at the preſent day, never attempted to introduce any plan of marine juriſprudence. Nay, this idea is carried farther by ſome writers, who declare, and I believe with truth,

Schomberg's Obſervations on the Rhodian laws.

truth, at leaſt we can diſcover nothing to the contrary, that the *Romans* did not even take the pains to digeſt the materials which they had borrowed; and that whilſt they carried every other branch of law to the higheſt pitch of accuracy and refinement, they were content to ſtand indebted to one of their own provinces both for the form and matter of their maritime code.

The *Romans*, it is true, after the firſt *Punick* war, conſtantly maintained a fleet; but long after that time, even in the year of the city 563, it was obſerved of them, that they were very unſkilful in the art of navigation. One of their own hiſtorians, who flouriſhed at the time of the ſecond *Punick* war, and who was tutor to the great *Scipio*, juſtly remarks, that at no period did they ever make any figure at ſea as a commercial power. Even when they arrived at their higheſt perfection in naval ſkill, their fleets were never employed for the purpoſes of trade, in the diſcovery of new ſtates, or eſtabliſhing commercial intercourſe with thoſe they already knew. The greateſt extent of their commerce was to bring to the market of *Rome* that corn, which they collected in the various granaries of *Sicily*, *Africa*, and *Egypt*. Upon all other occaſions the buſineſs of their fleet was to overawe the conquered, and to tranſport to *Rome* the ſpoils of ruined provinces. In ſuch a ſtate of commerce, it is impoſſible that inſurances could exiſt; and we have already quoted the opinion of a reſpectable author to ſhew that they were unknown.

Polybius.

Dr. Taylor, ut ſupra.

There

There are ſeveral reaſons applicable to all the ancient maritime powers, which ſeem to prove to demonſtration, that inſurances were not in uſe. We have ſeen, that inſurances are only introduced where commerce is widely extended. The commerce of the ancients, compared with modern times, could not be very conſiderable, as it was chiefly confined within the *Mediterranean*, *Egean*, and *Euxine* ſeas; to which they were compelled more from neceſſity than inclination. *Carthage* in all her glory had not arrived at any great degree of perfection in the art of ſhip building. Veſſels of the beſt conſtruction at that time could only be navigated with oars, or when they had a fair wind on a ſmooth ſea: they might be built of green timber; and in caſe of a ſtorm, could run aſhore under any cover, or upon any beach that was free from rocks: in ſhort, they were merely gallies, and were managed with the greater difficulty on account of the poſition of the ſails, and the mode of rigging practiſed in thoſe days. This could not fail of proving a conſiderable obſtacle to the extenſion of commerce. But when we conſider, in addition to the bad conſtruction of their ſhips, that the ancients were utterly ignorant of that unerring guide, the mariner's compaſs, (the honour of inventing which was reſerved for more modern times) by reaſon of which they durſt not venture out of ſight of land, for fear of being overtaken by tempeſts, and being left at large in the boundleſs ocean, their commerce could not have been great; although we are even led to admire the progreſs which they made in commercial affairs. It is true, that many diſtant naval expeditions were made under all theſe diſadvantages,

Anderſon's Hiſt. of Commerce.

Monteſq. Eſprit des loix, liv. 21. ch. vi.

disadvantages, which often proved fatal to the adventurers. (*a*) These expeditions, however, could add little or nothing to their maritime or geographical skill, in which the ancients were certainly very deficient, on account of the necessity they were always under of coasting the shores, for want of a better guide; and indeed, the shores were the only compass. These observations are not intended to detract from that merit, which has been already allowed to the ancients for their naval exertions; because they are founded merely on a comparison of their powers and knowledge in those arts with the improvements of the moderns, and are adduced to shew that, under such disadvantages and obstacles to the extension of their trade and commerce, it was impossible that insurances could be at all known to the ancient world. (*b*)

Montesq. vol. ii. ch. 6.

M. *Emerigon* agrees, that the contract of insurance, as it is understood at this day, was not in use amongst the *Romans*; but he thinks he discovers some traces of it in the history of that people. The first instance given by this learned writer is this, that about the time of the second *Punick* war, those who had undertaken to supply the troops in *Spain* with provisions and military stores, made it a previous condition that the republic should be at the hazard of exporting them, according to the words of

Preface to his work, p. 4.

(*a*) Huet, Bishop of Avanches, in his very instructive and entertaining treatise on the commerce and navigation of the ancients, has with infinite labour and accuracy collected the most remarkable facts on this head. Ch. 8.

(*b*) See note (*a*) page 10.

of *Livy*, "*Ut quæ in naves imposuissent, ab hostium,* "*tempestatisve vi, publico periculo essent.*" But with all deference to so great a name, this seems to bear no resemblance to the contract of insurance; for it is nothing more than every well regulated state is bound to do by the ties of natural justice. It is equitable and right, that those, who, in times of public danger, appropriate their private wealth to the advancement of the public service, should be reimbursed from the purse of the state for the private losses they may sustain. This indeed is the rule of conduct between man and man: for when one man purchases goods of another to be sent abroad, was it ever supposed that the seller was to run the risk of the voyage; or that if the goods perished, he was never to be paid? If such a doctrine were to prevail in any country, the state could only be supplied with necessaries in time of war, by means of extortion, rapine, and violence.

Livy, lib. 23. cap. 49.

Another instance given by *Emerigon* is a story, which we find recorded by *Livy*, of some men who were charged with the care of exporting provisions for the army, and who, *quia publicum periculum erat a vi tempestatis in iis, quæ portarentur ad exercitus*, endeavoured by fraud to destroy the ship, and then told the directors of the state, that many very valuable articles were on board; whereas they had taken care to send out very old, rotten ships, in which were a few commodities, and those of small value. That part of this story which is material to the present inquiry, has already met with an answer in what was said upon the last quotation; and the propriety of a government's indemnifying those

Traité des Assur. loc. cit. Livy, lib. 25. cap. 3.

those who might suffer in the public service, is not at all altered by the misconduct of some individuals. (*a*)

The next instance is from one of *Cicero*'s epistles, and is of a different nature from those last mentioned; because here *Cicero* seems to wish that the property in question should be secured, not only for himself, but also for the people of *Rome*. *Cicero*, having gained a victory in *Cilicia*, and the civil war between *Cæsar* and *Pompey* being then a matter almost unavoidable, wrote to *Caninius Sallustius* at *Laodicea*, in which letter he uses these words: "*Laodiceæ me prædes accepturum arbitror omnis pecuniæ publicæ, ut et mihi et populo cautum sit sine vecturæ periculo.*" From this passage it is inferred that *Cicero* alludes to an insurance. I own, from the meaning of the word *prædes*, and from the situation of affairs at *Rome*, it seems as if *Cicero* wished rather to find some secure and substantial person at *Laodicea*, in whose care and custody he might leave this money till more peaceable times; and it is very unlikely that in such a troublesome conjuncture he should be desirous of bringing a great treasure to the scene of faction and confusion, especially as, in a letter to his friend *Atticus*, he declares himself at a great loss to know what line of conduct he ought to pursue. But even if he wished to bring it to

Epistolæ ad Familiares, lib. 2. epist. 17.

Ferguson's hist. of the Rom. Rep. book 4. ch. 5.

Cicero ad Atticum, lib. 7. epist. 1.

(*a*) It has been truly observed by Mr. Millar (for an account of whose work upon insurances see the preface to the second edition) that in these instances from the Roman historians, no mention is made of a premium paid by the merchant for the hazard undertaken; and that they are rather to be considered as examples of a bounty offered by the public, than of a mutual contract.

to *Rome*, the mode he proposed seems more like the modern bill of exchange, than a policy of insurance. (*a*) Besides, unless this species of contract was at that time tolerably well understood, *Sallust*, the person to whom he wrote, would have found considerable difficulty in comprehending his meaning from the single sentence in his letter which has been mentioned; and if it were well known, is it possible to suppose it would not have obtained a place in their code of laws?

Molloy, Malyne.

But the passage upon which those, who contend for the antiquity of this branch of commerce, have chiefly relied, is one to be found in *Suetonius*, in the eighteenth chapter of his life of *Tiberius Claudius*, the fifth emperor of *Rome*. "*Negotiatoribus certa* "*lucra proposuit, suscepto in se damno, si cui quid per* "*tempestates accidisset.*" This sentence wholly unconnected seems to convey such an idea; but we must attend to the context in order to understand it. This relates merely to the corn trade; for as the *Roman* territory was not sufficient to supply enough for the consumption of the city, it became absolutely necessary to give great encouragement to this branch of commerce: nay, it was a political, not a mercantile concern; for the very existence of the empire

(*a*) Since I published the first edition of this work I have looked into Melmoth's translation of Cirero's epistles; and I am happy to find, that, without knowing I had such an authority, I have put the same sense upon this passage which that elegant translator had done before me. The whole sentence is translated thus: "I purpose to leave the money at Laodicea, which shall arise "from the sale of those spoils, and *to take security* for its being "paid in Rome; in order to avoid the hazard, both to myself "and the Commonwealth, of conveying it in specie."

empire depended upon it. It was this circumſtance which induced the emperor to pay ſuch regard to this branch of trade, to propoſe bounties, and to confer certain privileges, the *certa lúcra*, of which *Suetonius* ſpeaks, upon thoſe who would venture out to ſea for the public ſervice in the midſt of winter. Dr. *Taylor* tells us, that a private conſideration alſo had ſome weight with *Claudius* upon this occaſion; for that once, in a great ſcarcity of proviſions, he was attacked in the forum by the populace, and ſo diſagreeably treated with abuſe, and cruſts of ſtale bread, that he with great difficulty eſcaped through ſome private paſſage; from which time he made it his great care and concern to get corn imported, even in the winter. As to the riſk, which *Suetonius* ſays the emperor took upon himſelf, it is to be obſerved, that although the ſhips were private property, yet they would not have gone to ſea in the dangerous ſeaſons they did, had it not been for the public ſervice, and to provide proviſions for the uſe of the whole city. This being the caſe, we have already ſhewn, that it would be contrary to the firſt principles of juſtice and equity, and to the practice followed at this day by all governments which are founded on juſt principles, to allow ſuch loſſes to fall upon individuals. (*a*) From what has been ſaid it appears evident, that the *Romans* had no knowledge of inſurances; in addition to which, both *Grotius* and *Bynkerſhoek* have expreſsly declared, that among

Civil Law, p. 499.

Grotius de Jure Belli, lib. 2. cap. 12. ſ. 3. Bynk. quæſt. Juris Publici, lib. 1. cap. 21.

(*a*) The obſervations here made ſeem, upon examination, to be agreeable to the ideas of Dr. *Taylor*, the preſident *Monteſquieu*, and Mr. *Schomberg*, upon the ſame ſubject. See alſo the opinion of a learned civilian, *Langenbeck* of *Hamburgh*, in *Magen's* Eſſay on Inſurances. Vol. i. p. 1.

among the ancients this contract was unknown; the latter of whom uses these expressions: "*Adeo tamen ille contractus olim fuit incognitus, ut nec nomen ejus, nec rem ipsam in jure Romano deprehendas.*" (*a*)

But to whatever degree of excellence the *Romans* attained either in literature, commerce, or any of the refined arts, they all visibly declined when the *Roman* empire was over-run by the barbarians; or, perhaps it may be said with greater propriety, that they were overwhelmed and lost with that power which had raised them to be the object of public attention and notice. For in times of public ruin and desolation, when war rears its standard, lays waste cities, and tramples on the noblest improvements, it is impossible for commerce to hold its station,

(*a*) By a late work of *M. De Pauw*, entitled *Recherches Philosophiques sur les Grecs*, it is manifest that the *Athenians* were well acquainted with the nature of bills of exchange; and this learned foreigner seems to think it a matter of uncertainty whether the insurances of ships was ever practised among them: but he says it is clear that barratry was not unknown to them. I am inclined, however, to think with *Grotius* and *Bynkershoek*, that this contract was as much unknown to that great people as to the rest of the ancient world. If this had not been the case, can it be supposed that we should find no trace of it in their history, the speeches of their orators, or their laws? Is it not as likely to have been mentioned as bills of exchange; and particularly when barratry was mentioned, if this contract had had an existence, would it not have been stated, on whom the loss was to fall? Besides, the instance given of barratry by *M. De Pauw* is not what we call barratry in *England*; for the case put is a case of fraud committed by the owners, who, by the law of *England*, cannot commit barratry, *which is a criminal act of the captain, to the prejudice of his owners, and without their privity or consent.*

tion, or to flourish in the midst of contention and tumult.

It is the observation of a profound modern historian, that there is an ultimate point of depression, as well as of exaltation, from which human affairs naturally return in a contrary progress, and beyond which they seldom pass in their advancement or decline. This was the case with respect to commerce. When the repeated incursions of the Barbarians had ravaged the *Roman* empire, and had checked every liberal improvement, some people, forced by necessity, or led by inclination, took shelter in a few marshy islands that lay near the coast of *Italy*, and which would never have been thought worth inhabiting in time of peace. This happened in the sixth century; and at the first settling of these wanderers, they had certainly no other object in view, than that of living in a tolerable degree of security from their enemies, and of procuring a moderate subsistence. As these islands were divided from each other by narrow channels, and those channels were so encumbered by shallows, that it was impossible for strangers to navigate them, they found that security which they wished; and by uniting among themselves for the sake of improving their condition, they became in the eighth century a well established republic. This, though it may appear strange, was the origin of the famous republic of *Venice*, which soon became a great commercial power; for, from the first moment that those people took possession of the islands, necessity made them extremely attentive to commerce; the first beginning of which was naturally fishing. Next to

Hume's Hist. of England.

Anderson's History of Commerce, fol. vol. i. p. 19, 20.

fiſhing, they began to trade in ſalt, many pits of which were diſcovered in their own iſlands; and at laſt their city gradually became the magazine for the merchandize of the neighbouring continent on all ſides, and they themſelves the general carriers of *Europe*. Thus to the people of *Italy*, and to thoſe of *Venice* and *Genoa* in particular, we are to attribute the re-eſtabliſhment of commerce. Of the cauſes which contributed to its revival, it remains to ſpeak.

Various cauſes concurred to revive the ſpirit of commerce, and to renew, in ſome degree, that intercourſe between nations, which, during the period of *Gothic* ignorance and barbarity, had been much interrupted. The religious wars of the eleventh century, called the Cruſades, by leading many from every part of *Europe* into *Aſia*, opened an extenſive communication between the Eaſt and Weſt; and though the avowed purpoſe of theſe expeditions was conqueſt, and not commerce; though the iſſue of them proved as unfortunate, as the motives of undertaking them were wild and enthuſiaſtic, yet their commercial effects were beneficial and laſting. For the firſt armies, which ranged themſelves under the banner of the Croſs, having been led through a vaſt extent of country, and having ſuffered ſo much from the length of the march, and the barbariſm and inhoſpitality of the people inhabiting thoſe countries through which they travelled, others were deterred from taking the ſame courſe; and choſe rather to go by ſea, than encounter ſo many hardſhips. *Venice*, *Genoa*, and *Piſa*, furniſhed the tranſports to convey the troops: and it

Robertſon's View of Society, &c.

it is reported, that the ſums were immenſe which they received merely for freight. Beſides this, the Cruſaders contracted with them for ſupplies of military ſtores and proviſions; their fleets hovered on the coaſt; and by ſupplying the army with whatever was wanting, they engroſſed all the advantages ariſing from this branch of commerce. Theſe States were alſo benefited by the ſucceſs which attended the arms of theſe religious and enthuſiaſtic heroes; for there are charters yet extant, containing grants to the *Venetians*, *Piſans*, and *Genoeſe*, of great privileges in the various ſettlements, which the Chriſtians had gained in *Aſia*. When the Cruſaders ſeized *Conſtantinople*, the *Venetians*, who had planned the enterprize, transferred to their own State many of the valuable branches of commerce, which had formerly centered in *Conſtantinople*. Another great cauſe of the revival of commerce, was the invention of the Mariner's Compaſs, which, by rendering navigation more ſecure, as well as more adventurous, facilitated the communications between remote nations, and brought them nearer to each other. The honour of this invention, ſo beneficial to mankind, has been claimed by the *French*; and their claim has been allowed by ſeveral authors, and maintained by a celebrated writer of their own. In this opinion perhaps national partiality may have ſome weight. Moſt authors, however, agree that the inventor was *Flavio de Gioia*, a native of *Amalfi*, an ancient commercial city in the kingdom of *Naples*. (*a*)

Huét Traité du Commerce des Anciens, cap. 10. Anderſ. Hiſtory of Commerce, fol. edit. vol. i. p. 144.

It

(*a*) It appears from *Anderſon*, that ſome people had ſuppoſed that the conqueſts of *Charlemagne* in *Italy*, towards the end of the 8th century, and his ſubſequent eſtabliſhment of Chriſtianity

Anderſon's introd. fol. edit. p. 7.

It is evident, that almoſt all the commerce of *Europe*, in thoſe days, centered amongſt the *Italians*. As they at that time carried on and eſtabliſhed a regular trade with the Eaſt in the ports of *Egypt*, and drew from thence all the rich produce of *India*; it is reaſonable to ſuppoſe, that, in order to ſupport ſo extenſive a commerce, theſe induſtrious and ingenious people were the firſt who introduced inſurances into the ſyſtem of mercantile affairs. It is true, there is no direct authority to warrant a poſitive aſſertion, that they were the inventors of this kind of contract: but it is certain, that the knowledge of it came with them into the different maritime States, in which parties of them ſettled: and when it is admitted that they were the carriers, manufacturers, and bankers of *Europe*, it is probable that they alſo led the way to the eſtabliſhment of a contract, which is ſo eſſentially neceſſary to the ſupport and cultivation of commerce. It has, however, been aſſerted by writers of the *French* nation, (*a*) that inſurance dates its origin in the year 1182, and that it was introduced by the *Jews*, who were baniſhed from *France* about that period, and who took that method to facilitate and ſecure the removal of their effects. They proceed to ſay, that the *Lombards*, who were not idle ſpectators of this contrivance,

Monſ. Savary Dict. Univ. Le Guidon, c. 1. art. 1.

Chriſtianity in the Weſtern and Northern parts of *Germany*, contributed greatly to the revival of commerce. In what I have ſaid upon this ſubject, I choſe rather to follow the ſteps of a very elegant and profound hiſtorian of modern times. *Robertſon*'s View of Society, &c.

(*a*) *Anderſon* ſays, the *Jews* were baniſhed from *France* in 1143. *Anderſon*'s Hiſtory of Commerce, vol. i. p. 82. But I believe ſuch an event twice took place in that kingdom.

contrivance, adopted it, and in a ſhort time improved it conſiderably. It is not very neceſſary to inquire into the truth of this fact, nor indeed are there materials to enable us to do ſo: but it is obſervable that the Preſident *Monteſquieu* mentions that the *Jews* upon this occaſion invented bills of exchange; but does not ſay a ſyllable of policies of inſurance. It is agreed, however, that if the *Lombards* were not the inventors, they were at leaſt the firſt who brought the contract of inſurance to perfection, and introduced it to the world. (*a*) Eſprit des Loix, liv. 21. c. 16.

Before we come to conſider the amazing improvements which have taken place, with reſpect to this branch of commerce, in our own country, in theſe days, it will be expected that ſome notice ſhould be taken of thoſe maritime codes, and naval regulations, which have diſtinguiſhed the modern, no leſs than the laws of *Rhodes* did the ancient world.

To the people of *Amalfi* we are indebted as well for the firſt code of modern ſea laws, as for the invention of the compaſs. We learn from *Anderſon*, that the city of *Amalfi*, ſo long ago as the year 1020, was ſo famous for its merchants and ſhips, that its inhabitants at that time obtained from the Caliph of *Egypt* a ſafe conduct, to enable them to trade Vol. i. p. 58.

(*a*) I am aware that ſeveral learned men are of opinion, that inſurances were of an earlier date than is here aſcribed to them. On a ſubject where ſo much obſcurity muſt neceſſarily exiſt, I am by no means tenacious of my opinion; but the inclination of my mind is to adhere to the idea that the *Lombards* were the inventors. See alſo Mr. *Millar*'s Introduction.

trade freely in all his dominions; and they also received from him several other distinguished privileges. It was towards the close of that century, that they promulgated their system of marine law, which, from the place of its compilation, received the denomination of *Tabula Amalfitana*. This table superseded in a great measure the ancient *Jus Rhodianum*; and its authority was acknowledged by all the States of *Italy*, for some centuries. But as trade increased very rapidly in other cities on the coast of the *Mediterranean* sea, they became unwilling to receive laws from a neighbouring State, which they now equalled, if not surpassed, in the extent of their naval establishments. Every one, therefore, began to erect a tribunal, in order to decide all controverted points, according to laws peculiar to itself; but still referring, in matters of higher moment, to the former rule of action, the *Amalfitan* code. From such a variety of laws, as must necessarily be the consequence of each of the *Italian* States becoming its own legislator, so much disorder and confusion arose, that general convenience at last compelled them to do that, which jealousy of each others power and growing commerce would for ever have prevented them from effecting; and at a general assembly it was agreed to digest the laws of all the separate communities into one body. Every regulation, therefore, which was thought to be founded in justice, either in the laws of *Marseilles*, *Pisa*, *Genoa*, *Venice*, or *Barcelona*, was collected into one mass, and published in the 14th century, under the title of *Consolato del Mare*. A *French* writer *Sur la Saisie des Batimens neutres*, speaks of this production in a very unfavourable way; and

Hubner.

and calls it a rude ill-formed mafs of maritime and pofitive regulations, of ordinances of the middle ages, and of private decifions. Indeed when we confider that this was a compilation from the various regulations of fo many different States, it could not excite much furprife, if it really merited the cenfure of this author. But upon examination, it is a work of confiderable merit; the decifions it contains are founded on the laws of nations; it has been received and allowed to have the force of law in every part of *Italy;* and it is the fource from whence the people of that country, as well as thofe of *Spain* and *France*, have been faid to derive many of their beft marine regulations. Unfortunately too, *Emerigon* has difcovered, that becaufe one of the chapters in the *Confolato del Mare* overturns fome favourite fyftem of this learned author, he is out of humour with the whole compofition. One thing, however, is clear, that neither the *Confolato del Mare*, nor the *Amalfitan* code, upon which it is founded, contains any thing upon infurance law, fo that we have here another confirmation of the idea, that this contract was not a production of very ancient times. (*a*)

Vinnius in Peckium, 190.

Emerigon, preface, p. 8.

The fpirit of commerce was not, however, confined to the South parts of *Europe;* it now began to extend itfelf among the inhabitants of the Weftern coafts. But whatever maritime regulations they might have eftablifhed among themfelves, they were

(*a*) In what I have faid upon the *Amalfitan* code, I have found myfelf extremely indebted to Mr. *Schomberg*'s very ingenious obfervations upon that fubject, in his treatife on the maritime laws of *Rhodes*.

were found not to be sufficiently extensive for the commercial intercourse which began to take place in those countries in the course of the 12th century. Accordingly, about the year 1194, *Richard* the First, king of *England*, on his return from his wild expedition to the *Holy Land*, having staid to repose himself for some time at the isle of *Oleron*, in the *Bay* of *Biscay*, an island which he inherited in right of his mother, whose portion it was in marriage with his father *Henry* the Second, gave orders for the compilation of a maritime code. Some authors suppose that the hardships and dangers, to which, in the course of his expedition, he saw adventurers by sea were exposed, induced him to promulgate a law, by which their condition might be rendered more comfortable.

Schomberg's Observ. on the Rhodian Laws.

Others imagine, and probably their supposition is better founded, that the great intercourse between his *English* and *French* subjects, and their allies, required a certain general system of sea law, for the more speedy and impartial determination of all disputes which might occasionally arise.

Sir Philip Meadow's Observ. on the Dom. of the Sea, c. 4.

The laws of *Oleron*, therefore, which are in substance but an abstract of the old *Rhodian* laws, with some additions and alterations, accommodated to the practice of that age, and the customs of the Western nations, were proposed as a common standard and measure for the more equal distribution of justice amongst the people of different governments. These excellent regulations were so much esteemed, that they have been the model on which all modern sea laws have been founded; and two distinguished nations have contended for the honour of their production. *France*, jealous of the lustre which the *English* justly derive from the production of of this code, with much anxiety claims this honour to herself; and very distinguished authors have stood forth the champions of her claim. The substance of their argument is, that *Eleanor*, wife of *Henry* 2d king of *England*, and Duchess of *Guyenne*, returning from the *Holy Land*, and having seen the beneficial effects of the *Consolato del Mare*, ordered the first draught of the judgments or laws of *Oleron* to be made: *that her son Richard the First, returning from the same expedition, enlarged and improved* what his mother had begun: that they were certainly intended for the use of the *French* merely, because they were written in the old *Gascon French*, without any mixture of the *Norman* or *English* languages: that they constantly refer for examples of voyages to *Bourdeaux*, *St. Malo*, and other seaports in *France*; never to the *Thames*, or to any port of *England* or *Ireland*: and that they were made by a Duchess and Duke of *Guyenne*, for *Guyenne*, and not for their kingdom of *England*. One of these learned writers adds a reason, which he thinks very conclusive, to prove that these laws were of *French* extraction; namely, that, from their first appearance, their decisions have been treated with extreme respect in the courts of *France*.

Cleirac Coutumes de la Mer, p. 2. Valin. Emerigon.

Valin.

In these days, it is very immaterial whether *France* or *England* is entitled to the honour they respectively claim, and I shall not tire the reader with any argument upon the point. (*a*)

Anderson.

(*a*) For the arguments in favour of the *English* claim, the reader may cousult *Selden*'s *Mare Clausum*, lib. 2. cap. 24. Mr. Just. *Blackstone*'s Commentaries, vol. i. page 418. *Schomberg*'s Observations, page 88.

Vol. i. p. 454. *Anderſon* in his hiſtory of commerce has expreſsly ſtated, but he does not adduce any authority in ſupport of his opinion, that the laws of *Oleron* treat of inſurances. I have read them repeatedly with the direct view of diſcovering whether inſurances were of ſo ancient a date : but I have not found a ſingle word which could induce me to ſubſcribe to ſuch an aſſertion. In confirmation of my opinion, *Emerigon*, ſpeaking of theſe laws, has obſerved, "*Il n'y* "*eſt pas dit le mot du contrat d'Aſſurance, qui apparem-* "*ment n'etoit pas encore alors en uſage.*"

Preface, p. 11.

But while we pay due reſpect and veneration to thoſe maritime regulations which diſtinguiſhed the Southern and Weſtern parts of *Europe*, it would be improper ſilently to paſs over the laws, which were ordained by an induſtrious and reſpectable body of people, who inhabited the city of *Wiſbuy*, famous for its commerce, and renowned on the ſhores of the *Baltic*. The merchants of this city carried on ſo extenſive a trade, and gave themſelves up ſo entirely to commerce, that they muſt doubtleſs have found a great inconvenience in having no maritime code, to which they could refer to decide their diſputes. To ſuch a cauſe we are probably indebted for thoſe laws and marine ordinances, which bear the name of *Wiſbuy*, which were receiv-ed by the *Swedes*, at the time they were compoſ-ed, as a juſt and equitable rule of action, and which were long reſpected (and for aught I know, are to this day obſerved) by the *Germans*, *Swedes*, *Danes*, and by all the Northern nations ; although the city in which they received their origin, has long dwindled into inſignificancy and contempt. At

Cleirac Us et Coutumes de la Mer, Emerigon, Pref.

At what time these laws were compiled is a matter of dispute; and different writers have adopted different periods, in order to answer their own particular ends, or to advance the honour of that age which it happened to be their business to extol. The writers of the North pretend that *Wisbuy* was a great commercial city, in the 9th century; from whence they argue, that their laws must be of very high antiquity; that they were the model, from which those of *Oleron* were copied, and that they were received and acknowledged by all nations in *Europe*, even to the Straits of *Gibraltar*. On the other hand it is answered, and with much strength of reasoning, that the Northern code is a transcript from that of *Oleron*, although it contains several additions: for it has been shewn, that the laws of *Oleron* were promulgated by *Richard* the First about the close of the twelfth century, at which time, as appears by the report of a *Swedish* historian, the city of *Wisbuy* was not built, nor for near a century afterwards; that the inhabitants were merely strangers collected together from different parts, who, so far from having any power or influence over their neighbours, were not absolute masters of their own city. Besides, if their laws had been prior to those of *Oleron*, we should have found in the latter some regulations respecting insurances; because a copyist never would have omitted so material a branch of commercial legislation, the laws of *Wisbuy* having expressly mentioned insurances, and provided, that if the merchant obliged the master to insure the ship, the merchant shall be obliged to insure the master's life against the hazards of the sea.

Cleirac, 4.

Olaus Magnus, lib. 10. cap. 16.

Art. 66.

Afterwards,

Robertſon's View, vol. i. p. 351. quarto edit. Emerigon, pref. p. 12.

Afterwards, towards the cloſe of the fifteenth century, we find from hiſtory, that many conſiderable regulations were made at *Barcelona* in *Spain*, reſpecting marine inſurances.

Schomb. Obſerv. 106.

Robertſon's View of Society.

But if the laws of *Wiſbuy* were not prior to thoſe of *Oleron*, yet it is much to their honour, and ſhews in what eſtimation they were held in the greateſt part of *Europe*, that after having for a long courſe of time enjoyed the higheſt authority in all the Northern tribunals for maritime affairs, they were thought worthy of being adopted as the baſis of the ordinances of the *Hanſeatic League*. Of this ancient and famous confederacy it will be ſufficient in this place to obſerve, that it began about the thirteenth century, and originated with the cities of *Lubeck* and *Hamburgh*, which were obliged to enter into a league of mutual defence, in order to protect themſelves againſt the nations round the *Baltic*, who were extremely barbarous, and infeſted that ſea with their piracies. Theſe two cities derived ſuch advantages from their union, that other towns acceded to the confederacy, and in a ſhort time, eighty of the moſt conſiderable cities, ſcattered through thoſe countries, which ſtretch from the bottom of the *Baltic* to *Cologne* upon the *Rhine*, joined in the famous *Hanſeatic League*; which became ſo formidable, that its alliance was courted, and its enmity dreaded by the moſt powerful monarchs. This aſſociation, it is ſaid, formed the firſt ſyſtematic plan of commerce known in *Europe*: but notwithſtanding this, they did not for a long time publiſh any maritime code, but were entirely governed by thoſe of *Oleron* and *Wiſbuy*. At a general

general meeting, however, held at *Lubeck* in the year 1614, it was agreed to extract from those compilations whatever should be thought most useful, and that it should in future be the rule of decision in every contested point. It was prior to this time, about the fourteenth century, that the members of this league were in their greatest spendour; their commerce was at its height; they supplied the rest of *Europe* with naval stores, and they pitched upon different towns, the most eminent of which was *Bruges* in *Flanders*, where they established staples, in which their commerce was regularly carried on. The sovereigns of *Europe* looked up to the *Hanseatic League* with esteem and admiration, and the kings of *France* and *England* granted them considerable privileges. But when this union had rendered them rich and powerful, they grew arrogant and overbearing, which induced the princes, whom they had offended, to take a closer and more accurate view of the danger which might arise from such a confederacy, and of the advantages which might accrue to themselves from the possession of their trade. These causes at last concurred to effect the decay of this alliance, which however is not wholly dissolved at this day; as the cities of *Lubec*, *Hamburgh*, and *Bremen*, maintain sufficient marks of that splendour and dignity with which this confederacy was anciently distinguished.

Kuricke Comm. Schomb. Observ.

Robertson's View, &c. Ander. Hist. of Comm.

Hume's Hist. of England, vol. iv. p. 348, 349.

Having thus taken a brief but comprehensive view, of the most considerable maritime states both of ancient and modern times, I forbear to go more at length into the history of several governments, which have published naval regulations for the direction of of their own ſubjects; becauſe they are only binding within their own particular diſtricts: they are very ſimilar to thoſe about which ſo much has been already ſaid; they are all collected by *Magens* in the ſecond volume of his Eſſay on inſurances, and are occaſionally referred to in the courſe of the enſuing work. Beſides, I haſten to give an account of the vaſt improvements, which have been made in this country within theſe laſt thirty years, with reſpect to inſurances, and which are the main object of this inquiry. It would, however, be improper in a work of this nature, entirely to paſs over the *French* nation, the maritime ſtrength of which has of late years conſiderably increaſed; and whoſe writers upon commercial affairs would reflect honour upon any country.

Few people underſtand the theory of commerce better than our neighbours on the Continent; and yet they have not in practice come up to what might have been expected. It is true that *France* from her ſituation, from the bent of her people to certain manufactures, from the happineſs of her ſoil, and her natural advantages, muſt be always poſſeſſed of a great internal and external trade, which muſt add greatly to her wealth, and render her the moſt reſpectable power on the Continent of *Europe*. But the *French* do not naturally poſſeſs that undaunted perſeverance, which is neceſſary for commerce and colonization. It is beſides a great diſadvantage to the commerce of *France*, that as its government is military, the profeſſion of a merchant is not ſo honourable as in *England*, ſo that the *French* nobility think that it would be beneath

them

them to attend to the drudgery of trade, and that it would degrade their anceſtry to allow any of their ſons to follow the buſineſs of a merchant. The conſequence of this is, that the church, the law, and the army, are ſtocked with the members of noble families; and the counting-houſe is by them entirely deſerted. At one period, indeed, there was an appearance that *France* would make as illuſtrious a figure amidſt the powers of *Europe* in trade, as ſhe then did as a warlike nation. The period, to which I allude, was under the adminiſtration of the famous *Colbert*, who, next to *Henry* the Great, may juſtly be ſtyled the father of the *French* commerce and manufactures. This illuſtrious man, who was of *Scotch* extraction, deſcended of a family no way conſiderable by its ſplendour or antiquity, raiſed himſelf by his activity, diligence, and knowledge of commerce, to the firſt offices under the government of *France*. Being appointed to the ſuperintendance of the finances, he propoſed ſuch regulations as brought about the purpoſe he intended, the orderly and frugal management of them; and eſtabliſhed the trade of *France* with the *Eaſt* and *Weſt Indies*, from which ſhe has reaped conſiderable benefits. He alſo patronized and encouraged the liberal arts and ſciences, reformed the courts of juſtice, and introduced many important regulations, which regarded the order of ſociety. But in 1669, when appointed ſecretary of ſtate, and entruſted with the management of affairs relating to the ſea, he had a full opportunity of exerting thoſe talents, which he ſo eminently poſſeſſed, and for the exertions of which his name has been tranſmitted with ſo much honour to poſterity. In order

Vie de Colbert.

to gain a proper inſight into the true effects of commerce upon the various nations of the world, and the advantages of ſome particular branches of trade, he procured and employed learned and diligent men to inquire into the commercial hiſtories of cities long ſince deſtroyed, and the nature of the climate, ſoil, and productions of the countries then riſing into notice. It was to this ſpirit of inquiry in this famous ſtateſman, that the world is indebted, as appears from the dedication, for that very maſterly performance upon the commerce and navigation of the ancients, written by *Huet* biſhop of *Avranches* and *Soiſſons*, who is juſtly entitled to a high rank among men of letters. *Colbert* having thus made uſe of the labours of others in order to gain uſeful information, undertook to reſtore the navy and commerce of *France*; and he completed all his ſervices by the publication of that excellent body of Sea laws, known by the name of the Ordinances of *Lewis* the 14th, which comprehend every thing relating to naval or commercial juriſprudence; and of which the doctrine of inſurances forms a conſiderable part. To its merits all *Europe* has borne teſtimony; and the name of *Colbert* muſt ever be mentioned with reſpect, when the ordinances of *Lewis* the 14th are the ſubject of converſation. *(a)*

Huët Hiſt. du Commerce et de la Navigation des Anciens, pref.

Vie de Colbert.

L'Honneur Francois, tom. 7, p. 302.

This

(a) It was under the adminiſtration of *Colbert*, that the *French* laid the foundation of *Quebec* on the banks of the river *St. Lawrence*; and he performed a work, which, ſays a *French* hiſtorian, even in the eyes of *Richelieu*, ſeemed to ſurpaſs human power; and that was to effect a junction between the *Atlantic* and the *Mediterranean* by means of a canal, the execution of which attracted the admiration of *Europe*, and added much to the ſplendour of *French* commerce.

L'Honneur Francois, par M. de Sacy, tom. 7. p. 302.

This ordinance has had the good fortune to meet with a laborious commentator in *Valin*, who, being thoroughly ſenſible of the advantages which his country muſt neceſſarily derive from ſuch an excellent code, has, with a degree of labour and induſtry which excite our admiration, and which are highly deſerving of imitation, placed it in the moſt favourable point of view; has cleared up every obſcurity, by tracing theſe laws to their ancient ſources, and by a full inveſtigation of old ordinances, and the deciſions of former tribunals, has added much to the maſs of learning upon ſubjects of this nature. But of all the ſources, from which modern *French* legiſlators could derive the moſt eſſential information, the famous treatiſe called "*Le Guidon*" was the chief. This tract was republiſhed by *Cleirac*, who pays a due compliment to its merits, in his work upon the Uſages and Cuſtoms of the Sea: and although in its ſtyle and manner it certainly ſavours of the ruſt of antiquity; yet it contains the true principles of naval juriſprudence. If the ſtyle be antiquated, and the text be corrupted in ſome places, yet the treatiſe is ſtill valuable by the wiſdom, which ſhines through the whole, and the number of deciſions, which it contains.

Cleirac, p. 213.

Upon this occaſion let me not forget to take proper notice of two very modern and diſtinguiſhed *French* writers, M. *Pothier* and M. *Emerigon*. The former of theſe has written admirable diſſertations upon every ſpecies of expreſs and implied contracts, and amongſt the reſt upon that of inſurance; he has conſidered his various ſubjects with ſo much

Pothier, 3. tom. duod. p. 1.

clearnefs, and perfpicuity, and has produced fo many appofite examples in fupport of the pofitions he advances, that they greatly contribute to the advancement of the knowledge of this branch of jurifprudence. His ftyle is at the fame time manly, neat, and claffical; and well fuited to didactic difcourfes.

Traité des Affurances.

M. *Emerigon* has, in his work, confined himfelf to the confideration of marine infurances, and to the contract of bottomry only. This being the cafe, he has gone into thofe fubjects much more at length than any former *French* writer; and has with infinite labour, unwearied ftudy and reflection, collected the decifions and authorities, applicable to the purpofe of his work. This learned foreigner, I underftand, holds a diftinguifhed rank among the advocates of his own country: and his treatife upon infurances will by no means diminifh his fame.

We have feen, that the naval reputation of the *Englifh* was arrived at a great height in the twelfth century, for the laws of *Oleron*, of the merits of which much has been faid, were at that time compiled by an *Englifh* monarch, and received here as the regulator of naval affairs. The progrefs of commerce, however, in this country, was not anfwerable to fo aufpicious a beginning; for in the reign of *Edward* the Third, upwards of a century afterwards, commerce and induftry were at a very low ebb. That monarch, ftruck with the flourifhing ftate of the Northern provinces, which have been already defcribed, and perceiving the true caufe of their

Hume's Hift. of Eng. oct. edit. vol. ii. p. 494.

their profperity, endeavoured to excite a fpirit of induftry among his fubjects, who feemed to be blind to the advantages of the fituation, and ignorant of thofe fources, from which they might derive wealth and opulence. So far were they lulled by ignorance and indolence, that they did not even attempt thofe manufactures, the materials of which they themfelves fupplied to foreigners. Notwithftanding the endeavours of *Edward*, and the many wife eftablifhments propofed and encouraged by him, it was not till the reign of *Elizabeth*, that the *Englifh* began to difcover their true interefts, and the arts by which they were to obtain that pre-eminence and rank, which they now hold among commercial nations. This flow progrefs of commerce in this country may be accounted for, on various grounds. During the *Saxon* heptarchy, *England* was fplit into many kingdoms, perpetually at variance with each other; it was expofed to the fierce incurfions of the Northern pirates; it was funk in barbarity and ignorance; and confequently was in no condition to cultivate commerce, or to purfue any fyftem of wife or ufeful policy. To this fucceeded the *Norman* conqueft, and all the confequences of a feudal government, military in its nature, hoftile to commerce, and the arts and refinements of a liberal and civilized people. Scarce had the nation recovered from the fhock occafioned by this revolution, when it was engaged in fupporting its monarch's pretenfions to the *French* crown, and it long continued to wafte its vigour and wealth in wild endeavours to conquer that country. To this we may add the deftructive civil wars between the houfes of *York* and *Lancafter*, which

Robertfon's View of Society, &c.

which long deluged the kingdom with blood; and to which a period was at last happily put by the union of their several titles to the crown, in the person of *Henry* the Eighth. The reformation then took place under that monarch, and it was not till the reign of *Elizabeth*, that the feuds and dissensions which such an important event was likely to occasion, began to subside. During her long reign, and her wise and prudent administration of government, commerce began to rear its head, and found shelter and protection from the managers of public affairs. From this short sketch, it is not much to be wondered at, that *England* was one of the last nations of *Europe*, which availed herself of her great commercial advantages: but she has since made ample amends for her long continued indolence and inactivity, by the amazing extent of her commerce, and the wise laws and regulations to be found in her system of maritime jurisprudence.

While commerce continued in this weak and languid state, it cannot be supposed that insurances, which spring from commerce, were at all encouraged or understood. It is true, the *Lombards* came into *England* in the 13th century, and it is universally agreed, that whatever may have been the origin of insurances, they were introduced into *England* by that active and industrious people. This idea is countenanced and confirmed by the clause to this day inserted in all policies of insurance "that "this writing or policy of assurance shall be of as "much force and effect as any writing heretofore "made in *Lombard-Street*, &c." the place where these *Italians* are known to have taken up their residence,

1 Anderson's Hist. of Com.

Vide the Appendix, No. 1.

ſidence, and caried on their trade. The preamble to the ſtatute of Queen *Elizabeth*, which will be preſently mentioned, ſpeaks of inſurances, as having exiſted time out of mind in this kingdom. Be this as it may, it is certain that prior to the reign of that princeſs very few inſurances had been effected: or, if effected, no queſtion had ever ariſen upon them in any of the ſuperior courts. So little were the judges acquainted with the nature of the contract, that ſo late as the 30 and 31 of *Elizabeth*'s reign, it became a queſtion where an action upon a policy of inſurance ſhould be tried, the policy having been effected in *London*, and the ſhip detained in the river *Soane* in *France*. The policy was on a ſhip from *Melcombe Regis*, in the county of *Dorſet*, to *Abbeville* in *France*. The plaintiff declared, that the ſhip, in failing towards *Abbeville*, *to wit*, in the river of *Soane*, was arreſted by the king of *France*. The parties came to iſſue upon the queſtion, whether the ſhip was ſo arreſted or not: and it was tried before Lord Chief Juſtice *Wray*, in the city of *London*; and a verdict was found for the plaintiff. In arreſt of judgment it was moved, that this iſſue ariſing merely from a place *out of the realm*, could not be tried in *London*. But it was reſolved by the court, that this iſſue ſhould be tried where the action was in this caſe brought; for the promiſe which is the ground and foundation of the action, was made in *London*; and the arreſt now in iſſue, is not the ground of the action, which is founded on the *aſſumpſit*, and the arreſt is the breach of the *aſſumpſit*.

6 Coke Rep. 47 b.

This

This is the moſt ancient caſe I have been able to find upon the ſubject of inſurances; and I thought proper to inſert it here, as the beſt proof, that, prior to the reign of *Elizabeth*, this contract could have been very little, if at all known. We have ſeen, however, that under *Elizabeth*, the genius of *England* began to diſplay itſelf: about which time alſo, the legiſlature began to think the regulation of matters of aſſurance an object well worthy their moſt ſerious attention; and it cannot but afford us much pleaſure to find, that even in that early age, the true principles, upon which this ſpecies of contract is founded, and upon which it ought to be protected and encouraged in a commercial nation, were clearly and fully underſtood. In the preamble to an act of parliament, paſſed in the 43d year of the reign of Queen *Elizabeth*, concerning matters of aſſurance uſed amongſt merchants, the ſenſe of the legiſlature upon the ſubject is expreſſed with clearneſs and perſpicuity. After reciting that it has ever been the policy of this nation to encourage trade, and that policies of aſſurance have exiſted time out of mind, it goes on to ſtate the advantages to be derived from their encouragement in a commercial nation. "By means of "which policies of aſſurance, it cometh to paſs "upon the loſs or periſhing of any ſhip, there "followeth not the undoing of any man, but the "loſs lighteth rather eaſily upon many, than heavy "upon few, and rather upon them that adventure "not, than upon thoſe who do adventure, where-"by all merchants, eſpecially thoſe of the younger "ſort, are allured to venture more willingly, and "more freely."

43 Eliz. ch. 12.

The

The purpose of that statute was, to erect a particular court for the trial of causes, relative to policies of insurance, in a summary way; and to that end the statute ordained, that a commission should issue yearly, directed to the Judge of the *Admiralty*, the Recorder of *London*, two doctors of the civil law, two common lawyers, and eight merchants, empowering any five of them to hear and determine all such causes, arising in *London*; and it also gave an appeal from their decision, by way of bill, to the court of Chancery. But this statute not entirely answering the intention of the legislature, some further regulations were made by a subsequent statute: such as the reduction of the number necessary to constitute a quorum. I forbear entering at length into this matter, the court erected by these statutes being now entirely disused. The reasons of this may be collected from some few decisions in our reporters: but one appears on the face of the statute itself; namely, that its jurisdiction was not sufficiently extensive, being confined to such causes only *as arose in London*.

13 and 14 Car. 2. ch. 23.

By a case reported in *Style* we find, that a prohibition issued to the court of Policies of Insurance, to prevent it from proceeding in a case of insurance upon a life, the Court of King's Bench being of opinion, that the statute only meant to give the court below cognizance of *such contracts* only as related to *merchandize*.

Bendir v. Oyle, Style, 166.

In another case it seemed to be the opinion of the Court of King's Bench, that the jurisdiction of this newly erected court did not extend to suits brought

Dalbie v. Proudfoot, 1 Shower, 396.

brought by the affurer againft the affured; but only to fuch as were profecuted by the latter againft the former. It is true, in Sir *Bartholomew Shower's* note of the cafe, no decifion appears to have been made; but a rule to fhew caufe why a prohibition fhould not iffue, was obtained; and no notice is afterwards taken of it, although the learned reporter was himfelf the counfel in the caufe, who had obtained the original rule.

Came v. Moy, 2 Siderfin, 121.

But a cafe reported in *Siderfin*, feems to have ftruck a more fevere blow at the exiftence of this court than any of thofe cafes I have mentioned; for it was there held, that it was no bar to an action upon a Policy of Infurance at the common law to fay, that the plaintiff had fued the defendant for the fame caufe in the court erected by the ftatute of *Elizabeth*, and that his fuit was there difmiffed.

Lex Merc. Red. 4th edit. p. 292.

Thefe caufes co-operating, together probably with fome inftances of partiality in the judges, this court fell into difufe, no commiffion having iffued for many years; but infurance caufes are now decided, like all other queftions of property, and by that mode of trial moft agreeable to the nature of our conftitution, by a trial in a court of common law.

It has been much the fafhion of late years to infift upon the advantages which the trading part of the nation would derive from the eftablifhment of fome equitable and amicable judicatory for the trial of all difputed points in matters of infurance.

ſurance. This is only another proof of the weak-neſs and fallibility of the human mind, which is never ſatisfied with the enjoyments within its reach, however excellent they may be; but pants after thoſe of foreign growth. Thus, a people, who are poſſeſſed of a ſpecies of trial, the beſt calcu-lated for the diſcovery of truth, and the advance-ment of juſtice, and which has excited the ad-miration of the world, are deſirous of parting with ſuch an advantage for a mode of trial, which is very unſatisfactory.

The court erected by the ſtatute of *Elizabeth*, and which has now fallen into diſuſe, is perhaps one of the ſtrongeſt arguments, that can be adduced to prove, that ſuch a judicature is not congenial to the ſpirit and diſpoſition of *Britons*, nor well adapted for the purpoſes of its inſtitution. It is univerſally agreed by all writers upon juriſpru-dence, that nothing tends ſo much to the elucida-tion of truth, and the detection of fraud, as the open *viva voce* examination of witneſſes, in the preſence of all mankind; before judges, who from their knowledge of books and men, acquired by long ſtudy and experience, are well qualified to diſcriminate and decide between right and wrong; and before twelve upright citizens, who have an opportunity of obſerving the appear-ance, countenance, inclination, and deportment of thoſe, who are thus examined upon oath. Beſides the ſubjects of thoſe ſtates, which have eſtabliſhed theſe equitable tribunals, ſenſible of the ſuperior advantages of the *Engliſh* inſtitution, feeling that in great mercantile queſtions, the greateſt atten-

tion

tion is paid to the eternal and immutable principles of reaſon, and that all men, whether natives or foreigners, here meet with an equal meaſure in the adminiſtration of juſtice, fly to this country to make their contracts of inſurance, that in caſe of a diſpute, they may have the benefit of its laws. Did it fall within the compaſs of this inquiry, I could relate many caſes, of the truth of which I have not the ſmalleſt reaſon to doubt, which would ſerve to ſhew the idea entertained by foreigners of our mercantile juriſprudence, and the high repute and eſtimation in which our judges are juſtly held by the *European* nations.

But though the court of Policies of Aſſurance has been long diſuſed; though it is near a century ſince queſtions of this nature became chiefly the ſubject of common law juriſdiction; yet, I am ſure I rather go beyond bounds, if I aſſert that in all our reporters from the reign of Queen *Elizabeth*, to the year 1756, when Lord *Mansfield* became Chief Juſtice of the King's Bench, there are 60 caſes upon matters of inſurance. Even thoſe caſes, which are reported, are ſuch looſe notes, moſtly of trials at *Niſi Prius*, containing a ſhort opinion of a ſingle judge, and very often no opinion at all, but merely a general verdict, that little information can be collected upon the ſubject. From hence it muſt neceſſarily follow, that as there have been but few poſitive regulations upon inſurances, the principles, on which they were founded, could never have been widely diffuſed, nor very generally known.

This

This was owing to some defects, which were discoverable in the proceedings in our courts, and in the delays and expenses which suitors experienced; so that they rather chose to submit to their first loss, than be harrassed by the delays of the law, or be at the expense of trying a question, of which the decision might perhaps be of less moment to the individual than to the public. These defects were so glaring, that it was one of the first acts of Lord *Mansfield*'s administration to apply a remedy; and his labours have been happily attended with such success, that they have been of essential service to the nation in general, considered in a commercial light, and have excited the applause and approbation of *Europe*.

Before the time of this venerable judge, the legal proceedings, even on contracts of insurance, were subject to great vexations and oppressions. If the underwriters refused payment, it was usual for the insured to bring a separate action against each of the underwriters on the policy, and to proceed to trial on all. The multiplicity of trials was oppressive both to the insurers and insured; and the insurers, if they had any real point to try, were put to an enormous expense, before they could obtain any decision of the question which they wished to agitate. Some underwriters, who thought they had a sound defence, and who were desirous of avoiding unnecessary costs or delay to themselves or the insured, applied to the court of King's Bench to stay the proceedings in all the actions but one, undertaking to pay the amount of their subscriptions

with

with costs, if the plaintiff should succeed in the cause which was tried; and offering to admit on their part every thing, which might bring the true merits of the case before the court and jury. Reasonable as this offer was, the plaintiff, either from perverseness of disposition, or the illiberality and cunning of his advisers, refused his consent to the application. The court did not think themselves warranted to make such a rule without his consent; but Mr. Justice *Denison* intimated that if the plaintiff persisted, against his own interest, in his right to try all the causes, the court had the power of granting imparlances in all but one, till there was an opportunity of trying that one action. Lord *Mansfield* then stated the great advantages resulting to each party by consenting to the application which was made; and added, that if the plaintiff consented to such a rule, the defendant should undertake not to file any bill in equity for delay, nor to bring a writ of error,(*a*) and should produce all books and papers, that were material to the point in issue. This rule was afterwards consented to by the plaintiff, and was found so beneficial to all parties, that it is now grown into general use, and is called The Consolidation Rule. Thus on the one hand, defendants may have questions of real importance tried at a small expense; and plaintiffs are not delayed in their suits by those arts, which have too frequently been resorted to,

2 Barnard. B. R. 103.

(*a*) The Court of Common Pleas were unanimously of opinion, after consideration, that a defendant who had entered into the consolidation rule, could not bring a writ of error at all, although there be manifest error upon the record. *Camden.* v. *Edie*, 1 H. Blac. Rep. 21.

to, in order to evade the payment of a juſt demand.

In former times, the whole of the caſe was left generally to the jury, without any minute ſtatement from the bench of the principles of law, on which inſurances were eſtabliſhed; and as the verdicts were general, it is almoſt impoſſible to determine from the reports we now ſee, upon what grounds the caſe was decided. Nay, even if a doubt aroſe in point of law, and a caſe was reſerved upon that doubt, it was afterwards argued in private at the chambers of the judge who tried the cauſe, and by his ſingle deciſion the parties were bound. Thus, whatever his opinion might be, it never was promulgated to the world; and could never be the rule of deciſion in any future caſe.

Lord *Mansfield* introduced a different mode of proceeding; for in his ſtatement of the caſe to the jury, he enlarged upon the rules and principles of law, as applicable to that caſe; and left it to them to make the application of thoſe principles to the facts in evidence before them. So that if a general verdict were given, the grounds on which the jury proceeded might be more eaſily aſcertained. Beſides, if any real difficulty occurred in point of law, his Lordſhip adviſed the counſel to conſent to a ſpecial caſe. In a ſpecial caſe, the facts are either admitted by the parties, or if they are diſputed, are proved; and then the judge takes the opinion of the jury upon thoſe facts, reſerving the queſtion of law to be agitated elſewhere. Theſe caſes are afterwards argued, not before the judge in private, but in open court

court before all the judges of the bench from which the record comes. Thus nice and important queſtions are now not haſtily and unadviſedly decided; but the parties have their caſe ſeriouſly conſidered and debated by the whole court; the deciſion becomes notorious to the world; it is recorded for a precedent of law ariſing from the facts found, and ſerves as a rule to guide the opinions of future judges.

It had alſo been the cuſtom, when caſes were reſerved, to leave it to the council on both ſides to draw them up at their leiſure. This introduced conſiderable delays; for every fact became again a ſubject of diſpute; and frequently from the hurry of buſineſs and other avocations of the counſel, the caſe was neglected for a conſiderable time, before it was ready for the inſpection of the court.

Now, whenever a caſe is reſerved, the judge himſelf dictates to the clerk of the court the facts which ought to be ſtated, and the queſtion upon which the opinion of the court is required: and in addition to this, Lord *Mansfield*, whoſe rules are now the ſubject of our inquiry, ordered, that all caſes ſo reſerved muſt be ſet down for argument within the firſt four days of the term following the trial; otherwiſe the judgment muſt be entered according to the finding of the jury.

One additional improvement in the proceedings remains to be mentioned. Before Lord *Mansfield*'s time, it was almoſt a matter of courſe not to decide any caſe, without hearing two arguments upon it: but

but in the very firſt cauſe, which is reported of his Lordſhip's deciſions, he expreſſed himſelf to this effect: "Where we have no doubt, we ought not to "put the parties to the delay and expenſe of a far- "ther argument, nor leave other perſons, who may "be intereſted in the determination of a point of "a general nature, unneceſſarily under the anxiety of "ſuſpenſe." When we add to theſe wiſe regulations the conſideration that Lord *Mansfield*, during his long adminiſtration of juſtice, has given up a great part of his time, and has employed his talents in the elucidation of thoſe points, which tend to fix the ſyſtem of mercantile juriſprudence upon the ſureſt grounds, we need not wonder that that part of it, which relates to marine inſurances, has attained to its preſent ſtate of perfection. Raynard v. Chaſe, 1 Burrow 5.

A complete ſyſtem of juriſprudence cannot be ſuddenly erected: but there is rather matter to excite our wonder that ſo much has been done in this reſpect within the laſt 30 years, than ground to complain that little has been effected. It is the boaſt of this age, that in it the great foundations of marine juriſprudence have been laid, by clearly developing the principles on which policies of inſurance are founded, and by happily applying thoſe principles to particular caſes. It will be the buſineſs of the following work, which profeſſes to lay down a ſyſtem of the law as it now ſtands, to point out, amongſt other things, the improvements which have been made by the legiſlature from time to time on the ſyſtem of inſurances, by many wiſe ſtatutes and ſalutary reſtrictions; and to prove, that the learned judges of the courts both of law and equity, by their liberal and equitable conſtructions of thoſe ſtatutes, and by adopting the true principles of commerce in their deciſion of the many intricate caſes, which have been brought before them, have added another pillar to that beautiful ſtructure of rational juriſprudence, which has deſervedly acquired the admiration of mankind.

CHAPTER THE FIRST.

OF THE POLICY.

CHAP. I.

POLICY is the name given to the inſtrument, by which the contract of indemnity is effected between the inſurer and inſured; and it is not, like moſt, contracts, ſigned by both parties, but only by the inſurer, who on that account, it is ſuppoſed, is denominated an underwriter. Notwithſtanding this, there are certain conditions, of which we ſhall hereafter have occaſion to ſpeak, to be performed as well by the perſon not ſubſcribing, as by the underwriter, otherwiſe the policy will be void. Of policies there ſeem to be two kinds, *valued* and *open* policies; and the only difference between them is this, that in the former, goods or property inſured are valued at prime coſt at the time of effecting the policy; in the latter, the value is not mentioned: that in the caſe of an open policy, the real value muſt be proved; in a valued policy it *is agreed*, and is juſt as if the parties had admitted it at the trial. 2 Burr. 1117.

Although policies of aſſurance are not to be ranked with ſpecialty contracts, not being under ſeal, yet they have always been held as ſacred agreements and of the firſt credit: ſo much ſo, that when once they are underwritten, they can never be altered by any authority whatever; becauſe it would open a door to an infinite variety of frauds, and introduce uncertainty into a ſpecies of contract, of which certainty and preciſion are the moſt eſſential requiſites. Skinn. 54.

In a caſe before Lord Chancellor *Hardwicke*, this doctrine was admitted in its full extent. The plaintiff had inſured a ſhip at and from *London* to *Oſtend*, from thence to *Rotterdam*, from thence to the *Canaries*, warranted an *Oſtend* ſhip, which ſhip was afterwards taken. The bill was brought to have the policy rectified, for that the intention of the parties was miſtaken therein, which was, that the warranty was too general, and that the voyage ſhould have been ſtated to take place from *Oſtend* only, and not from *London*. The evidence in this caſe was the depoſition of *Knox*, the agent for the company; who depoſed, that the

Henkle v. The Royal Exch. Aſſur. Company. 1 vez. 317.

[2]

CHAP. I. plaintiff applied to him to insure the ship, and that he believed the plaintiff told him, she was, or had been an *English* ship, and might say something concerning the manner or intent of making her an *Ostend* ship; but that his answer was, that he would not enter into the manner, but that if the plaintiff would warrant her to be an *Ostend* ship, he would insure; and that on those terms, and no other, the agreement was made. There was the evidence of another person, who varied from *Knox*; in addition to which it was said, there was the evidence arising from circumstances, for that it was impossible for the plaintiff to intend to insure her as an *Ostend* ship, she being then in *London*, and could not be an *Ostend* ship without going to *Ostend*; for which proof was read that it was necessary she should be registered.

Lord Chancellor.—"The first question is, whether it sufficiently appears to the court, that this policy, which is a contract in writing, has been framed contrary to the intent and real agreement. It is certain, that to come at that, there ought to be the strongest proof possible, for the agreement is twice reduced into writing in the same words, and must have the same construction; and yet the plaintiff seeks, contrary to both these, to vary them, and that in a case where his witnesses vary from each other. The single deposition, upon which it depends, is very uncertain; and imports that they relied on the plaintiff's warranty, leaving the transaction relating to the manner of making her an *Ostend* ship entirely to himself. His Lordship, therefore, as there was no evidence to vary the contract from the written words, ordered the bill to be dismissed."

At the same time it must be observed, that cases frequently may, and do exist, in which a policy, upon proper evidence, may be altered, without any violation of the
[3] principles above laid down, and which has been often done by the courts both of law and equity; for let it be remembered once for all, that in questions of insurance, which is a contract founded upon broad equitable principles, courts of common law are bound by the same rules of decision as courts of equity. After signing, policies are likewise frequently

quently altered by *consent* of the parties, and such policies are good, agreeably to the maxim, *consensus tollit errorem*. CHAP. I.

An instance of the former kind of alteration of a policy occurs in the chancellorship of Lord *Hardwicke*, to whose decision we last referred. The insurance was upon the ship five hundred pounds, and the policy stated, that the adventure was to commence immediately *from the departure of the ship from Fort St. George to London*. The bill was brought by the plaintiff, suggesting that the owner had employed a Mr. *Halhead* to insure the ship with the defendants, to commence *from her arrival at Fort St. George*; that a label, agreeable to those instructions, with all the particulars of the agreement, had been entered in a book, and subscribed by *Halhead*, and two of the directors of the company; that by a *mistake* the policy was made out different from the label; that the ship being lost in the Bay of *Bengal*, *after* her arrival at *Fort Saint George*, but *before* her departure for *England*, the company refuse to pay; upon these suggestions, the plaintiff prayed that the mistake might be rectified, and that the company might be ordered to pay five hundred pounds with interest.

Motteux v. the Gov. and Comp. of the London Assurance. 1 Atkyns 545.

His Lordship was of opinion, that the label was a memorandum of the agreement, in which the material parts of the policy were inserted; that, although the policy was ambiguous, the label made it clear; and as it was only a mistake of the clerk, it ought to be rectified according to the label.

In an action upon a policy of insurance, and *non assumpsit* pleaded, the facts were, that *Stubbs*, a broker, had instructions to procure an insurance on goods on board the *Mary Galley, of Saint Christopher's, Captain A. Hill, commander*: that *Stubbs*, in writing the policy, by mistake, made the insurance on the *Mary, Captain Haslewood, commander*, which was subscribed by the defendant: that the *Mary Galley* was lost, and then *Stubbs* applied to the insurers to consent to alter the policy, to which they agreed. It was urged, that on account of the alteration, the defendant should have an increase of premium, the ship *Mary* being stouter than the *Mary Galley*. But *Holt*, chief justice, ruled,

Bates v. Grabham. Salk. 444.

[4]

CHAP. I.

ruled, that the action well lay upon the policy, and that the mistake might be set right.

A policy of insurance, when effected, becomes the property of the insured: and if it be *wrongfully* withheld, either by the broker employed by him to effect it, or by any other person to whose hands it may happen to come, he may maintain an action of trover for it, as well as for any other species of property.

Harding v. Carter and another. Sittings at Guildhall, Easter Vacation, 1781.

Thus an action of trover was brought against the defendants for two policies of insurance. The defendants were brokers, who had written to the plaintiff, the master of a vessel, that they had got two policies effected; the one on account of the plaintiff's cloaths and wages, the other on account of the owners, and that the underwriter was Mr. *Newnham*. A loss having happened, the defendants produced a policy, underwritten by one *J. S.* only insuring the ship, in which the plaintiff had no interest.

Lord *Mansfield*.—"I shall consider the defendants as the actual insurers, and therefore the plaintiff must prove his interest and loss. The defence set up was, that the letter above stated in evidence was written by the defendant's clerk through mistake; and it was said, that trover could not be maintained for that which never existed: but his Lordship would not suffer the defendants now to contradict their own representation; and the plaintiff accordingly had a verdict to the amount of his interest, the premium being deducted."

It is material to observe, that policies of insurance, though called *written* instruments, are, for the convenience of trade, and the dispatch of business, generally printed, leaving blanks for the insertion of names, and all other requisites. This being the case, it is frequently necessary to insert written clauses, in order to express the meaning of the parties to the contract, which, from some particular [5] circumstances, the printed form may not sufficiently explain. These written clauses and conditions, thus inserted, are to be considered as the real contract; the court will look to them to find out the intention of the parties, and will consequently suffer such conditions to control the printed words in policies of insurance.

Having

CHAP. I.

Having premifed thus much of policies in general, it may be proper to confider this fubject in a threefold point of view: Firft, what perfons may be infurers; Secondly, what things may be infured; Thirdly, what the requifites of a policy are.

1ft. What perfons may be infurers. It fhould feem, that by the common law and ufage of merchants, any perfon whatever might be an infurer, however unable he might be, from poverty to make up the loffes infured againft, provided the merchant was weak enough to truft to fuch a fecurity. In procefs of time, however, there were fo many who made a fhew of great wealth, in order to deceive the honeft and unfufpicious trader out of his premiums, and who were in infolvent circumftances, that it became an object of national concern, and parliamentary interference. The mifchiefs then exifting in this branch of trade, and the dangerous confequences thence arifing to the intereft of the country, are to be collected from the preamble of the ftatute, which paffed in the reign of *George* the First, to remedy thefe evils, and which has in fome, though not in any great degree, reftrained the rule of the common law as to the unlimited right any man or body of men had to become infurers. "Whereas it has been found by expe- 6 Geo. I. c. 18.
"rience, that many particular perfons, after they have re-
"ceived large premiums or confideration monies for or
"towards the infuring of fhips, goods, and merchandizes at
"fea, have become bankrupts, or otherwife failed in an-
"fwering or complying with their policies of affurance,
"whereby they were particularly engaged to make good,
"or contribute towards the loffes which merchants and
"traders have fuftained, to the ruin and impoverifhment of
"many merchants and traders, and to the difcouragement
"of adventurers at fea, and to the great diminution of the
"trade, wealth, ftrength, and public revenues of the king-
"dom: And whereas it is conceived, that if two feveral
"and diftinct corporations, with a competent joint ftock to
"each of them belonging, and under proper conditions, [6]
"reftrictions and regulations, were erected and eftablifhed
"for affurance of fhips, goods, or merchandizes at fea, or
"going to fea, (exclufive of all or any other corporations

"or

CHAP. I.

"or bodies politic already created, or hereafter to be "created, and likewife exclufive of fuch focieties or part-"nerfhips as now are, or may hereafter be entered into for "that purpofe) feveral merchants or traders, who adven-"ture their eftates, or part of their eftates, in fuch fhips, "goods, and merchandizes, at fea, or going to fea, (efpec-"ially in remote or hazardous voyages) would think it "much fafer for them to depend upon the policies or af-"furances of either of thofe two corporations, fo to be "erected and eftablifhed, than on the policies or affurances "of private or particular perfons." The ftatute then goes on to authorize his majefty to grant charters to two diftinct companies or corporations, for the infurance of fhips, goods, and merchandizes, at fea, or going to fea, and for lending money on bottomree. The ftatute alfo enacts that the corporations may purchafe lands to the amount of one thoufand pounds *per annum*, may have a common feal, and may be capable to fue and be fued at law; that each corporation fhall provide a fufficient ftock of ready money to fatisfy and difcharge all juft demands, arifing upon their policies of infurance; and in cafe of refufal, the parties infured may bring their action againft the corporation, and fhall

8 Geo. I. c. 15. f. 25. 11 Geo. I. c. 30. f. 43.

recover *double* damages and cofts. This claufe, however, giving double damages, was afterwards thought by the legiflature to be hard and oppreffive; and therefore, by a claufe in a fubfequent ftatute, thefe corporations were allowed to plead the general iffue to any action brought

Vide Poft. c. 20.

againft them; and the jury, in eftimating the damages, as well with refpect to them as any other perfons, were left to their own difcretion.

After feveral other claufes for the internal regulation of thefe corporations, the ftatute of the fixth of *Geo.* the Firft goes on to prohibit any other fociety or partnerfhip whatfoever from making infurances, or lending money on bottom-

Sec. 12.

ree. "And be it enacted, that from and after the grant-"ing or making the faid charters or indentures for erect-"ing the two corporations before mentioned, and paffing "the fame under the great feal, for and during the contin-"uance of the faid corporations refpectively, or either "of them, all other corporations or bodies politic, be-

"fore

" fore this time erected or established, or hereafter to be " erected or established, whether such corporations or " bodies politic, or any of them, be sole or aggregate, and " all such societies and partnerships as now are, or here- " after shall or may be, entered into by any person or per- " sons, for assuring ships or merchandizes at sea, or for " lending money on bottomree, shall, by force and virtue " of this act, be restrained from granting, signing, or un- " derwriting any policy of assurance, or making any con- " tracts for assurance of or upon any ship or ships, goods, " or merchandizes, at sea, or going to sea, and for lending " any monies by way of bottomree as aforesaid: and if " any corporation or body politic, or persons acting in " such society or partnership (other than the two corpo- " rations intended to be established by this act, or one of " them) shall presume to grant, sign, or underwrite, after " the twenty-fourth day of *June* 1720, any such policy " or policies, or make any such contract or contracts for " assurance of or upon any ship or ships, goods or mer- " chandizes, at sea or going to sea, or take or agree to " take any premium or other reward for such policy or " policies, every such policy and policies of assurance of " or upon any such ship or ships, goods or merchandizes, " shall be *ipso facto* void, and all and every such sum or " sums so signed and underwritten in such policy or poli- " cies shall be forfeited, and shall and may be recovered, " one half to the use of his majesty, the other to that of " the informer, by action: and if any corporation or " bodies politic, or persons acting in such society or part- " nership, other than the two corporations intended to be " erected by this act, or one of them, shall presume to " lend, or agree to lend, or advance, by themselves or " any others on their behalf, after the said twenty-fourth " day of *June* 1720, any money by way of bottomree " contrary to this act, the bond or other security for the " same shall be *ipso facto* void, and such agreement shall be " adjudged to be an usurious contract, and the offenders " therein shall suffer as in cases of usury: nevertheless it " is intended and hereby declared, that any private or par- " ticular person or persons shall be at liberty to write or

" underwrite

CHAP. I.

" underwrite any policies, or engage himſelf or herſelf in " any aſſurance of, for, or upon any ſhip or ſhips, goods " or merchandizes at ſea, or going to ſea, or may lend mon- " ey by way of bottomree, as fully and beneficially, as " if this act had never been made, ſo as the ſame be not " on the account or riſque of a corporation or body poli- " tic, or upon the account or riſque of perſons acting in a " ſociety or partnerſhip for that purpoſe as aforeſaid."

Sullivan v. Greaves. Sittings after Eaſter 1789.

Upon this clauſe of the ſtatute, a queſtion lately aroſe at *Guildhall.* It was an action brought againſt the defendant to recover a ſum of money received by him from one *Briſtow* to the plaintiff's uſe. The plaintiff was an underwriter, and the defendant was a broker; and a loſs having happened upon a policy underwritten by the plaintiff, he had been obliged to pay it: but *Briſtow,* having agreed to take half the plaintiff's riſk, had paid his moiety of the loſs into the hands of the defendant, to recover it from whom this action was brought.

Lord *Kenyon,* C. J.—"I am of opinion that the plaintiff cannot recover; for this is clearly a partnerſhip within the act of parliament. If a ſingle name appears upon the policy, as in this caſe, the inſurer ſhall never be allowed, if a loſs happen, to defeat a *bonâ fide* inſurance, by ſaying to an innocent perſon, there was a ſceret partnerſhip between another and myſelf; and therefore the policy is void. But here the plaintiff is himſelf the underwriter, who comes to enforce an illegal contract: it is a partnerſhip *pro hac vice*: and this party cannot apply to a Court of Juſtice to enforce a contract founded in a breach of the law."

No motion was ever made to ſet aſide the nonſuit; but two or three days after, Lord *Kenyon* took occaſion to mention to the Bar, that he had ſtated the caſe to the other Judges of the Court of *King's Bench,* who were unanimouſly of the ſame opinion with his Lordſhip.

Mitchell and others, aſſignees of Robertſon a bankrupt, v. Cockburn, aſſignee of Tyler a bankrupt, 2 H. Blac. Rep. in C. P. 379.

In a very modern caſe, the deciſion in *Sullivan* v. *Greaves* came under diſcuſſion in the court of *Common Pleas,* and the opinion given by Lord *Kenyon* was confirmed by the unanimous opinion of that Court.

The facts were, that the two bankrupts were engaged in a partnerſhip for the inſurance of ſhips, which was carried

on

on in the name of *Robertson*, who, at the time of his bankruptcy, had paid a much larger ſum for loſſes than he had received for premiums; and to recover a moiety of this ſum from *Tyler*'s eſtate was the object of this action. The Lord Chief Juſtice *Eyre* having nonſuited the plaintiffs at the trial, and a motion having been made to ſet the nonſuit aſide, the learned Judges, after argument at the bar, delivered their opinions.

Ld. Ch. J. *Eyre*.—"This queſtion depends on the true conſtruction of the ſtat. 6 *Geo.* 1. c. 18. By that act, the two corporations became the purchaſers of the excluſive privilege of inſuring on a joint ſtock; and to give effect to that privilege all other perſons are prohibited from inſuring on a joint ſtock. Now it appears clearly on the firſt view, that the proviſions of the act are at an end, if a perſon, by merely inſuring in his own name, can have the advantage of a joint capital, which the act meant to prohibit. This partnerſhip therefore is contrary to the ſpirit of the act; and it is alſo contrary to the letter of it. The 12th ſection directs, that all ſocieties, &c.* This does not at all go to confine the meaning of the legiſlature to an avowed partnerſhip, inſuring publickly in their own names; but the object is to prevent any other joint ſtock being embarked in inſuring. This being ſo, the conſequence unavoidably is, that no contract can ariſe directly out of ſuch a proceeding, ſo as to be the foundation of an action."

Mr. *J. Heath*.—"I am of the ſame opinion. It ſeems to me that the object of the ſtatute would be totally defeated, if it were to extend only to thoſe policies, in which the names of all the partners were inſerted. It expreſsly declares, that every policy ſubſcribed by any perſon acting in a partnerſhip ſhall be abſolutely null and void, though it may be true that the party ſubſcribing, ſhall be eſtopped from ſetting up a ſecret partnerſhip to defeat a *bonâ fide* inſurance. And the reaſon is obvious; trade is carried on according to the capital employed. Now the inſurances would run to the extent of the capital, in whatever name the policy might be ſubſcribed. The

* Vide ſupra, p. 6.

CHAP. I. The object therefore of the ſtatute was to prevent the employment of a joint capital, which would afford the greateſt competition with the eſtabliſhed corporations."

Mr. *J. Rooke.*—"As to the ſecond point, I agree that if the contract be illegal, no action can ariſe out of it. But as to the firſt queſtion, whether this contract were illegal or not, I muſt confeſs I had great doubts, till I heard the opinions of my Lord Chief Juſtice and my brother *Heath*, and alſo the caſe cited from *Park's Inſurance*, for it ſeemed to me that the ſtatute only meant to prohibit inſurances where both parties knew that a partnerſhip exiſted, but not where there was a ſleeping partnerſhip. But I was very much ſtruck with the obſervations of my brother *Heath*, that the extent of the inſurance would be in proportion to the capital employed, and if there were an increaſed capital, there would be an increaſed rivalſhip with the corporations. Whatever doubts therefore I had, I ſubmit to the authority of the other Judges."

Booth v. Hodgſon, 6 Term Rep. 405, Acc.

Rule for ſetting aſide the nonſuit was diſcharged.

Sec. 24. 26. 28. There are clauſes, in a ſubſequent part of the ſtatute, ſecuring to the *South Sea* and *Eaſt India* Companies all the rights and privileges which they had enjoyed previous to the paſſing of that act, and the right of lending money on bottomree to the captains of their own ſhips.

This ſtatute is the only poſitive regulation to be found in the law of this country, with reſpect to what perſons ſhall, or ſhall not be inſurers. By virtue of that regulation, the two offices under the names of the *Royal Exchange Aſſurance* [9] Office, and the *London Aſſurance* Office were created and eſtabliſhed, by charter of *George* the Firſt, under the great ſeal of *Great Britain*, bearing date the twenty-ſecond day of *June*, in the ſixth year of his reign; and they ſtill continue offices for the inſurance of property. The legiſlature having thus anxiouſly provided for the ſecurity of thoſe merchants, who might be deſirous of carrying on an extenſive trade, but who were deterred from doing ſo, through fear of the inſolvency of underwriters, having ſtipulated with the company that they ſhould have ſufficient funds for the payment of all demands

mands that might be made, and, at the fame time, allowing to private underwriters the full liberty of infuring to any amount with thofe who were fatisfied to truft to their private fecurities only; it is not to be wondered at, that the bufinefs of infurance increafed to a degree almoft inconceivable. Indeed, any perfon, fince this ftatute, may infure as at the common law, with this fingle exception, that any policy fubfcribed by a private firm or partnerfhip, is abfolutely void.

2dly. What things may be infured. I beg leave here to premife, that I do not mean at prefent to go into the great queftion of infurance, *upon intereft or no intereft*, having referved that for the fubject of a diftinct chapter. My defign in this place is only to fhew, what kinds of property are the fubject of infurance, upon fuppofition that every perfon, making infurance, is interefted in the goods as the law requires.

The moft frequent fubjects of infurance are fhips, goods, merchandizes, the freight or hire of fhips: alfo houfes, ware-houfes, and the goods laid up in them from danger by fire, and infurance on lives. Of the two laft of which, more will be faid hereafter. But although infurances upon fuch property as we have juft enumerated, moft frequently occur in practice; yet in the law books we meet with cafes which can hardly fall within any of thofe defcriptions. 1 Magens 4. See poft. chap. 22 and 23.

Thus bottomree and *refpondentia* are a particular fpecies of property which may be the fubject of infurance. But then it muft be particularly expreffed in the policy to be *refpondentia* intereft; for under a general infurance on *goods*, the party infured cannot recover money lent on bottomree. Such has been, and is at this day, the eftablifhed ufage of merchants.

This was folemnly decided in an action upon a policy of infurance "upon *goods and merchandizes*, loaden, or to be [10]

"loaden

CHAP. I.

Glover v. Black, 3 Burrow 1394. and 1 Blackstone Rep. 405.

"loaden aboard the *Denham*, *William Tryon*, commander, "at and from *Bengal*, to any ports or places whatsoever in "the *East Indies*, until her safe arrival in *London*." The evidence appeared to be, that before the signing of the policy, the plaintiff had lent Captain *Tryon*, *upon the goods*, then loaden, and to be loaden on board the said ship, on account of the said Captain *Tryon*, the sum of seven hundred and sixty-four pounds, at *respondentia*, for which a bond was executed in the usual form: that the ship, at the time of the loss, had goods and merchandizes on board, the property of Captain *Tryon*, of greater value than all the money he had borrowed: that the ship was afterwards burnt, and all the goods and merchandizes were totally consumed and lost. Upon these facts, the question was, whether the plaintiff could recover. This case was twice argued at the bar; the court took time to consider it, and were unanimous in their determination.

Lord *Mansfield*.—"I inclined, at the trial, and since upon the argument, to support this insurance, being convinced that it is fair, and that the doubt has arisen by a slip in omitting to specify (as it was intended to have been done) that this was a *respondentia* interest. The ground of supporting this insurance, if it could have been supported, was a clause of the 19 *G.* 2. c. 37. *s.* 5. which, as to the purpose of insurance, considers the borrower as having a right to insure only for the surplus value, over and above the money he has borrowed at *respondentia*. Yet we are all satisfied that this act of parliament never meant, or intended to make, any alteration in the manner of insurances; its view was to prevent gaming or wagering policies, where the insurer had no interest at all; and if the lender of money at *respondentia* were to be at liberty to insure for more than his whole interest, it would be a gaming policy; for it is obvious, that if he could insure all the goods, and insure his *respondentia* interest besides, this would amount to an insurance beyond his whole interest. In describing *respondentia* interest, the act gives the lender *alone* a right to make insurance on the money

[11]

money lent : fo that the act left it on the practice. I have looked into the practice, and I find that bottomree and *refpondentia* are a *particular fpecies* of infurance in themfelves, and have taken a particular denomination. I cannot find even a *dictum* in any writer, foreign or domeftic, that the *refpondentia* creditor may infure upon the *goods, as goods*. I find too, by talking with intelligent perfons very converfant in the knowledge and practice of infurances, that they always do mention *refpondentia* intereft, whenever they mean to infure it. It might be greatly inconvenient to introduce a practice *contrary to general ufage*, and there may be fome opening to fraud if it be not fpecified. The ground of our refolution is, "That it is now eftablifhed, as the law and practice of "merchants, that *refpondentia* and bottomree muft be fpeci-"fied and mentioned in the policy of infurance."

It is to be obferved, that in this judgment the court confined itfelf entirely to the cafe then before it, but did not mean to decide, that a perfon, having a fpecial intereft in goods, could not recover under an infurance upon goods generally. Lord *Mansfield*, indeed, exprefsly faid, at the conclufion of his argument, that they did not mean to determine, that no fpecial intereft in goods might be given in evidence, in other cafes than in thofe of *refpondentia* and bottomree, if the circumftances of the cafe fhould happen to admit of it. The lien which a factor, to whom a balance is due, has upon the goods of his principal, comes under the exception taken by the court; and an infurance upon fuch an intereft feems to have been admitted, if not abfolutely held, to be good, in the cafe of *Godin* v. *London* Affurance Company, which will be fully ftated in that part of this work, which treats of double infurances.

3 Burr. 1401.

1 Burr. 489.

But although the cafe of *Glover* and *Black* is certainly good law, yet it has fince been ruled, that money expended by the captain for the ufe of the fhip, and for which *refpondentia* intereft was charged, may be recovered under an infurance on *goods, fpecie, and effects*, provided the ufage of the

CHAP. I.

the trade, which in matters of insurance is always of great weight, sanctions it.

Gregory v. Christie, B. R. Trinity, 24 Geo. III.

[12]

Thus in an action upon a policy of insurance *on goods, specie, and effects*, of the plaintiff, who was also the captain on board the ship, the plaintiff claimed under that insurance, money expended by him in the course of the voyage for the use of the ship, and for which he charged *respondentia* interest.

Lord *Mansfield*, after delivering his opinion upon another point, which arose in the cause, and which will be mentioned in another part of this work, said, as to the second question, whether the words "*goods, specie, and effects*" extended to this interest, I should think not, if we were only to consider the words made use of. But here there is *an express usage*, which must govern our decision. A great many captains in the *East India* service swear, that this kind of interest is always insured in this way, and I observe the person here insured is the *captain*.

1 Magens 18.

By the marine regulations of most, if not of all, the trading powers in *Europe*, insurances upon the wages of seamen are forbidden; a regulation founded in wisdom and sound policy. In *Great Britain*, a great and commercial nation, such an ordinance is particularly necessary, and it is agreeable to the policy of the general law of that country, by which it is declared, "That no master or owner of any "merchant ship shall pay to any seaman, beyond the seas, "any money or effects on account of wages, exceeding one "moiety of the wages due, at the time of such payment, "till such ship shall return to *Great Britain* or *Ireland*." By this salutary law, the sailors are interested in the return of the ship; they will, on that account, be prevented from deserting it when abroad, from leaving it unmanned, and in times of danger, arising either from perils of the sea, or the attacks of an enemy, will be more anxious for its preservation. But these good effects would be entirely defeated, if

8 Geo. 1. ch. 24. f. 7.

if insurance on their wages were to be permitted; for to whatever cause the loss might be attributed, they would still be secure. However, it should seem, that this regulation does not mean to prevent mariners from insuring those wages, which they are entitled to receive abroad, or goods which they have purchased with those wages in order to bring them home; but, in such a case, they are to be considered in the same light with other men. 1 Magens 19.

In an action upon a policy of insurance upon *Fort Marlborough*, otherwise *Bencoolen*, in the *East Indies*, for twelve calendar months, from the first of *October* 1759, to the first of *October* 1760, against any *European* enemy, for the benefit of the governor, it was doubted by the learned chief justice who tried that cause, whether a policy against the loss of *Fort Marlborough* for the benefit of the governor was good, upon the principle which does not allow a sailor to insure his wages. But afterwards, when he came to deliver the opinion of the court upon all the points in that cause, after mentioning this doubt, which had occurred to his mind, he went on thus: "But considering that this place though "called a fort, was really but a factory or settlement for trade; "and that he, though called a governor, was really but a mer-"chant; considering too, that the law allows a captain of "a ship to insure goods which he has on board, or his share "in the ship, if he be a part owner; and the captain of a "privateer, if he be a part owner, to insure his share; con-"sidering too, that the objection could not, upon any "ground of justice, be made by the insurer, who knew him "to be the governor at the time he took the premium; and "as with regard to principles of public convenience, the "case so seldom happens, (I never knew one before) any "danger from the example is little to be apprehended; I did "not think myself warranted, upon that point, to nonsuit "the plaintiff; especially too, as the objection did not come "from the bar. Though this point was mentioned, it was "not insisted upon at the last trial; nor has it been seriously "argued, upon this motion, as sufficient alone to vacate the "policy: and if it had, we are all of opinion, that we are "not warranted to say, that it is void upon that account."

Carter v. Boehm, 3 Burr. 1905. and 1 Blackst. 593.

[13]

Lord Mansfield.

CHAP. I.

It has long been a queſtion, how far inſurances upon the ſhips or goods of enemies are politic or legal. Upon the continent of *Europe* it ſhould ſeem, that they are in general abſolutely prohibited, under penalty of the inſurance being void, and the delinquent's forfeiting the ſum, to which he had ſubſcribed. Theſe laws have been paſſed from an idea, that ſuch inſurances are prejudicial to the intereſt of the country tolerating ſuch contracts, by enabling an enemy to continue his trade, on account of the [14] degree of protection thus afforded him againſt the maritime ſtrength of the nation making the inſurance. In *England*, till very lately, this queſtion has been undecided: but the court of King's Bench have, in two very modern inſtances, been unanimouſly of opinion that ſuch inſurances are illegal and abſolutely void. I ſhall, however, when I come to the chapter on illegal voyages, ſtate the arguments on both ſides of this important queſtion. In this place I ſhall only obſerve, that in the year 1748, a bill was introduced into parliament, "to prevent aſſurances on ſhips belonging to *France*, and on merchandizes and effects laden "thereon, during the then exiſting war with *France*." That bill was oppoſed on principles of policy and expediency, by the two greateſt lawyers and moſt eminent ſpeakers of that age, the Honourable *William Murray* and Sir *Dudley Ryder*; but the legiſlature thought proper to paſs the bill into a law, inflicting a penalty of 500 *l.* upon the perſons making ſuch inſurances, and alſo declaring the policy to be void.

Ord. of Stockholm. Bynkerſhoek's Queſt. Juris. pub. lib. 1. c. 21. p. 153.

Brandon v. Neſbitt, and Briſtow v. Towers. 6 Term. Rep. 23 and 35.

Deb. in Houſe of Com. by Debrett, vol. ii. p. 171.

21 Geo. II. c. 4.

The exiſtence of that act, however, was limited by the duration of the then war. But in the preſent war a ſimilar legiſlative proviſion has been made, declaring that inſurances in the act mentioned ſhall not only be void, but the offending perſon ſhall be impriſoned three months. This ſtatute is alſo temporary; but the deciſions above alluded to, and which will be fully quoted hereafter, have determined that all inſurances upon the property of an open enemy are void, independent of the acts of parliament.

33 Geo. III. c. 27. ſ. 4.

ment. It is not to be diſſembled that theſe deciſions are rather in oppoſition to the ſentiments of Lord *Mansfield* and Lord *Hardwicke*: for although the caſe does not ſeem ever to have come for a judicial opinion before them, yet it is evident, from what they have declared both in parliament and on the bench, that on principles of expediency, those illuſtrious men were inclined to ſupport ſuch inſurances, although it ſhould ſeem, with all deference to ſuch names, that even the expediency of the meaſure may greatly be doubted.

1 Vez. 320. Giſt v. Maſon. Sittings at Guildhall, Mich. Vac. 1785.

One ſpecies of inſurance on foreign ſhips or goods was prohibited by ſtatute, with a view to ſecure to the *Eaſt India* company the ſole trade to and from the *Eaſt Indies*, and other places, beyond the *Cape of Good Hope*. The ſtatute, after reciting, that to admit of inſurances on the ſhips or veſſels of foreigners trading to the *Eaſt Indies*, may be a means of encouraging his majeſty's ſubjects to ſhare with foreigners, in eſtabliſhing new ſocieties or companies for carrying on the ſaid trade in the dominions of foreign ſtates or princes, enacts, "That no inſurances ſhall "be made, or money lent on bottomree, on foreign ſhips "or goods, bound to or from the *Eaſt Indies*, under the "forfeiture of treble the ſum inſured or lent." It contains an exception, however, in favour of inſurances made, or to be made, on ſhips of the ſubjects of ſuch ſovereigns as carried on a trade with that part of the world previous to the month of *October* 1748. This act was to be in force for ſeven years. Whether upon a trial it was found to be a politic or wiſe regulation, I have not been able to diſcover: but the preſumption is to the contrary; as it does not appear from the ſtatute book, that this act of parliament was continued, or that it was revived by any ſubſequent ſtatute.

25 Geo. II. c. 26.

[15]

3dly. Of the requiſites of a policy. The form of a policy, now uſed in *London*, is nearly the ſame which was adopted two hundred years ago, as may be collected from

 Malyne,

CHAP. I. *Malyne*; but its antiquity cannot preserve it from just censure, it being very irregular and confused, and frequently ambiguous, from making use of the same words in different senses.

Malyne 108. 2 Burr. 1555.

The essentials in the contract of insurance are: First, the name of the person for whom the insurance is made: Secondly, the names of the ship and master: Thirdly, whether they are ships, goods, or merchandizes, upon which the insurance is made: Fourthly, the name of the place where the goods are laden, and whither they are bound: Fifthly, the time when the risk begins, and when it ends: Sixthly, all the various perils and risks which the insurer takes upon himself: Seventhly, the consideration, or premium, paid for the risk or hazard run: Eighthly, the month, day, and year, on which the policy is executed: Ninthly, the stamps required by act of parliament. Of each of these in their order.

First, Of the name of the person insured. It was formerly very much the practice to effect policies of insurance, *in blank* as it was called, that is, without specifying the names of the persons, for whose use and benefit, or on whose account such insurances were made; a practice, which had been found in many respects to be mischievous, and productive of great inconveniences. These evils were remedied at a very early period in *Genoa* and *France* by the marine ordinances of those countries, which required the name of the person insured to be inserted in the policy, and whether he was to be considered in the capacity of principal or factor. In *England* a similar regulation took place in the year 1774, with respect to insurances upon lives; but it was not till the year 1785, that any provision was made for this evil in policies upon ships and merchandizes.

2 Magens 65. 169.

14 Geo. III. c. 48.

[16]

The statute declares, "That from and after the fifth day "of *July* 1785, it shall not be lawful for any person or "persons, who reside in *Great Britain*, to make, or cause

25 Geo. III. c. 44.

"to

" to be made, any policy or policies of insurance upon his, " her, or their interest in any ship or ships, or any goods, " merchandizes, effects, or other property, without insert- " ing in such policy or policies, *his, her, or their own* " *name or names*, as the person interested therein, or the " *name or names of the person or persons*, who shall effect " the same, *as the agent or agents* of the person or persons " so really interested therein, or for whose use or benefit, " or on whose account, such policy or policies is or are " underwrote: and that it shall not be lawful for any per- " son or persons, who shall not live or reside in *Great* " *Britain*, to make, or cause to be made, any policy or " policies of assurance upon his, her, or their interest in " any ship or ships, or on any goods, merchandizes, ef- " fects, or other property, without inserting in such pol- " icy or policies the name or names of the agent or agents " of the person or persons so really interested therein, and " for whose use or benefit, or on whose account, the same " is or are so made and underwrote: and that every policy " or policies of assurance, made or underwrote contrary to " the true intent and meaning hereof, shall be null and void " to all intents and purposes."

See Cox and another, Executors, v. Parry. 1 Term Rep. 464. in which it was held that the Executors could not recover, because, amongst other grounds, the name of their Testator was not inserted in the policy.

Upon the statute just recited, a question of some consequence very soon arose, namely, Whether, when the agent effects a policy for the principal residing abroad, it be necessary to insert his name in the policy, *as agent*. Upon a debate, it was held, that if it be not stated, that he effected the policy, *as the agent* of the principal, the policy will be void within the statute. Another question also occurred in the same cause, Whether it was not the intention of the legislature, when the principal resided abroad, that the agent should live in *England*. It did not become necessary for the court to decide the latter question; but the leaning of the judges clearly was in the affirmative. The case was thus:

An

CHAP. I.

Pray and others verf. Edie, 1 Term Rep. p. 313. for Trinity, 26 Geo. III.

An action was brought upon a policy of infurance on a ship and its cargo from *Sunbury*, in *Georgia*, to *Amfterdam*; and it was agreed, that a verdict fhould be taken for the plaintiffs, and that the defendant's counfel fhould have the liberty of moving the court to fet it afide, and enter a verdict for the defendant, (without cofts) if, upon the conftruction of the 25th of *George* the Third, chap. 44. the court fhould be of opinion, that the plaintiffs were not entitled to recover. At the trial before Mr. Juftice *Buller* it appeared, that the plaintiffs lived in *Georgia*, and had formerly been owners of the veffel, but, before *May* 1785, had transferred their property in her to one *Pierce*, who refided in the fame country. The names of the plaintiffs were at the head of the policy, which was underwritten by the defendant in *September* 1785; and the declaration ftated, that they made it for the benefit of *Pierce*, in whom the intereft was averred to be. Upon thefe facts the two queftions arofe: Firft, Whether when an agent effects a policy for his principal refiding abroad, the ftatute requires that fuch agent's name fhould be inferted, *eo nomine*, as agent? Secondly, Whether, under the fame act, it be neceffary that the agent fhould live in *England* when the principal was abroad?

Lord *Mansfield*.—" Whatever doubts I may have in my own mind with refpect to the policy and expedience of this law, yet as long as it continues in force, I am bound to fee it executed according to its meaning; and however I may think that this is not a commendable defence in the underwriter, yet that is a matter for his confideration, and not for mine. I have not a particle of doubt as to the true conftruction of this act. Let us confider what are the mifchiefs intended to be remedied, and the provifions of the act for remedying them. The preamble recites, that great inconveniencies had arifen from omitting to infert in policies of infurance, the names of the perfons for whofe benefit, or on whofe account, fuch policies were effected. That is the mifchief: and it is remedied by enacting, that if *the principal*

principal resides in England, his *own* name shall be inserted, or what amounts to the same thing, the name of his *agent*, *eo nomine*, *as agent for him*. If the agent were not to be named in the policy, in the capacity of *agent for the insured*, the public would still be left ignorant who the insured was; and the principal intention of the act would be defeated. Then as to the case of the insured *living abroad*, who *cannot insure in his own name*, there can be no doubt but that the name of his agent must be inserted, *eo nomine*, *as agent*. I am also strongly inclined to think, that the other objection, with regard to the residence of the agent, is good; but it is not necessary to give a direct opinion on that point." [18]

Mr. Justice *Buller*.—"It seems to me to have been the intention of the legislature, that the name of the agent, who effects the policy for his principal residing abroad, should be inserted in the policy, *quasi agent for such person*. For the word "agent," in the second clause, is to be understood in the same sense as it is taken in the first; and I have as little doubt that the meaning of the act is, that such agent should reside in *Great Britain*.

Mr. Justice *Willes* and Mr. Justice *Ashhurst* were of the same opinion: and the rule was made absolute.

If there are more persons interested than one, it is absolutely necessary that the names of all should be inserted, otherwise the policy is void: Nor will any other description answer the design of the statute. Thus in a case, where there were several plaintiffs, the policy was made "*In the name of Mr. William Wilton and the rest of the* "*owners*," Mr. Justice *Buller* held the policy was void under the statute.

Wilton and others v. Reafton, B R. at Guildhall Sittings after Michaelmas 1787.

The decisions, which have been made upon this statute have now become very immaterial; and are only preserved to shew the complete history of that branch of the law, which

CHAP. I. which we are difcuffing: for fuch mifchiefs and inconveniencies were found to arife to perfons interefted in fhips 28 Geo. III. ch. 56. or veffels from that act of parliament; that by a fubfequent ftatute, it was wholly repealed. But it was not deemed expedient again to allow of policies in blank; and therefore the fame ftatute declared, "That it fhould not be "lawful, from and after the paffing of that act, for any "perfon or perfons, to make or effect, or caufe to be "made or effected, any policy of affurance on any fhip or "veffel, or upon any goods, merchandizes, effects, or "other property whatfoever, without firft inferting, or "caufing to be inferted in fuch policy, the name or names, "or the ufual ftile and firm of dealing of one or more of [19] "the perfons interefted in fuch affurance; or without, in-"ftead thereof, firft inferting the name or names of the "ufual ftile and firm of dealing of the confignor or con-"fignors, confignee or confignees, of the goods or prop-"erty fo to be infured; or the name or names, or the ufual "ftile and firm of dealing of the perfon or perfons refid-"ing in *Great Britain*, who fhall receive the order for and "effect fuch policy, or of the perfon or perfons who fhall "give the order or directions to the agent or agents imme-"diately employed to negociate or effect fuch policy. The "ftatute further declares that every policy made or under-"wrote contrary to the true intent and meaning of this "act, fhall be null and void to all intents and purpofes."

French v. Backhoufe. 5 Bur. 2727. Previous to the paffing of either of thefe acts it was held, that the hufband of a fhip had no right to infure for any part-owner, without his particular direction; nor for all the owners in general, without their general direction, or fomething equivalent to it.

Secondly, of the names of the fhip and mafter. I do not find any exprefs regulation of this matter in *England*; but it feems to be neceffary, by the law and ufage of merchants, to infert the names of the fhip and mafter, in order to fix with precifion the bottom upon which the adventure

CHAP. I.

ture is to be made, and the captain, by whoſe direction the ſhip is to be navigated, becauſe, according to the degree of ſtrength and ſufficiency of the one, and the ſkill, ability, and knowledge of the other, the riſk is increaſed or diminiſhed; and ſo alſo probably will the amount of the premium be regulated. The uſage of the merchants of *England* in this reſpect is agreeable to the expreſs laws and regulations of other maritime ſtates upon this point. Sometimes, however, there are inſurances generally "*upon any ſhip or ſhips*" expected from a particular place: and although it is more accurate to inſert the name of the captain, I would not be underſtood to aſſert, as no deciſion has been made, that if a different captain came in the ſhip from that whoſe name is mentioned in the policy, it would therefore be void; eſpecially as the policy always contains the words "or whoſoever elſe ſhall go for maſter in the ſaid ſhip."

Ord. of Lew. 14 tit. Inſurance, art. 3. Ord. of Amſterdam, ſ. 2.

[19 *a*]

Since the publication of the two former editions of this work, the validity of theſe inſurances *upon ſhip or ſhips* was very elaborately diſcuſſed in the court of Common Pleas, and the judgment of the court, conſiſting of Lord Chief Juſtice *Eyre*, Mr. Juſtice *Buller*, Mr. Juſtice *Heath*, and Mr. Juſtice *Rooke*, was unanimous in their favour; and that the aſſured had a right to cover by ſuch policy whatever ſhip he thought proper, that fell within the terms of it. The facts of the caſe were theſe—On the 24th *May* 1793, *Freeland* and *Rigby*, merchants at *St. Vincents*, wrote to the plaintiffs, merchants at *Liverpool*, who were alſo partners in a houſe of the ſame name at *Grenada*, requeſting them to get 1,260 *l.* inſured on 70 bales of cotton ſhipped on board the *Elizabeth*, from *Grenada* to *England*, and alſo 1,300*l.* on another cargo of cotton and other goods, which they intended to ſhip on board *ſome other ſhip* that ſhould ſail with the firſt convoy, and therefore directed the latter inſurance to be *on ſhip or ſhips*. The plaintiffs accordingly, by their broker, inſured 1,260 *l.* on board the *Elizabeth* in *London*, and 1,300 *l.* on board *ſhip or ſhips*, viz. 700 *l.* at *Liverpool*, and 600 *l.* in *London*. The policy for 700 *l.* of

Kewley and another v. Ryan, 2 H. Blackſt. Rep. p. 343. See this caſe again quoted for another point, poſt. c. 17. p. 316.

CHAP. I.

of which the defendant underwrote 50 *l.* and on which the action was brought, was *at and from Grenada to Liverpool*, on any kind of goods as intereſt ſhould appear, *in ſhip or ſhips on account of Freeland and Rigby*, warranted to ſail on or before the 1ſt of *Auguſt* 1793, and to return 3 *per cent.* if the ſhip ſailed with convoy bound to *Great Britain*, and arrived, &c. without any exception of the goods on board the *Elizabeth*. The policy for 600 *l.* effected in *London*, was alſo *on ſhip or ſhips*, at and from *Grenada* to *Liverpool*, but with an exception of 1,260 *l.* "on 70 bales of "cotton *per Elizabeth, Crettin*," the ſame underwriters in *London* having before ſubſcribed the policy on the *Elizabeth*. But the plaintiffs did not communicate to the underwriters at *Liverpool*, the Letter of *Freeland* and *Rigby*, directing an inſurance on the *Elizabeth*, nor any circumſtance reſpecting the goods ſhipped on board the *Elizabeth*, and the inſurance made on that ſhip. The *Elizabeth* ſailed early in *June*, and arrived ſafe at *Liverpool* in *Auguſt* 1793. The *Heart of Oak*, on board of which *Freeland* and *Rigby* had ſhipped their ſecond cargo of cotton, &c. ſailed the latter end of *July*, bound for *Liverpool*, but with a deſign *formed before the commencement of the voyage* (as appeared by clearances, and was admitted on all ſides) to touch at *Cork* in her way to *Liverpool*, but was totally loſt before ſhe arrived at the dividing point. The defendant pleaded the general iſſue, and a tender of 1 *l.* 10 *s.* on account of the ſafe arrival of the *Elizabeth*, which plaintiff took out of court, and obtained a verdict for 48 *l.* 10 *s.*

A rule having been obtained to ſhew cauſe, why there ſhould not be a new trial on ſeveral grounds, the court diſcharged the rule, declaring as to this point, that the legality of the policy on *ſhip or ſhips* was too well eſtabliſhed, both by uſage and authority, to be diſputed: As to the ſecond, that the aſſured had clearly a right to apply ſuch an inſurance to whatever ſhip he thought proper, within the terms of it; for which the caſe of *Henchman* v. *Offley*, was an authority.

B. R. Michael. 23 Geo. III. See that caſe fully reported. 2 H. Black. Rep. 345. Note (*a*).

It

It has alſo been held, that the owners of goods inſured by the act of ſhifting the goods from one ſhip to another, do not preclude themſelves from recovering an average loſs arifing from the capture of the ſecond ſhip, if they acted from neceſſity, and for the benefit of all concerned.

Plantamour v. Staples, 1 Term R. 611. note(*a*) upon a caſe reſerved.

Thirdly, whether they are ſhips, goods, or merchandizes, upon which the inſurance is made, is a fact which muſt be ſtated. It is abſolutely neceſſary that there ſhould be a ſpecification upon which of theſe the underwriter inſures; becauſe otherwiſe it would be impoſſible to know, whether, in any inſtance, he is liable or not to the loſs ſuſtained. But it is another queſtion, whether, in policies upon goods, it be neceſſary to declare the particulars. The practice, I believe, is very unſettled. It is the opinion, however, of a very reſpectable merchant, that the particulars of goods ſhould be ſpecified, if poſſible, by their marks, numbers, and packages, rather than that they ſhould be included under the general denomination of merchandize; or that if it be agreed to inſert them when known to the inſured, care ſhould be taken not to omit it, as ſuch ſpecification prevents much trouble in proving to the inſurer the particular goods inſured, which are, more or leſs, ſubject to damage. But this mode of particularizing property is only adviſeable to be done, or, indeed, can only be done when the riſk commences at home; becauſe, when goods are coming from abroad, it is better to inſure under general expreſſions, on account of the various caſualties, which may happen to obſtruct the purchaſe of the commodities intended to be ſent. It may be proper here to mention, that there are certain kinds of merchandize, which are of a periſhable nature, and liable to early corruption; on account of which, the underwriters of *London* have inſerted a memorandum at the foot of their policy, by which they declare, that in inſurances upon corn, fiſh, ſalt, fruit, flour, and ſeed, they will not be anſwerable for any partial loſs, but only for general averages, except the ſhip be ſtranded. That in inſurances on ſugar, tobacco, hemp, flax, hides, and

1 Magens 8.

Vide the Append. No. 1.

CHAP. I.

and ſkins, they conſider themſelves free from partial loſſes, not amounting to *five per cent.* and that on all other goods, as well as on the ſhip and freight, if the partial loſs be under *three pounds per cent.* unleſs it ariſe from a general average, or the ſtranding of the ſhip, they alſo conſider themſelves diſcharged.

[21]

Per Buller Juſtice in Cocking, v. Fraſer. B. R. Eaſt. 25 Geo. III. vide Poſt.

This clauſe was introduced in the year 1749, in order to prevent the underwriters from being haraſſed by trifling demands, which muſt neceſſarily have ariſen upon every inſurance of this kind, on account of the periſhable nature of the cargo. The form of this memorandum was univerſally uſed, as well by the two inſurance companies, as by private underwriters, till the year 1754, when Lord Chief Juſtice *Ryder* ruled, and a ſpecial jury, agreeably to his direction, decided, that a ſhip, having run a-ground, was a ſtranded ſhip within the meaning of the memorandum; and that although ſhe got off again, the underwriter was liable to an *average or partial loſs* upon damaged corn. This deciſion induced the two companies to alter the memorandum, by ſtriking out the words, "*or the ſhip be ſtranded*;" ſo that now they conſider themſelves liable to no loſſes, which can happen to ſuch commodities, except general averages and total loſſes: but the old form is ſtill retained by the private inſurers.

Cantillon v. Lond. Aſſur. Comp. mentioned, 3 Burr. 1553.

What ſhall be conſidered as loſſes within the meaning of this memorandum, will be the ſubject of future inveſtigation; my deſign at preſent being only to enumerate the eſſentials of a policy, and the reaſon and origin of them, as far as I have been able to trace them.

There are, however, ſome kinds of property, which do not fall under the general denomination of goods in a policy; and for the loſs of which the underwriters are not anſwerable, unleſs they are ſpecifically named.

Roſs v. Thwaite, Sit. after Hill. 16 Geo. III. at Guildh.

An action was brought upon a policy of inſurance of the captain's goods for ſix months certain. The loſs proved

proved was chiefly for goods lashed on deck, and the captain's cloaths, and the ship's provisions. It was proved by an underwriter and a broker, that none of those things are within a general policy on goods; for the risk was greater as to goods lashed on deck than other goods: and a policy on goods means only such goods as are merchantable, and a part of the cargo. They also swore that when goods like the present are meant to be insured, they [22] are always insured by name; and the premium is greater.

Lord *Mansfield* said, he thought it consistent with reason, and understood the usage to be so: therefore he advised the plaintiff to withdraw a juror, the premium having been paid into court, to which he consented.

It is a question whether a cargo of dollars, or other coin, jewels, *&c.* if lost, be recoverable under a policy upon goods and merchandizes generally: and I can find no printed case, where the question has been at all discussed in *England*. In one case, *Da Costa* v. *Firth*, the subject matter of the insurance was bullion, and the policy was general on goods and merchandizes: but no objection was taken on that ground, nor was the point ever argued. By the ordinances of several foreign states, *Middleburg*, *Amsterdam*, *Konigsberg*, and others, it is *specially* declared, that money shall not be recovered under the denomination of goods or merchandize; but the insurance must, in the policy, be expressed to be upon money to render it valid. The book, in which the ordinances above referred to are collected, states explicitly that gold and silver, coined and uncoined, pearls and other jewels, may be insured at *London* and *Hamburgh*, and several other places, under the general expression of merchandize.

4 Burr. 1966.

2 Magens 71, 89, 131, 187.

1 Magens 10.

Roccus, in his treatise upon insurances, concurs in the latter opinion, and quotes *Santerna* upon the subject; he draws a distinction, upon the merits of which I do not presume to decide, between money or jewels, for the purposes

CHAP. I.

See Post. p. 127, 129.
Roccus Not. 17.

poses of commerce, which constitute part of the cargo, and such as are merely personal, and for private purposes; the former being clearly liable to contribute to a general average, but not the latter. His words are these: "*Assecurans* "*merces in talem navem immissas, intelligitur assecurare pecuni-* "*am, aurum, argentum, gemmas, margaritas, et annulos in* "*dicta navi existentes, quæ omnia, appellatione mercium, in na-* "*vem immissarum, comprehenduntur, licet expressa non fuissent.* "*Santerna declarat, quod si pecuniæ, margaritæ et annuli erant* "*destinati ad vendendum vel mercandum alias merces, tunc ap-* "*pellatione mercium veniunt, et in assecuratione comprehendun-* "*tur, et loco mercium habentur: vocat dictas res merces, cum* "*occasione earum, habeat locum contributio, sicut aliarum, rerum,* "*ne in istis assecurationibus mercatorum potius apices juris,* "*quam veritas observari videantur: et tandem, quia largè* "*comprehenduntur omnes res, quæ sunt destinatæ ad negotian-* "*dum, et facit etiam, quod confiscatio mercium navis extenditur* "*etiam ad pecuniam numeratam.*" I forbear to draw any conclusion from these premises, which is the plan I have uniformly adopted, where there is no adjudged case upon the question.

Fourthly, The name of the place at which the goods are laden, and to which they are bound.

This has been always held to be necessary in policies, at least for upwards of two hundred years; and must be so, on account of the evident uncertainty which would follow from a contrary practice, as the insurer would never know what the risk was, which he had undertaken to insure.

Molloy, b. 2. c. 7. s. 14.

Molloy has laid down this doctrine, that if a ship be insured from *London* to , a blank being left by the lader of the goods to prevent a surprize by an enemy, and if, in her voyage she happen to be cast away, though there be private instructions for her port, yet the insured must sit down with his loss, by reason of the uncertainty. In support of his opinion, he cites the case of Monsieur

Monfieur *Gourdan*, governor of *Calais*, which was decided by commiffioners of affurance at *Rouen* againft the affured, becaufe, although the bills of lading truly declared the quantity and quality of the goods, the port of the fhip's difcharge was left a blank, on account of the war, which was then exifting. Such alfo is now the law and ufage of merchants.

CHAP. I.

It is alfo cuftomary to ftate in the policy at what port or places the fhip may touch and ftay during the voyage, fo that it fhall not be confidered as a deviation to go to any of thofe places.

Fifthly, The time when the rifk commences, and when it ends. In moft of the commercial countries abroad, it is particularly expreffed, either in their ordinances or policies, and fometimes in both, that the rifk of the infurers fhall commence, the moment the goods quit the fhore, and fhall continue till they are landed at the place of their deftination: and that the infurer not only runs the rifk in the fhip named in the policy, but alfo in all the boats or lighters, that fhall be employed in carrying the goods aboard, and alfo in fetching them afhore. But the cuftom of this country is very different, for the *Englifh* policies exprefsly declare, that "the adventure fhall begin upon "the faid goods and merchandizes *from the loading thereof* "*on board the faid fhip*, and fo fhall continue until the faid "fhip, goods, and merchandizes fhall be arrived at L. "and upon the faid fhip until fhe hath moored at anchor "24 hours in good fafety; and *upon the goods till the fame* "*be there fafely difcharged and landed.*" From thefe words, it is obvious, that infurers are not anfwerable for any accidents, which may happen to the goods in lighters or boats going aboard, *previous* to the voyage; yet as the policy fays, the rifk fhall continue *till the goods are fafely landed*, it feems no lefs obvious, that where fhips cannot come clofe to the quay in order to unload, the infurer continues refponfible for the rifk to be run in carrying the goods

Ord. of Antwerp, Amfterdam, France, Spain, and Copenhagen.

[23]

Vide Appendix, No. 1.

As to continuance of the rifk *upon the fhip*, fee c. 2. page 31.

CHAP. I.

goods in boats to the ſhore. If there be a loſs, however, in theſe caſes, the accident muſt have happened while the goods were in the boats or lighters belonging to the ſhip; for then it is conſidered as a continuance of the ſame ſhip and voyage. But in a caſe where the owner of the goods brought down his own lighter, received the goods out of the ſhip, and before they reached land, an accident happened, whereby the goods were damaged, a ſpecial jury of merchants, under the expreſs direction of Lord Chief Juſtice *Lee*, found that the inſurer was diſcharged, although the inſurance was upon goods to *London*, and *till the ſame ſhould be ſafely landed there*.

Sparrow v. Carruthers, 2 Stra. 1236.

By the ordinances laſt referred to, the number of days, in which people are obliged to unload their goods, is ſtipulated; but in *England* no expreſs time is fixed, the owners being left to their own diſcretion, provided there is no unreaſonable delay, which muſt always depend upon circumſtances.

1 Magens 47.

The riſk on the body of a ſhip, according to the form of the policy received in practice, is to commence in general, "from *her beginning to load at* and ſo "ſhall continue and endure *until the ſaid ſhip ſhall arrive* "*at* and hath there been moored at anchor

[24]

"twenty-four hours in good ſafety." But this mode of ſtating the commencement of the riſk muſt commonly be applied only to inſurances on ſhips outward bound; for when inſurance is made on the homeward riſk, the beginning of the adventure is ſometimes ſtated to be "immediately from and after her arrival at the port abroad;" at other times, "from the departure;" and in ſhort, it is ſo variable, that nothing certain can be ſaid upon the point, depending, as it always has, and always muſt, upon the inclinations of the inſured, as expreſſed in the contract.

Sixthly, Of the various perils and riſks, againſt which the underwriter inſures. Theſe muſt always be inſerted in in all policies, and indeed the words now ufed are fo comprehenfive, that in the opinion of *Molloy*, all thofe curious queftions, which occafioned much debate and controverfy among the lawyers of former days, are now finally fettled. Be this as it may, it is certain, that there is hardly any event which the imagination can form, as likely, in the common courfe of things, to happen to any fhip, that is not amply provided for by the policies now ufed by underwriters. They undertake to bear "all perils of the feas, "men of war, fire, enemies, pirates, rovers, thieves, jet-"tifons, letters of mart, and counter mart, furprifals, "takings at fea, arrefts, reftraints and detainments of all "kings, princes, and people, of what nation, condition, "or quality foever; barratry of the mafter and mariners, "and all other perils, loffes, and misfortunes, that have "or fhall come to the hurt, detriment, or damage of the "faid goods and merchandizes, and fhip, or any part "thereof." But although the words, defcriptive of the hazards run by the infurers, be fo very large and comprehenfive, it fhould feem that a great difference is to be made between the damage fuftained by goods from injuries *on board* a fhip, and that which occurs by external accidents; that the infurer is liable in the latter cafe cannot admit of a doubt, but as the former may proceed from the bad ftowage of the goods, or from their being expofed to wet; and as they are neglects attributable to the mafter; the fhip and not the infurer ought to be anfwerable. Upon this point, however, I find no cafe in the reports, and therefore I ftart it rather as a doubt in my own mind, than as prefuming to hint at an opinion. In *Malyne* it is faid, that if there be thieves on fhip-board among themfelves, the mafter of the fhip is to anfwer for that, and to make it good, fo that the infurers are not to be charged [25] with any fuch lofs, for he fuppofes the word "thieves" to mean *affailing thieves* only, for fo he terms them. It is certain, that a modern ftatute gives fome countenance to this idea, by the preamble to which it appears, that previous to the period of paffing that act, the owners of

Book 2. c. 7. f. 7.

See the Appendix.

1 Magens 50.

Malyne, c. 25. Lex. Merc. Red. 4th edit. p. 295.

7 Geo. II, c. 15.

CHAP. I. the ſhip were liable to the proprietors of the goods for any embezzlement, ſecreting, or making away with, of the goods, by the maſter or the mariners, or with their privity, to whatever amount the value might be: by that ſtatute however, the meaſure of the reſponſibility is to be the value of the ſhip and freight. (*a*) To be ſure, it is not a neceſſary conſequence, that becauſe the owner is liable in ſuch a caſe, therefore the inſurer, if an inſurance has been made, muſt be diſcharged, eſpecially as the underwriter expreſsly undertakes, by the terms of the policy, to anſwer for the barratry of the maſter and mariners. *Roccus*, however, is of opinion, that when a theft is committed *on board* the ſhip, and ſome goods have been ſtolen, then the inſurers are not bound, becauſe the owner of the goods, as much as in him lies, is obliged to take care of them; and if they are ſtolen, while in the veſſel, this cannot be called an *accident*, but has happened through the *negligence* of thoſe, who did not take proper care of them. He adds, that the maſter or owners being liable is an additional reaſon for this regulation, becauſe the maſter of the ſhip is held anſwerable for thefts committed therein, as by receiving the goods on board, he enters into a tacit agreement to deliver them ſafe and whole. It was thought proper thus to ſtate the opinion of this learned writer upon the ſubject, on account of the total ſilence of the law of *England* in this reſpect; though his reaſoning upon this ſubject is by no means concluſive as to *Engliſh* inſurances, on account of the terms of the contract.

Roccus de aſſecurationibus, Not. 42.

But that the underwriter is liable for a robbery of the goods inſured, when committed by thieves from without, cannot be doubted; as thieves are a peril expreſsly inſured by the policy.

Harford v. Maynard, bef. Lord Mansfield at Guildhall, Hil. Vac. 1785. Molloy, b. 2. c. 7. ſ. 5.

In

(*a*) By a ſubſequent ſtatute, 26 *Geo.* III. ch. 86. the owner's reſponſibility is limited to the value of the ſhip and freight, even in caſes of *external* robbery, without the privity of the maſter or mariners: and by the 2d ſection, owners are wholly exempted from any loſs occaſioned by fire.

CHAP. I.

In addition to the various riſks above enumerated, which the underwriters take upon themſelves, it is frequently the practice, to inſure her *loſt or not loſt*, which is certainly very hazardous; becauſe if the ſhip ſhould be loſt at the time of the inſurance, ſtill the underwriter, provided there be no fraud, is liable. The premium is, however, great in proportion, depending upon the circumſtances ſtated to ſhew the probability or improbability of the ſhip's ſafety. Theſe words "*loſt or not loſt*," are peculiar to *Engliſh* policies, not being inſerted in the policies of foreign nations. Roccus Not. 51. 5 Burr. 2803.

[25 *a*]

There is one caſe, in which, by act of parliament, the underwriters are prevented from undertaking certain of the riſks mentioned in the printed policies, and that is, upon cargoes of ſlaves. The acts of parliament upon this ſubject are annual acts, for regulating the ſhipping, and carrying ſlaves in *Britiſh* veſſels from the coaſt of *Africa*: but they have now been continued for ſeveral years, and, on account of the benefits derived to the ſlaves from the humanity of thoſe proviſions, are likely to be continued. With a view, therefore, to procure better treatment, when in health, and a greater degree of care and attention when in ſickneſs, for the objects of this traffic, the legiſlature has provided, that though the uſual printed words may remain on the face of the policy, that no loſs or damage ſhall thereafter be recoverable on account of the *mortality* of ſlaves, *by natural death or ill treatment*, or loſs *by throwing overboard* of ſlaves on any account whatever, or loſs or damage by reſtraints and detainments, by kings, princes, people, or inhabitants of *Africa*, where it ſhall be made appear that ſuch loſs or damage has been occaſioned though any aggreſſion for the purpoſe of procuring ſlaves, and committed by the maſter of any ſuch ſhip, or by any perſon or perſons commanding any boat or boats, or party or parties of men belonging to any ſuch ſhip, or by any perſon or perſons acting by the direction of any ſuch maſter or commander reſpectively. 34 Geo. III, c. 80. ſ. 10. continued by 35 Geo. III, c. 90.

Seventhly,

CHAP. I.

Seventhly, The confideration or premium for the rifk or hazard run: This is the moft material part of the policy, becaufe it is the confideration of the premium received, that makes the underwriter liable to the loffes that may happen. In *Englifh* policies it is always expreffed to have been received at the time of underwriting; "we the "affurers confeffing ourfelves paid the confideration due "unto us for this affurance by the affured." This being fubfcribed by the underwriter, it is proper to inquire whether, if the premium were not actually paid at the time, he could afterwards maintain an action for it againft the *affured*, who might then produce his fubfcription, as evidence againft himfelf. One old cafe has been found upon the fubject, but that is by no means fatisfactory. It was an action of affumpfit, and the plaintiff declared that the defendant was indebted to him in twenty pounds, for a premium upon a policy of infurance on fuch a fhip. The defendant demurred *fpecially*, becaufe the plaintiff did not fhew the confideration certainly, what the premium was, or how it became due: but the objection was not allowed, for this is as good as an *indebitatus pro quodam falario*, which has been adjudged good. Here, however, is no decifion upon the merits, nor does it appear, whether the defendant was the broker or the infured himfelf. It is true, in practice, policies in general are effected by the intervention of a broker; and by the ufage of trade, open accounts are kept between the infurers and brokers, in which cafe, the underwriter may have an action againft the broker for premiums received to his ufe. In one cafe, indeed, the queftion did arife, though nothing was done upon it.

Fowk v. Pinfacke, 2 Lev. 153.

It was an action by the infurer againft the owners, who in this cafe acted, without the intervention of a broker, for money had and received to his ufe. The cafe was decided upon other grounds, for which it will be mentioned more at length hereafter; but juft before the verdict was given, it was objected, that this action would not lie for premiums againft the *infured themfelves*. Lord *Mansfield* however,

Gift v. Mafon, Mich. Vac. 1785, at Guildh.

however, thought the objection came too late, and would not, at that stage of the cause, when the jury were ready to give their verdict, enter into it.

CHAP. I.

In an action brought by the assignees of a broker against the assured, for premiums paid by the bankrupt to the underwriters, the question came collaterally before the court: [27] but I do not find that any point was reserved, and the verdict was general. However, upon all the cases it seems that the broker alone is the debtor to the underwriter.

Airy and others, Assignees of Milton v. Bland, Trin. Sitt. at Guildhall, 14 Geo. III.

It was an action brought by the plaintiffs, as assignees of *Milton*, who was a broker at *Newcastle*, and who had procured an insurance to be effected by different persons for the defendant. The declaration stated, that in consideration that the bankrupt would procure an insurance to be made on the ship *Jason*, and would procure six hundred pounds to be insured thereon by good and sufficient persons, the defendant promised that he would pay the bankrupt the premiums, and a reasonable sum for his trouble. The first question was, whether credit was given by the underwriters to the assured or to the broker, where the premium was not paid down at the time the assurance was made. *Milton*, the bankrupt, swore, that in *May* 1764, he was told by the underwriters that they should look upon him as their debtor, and that they would have nothing to do with the insured, which was considered at *Newcastle*, as the *London* practice: that from that time he had always acted on this plan, and had paid, since that time, one thousand pounds to underwriters, which he had never received. His commission was five *per cent.* *London* insurance brokers were then called, who said, they understood the underwriters looked to them only; and that the underwriters did not once in ten times know who the insured were; and that in case of failure, the underwriter came upon the effects of the broker; the broker upon those of the insured.

Lord

CHAP. I.

Lord *Mansfield* said,—"The plaintiff's case is stronger than referring to the general usage in *London*; for they act by a specific rule, which they suppose to be the rule in *London*: and if the usage in *London* were doubtful, still the plaintiffs would be entitled to recover."

There was a verdict for the plaintiffs.

1 Mag. 84.

Eighthly, The day, month, and year, on which the policy is executed. This insertion seems very necessary, because by comparing the date of the policy with the date of facts which happen afterwards, or are material to be proved, it will frequently appear, whether there is any reason to suspect fraud or improper conduct on the part of the insured.

[28]

The ninth and last requisite of a policy of insurance, is, that it be duly stamped.

35 Geo. III, c. 63.

By several acts of parliament, passed in this and the preceding reigns, various duties had been imposed upon policies of insurance; but by an act passed in the 35th year of *Geo.* III. for the purpose of imposing a new duty on marine insurances, it was by the 24th section of the statute positively declared, that all former duties on that species of insurance, should, from and after the 5th day of *July* 1795, cease and determine, and be no longer paid or payable. By the 2d section of the act it is declared that the duty thereby imposed shall not extend, or be construed to extend to insurances on lives or insurances from losses by fire.

Section 1.

"For every skin, or piece of vellum, or parchment, or "sheet of paper, on which any insurance upon any ship "or ships, goods or merchandize, or upon any other "property, or interest whereon insurances may lawfully "be made, shall be engrossed, written or printed, the stamp "duties following upon the sums insured; that is to say, "Where the sum to be insured shall amount to one hundred pounds, a stamp duty of two shillings and sixpence, "and so progressively for every sum of one hundred pounds

"insured;

"insured; and where the sum to be insured shall not "amount to one hundred pounds, a like stamp duty of two "shillings and sixpence; and where the sum to be insured "shall exceed one hundred pounds, or any progressive "sums of one hundred pounds each, by any fractional part "of one hundred pounds, a like stamp duty of two shillings "and sixpence for each fractional part of one hundred "pounds: and that upon all and every insurances or in-"surance, where the premium, or consideration in the nature "of a premium, actually and *bonâ fide* paid, given, or "contracted for, shall not exceed the rate of ten shillings, "there shall be paid the following duties; (that is to say) "where the sum so to be insured shall amount to one hun-"dred pounds, a stamp duty of one shilling and three-pence, "and so progressively for every sum of one hundred pounds "so insured; and where the sum so to be insured shall not "amount to one hundred pounds, a like stamp duty of one "shilling and three-pence; and where the sum so to be "insured shall exceed one hundred pounds, or any pro-"gressive sums of one hundred pounds each, by any *frac-"tional* part of one hundred pounds, a like stamp duty of one "shilling and three-pence for such fractional part of one "hundred pounds; which several duties shall be payable "and paid by the assured in such insurances respectively."

"Provided always, and be it further enacted, That upon "all and every such insurances or insurance, where the pre-"mium, or consideration in the nature of a premium, "actually and *bonâ fide* paid, given, or contracted for, shall "not exceed the rate of ten shillings *per centum* on the sum "insured, it shall be lawful, in all cases where the sum in-"sured shall amount to two hundred pounds or upwards, "to use stamps of two shillings and sixpence for every two "hundred pounds of the sum insured, instead of stamps of "one shilling and three-pence for every one hundred "pounds of the like sums so insured." Section 4.

"And

CHAP. I.

Section 11. "And be it further enacted by the authority aforesaid, "That every contract or agreement which shall be made "or entered into for any insurance, in respect whereof "any duty is by this act made payable, shall be engrossed, "printed, or written, and shall be deemed and called *A "Policy of Insurance*; and that the premium, or con- "sideration in the nature of a premium, paid, given, or "contracted for, upon such insurance, and the particular "risk or adventure insured against, together with the "names of the subcribers and underwriters, and sums "insured, shall be respectively expressed or specified in or "upon such policy, and in default thereof every such in- "surance shall be null and void to all intents and pur- "poses whatever."

Section 12. "And be it further enacted by the authority aforesaid, "That no policy of insurance upon any ship, or upon any "share or interest therein, shall be made for any certain "term longer than twelve calendar months; and every "policy which shall be made for any longer term shall be "null and void to all intents and purposes."

Section 10. The 10th section of the statute provides for an allowance to be made under certain circumstances by the commissioners, where the sums insured on homeward voyages shall be found to exceed the interest of the assured.

Section 13. The 13th section provides that nothing contained in the act shall prohibit the making of any alteration which may lawfully be made in the terms or conditions of any policy of insurance, duly stamped as aforesaid, after the same shall have been underwritten, or to require any additional stamp duty by reason of such alteration, so that such alteration be made before notice of the determination of the risk originally insured, and the premium or consideration originally paid or contracted for shall exceed the rate of 10*s*. *per cent.* on the sum insured, and so that the thing insured shall remain the property of the same person or persons, and

and so that such alteration shall not prolong the term insured beyond the period allowed by this act (see sect. 12.) and so that no additional or further sum shall be insured by reason or means of such alteration. CHAP. I.

By this section, a penalty of 500*l.* is imposed both on the persons procuring, and the brokers effecting insurances on policies not duly stamped; and the latter can neither demand their brokerage, nor the money expended for premiums; and by the 17th section, every underwriter subscribing such illegal policy is also liable to a like penalty of 500*l.*

Section 15.

Section 16.

By the ordinances of *France*, and other maritime countries, all policies of insurance must be registered; but no such regulation prevails in *England*, either by the law, or in practice.

[29]

Ord. of France, Article 69. Tit. Assurance.

CHAPTER THE SECOND.

Of the Construction of the Policy.

CHAP. II.

A POLICY of insurance, being a contract of indemnity, and being only considered as a simple contract, must always be construed, as nearly as possible, according to the intention of the contracting parties; and not according to the strict and literal meaning of the words. The mercantile law, in this respect, is the same in every part of the world; for from the same premises, the sound conclusions of reason and justice must ever be the same. Thus as the benefit of the insured, and the advancement of trade, are the great objects of insurance, policies are to be construed largely, in order to attain those ends: for it would be absurd to suppose, that when the *end* is insured, the ordinary and usual means of attaining it can possibly be excluded; whatever, therefore, is done, by the master of the ship, in the usual course, necessarily, *et ex justâ causâ*, although a loss happen thereon, the underwriter shall be answerable.

1 Burr. 347. Roccus Not. 18.

1 Burr. 348.

But, in the construction of policies, no rule has been more frequently followed than the *usage* of trade, with respect to the particular voyages or risks, to which the policy relates; and in the cases about to be quoted in support of these principles, it will be found, that the learned judges have always called in the usage of trade, as the ground, upon which the construction turns.

In stating the different cases upon this subject, as the point is nearly the same in all, the order of time, in which they were determined, is that which will be pursued, in order to prevent confusion.

Anonymous, Skinn. 243.

The first to be mentioned is an anonymous case in the time of *James* the second; but it is from a reporter of very good authority. A policy of insurance shall be construed to run until the ship shall have ended, and be discharged of her voyage; for arrival at the port, to which she was bound, is not a discharge *till she is unloaded*: and it was so adjudged by the whole court, upon a demurrer.

But although this construction may be perfectly right, where the policy is general from *A.* to *B.* yet if it contain the words usually inserted "*and till the ship shall have moored* "*at anchor twenty-four hours in good safety,*" the underwriter is not liable for any loss, arising from seizure after she has been twenty-four hours in port; though such seizure was in consequence of an act of barratry of the master *during the voyage*: for, if it were extended beyond the time limited in the policy, it would be impossible to lay down any fixed rule, and all would be uncertainty and confusion.

This was decided in an action on a policy of insurance on the ship *Hope* from *Hamburgh* to *London*, subscribed by the defendant for two hundred pounds at one guinea *per cent.* At the trial before Mr. Justice *Buller*, at *Guildhall*, a verdict was found for the plaintiffs, subject to the opinion of the court, upon the following case: that the plaintiffs were interested in the ship to the amount of the sum insured. That in the course of the voyage, the master committed barratry by smuggling on his own account, by hovering and running brandy on shore in casks under sixty gallons. That on the first of *September* 1785, *the ship arrived in safety at her moorings in the river Thames, and remained there in safety till the twenty-seventh of the said month of September,* when she was seized by the revenue officers for the smuggling before stated. That about three weeks after the seizure, the plaintiffs informed the underwriters thereof; and that they would hold them liable on the policy. That on the twentieth of *October*, the plaintiffs presented a petition to the commissioners of his majesty's customs, in which they imputed all the blame (which was certainly the truth) to the captain, and praying that their vessel might be restored, on paying something to the seizing officer. The answer was, "that

Lockyer and others v. Offley, 1 Term Reports, p. 252.

CHAP. II.

" that the profecution muft proceed, as the fhip had been " guilty of a grofs violation of the laws, but that the own- " ers fhould be at liberty to compound, according to the " rules of the Exchequer." That the fhip was appraifed at the fum of three hundred and forty-five pounds, and by [32] the courfe of the court of Exchequer, the fhip would have been reftored to the plaintiffs, upon the payment of two hundred and thirty pounds, befides cofts and charges, which would altogether have amounted to three hundred and twenty-nine pounds nine fhillings and feven-pence. That in *November*, a notice was indorfed on the policy, binding the underwriters for all cofts and charges expended about the recovery of the fhip. That this was fhewn to the underwriters, who refufed to fubfcribe it.

This cafe was fully argued, in the abfence of Lord *Manffield*, and the court having taken time to deliberate, Mr. Juftice *Willes* pronounced their unanimous opinion. " There is no doubt in this cafe, but that the mafter was " guilty of barratry, by fmuggling on his own account, " without the privity of his owners. Many definitions of " barratry are to be found in the books, but perhaps this " general one may comprehend almoft all the cafes: barra- " try is every fpecies of fraud or knavery in the mafter of " the fhip, by which the freighters or owners are *injured*; " and in this light a criminal or wilful deviation is barratry, " if it be without their confent. The general queftion here " is, whether, as the lofs, which was occafioned by the bar- " ratry of the mafter, did not happen *during the continuance* " *of the voyage*, the infurers are liable? I muft own this ap- " pears to me to be a novel queftion, and not to have been " decided by any former determinations. Difficulties occur " on both fides in laying down any rule. The firft thing to " be obferved is, that the policy, by the terms of it, is an un- " dertaking *for a limited time*, during the voyage from *Hamburgh* to *London*, *till the fhip has moored twenty-four hours* " *in fafety*; and the fhip was not actually feized till near a " month afterwards. But it has been faid that under the

" 24th

" 24th of *George* the third, chap. 47. and the excise laws, the " forfeiture attaches the moment the act is done, and that " the barratry was committed *during the voyage.* It may be " so as to some purposes, as to prevent intermediate altera- " tions or incumbrances; but I think the *actual* property is " not altered *till after the seizure,* though it may be before " condemnation. I will put this case; suppose, before the " seizure of the ship, she had gone another voyage, and on " her return had been seized, would the crown be entitled " to an account of her earnings, after deducting the expen- [33] " ses of the outfit? surely not. Till the seizure, it was not " certain that the officers of the crown knew of the illicit " trade carried on by the master, or whether they would " take advantage of the forfeiture. It would be a dange- " rous doctrine to lay down, that the insurer should, in all " cases, be liable to remote consequential damages. This " has been compared to a death's wound received during the " voyage, which subjected the ship to a subsequent loss. To " this point the case of *Meretony* v. *Dunlop,* seems very ma- " terial. That was an insurance on a ship for six months; Easter 23. Geo. III, B. R. " and three days before the expiration of the time, she re- " ceived her death's wound, but by pumping, was kept afloat, " till three days after the time: There the verdict, under the " direction of Lord *Mansfield,* was given for the insurer; and " it was afterwards confirmed by the court. I will put " another case: suppose an insurance upon a man's life for " a year, and some short time before the expiration of the " term, he receives a mortal wound, of which he dies after " the year, the insurer would not be liable. The case of Vide post, c. 5. " *Vallejo* v. *Wheeler* was cited for the plaintiff, but that does " not conclude this question, for there the ship was lost " *during the voyage.* It was also argued, that this ship, even " in the hands of a fair purchaser, would be liable to the " forfeiture. I do not know that it ever has been so " decided; it may depend on circumstances, such as length " of possession, laches in seizing, or other matters. But sup- " pose the law to be so, it does not follow from thence, " that though the ship *is always liable to confiscation,* that the

" insurer

CHAP. II.

" insurer at any distance of time, is answerable for the loss, " under a limited undertaking. And this brings me to that " part of the case, which weighs most with the court, in fa- " vour of the defendant, and to which it does not appear to " us that any satisfactory answer has beeen given. It was " agreed in the argument, that the custom-house officers " might seize for the forfeiture within three years after the " fact committed; and that the attorney-general might file " an information, at any time whilst the ship was in being. " Is the insurer during all this time to continue liable? " Suppose the ship had gone several voyages afterwards; [34] " and suppose a partial loss paid, and the underwriter's name " struck off, shall an action be afterwards brought upon the " policy? His accounts could never be settled, nor could he " be finally discharged, whilst the ship was in existence; " such a position would be monstrous, and attended with " infinite inconvenience. There must be some certain and " reasonable limitation in point of time laid down by the " court, when the insurer shall be released from his en- " gagement. If he be liable for a month, he may be for a " year, and so on. We all think that the law of insurances " would be left unsettled, and in much confusion, if any " other time were allowed, than that prescribed by the " policy, namely, *the continuance of the voyage, and the ship's* " *mooring twenty-four hours in safety*." Judgment for the defendant.

Lethulier's Case, 2 Salk. 443.

In an action upon a policy of insurance by the defendant at *London*, insuring a ship from thence to the *East Indies*, warranted to depart with convoy, the declaration shewed, that the ship went from *London* to the *Downs*, and from thence with convoy, and was lost. After a frivolous plea and demurrer, the case stood upon the declaration, and it was objected, that there was a departure without convoy. But by the court, the clause " warranted to depart with convoy," must be construed according to the usage among merchants, that is, from such place where convoys are to be had, *as the Downs*.

It

CHAP. II.

It is true, Lord Chief Justice *Holt* differed from the rest of the court, being of opinion that it was no part of the law of merchants to take convoy in the *Downs*. His lordship's opinion, however, although it is one of the first legal authorities, is certainly contradicted by practice, it being almost the invariable custom for the convoy to meet the merchant ships only in the *Downs*.

See Gordon v. Morley, post, p. 36.

Case upon a policy of insurance, which was to insure the *William* galley in a voyage from *Bremen* to the port of *London*, warranted to depart with convoy. The case was, the galley set sail from *Bremen*, under convoy of a *Dutch* man of war to the *Elbe*, where they were joined by two other *Dutch* men of war, and several *Dutch* and *English* merchant ships, whence they sailed to the *Texel*, where they found a squadron of *English* men of war and an Admiral. After a stay [35] of nine weeks, they set sail from the *Texel*; the galley was separated in a storm, taken by a *French* privateer, and retaken by a *Dutch* privateer, and paid eighty pounds salvage. It was ruled by *Holt*, Chief Justice, that the voyage ought to be according to *usage*, and that their going to the *Elbe*, though out of the way, was no deviation; for till after the year 1703, (prior to which time this policy was made) there was no convoy for ships directly from *Bremen* to *London*. Verdict for the plaintiff.

Bond v. Gonsales, 2 Salk. 445.

The ship *Success* was insured "*at and from Leghorn to the* "*port of London, and till there moored twenty-four hours in* "*good safety*." She arrived the 8th of *July* at *Fresh Wharf* and moored, but was the same day served with an order to go back to the *Hope* to perform a fourteen days quarantine. The men upon this deserted her, and on the 12th of the month the captain applied to be excused going back, which petition was adjourned to the twenty-eighth, when the regency ordered her back: and on the thirtieth, she went back, performed the quarantine, and then sent up for orders to air the goods; but before she returned, the ship was burnt on the

Waples v. Eames, 2 Stra. 1243.

the twenty-third of *Auguſt*, and now the queſtion was, whether the inſurer was liable?

Lord Chief Juſtice *Lee* ruled, that though the ſhip was ſo long at her moorings, yet ſhe could not be ſaid to be there in *good ſafety*, which muſt mean the opportunity of unloading and diſcharging; whereas here ſhe was arreſted within the twenty-four hours, and the hands having deſerted, and the regency taken time to conſider the petition, there was no default in the maſter or owners; and it was proved, that till the fourteen days were expired, no application could be made to air the goods; whereupon the jury found for the plaintiff.

[35 *a*]

Minett v. Anderſon. Peake 211. Sitt. after Hil. 34 Geo. III.

So where the ſhip *Hercules* was inſured from *Bilboa* to *Rouen*, and till 24 hours moored in ſafety there. The ſhip arrived, an embargo having been previouſly laid on all *Engliſh* veſſels in that port. The captain went on ſhore the day he arrived, and the next day the embargo was laid on his ſhip.—He was afterwards permitted to land his cargo, which he delivered to his conſignees, but the ſhip was *detained as a prize*, and the captain and crew allowed ſubſiſtence as priſoners of war, from the time of their arrival.

Lord *Kenyon*.—"She was as much within the power of the enemy, as if a guard had been put on board the moment ſhe arrived. She could not be ſaid to be 24 hours, or a minute, *moored in ſafety*, as far as relates to theſe plaintiffs, for immediately on her entering the port, ſhe was to all intents and purpoſes captured by the French." Verdict for the plaintiffs.

Angerſtein v. Bell. Sitt. at Guildh. after Trin. 1795.

But where a ſhip had arrived at the wharf, where ſhe intended to unload, on the 12th *January*, and was laid on the outſide of the tier, there being no room to lay her in the inſide; where the ſails were unbent, top-maſts ſtruck, three anchors out, and ſhe was alſo laſhed to another ſhip, and

and ſo continued till the 19th, when ſeveral ſhips and a quantity of ice drove athwart her ſtern, forced her adrift, and ſhe was wholly loſt. Lord *Kenyon* was of opinion that ſhe was completely moored upon the 12th, and as the accident did not happen till above 24 hours after that time, the plaintiff was nonſuited.

In an inſurance upon *freight*, if an accident happens to the ſhip before any goods are put on board, which prevents her from ſailing, the inſured upon the policy cannot recover the freight which he would have begun to earn, if the goods had been ſhipped. The circumſtances of the caſe were theſe;

Tonge v. Watts, 2 Stra. 1251.

The plaintiff inſured *on ſhip and freight*, at and from *Jamaica* to *Briſtol*. A cargo was ready to put on board: but the ſhip being careening, in order for the voyage, a ſudden tempeſt aroſe, and ſhe and many others were loſt. [36] The rigging and parts of her were recovered and ſold, and the defendant paid into court as much as, upon an average, he was liable to for the loſs of the ſhip: but the plaintiff inſiſted to be allowed ſix hundred pounds for the freight the ſhip *would have earned* in the voyage, if the accident had not happened. But, as the goods were not actually on board, ſo as to make the plaintiff's right to freight commence; Lord Chief Juſtice *Lee* held, he could not be allowed it, and he was nonſuited.

Montgomery v. Eggington, 3 Term R. 362.

But if the policy be a valued policy, and part of the cargo be on board when ſuch accident happens, the reſt being ready to be ſhipped, the inſured may recover to the whole amount. This was ſo decided in an action brought by the aſſured on a policy on freight, valued at fifteen hundred pounds: in fact, only five hundred pounds worth of freight was on board when the ſhip was driven from her moorings and loſt: but goods, to the amount of the reſt of the freight were ready to be ſhipped, and were lying on the quay for that purpoſe at the time.

CHAP. II.

Lord *Kenyon*, Chief Justice, before whom the cause was tried, told the jury, that the question for their consideration was, whether this was a mere colourable insurance and a gaming policy, or whether it was a *bonâ fide* transaction: if the latter, the assured was entitled to recover for the whole value in the policy. The jury found the whole sum. The defendant's counsel obtained a rule for a new trial, which he afterwards abandoned, the court being strongly of opinion against him.

[36 *a*]
Thompson v. Taylor, B. R. Mich. 36 Geo. III. 6 Term. R. 478.

So also in an *open* policy on freight, *at and from London and Teneriffe to any of the West India islands*, (*Jamaica* excepted) the underwriters were held liable to pay the insurance, though the ship sailed from *London* in ballast, and was captured before her arrival at *Teneriffe*, where the cargo was to be put on board. But, as the ship was under a charter party *to depart out of the river Thames, and proceed to Teneriffe, and there to load and receive on board from the freighters* 500 *pipes of wine, to be delivered in the West Indies, for the freight of which* 500 *pipes the freighters covenanted to pay* 35 *s. the pipe*; the court held that the instant the ship departed from the *Thames*, the contract for freight had its inception, and the plaintiff was entitled to recover. At the trial, the plaintiff had obtained a verdict, and the case was afterwards brought before the court upon a motion to enter a nonsuit. After argument at the bar,

Lord *Kenyon* said—"When this case came on at *nisi prius*, I thought the plaintiff was not entitled to recover; because I considered it as similar, in every respect, to that of *Tonge v. Watts*; and had it been so, my judgment now would have gone with that case. But this case depends upon its own peculiar circumstances. It is admitted, that if this contract had an inception, that the right to freight then commenced, and the policy attached. Now by the charter party there was an inception of the contract, by the departure from the *Thames*; for the covenant in the charter party was to go from the port of *London*. In the case from

from *Strange*, the inception of the contract would have been by taking the goods on board, which not being done, the insurance did not attach. In the case of *Montgomery v. Eggington*, there was an inception of the contract, and plaintiff recovered. The case in *Strange* importantly differs from this; but I am now completely satisfied, though the case is new, that the plaintiff ought to recover."

Mr. Justice *Grose*.—" In this case the freight begins to run in consequence of the ship's departure from *London*; the plaintiff therefore has an interest in the voyage. But in *Tonge v. Watts*, the voyage was not begun, nor were the goods on board."

Mr. Justice *Lawrence*.—" I think this plaintiff had an insurable interest; for it seems to me equally as strong an interest as the profits to arise from a cargo of molasses, which have been held to be an insurable interest. It is said that the plaintiff had a mere right of action against the freighter; and if he had not provided a cargo, though the plaintiff might recover against the freighter for breach of contract, yet he could not recover against the underwriters. It is true an insurance on freight could not have been recovered, if the ship had proceeded to the *West Indies* without one. But here, by a peril in the policy, the assured is prevented from earning a specific freight; and therefore the rule for entering a nonsuit must be discharged."

See post, 267.

Gordon v. Morley. Campbell v. Bordieu. 2 Stra. 1265.

On an insurance from *London* to *Gibraltar*, warranted to depart with convoy; it appeared there was a convoy appointed for that trade at *Spithead*, and the ship *Ranger* having tried for convoy in the *Downs*, proceeded for *Spithead*, and was taken in her way thither. The insurers resisted the demand of indemnity, alleging, that as there was a *French* war, the ship should not have ventured through the *Channel*, but have waited for occasional convoy. Lord Chief Justice *Lee*, however, was of opinion, that

CHAP. II.

that the ſhip was to be conſidered as under the defendant's inſurance to a place of general rendezvous, according to the interpretation of the words, *warranted to depart with convoy*, *Salk.* 443, 445, and if the parties meant to vary the inſurance from what is *commonly* underſtood, they ſhould have ſtated it. Two ſpecial juries of merchants found their verdicts agreeably to that direction.

Vide ſupra.

[37]

Motteux and others, v. the Gov. and Comp. of London Aſſur. 1 Atk. 545.

This caſe has already been mentioned, on account of an alteration made in the policy after the time of underwriting; it ſhall now, however, be conſidered wholly independent of that circumſtance. It was a bill filed in the court of Chancery, which ſtated, that the ſhip *Eyles*, late in the *Eaſt India* Company's ſervice, was, in the year 1732, at *Bengal*, at which time the owner employed *I. H.* to inſure the ſhip in the *London* Aſſurance Office for five hundred pounds. The adventure thereon was to commence *from her arrival at Fort Saint George*, and thence to continue till the ſaid ſhip ſhould arrive in *London*, and that it ſhould be lawful for the ſaid ſhip, in the ſaid voyage, to ſtay at any ports or places without prejudice, and that the ſhip was, and ſhould be rated *at intereſt or no intereſt*, without farther account: in conſideration whereof, *I. H.* paid fifteen pounds premium. *The Eyles* came to *Fort Saint George* in *February* 1733, in her way to *England*; but being leaky, and in a very bad condition, upon the unanimous advice of the governor, council, commanders of ſhips, *&c.* ſhe ſailed to *Bengal* to be refitted, and after being ſheathed, in her return upon her homeward-bound voyage, ſhe ſtruck upon the *Engilee* ſands and was loſt. Evidence was read on the part of the plaintiffs to prove, that *Bengal* was the moſt proper place to refit, and that ſhe went thither for that reaſon; that this was a voyage of neceſſity, and not a trading voyage, for ſhe took nothing on board, but water, proviſion, and ballaſt.

Lord Chancellor *Hardwicke*.—" As to the queſtion, whether there has been a breach, or, in other terms, a loſs,

loſs, within the meaning of this policy, the general principles laid down by the plaintiff's council are right, that ſtreſs of weather, and the danger of proceeding on a voyage, when a ſhip is in a decayed condition, are to be conſidered. In ſuch a caſe, if ſhe went to the neareſt place, I ſhould conſider it equally the ſame as if ſhe had been repaired at the very place from which the voyage was to commence, according to the terms of the policy, and no deviation."

[38] It is a very material circumſtance, that the governor ordered the lading to be taken out, to ſhew the neceſſity of the ſhip's being repaired, but there is not a ſyllable of proof why ſhe might not have been equally well repaired at *Fort Saint George*. There is one part of this caſe which diſtinguiſhes it from all others whatever, and that is, as to the certain time the voyage was to commence. The fact is, the ſhip was loſt in *July* 1733, three weeks before the time of making this policy, ſo that clearly the ſhip was not at *Fort Saint George* at the time the agreement was made; and therefore it is a material queſtion, whether it comes within the agreement. His Lordſhip directed an iſſue to try, whether the loſs in *July* 1733, was a loſs during the voyage, and according to the adventure agreed upon; which iſſue was afterwards found for the plaintiffs upon a trial in the Common Pleas.

In an action upon a policy of inſurance, before Lord Chief Juſtice *Hardwicke*, it has been held, that the words " at and from *Bengal* to *England*," meant *the firſt arrival* at *Bengal*; and it was agreed, that when ſuch words are uſed in policies, *firſt arrival* is always implied and underſtood. 1 Atk. 548.

It has likewiſe been held, that when a ſhip is inſured *at and from a place*, and it arrives at that place, as long as the ſhip is preparing for the voyage upon which it is inſured, the inſurer is liable: but if all thoughts of the voyage be laid Chitty v. Selwin, 2 Atk. 359.

CHAP. II.

laid aside, and the ship lie there five, six, or seven years, with the owner's privity, it shall never be said the insurer is liable; for it would be to subject him to the whim and caprice of the owner.

Camden v. Cowley, 1 Black. 417.

This was an action on a policy of insurance on a ship, at and from *Jamaica* to *London*. The ship had also been insurfrom *London* to *Jamaica* generally, and was lost in coasting the island, after she had touched for some days at one port there, but before she had delivered all her outward-bound cargo at the other ports of the island. This was an action on the homeward policy; and in order to shew when the homeward bound risk commenced, it was necessary to shew at what time the outward-bound risk determined; and the [39] jury, which was special, after an examination of merchants as to the custom, by their verdict decided, that the outward risk ended, when the ship had moored in any port of the island, and did not continue till she came to the last port of delivery.

1 Black. 418.

In the *Trinity* term following, a motion was made for a new trial, but it was refused; because it had been thoroughly tried and no new light could be thrown upon it, although Lord *Mansfield* said, the inclination of his opinion at the trial was the contrary way. Mr. Justice *Wilmot* thought, the construction put upon the policy by the jury was the right one.

Barrass v. The London Assurance. Sittings after Hilary 1782, at Guildhall.

In a similar case Lord *Mansfield* laid down the same doctrine to the jury, namely, that the outward risk *upon the ship* ended twenty-four hours after its arrival in the first port of the island to which it was destined: but that the outward policy *upon goods* continued till they were landed.

Leigh v. Mather, Sittings at Guildhall, after Michaelmas Term, 1795.

The doctrine contained in the two last cases has met with material confirmation in a very modern decision. It was an action upon a policy of assurance on *the ship Palliser*, and *on goods* on board thereof, on a voyage *at and from Georgia to Jamaica*. The ship arrived in *Montego Bay*, and *moored* at *at anchor*, and there alſo the agent of plaintiff ſold and *delivered* the greateſt part of the cargo to Meſſrs. *Adams* and *Hatton* merchants there. The captain then entered into a charter party with *Adams* and *Hatton*, to proceed from thence to *St. Anne's*, and there to take in a cargo for *London*. After unloading the greateſt part of the cargo at *Montego Bay*, and remaining there a month, it was verbally agreed that the remainder of the cargo (which was lumber) ſhould be carried as ballaſt to *St. Anne's*, and accordingly the veſſel, after taking in ſome fuſtic, proceeded towards *St. Anne's*, but was wrecked and never arrived there. For the plaintiff it was urged, that in ſuch an inſurance, the ſhip might go from port to port; and that, at all events, the goods were protected by the policy, *till they were all diſcharged and ſafely landed.*

Lord *Kenyon* was clearly of opinion, and was confirmed in that opinion by a Special Jury, to whom his Lordſhip particularly referred upon this occaſion, that the riſk *on the ſhip* ceaſed, *after ſhe had been moored at anchor twenty-four hours* in the *firſt port* of the iſland, *for the purpoſe of unloading*: and the facts diſcloſed in this caſe having manifeſted that *Montego Bay* was alſo the original deſtination of the cargo, and that its not being wholly delivered there was only prevented by a new agreement, *the goods* cannot be recovered under this policy of inſurance. A ſhip inſured to *Jamaica* generally cannot be permitted to go round the whole iſland, from port to port, for the purpoſe of unloading her cargo, eſpecially where, as in this caſe, the owner of ſhip and goods is the ſame perſon. The plaintiff was nonſuited.

But the great and leading caſes, upon queſtions of conſtruction, are two, *Tiernay* v. *Etherington*, and *Pelly* v. the *Royal Exchange* Aſſurance company; the former determined by Lord Chief Juſtice *Lee*, and the latter by Lord *Mansfield*. In theſe caſes, the principles, which are to be obſerved in the conſtruction of policies, are ſo fully conſidered, and the application of them to the particular circumſtances of the different

CHAP. II.

ferent cafes is made with fo much accuracy and perfpicuity, that they are to be regarded as the pole ftar to direct our inquiries upon all fimilar occafions.

Tiernay v. Etherington, before Lee Chief Juftice 5 Mar. 1743. 1 Burr. 348.

The firft of thefe caufes, was an action upon a policy of infurance "on goods, in a *Dutch* fhip, from *Malaga to Gibraltar*, and at and from thence to *England* and *Holland*, "both, or either: on goods, as hereunder agreed, beginning "the adventure from the loading, and to continue till the "fhip and goods be arrived at *England* or *Holland*, and "there fafely landed." The agreement was, "that upon "the arrival of the fhip at *Gibraltar*, the goods might be "unloaded, and re-fhipped in one or more *Britifh* fhip or "fhips for *England* and *Holland*, and to return one *per cent*, if difcharged in *England*." It appeared in evidence, that when the fhip came to *Gibraltar*, the goods were unloaded, and put into a *ftore fhip*, (which it was proved was [40] always confidered as a warehoufe) and that there was then no *Britifh* fhip there. Two days after the goods were put into the ftore fhip, they were loft in a ftorm. The queftion was, whether this was a lofs within the conftruction of the policy.

Lee, Chief Juftice.—"It is certain, that in the conftruction of policies, the *ftrictum jus* or *apex juris*, is not to be laid hold of: but they are to be conftrued largely for the benefit of trade, and for the infured. Now it feems to be a ftrict conftruction, to confine this infurance only to the unloading and re-fhipping, and the accidents attending that act. The conftruction fhould be according to the courfe of trade in this place; and this appears to be the ufual mode of unloading and re-fhipping in that place, *viz.* that when there is no *Britifh* fhip there, then the goods are kept in ftore fhips. Where there is an infurance on goods on board fuch a fhip, that infurance extends to the carrying the goods to fhore in a boat. So, if an infurance be of goods to fuch a city, and the goods are brought in fafety to fuch a port, though diftant from the city, that is a compliance with the policy; if if that be the usual place to which the ships come. Therefore, as here is a liberty given of unloading and re-shipping, it must be taken to be an insuring under such methods as are proper for unloading and re-shipping. There is no neglect on the part of the insured, for the goods were brought into port the nineteenth, and were lost the twenty-second of *November*. This manner of unloading and re-shipping is to be considered as the necessary means of attaining that, which was intended by the policy; and seems to be the same, as if it had happened in the act of unshipping from one ship into another. And as this is the known course of the trade, it seems extraordinary, if it was not intended. This is not to be considered as a suspension of the policy; for as the policy would extend to a loss, happening in the unloading and re-shipping from one ship to another, so any means to attain that end come within the meaning of the policy." The plaintiff had a verdict.

Afterwards a new trial was moved for; but it was refused by *Lee* Chief Justice, Mr. Justice *Chapple*, and Mr. Justice *Denison*, against the opinion of Mr. Justice *Wright*. Easter Term, 1743.

[41]

Pelly v. The Governor and Com. of the Royal Exchange Assur. 1 Burr. 341.

The next of these causes came before the court upon a case reserved for their opinion, after a trial and verdict for the plaintiff, at *Guildhall*, before Lord *Mansfield*. It was an action of covenant upon a policy of insurance.

The case states, that the plaintiff, being part owner of the ship *Onslow*, an *East India* ship, then lying in the *Thames*, and bound on a voyage to *China*, and back again to *London*, insured it "at and from *London*, to any ports or places beyond "the *Cape of Good Hope*, and back to *London*, free from "average under ten *per cent.* upon the body, tackle, appa-"rel, ordnance, munition, artillery, boat, and other fur-"niture of and in the said ship: beginning the adventure "upon the said ship from and immediately following "the date of the policy, and so to continue and endure "until the ship shall be arrived as above, and there anchored

"twenty-

CHAP. II.

"twenty-four hours in good ſafety." The perils mentioned in the policy were the common perils, *viz.* "of "the ſeas, men of war, fire, *&c.*" The ſhip arrived in the river *Canton*, in *China*, where ſhe was to ſtay to clean and refit, and for other purpoſes. Upon her arrival there, the ſails, yards, tackle, cables, rigging, apparel, and other furniture, were by the captain's order, taken out of her, and put into a warehouſe, or ſtorehouſe, called a bank-ſaul, built for that purpoſe on a ſand bank, or ſmall iſland, lying in the ſaid river, near one of the banks called *Bank-ſaul Iſland*, in order to be there repaired, kept dry, and preſerved, till the ſhip ſhould be heeled, cleaned and refitted. Some time after this, a fire broke out in the bank-ſaul, belonging to a *Swediſh* ſhip, and communicated itſelf to another bank-ſaul, and from thence to that belonging to the *Onſlow*, and conſumed the ſame, together with all the ſails, yards, *&c.* belonging to the *Onſlow* that were therein. The caſe ſtates further, that it was the *univerſal and well-known uſage*, and has been ſo for a great number of years, for all *European* ſhips, which go a *China* voyage, except *Dutch* ſhips, (who for ſome years paſt have been denied this privilege by the *Chineſe*, and who look upon ſuch denial as a great loſs) when they arrive near this *Bank-ſaul Iſland*, in the river *Canton*, to unrig the ſhips, and to take out their ſails, yards, tackle, cables, rigging, apparel, and other furniture; and to put them on ſhore in a bank-ſaul, built for that purpoſe on the ſaid iſland, (in the manner that had been done by the captain
[42] of the *Onſlow*, on the preſent occaſion) in order to be repaired, kept dry, and preſerved, until the ſhips ſhould be heeled, cleaned, and reſitted. The caſe adds, that ſo doing is prudent, and for the common and general benefit of the owners of the ſhip, the inſurers, and inſured, and all perſons concerned in the ſafety of the ſhip. The ſhip arrived from her ſaid voyage in the *Thames*, having been again rigged, and put in the beſt condition the nature of the place and circumſtances of affairs would permit. The queſtion for the opinion of the court was, whether the inſurers are liable to anſwer for this loſs, ſo happening upon the bank-ſaul, within the intent and meaning of this policy.

The court, after a ſolemn argument, took time to conſider the queſtion, and then Lord *Mansfield* delivered the unanimous opinion of the court for the plaintiff.

Lord *Mansfield*.—"By the expreſs words of the policy, the defendants have inſured the tackle, apparel, and other furniture of the *Onſlow*, from *fire* during the whole time of her voyage, until her return in ſafety to *London*, without any reſtriction. Her tackle, apparel, and furniture, were inevitably burnt in *China*, during the voyage, before her return to *London*. The event then, which has happened, is a loſs within the general words of the policy; and it is incumbent upon the defendant to ſhew, from the manner, in which this misfortune happened, or from other circumſtances, that it ought to be conſtrued a peril, which they did not undertake to bear. If the chance be varied, or the voyage altered, by the fault of the owner or maſter of the ſhip, the inſurer ceaſes to be liable; becauſe he is only underſtood to engage that the thing ſhall be done ſafe from fortuitous dangers, provided due means are uſed by the trader to attain that end. But the maſter is not in fault, if what he did was done in the uſual courſe, and for juſt reaſons. The inſurer, in eſtimating the price at which he is willing to indemnify the trader againſt all riſks, muſt have under his conſideration the nature of the voyage to be performed, and the uſual courſe and manner of doing it. Every thing done in the uſual courſe muſt have been foreſeen, and in contemplation at the time he engaged: he took the riſk, upon a ſuppoſition, that what was uſual or neceſſary ſhould be done. In general, what is uſually done by a ſhip, with ſuch a cargo, in ſuch a voyage, is underſtood to be referred to by every policy, and to make a part of it, as much as if it were expreſſed. The uſage when foreſeen, is rather allowed to be done, than what is left to the maſter's diſcretion, upon unforeſeen events: yet if the maſter, *ex juſtâ causâ*, go out of the way, the inſurance continues. Upon theſe principles it is difficult to frame a queſtion, which can ariſe out of this caſe, as ſtated. The only objection is, that they were [43]

burnt

CHAP. II.

burnt in a bank-ſaul, and not in the ſhip; upon land, not at ſea, or upon water: and being appertinent to the ſhip, loſſes and dangers aſhore could not be included. The anſwer is obvious: Firſt, the words make no ſuch diſtinction: Secondly, the intent makes no ſuch diſtinction. Many accidents might happen at land, even to the ſhip. Suppoſe a hurricane to drive it a mile on ſhore; or an earthquake may have a like effect; ſuppoſe the ſhip to be burnt in a dry dock, or ſuppoſe accidents to happen to the tackle upon land, taken from the ſhip, while accidentally and occaſionally refitting, as on account of a hole in its bottom, or other miſchance; theſe are all poſſible caſes. But what might ariſe from an accidental repair of the ſhip, is not near ſo ſtrong, as a certain, neceſſary conſequence of the ordinary voyage, which the parties could not but have in their direct and immediate contemplation. Here the defendants knew that the ſhip muſt be heeled, cleaned, and refitted, in the river of *Canton:* they knew that the tackle would then be put in the bank-ſaul: they knew that it was for the ſafety of the ſhip, and prudent that they ſhould be put there. Had it been an accidental neceſſity of refitting, the maſter might have juſtified taking them out of the ſhip, *ex juſtâ cauſâ:* but deſcribing the voyage is an expreſs reference to the uſual manner of making it, as much as if every circumſtance was mentioned. Was the chance varied by the fault of the maſter? It is impoſſible to impute any fault to him. Is this like a deviation? No: 'tis *ex juſtâ cauſâ*, which always excuſes. Had the inſurers in this caſe been aſked, whether the tackle ſhould be put in the bank-ſaul, they muſt, for their own ſakes, have inſiſted that it ſhould. They would have had reaſon to complain, if from their not being put there a miſfortune had happened. In ſuch a caſe, the maſter would have been to blame, and by his fault would have varied the chance. They have taken a price for ſtanding in the plain-
[44] tiff's place, as to any loſſes he might ſuſtain in performing the ſeveral parts of the voyage, of which this was known and intended to be one. Therefore, we are all of opinion, that in every light, and in every view of this caſe, in rea-

ſon

ſon and juſtice, and within the words, intent, and meaning, of this policy, and within the view and contemplation of the parties to the contract, the inſurers are liable to anſwer for this loſs.

This caſe has ſince been confirmed by Lord *Kenyon* and the whole court of King's Bench.

Brough v. Whitmore, 4 Term R. 206. See poſt, p. 56. for another point.

So alſo in another caſe, the ſame principles were adhered to, and the ſame rule of deciſion was adopted. The inſurance was upon the ſhips the *Hope* and the *Anne*, at and from *Dartmouth* to *Waterford*, and from thence to the port, or ports, of diſcharge, on the coaſt of *Labrador*, with leave to touch at *Newfoundland*, and upon any kinds of goods and merchandizes; and alſo on the ſhips, till they ſhould be arrived at their port of diſcharge, and ſhould have moored at anchor *twenty-four hours, and on the goods until the ſame ſhould be there diſcharged and ſafely landed.* By a clauſe in the policy, money advanced to the fiſhermen was inſured. The *Anne* arrived ſafe on the coaſt of *Labrador* on the 22d of *June*, and the *Hope* on the 14th of *July*, 1778. From the time of their arrival, the crews were employed in fiſhing, and had taken out none of their cargoes, except at leiſure hours (partly on *Sundays*) ſuch things as were immediately wanted. On the 13th of *Auguſt*, an *American* privateer entered the harbour and took both the veſſels, there being at that time nobody on board either of them. The action was brought to recover the value of the goods. The defence was, that there had been an unneceſſary delay in unloading the cargoes, in conſequence of which they had been expoſed to capture, and that the underwriters ought not to be liable for what had happened from the negligence of the inſured. The plaintiffs reſted their caſe on the words of the policy, and the uſage of the trade. They called the captain of the *Anne*, who ſwore, that he had been the ſame voyage three times in the three laſt years, and that they had proceeded in the ſame manner during each of the voyages; that he did not think the plaintiffs had

Noble and others v. Kennoway. Dougl. 492.

CHAP. II.

had warehouses sufficient to have held the goods if they had been landed; and that there were no settlements on the coast of *Labrador*, but those belonging to the plaintiffs. [45] One of the sailors swore to the same effect. The plaintiffs then called one *French*, to prove the custom of the *Newfoundland* trade. This evidence was objected to; but Lord *Mansfield* admitted it, and the witness swore, that, in the *Newfoundland* trade, it is customary to keep their goods on board several months, and that sometimes they have part of their homeward cargo of fish, and part of their old cargo on board, at the same time. That the first object is to catch fish, and they unload only at times when they cannot fish. The old cargo being chiefly salt and provisions, it is taken out gradually for curing the fish, and for consumption. The testimony of this witness was confirmed by one *Newman*. Neither *Newman* nor *French* had been at *Labrador*. Mr. *Hunter* was then called, who proved, that, some years since, he used to send vessels of his own, and also chartered vessels to *Labrador*, and that it was usual, in chartering vessels, to stipulate, that they should have sixty days allowed for discharging. That he apprehended they were oftentimes longer in fact, and that it was not so easy to discharge a cargo at *Labrador*, as at *Newfoundland*. Upon this evidence a verdict was found for the plaintiffs, and in the subsequent term the defendant moved to set it aside, which was not granted.

Lord *Mansfield*.—"The trade of fishing on the coast of *Newfoundland*, especially from the west of *England*, has been known and practised for many years. Since the treaty of *Paris*, a new trade has been opened to *Labrador*. The insurance here is on the ships, and *on the goods till landed*. The defendant says, the plaintiffs have been guilty of an unreasonable delay in landing. That question was to be tried by the jury, and could only be decided, by knowing the usual practice of the trade. Every underwriter is presumed to be acquainted with the practice of the trade he insures, and, *that*, whether it is recently established lifhed or not. If he does not know it, he ought to inform himfelf. It is no matter if the ufage has been only for a year. This trade has exifted, and has been conducted in the fame manner for three years. It is well known, that the fifhery is the object of the voyage, and the fame fort of fifhing is carried on in the fame way at *Newfoundland.* I ftill think the evidence on that fubject was properly admitted, to fhew the nature of the trade. The point is not analogous to a common law cuftom."

Mr. Juftice *Buller.*—" I think there was fufficient evidence, without calling in aid the ufage of the *Newfoundland* trade; for it appeared, on the face of the policy, that the fifhery was the purpofe of the voyage: but I think the evidence objected to was properly admitted. If it can be fhewn, that the time would have been reafonable in one place, that is a degree of evidence to prove, that it was fo in another. The effect of fuch evidence may be taken off, by proof of different circumftances. It is very true, that the cuftom of one manor is no evidence of the cuftom of another; that has been determined in many cafes: but the point here is very different; it is a queftion concerning the nature of a particular branch of trade." [46]

The rule was difcharged.

Although the decifions in all the above caufes, notwithftanding the vaft variety of circumftances that are to be found in them, are fo uniform in principle; and although we find, that the learned judges make a conftant reference to the ufage of trade; yet in no inftance whatever has this been fo apparent as in the cafes of infurance upon *Eaft India* voyages, in which the infurers have been held liable, not only for events which may poffibly happen from the port of difcharge to that of delivery; but alfo for all intermediate, or country voyages, upon which the fhip may be difpatched by the order of the council of any of the *Eaft India* Company's fettlements abroad.

It

CHAP. II.

It is not that in these cases, the judges have given a greater latitude to the usage of trade, than in any other; but because from the great variety of cases that have arisen upon the subject, the usage with regard to the *East India* voyage is more notorious, and better established than in those where the question has but seldom occurred. The grounds and reasons of such decisions seem to have been the terms in which all the printed charter parties of the *East India* Company are conceived. By those charter parties, liberty is given to prolong the ship's stay for a year; besides which, it is very common by a new agreement to detain her a year longer: and the longer a ship is kept, it is the more beneficial to the owners. The words of the policy, too, are adapted to this usage, being without limitation of time or place, and without any reference to [47] the first voyage particularly mentioned in the charter party. These charter parties, being printed, are matter of public notoriety; and are so generally and universally known, or may be so, by an inquiry at the *India House*, that the chance of her stay is always one of the risks insured: and both the insured and insurer must be supposed to be fully apprized and sufficiently conusant of it. Indeed, the understanding of the policy depends so much on the course and usage of the *East India* trade, that it seems to be contradictory to the policy to say, that the underwriter did not underwrite for a country voyage.

All these principles were fully laid down by Lord *Mansfield* in a very few years after he took upon him the administration of justice in this country; and they have been frequently recognized, and invariably pursued in a multitude of decisions upon such policies since that time. The learned chief justice, when he laid down these rules, as the ground of his then opinion, and as the guide of future decisions, said, he did so, because the court esteemed this to be the most convenient way of determining the question: for whoever should thereafter insure on an *East India* ship would know, that he insured the contingencies, and might

might take proper precautions againſt them, if he pleaſed. Whereas if every perſon ſhould be obliged to open to the inſurer all the grounds of his expectations about the ſhip's continuance in the *Eaſt Indies*, or coming to *England*, it might produce great litigation and confuſion in caſes ariſing upon theſe policies. CHAP. II.

The caſes, in which theſe principles were ſettled, were the nine cauſes tried upon the ſhip *Winchelſea* an *Eaſt India-man*; in all of which the policies were the ſame, the parties only being different; and all of which were at firſt tried with various ſucceſs; but the nine verdicts were ultimately uniform for the plaintiffs, the inſured, againſt the underwriters. Salvador v. Hopkins, 3 Burr. 1707.

The charter party was in the uſual printed form, and contained a clauſe, empowering the company's ſervants abroad to detain the ſhip a year longer, if they pleaſed, than the time originally limited by the charter party. The inſurance was in theſe words, "at and from *Bengal*, to "any ports or places whatſoever in the *Eaſt Indies*, *China*, "*Perſia*, or elſewhere, beyond the *Cape of Good Hope*, [48] "forwards and backwards, and during her ſtay at each "place, until her arrival at *London*, on money, *&c.*" On the twenty-fifth of *March* 1762, the ſhip failed; on the nineteenth of *September*, in the ſame year, ſhe arrived at *Bombay*; and early in the *November* following, ſhe left *Bombay* the firſt time. The ſhip arrived at *Calcutta* in *Bengal*, on the fifth of *March* 1763; and on the twenty-eighth of the ſame month, the preſident and council of *Bengal* entered into a new agreement with the captain, reciting, that the charter party would expire on the eleventh of *February* 1764, but that the preſident and council, finding it expedient to detain the ſhip in *India*, and being deſirous of having the time limited in the charter party prolonged, *&c.* the indenture therefore witneſſeth, that the captain lets the ſhip to freight for one whole year from the ſaid eleventh of *February* 1764. The ſhip ar-

CHAP. II. rived at *Bombay* a second time in *July* 1763: in *December* following, she again sailed for *Bengal*, and arrived there early in 1764: on the nineteenth of *March* in that year she left *Bengal*, in order to proceed for *Bombay*, and on the twenty-first of that month, subsequent to the expiration of the old charter party, the ship was lost. On the third of *April* 1764, Mr. *Hume*, the plaintiff in several of these actions, received a letter from the captain, dated the fourteenth of *April* 1763, inclosing a copy of the new agreement; which letter was publickly read in a coffee-house. The next day after the receipt of the letter, some insurances were made by Mr. *Hume*. On the seventeenth of *July* 1764, other insurances were effected by Mr. *Hume*, and all the other insurances were made, after the captain's letter, of the fourteenth of *April* 1763, had been received and publickly read in a coffee-house.

3 Burr. 1713.

The court, after laying down all those principles above stated, respecting the notorious usage of this branch of trade, enlarged upon the circumstances peculiarly distinguishing these causes. "No mention was made, or "question asked, at the time of underwriting, when the "ship was chartered; when she sailed from *England*; when "she arrived in *India*; whether she was detained a year "according to the proviso in the charter party: and yet "her continuance in the *East Indies* depended upon all "these facts. If they ought necessarily to be disclosed, "the policy was void, to the knowledge of the under- [49] "writers, at the time they took the premium. The evi- "dence in all the causes was very strong, that her staying "a year longer, if known, would not have varied the "premium. This ship was insured at the same premium "after the prolongation of her stay in *India* was known. "None of the defendants desired to be off, after they "knew that an account of the new agreement had been "received in *England* upon the third of *April* 1764, "which was notorious to them all, before the intelligence "of her loss, which came in the *October* following. So "that

"that if there had been any force in the objection, it "would have been waved by the acquiescence of the "underwriters, after they were fully apprized of the "whole."

Gregory v. Christie, B. R. Trinity 24 Geo. III.

So also, in an action upon a policy "on the goods, "specie, and effects, of the plaintiff, on board the ship on "her voyage from *London* to *Madras* and *China*, with "liberty to touch, stay, and trade, at any ports or places "whatsoever," a similar question arose upon the following facts. When the ship arrived at *Madras*, she was too late to go to *China* that year; upon which she was employed by the council there to go from *Madras* to *Bengal* to fetch rice, which voyage she performed once, and, in attempting to perform it a second time, was lost. The jury found a verdict for the plaintiff.

Vide supra, c. 1, p. 11. where the other point is stated.

A new trial was afterwards moved for on two grounds, one of which only is material here, *viz.* that these intermediate voyages were not insured under the policy; for that the words "to touch, stay, and trade at any ports or "places whatsoever" only meant, to give a license to stay at such places, as it should be necessary to stop at *in the course of the voyage.*

Lord *Mansfield.*—"To understand this policy you must refer to the course of trade, to which it relates. What is the course of trade with the *East India* Company? If an *India* ship come to *Madras* too late in the season to proceed to *China*, the council employs her in an intermediate voyage. It is beneficial to all parties so to employ her; the underwriters are perfectly well acquainted with this usage, and are bound to take notice of it. Before the year 1780, it was usual to insure both the outward and homeward bound voyage in one policy, and then the [50] words "*backwards and forwards*" were inserted: but since that time, they have separated the insurance, and insure the outward voyage in a distinct policy. The policy in

 question

CHAP. II. queſtion differs from others; becauſe it contains a permiſſion to *trade*, as well as to *touch and ſtay*, at any ports or places, which is not uſual in policies of this nature: for in general they only permit them to *touch and ſtay*, which words can only be intended to give a permiſſion ſo to do, if neceſſity oblige them; but to *touch, ſtay, and trade*, are words ſo large, that they ſeem to include the intermediate voyage. It would narrow the conſtruction very much, indeed, to ſay, that the policy relates to thoſe places *only*, at which they ſhall ſtop *in* the voyage. The words made uſe of certainly take in the intermediate voyage; and the uſage of trade confirms this conſtruction." The conſequence of this opinion was, that the verdict of the jury was held to be right.

Farquharſon v. Hunter, B. R. Hilary 25 Geo. III.

So alſo, in an action on a policy of inſurance upon the ſhip *Blandford*, "at and from *London* to *Madras* and *Bengal*, beginning the riſk upon the ſaid ſhip, &c. at *London*, "and ſo to continue till the arrival of the ſaid ſhip at *Madras* "and *Bengal*, with liberty to touch and ſtay at any port "or place in this voyage:" the facts were theſe. The *Blandford* arrived at *Madras*, where her cargo was unloaded by order of the preſidency; ſhe was then ſent for rice to *Viſagipatnam*, and by an entry in the council book, her voyage to *Bengal* is ſaid to be poſtponed. That part of her outward-bound cargo, which was intended for *Bengal*, was ſent thither in the *Lord Mulgrave*, and afterwards the *Blandford* was ſent to *Bengal* in ballaſt, and was taken in the paſſage; for which loſs this action was brought. At the trial, Lord *Mansfield* thought the words in the policy would not admit of ſuch a latitude of conſtruction, as to take in the intermediate voyage, the words being much narrower than thoſe in *Gregory* v. *Chriſtie*: upon which the plaintiff was nonſuited.

However, in the following term, when a motion was made to ſet aſide the nonſuit, his lordſhip ſaid, "This is "a policy on the ſhip: it is an *India* voyage: and the "uſage

[51]

"usage as to the intermediate voyages is notorious to both "parties; and the contract refers to it. The insurance "here is from *London* to *Madras* and *Bengal*. What "is the usage of the trade? That when the ships arrive "at *Madras*, the council may send them elsewhere."— The other judges concurred; and the rule for setting aside the nonsuit was made absolute.

From these cases it is evident, that in the construction of *East India* policies, whether the words be large and comprehensive, as in *Salvador* v. *Hopkins*, and *Gregory* v. *Christie*; or restrained and limited, as in the last case, the usage of trade shall always be considered, and the intermediate or country voyages held to be insured. At the same time, though the general rule be so, the parties contracting may, by their own agreement, prevent such a latitude of construction; and so Lord *Mansfield* said in *Salvador* v. *Hopkins*. In order to do this, it is not necessary that express words of exclusion should be inserted in the policy; but if, from the terms used, the court can collect that such was the intention of the parties, that construction, which is most agreeable to their intention, shall most assuredly prevail.

Thus, in an action upon a policy, the voyage insured was described in these words: "at and from *Port L'Orient* "to *Pondicherry*, *Madras*, and *China*, and at and from thence "back to the ship's port or ports of discharge in *France*, "with liberty to touch, *in the outward or homeward bound* "*voyage*, at the isles of *France* and *Bourbon*, and at all or "any other place or places what or wheresoever." In a subsequent part of the policy, there was this clause, "and "it shall be lawful for the said ship *in this voyage*, to pro-"ceed and sail to, and touch and stay at any ports or "places whatsoever, as well on this side, as on the other "side of the *Cape of Good Hope*, without being deemed a "deviation." The ship arrived at *Pondicherry*, and after remaining there one month, she failed for *Bengal*, instead of

Lavabre v. Wilson and Lavabre Walter, Douglas 284.

CHAP. II. of going to *China*: having wintered at *Bengal*, and received considerable repairs, she returned to *Pondicherry*; and having taken in a homeward-bound cargo, proceeded in her voyage back to *L'Orient*, but was taken by the *Mentor* privateer. The question in that case, as far as it is material to us in this part of our work, was whether the voyage to *Bengal* was insured within the construction of this

Mr. Douglas. policy. The reporter of this case says, it was insisted, in the opening for the plaintiffs, that, under the general lib-

[52] erty given by the policy, of touching at all places whatsoever, the vessel might go to *Bengal*, which, by the operation of those words, was as much part of the voyage, as if it had been expresly named.—Lord *Mansfield*, however, having intimated a clear opinion, that the general words were, by the expressions of "*in the outward or homeward* "*bound voyage*," and "*in this voyage*," qualified and restrained so as to mean all places whatsoever in the usual course of the voyage "*to and from the places mentioned in* "*the policy*," this ground was immediately abandoned, and never farther mentioned by the council for the plaintiffs in the progress of these causes.

But although the judges have been thus liberal in their constructions of this contract, and have gone as far as possible to effectuate the intention of the parties; yet they have never extended those equitable principles to such a length as to say, that when a man has insured one species of property, he shall recover damage, which he has suffered by the loss of a description of property, different from that named in the policy. Thus a man, who has insured a cargo of goods, cannot recover under such a policy, the freight, which he has paid for the carriage of that cargo; nor shall it be permitted to an owner of a ship, who insures the *ship merely*, to demand satisfaction for the loss of mer-

See post, 53. chandize laden thereon, or to ask from the insurers *extraordinary wages paid to the seamen, or the value of provisions consumed*, by reason of the detention of the *ship* at any port, longer than was expected.

Such

CHAP. II.

Such attempts have, indeed, been made, but they have always been reſiſted: for to admit of ſuch demands would introduce an infinite variety of frauds, and would be repugnant to the moſt ſettled maxims of inſurance law, and to the conſtant practice and uſage of trade. In *Molloy* it is ſaid, that if a merchant inſure a ſhip generally, and the ſhip then happen to be laden, and if it afterwards miſcarry, the inſurer ſhall not anſwer for the goods, but only for the ſhip. This poſition ſtands uncontradicted by any foreign writer, ancient or modern, and is ſupported by ſeveral deciſions of the firſt authority in this country.

Molloy b. 2. c. 7. ſ. 8.

Roccus de Aſſecur. Not. 16.

[53]

Fletcher and others v. Poole, Sitt. after Eaſt. 1769, before Lord Mansfield at Guildhall.

In an inſurance *upon the ſhip Tartar* at and from *London* to *Newcaſtle*, and *Marſeilles*, and at and from *Marſeilles* to her diſcharging port or ports in the *Weſt Indies*, (*Jamaica* excepted) the facts were, that the ſhip being diſtreſſed, bore away for *Minorca*, and put into *Port Mahon*, where the captain obtained leave from the vice admiralty court to have his ſhip ſurveyed, in conſequence of which, ſhe was long detained; and the action was brought to recover the extraordinary wages, and the proviſions expended during the detention for theſe repairs.

Lord *Mansfield* was of opinion, that ſuch articles as ſailors wages and proviſions expended, while a ſhip is detained to refit, can never be allowed as a charge againſt the inſurer *on the ſhip*; and a verdict was accordingly given for the defendant.

Baillie v. Moudigliani, B. R. Hill. 25 Geo. III.

In another cauſe, after a trial at *Guildhall*, a ſpecial caſe was reſerved for the opinion of the court, ſtating, that this was an action upon a policy of inſurance *on goods* at and from *Nevis* to *Briſtol*. The ſhip ſailed from *Nevis*; but, before her arrival at *Briſtol*, ſhe was captured and taken into *Morlaix*, and there condemned. An appeal was lodged in the parliament of *Paris*, where the ſentence was reverſed, and the ſhip and cargo were decreed to be reſtored. Before the ſentence of reſtitution, the ſhip and

cargo

CHAP. II.

cargo had been fold; but the money was paid, the charges of profecuting the appeal being deducted. The defendants have paid all the charges of the fuit, and the falvage, except the fum now in demand, which was paid by the plaintiffs, as owners of the goods to the owner of the fhip for *freight pro ratâ itineris:* and for which *freight* this action is brought on the policy *on goods*.

After time taken to deliberate, Lord *Mansfield* delivered the unanimous opinion of the court for the defendants: the *item* now in litigation, his lordfhip faid, is that which was paid for freight, by the owner of the cargo to the proprietor of the fhip *pro ratâ itineris*. The queftion is, whether he can charge thefe underwriters for it. As between the owners of the fhip and cargo, in cafe of a total lofs, no freight is due: but as between them no lofs is total, where part of the property is faved, and the owner [54] takes it to his own ufe. In this cafe, the value of the goods was reftored in money, which is the fame as the goods; and therefore freight was certainly due *pro ratâ itineris*. But as between the owners of the goods, and the underwriters *upon the cargo*, the latter have nothing to do with the *freight*. The owner of the fhip has a lien for his freight; but in a total lofs, literally fo called, no freight is due. In cafe of a lofs, total in its nature, with falvage, the owner may either take the part faved, or abandon: but in neither cafe, can he throw the freight upon the underwriters; becaufe they have not engaged to indemnify him againft it.

Eden v. Poole, Sitt. after Hil. 1785.

This alfo was an action on a policy of infurance, which was on the *fhip and goods* from *Oftend* to *Dominique*. The following facts appeared in evidence: that the fhip met with bad weather, and was in great diftrefs: that the crew threatened to take the command from the captain, unlefs he would make for the firft port: that he then went to *Ferrol* to repair his fhip, and by the time the repairs were finifhed, the crew forfook her: that he then got another

another crew, and at the moment he was going to ſail, the *Spaniſh* governor ſtopped him: that after a detention of 37 days, ſhe was diſcharged, and then arrived at *Dominique*. This action was brought for the expenſe incurred by wages, proviſions, &c. during the demurrage at *Ferrol*. On the part of the inſurer it was contended, and ſo held by Mr. Juſtice *Buller*, who preſided upon that trial, that the freight, and not the ſhip, is liable for this loſs, and that the charge of demurrage could not be allowed upon this policy. The plaintiff was nonſuited.

Agreeably to the above doctrine, there is a modern decision of the whole court of King's Bench. That alſo was an action on a policy of inſurance, on the ſhip *Dumfries*, at and from *London* to *Africa*, during her ſtay and trade there, and at and from thence to her port or ports of diſcharge in the *Britiſh Weſt India* iſlands, to recover a partial loſs. The facts were, that this ſhip, in the courſe of the laſt war, after performing her voyage to *Africa*, in coming from thence laden with ſlaves to the *Weſt Indies*, touched at *Barbadoes* in *December* 1781, for the purpoſe of watering, at which iſland an embargo was laid on all ſhips, by order of Lord *Hood*, the commander in chief upon that ſtation; and the veſſel was detained a conſiderable time. The captain applied for leave to depart; but was refuſed: whereupon he attempted to ſail away privately in the night, but was purſued by the the *Salamander* ſloop of war, and after a ſlight engagement, he was brought back, the *Dumfries* not having ſuſtained any damage, for which the underwriters could be charged, on account of a clauſe, exempting them from partial loſſes, not amounting to 3 *per cent.* Lord *Hood*, in conſequence of this breach of embargo, upon her return took almoſt all the men out of the *Dumfries*, diſperſed ſome of the crew among the ſhips of war, the captain and the reſt of the crew were confined; and the ſhip was detained at *Barbadoes* till the *April* following. This detention, however, was not proved to have ariſen ſolely from the embargo, as

Robertſon v. Ewer, B. R. Hil. 26 Geo. III. 1 Term Reports, p. 127.

[55]

CHAP. II. as it appeared, that, for some part of the time, the small-pox prevailed among the slaves, and that the embargo was frequently taken off and renewed between *December* and *April*. The action was brought to recover from the insurer *upon the ship*, the additional *wages* paid to the seamen, and the *charges for provisions*, during this detention.

Mr. Justice *Buller* was of opinion, at the trial, that the only damages proved, being items for seamen's wages, provisions, and demurrage, during the detention, could not be recovered under this policy on the ship only. To make the underwriter liable, there must be a loss of the ship, for the policy is on the body of the ship only; and if she arrive safe at her port of delivery, be the voyage ever so long, you cannot recover under such a policy; if, indeed, she be in such a state as to prevent her from completing her voyage, it is certainly a loss. The plaintiff was nonsuited.

In the following term a motion was made to set aside the nonsuit, which, after argument, was refused by the whole court to be done, and, upon that occasion, Lord *Mansfield* said, "There is no authority to shew, that on this policy, the insured can recover for such a loss; but it is contrary to the constant practice. On a policy on a *ship*, sailors wages or provisions are never allowed in settling the damages. The insurance is on the *body of the ship*, tackle, and furniture; *not on the voyage or crew*. In this case it is
[56] admitted, that there was no damage done to the ship, tackle, or furniture; and therefore I think the direction was right, and that the plaintiff ought not to recover."

Mr. Justice *Buller*.—"I take it to be perfectly well settled, that you are not to recover on a policy on the body of the ship for seamen's wages or provisions; these are not the subject of the insurance. The case put at the bar proves the rule. For if the ship had been detained in consequence of any injury which she had received in a storm, though the

underwriter

underwriter must have made good that damage, yet you could not have come upon him for the amount of wages or provisions, during the time she was so repairing. Here the ship itself is safe; and the court only look to the thing itself, which is the subject of insurance; and the wages and provisions are no part of the thing insured."

The doctrine contained in the preceding cases was much discussed, and by some supposed to be considerably shaken by a decision of the court of King's Bench in the year 1791; where it was unanimously held by the learned judges, that *provisions* sent out in a ship for the use of the crew are protected by a policy of insurance on the *ship and furniture*. In the argument of that case, the judges at first thought it fell within the principle of decision in *Robertson* v. *Ewer*, which they were determined to support: but the grounds of distinction between the two decisions are stated with so much clearness and perspicuity, and the effect of usage upon this species of contract so well ascertained, that I feel it my duty not to abridge the arguments adopted by the court.

It was an action on a policy of insurance on an *East India* and *China* ship, and on the tackle, ordnance, ammunition, artillery, and *furniture of the ship*. At the trial before Lord *Kenyon* at *Guildhall*, it appeared that while the ship was lying off *Bank-saul Island* in the river *Canton*, it became necessary to refit her, for which purpose the *stores and provisions* were taken out of her, and put into a warehouse, called a bank-saul, and that while they were in the warehouse, they were destroyed by an accidental fire. It was admitted that the policy covered all the articles but the provisions, which were merely for the use of the ship's crew: but if those provisions were not protected by the policy, then there was not an average loss of 3*l*. *per cent*. It was considered in the same light, as if the accident had happened on board the ship. For the defendant it was contended, that the provisions were not protected by the insurance;

Brough v. Whitmore, 4 Term Rep. 206.

See ante, page 41.

CHAP. II. ance; but one of the jury ſaid, it had been determined in Lord *Mansfield*'s time, that they were included under the word *furniture*, under which deciſion the merchants had ſince acquieſced; on which the plaintiffs obtained a verdict.

A motion, founded upon this objection, was afterwards made to ſet aſide the verdict, and an inquiry was ordered reſpecting the caſe alluded to by the juryman; and the argument was fully entered into at the bar.

Lord *Kenyon*, after obſerving on the looſe and ambiguous terms of policies of inſurance, ſaid, "The queſtion here ariſes on the meaning of the word "*furniture*;" one of the jurymen ſaid, and in that he is now confirmed, that according to the underſtandings of thoſe who enter into theſe contracts, it includes *the proviſions for the uſe of the crew*. Now, among the ſeveral accidents, againſt which the defendant inſured, *are perils by fire*; and this ſhip being at *Canton*, it became neceſſary to refit her, and to take out all her goods, and land them on this iſland, where the accident happened; by which theſe proviſions, with the reſt of the goods, were burned; and there is no doubt but that the loſs on this iſland muſt be conſidered in the ſame light as if it had happened on board the ſhip itſelf. This was determined in *Pelly* v. *The Royal Exchange Aſſurance Company*. Then if theſe proviſions be inſured as part of the out-fit of the ſhip, and they were conſumed by one of the perils inſured againſt, there is an end of the queſtion; a loſs has happened within the meaning of the policy; and conſequently the defendant is liable. But it was ſaid in the argument that the inſtant any of the proviſions were conſumed on board, there could not be a total loſs: but the ſhort anſwer to that is, that that comes within the wear and tear of the ſhip, and it might as well be ſaid that if a maſt were a little injured there could not be a total loſs. If this deciſion were to militate againſt any determination, or even an *obiter dictum*, of Lord *Mansfield*, I ſhould have heſitated for ſome

time

time before I delivered my opinion. But the cafe of *Robertfon* v. *Ewer* is clearly diftinguifhable from the prefent; here the goods were confumed by an accident by fire on board the fhip, (for the ifland was for this purpofe equivalent to the fhip) and within the meaning of the policy of infurance: but in that cafe they were confumed *by the Negroes during a detention* of the fhip.

Mr. Juftice *Afhhurft.*—" The cafe cited is not like the prefent, for the reafon given; and I think that this lofs comes within the terms of the policy. It is an undertaking to infure againft all accidents which will prevent the provifions being applied to the purpofe for which they were intended. Thefe provifions were part of the out-fit; they were confumed by fire, (one of the accidents againft which the defendant infured) and confequently could not be applied to the purpofe for which they were put on board."

Mr. Juftice *Buller.*—" I am clearly of opinion that the underwriters on the body and furniture of the fhip are liable to pay the amount of thefe provifions, which were bought to replace thofe, which were confumed by an accident within the meaning of the policy. Without commenting on the words of the policy, it is fufficient to fay that a policy of affurance has at all times been confidered in courts of law as an abfurd and incoherent inftrument; but it is founded on ufage, and muft be governed and conftrued by ufage. Now it is perfectly clear that in every inftance, where loffes have been fettled, the provifions put on board the veffel when fhe failed, have been confidered as part of the fhip. The value is taken in this way; the underwriters have a right to go and fee the fhip, to examine the value of the hull, the mafts, and the provifions; the value of the fhip alone comprehends all thefe articles; but though the underwriters have a right to examine the fhip itfelf, in point of fact they do not, becaufe they know, from experience, the quantity of provifions neceffary for the crew for the intended voyage; and if that value be ftated to them in the ordinary

CHAP. II. ordinary way, they ſign their names immediately without making further inquiries. Then if the proviſions be included in a policy on the ſhip, and the ſhip and all the proviſions be loſt, the underwriters muſt make good the whole loſs, whether it be a valued or an open policy. But it has been ſaid that, if an accident happen after ſome of the proviſions are conſumed, the underwriters are entitled to a deduction to the amount of ſuch proviſions: I will anſwer this, firſt, as the argument applies to a valued, and then to an open policy. As to the firſt; from the nature of the policy, the proviſions are not inſured againſt all events; they are only inſured againſt particular riſks. Again, there is nothing from which there can be ſalvage; if the body of the ſhip and every thing on board be ſunk, or burned, there can be no ſalvage. And, in the caſe of an open policy, the inſured muſt prove by evidence what was the value of the whole, and then the ſame reaſons apply as in the caſe of a valued policy. With reſpect to the caſe of *Robertſon* v. *Ewer*, which has been relied on; I thought at firſt that it applied ſtrongly to the preſent; and if I ſtill entertained the ſame opinion, I would not on account of any uſage to the contrary among underwriters, overturn a ſolemn determination of this court: but that caſe, and the two others there mentioned, are clearly diſtinguiſhable from the preſent. In all thoſe the inſured wiſhed to charge the underwriters with the amount of the proviſions conſumed, during the time when the ſhips were detained. Of thoſe therefore it is ſufficient to ſay that an inſurance is *on the ſhip for the voyage*: but, during a detention, the ſhip is not proceeding; and therefore the underwriters are not liable. This caſe alſo differs from that of *Robertſon* v. *Ewer*, in another circumſtance; there the proviſions were conſumed by the ſlaves on board, and not by the ſhip's crew, and the ſlaves are conſidered as part of the cargo. The words of Lord *Manſfield* in that caſe muſt be taken with a reference to the caſe then before him: He was then ſpeaking of a charge for proviſions uſed during the detention of the ſhip, and for the maintenance of the ſlaves; and he ſaid, "there is no autho-

"rity

" rity to shew that, on *this* policy, the insured can recover " for *such a loss*; but it is contrary to the constant practice." Then he proceeded to say, on a policy on a ship, sailors' wages or provisions are never allowed in settling the damages. Now, even if those latter words be taken in their general sense, and not confined to the case immediately before the court, they are accurate; for " provisions" *eo nomine* are not taken into consideration. In general, the captain of a ship takes on board provisions sufficient for the voyage; and, if he be detained in any port, and he be a prudent man, he will not use what are called the ship's stores during his detention, but he will buy others for immediate consumption during the detention, because he cannot but know that he has the same length of voyage to perform that he had before he was detained: it makes no difference however to the underwriters whether he do so or not; for if the captain be obliged to purchase other stores for the remainder of the voyage, the underwriters are not answerable for these, but only for those which were on board at the time of the insurance, since they only formed a part of the value of the ship. On the whole therefore I am of opinion that there should be no new trial. The cases cited are distinguishable from the present; the usage of merchants, as to the construction of these instruments, stands unimpeached, and therefore it must prevail in this case."

Mr. Justice *Grose* agreed, and the rule was discharged.

Hoskins v. Pickersgill, B. R. Easter, 23 Geo. III.

In an insurance upon a *Greenland* ship, it became a question, whether the *lines and tackle* employed in the fishery in those seas could be recovered under a policy made upon *the ship, tackle and furniture*, &c. This case came before the court, upon a motion for a new trial, and the judges were unanimously of opinion, that they were not protected by the policy, not being part of the *ship's* tackle or furniture.

It is also necessary, in order to entitle the insured to recover, that the loss, which has happened, be a direct and immediate

CHAP. II.

mediate confequence of the peril infured, and not a remote one. This doctrine was laid down in a cafe before Lord *Mansfield*, and the decifion of the jury was agreeable to the principle ftated by the Chief Juftice.

Jones v. Schmoll, Guild. Tr. Vac. 1785, 1 Term Rep. p. 130. Note (*a*)

It was an action on a policy of affurance "at and from "*Briftol* to the coaft of *Africa*, during her ftay and trade "there, and from thence to her port or ports of difcharge in "the *Weft Indies*." There was a memorandum on the pol-"icy, that the affurers are not to pay any lofs that may "happen in boats during the voyage (mortality by natural "death excepted) and not to pay for mortality by mutiny, "unlefs the fame amount to 10*l.* *per cent.* to be computed "on the firft coft of the fhip, out-fit, and cargo, valuing "negroes fo loft at 35*l.* per head." The demand upon the policy was the lofs of a great many flaves by mutiny. The evidence of the captain was, that he had fhipped 225 prime flaves on board: that on the third of *May*, before he failed from the coaft of *Africa*, an infurrection was attempted; that the women feized him on the quarter deck, and endeavoured to throw him overboard, but he was refcued by the crew; that the women and fome men threw themfelves down the hatchway, and were much bruifed. That he fent the ringleader on fhore, and twelve men and a woman after- [57] wards died of thofe bruifes, and from abftinence: that on the 22d of *May* there was a general infurrection, the crew were forced to fire upon the flaves, and attack them with weapons, it being a cafe of imminent neceffity. Several flaves took to the fhip's fides, and hung down in the water by the chains and ropes, fome for about a quarter of an hour, three were killed by firing, and three were drowned, the reft were taken in, but they were too far gone to be recovered; many of them were defperately bruifed, many died in confequence of the wounds they had received from the firing during the mutiny, fome from fwallowing falt water, fome from chagrin at their difappointment, and from abftinence; feveral of fluxes and fevers; in all to the amount of 55. The underwriter had paid at the rate of 15 *per cent.* for 19, who

who were either killed during the mutiny, or had afterwards died of their wounds. Another consequential damage was stated, that the mutiny had lessened the remaining slaves in the estimation of the planters, and reduced their price.

CHAP. II.

Lord *Mansfield* said, " as to the latter loss, I think the underwriter is not answerable for the loss of the market, or the price of it : that is a remote consequence, and not within any peril insured against by the policy.

" The question for the jury will be, whether any of those who died by any other means, except by being fired upon, or in consequence of the wounds and bruises which they received during the struggle, are within the meaning of the policy, which insures against damage by mutiny. This policy is in the common form, and if it were not for the memorandum, I should say, the case was not within the instrument. But as it now stands it is very clear, that those who were killed by the firing, or died in consequence of their wounds, are within the policy; the other complicated cases must be left to the jury. The first class, such as were killed in the fray, certainly come within the meaning of the policy ; and the second class also, those who died of the wounds they received. The third class are, I think, as clearly not within it, such as being baffled in their attempts, in despair chose a mode of death, by fasting, or died through despondency : that is not mortality by mutiny, but the reverse, for it is by *failure of mutiny*. [58] The great class are such as received some hurt by the mutiny, but not mortal, and died afterwards of other causes, as those who swallowed water, jumped overboard, *&c*. This is the great point."

The jury found, that all who were killed in the mutiny, or died of their wounds, were to be paid for. That all those who died of their bruises, which they received in the mutiny, though accompanied with other causes, were to be paid for. That all who had swallowed salt water, and died in consequence thereof, or who leaped into the sea, and hung upon the

CHAP. II. the sides of the ship, without being otherwise bruised, or who died of chagrin, were not to be paid for.

In the construction of policies of insurance for time (*a*), which are very frequent, the same liberality, equity, and good sense, have always prevailed, as in all other insurances: and the courts have gone, as far as possible, to decide according to the intention of the parties.

Syres and others v. Bridge, Doug. 509.

In an action on a policy of insurance on the ship *Mary*, a letter of marque, the words of the policy were, "at and "from *Liverpool* to *Antigua*, *with liberty to cruise six weeks*, "and to return to *Ireland*, or *Falmouth*, or *Milford*, with any "prize or prizes." This ship having been taken, this action was brought, and came on to be tried before Baron *Hotham* at *Lancaster*, when a verdict was found for the plaintiffs.

Upon a motion for a new trial, the material parts of the evidence were, that the policy was made on the 9th of *February* 1779, and there was no time fixed in it for the commencement, or the duration of the voyage. The captain of the ship, being called on the part of the plaintiffs, swore that he in fact sailed from *Liverpool* on the 28th of *February*: he was five days before he cleared the land; and he proceeded on his direct voyage till the 14th of *March*, chasing, however, at different times, from the 7th to the 14th, at which time he began his cruise, giving notice thereof to the crew, and ordered a minute of it to be entered in the log-book, which was done. From the 14th of *March*, he continued cruising about the same latitude till the 17th or 18th of *April*; when he discontinued the cruise, of which he also gave notice, [59] intending to go to the *Burlings*, off *Lisbon*, in the course of his voyage. On the 23d he renewed the cruise, of which he gave notice as before, and ordered a minute, to that purpose, to be entered in the log-book. From that time he continued cruising till the 28th of *April*, when he was taken by an

(*a*) By a late act of parliament 35 Geo. III. c. 63. s. 12. no policy upon any ship, or interest therein, shall be made for any longer term than 12 calendar months. See ante, p. 28.

an *American* privateer. Many witneſſes were examined, ſome of whom thought, that the liberty of cruiſing given by the policy, meant ſix ſucceſſive weeks; others conceived, that if the ſeparate times of cruiſing, when added together, ſhould not exceed the ſpace of ſix weeks, the terms of the inſurance would be complied with: but none of them could prove any uſage, as none of the witneſſes ever knew a caſe exactly circumſtanced like the preſent.

Lord *Mansfield*.—"This was merely a queſtion of conſtruction, on the face of the policy, and unleſs an uſage could have been ſhewn in favour of this deſultory cruiſing, calling witneſſes to ſupport it, was calling them to ſwear to mere opinion. None of thoſe produced knew of any inſtance; and therefore, their evidence ought not to have been received. Yet, I dare ſay, their teſtimony had great weight with the jury. The meaning of words depends upon the ſubject. The inſtructions were not read, but they ſhew the meaning very clearly, for they run thus: "To cruiſe ſix "weeks, and *then* proceed to *Antigua*." There can be no general rule. Here the ſubject matter, in my opinion, is deciſive to ſhew, that the ſix weeks meant one continued period of time. A cruiſe is a well known expreſſion for a connected portion of time. There are frequently articles for a month's cruiſe, a ſix weeks cruiſe, *&c.* Such a liberty, as in this caſe, to a letter of marque, is an excuſe for a deviation. But what is contended for by the plaintiffs is impoſſible in practice. Suppoſe the ſhip returns *directly back*, cruiſing for the ſpace of a week. She may then perhaps take three weeks to return to where ſhe had been. Can ſhe then renew the cruiſe, return again, and ſo repeatedly? The voyage, in that way, might laſt for years. But the true meaning is, "I will excuſe a deviation for ſix weeks." The inſtructions, although it happens they were not read, ſtrike me much. Another argument: Six weeks is a continuation, a congregate denomination of time. If they had meant ſeparate days, they would have ſaid forty-two days." [60] The rule for a new trial was made abſolute.

CHAP. II.

Having said thus much of construction in general, by which it appears, that the material rules to be adhered to are, the intention of the parties entering into the contract, and the usage of trade; it will be proper to consider more particularly, what shall be construed a loss within the meaning of the policy. This mode of treating the subject naturally leads us to consider losses by perils of the sea; losses by capture, and by detention of princes or people; and losses by the barratry of the masters or mariners; which are the great divisions of perils insured, and which will furnish materials for the three following chapters.

CHAPTER THE THIRD.

Of Loſſes by Perils of the Sea.

THE ſubject matter of this chapter may be reduced to a very ſmall compaſs; as very few queſtions have ever been agitated in the *Engliſh* courts of law upon this point. It may, in general, be ſaid, that every thing which happens to a ſhip, in the courſe of her voyage, by the immediate act of God, without the intervention of human agency, is a peril of the ſea. Thus in an inſurance againſt perils of the ſea, every accident happening by the violence of wind or waves, by thunder and lightning, by driving againſt rocks, by the ſtranding of the ſhip, or by any other violence which human prudence could not foreſee, nor human ſtrength reſiſt, may be conſidered as a loſs within the meaning of ſuch a policy: and the inſurer muſt anſwer for all damages ſuſtained, in conſequence of ſuch accident. But if a ſhip be driven by ſtreſs of weather on an enemy's coaſt, and is there captured, it is a loſs by capture, and not by perils of the ſea. This was ruled by Lord *Kenyon* in an action on a policy againſt capture only, and the ſhip was driven by a hard gale of wind on the coaſt of *France*, and was there captured, but ſhe did not receive any damage by the wind. Lord *Kenyon* ſaid, this was clearly a loſs by capture, for had ſhe been driven on any other coaſt than that of an enemy, ſhe would have been in perfect ſafety. The plaintiff had a verdict.

CHAP. III.

1 Shower 323. Roccus. Not. 64.

Green v. Elmſlie, Peake 212.

In caſes where the loſs is not total, but only partial, ariſing from a leak, from the ſtranding of the ſhip, or from the loſs of her maſts, cables, or rigging, the inſurers upon the cargo are liable to reſtore the value of all the damaged goods, and the underwiter upon the ſhip is alſo anſwerable for all the injury which ſhe has ſuſtained.

1 Magens 52. 76.

In

CHAP. III

2 Roll. Abr. 248. pl. 10. Comberbatch, 56.

In charter parties, if the veſſel freighted was robbed or taken by pirates, that was held to be a loſs within the meaning of the words "perils of the ſea." It is alſo ſaid, that the ſame rule of conſtruction prevails as to policies of aſſurance. That poſſibly might and would be the true conſtruction upon thoſe words: but as it is now the univerſal cuſtom to inſure againſt the attacks of pirates, by expreſs words inſerted in the policy, that queſtion can now hardly ariſe.

Although the courts in this caſe, as in all others, will endeavour to give effect to this ſpecies of contract, by a liberal [62] and equitable conſtruction; yet they will be cautious not to extend the principle ſo far, as to ſay, that the acts of the parties ſhall be made to operate beyond their intention; and therefore they will attend to the words of the contract, and ſee that the loſs, which has proved to have happened, is really one of thoſe riſks againſt which the underwriter has inſured.

Gregſon v. Gilbert, B. R. Eaſter, 23 Geo. III.

An action was brought upon a policy of inſurance for the value of certain ſlaves, inſured by that policy. The declaration ſtated, "that by perils of the ſea, contrary winds, currents, and other misfortunes, the voyage was ſo much retarded, that a ſufficient quantity of water did not remain for the ſupport of the ſlaves, and other people on board, and that certain of the ſlaves, mentioned in the declaration, periſhed for want of water." The facts, appearing in evidence, were, that the ſhip, being bound from *Guinea* to *Jamaica*, had miſſed the iſland, and the crew were reduced to great diſtreſs for want of water: that the captain conſulted with the crew, and it was unanimouſly agreed upon that ſome of the ſlaves ſhould be thrown overboard, in order to preſerve the reſt: that at the time this reſolution was formed, there remained but one day's full allowance of water, at two quarts *per* man. The jury, upon this evidence, found a verdict for the plaintiff, with damages at 30*l.* a head for every ſlave thrown overboard.

A motion was afterwards made for a new trial, upon the ground, that this was not a loſs by perils of the ſea. CHAP. III.

Lord *Mansfield*.—"This is a very uncommon caſe, and deſerves a further conſideration. There is great weight in the objection, that the loſs is ſtated, by the declaration, to have ariſen from the perils of the ſea, and that the currents, *&c.* had made the ſhip foul and leaky. Now does it appear by evidence, that the ſhip was foul and leaky? On the contrary, the loſs happened by miſtaking *Jamaica* for another place. Beſides, a fact has been mentioned by the council of throwing ſome overboard *after* the rain fell; a fact, which is not agreed on by both ſides, though a very material one."

Mr. Juſtice *Buller*.—"The declaration does not, in any part of it, ſtate the loſs, which has been the occaſion of this demand; and it would be very miſchievous, if we were to overturn this objection. Suppoſe, for a moment, that the underwriters, in ſome caſes, are liable for the miſtake of the captain, yet, if they are not liable in others, the nature of the loſs muſt be ſtated in the declaration, that the defendant may have an opportunity of moving in arreſt of judgment, if it be not ſufficiently alleged. But it would be impoſſible for the defendant in this caſe to move in arreſt of judgment; for the facts of the caſe, as proved, are different from thoſe ſtated in the declaration. The point of law in arreſt of judgment can only be argued from the facts ſtated on record; and the declaration in this caſe ſtates the loſs of the plaintiff to have happened by perils of the ſea." The rule for a new trial was made abſolute, on payment of coſts. [63]

If a ſhip has been miſſing, and no intelligence received of her within a reaſonable time after ſhe ſailed, it ſhall be preſumed that ſhe has foundered at ſea.

The

CHAP. III.

Greenv. Brown. 2 Stra. 1199. The ſhip *Charming Peggy* was inſured in 1739, from *North Carolina* to *London*, with a warranty againſt captures and ſeizures, and in an action the loſs was laid in the declaration to be by ſinking at ſea. All the evidence given was, that ſhe failed out of port on her intended voyage, and had never ſince been heard of. Several witneſſes proved, that, in ſuch a caſe, the preſumption is, that ſhe periſhed at ſea, all other ſorts of loſſes being generally heard of. It was inſiſted for the defendant, that as captures and ſeizures were excepted, it lay upon the plaintiff to prove, that the loſs happened in the particular manner declared on. But Lord Chief Juſtice *Lee* ſaid it would be unreaſonable to expect certain evidence of ſuch a loſs, where every body on board is preſumed to be drowned: and all that can be required is the beſt proof the nature of the caſe admits of, which the plaintiff has given. He therefore left it to the jury, who found according to the plaintiff's declaration.

Newby v. Read, Sittings after Michaelmas, 3 Geo. III. The ſame doctrine was held in a more modern caſe before Lord *Mansfield*. It was an action of covenant on a deed, in the nature of a policy of inſurance, by which the defendant was bound to inſure againſt any loſs happening before

[64]

the 30th of *November* 1762, free from average. The ſhip ſailed from *Newcaſtle* to *Copenhagen*, which is uſually about ten days voyage. She was ſoon after taken by a *French* privateer, but ranſomed; and ſhe then proceeded on her voyage to *Copenhagen* (as was proved by the ranſomers) in a bad condition. She was never heard of afterwards, though all due diligence had been uſed; and ſeveral ſhips, which ſailed after her, were proved to have arrived ſafe at *Copenhagen*.

Lord *Mansfield* told the jury, that this evidence was a ſufficient ground to preſume that ſhe periſhed at ſea, unleſs the contrary appeared. The jury accordingly found for the plaintiffs.

I have

I have not been able to find any regulation in the law of *England*, or the usage of merchants, fixing a limited time, within which the assured may demand payment for his loss, in case no accounts arrive of the ship, upon which insurance is made. Indeed, from the nature of the thing, what shall be a reasonable time, in such cases, must always depend upon a variety of obvious circumstances. I understand, however, a practice has prevailed among insurers, which seems reasonable enough, that a ship shall be deemed lost, if not heard of in six months after her departure, (or after the time of the last intelligence from her) for any part of *Europe*; and in twelve months, if for a greater distance. The only objection to such a practice is, that the latter period does not seem sufficient in *India* voyages. However, that is a matter for the insurer's consideration; Salk. 22. and even if he should pay the money under a mistake, supposing the ship lost, when it really is not, he might, as we shall see hereafter, if the insured were unwilling to refund, recover it back, in an action for money had and received to his use. Vide post, c. 20.

In *Spain* and *France*, this matter, however, is not left to uncertainty; but the time, within which such *losses* may be demanded, is fixed and ascertained by express regulations. By the ordinances of the former, if any ship insured on going to, or coming from the *Indies*, is not heard of in a year and a half after her departure from the port where she loaded, it is declared that she is, and shall be deemed lost: by those of the latter it is said, that if the insured receive no news of his ship, he may, at the expiration of a year for common voyages, reckoning from the day of the departure, and after two years for those at a greater distance, make his cession to the underwriters, and demand payment, without being obliged to produce any certificate of the loss.

2 Magens 33.

[65]

2 Magens 177. Ord. of Lewis 14. f. 31. art. 58.

CHAPTER THE FOURTH.

Of Loffes by Capture and Detention of Princes.

CHAP. IV.

CAPTURE, as applied to the fubject of marine infurances, may be faid to be a taking of the fhips or goods belonging to the fubjects of one country, by thofe of another, when in a ftate of public war. What fhall be confidered as a capture, fo as to render an infurer liable under a policy, infuring againft captures, has now become a queftion of very little difficulty.

2 Burr. 694. 1ft point in Gofs v. Withers.

The law upon this fubject is pefectly fettled in *England*, between the infurer and the infured; and it is this, that the fhip is to be confidered as loft by the capture, though fhe be never condemned at all, nor carried into any port or fleet of the enemy: and the infurer muft pay the value. If, after a condemnation, the owner recover or retake her, the infurer can be in no other condition, than if fhe had been retaken or recovered before condemnation. The infurer runs the rifk of the infured, and undertakes to indemnify; he muft therefore bear the *lofs*, actually fuftained, and can be liable to no more. So that if, after condemnation, the owner recovers the fhip in her complete condition, but has paid falvage, or been at any expenfe in getting her back, the infurer muft pay the lofs fo actually fuftained. No capture by the enemy can be fo total a

2 Burr. 696.

lofs, as to leave no poffibility of recovery. If the owner himfelf fhould retake at any time, he will be entitled; and by late acts of parliament, if an *Englifh* fhip retake the veffel captured, either before or after condemnation, the owner is entitled to reftitution upon ftated falvage. This chance does not, however, fufpend the demand for a total lofs upon the infurer: but juftice is done, by putting him in the place of the infured, in cafe of a recapture.

29 Geo. II. c. 34. f. 24. 33 Geo. III. c. 66. f. 42.

Thefe

These principles, which are agreable to the ideas of foreign writers, were settled by Lord *Mansfield*, and the whole court of King's Bench, in *Goss* against *Withers*, (which will be cited at length when we come to treat of abandonment) and which have never since been disputed. It has likewise been held, that where a capture has been made, whether it be legal or not, the insurers are liable for the charges of a compromise made *bonâ fide*, to prevent the ship from being condemned as prize. It is true, the only case I have been able to find where this point came directly in question is a *nisi prius* note; but when we consider the high authority from which this doctrine is taken, and that the thing in itself is not at all repugnant to the general principles of the law of insurance, it certainly has a claim to our attention.

2 Burr. 683.

Rocci Selecta responsa. Resp. 34.

Berens v. Rucker. 1 Black. 313.

It was an action on a policy of insurance on a *Dutch* ship, called the *Tyd*, and its cargo, at and from *Saint Eustatius* to *Amsterdam*, warranted a *Dutch* ship, and the goods *Dutch* property, and not laden in any *French* port in the *West Indies*. The cargo was worth 12,000*l.* and was insured at a premium of fifteen guineas *per cent.* which was advanced to this high rate, on account of the number of captures made by the *English*, of neutral vessels, on suspicion of illicit trade, and the detention of those vessels, by the proceedings in the courts of admiralty. The defendant underwrote 82*l.* of the plaintiff's, for a premium of 12*l.* 18*s.* 3*d.* In *May* 1758, the ship was at *Saint Eustatius*, taking in her cargo, which consisted of sugar and indigo, and other *French* commodities, which were put on board her, partly out of barks from sea, partly from the shore of the island. On the 18th of *June* 1758, she sailed on her voyage; on the 27th she was taken by an *English* privateer, and carried into *Portsmouth*. On the 1st of *August*, the sailors were examined upon the standing interrogatories, prescribed by the statute 29 *Geo.* II. *c.* 34. and the captain entered his claim in the Admiralty court. In *October* 1758, the claimants were cited to specify what part of the goods was

CHAP. IV. was taken from the ſhore of *Saint Euſtatius* and what from the barks. Citation was continued from court to court till *February* 1759, when an interlocutory decree was pronounced for the contumacy of the claimants in not ſpeci-
[68] fying, and that therefore the goods ſhould be preſumed *French* property. There was an appeal to the lords commiſſioners of prizes: but as many cauſes ſtood before it, as the market was very high, and as the cargo was in part periſhable, the agent of the owners agreed with the captors to give them 800*l.* and coſts, to obtain the reverſal of the ſentence. The reverſal was had by conſent, and, in order to give coſts to the captor, it was decreed by conſent, that there was a ſufficient cauſe for ſeizure; and thereupon coſts were decreed to the captors, and reſtitution of the cargo to the owners was alſo ordered. The ſhip, when reſtored, proceeded to *Amſterdam*; and after her arrival there, the Chamber of Inſurances in that city ſettled the average of the plaintiff towards the loſs and expenſes at 14*l.* 3*s.* 8*d.* occaſioned by the capture, detention, and litigation; and for this ſum the action was brought.

Lord *Mansfield.*—"The firſt queſtion is, whether this was a juſt capture? Both ſentences are out of the caſe, being done and undone by conſent. The capture was certainly unjuſt. The pretence was, that part of this cargo was put on board off *Saint Euſtatius*, out of barks, ſuppoſed to come from the *French* iſlands, and not loaded immediately from the ſhore. This is now a ſettled point by the Lords of Appeal, to be the ſame thing as if they had been landed on the *Dutch* ſhore, and then put on board afterwards; in which caſe there is no colour for ſeizure. The rule is, that if a neutral ſhip trade to a *French* colony, with all the privileges of a *French* ſhip, and is thus adopted and naturalized, it muſt be looked upon as a *French* ſhip, and is liable to be taken. Not ſo, if ſhe have only *French* produce on board, without taking it in at a *French* port; for it may be purchaſed of neutrals.

Second

Second queſtion is, whether the owners have acted *bonâ fide*, and uprightly, as men acting for themſelves, and upon a reaſonable footing; ſo as to make the expenſes of this compromiſe a loſs to be borne by the inſurers. The order of the judge of the Admiralty to ſpecify was illegal, contrary to the marine law and the act of parliament, which is only declaratory of the marine law; becauſe if they had ſpecified, it could be of no conſequence, according to the rule I before mentioned. The captors were, however, in poſſeſſion of a ſentence, though an unjuſt [69] one: and a court of appeal cannot, or ſeldom does, upon a reverſal, give coſts or damages, which have accrued ſubſequent to the original ſentence; for theſe damages ariſe from the fault of the judge, not of the parties. Under all theſe circumſtances, therefore, the owners did wiſely to offer a compromiſe. The cargo was worth 12,000 *l.* the appeal was hazardous; the delay certain. The *Dutch* deputy in *England* negotiated the compromiſe; the Chamber of Commerce at *Amſterdam* ratified it, and thought it reaſonable. Had the whole ſentence been totally reverſed, the coſts muſt have ſat heavy on the owners. I therefore think the inſurers liable to anſwer this average loſs, which was ſubmitted to, in order to avoid a total one." The jury found for the plaintiff, agreeably to the above direction (*a*).

CHAP. IV.

But though the law upon this ſubject is ſo clearly defined, that at this day it ſeems almoſt impoſſible to raiſe a queſtion, yet it formerly occaſioned much doubt and litigation, what effect a recapture might have upon this kind of contract; and how long it was neceſſary for goods to remain in the hands of the enemy, in order to diveſt the original proprietor of his property in caſe of a recapture.

All theſe doubts are now entirely removed, and can never again be agitated in this country, between an inſurer and

(*a*) In Tyſon v. Gurney, 3 Term R. 477. this caſe was quoted without contradiction; and the point, in ſupport of which it was adduced, was held accordingly.

CHAP. IV. and insured; Lord *Mansfield*, for himself and his brethren, having declared, in giving judgment in *Goss* v. *Withers*, that 2 Burr. 695. these questions could never have been started in policies *upon real interest*, because, as we have seen, they never could Vide beginning of this Chap. have varied the case. But wager policies gave rise to them; for it was necessary to set up a total loss, as between third persons, for the purpose of their wager, though *in fact* the ship was safe, and restored to the owner. His 2 Burr. 1198. 19 Geo. II. c. 37. Lordship laid down the same doctrine in *Hamilton* v. *Mendez*; the consequence of which is, that as wager policies are now expressly prohibited by statute, these questions can never arise upon a policy of insurance.

2 Burr. 693. The only two possible cases, in which they can be material, are: 1st, Between the owner and a neutral person [70] who has bought the capture from the enemy: and, 2dly, Between the owner and recaptor: But whatever rule ought to be followed in favour of the owner, against a recaptor or vendee, it can no way affect the insurance between the insurer and insured.

Notwithstanding this point is now, as far as relates to our present inquiry, no longer a subject of uncertainty, it cannot but afford pleasure to the mind, and, I trust, it will not be considered as impertinent, to trace the opinion of foreign writers upon this question, and to state briefly several cases which have been decided in our courts of law here, upon capture and recapture, previous to the statute of 19 *Geo.* II.

It seems to be generally agreed by foreign writers, that it is not every taking and subsequent possession under that taking, which will constitute a capture in the legal sense of the word, or make it become the property of the captor; but that there must be a firm possession. In this they all agree; but what shall be such a possession, as to vest the absolute property in the captor, is so much a matter of doubt, that it is difficult to find two writers of the same opinion.

opinion. Upon this ſubject, various lines have been drawn by arbitrary rules, partly from policy, to prevent too eaſy diſpoſitions to neutrals; and partly from equity, to extend the *jus poſtliminii* in favour of the owner. And it is not to be wondered at, that there is ſo great an uncertainty and variety of notions amongſt the writers on this ſubject, about fixing a poſitive boundary by the mere force of reaſon, where the ſubject matter is arbitrary, and not the object of reaſon alone.

CHAP. IV.

2 Burr. 693.

Grotius is of opinion, that the captor ſhall be ſaid to have the property in him, as ſoon as the former owner ſhall have loſt the hope of recovery, and the ability to purſue, and that property ſhall then be ſaid to be *taken*, when it is brought within the enemy's fortreſs. Whence it follows, as a conſequence, that in marine captures, the capture ſhall be deemed complete, when the ſhips or goods taken ſhall be brought within the harbour or ports of the enemy, or to that place where their whole fleet is ſtationed; for then the recovery may be deſpaired of. But, by a more recent law, introduced among the *European* nations, it ſeems, that, that only is deemed a capture, which has been twenty-four hours in the poſſeſſion of the captor. [71] The former part of this opinion, I find, was adopted in a caſe in *March*'s Reports, where it is ſaid, that the property is not altered, unleſs it be brought *infra præſidia* of the enemy: and ſome nations have made twenty-four hours quiet poſſeſſion by the enemy, the criterion of their judgment. Thus, by the ordinances of *Lewis* the fourteenth, it is declared, that if any of the ſhips of *French* ſubjects be retaken from their enemies, after having been twenty-four hours in their hands, they ſhould be good prize; and if it be before twenty-four hours, they ſhall be reſtored to the owners, with all that is in them, and one third ſhall be given to the ſhip that retakes them. *Bynkerſhoek*, however, ſtates the opinion of *Grotius*, controverts it with much ability, and ſeems to think, that the *ſpes recuperandi* is the ground on which the queſtion is to be decided. He mentions

Grotius de jure belli, lib. 3. c. 6. ſ. 3.

March 110.

Ord. of Lew. ſ. 34. art. 8.

Bynkerſhoek quæſt. publ. juris, lib. 1. c. 4.

CHAP. IV. mentions the opinion of ſome writers, who think that it is neceſſary for the ſhip to have arrived in the enemy's port, to have been condemned, to have ſailed out again, and arrived in a friend's port, before the property can be ſaid to be changed. *Roccus* rather ſtates the various opinions of others, than aſſerts one of his own; but he ſeems to lean to the idea, that it is neceſſary to bring the ſhip within the confines of the captor, and to keep it there a night in ſafe cuſtody. But as was ſaid by Lord *Mansfield*, all theſe circumſtances are very arbitrary, and therefore are generally exploded.

Roccus Not. 66. 2 Black. Com. 401.

2 Burr. 694.

2 Burr. 694.

By the marine law of *England*, as practiſed in the court of Admiralty, previous to the paſſing of any act of parliament, which commanded reſtitution, or fixed the rate of ſalvage, it was held, that the property was not changed ſo as to bar the owner in favour of a vendee or recaptor, till there had been a ſentence of condemnation. Agreeably to this principle, judgment was given in that court, decreeing reſtitution of a ſhip retaken by a privateer, though ſhe had been fourteen weeks in the enemy's poſſeſſion. Another caſe alſo, upon the ſame principle, was decided againſt the vendee after a long poſſeſſion, two ſales, and ſeveral voyages.

Thus ſtands the marine law of *England*, by which it appears, that the *jus poſtliminii* continues till condemnation, which, by the acts of parliament, about to be quoted, is extended, and now continues for ever.

[72]

By the ſtatutes of the 13th *Geo.* II. c. 4. and 29th *Geo.* II. c. 34. ſhips or veſſels of his majeſty's ſubjects, which had been captured by the enemy, and were retaken, either by men of war or privateers, were decreed to be reſtored to the original owners, upon paying for ſalvage the ſums mentioned in the ſtatutes, and the quantum of ſalvage to be paid to privateers was made to depend upon the length of time which the re-captured veſſel had been in the enemy's my's hands; such salvage, however, never being allowed to exceed a moiety of the value. CHAP. IV.

By the last prize act this distinction is abolished, and the rate of salvage payable in all cases is fixed to one-eighth of the value, if the re-capture is made by any of his majesty's ships, and to one-sixth, if by a privateer, or other ship. 33 Geo. III. c. 66.

The words of this clause of the statute are, "that if "any ship or vessel, or boat taken as prize, or any goods "therein, shall appear and be proved, in any court of "admiralty having a right to take cognizance thereof, to "have belonged to any of his majesty's subjects of *Great* "*Britain* or *Ireland*, or any of the dominions and territo-"ries remaining and continuing under his majesty's pro-"tection and obedience, which were before taken or sur-"prized by any of his majesty's enemies, and at any time "afterwards again surprized and retaken by any of his maj-"esty's ships of war, or any privateer, or other ship, "vessel, or boat, under his majesty's protection and obe-"dience, that then such ships, vessels, boats, and goods, "and every such part and parts thereof as aforesaid, for-"merly belonging to such his majesty's subjects, shall in all "cases (save in such as are hereafter excepted) be adjudged "to be restored, and shall be, by decree of the said court "of admiralty, accordingly restored to such former owner "or owners, or proprietors, he or they paying for and in "lieu of salvage (if retaken by any of his majesty's ships) "one-eighth part of the true value of the ships, vessels, "boats, and goods respectively, so to be restored, which "said salvage of one-eighth shall be answered and paid to "the flag officers, captains, officers, seamen, marines, and "soldiers, in his majesty's said ship or ships of war, to be "divided in such manner as before in this act is directed "touching the share of prizes belonging to the flag offi-"cers, captains, officers, seamen, marines, and soldiers, "where prizes are taken by any of his majesty's ships of s. 42.

CHAP. IV.

"war; and if retaken by any privateer, or other ſhip, "veſſel, or boat, one-ſixth part of the true value of the "ſaid ſhips, veſſels, boats, and goods; all which pay- "ments to be made to the owner or owners, officers and "ſeamen of ſuch privateer, or other ſhip, veſſel, or boat, "ſhall be without any deductions, and ſhall be divided in "ſuch manner and proportions as ſhall have been agreed "on by them as aforeſaid; and in caſe ſuch ſhip, veſſel, "or goods, ſhall have been retaken by the joint operation "or means of one or more of his majeſty's ſhips, and one "or more private ſhip or ſhips, then the judge of the High "Court of Admiralty, or other court having cognizance "thereof, ſhall order and adjudge ſuch ſalvage to be paid "to the re-captors, by the owner or owners of ſuch re- "taken ſhip, veſſel, or goods, as he ſhall, under the cir- "cumſtances of the caſe, deem fit and reaſonable, which "ſalvage ſo to be adjudged ſhall be accordingly paid by "the owners of ſuch retaken ſhip, veſſel, or goods, to "the agents of the re-captors, in ſuch proportions as the "ſaid court ſhall adjudge; but if ſuch ſhip or veſſel ſo re- "taken ſhall appear to have been, after the taking by his "majeſty's enemies, by them ſet forth as a ſhip or veſſel "of war, the ſaid ſhip or veſſel ſhall not be reſtored to "the former owners or proprietors, but ſhall in all caſes, "whether retaken by any of his majeſty's ſhips, or by any "privateer, be adjudged lawful prize for the benefit of the "captors."

From hence it is clear, that by the marine law received and practiſed in *England*, there is no change of property, in caſe of a capture, before condemnation, and that now by the act of parliament juſt recited in caſe of a re-capture, the *jus poſtliminii* continues for ever, unleſs the ſhip ſo retaken ſhall appear to have been ſet forth by his majeſty's enemies as a ſhip of war, in which caſe ſhe ſhall be deemed good prize to the re-captors. However, as has been already ſaid, the change of property is not at all material as between the inſurer and inſured, upon policies of real intereſt,

interest, which are the only policies that can now by law be effected.

I proceed then to state the cases, which were determined upon this point, on wager policies, previous to the act of parliament, prohibiting such insurances.

[73]

The first case is one in the 10th year of Queen *Anne's* reign, in which the facts upon a special verdict appeared to be, that the plaintiff had insured a certain sum of money upon a ship, called the *Ruth*, in a certain voyage, *in which ship the plaintiff was found not to be at all interested*. It happened that this ship was taken by the enemy, and kept in their possession for nine days, and then before it was carried *infra præsidia*, it was retaken by an *English* man of war. Upon these facts, the question was, whether or not this was such a taking as should enable the plaintiff to recover the sum insured against the defendant.

Assievedo v. Cambridge, 10 Mod. 77.

After argument, the court seemed to think (but a second argument was ordered, which does not appear from any reporter ever to have been made) that the defendant was entitled to judgment.

Upon this case Lord *Mansfield* has observed, that the man of war, which retook the ship, brought her into the port of *London*, and restored her to the owner upon reasonable redemption; that this appears from the special verdict, although it is not stated in the printed case; and then, as the owner did not abandon the ship, he could only have come upon the insurers for the redemption; and no question could have arisen upon the change of property. Besides, the policy being interest or no interest, without benefit of salvage, the question arose upon the terms and meaning of the wager. But that case was not determined.

2 Burr. 695.

This also was an action of *assumpsit* on a policy of insurance, where the defendant insured the plaintiff, *interest or*

Depaiba v. Ludlow, Comyn's Rep. 360.

CHAP. IV.

or no intereſt, againſt all enemies, pirates, takings at ſea, and all other damages whatſoever. And upon trial it appeared, that the ſhip was taken by a pirate of *Sweden*, and was in his poſſeſſion for nine days, and was then retaken by an *Engliſh* man of war, and after the ſuit commenced, was brought into *Harwich*. The queſtion was, whether, in ſuch a caſe, the defendant was reſponſible.

[74] It was determined for the plaintiff. But although it was objected, that the inſurer was only reſponſible, where the plaintiff had a property, and that the term of inſuring, *intereſt or no intereſt*, was introduced ſince the revolution; yet it was ſaid, that ſuch inſurance was good, and the import of it is, that the plaintiff has no occaſion to prove his intereſt, and that the defendant cannot controvert it. And though the ſhip was here retaken, yet the plaintiff received a damage, for his voyage was interrupted; and the queſtion is not, whether the plaintiff had his ſhip, and did not loſe his property, but what damage he ſuſtained.

2 Burr. 695.

Lord *Mansfield* has alſo obſerved upon this caſe, that it was a wager policy, and the property could not be changed, for there was then no war, or declaration of war; that the court held, that as the ſhip was once taken in fact, the event had happened, though ſhe was afterwards recovered. His Lordſhip ſaid, that the ſame obſervations were applicable to the caſe of *Pond* v. *King*.

Pond v. King, 1 Wilſ. 191. and Lex Merc. red. 4th edit. 302.

That was an action on a policy of inſurance upon the *Salamander* privateer (of which the plaintiff was part owner) from the *Downs* to any port or place where ſhe ſhould ſail for three months from the 1ſt of *December* 1744, *intereſt or no intereſt*, free from average, and without benefit of ſalvage; the inſurance was againſt ſuch perils as are uſually mentioned in policies: the breach aſſigned is, that the *Salamander* was taken by a *French* ſhip of war within the three months, and was wholly loſt, whereby ſhe could not proſecute her voyage or cruiſe. The jury found a ſpecial verdict,

verdict, stating, that the *Salamander* was taken by a *French* ship of war within the three months; that 117 of her men were taken out of her, and carried into *France*, and her guns taken out, and that she remained in the possession of the enemy from four o'clock in the afternoon of the 2d of *February* till five o'clock in the afternoon of the 5th of *February*; that before she was carried into any port, she was retaken by an *English* privateer, and by the captain of the privateer kept eight days upon the high seas without sailing, and at the end of eight days the captain of the privateer took a *French* prize, and, together with her and the *Salamander*, endeavoured to come into some *English* port, but the wind not permitting, he carried them into *Lisbon*; that the *Salamander* remains there for the benefit of those to whom she belongs; that the plaintiff is interested, exceeding the sum insured; that the ship was prevented from finishing her three months cruise by the capture, but that she was a living ship at the end of three months; that *Lisbon* is a neutral port; that the master of the privateer obtained a decree in the Court of Admiralty at *Gibraltar*, that the ship should be restored to the owners, on payment of one third part for salvage. [75]

Lord Chief Justice *Lee*, after two arguments, delivered the unanimous opinion of the whole court:—" The question is, whether the capture of this ship, which was never carried *infra præsidia hostis* before she was retaken, and upon the matter as found by the verdict, shall be considered as a total loss, so as to entitle the insured to recover the whole sum insured. And although by the civil law it may not perhaps be adjudged a total loss, yet the rules of that law are not to govern us, but we must give our judgment according to the common law of *England*, and upon this agreement between the parties, whose intention appears, and must guide us. By the civil law, there must be a total loss to entitle the assured to recover, but the policy in this case extends to captures and other accidents. The meaning of the parties here is plain; the insured paid his premium in

CHAP. IV.

in consideration of the insurer's undertaking, that the *Salamander* should cruise safely during three months; the jury have found that she was disabled from prosecuting her cruise for three months. We are all of opinion for the plaintiff, and that this is not an average, but a total loss to the insured: the insurance is to be understood for the voyage of three months, and in common sense it cannot be otherwise; so that as soon as the voyage is broken or interrupted, it is at an end. Safety during the three months is what is meant; but it appears that the ship was taken and detained within that time, and that the plaintiff was hindered in his cruise; and this, by our law, is a total loss to the plaintiff. I have avoided saying any thing whether this was a prize or not, as having never been carried *infra præsidia hostis*, because we are all of opinion, that this is a total loss." Judgment for the plaintiff.

Spencer v. Franco coram Lord Hardwicke, Dec. 1736. Lex Merc. red. 4th edit. p. 316.

[76]

In the case of *Spencer* v. *Franco*, the plaintiff had caused himself to be insured on the *Prince Frederick*, from *Vera Cruz* to *London*, *interest or no interest*, free of average, and without benefit of salvage. The ship was afterwards seized by order of the viceroy of *Mexico*, and the *Spaniards* turned her into a man of war, called the *Saint Philip*, and sent her as commodore, with a squadron of *Spanish* men of war, to the *Havannah*, they having first taken out the *South Sea* Company's arms, and made several alterations in her, and there was a war between *England* and *Spain*, and *Gibraltar* was actually besieged by the *Spaniards*. The defendants proved the signing of preliminary articles of peace before the seizure of the ship, and therefore insisted, that this seizure did not alter the property, and consequently the defendants were not liable: for if the property was not altered, this insurance made by the plaintiff, who had no interest, cannot bind, as nothing comes within the policy but a total loss: and though there be those general words in the policy, *restraint, or detainment of princes*, Lord Chief Justice *Hardwicke* declared, that a war might begin without an actual declaration or proclamation, as in this

this case, by laying siege to *Gibraltar*, a garrison town; that as a war may begin by hostilities only, so it may end by a cessation of arms; and these preliminary articles being signed before the seizure of the ship, and there being a cessation of arms, he thought the ship being taken afterwards, not to be a taking by enemies, unless the jury took the caption to begin from the time the *South Sea* arms were seized, which was before the articles: that supposing the ship not taken by enemies, whether his detention for near the space of a year was, in this sort of policies, *viz. interest or no interest*, a detention within the policy; or whether in such policies the insurers are ever liable, but in case of a total loss; and if so, this ship being afterwards restored, then he directed the jury to find for the defendants, which they accordingly did.

In another case, the insurance was on goods by the *Dursley* galley, *interest or no interest*, at and from *Jamaica* to *Bristol*. In her passage she was taken by a *Spanish* privateer, and carried into *Mores*, a port in *Spain*, kept eight days, and then cut out by an *English* ship. The plaintiff insisted, that this insurance, though on goods, was to be considered as a wager on the bottom of the ship; and therefore brought his action for a total loss. The defendant said, that by the stat. of 13 *Geo.* II. *c.* 4. the ship is to be restored to the owners upon paying salvage, and consequently this is only an average loss; and the plaintiff can only recover upon a total one. Lord Chief Justice *Lee* held, that the plaintiff ought to recover: for this is a wager upon a total loss in the voyage, and here has happened one; for being carried into port and detained eight days makes one. Where the policy is, "*interest or no interest*," the provisions of the act in cases of valued policies cannot take place. The act does not declare that the property is not gone by such a capture, but only provides for restoring the ship to whom it did, and shall be proved to have belonged. He said, it might be otherwise, where the ship was recaptured, before it was carried *infra præsidia*,

Dean v. Dicker, 2 Stra. 1250.

[77]

CHAP. IV. *sidia*, or in case of goods actually on board, and upon a valued policy.

Whitehead v. Bance, B. R. Mich. 1749. An insurance was made on the *Dispatch* galley, *interest or no interest*, free of average, *&c.* from *Jamaica* to *Hull*. In her voyage she was taken by a *French* privateer; and carried to *Hamburgh*, and after being twelve days in the hands of the enemy, she was retaken by an *English* ship, and brought to *London*, where she was adjudged to be restored to the owner, paying salvage. The owner sold the ship, and paid the salvage. An action being brought on the policy, it was held to be a loss of the voyage; and a verdict was given accordingly.

These cases have been laid before the reader, without any comments, except such as have occurred from time to time to Lord *Mansfield*, as he has had occasion to mention them; and it was the less necessary to observe upon each particular case, as one general observation is applicable to all, namely, that they were not policies upon *real interest*. Let it suffice then to repeat, that, at this day, in cases of capture, the underwriter is immediately responsible to the insured. But if the ship be recovered before a demand for indemnity, the insurer is only liable for the amount of the loss actually sustained at the time of the demand: or if the ship be restored at any time subsequent to the payment by the underwriter, he shall then stand in the place of the insured, and receive all the benefits and advantages resulting from such restitution. All these regulations certainly have their foundation in the great principles of equity and justice; an observation which must be obvious to every one who recollects, that a policy of insurance is nothing more than a contract of indemnity.

[77 *a*] 33 Geo. III. c. 66. s. 44. Before the subject of capture and recapture is closed, it may be proper to mention, that by the late prize act, if a ship be retaken before she has been carried into an enemy's port, it shall be lawful for her, with consent of the recaptors, to prosecute her voyage, and it shall not be necessary for the recaptors to proceed to an adjudication till six months, or till her return to the port from which she sailed; and it shall be lawful for the master, owners, &c. with consent of the recaptors, to unliver and dispose of the cargo before adjudication: and in case the vessel shall not return directly to the port from which she sailed, or the recaptors shall have had no opportunity of proceeding to adjudication within the six months, on account of the absence of the said vessel, the Court of Admiralty shall, at the instance of the recaptors, decree restitution to the former owners, paying salvage, upon such evidence as to the said court, under all the circumstances of the case, shall appear reasonable, the expense of such proceeding not to exceed the sum of fourteen pounds. CHAP. IV.

[78]

Having thus endeavoured to explain the nature of captures by an enemy, as far as they affect the subject of insurances, I proceed now to treat of losses arising from another species of capture, namely, by detention; a part of our inquiry which will not demand a long or tedious discussion. The underwriter, by the express terms of his contract, is answerable for all loss or damage arising to the insured, "*by the arrests, restraints, and detainments of* "*all kings, princes, and people, of what nation, condition, or* "*quality whatsoever.*"

The only question then is, what shall be considered as such detention: and indeed the words used are so large and comprehensive, as hardly to admit of a doubt even upon that head. The learned *Roccus* is of opinion "*ut si* "*merces captæ a potestate, seu judice justitiam administrante* "*in illo loco, aut a populo, aut ab aliâ quâcunque personâ* "*per vim, absque pretii solutione, tenentur assecuratores sol-* "*vere æstimationem dominis mercium, factâ prius per dominos* "*mercium cessione ad beneficium assecuratorum pro recuperan-* "*dis illis mercibus, vel pretio ipsorum a capientibus.*" In another place he says, "*Regis & principis factum connume-* Roccus de assec. Not. 54. Not. 65.

"*ratur*

CHAP. IV.

"*ratur inter casus fortuitos ; ideo si rex et princeps retineant* "*navem oneratam frumento ex causâ penuriæ, quapropter* "*navis non potuerit frumenta asportare ad locum destinatum,* "*tenentur assecuratores.*"

Malyne 110.

Malyne lays down the law to be, that the insurers are liable for all losses by arrests, detainments, *&c.* happening both in time of war and peace, committed by the public authority of princes. And Lord *Mansfield* has said, that the insured may abandon in case merely of an arrest or embargo by a prince, not an enemy; and consequently such an arrest is a loss within the meaning of the word *detention.*

2 Burr. 696.

Nesbitt and another v. Lushington, 4 Term R. 783.

What the word "*people,*" in this clause of a policy of insurance, means, has lately been judicially settled in a case, where the declaration claimed a loss of corn, occasioned *by the unlawful arrest, restraint, and detention of people to the plaintiffs unknown.* The facts upon this part of the case were, that the ship being forced into *Elly Harbour,* in *Ireland,* and a great scarcity of corn happening to be there at that time, the people came on board in a tumultuous manner, took the government of the vessel from the captain and crew, weighed her anchor, by which she drove upon a reef of rocks, and would not leave her, till they had compelled the captain to sell almost all the corn considerably below the invoice price. The word *people,* it was contended at the bar, meant individuals of a nation as opposed to magistrates or rulers.

Lord *Kenyon.*—"That which happened in this case does not fall within the meaning of "arrests, restraints, and detainments of kings, princes, and people." The meaning of the word *people* may be discovered here by the accompanying words, *noscitur a sociis* ; it means, "*the ruling* "*power of the country.*"

Mr. Justice *Buller.*—"I cannot agree with the construction put at the bar upon the word, *people* ; it means *the supreme power; the power of the country*, whatever it may be. This appears clear from another part of the policy; for where the underwriters insure against the wrongful acts of individuals, they describe them by the names of "*pirates*, "*rogues*, *thieves*:" then having stated all the individual persons, against whose acts they engage, they mention other risks, those occasioned by the acts of "kings, princes, and *people*, of what nation, condition, or quality soever." Those words, therefore, must apply to *nations* in their collective capacity."

An embargo is an arrest laid on ships or merchandize by public authority, or a prohibition of state commonly issued to prevent foreign ships from putting to sea in time of war, and sometimes also to exclude them from entering our ports. This term has also a more extensive signification, for ships are frequently detained to serve a prince in an expedition, and for this end have their loading taken out, without any regard to the colours they bear, or the princes to whose subjects they belong. The legality of such a measure has been doubted by some, but it is certainly conformable to the law of nations, for a prince in distress to make use of whatever vessels he finds in his ports, that may contribute to the success of his enterprise. Embargoes laid on shipping in the ports of *Great Britain*, by royal proclamation, *in time of war*, are strictly legal, and will be equally binding, as an act of parliament, because such a proclamation is founded on a prior law, namely, that the king may prohibit any of his subjects from leaving the realm. But in times of peace the power of the king of *Great Britain* to lay such restraints is doubtful; and therefore where such a proclamation issued in the year 1766, against the words of a statute then in force, although absolutely necessary for the prevention of a dearth in this country, it was thought prudent to procure an act of the legislature to indemnify those who advised, or who acted under, that proclamation.

Lex Merc. red. 4th edit. 260.

[79]

Grot. de jure belli, lib. 2. cap. 2. s. 10. 1 Black. Com. 270.

7 Geo. III. c. 7.

In case of detention by a foreign power, which in time of war may have seized a neutral ship at sea, and carried it into port

1 Magens 67.

CHAP. IV.

port to be searched for enemy's property, all the charges consequent thereon must be borne by the underwriter: and whatever costs may arise from an improper detention, must always fall upon them.

Salucci v. Johnson, B. R. Hil. 25 Geo. III.

This was held by *Willes*, *Ashhurst*, and *Buller*, justices, in the absence of Lord *Mansfield*, in a case, the circumstances of which are as follows: It was an insurance on the ship *Thetis*, a neutral ship; and upon the trial, a special case was reserved for the opinion of the court, stating, that the plaintiffs were *Tuscan* subjects, resident at *Leghorn*, sole owners of the ship *Thetis*, which sailed from *Leghorn*, and was captured by a *Spanish* ship off the coast of *Barbary*, with neutral goods on board, consigned to *London*. She was condemned as prize in the court of Vice Admiralty in *Spain*, which sentence was reversed; but upon another appeal to a superior court, the latter sentence was also reversed, and the former confirmed. The grounds of condemnation were two: 1st. That the ship *Thetis* refused to be searched, and resisted with force, having fired at the *Spanish* ship: 2dly. That she had no charter party on board. The captain of [80] the *Thetis* answered these two grounds: 1st. that he resisted and fired, because the *Spaniard* hailed him under false colours: 2dly. that he had taken the goods on board by the piece, and had not freighted his ship to any individual; in which case a manifesto was sufficient without a charter party. The sentence of the last court of appeal, although it condemns, admits the neutrality, for it states the vessel to be "*a* "*Tuscan ship.*" The last ground relative to the charter party was not insisted upon. Upon the other, the three learned judges above mentioned were of opinion, that a neutral ship is not obliged to stop to be searched; that the captain had not been guilty of barratry; that the searcher stops a neutral ship at his peril; that this was to be considered as a case of improper detention, and consequently that the plaintiff upon this policy was entitled to recover.

But

But though an underwriter is liable for all damage ariſing to the owner of the ſhip or goods from the reſtraint or detention of princes, yet that rule ſhall not be extended to caſes where the inſured ſhall navigate againſt the laws of thoſe countries, in the ports of which he may chance to be detained, or to caſes where there ſhall be a ſeizure for non-payment of cuſtoms. This was ſo ruled by Lord Commiſſioner *Hutchins* in Chancery, in the year 1690; and the reaſon of it is obvious, becauſe there is a groſs fraud on the part of the owner of the property inſured; and no man ſhall take advantage of his own miſconduct. If indeed any of thoſe acts were committed by the maſter of the ſhip, without the knowledge of the inſured, the underwriter would be liable, if not for loſſes by detention, at leaſt for a loſs by the barratry of the maſter, to which ſuch conduct would moſt certainly amount.

2 Vern. 176.

Vide the next chapter.

It has been a queſtion, whether the inſurers are liable for the payment of damage ariſing by the detention or ſeizure of ſhips by the government of the country, in whoſe ports the ſhip loads. Till lately there was only one common law caſe where this point was expreſsly in iſſue, and that was not decided.

In evidence upon the trial in an action upon a policy of inſurance, the caſe appeared to be, that the inſurer agreed to inſure the ſhip from her arrival at ——— in *Jamaica* during her voyage to *London*; and an embargo was laid upon the ſhip, by the government; who afterwards ſeized the ſhip, converted her into a fire-ſhip, and offered to pay the owners. The queſtion was, if this would excuſe the inſurers? *Holt*, Chief Juſtice, ſeemed to incline, that it would not, and that this was within the words, *detention of princes, &c.* but he gave no abſolute opinion, the cauſe having been referred to three of the jury.

Green v. Young, 2 Ld. Raym. 840. 2 Salk. 444.

[81]

The very general words made uſe of in policies go to ſupport the idea entertained by Lord *Holt*, and although till lately

CHAP. IV. lately there was no case where this point was expressly considered, yet it seems to have been taken as settled in many Vide ante, p. 54. cases, which have come before the court. One instance immediately occurs, in the case of *Robertson* v. *Ewer*, which was cited in a former chapter. There an embargo had been laid by Lord *Hood* on all shipping at *Barbadoes*; and it does not appear to have been doubted or questioned at the bar; that the insurer was liable for any loss which might have been sustained by such detention, provided the loss had 2 Magens 176. happened to any of the property specifically insured. It is true, that it is declared by the ordinances of *France*, "that "if any ship be stopped by our orders in any of the ports "of our kingdom *before the voyage be begun*, the insured shall "not, on account of this detention, abandon or cede their 2 Magens 417. "effects to the insurers." A similar regulation is to be found in *Bilboa*, by which it is ordained, "that if any ship "or ships insured, with or without goods, shall be detained "by his majesty's orders in the ports of these kingdoms of "*Spain, before the commencement of the voyage she is bound on*, "it shall be judged that no cession can be made of them, "but rather the insurance in such case ought to be held "null." If these ordinances, when they use the words, "commencement of the voyage," mean commencement of the risk insured, they agree with the laws of *England* (a); because the underwriter can never be answerable for any thing happening before that period: but when the risk insured is "at and from," if the ship be detained in the loading port, by order of the state, before her departure for the voyage, but after the risk commenced, the insurer by our law is liable for the damage occasioned by such detention, as the [81 a] words in the policy do in themselves import no restriction to restraints and embargoes by foreign or hostile powers only.

This

(a) The French policies on the ship always attach only from the day the ship sails, unless the parties vary the general rule by a particular agreement. See the ordinances in 2 Magens 168, 169.

This queſtion came on lately for conſideration in the court of King's Bench; and was unanimouſly decided in favour of the aſſured, after two arguments at the bar. But the learned judges deſired not to be conſidered as deciding upon the effect of an embargo laid on by our own ſovereign upon ſhips loading in this country. The queſtion came before the court upon a ſpecial caſe reſerved for its opinion, upon the trial of an action on a policy of inſurance on three ſhips, the *Adelaide*, *Adele*, and *Victor*, their ſtores, boats, and fiſhing materials, &c. upon two of them at and from *L'Orient*, and upon the third, at and from and after her arrival at *L'Orient*, and on all of them, "to all ports, ſeas, "and places whatſoever, beyond and on this ſide the Capes "of *Good Hope* and *Horn*, on the ſouthern whale and ſeal "fiſhery and trade, and until the ſhip's arrival back at "*L'Orient*." The loſs is ſtated by the declaration to have happened by the ſhips and their ſtores and proviſions being, by authority of certain perſons exerciſing the powers of government in *France*, at *Port Louis* with reſpect to one, and at *L'Orient* with reſpect to the two others, arreſted and reſtrained from further proſecuting their voyages, and that they had thence hitherto been prevented and reſtrained therefrom under and by virtue of ſuch reſtraint. The caſe ſtated that the ſhip *Adelaide* failed from the port of *L'Orient* on the voyage inſured, but was obliged to put back by ſtreſs of weather into *Port Louis*; and whilſt ſhe lay there, and the ſhips *Adele* and *Victor* were preparing for the voyages in the policies mentioned, and before the neceſſary paſſports and clearances could be obtained, on the 5th *Feburary* 1793, an embargo was laid on all veſſels in thoſe ports. That the *Adelaide* was brought back to *L'Orient*, and the periſhable ſtores of all the three ſhips ſold; and the ſaid three veſſels with the reſt of the ſtores now remain at *L'Orient*, under the embargo, which has continued ever ſince on all ſhips deſtined on long voyages; and none have ſince been permitted to ſail, except thoſe in government ſervice or upon ſhort coaſting voyages. The *Adele* and *Victor* had entered outwards upon the voyages inſured, when the embargo came; and

Rotch v. Edie, very fully reported in 6 Term Rep. 413.

CHAP. IV.

and that alone prevented the ſhips from failing. That notice of abandonment was given to the underwriters on 27th *Feb.* 1793, and a total loſs claimed; and the like notice and claim were repeated in *Auguſt* 1793 (*a*).

Lord *Kenyon*.—"I have looked into all the caſes which have been cited, and I have alſo conſidered the paſſages collected from foreign writers, and the moſt reſpectable of them ſeem to me to coincide with the conſtruction, which an *Engliſh* court of juſtice would put upon ſuch an inſtrument as the preſent. This plaintiff is under no diſability to ſue, and the defendant has entered into an engagement to indemnify him againſt arreſts, reſtraints, and detainments of all kings, princes, and people, of what nation, condition, or quality ſoever. By this peril, the ſhip has been detained near three years, and the voyage is defeated: but the plaintiff is to be told this is not a loſs within the policy. No common man reading the words of the policy could doubt upon the queſtion: and it is by artificial reaſoning only collected by great reading from foreign authors that his claim can be repelled. But in truth, when examined, the reſearch turns out to be all one way, and that is in favour of the plaintiff. *Roccus*, *Le Guidon*, *Green* v. *Young*, from Lord *Raymond*, are all one way: and although Lord *Holt* is ſaid not to have given an abſolute opinion, every thing that fell in judgment from that great man is deſerving of the higheſt attention. Lord *Mansfield* too has given an opinion upon the very point (2 *Burr.* 696, and ante, p. 78;) and when to this current of authorities we add the words of the policy itſelf, it is perfectly clear. Suppoſe war had been declared, and the ſhip had been detained in port as a prize, could there have been a doubt? and I can ſee no difference between the caſes."

The

(*a*) Some other facts were ſtated; but as the effect of them was to ſhew that the plaintiff was either an alien enemy, or in partnerſhip with an alien enemy; and as the facts did not ſupport the argument which was to be raiſed upon them, and did not form an ingredient in the judgment of the court, I forbear to ſtate them.

The other judges delivered their opinions *feriatim*, concurring unanimoufly with his Lordfhip; and there was judgment for the plaintiff.

By what has been faid it appears, that before the infured can recover againft the underwriter in cafes of detention, he muft firft abandon to the infurers his right, and whatever claims he may have to the goods infured. This point will be fully treated of in the chapter of abandonment. It will be fufficient here to remark, that in moft of the countries on the continent, the time for abandonment in fuch cafes is fixed to a limited period after the event has happened. In *Bilboa* and *France* the ceffion muft be made within fix months, if the lofs has happened in any part of *Europe*; and within a year, if in a more diftant country. A fimilar regulation as to time is eftablifhed by the ordinances of *Middleburgh* in *Zealand*. By the law of *England*, there is no pofitive rule on this fubject, confequently an infured has a right to abandon immediately upon hearing of the detention. But it fhould feem, that in order to prevent the underwriters from being haraffed, the infured ought to make his election, whether he will abandon or not, within a reafonable time; and what that fhall be, muft in general depend upon the circumftances of the cafe.

2 Magens 175. 416.

2 Magens 23.

See the cafe of Mitchell v. Edie, poft. ch. 9. p. 172. where this point has been confidered and fettled.

CHAPTER THE FIFTH.

Of Losses by the Barratry of the Master or Mariners.

CHAP. V.

IT does not seem to have been any where precisely ascertained, from what source the term *barratry* has been derived.

Indeed the derivations of barratry have rather tended to confound, than to throw any light upon the subject: for its root has been so frequently altered, according to the caprice of the particular writer, that it is impossible to decide which is the true one. The *English* however, most probably have taken it from the *French*, *barrateur*, which is to be traced to the *Italians*: but where the latter found this word is a thing by no means clear.

Cowp. 154. Whatever the derivation may be, the word seems to have been originally introduced into commercial affairs by the *Italians*, who were the first great traders of the modern world. In the *Italian* dictionary, the word *barratrare* means to cheat; and whatsoever is done by the master, amounting to a cheat, a fraud, a cozening, or a trick, is barratry in him. *Postlethwaite*, in his dictionary of trade and commerce, defines *barratry* thus: "barratry is committed when the master of the "ship, or the mariners, cheat the owners, or insurers, wheth-"er it be by running away with the ship, sinking her, de-"serting her, or embezzling the cargo." In another place, the same author observes, "one species of barratry in a "marine sense is, when the master of a ship defrauds the "owners or insurers, by carrying a ship a course different "from their orders." These definitions are so very comprehensive, that they seem to take in every case of barratry, known to the law of *England*, as far as we can collect the principles from the several cases that have been decided. From a review of those cases, and they are but few, it

1 vol. p. 214.

1 vol. 136.

1 Stra. 581.

it appears that any act of the master, or of the mariners, which is of a criminal nature, or which is grossly negligent, tending to their own benefit, to the prejudice of the owners of the ship, without their consent or privity, is barratry. 2 Stra. 1173. Cowp. 143. 1 Term Rep. 323.

It is not necessary, in order to entitle the insured to recover for barratry, that the loss should happen *in the act of barratry*; that is, it is immaterial, whether it take place *during* the *fraudulent* voyage, or *after* the ship has returned to the regular course; for the moment the ship is carried from its right track with an evil intent, barratry is committed. Cowp. 155.

But the loss, in consequence of the act of barratry, must happen *during the voyage insured*, and within the time limited by the policy, otherwise the underwriters are discharged. Thus, if the captain be guilty of barratry by smuggling, and the ship afterwards arrive at the port of destination, and *be there moored at anchor twenty-four hours in good safety*; the underwriters are not liable, if, after this, she should be seized for that act of smuggling. Lockyer v. Offley, 1 Term Rep. p. 252. Vide ante, ch. 2. p. 31.

From the above descriptions of barratry, it will appear, that if the act of the captain be done with a view to the benefit of his owners, and not to advance his own private interest, no barratry has been committed. I have said, that to constitute barratry, it must be without the knowledge or consent of the owners; because nothing can be so clear as this, that no man can complain of an act done, to which he himself is a party. But it is material to consider, in what sense the word owner is to be understood, in this definition. It has been argued, that if *A.* be the owner of a ship, and let it out to *B.* as freighter, who insures it for the voyage; and if the deviation be with the knowledge of *A.* though unknown to *B.* the insurer is discharged. But the court over-ruled that argument, and said, that in order to discharge the insurer from the loss by barratry, it must appear, that the act done was by the consent, or with the privity of the owner, *pro hâc vice*, that is, the freighter, the person insured. Cowper 154.

CHAP. V.

These principles being advanced, it will now be sufficient to shew that they are supported and established by the cases which have been decided. But before they are quoted, it will be proper to observe, that by the positive regulations [85] of *Middleburgh*, *Amsterdam*, *Hamburgh*, and other countries in *Europe*, the underwriters are universally held to be answerable for losses arising by the barratry of the master or mariners. By the ordinances of *Rotterdam*, the owners of ships are prohibited from making insurances against the barratry of the masters, whom they themselves shall appoint; but they may insure against their neglect, and also against the villainy of the sailors, and of such masters, as may happen to succeed to the command of the ship in foreign parts, without the knowledge of the owners, on account of the decease or absence of the master originally appointed. No such rule prevails in the law of *England*; but the insurer undertakes generally and by express words inserted in the policy, to indemnify the owner of the ship or cargo against all losses which he may happen to sustain by the barratry of the master or mariners, even though the master should have been appointed by himself: a circumstance which is rather singular, for the insurer to undertake for the conduct of a man whom he can neither appoint nor dismiss.

2 Magens 73. 130. 215.

2 Magens 89.

Knight v. Cambridge. 2 Ld. Raym. 1349. 1 Stra. 581.

In an action upon the case on a policy of insurance, on the ship *Riga Merchant*, "at and from *Port Mahon* to *London*, against the barratry of the master (among other "things,) and all other damages, dangers, and misfortunes "which should happen to the prejudice and damage of the "said ship," the breach assigned in the declaration was the loss of the ship "*by the fraud and negligence*" of the master. The plaintiff had judgment in the court of Common Pleas. The defendant brought a writ of error, and it was contended by his counsel, that the words, "*fraud and negligence*," used in the declaration, were more general than the word *barratry*; and that the breach should have been express, that the ship was lost by the barratry of the master: that if the word

word *barratry* do import fraud, yet it does not import neglect; and the fact here alleged is, that the ſhip was loſt by the fraud and negligence of the maſter. CHAP. V.

But the court were unanimouſly of opinion, that there was no occaſion to aver the fact in the very words of the policy; but that if the fact alleged came within the meaning of the words in the policy, it would be ſufficient. Barratry imports fraud; and he that commits a fraud, may properly be ſaid to be guilty of a neglect, *viz.* of his duty. [86] Barratry of a maſter is not to be confined to the maſter's running away with the ſhip; but it extends to any fraud of the maſter. The end of inſuring is to be ſafe in all events; and, it would be very prejudicial if we were to make loopholes to get out of theſe policies. The judgment was affirmed.

In another caſe, the ſhip the *Gothick Lyon* being advertiſed to go to *Marſeilles*, goods were ſhipped on board her on behalf of the plaintiff; and a bill of lading was ſigned by the maſter, whereby he undertook to go ſtraight to *Marſeilles*, and the defendant underwrote a policy from *Falmouth* (where the goods were taken in) to *Marſeilles*. Before the ſhip departed from the port of *London*, another advertiſement was publiſhed for goods to *Genoa*, *Leghorn*, and *Naples*; and the plaintiff's agent was told, that it was intended to go to thoſe ports firſt, and then come back to *Marſeilles*; but he inſiſted that his bargain was to go directly to *Marſeilles*; and, he would not conſent to let her paſs by *Marſeilles*, or alter his inſurance. Stamma v. Brown. 2 Stra. 1173.

The ſhip, however, did paſs by *Marſeilles*; and after delivering her cargo at the other ports, ſet out on her return for *Marſeilles* with the plaintiff's goods; but in a voyage thither, was blown up in an engagement with a *Spaniſh* ſhip. In an action upon the policy, the breach aſſigned was a loſs by the barratry of the maſter.

Lord

CHAP. V. Lord Chief Juſtice *Lee* told the jury, that this voyage, being againſt the expreſs agreement to go firſt to *Marſeilles*, ſeemed to be more than a common deviation, as it was a formed deſign to deceive the contractor. He compared it to the caſe of ſailing out of port without paying the duties, whereby the ſhip was ſubjected to forfeiture, and which has been held to be barratry.

The jury ſtaid out ſome time, and upon their return, aſked the Chief Juſtice, "Whether, if the maſter were to have no benefit to himſelf by paſſing by *Marſeilles*, and went only to the other places firſt for the benefit of his owners, that would be barratry?" and the Chief Juſtice having anſwered, "No," they found for the defendant.

[87] A new trial being moved for, the caſe was argued; and all the judges of the King's Bench were of opinion, that the verdict was right: for the maſter has acted conſiſtent with his duty to his owners; and the plaintiff's agent knew of the intended alteration before the goods were put on board, and might have refuſed to ſhip them, or have altered the inſurance. The court alſo held, that to conſtitute barratry, there muſt be ſomething of a criminal nature, as well as a breach of contract; and, that as the breach was aſſigned upon the barratry only, it was not ſupported by the evidence. So the defendant had judgment.

Elton v. Brogden. 2 Stra. 1264. In Sir *John Strange*'s Reports we find another caſe upon the ſubject of barratry. The ſhip *Mediterranean* went to ſea in the merchants' ſervice, having alſo a letter of marque; and was inſured by the defendant, being bound from *Briſtol* to *Newfoundland*. In her voyage ſhe took a prize, returned with it to *Briſtol*, and received back a proportionable part of the premium. Another policy was then made, and the ſhip ſet out, the captain having firſt received expreſs orders from the owners that if he took another prize, he ſhould put ſome hands on board ſuch prize, and ſend her to *Briſtol*; but that the ſhip in queſtion ſhould proceed with the mer-

chant's

chant's goods. Another prize was taken in the due courſe of the voyage; and the captain gave orders to ſome of the crew to carry the prize to *Briſtol*, and deſigned to go on to *Newfoundland*: but the crew oppoſed him, and inſiſted that he ſhould go back, though he acquainted them with his orders: upon which he was forced to ſubmit, and, on his return, his own ſhip was captured, but the prize got in ſafe.

In an action againſt the inſurers, it was inſiſted, that this was ſuch a deviation as diſcharged them. But Lord Chief Juſtice *Lee* and the jury held, that this deviation was excuſed by the force upon the maſter, which he could not reſiſt, and therefore fell within the plea of neceſſity, which had always been allowed. The plaintiff's counſel thought it was barratry; but the Chief Juſtice was of opinion, that it did not amount to that, as the ſhip was not run away with, in order to defraud the owners. But as this was a caſe not of wilful deviation, but of a deviation through neceſſity; the inſurers were held to be anſwerable, and the plaintiff had a verdict for the ſum inſured.

Theſe are all the common law caſes, which are to be found on the ſubject of barratry, during a long ſeries of years, *viz.* from the firſt origin of inſurances, till the year 1774, when a caſe aroſe, in which all the doctrine on this head was fully conſidered. [88]

Vallejo and another v. Wheeler, Cowp. R. 143.

It was an action on a policy of inſurance upon goods on board the *Thomas* and *Matthew*, from *London* to *Seville*. The policy was made in the common form, with liberty to touch at any ports or places, &c. The loſs was aſſigned different ways in the declaration: Firſt, by ſtorms and perils of the ſea, in conſequence of which, the ſhip was obliged to go to *Dartmouth* to be repaired; and, that afterwards a further loſs happened by ſtorms, &c. Secondly, that it happened by ſtorms and perils of the ſeas in the voyage

CHAP. V.

voyage generally; and Thirdly, by the *barratry* of the maſter.

The cauſe was tried before Mr. Juſtice *Aſhhurſt* at *Guildhall*, at the ſittings after *Eaſter* term 1774, by a ſpecial jury. On the trial it was proved, that this ſhip was put up as a general ſhip from *London* to *Seville*; and was let to freight to one *Darwin*, to whom ſhe was chartered by *Brown* the captain: that it is the courſe of veſſels going on this voyage, to ſtop at ſome port in the weſt of *Cornwall*, to take in proviſions: that this ſhip having taken her cargo on board, ſailed from *London* to the *Downs*: that while ſhe lay there, all the other ſhips bound to the weſtward bore away; but ſhe ſtaid till the night after, and then ſailed to *Guernſey*, which was *out of the courſe of the voyage*: that the captain went there for his own convenience, to take in brandy and wine on his *own account*; after which he intended to proceed to *Cornwall*: that the night after the ſhip quitted *Guernſey* ſhe ſprung a leak, which obliged her to put into *Dartmouth*. When ſhe was refitted, ſhe ſet ſail again and proceeded for *Helford* in *Cornwall*, where it was always intended ſhe ſhould ſtop to take in proviſions; but in her way ſhe received further damage, and on her arrival there, was totally incapable of proceeding on the voyage, and the goods were much damaged. It was attempted on the part of the defendant to prove, that one *Willes* was the owner of the ſhip: that the voyage to *Guernſey* was on his account, and that the goods taken on board there were his
[89] property: but this evidence went little further than information and belief, except that it was proved, that when the ſhip arrived at *Helford*, the wine was delivered to him in his cellar. The learned judge directed the jury, that if the going to *Guernſey* was *without the knowledge of Darwin*, it was barratry, and they ought to find for the plaintiff; but if done with his knowledge, then it was not barratry: that if they ſhould be of opinion, that it was without the knowledge of *Darwin*, he deſired them to ſay, whether they

they thought it was with the knowledge of *Willes* or not. The jury found a verdict for the plaintiff, and said, they thought the going to *Guernsey* was without the knowledge of *Darwin*, whom they looked upon to be the true owner; but they were of opinion, it was with the knowledge of *Willes*.

A motion was afterwards made for a new trial; and the case, being a question of great consequence to the mercantile world, was twice argued at the bar; after which the judges were unanimously of opinion, that the plaintiff was entitled to recover, but they delivered the reasons of their judgment *seriatim*.

Lord *Mansfield*.—"The ground of the motion for a new trial in this case is, that under the circumstances, as they were given in evidence to the jury, the carrying the ship to *Guernsey*, was merely a *deviation*, but not *barratry*. Much more stress was laid at the trial, than in either of the arguments, upon this fact; namely, that the deviation being with the knowledge of *Willes*, the owner (though not owner *pro hâc vice)* of the ship, it could never be barratry; and therefore, the jury were pressed to say, whether it was with the consent of *Willes* or not; and they said, "It was." To be sure nothing is so clear, as that if the owner of a ship insure, and bring an action on the policy, he can never set up as a crime a thing done by his own direction or consent. It was therefore a material fact to proceed upon, if *Willes* had had any thing to do in the case; but he had not. It appeared to me that the nature of barratry had not been judiciously considered, or defined in *England* with accuracy. In all mercantile transactions, the great object should be certainty: and therefore, it is of more consequence that the rule should be certain, than whether the rule is established one way or the other; because [90] speculators in trade then know upon what ground to proceed." His lordship then stated the three cases above quoted from *Strange*; and after giving a definition of the word barratry,

CHAP. V.

barratry, he proceeded thus : "In this cafe, the underwriter has infured againft all barratry of the mafter ; and we are not now in a cafe where the owner or freighter is privy to it : if we were, it is evident, that no man can complain of an act, to which he is himfelf a party. In this cafe, all relative to *Willes* may be laid out of it : he is originally the owner ; but not the infurer here. *Darwin* was the freighter of the fhip, and the goods that were on board were his : if any fraud be committed on the owner, it is committed on *Darwin*. The queftion then is, What is the ground of complaint againft the mafter ? He had agreed to go on a voyage from *London* to *Seville* ; *Darwin* trufts he will fet out immediately, inftead of which the mafter goes on an iniquitous fcheme, totally diftinct from the purpofe of the voyage, to *Seville* : that is a cheat and a fraud on *Darwin*, who thought he would fet out directly ; and whether the lofs happened in the act of barratry, that is *during* the fraudulent voyage, or *after*, is immaterial, becaufe the voyage is equally altered, even though there is no other iniquitous intent. But in the prefent cafe, there is a great deal of reafon to fay, that the lofs fuftained was in confequence of the alteration of the voyage. The moment the fhip was carried from its right courfe, it was barratry ; and here the lofs happened immediately upon the alteration. Suppofe the fhip had been loft *afterwards*, what would have been the cafe of the infured if he were not fecured againft the barratry of the mafter ? He would have loft his infurance by the fraud of the mafter ; for it was clearly a deviation, and the infured cannot come upon the underwriters for a lofs, in confequence of a deviation. Therefore, I am clearly of opinion, that this fmuggling voyage was barratry in the mafter."

Mr. Juftice *Afton*.—"I wonder that there fhould remain a doubt at this day, what is meant by barratry in the mafter. In different ordinances different terms are ufed ; but they all have the fame meaning. In one of the ordinances of *Stockholm*, it is called "knavery of the mafter or mariners ;"

ners;" and the facts stated here, clearly fall within that description. Where it is a deviation with the consent of the *owner of the vessel*, and the master is not acting for his own private interest; in such case it is nothing but a deviation with the consent of the owner, and the underwriter is excused. In this case, the hull of the ship belonged to *Willes*; but he had nothing to do with it, having chartered it to *Darwin*: the jury therefore did right in considering *Darwin* the owner *pro hâc vice*. Having considered him in that light, the conduct of the master was clearly barratry; for he was acting for his own benefit, without intending any good to his owner, and without his consent and privity. Nobody knows when the first commencement of the injury happened; but most probably, on the return of the ship to *Dartmouth* from *Guernsey*, where he had been for the purpose of smuggling. Therefore, I am clearly of opinion, that this change of the voyage for an iniquitous purpose, was barratry; which is not confined to the running away with the ship, but comprehends every species of fraud, knavery, or criminal conduct in the master, by which the owners or freighters are injured."

Mr. Justice *Willes*.—"The only doubt I had in this case was, at what time the loss happened: and I think it may reasonably be said to have happened in consequence of the smuggling voyage: for if the ship had proceeded on her first intended course, she would have escaped the storm. Though this was a deviation, yet it is a fair and just rebutter to say, that it was barratry in the master, which is a peril insured against by the policy."

Mr. Justice *Ashhurst* continued of the same opinion, which he held at the trial; and the rule for a new trial was discharged by the unanimous opinion of the whole court.

In another case, which has already been twice cited for another purpose, Mr. Justice *Buller*, who tried that cause, seemed

Robertson v. Ewer. Vide the last chapter.

CHAP. V.

seemed to think, that the breach of an embargo was an act of barratry in the master.

Ross v. Hunter, 4 Term R. 33. See post. p. 94. for another point.

In a subsequent case, which was an action on a policy on goods on board the *Live Oak*, whereof *Joseph Rati* was master, at and from *Jamaica* to *New Orleans*, it appeared, that the ship was put up as a general ship at *Jamaica* in 1783; that she sailed on the voyage insured in *May* 1783, and arrived in *June* following at the mouth of the river *Mississippi*, which leads up to *New Orleans* in *Spanish America*, at the distance of about 35 leagues. When the captain had got thus far he dropped anchor, and went in his boat up the river to *New Orleans*, and on his return, without carrying the ship to her port of destination, stood away for the *Havannah*, after which he was never heard of. It appeared that he had a private adventure of negroes of his own on board, which there was reasonable evidence for supposing he intended to have disposed of at *New Orleans*; but finding it difficult to do so, on account of a prohibition to import them into the *Spanish* government, he went to the *Havannah*. The jury found for the plaintiff on the count in the declaration, charging the barratry of the master; and the whole court of King's Bench, upon a motion for a new trial, were of opinion, that the facts stated amounted clearly to the crime of barratry.

Moss v. Byrom. 6 Term R 379. See post. p. 299.

So also it has been held by the Court of King's Bench, that if the captain of a ship, contrary to the instructions of his owner, cruize for and take a prize, and the vessel is afterwards lost in consequence of it, he is guilty of barratry, even though he libel his prize in the Court of Admiralty in the name of himself and his owner; and though the owner had procured a letter of marque, solely with a view to encourage seamen to enter, and without any intention of using it for the purpose of cruising; for whatever is done by the captain to defeat or delay the performance of the voyage, is barratry in him, it being to the prejudice of his owners; and though the captain might conceive that what

what he did was for the benefit of his owner, yet if he acted contrary to his duty to them, it is barratry. CHAP. V.

In the case of *Vallejo* v. *Wheeler*, it was settled, that the freighter of the ship is to be considered as the owner for that voyage: and it seems also clearly settled by the same case, that if an act be committed with the consent of the owners of the ship, that cannot be barratry. It was, however, in a very late case, insisted upon at the bar, that an act of the captain, without the consent of the owners of the goods, who were the insured, *though with the consent of the owners of the ship*, was barratry, so as to charge the underwriters. But this argument was over-ruled by the court; and could not have been admitted without overturning all former decisions upon the subject. Barratry implies something contrary to the duty of master and mariners, *in the relation in which they stand to the owners of the ship*; and although they may make themselves liable to the owners of the goods for misconduct, yet not for *barratry*, which can be committed against the owners of the ship, and them only. [92]

The case, in which this point was settled, was an action on a policy of insurance, made by *Hague* before he became a bankrupt, *on goods* laden in the ship *Rachette* (otherwise the *Bellona*) for a voyage from *London* to *Rochelle*, subscribed by the defendant for 120 *l.* at 1 *l.* 10 *s.* *per cent.* premium. The cause was tried at *Guildhall* before Mr. Justice *Buller*, when a verdict was found for the plaintiff, subject to the opinion of the court, upon the following case: That the bankrupt shipped on board the vessel in question goods to the amount of 1,800 *l.* for *Rochelle*. That the captain, *by the instigation and direction of Messrs. Le Grands, the owners of the ship, went with the ship and cargo to Bourdeaux, instead of Rochelle*, where the cargo was sold by the agent of *Le Grands*. That a petition was presented by the plaintiffs to the lieutenant-general of the Admiralty of *Guienne*, stating the whole of the transaction between the

Nutt & others, assignees of Hague v. Bourdieu, 1 Term Rep. 323.

CHAP. V. the bankrupt and the owners and captain; that in order to procure a landing at *Bourdeaux*, their original deſtination being to *Rochelle*, falſe bills of loading were made out by the captain, at the inſtigation of *Le Grand:* the petition concluded with a prayer for relief. In conſequence of this petition, a decree was paſſed, declaring *René Guiné* (captain) *guilty of the crime of barratry of the maſter*, for having ſigned falſe bills of lading, *&c.* for reparation whereof, it ſentenced him to perpetual ſervice in the gallies. It alſo declared *Dominique Le Grand* guilty and convicted *of having been an inſtigator and accomplice of the ſaid barratry* of the maſter, and adjudged him to five years ſer-[93]vitude in the gallies: and alſo decreed, that the ſaid *René Guiné* and *Le Grand* ſhould pay to the plaintiffs the amount of their loſs, and all charges and coſts. The queſtion on this caſe, is, Whether the plaintiffs were entitled to recover againſt the inſurers? After the firſt argument,

Lord *Mansfield* ſaid, "that with regard to the ſentence which had been paſſed abroad, and which had declared the maſter and owner to have been guilty of barratry, it was entirely out of the queſtion. That, though it was a moſt righteous judgment, yet that it was no part of the conſideration of the court there, what was meant by barratry in an *Engliſh* policy. The queſtion was left entirely open. That their idea of barratry was manifeſtly different from the conſtruction put upon that word in our own courts, for they had found the *owner* guilty of barratry, which was entirely repugnant to every definition of barratry, which had ever been laid down in an *Engliſh* court of juſtice."

A few days afterwards the court declared, that they had not the ſmalleſt doubt as to the preſent queſtion, and therefore thought it very unneceſſary to hear a ſecond argument.

Lord *Mansfield* delivered the opinion of the court.

All

CHAP. V.

All queſtions upon mercantile tranſactions, but more particularly upon policies of inſurance, are extremely important, and ought to be ſettled. The general queſtion here, is on the conſtruction of the word *barratry* in a policy of inſurance. It is ſomewhat extraordinary that it ſhould have crept into inſurances, and ſtill more, that it ſhould have continued in them ſo long; for the underwriter inſures the conduct of the captain, whom he does not appoint, and cannot diſmiſs, to the owner, who can do either. The point to be conſidered is, Whether barratry, in the ſenſe in which it is uſed in our policies of inſurance, can be committed againſt any but the owners of the ſhip? It is clear, beyond contradiction, that it cannot; for barratry is ſomething contrary to the duty of the *maſter and mariners*, the very terms of which imply, that it muſt be in the relation in which they ſtand to the *owners of the ſhip*. The words uſed are *maſter* and *mariners*, which are very particular. *An owner cannot commit barratry.* He may [94] make himſelf liable by his *fraudulent conduct* to the owner of the goods, but not *as for barratry.* And, beſides, barratry cannot be committed againſt the owner, *with his conſent*: for though the owner may become liable for a civil loſs by the miſbehaviour of the captain, if he conſents, yet that is not *barratry*. Barratry muſt partake of ſomething criminal, and muſt be committed *againſt the owner* by the *maſter* or *mariners*. In the caſe of *Vallejo* and *Wheeler*, the court took it for granted, that barratry could only be committed againſt the owner of the ſhip. The point is too clear to require any further diſcuſſion.

The *poſtea* was delivered to the defendant.

It is clear that if the owner be alſo the maſter of the ſhip, any act, which in another maſter would be conſtrued barratry, cannot be ſo in him; becauſe ſuch doctrine would militate againſt one of the rules laid down in a former part of this chapter; namely, that no man ſhall be allowed to derive a benefit from his own crime, which he would

CHAP. V. would do, were he to recover against the insurers for a loss, occasioned by his own act. But where the person, who acts as master of the ship, is proved to have carried her out of her course for fraudulent purposes of his own, that is *primâ facie* evidence of barratry, so as to entitle the assured to recover against the underwriter, without requiring him to prove *negatively* that such captain was not the owner, or shewing who really was so. The fact of his being owner must be established by the underwriter, in discharge of whom it is to operate.

Ross v. Hunter, 4 Term R. 33. See ante, p. 91.

This rule respecting the same person being both owner and master has been extended in the Court of Chancery to a case where such an owner and master, after mortgaging his ship, had committed barratry; and when the mortgagee brought an action at law against the insurer to recover damages for the loss which he had sustained by this act of barratry, the court, still considering the mortgagor as the owner, granted an injunction.

Lewin v. Suasso, Chancery, 16 Geo. II. Postlethw. Dictionary, 1 vol. 147.

The facts of that case were these. The plaintiff in equity, having been sued at law upon a policy of insurance against the barratry of the master, which was also the loss assigned in the declaration, brought his Bill in Chancery to be relieved, and for an injunction. The voyage insured was from *London* to *Marseilles*, and from thence to some port in *Holland*. The master sailed with the ship to *Marseilles*, and then, instead of pursuing his voyage, sailed to the *West Indies*, where he sold his ship, and died insolvent. The plaintiff, by his bill, suggested, that *Matthews*, the master, was also the owner of the ship: that he had, before the voyage, entered into a bottomry bond to the defendant [95] for 200*l.* and afterwards, by a bill of sale, had assigned over his interest in the ship to the defendant, as a security for the 200*l*: that *Matthews* was, nevertheless, in equity, to be considered as owner of the ship, though in law the ownership and property would be looked upon to be in the defendant; and that the owner of a ship could not, either in in law or equity, be guilty of a barratry concerning the ſhip; and therefore, he prayed an injunction, and that the policy might be delivered up. The matters of fact being confeſſed by the anſwer, an injunction was moved for on the principle, that a morgagor is to be conſidered in equity as the owner of the thing mortgaged; and that *Matthews*, the maſter, being owner, could not be guilty of barratry. CHAP. V.

Lord *Hardwicke*.—"Barratry is an act of wrong done by the maſter againſt the ſhip and goods; and this being the caſe of a ſhip, the queſtion will be, Who is to be conſidered as the owner? Several caſes might be put, where barratry may be aſſigned as the breach of an inſurance; and barratry or not, is a queſtion properly determinable at law: but in this caſe it is not ſo, for courts of law will not conſider a mortgagor as having any right or intereſt in the thing mortgaged; and a man may frequently come into equity for relief in reſpect of a part only of his caſe. It might, indeed, be conſidered at law, whether what the maſter has done, whether he be owner or not, did not amount to a breach of contract as maſter, and ſo to a barratry: it may likewiſe be ſo conſidered in this court. But at law a defendant cannot read part of a plaintiff's anſwer to a bill filed againſt him here; the whole anſwer muſt be read, which has often been a reaſon for this court to interpoſe by injunction upon a plaint at law; and conſidering the mixed nature of this caſe, I think an injunction ought to be granted."

Havelock v. Hancil upon Demurrer, 3 Term R. 277.

Even if the parties inſert in the policy that the inſurance ſhall be upon the ſhip *in any lawful trade*, if the captain commit barratry by ſmuggling, the underwriters are anſwerable. For otherwiſe the word *barratry* ſhould be ſtruck out of the policy; and moſt clearly the ſtipulation in the policy reſpecting the employment of the ſhip in a lawful trade, muſt mean, as was ſaid by Lord *Kenyon* in delivering the unanimous opinion of the Court, *the trade* on which ſhe is ſent by the owners.

CHAP. V.

Hitherto we have confidered barratry only, as it affects the rights of the infurer and infured, which is certainly the material point of view in our prefent inquiry: but, before we come to the conclufion of this chapter, it will be proper to take notice of thofe pofitive regulations, which exift in this and other countries, for the punifhment of thofe who are guilty of fome of the more heinous acts of barratry.

2 Magens 77. 112. 215.

By the ordinances of *Middleburgh*, *Rotterdam*, and *Hamburgh*, if any act of barratry be committed by the mafter, various degrees of punifhment, fometimes amounting even to death, are inflicted upon him, proportioned to the enormity of his guilt.

We do not find that any punifhment was exprefsly provided, by the law of *England*, for offences of this nature, till the reign of Queen *Anne*, at which time, as may be collected from the preamble of the ftatute, the wilful cafting away, burning or deftroying of fhips by the mafter or mariners, was become very frequent.

1 Anne, ftat. 2. c. 9. f. 4.

To prevent thefe evils that ftatute ordains, "that if any "captain, mafter, mariner, or other officer belonging to "any fhip, fhall wilfully caft away, burn, or otherwife "deftroy the fhip unto which he belongeth, or procure "the fame to be done to the prejudice of the owner or "owners thereof, or of any merchant or merchants that "fhall load goods thereon, he fhall fuffer death as a "felon."

4 Geo. I. c. 12. f. 3.

Upon trial this act was found not to be fufficiently extenfive; and therefore, by a fubfequent ftatute, it was declared, "that if any owner of, or captain, mafter, mariner, "or other officer belonging to any fhip, fhall wilfully caft "away, burn, or otherwife deftroy the fhip of which he "is owner, or unto which he belongeth, or in any man-"ner direct or procure the fame to be done, to the preju-

"dice

"dice of any perſon or perſons that ſhall underwrite any "policy or policies of inſurance thereon, or of any mer- "chant or merchants that ſhall load goods thereon, he "ſhall ſuffer death." CHAP. V.

By a ſubſequent ſtatute it was afterwards enacted, "that "if any owner of, or captain, maſter, officer, or mariner "belonging to any ſhip or veſſel, ſhall wilfully caſt away, "burn, or otherwiſe deſtroy the ſhip or veſſel of which he "is owner, or to which he belongeth; or in any wiſe direct "or procure the ſame to be done, with intent or deſign to "prejudice any perſon or perſons that hath underwrote, or "ſhall underwrite any policy or policies of inſurance there-"on, or of any merchant or merchants that ſhall load "goods thereon, or of any owner or owners of ſuch ſhip "or veſſel, the perſon or perſons offending therein, being "thereof lawfully convicted, ſhall be deemed and adjudged "a felon or felons, and ſhall ſuffer, as in caſes of felony, "without benefit of clergy." 11 Geo. I. c. 29. ſ. 6. [97]

The following ſection directs, that if the offence be committed within the body of a county, the ſame ſhall be tried as all felonies are in the common law courts: but if upon the high ſeas, then to be tried agreeably to the directions of the 28th H. 8. c. 15. 7th Section.

Theſe are the only poſitive regulations, known to the law of *England*, for the puniſhment of thoſe who wilfully, deſtroy ſhips to the prejudice of ſuch perſons as are intereſted in their preſervation.

CHAPTER THE SIXTH.

Of Partial Loſſes, and of Adjuſtment.

CHAP. VI.

HAVING, in the preceding chapters, treated fully of the different kinds of loſſes, for which the underwriters are anſwerable, the ſubject naturally leads one to conſider, when loſſes ſhall be ſaid to be total, and when partial or *average*, as they have been moſt commonly denominated. When we ſpeak of a total loſs, we do not always mean to ſignify, that the property inſured is irrecoverably loſt or gone: but that, by ſome of the perils mentioned in the policy, it is in ſuch a condition, as to be of little uſe or value to the inſured, and ſo much injured, as to juſtify him in abandoning to the inſurer, and in calling upon him to pay the whole amount of his inſurance, as if a total loſs had actually happened. But the idea of a total loſs, in this ſenſe of the word, is ſo intimately blended and interwoven with the doctrine of abandonment, that it will add much to clearneſs and preciſion, to defer what may be ſaid on this ſubject, till we come to the chapter on abandonment. In this place it will be ſufficient to remark, that in caſe of a total loſs, properly ſo called, the prime coſt of the property inſured, or the value mentioned in the policy, muſt be paid by the underwriter; at leaſt, as far as his proportion of the inſurance extends. This is evident from the nature of the contract; for the inſurer engages, as far as to the amount of the prime coſt, or value in the policy, that the thing inſured ſhall come ſafe: he has nothing to do with the market; he has no concern in any profit or loſs which may ariſe to the merchant from the ſale of the goods. If they be totally loſt, he muſt pay the prime coſt, that is, the value of the thing he inſured, at the *outſet*; he has no concern in any ſubſequent value. So, likewiſe, if part of the cargo, capable of

2 Burr. 1170.

a ſeveral

a ſeveral and diſtinct valuation at the outſet, be totally loſt; as if there be one hundred hogſheads of ſugar, and ten happen to be loſt, the inſurer muſt pay the prime coſt of thoſe ten hogſheads, without any regard to the price, for which the other ninety may be ſold. Thus much at preſent for total loſſes. CHAP. VI. [99]

The ſubject of this and the following chapter, ſeems to be of all others the moſt intricate and perplexing, in the whole law of inſurance; an intricacy, which ariſes from ſeveral cauſes. In the firſt place, the ſubject of average has very ſeldom fallen under the cognizance of courts of judicature in this country; conſequently there are very few adjudged caſes to be found. In this ſcarcity of ſettled principles, recourſe muſt be had to the writers of foreign nations, and to ſuch of our own as have written upon commerce in general: but the reſearch is by no means attended with ſatiſfaction, much leſs with conviction. Another ſource of perplexity upon this ſubject is, the irregularity and confuſion, which we meet with, in the preſent form of policies of inſurance. Ambiguities frequently ariſe in them, by uſing the ſame words in different ſenſes; and, in no inſtance, is this abſurdity more glaring than in the uſe of the word average. This word in *policies* has two ſignifications; for it means "*a contribution to a general loſs*;" and it alſo is uſed to ſignify "*a particular partial loſs*." In commercial affairs, indeed, it has no leſs than four different meanings: and therefore, it cannot be wondered at, if much confuſion of ideas has ariſen upon the ſubject. In order to prevent that, if poſſible, in the ſubſequent part of this work, I ſhall here endeavour to diſtinguiſh between the four different ſenſes of the word "average;" and wherever I ſhall have occaſion in future to ſpeak of a damage ariſing to goods or other property, not total, except when I am reciting the words of a policy, I ſhall take the liberty of calling it, as I have already done at the head of this chapter, a *partial*, not an *average* loſs. 3 Burr. 1555.

When

CHAP. VI.

Lex. Merc. red. 147. When goods or merchandizes carried by fea, are thrown over-board in a ftorm, for the purpofe of lightening the fhip; the owners of the fhip and of the goods faved contribute for the relief of thofe, whofe goods are ejected, in fuch a manner, that all, who profited by the lightening of the fhip, may bear a proportional lofs of the goods, thus thrown overboard for the common fafety. This con- [100] tribution is what is called general or grofs average; the full difcuffion of which will be the bufinefs of the next chapter.

Small or petty averages are the next fpecies; and, as thefe never fall upon the underwriters, I fhall here fet down all that is neceffary upon that fubject. (Magens 72.) Petty average confifts in fuch charges and difburfements, as, according to occurrences, and the cuftom of every place, the mafter neceffarily furnifhes for the benefit of the fhip and cargo, either at the place of loading or unloading, or on the voyage. Thefe charges are lodemanage, which, as it appears by *Cowel's* interpreter, means the hire of a pilot for conducting a veffel from one place to another; (Cowel, 2 Mag. 180. 278.) towage, pilotage, light-money, beaconage, anchorage, bridge-toll, quarantine, river charges, fignals, inftructions, paffage money by caftles, expenfes for digging a fhip out of the ice when frozen up, that it may be brought into a proper harbour; and at *London*, by cuftom, the fee paid at *Dover* pier. Thefe feem to be all the articles which come under the denomination of petty or accuftomed average, as well in this as in foreign countries.

Mag. 72. For thefe charges, the infurers are never anfwerable; but one third of the expenfes is borne by the fhip, and two thirds by the cargo. But in order to difcharge the infurer, it muft appear, that the difburfements were ufual and cuftomary in the voyage; for if they were incurred for any extraordinary purpofe, or in order to relieve the fhip and cargo from fome impending danger, they fhall then be reputed a general average, and confequently be a charge

charge on the infurer. In lieu of thefe petty averages, it has become ufual at fome places to pay 5 *per cent.* calculated on the freight, and 5 *per cent.* more for primage to the captain.

CHAP. VI.

1 Mag. 72.

Another fpecies of average, in matters of commerce, is that which we are accuftomed to meet with in bills of lading, "paying fo much freight for the faid goods, with "primage and *average* accuftomed." In this fenfe it fignifies a fmall duty, which merchants, who fend goods in the fhips of other men, pay to the mafter over and above the freight, for his care and attention to the goods fo entrufted to him. This kind of average may alfo be laid out of the prefent inquiry, as it is too infignificant a charge to fall upon the underwriter.

Jacob's Law Dict. title Average.

[101]

Having thus difpofed of the different kinds of average, fo as to prevent a confufion of ideas, we fhall now proceed to the main fubject propofed, namely, what fhall be confidered as a partial lofs? how fuch a lofs fhall be adjufted, and in what proportion it fhall be paid. I faid, at the beginning of this chapter, that thefe were queftions of intricacy; and fo moft undoubtedly they formerly were: but much light has been thrown upon them by Lord *Mansfield*, in his elaborate and very learned argument in the cafe of *Lewis* v. *Rucker*; and, as that cafe has been frequently recognized, and has ever fince been looked up to, as the rule and ftandard of decifion, upon fimilar occafions, I have drawn moft of my ideas upon this fubject from the reafoning there made ufe of by his lordfhip in delivering the opinion of the court.

2 Burr. 1167.

Partial lofs, *ex vi termini*, implies a damage, which the fhip may have fuftained in the courfe of her voyage, from any of the perils mentioned in the policy: when applied to the cargo, it alfo means the damage which goods may have received, without any fault of the mafter, by ftorm, capture, ftranding, or fhipwreck, although the whole, or the greater part thereof may arrive in port. Thefe partial loffes fall upon

CHAP. VI.

2 Burr. 1172.

upon the owners of the property ſo damaged, who muſt be indemnified by the underwriter. For if the goods arrive, but leſſened in value through damage received at ſea, the nature of an indemnity ſpeaks demonſtrably, that it can only be effected by putting the merchant in the ſame condition in which he would have been if the goods had arrived free from damage.

Vide the Appendix, No. 1.

The underwriters of *London* expreſsly declare, as appears from a memorandum at the foot of the policy, that they will not anſwer for partial loſſes not amounting to 3 *per cent.* This clauſe was introduced into *Engliſh* policies about the year 1749, having long before that time been generally uſed in almoſt all the trading countries in *Europe*; and it was intended to prevent the underwriters from being continually haraſſed by trifling demands. But at the ſame time, that they provide againſt trifling claims for partial loſſes, they [102] undertake to indemnify againſt loſſes, however inconſiderable, that ariſe from a general average; becauſe that can never happen but in caſes of imminent danger, when it is for the common intereſt that ſuch expenſes ſhould be incurred.

1 Magens 73.

It has been obſerved by a very ſenſible merchant, who has written upon inſurances, that almoſt all the ordinances ſeem deficient, in not fully explaining in what caſes, and in what manner the damage ariſing from a partial loſs, ſhall be deemed to exceed 3 *per cent.* To illuſtrate his meaning, he ſtates this caſe. Suppoſe, ſays he, a merchant has ſhipped 101 cheſts of goods, of which, on arrival, three cheſts are, by the ſea, or by ſome accident, ſo ſpoiled as to be worth nothing; if the damage be calculated as on the whole value of 101 cheſts, it will not exceed 3 *per cent.* and it is thought by moſt inſurers not to be recoverable, in ſuch a caſe, by the inſured: eſpecially if the inſurance be made without expreſsly declaring in the policy the particular ſum inſured on each cheſt. The foundation of this opinion is, that it is conſidered as one entire inſurance, and not a diſtinct inſurance on each cheſt.

This

This is a point, which at first view may seem to fall within a case laid down by Lord *Mansfield*. "If," said his lordship, "the cargo be totally lost, the underwriter must pay the value of the thing he insured. So, if part of the cargo, capable of a several and distinct valuation at the outset be *totally* lost; as if there be 100 hogsheads of sugar, and ten happen to be lost, the insurer must pay the prime cost of those ten hogsheads, without any regard to the price for which the other 90 may be sold." So it has been supposed in the case put by *Magens*, the three chests of goods are as capable of a distinct and several valuation, as the three hogsheads of sugar; and consequently are to be paid for, as for a total loss. But Lord *Mansfield* is putting a case merely to shew, that the market price is not at all to be considered in charging the insurer; and his lordship certainly had not in his contemplation the case put by *Magens*. 2 Burr. 1170.

As clearness and precision are necessary upon all subjects, and more especially upon this, it will be proper to observe, that when we speak of the underwriter being liable to pay, [103] whether for total or partial losses, it must always be understood, that they are liable only in proportion to the sums which they have underwritten. Thus, if a man underwrite 100*l.* upon property valued at 500*l.* and a total loss happen, he shall be answerable for 100*l.* and no more, that being the amount of his subscription: if only a partial loss, amounting to 60*l.* or 70*l.* *per cent.* upon the whole value; he shall pay 60*l.* or 70*l*, being his proportion of the loss.

When a total loss happens, the insured is entitled to recover against the underwriter, as soon as he has proved the value of the thing insured: but when the value is inserted in a policy, the insurer, by allowing such insertion, has admitted the value to be as stated; and nothing remains but to prove, that the goods insured were actually on board the ship. It is only in cases of total loss that any difference consists between a valued, and an open policy: in the former case the value is ascertained; in the latter, it must be proved. 1 Magens 35. Vide ante, c. 1. p. 1.

But

CHAP. VI. But where the loss is partial, the value in the policy can be no guide to ascertain the damage; which then necessarily becomes a subject of proof, as much as in the case of an open policy.

When a partial loss happens, the first inquiry which naturally arises is this; for what does the insurer undertake to indemnify the owner, in case of a partial loss? To answer this question, regard must be had to the nature of the contract, between the underwriter and the merchant. What is the nature of the contract? That the goods shall come safe to the port of delivery; or if they do not, that the insurer will indemnify the owner to the amount of the value of the goods stated in the policy. Wherever then the property insured is lessened in value, by damage received at sea, justice is done by putting the merchant in the same condition (relation being had to the prime cost or value in the policy) which he would have been in, if the goods had arrived free from damage; that is, by paying him such a proportion of the prime cost or value in the policy as corresponds with the proportion of the diminution in value occasioned by the damage. The question then is, how is the proportion of damage to be ascertained? It certainly cannot be by any measure taken from the prime cost: but it may be done in this way. Where an entire thing, as one hogshead of sugar happens to be spoiled, if you can fix, whether it be a third, a fourth, or a fifth worse, then the damage is ascertained to a mathematical certainty. How is this to be found out? Not by any price at the port of discharge; but it must be at the port of *delivery*, where the voyage is completed, and the whole damage known. Whether the price at the latter be high or low, it is the same thing; for in either case it equally shews, whether the damaged goods are a third, a fourth, or a fifth worse than if they had come sound: consequently, whether the injury sustained be a third, fourth, or fifth of the value of the thing. And as the insurer pays the whole prime cost, if the thing be wholly lost; so if it be only a third, fourth, or fifth worse, he pays a third,

2 Burr. 1172, 1173.

2 Burr. 1170.

[104]

a third, fourth, or fifth, not of the value for which it sold, but of the value stated in the policy. And when no valuation is stated in the policy, the invoice of the cost, with the addition of all charges, and the premium of insurance, shall be the foundation, upon which the loss shall be computed.

CHAP. VI.

1 Magens 37.

This rule of ascertaining damage, occasioned by a partial loss, seems to be fraught with so much good sense, to be so very comprehensive, and so intelligible to every understanding, that it will now be only necessary to shew, that the decided cases have been agreeable to that rule; first requesting the reader to bear in mind, what has already been mentioned, namely, that the value upon which the foregoing calculation rests, is the prime cost of the commodity, wholly independent of the rise or fall of the market, or the schemes or speculation of the merchant.

Dick and another v. Allen, at Guildh. after Mich. Term, 1785.

In an action upon a policy of insurance to recover an average loss upon goods, Mr. Justice *Buller* observed, that in such cases, whether the goods arrived to a good or bad market was immaterial; for the true way of estimating the loss was to take them at the fair invoice price (*a*).

Lewis and another v. Rucker, 2 Burr. 1167.

A rule having been obtained by the plaintiffs, who were the insured, for the defendant (the insurer) to shew cause, why a verdict, obtained by him, should not be set aside, and a new trial had;

[105]

The court, after hearing the matter fully debated, took time to advise, and their unanimous opinion was delivered to the following effect.

Lord *Mansfield*.—" This was an action brought upon a policy, by the plaintiffs, for Mr. *James Bourdieu*, upon the goods on board a ship, called the *Vrow Martha*, at and from *St. Thomas Island* to *Hamburgh*, from the loading at *St. Thomas Island*, till the ship should arrive, and land the goods at *Hamburgh*.

(*a*) Neither does the underwriter insure against any loss that may arise from the difference of exchange. *Thellusson* v. *Bewick*. Sittings after *Michaelmas* 34 *Geo.* III. *Espinasse*, p. 77.

CHAP. VI. *Hamburgh*. The goods, which consisted of sugars, coffee and indigo, were valued; the clayed sugars at 30*l*. *per* hogshead; the *Muscovado* sugars at 20*l*. *per* hogshead; and the coffee and indigo were likewise respectively valued.— The sugars were warranted free from average (that is partial loss) under 5*l*. *per cent*; and all other goods free from average under 3*l*. *per cent*. unless general or the ship be stranded.

In the course of the voyage the sea water got in; and when the ship arrived at *Hamburgh*, it appeared that every hogshead of sugar was damaged. The damage the sugars had sustained, made it necessary to sell them immediately; and they were accordingly sold; but the difference between the price which they brought, on account of the damage, and that which they might then have been sold for at *Hamburgh*, if they had been sound, was as 20*l*. 0*s*. 8*d*. *per* hogshead is to 23*l*. 7*s*. 8*d*. *per* hogshead: (that is, if sound, they would have been worth 23*l*. 7*s*. 8*d*. *per* hogshead; as damaged, they were only worth 20*l*. 0*s*. 8*d*. *per* hogshead.)

The defendant paid money into court, by the following rule of estimating the damage: he paid the like proportion of the sum, at which the sugars were valued in the policy, as the price of the damaged sugars bore to sound sugars at *Hamburgh*, the port of delivery. All this was admitted at the trial; though perhaps upon an accurate computation, there may be a mistake of about 17*s*. on the money paid in. But no advantage was attempted to be taken of this slip; it was admitted, that the money paid in was sufficient, if the rule, by which the defendant estimated the loss, was right: and the only question was, by what measure or rule the damage, upon all the circumstances of the case, ought to be estimated.

[106] To distinguish this case, under its particular circumstances, out of any general rule, the plaintiff's counsel called Mr. *Samuel Chollett*, clerk to Mr. *Bourdieu*, who proved, that

that upon the 15th of *February*, the time of the insurance, sugars were worth at *London* and *Hamburgh*, 35*l.* a hogshead; that the proposal of a congress to be holden, and the expectation of a peace, had, on a sudden, sunk the price of sugars: that before the ship arrived at *Hamburgh*, and before he knew that the sugars had received any damage, Mr. *Bourdieu* had sent orders, that the sugars should be housed at *Hamburgh*, and kept till the price should rise above 30*l.* a hogshead: that he had many hundred hogsheads of sugar lying at *Amsterdam*, to which place he had sent the like orders; that the congress not taking place, *in fact* sugars rose 25 *per cent:* that what he sold of the sugars, which he had at *Amsterdam*, brought 30*l.* *per* hogshead, and upwards: that he might have sold these sugars at the same price, if they had been kept, according to his orders; and the only reason for which they were not kept was, because they were rendered perishable from the sea water, which had got in. Therefore, said they, the necessity of an immediate sale, and the consequence thereof, ought to be computed into the damage.

The special jury (amongst whom there were many sensible merchants) found the defendant's rule of estimation to be right, and gave their verdict for him. They understood the question very well, and knew more of the subject of it, than any body else present; and they formed their judgment from their own notions and experience, without much assistance from any thing that passed.

The counsel for the plaintiff, in the outset, chiefly rested upon the particular circumstances of this case. The defendant offered to call witnesses to prove the general usage of estimating the quantity of damage, when goods are injured.

I was at first struck with the argument, that the immediate necessity of selling in this case might be taken into consideration, as an exception to the general rule; and proposed that the cause might be left to the jury upon that point. But Mr.

CHAP. VI. Mr. *Winn* for the defendant argued, that the neceſſity of ſelling, and the conſequence thereof ought not to be regarded: and what he ſaid, had ſo much weight, that it very much changed my way of thinking.

There was nothing to ſum up; but the jury aſked, Whether I would give them any directions? I ſaid, I left it to them, "Whether the difference between the ſound "and the damaged ſugars, at the port of delivery, ought "to be the rule; or, whether the neceſſity of an immedi-"ate ſale, certainly occaſioned by the damage, and the loſs "thereby, ſhould be taken into conſideration." I told them, though, it had ſtruck me at firſt, this might be an exception; yet what the counſel for the defendant ſaid to the contrary, ſeemed to have great weight. The verdict was for the defendant; and a new trial was moved for.

No fact is now diſputed; the only queſtion is, whether the jury have eſtimated the damage by a proper meaſure. To make this matter more intelligible, I will firſt ſtate the rule, by which the defendant and the jury have gone; and then I will examine whether the plaintiff has ſhewn a better.

The defendant takes the proportion of the difference between ſound and damaged at the port of delivery, and pays that proportion upon the value of the goods ſpecified in the policy; and has no regard to the price in money, which either the ſound or the damaged goods bore in the port of delivery. He ſays, the proportion of the difference is equally the rule, whether the goods come to a riſing or a falling market. For inſtance, ſuppoſe the value in the policy to be 30*l.*; the goods are damaged, but ſell for 40*l.*: if they had been ſound, they would have ſold for 50*l.* The difference then between the ſound and damaged is a fifth; conſequently the inſurer muſt pay a fifth of the prime coſt, or value in the policy, that is 6*l.*: *e converſo*, if they come to a loſing market, and ſell for 10*l.* being damaged, but

but would have ſold for 20*l.* if ſound, the difference is one half: the inſurer muſt pay half the prime coſt, or value in the policy, that is 15*l.*

To this rule, two objections have been made. Firſt, that it is going by a different meaſure in the caſe of a partial, from that which governs in caſe of a total loſs; for upon a total loſs, the prime coſt, or value in the policy, muſt be paid. The anſwer to which objection is, that the diſtinction is founded in the nature of the thing. [108] Inſurance is a contract of indemnity againſt the perils of the voyage, to the amount of the value in the policy; and therefore, if the thing be totally loſt, the inſurer muſt pay the whole value which he inſured at the outſet. But where a part of the commodity is ſpoiled, no meaſure can be taken from the prime coſt to aſcertain the quantity of the damage ſuſtained. The only way is to fix, whether the thing be a third or fourth worſe than the ſound commodity; and then you pay a third or fourth of the prime coſt, or value of the goods ſo damaged.*

The next objection, with which this caſe has been entangled, is taken from the circumſtance of the policy in queſtion being a valued policy.

I am a little at a loſs to apply the arguments drawn from thence. It is ſaid, "that a valued is a wager policy, like "*intereſt or no intereſt*; and if ſo, there can be no partial "loſs, and the inſured can only recover as for a total loſs, "abandoning what is ſaved, becauſe the value ſpecified is "fictitious."

A valued policy is not to be conſidered as a wager policy, or like "*intereſt or no intereſt.*" If it were, it would be void,

* In Lord *Mansfield*'s argument, in anſwer to the firſt objection, I have taken the liberty of abridging much of what fell from his lordſhip, having already inſerted it, in the former part of the chapter, where I laid down the rules of deciſion upon this point.

CHAP. VI.

Vide post, c. 14.

void, by the statute of 19 *Geo.* II. c. 37. The only effect of the valuation, is fixing the amount of the prime cost, just as if the parties admitted it at the trial: but in every argument, and for every other purpose, it must be taken, that the value was fixed in such a manner, as that the insured meant to have an indemnity only, and no more. If it be undervalued, the merchant himself stands the insurer for the rest. If it be much overvalued, it must be done with a bad view, either to gain, contrary to the 19th of *George* the Second, or with some view to a fraudulent loss; therefore, the insured never can be allowed to plead in a court of justice, that he has greatly overvalued, or that his interest was merely a trifle.

[109] It is settled that upon valued policies, the merchant need only prove some interest to take them out of the 19th *Geo.* II.; because the adverse party has admitted the value: and if more proof were required, the agreed valuation would signify nothing. But if it should come out in proof, that a man had insured 2,000*l.* and had interest on board to the value of a cable only; there never has been, and, I believe, there never will be a determination, that, by such an evasion, the act of parliament may be defeated. There are many advantages from allowing valued policies: but where they are used merely as a cover to a wager, they would be considered as an evasion. To argue that there can be no adjustment of a partial loss upon a valued policy, is directly contrary to the very terms of the policy itself. It is expressly *subject to average*, if the loss upon sugars exceed 5 *per cent.*; and even if it were not subject to average, the consequence would be, that every partial loss must thereby become total; but only the event, to entitle the insured to recover, would not happen, unless there was a total loss. Consequently the plaintiff in this case would not be entitled to recover at all; for there is no colour to say that this was a total loss: besides the plaintiffs have taken the goods and sold them.

In

In oppofition to the meafure the jury have gone by, the plaintiffs contend, that they ought to be paid the whole value in the policy, upon one of two grounds.

1ft. Becaufe the general rule of eftimating fhould be the difference between the price the damaged goods fell for, and the prime coft or value in the policy. Here the damaged fold at 20 *l.* 0 *s.* 8 *d.* *per* hogfhead; and the underwriter fhould make it up 30 *l.* To this I anfwer, that it is impoffible that fhould be the rule: it would involve the underwriter in the rife or fall of the market: it would fubject him, in fome cafes, to pay vaftly more than the lofs; in others, it would deprive the infured of any fatisfaction, though there was a lofs. For inftance, fuppofe the prime coft or value in the policy 30 *l.* *per* hogfhead; the fugars are injured; the price of the beft is 20 *l.* a hogfhead; the price of the damaged is 19 *l.* 10 *s.* The lofs is about a fortieth, and the infurer would be to pay above a third. Suppofe they come to a rifing market, and the found fugars fell for 40 *l.* a hogfhead, and the damaged for 35 *l.* the lofs is an eighth, yet the infurer would be to pay nothing.

Vide fupra, Dick v. Allen, p. 104.

The 2d ground, upon which the plaintiffs contended that the 30 *l.* fhould be made up, is, that it appears the fugars would have fold for that price, if the damage from the fea water had not made an immediate fale neceffary. The moment the jury brought in their verdict, I was fatisfied that they did right, in totally difregarding the particular circumftances of this cafe: and I wrote a memorandum at *Guildhall*, in my note-book, that the verdict feemed to me to be right. As I expected that the other caufe upon the fame point would be tried, I thought a good deal upon the queftion, and endeavoured to get what affiftance I could, by converfing with fome gentlemen of experience in adjuftments. The point has now been fully argued at the bar; and the more I have thought, the more I have heard upon the fubject, the more I am convinced, that the jury did right to pay no regard to thefe circumftances.

CHAP. VI.

The nature of the contract is, that the goods ſhall come ſafe to the port of delivery, or if they do not, that the inſurer will indemnify the plaintiff to the amount of the prime coſt. If they arrive, but leſſened in value; in order to indemnify the owner, he muſt be put in the ſame condition, in which he would have been if the goods had arrived free from damage: that is, by paying ſuch proportion or *aliquot* part of the prime coſt, as correſponds with the proportion or *aliquot* part of the diminution in value occaſioned by the damage.

The duty accrues upon the ſhip's arrival and landing her cargo at the port of delivery: the inſured has then a right to demand ſatisfaction. The adjuſtment can never depend upon future events or ſpeculations. How long is he to wait? a week, a month, or year?

In this caſe, the price roſe: but if the congreſs had taken place, or a peace had been made, it would have fallen. The defendant did not inſure, that there ſhould be no congreſs or peace. It is true Mr. *Bourdieu* acted upon political ſpeculation, and ordered the ſugars to be kept till the price ſhould be 30 *l.* and upwards: but no private ſcheme or project of trade of the inſured can effect the inſurer; for he knew nothing of it. The defendant did not undertake that the ſugars ſhould bear a price of 30 *l.* a hogſhead. If ſpec-
[111] ulative deſtinations of the merchant, and the ſucceſs of ſuch ſpeculations were to be regarded, it would introduce the greateſt injuſtice and inconvenience: the underwriter knows nothing of them: the orders here were given after the policy was ſigned. But the deciſive anſwer is, that the inſurer has nothing to do with the price; and that the right of the inſured to a ſatisfaction ariſes immediately upon their being landed at the port of delivery.

We are of opinion, that the plaintiffs are not entitled to have the price, for which the damaged ſugars were ſold, made up 30 *l. per* hogſhead: and it ſeems to us as plain as any propoſition in *Euclid*, that the rule by which the jury have gone, is the right meaſure.

In

In a fubfequent cafe, which will hereafter be mentioned for another purpofe, Lord *Mansfield* faid, that the cafe of *Lewis* v. *Rucker*, fhould be the rule in all fimilar cafes, that is, wherever there was a fpecific defcription of cafks or goods: but in *Le Cras* v. *Hughes*, the property, which confifted in various goods taken from an enemy, was valued at the fum infured, and part was loft by perils of the fea; confequently the fame rule could not be adopted, on account of the nature of the thing infured. The only mode was to go into an account of the whole value of the goods, and take a proportion of that fum, as the amount of the goods loft.

CHAP. VI.

Le Cras v. Hughes, B. R. Eaft. 22 Geo. III. Vide poft, c. 14.

Since the 19th of *Geo*. II. the conftant ufage has been to let the valuation fixed in the policy remain, in cafe of a total lofs, unlefs the defendant can fhew that the plaintiff had a colourable intereft only, or that he has greatly overvalued the goods: but a partial lofs opens the policy. This cuftom, faid Lord *Mansfield*, was introduced by Lord Chief Juftice *Lee*, in a cafe of *Erafmus* v. *Banks*: and in another cafe of *Smith* v. *Flexney*, which happened about the fame period, the fame rule of decifion was adopted.

M. 21 Geo. II.

By the ordinances of *Hamburgh* it is declared, that in cafe of a damage to goods, the affured is not to open the damaged goods but in the prefence of the affurers or their deputies; but if time and circumftances do not give opportunity to call them, yet the goods muft not be opened, but in the prefence of a notary, and fome witneffes. I can find no fuch regulation in the law of infurance in *England*, nor do I underftand, that any fuch is adopted in practice. Indeed it feems to be needlefs; becaufe an affured, in order to entitle himfelf to recover for a partial lofs, muft prove by difinterefted witneffes, to the fatisfaction of the jury, the quantity of goods damaged in the courfe of the voyage. The parties may, however, infift upon being prefent.

2 Magens 228.

[112]

CHAP. VI.

Ord. of France, Stockholm, and Hamburgh. Vide Apppendix, No. 1.

It will be proper here to remark that ſome goods are of a periſhable nature; and therefore, when they are damaged by ſuch natural and inherent principle of corruption in themſelves, the underwriters, by the ordinances of moſt countries, are held to be diſcharged. The underwriters of *London* have, indeed, by expreſs words inſerted in their policy, declared, that they will not be anſwerable for any partial loſs happening to corn, fiſh, ſalt, fruit, flour, and ſeed, unleſs it ariſe by way of a general average, or in conſequence of the ſhip being ſtranded. This clauſe was introduced by the underwriters, to prevent the vexation of trifling demands, which muſt have ariſen in every voyage, on account of the very periſhable nature of thoſe commodities, which we have juſt had occaſion to enumerate. This form was formerly uſed by the two inſurance companies, as well as by the private inſurers, till the year 1754, when a ſhip having been ſtranded, and got off again, the inſured recovered a ſmall partial loſs againſt the *London* Aſſurance Company, ſince which period, the Companies have left out the words, "*or the ſhip be ſtranded;*" and are now only liable, in caſes of a general average; but the old form is ſtill retained by private inſurers.

Cantillon v. the London Aſſur. Comp. cited in 3 Burr. 1553.

Upon this clauſe there have been ſeveral determinations, in all of which it has been uniformly held, that the underwriters can in no caſe be anſwerable for a partial loſs to ſuch commodities: and that no loſs ſhall be deemed a total one, but the abſolute deſtruction of the thing inſured; for that while it ſpecifically remains, though perhaps wholly unfit for uſe, no loſs has hapened within the meaning of this memorandum. It may alſo be proper to premiſe that *corn* is a general term, and includes many particulars; peas and beans have been held to come within the meaning of the word.

Maſon v. Skurray. Vide poſt.

[113]

Journu v. Bourdieu, Sittings after Eaſter Term, 27 Geo. III.

But in a late trial at *Guildhall* in the Court of Common Pleas, Mr. Juſtice *Wilſon* was of opinion, that the term *ſalt* uſed in the memorandum did not include ſalt-petre.

An

CHAP. VI.

Wilson v. Smith, 3 Burr. 1550.

An action upon a policy of insurance was brought for the recovery of 56*l.* 19*s* 8*d.* *per cent.* being the damage received by a cargo of wheat on board the *Boscawen* insured at and from *Lancaster* to *Rotterdam*. The wheat was valued by agreement at 30*s.* *per* quarter. The policy was in the ordinary form, with the usual clause at the bottom, that corn, fish, fruit, *&c.* should be warranted free from average, unless general, or the ship be stranded. The defendant underwrote this policy for 100*l.* The defendant having pleaded the general issue, the cause came on to be tried; and a special case was reserved for the opinion of the Court, stating, that after the ship's departure from *Lancaster*, and before her arrival at *Rotterdam*, she met with a violent storm: that she was, by and through the force of winds and stormy weather, obliged to cut away, and leave her cable and anchor, for the safety of the ship and cargo; that she was also greatly damaged, and obliged to run to the first port to refit: that the expense of refitting the ship amounted to 38*l.* 15*s.* *per cent.* which the defendant in this case had paid, being a general average. The case then states, that the hatches were not opened at *Liverpool* (the place where she had gone to repair;) but the ship, being refitted, proceeded on her voyage, and arrived at *Rotterdam* where her cargo of wheat was landed: that upon her unloading it, it appeared that it had received damage by the said storm to the amount of 56*l.* 19*s.* 8*d.* *per cent.*

The single question was, upon the true construction and meaning of the words, "*free from average, unless general,* " *or the ship be stranded,*" whether the plaintiff could under the circumstances recover in this action for the damage of 56*l.* 19*s.* 8*d.* *per cent.* After two arguments, the Court gave judgment for the defendant.

Lord *Mansfield*.—" Policies of insurance, according to their present form, are very irregular and confused: an ambiguity arises in them from using the same words in different senses;

CHAP. VI. ſenſes; particularly, in the uſe of the word *average*. It is uſed to ſignify a contribution to a general loſs; and it is alſo uſed to ſignify a particular partial loſs.

But whether it be conſidered in one or other of theſe ſenſes, it will not avail the plaintiffs in this caſe. For if it here ſignify *contribution*, the inſurer is to be free from contribution, unleſs the contribution be general. If it ſignify *loſs*, then plainly it is warranted free from all particular loſs. The inſurer is liable to all loſſes ariſing from the ſhip being ſtranded; and in all caſes, where there is a general average: but all other partial loſſes are excluded by the expreſs terms of the policy.

The word "unleſs" means the ſame as "except;" and never can be conſtrued as a condition, in the ſenſe that the counſel for the plaintiffs would put upon the word "condition," namely, to be free from partial loſs, unleſs in two events, *viz.* a general average, or the ſtranding of the ſhip: but if either of thoſe events did happen, then to be liable to all other average. The words "free from average unleſs general," can never mean to leave the inſurer liable to any particular damage. It is clear then that the plaintiff ought not to recover; and that judgment ought to be given for the defendant."

Cocking v. Fraſer, B. R. Eaſt. 25 Geo. III. Vide ante, p. 31.

In a modern caſe a queſtion aroſe upon the memorandum. It was an action brought upon a policy of inſurance to recover againſt the underwriters for a total loſs of the cargo. The jury found a verdict for the plaintiff, ſubject to the opinion of the Court upon a ſpecial caſe.

The caſe ſtates, that the ſhip ſailed from *Newfoundland* on the 2d of *December* 1783, with a cargo of fiſh: that on the 11th they hove overboard 40 quintals for the general preſervation of the ſhip and cargo: that on the 20th, they threw over 20 quintals more for the ſame purpoſe. The

The ſhip had exceeding bad weather till her arrival at *Liſbon*, on the 10th of *January* 1784, the ſhip being bound to *Figara*. When ſhe arrived at *Liſbon*, a ſurvey was had at the requeſt of the captain, who was alſo the conſignee of the goods, by the Board of Health; and it appeared to them, and ſo the fact was, that the cargo was of *no value* through ſea damage. The ſhip did not proceed to *Figara*. The defendant has paid into Court the amount of the partial loſs ſuſtained by the ſhip, and alſo the general average upon the cargo. [115]

Lord *Mansfield*.—"Moſt litigations ariſe from improper ſtatements of caſes, and from not properly defining terms. This clauſe relative to fruit and fiſh, is now a very old one in policies of inſurance. The inſurer undertakes for all loſſes, except particular damage, unleſs the ſhip be ſtranded: he engages againſt a total loſs. What is a loſs? The total loſs of the thing inſured is the *abſolute deſtruction* of it, by the wreck of the ſhip. The fiſh may all come to port; though from the nature of the commodity, it may be damaged, it may be ſtinking: ſtill as the commodity *ſpecifically* remains, the underwriter is diſcharged."

The other judges concurred, Mr. Juſtice *Buller* obſerving, that from the firſt introduction of the clauſe in the year 1749, till the preſent time, the underwriter never has been held anſwerable but in caſes where there has been a total loſs of the commodity.

So alſo in an inſurance on fruit from *Liſbon* to *London*, it appeared that the ſhip was captured, and recaptured, brought into *Portſmouth*, and afterwards arrived at *London*: but the cargo, by the capture, recapture, and conſequent length of the voyage, had ſuſtained a damage of 80*l. per cent*. The aſſured, however, never heard of the capture till the ſhip was ſafe at *Portſmouth*, and then he offered to abandon.

M'Andrews v. Vaughan, Sittings at G. H. after Mich. 1793.

Lord

Lord *Kenyon*.—"As there has been no ftranding, there cannot be a recovery for a partial lofs. The queftion then is, Whether the affured can recover for a total lofs? Had the plaintiff heard of the capture only, he might have abandoned: but he hears nothing of the accident till the fhip is in fafety. The cargo arrives at the port of deftination; and though it is good for very little, yet it has invariably been held that the voyage muft either be loft, or the cargo, if it be one of thofe mentioned in the memorandum, muft be wholly and actually deftroyed to entitle the affured to recover." The plaintiff was nonfuited.

Nefbitt v. Lufhington, 4 Term.R.783.

The effect of the memorandum has been alfo very recently difcuffed by the whole Court, in an action on a policy on *wheat* and coals, the declaration ftating the lofs to be by *detention*. It appeared in evidence that the fhip was forced by ftrefs of weather into *Elly* Harbour in *Ireland*, and there happening to be a great fcarcity of corn there at that time, the people came on board the fhip in a tumultuous manner, took the government of her from the captain and crew, and weighed her anchor, by which fhe drove upon a reef of rocks, where fhe was ftranded, and they would not leave her till they had compelled the captain to fell all the corn (except about 10 tons) at a certain rate. The 10 tons were loft in confequence of the ftranding, by which it was damaged, and obliged to be thrown overboard. The fhip afterwards arrived with the reft of the cargo at the place of deftination. A verdict was found as for a total lofs. A motion was made for a new trial. There were other points in the caufe, one of which has been already confidered. As to this upon the memorandum,

See ante, p. 78.

Lord *Kenyon* faid—"This being a policy upon corn, the memorandum ftates that the underwriter will not be liable for any average, unlefs general, or the fhip be ftranded. And I am of opinion that this is not a general average; becaufe the whole adventure was never in jeopardy.

ardy. There is no pretence to ſay that the perſons, who took the corn, intended any injury to the ſhip or any other part of the cargo but the corn, which they wanted in order to prevent their ſuffering in a time of ſcarcity. Therefore the plaintiffs could never have called on the reſt of the owners to contribute their proportion, as upon a general average. On the meaning of the memorandum I have no doubt. The articles there enumerated are of a periſhable nature: as it might be difficult to aſcertain whether their being damaged aroſe from any accident, or from the nature of the articles themſelves, this memorandum is inſerted in all policies, to prevent diſputes; and by it the underwriters expreſsly provide they will not pay any average, unleſs general, or the ſhip be ſtranded. When a ſhip is ſtranded, then the underwriters agree to aſcribe the loſs to the ſtranding, as being the moſt probable occaſion of the damage, though that fact cannot be always aſcertained. Therefore here all the damage done to the cargo thrown overboard may be aſcribed to the ſtranding; but the objection is, that the declaration imputes the loſs to another cauſe."

Mr. Juſtice *Buller*.—"With reſpect to the objection, that this does not fall within the reaſon of the memorandum; there are only two inſtances, in which the owner may recover an average loſs on the articles there enumerated; either where the average is general, or where the loſs ariſes from the ſtranding of the veſſel. Now this cannot be ſaid to be a general average, for the reaſons already given. And as to the other inſtance of ſtranding, the plaintiffs are entitled to recover for any loſs occaſioned to the cargo in conſequence of the ſtranding, provided it be a direct and immediate conſequence of ſtranding: but they cannot recover for that which was taken by the mob; for that was not the conſequence of the ſtranding, but, on the contrary, the ſtranding was occaſioned by the mob coming on board for the corn. The rioters took poſſeſſion of the ſhip in order to get at the cargo: but this loſs cannot

CHAP. VI. cannot be afcribed to the ftranding. Suppofe the mob had taken out 100 quarters of corn before the fhip had been ftranded, and had ufed no threat to deftroy the whole, if it were not delivered to them, it is clear that the underwriters would not be liable. Then the fact of their taking the corn after fhe was ftranded is as much unconnected with that circumftance as if it had been before. But the lofs which happened to that part of the cargo which was thrown overboard, being afcribeable to the ftranding, and being a direct and immediate confequence of the peril infured againft, might have been recovered, had there been any count in the declaration applicable to a lofs by ftranding."

Boyfield v. Brown, 2 Stra. 1065.

There is indeed a cafe in Sir *John Strange*'s Reports, which feems to militate againft the above decifions.

Upon the execution of a writ of inquiry before Lord *Hardwicke*, when Chief Juftice, it appeared, that the defendant was an infurer to the amount of 200*l.* upon corn, the value of which was 217*l.*: that the corn was fo damaged in the voyage, that it fold for 67*l.* only, and the freight came to 80*l.* The queftion upon this cafe was, Whether, as the freight exceeded the falvage, this was not to be confidered as a total lofs?

The Chief Juftice was of opinion, that within the reafon of deducting the freight, when the falvage exceeds it; the plaintiff in this cafe, wherein it fell fhort, was entitled to have it confidered as a total lofs. The jury accordingly found for the plaintiff.

Upon this cafe it may be obferved, that it was decided prior to the introduction of the claufe, upon which fo much has lately been faid; and confequently, fuch a decifion can have no weight now, becaufe the law is altered
[116] on account of the agreement of the parties. Indeed the cafe I am about to cite was exactly fimilar in circumftances

to

to *Boyfield* v. *Brown*: but Lord *Mansfield* in his charge to the jury gave a very different direction, and the jury found accordingly.

It was an action brought on a policy of insurance on goods, on board the *Happy Recovery*, at and from *London* to *St. Augustine*, to recover for a total loss. The cargo was *peas*, which, in a former cause on the same policy, were held to fall within the general denomination of *corn*, in the memorandum at the foot of the policy. The peas arrived at the place of destination; but being much damaged, the produce of them was less by about three fourths than the freight, which, on account of the ship's arrival at the port of discharge, became due.

Mason v. Skurray, Sittings after Hilary Term, 1780, at Guildhall. Vide ante, 112.

The defence set up by the underwriter was, that if the goods mentioned in the memorandum arrive at the market, though a loss amounting to a total one has happened, the underwriters are not liable. Four or five witnesses conversant in settling losses upon policies being called, proved, that the usage was, in such cases, to hold the underwriter discharged.

Lord *Mansfield* told the jury, "this was a question of consequence, and it turned upon the general import of the exception: the witnesses examined have put it on that point; and they hold, that if the specific thing come to the port of delivery, the underwriter cannot be called on. How did this matter stand before the year 1749? When the policy was general, and operated as an indemnity, there was little difference between a total and a partial loss. His lordship here stated the determination of *Boyfield* v. *Brown*, which, he observed, was prior to the clause in question. But the cases now stand upon the memorandum, which is in very general words. The question is, Whether the usage has not explained the generality of the words? If it has, every man, who contracts for a policy under usage, does it, as if the point of usage were inserted in his contract

CHAP. VI.

tract *in terms*. The witnesses examined all swear it to be *understood*, that if the specific thing comes to the market, the memorandum warrants the insurer to be free from any demands for an average, or partial loss." The jury found for the defendant.

[117] Vide ante, c. 2. p. 53.

The case of *Boyfield* v. *Brown* has certainly been overturned by this decision, which was recognized as a proper determination in the case of *Baillie* v. *Modigliani*, before cited, where Mr. Justice *Buller* said, that the case in *Strange's* Reports had been expressly over-ruled by the Court in the case of *Mason* v. *Skurray*.

When the quantity of damage sustained in the course of the voyage is known, and the amount, which each underwriter upon the policy is liable to pay, is settled, it is usual for the underwriter to endorse on the policy, "*adjusted* "*this loss, at so much per cent.*" or some words to the same effect. This is called an adjustment.

It has been determined, that after an adjustment has been signed by the underwriter, if he refuse to pay, the owner has no occasion to go into the proof of his loss, or any of the circumstances respecting it. This, it is said, has been the invariable custom upon this subject; which seems perfectly just, as the underwriter has under his hand expressly admitted that the plaintiff has sustained damage to a certain amount. To be sure, if any fraud were discovered in obtaining the adjustment, that might be a ground for setting it aside: but supposing the transaction fair, as we must always do till proof is given to the contrary, the rule of not suffering the adjustment to be contradicted, is fair and equitable.

Hog v. Gouldney, Sittings after Trin 1745, at Guildhall, Beawes Lex Mer. 310.

An action was brought, by the plaintiff against the defendant, on a policy of insurance, which the latter underwrote in *November* 1743, on the ship *George* and *Henry*, captain *Bower*, at and from *Jamaica* to *London*, interest or no interest,

rest, free of average, and without benefit of salvage to the insurers, with a warranty annexed to the policy, that the ship should sail from *Jamaica*, with the fleet that came out under convoy of the *Ludlow Castle* man of war. The ship sailed with the fleet under that convoy, but was damaged so much, as to oblige her to bear away for *Charlestown*, where she was condemned and broken up. The plaintiff demanded his insurance; and all the underwriters, being satisfied of the truth of the case, paid their loss, except the defendant, who went so far as to settle it, and according to the custom upon these occasions, underwrote the policy in these [118] words, "adjusted the loss on this policy, at ninety-eight "pounds *per cent.* which I do agree to pay one month after "date, *London*, 5th *July*, 1745, *Henry Gouldney.*"

When the note became due, he insisted on fuller proof, particularly of the ship's sailing with convoy, and her condemnation: but as it always was the custom, after adjustment and a promise to pay, never to require any further proof, but to pay the loss; and Lord Chief Justice *Lee* being of opinion, that this was to be considered as a note of hand, and that the plaintiff had no occasion to enter into the proof of the loss, the jury found a verdict for the plaintiff. The same rule was pursued in the following year in another case, before Lord Chief Justice *Lee*, between *Hewitt* and *Flexney*. Beawes Lex Merc. 308.

The words used by Lord Chief Justice *Lee* are extremely large, and perhaps the true rule upon the subject may be better collected from the two following cases:

Case on a policy of assurance on ship and goods from *London* to *Shelburne*, in *Nova Scotia*. The policy had been adjusted by the defendant, at 50 *per cent.* and it was contended, that he was now bound by that adjustment. On the other hand, it was argued that the adjustment was not binding; and that if it were, it ought to have been declared upon specially. Rogers v. Maylor, Sittings after Trin. 1790.

Lord

CHAP. VI.

Lord *Kenyon* ſaid, that he did not think it neceſſary to declare on the adjuſtment ſpecially, that it was *primâ facie* evidence againſt the defendant; but if there had been any miſconception of the law or fact, upon which it had been made, the underwriter was not abſolutely concluded by it. This turned out to be the caſe; and there was a verdict for the defendant.

De Garron v. Galbraith, Sittings after Trin. 1795.

So in a ſtill later caſe, the plaintiff came down to trial, having no other evidence to produce but the adjuſtment; and the witneſs, who proved it, ſwore, that doubts, ſoon after they had ſigned it, aroſe in the minds of the underwriters, and they refuſed to pay; upon which Lord *Kenyon* ſaid, that under theſe circumſtances, the plaintiff muſt go into other evidence, which not being prepared to do, he was nonſuited. In the following term a motion was made to ſet aſide the nonſuit, upon the ground that an adjuſtment was *primâ facie* evidence of the whole caſe, and threw the *onus probandi* upon the underwriter, and that it amounted to more than proof of the defendant's ſubſcription to the policy.

Michaelmas Term, 36 Geo. III.

Lord *Kenyon.*—"I admit the adjuſtment to be evidence in the cauſe to a certain extent; but I thought at the trial, and ſtill think, that when the ſame witneſs, who proved the ſignature of the defendant to the adjuſtment, ſaid, that doubts, ſoon after the adjuſtment took place, aroſe in the minds of the underwriters, as to the honeſty of the tranſaction, and they called for further proof, the plaintiff ſhould have produced other evidence: and that by ſhutting the door againſt inquiry after an adjuſtment, would be putting a ſtop to candour and fair dealing amongſt the underwriters." The rule was refuſed.

Thelluſſon v. Fletcher, Dougl. 301.

The ſpirit of this rule was adopted in a very modern caſe, in an inſurance upon goods on board a *foreign ſhip*, "the "policy to be deemed ſufficient proof of intereſt in caſe of "loſs." The defendant ſuffered judgment to go againſt him

him by default; and on a motion to fet afide the writ of inquiry, the court of King's Bench faid, that although fuch a policy would be void in this country, by virtue of the ftatute of the 19th *Geo.* 2. *c.* 37, yet the ftatute did not extend to policies on foreign fhips: and in this cafe the underwriter, having fuffered judgment to go by default, has confeffed the plaintiff's title to recover; and the amount of that lofs was fixed, by his own ftipulation in the policy, and which he cannot now controvert.

CHAP. VI.

Vide poft, c. 14.

One rule relative to adjuftments remains ftill to be mentioned, which is, that if an infurer pay money for a total lofs, and in fact it be fo at the time of adjuftment; if it afterwards turn out to be only a partial lofs, he fhall not recover back the money fo paid to the infured. But fubftantial juftice is done, by putting him in the place of the infured, and giving him all the advantages that may arife from the falvage.

This rule was fettled by the King's Bench in the year 1766. It was an action on the cafe for 200*l.* upon an *indebitatus affumpfit*, for fo much money had and received to the ufe of the plaintiff. *Non affumpfit* was pleaded, and iffue joined. It was brought by the infurer againft the infured, to recover back what he had paid him. At the trial, a cafe was referved for the opinion of the court. The facts were; that a policy had been underwritten by the plaintiff, for the infurance of any of the packet boats that fhould fail from *Lifbon* to *Falmouth*, or fuch other port in *England* as his majefty fhould direct, for one whole year, commencing the 1ft of *October* 1763, and to continue to the 1ft of *October* 1764, inclufive, upon any kinds of goods and merchandizes whatfoever: and it was agreed, that the goods and merchandizes fhould be valued at the fum infured on fuch packet boat, without farther proof of intereft than the policy, and to make no return of premium for want of intereft being on bullion or goods. And in cafe of lofs or misfortune, the infured to be at liberty to fue, labour, and travel,

Da Cofta v. Firth, 4 Burr. 1966.

[119]

CHAP. VI. travel, for, in, and about the defence, ſafeguard, and recovery of the ſaid goods, or any part thereof, without prejudice to the inſurance, to the charges whereof the inſurers were to contribute, each one according to the rate and quantity of his ſum inſured. The conſideration paid by the inſured was 10 *per cent.* and in caſe of loſs they were to abate nothing. Then follows the uſual memorandum.

The caſe then ſtates, that the defendant had an intereſt in bullion, on board the *Hanover* packet, being one of the king's packets, between *Liſbon* and *Falmouth*: that on the 2d of *December* 1763, it was totally loſt off *Falmouth*, in a voyage between *Liſbon* and *Falmouth*; and the loſs was adjuſted in writing under the policy, in the words following:—

"Adjuſted a loſs on this policy at 100*l.* *per cent.* the "*Hanover* packet, captain *Sherborn*, being totally loſt at "*Falmouth*. Should any ſalvage hereafter be recovered, the "inſured promiſes to refund to the inſurer whatever he may "ſo recover, in ſuch proportion as the ſum inſured bears to "the whole intereſt. *London*, 23 *October* 1764, for *Richard* "*Seward*, *Michael Firth*."

The inſurer paid the whole money inſured, which was 200*l.* In *April* 1765, the iron trunk, which contained all the bullion, was fiſhed up; and thereby all the bullion was
[120] recovered without prejudice, and delivered to the defendant. The defendant's expenſe of ſalvage amounted to 63*l.* 8*s.* 2*d.* and deducting that ſum for ſalvage, the nett proportion of his ſhare came to 206*l.* 11*s.* 9*d.* The plaintiff's proportion thereof, in reſpect of his ſubſcription, amounted to 48*l.* 4*s.* which was paid into the court.

The queſtion was, whether the plaintiff was entitled to recover.

Vide poſt, c. 14. The court held, that this was a policy of a peculiar ſort; and that it was good within the exception of the 19th *George*

George 2. *c.* 37. which ſays, that certain policies of a particular form ſhall be void, except on effects from any port in *Europe*, or *America*, in the poſſeſſion of the crowns of *Spain* or *Portugal*. This is a mixed policy; partly a wager policy, partly an open one: it is a valued policy, and fairly ſo, without fraud or miſrepreſentation. Therefore the loſs having happened, the inſured is entitled to recover as for a total loſs. The inſurer agreed to the value; and cannot be allowed to diſpute it. The inſured has received the money for a total loſs; and there is no want of conſcience in retaining it. The caſes, cited at the bar, only tend to ſhew, that where it appears, *before* adjuſtment, to be but a *partial loſs*, the underwriter ſhall pay no more than the *real* damage: the reaſon of which deciſion is, that the inſured muſt ſhew the whole caſe, as it then ſtood. But in the preſent caſe, there was a total loſs *at the time* of the adjuſtment. The adjuſtment in this caſe makes an end of the queſtion. Here is a ſolemn abandonment, and a ſolemn agreement, "that the inſurers ſhall be content with ſalvage "in ſuch proportion as the ſum inſured bears to the whole "intereſt." There was a total loſs at the time of the adjuſtment (which is the ſame as if the damages had then been recovered in an action.) Here is no ſort of fraud, nor any thing that is againſt any law: and to refund more than in that proportion would be contrary to the underwriter's own agreement. Therefore the nett proportion only, in reſpect to the plaintiff's ſubſcription after deduction of ſalvage, ought to be returned, and that is paid into court. The *poſtea* was ordered to be delivered to the defendant.

CHAPTER THE SEVENTH.

Of General or Grofs Average.

CHAP. VII.

3 Burr. 1555.

AVERAGE, in that fenfe in which we are now to confider it, fignifies a contribution to a general lofs: but in order to fatisfy the reader, it will be neceffary to give a more particular defcription of it.

Magens 55.

Whatever the mafter of a fhip in diftrefs, with the advice of his officers and failors, deliberately refolves to do, for the prefervation of the whole, in cutting away mafts or cables, or in throwing goods overboard to lighten his veffel, which is what is meant by jettifon or jetfon, is in all places permitted to be brought into a general or grofs average; in which all who are concerned in fhip, freight, and cargo, are to bear an equal, or proportionable part, of the lofs of what was fo facrificed for the common welfare; and it muft be made good by the infurers in fuch proportions, as they have underwritten. In the works of writers upon commercial affairs, we very often meet with the word contribution, alfo fignifying the thing juft defcribed: and in a marine fenfe, average and contribution are fynonimous terms.

Beawes 147.

This obligation, which, by the laws of all the maritime countries in *Europe,* binds the proprietor of the goods or fhip faved to contribute to the relief of thofe whofe goods are thrown overboard, is founded on the great principle of diftributive juftice: for it would be hard that one man fhould fuffer by an act, which the common fafety rendered neceffary; and that thofe who received a benefit from that act fhould make no fatisfaction to him who had fuftained the lofs.

This obligation, which is tacitly entered into by all who have property at fea, was introduced by the *Rhodians.* Their

Their laws most equitably enacted, that all the property on board should contribute to this necessary and general loss; and in modern constitutions we find very little alteration in the doctrine of averages, from that established at *Rhodes*. Similar regulations were made by the laws of *Wisbuy*, and as I have already said, they are now become general. From *Molloy* we learn, that the *Rhodian* laws upon this subject were introduced into *England* by *William* the Conqueror.

CHAP. VII.

Leg. Rhod. s. 2. art. 9.

Laws of Wisbuy art. 20. L. 2. c. 6. s. 3.

Beawes is of opinion, that in order to make the act of throwing the goods overboard legal, three things must concur.

Beawes Lex Merc. 148.

1st, That what is so condemned to destruction, be in consequence of a deliberate and voluntary consultation held between the master and men.

2dly, That the ship be in distress, and that sacrificing a part be necessary in order to preserve the rest.

3dly, That the saving of the ship and cargo be actually owing to the means used with that sole view.

But of these the first and third propositions may be doubted, as the second point alone seems to be all that is necessary.

It appears also, by the laws of *Wisbuy*, that in an emergency of such a nature as to justify lightening the ship, it was necessary first to consult the owner of the goods or the supercargo: but if they would not consent, the merchandize might, notwithstanding their refusal, be ejected, if it appeared necessary to the rest of the people on board; a regulation evidently founded in necessity, to prevent a sordid individual from obstructing a measure so essential to the general safety.

Laws of Wisbuy, art. 20.

Laws of Oleron, art. 8.

If the ship ride out the storm, and arrive in safety at the port of destination, the captain must make regular protests,

Beawes 148. Molloy, l. 2. c. 6. s. 2.

CHAP. VII.

tests, and must swear, in which oath some of the crew must join, that the goods were cast overboard for no other cause, but for the safety of the ship and the rest of the cargo. And as the law has authorized such proceedings in these cases of imminent necessity, it will protect those who act *bonâ fide*, and will indemnify them against all consequences. Thus in an action of trespass against a man for throwing goods overboard, he pleaded specially, that it was done in a storm, in a case of necessity, *navis levandæ causâ*; and if that act had not been done, that the passengers must all have perished. The court held, that the plea was good, and the defendant had judgment.

Mouse's case, 12 Co. 63.

[123]

It is evident from one of the rules above stated, that there can be no contribution without the ejection of some goods, and the saving of others: but it is not always necessary for the purpose of contribution, that the ship should arrive at the port of destination.

Ord. Lew. 14. tit. Contribu. art. 15, 16. Ord. of Hamb. 2 Mag. 240. Ord. of Rotterdam, 2 Magens 98. But see page 122.

If the jettison does not save the ship, but she perish in the storm, there shall be no contribution of such goods as may happen to be saved; because the object, for which the goods were thrown overboard, was not attained. But if the ship, being once preserved by such means, and continuing her course, should afterwards be lost, the property saved from the second accident, shall contribute to the loss sustained by those whose goods were cast out upon the former occasion.

1 Mag. 56.

Magens, in his preliminary Essay on Insurances, advances a different doctrine, and contends, that if a ship be saved by throwing goods overboard, and afterwards perish by another calamity, the goods saved shall not contribute to the former loss. He puts a case to illustrate his meaning; but the ordinances above referred to, as will appear from the abstract of them in the preceding paragraph, directly contradict his positions, although he seems to have had those ordinances in view when he advanced them. It

was

was necessary to say thus much, because the doctrines of such an useful writer are often received implicitly; erroneous opinions are adopted and confirmed, because they are not accurately examined; and the more respectable the writer is, the greater is the danger which is to be apprehended. But what is still more remarkable, in the very next paragraph to that I last mentioned, he puts a similar case, in which he admits that the goods saved ought to contribute. 1 Mag. 57.

The writers upon this subject have stated with much minuteness and accuracy, the various accidents and charges, that will entitle the party suffering to call upon the rest for a contribution. I doubt whether it be necessary to be so particular in this place; because, we may gather in general [124] from the description given of average at the beginning of this chapter, that all losses sustained, and expenses incurred voluntarily and deliberately, with a view to prevent a total loss of the ship and cargo, ought to be equally borne by the ship and her remaining lading. Such for instance is the damage sustained, in defending a ship against an enemy or pirate: such is the expense of curing, and attendance upon the officers or mariners wounded in such defence: and such also is the sum which the master may have promised to pay for the ransom of his ship to any privateer or pirate, when taken. A master who has cut his mast, parted with his cable, or abandoned any other part of the ship and cargo, in a storm, in order to save the ship, is well entitled to this compensation: but if he should *lose* them by the storm, the loss falls only upon the ship and freight; because the tempest only was the occasion of this loss, without the deliberation of the master and crew, and was not done with a view to save the ship and lading. Upon the same principle it is, that by the naval laws of *Wisbuy*, which in this respect, as well as in many others, have been adopted by modern states, it was declared, that when a ship arrived at the mouth of a harbour, and the master, finding that his ship was too heavy laden to sail up, was obliged to put

Beawes Lex Merc. 148.
1 Mag. 64.
Beawes 148.
Art. 56.
Ord. of France & Rotterdam, 2 Magens 96. 183. Molloy tit. Average, f. 12.

CHAP. VII. put part of the cargo into hoys and barges; the owners of the ship and of the goods that remained, were obliged to contribute, if the lighters perished. But if the ship should be lost, and the lighters saved, the owners of the goods so preserved, were not to contribute to the proprietors of the 1 Mag. 56. ship and cargo lost. The difference is this, the lightening of the ship was an act of deliberation for the general benefit: whereas the circumstance of the lighters being saved, and the ship lost, was accidental, no way proceeding from a regard for the whole.

Beawes 148. Molloy, l. 2. c. 6. s. 8. It is not only the value of the goods thrown overboard that must be considered in a general average; but also the value of such as receive any damage by wet, *&c.* from the jettison of the rest.

Beawes 150. It is said, that if a ship be taken by force, carried into some port, and the crew remain on board to take care of and reclaim her, not only the charges of reclaiming shall [125] be brought into a general average; but the wages and expenses of the ship's company during her arrest, from the time of her capture, and being disturbed in the voyage. 1 Mag. 67. In this idea *Magens* concurs, and asserts, that such expenses are allowed as average in *London* as well as elsewhere. He denies, however, and as it seems, justly denies, that an allowance would be made under general average, for sailors wages and victuals, when they are under a necessity of performing quarantine, in which case the master would have been obliged to maintain and pay them, though his vessel had arrived only in ballast. But at the same time he admits, that charges occurring by an extraordinary quarantine shall be brought into a general average.

It has however been a considerable question, Whether the extraordinary wages and victuals expended during the detention by a foreign prince not at war, ought to be brought into a general average, so as to charge the underwriter? *Magens* and *Beawes* differ upon the point; the latter

latter being of opinion that it ſhould, the former that it ſhould not. In *England* there is no adjudged caſe, nor any regulation upon the ſubject; and therefore, the only mode by which this and ſimilar queſtions are to be decided, is to conſider, whether theſe expenſes were neceſſarily and unavoidably incurred, for the general ſafety of the ſhip and cargo.

Lord *Mansfield* ſeems to have been of that opinion in an action upon a policy of inſurance on a *ſhip*. It was brought to recover the amount of wages and proviſions expended during the time the ſhip went from *Bengal* to *Bombay* to repair. His lordſhip, as he has frequently done ſince upon ſimilar occaſions, decided againſt the action, being an inſurance on the ſhip only, and the item in queſtion being ſailors wages. But his lordſhip ſaid, there may be caſes, where exceptions to the general rule ſhould be allowed; but in order to conſider a caſe as excepted, it muſt be an expenſe abſolutely neceſſary, and ſuch as could not be avoided, owing to ſome of the perils ſtated in the policy.

Lateward v. Curling, G. H. Sittings after Trin. 1776.

Vide ante, p. 52. 54.

His lordſhip here ſeems to allude to a general average: but on a point, on which no authority can be adduced, I would not chooſe that Lord *Mansfield*'s words ſhould be ſuppoſed to convey an idea, which perhaps the ſpeaker never intended. It does not become me to hazard an opinion; and, therefore, I ſhall leave it as a matter undecided; only obſerving, that by the ordinances of *Lewis* the Fourteenth, the charges in ſuch a caſe ſhall be reputed general average, if the ſeamen be hired by the month; otherwiſe, if by the voyage.

[126]

Tit. Average Art. 7.

It may be proper before I cloſe this branch of my ſubject, to ſtate a paragraph I have met with, which confirms the idea, entertained by Lord *Mansfield*. "Though "it muſt be noted, ſays this author, that the charges of "unloading a ſhip, to get her into a river or port, ought "not to be brought into a general average; but they may "when

Beawes 150.

CHAP. VII. "when occasioned by an indispensable necessity to prevent the loss of ship and cargo. As when a ship is "forced by a storm to enter a port to repair the damage "she has suffered, if she cannot continue her voyage "without an apparent risk of being lost; in which case, "the wages and victuals of the crew are brought into "an average from the day it was resolved to seek a port "to refit the vessel, to the day of her departure from it, "with all the charges of unloading, reloading, anchorage, "pilotage, and every other expense incurred by this "necessity."

Da Costa v. Newnham, 2 Term R. 407. Since the first edition of this work, a question nearly similar came before the court of King's Bench, in which Mr. Justice *Buller* quoted the above passage from *Beawes*, as also the case of *Lateward* v. *Curling* in the preceding page: and although the learned judge thought it then unnecessary to decide the point here agitated, yet the leaning of his mind seemed to be in favour of the affirmative. This, however, was held by the whole court, that where a ship is obliged to go into port for the benefit of the whole concern, the charges of loading and unloading the cargo, and taking care of it, and the wages and provisions of *the workmen hired for the repairs*, become general average.

De leg. Rhod. f. 2. art. 8 Oler. art. 8. Wisb. art. 20. Molloy, l. 2. c. 6. f. 4. By the ancient laws of *Rhodes*, *Oleron*, and *Wisbuy*, the ship, and all the remaining goods, shall contribute to the loss sustained. The most valuable goods, though their weight should have been incapable of putting the ship in the least hazard, as diamonds or precious stones, must be valued at their just price in this contribution, because they [127] could not have been saved to the owners but by the ejection of the other goods. Neither the persons of those in the ship, nor the ship provisions, nor respondentia bonds, Vid. post. c. 21. Joyce v. Williamson. suffer any estimation; nor does wearing apparel in chests and boxes, nor do such jewels as belong to the person merely;

merely; but if the jewels are a part of the cargo, they must contribute. CHAP. VII.

Those who carry jewels by sea ought to communicate that circumstance to the master; because the care of them will be increased in proportion to their worth, to prevent their being thrown overboard pro·· ·scuously with other things: and hence their preservation will be a common benefit. 1 Mag. 63.

Both by law and custom, the wages of sailors are not to contribute to the general loss; a provision intended to make this description of men more easily consent to a jettison, as they do not then risk their all, being still assured that their wages will be paid. 1 Mag. 71.

The way of fixing a right sum, by which the average ought to be computed, can only be, by examining what the whole ship, freight, and cargo, if no jettison had been made, would have produced neat, if they had all belonged to one person, and been sold for ready money. And this is the sum whereon the contribution should be made, all the particular goods bearing their nett proportion. 1 Mag. 69.

In no respect whatever do the ordinances of foreign states differ so much, as in the manner of settling the contribution of the ship and freight. In some places, the ship contributes for the whole of her value and freight; in others for the half of her value, and one third of her freight: and again, in others, both ship and freight are to contribute for one half. By the laws of *Koningsberg*, *Hamburgh* and *Copenhagen*, the ship is to contribute for the whole of her value and freight. They also declare, that the value of the ship shall be that which she was worth when she arrived; and that from the freight a deduction shall be made of the men's wages, pilotage, and such other charges, as come under the name of petty average, of which it is customary every where, as we have before Ord. of Genoa and France. 2 Mag. 207. 237. 339. Vide the last chapter.

CHAP. VII. before obſerved, for the cargo to bear two-thirds, and the ſhip one.

The *Engliſh* writers upon commerce are totally ſilent in this reſpect; and therefore cuſtom muſt be our guide: and [128] I think from that we may collect, that the ſhip, freight,(*a*) and cargo, are to bear an equal and proportional part of what was ſo ſacrificed for the common good.

The ſea laws of different countries vary no leſs than upon the former queſtion, in fixing at what prices goods thrown overboard ſhall be eſtimated, and for what value thoſe ſaved are to contribute.

2 Mag. 100. 285. 339. By the ordinances of *Rotterdam*, *Stockholm*, and *Copenhagen*, if the accident, which occaſioned the general average, happened before half the voyage was performed, the jettiſon was to be eſtimated at prime coſt; but if after that period, then at the price for which ſuch goods would ſell, at the place of diſcharge, freight, duties, and ordinary charges deducted. Molloy, tit. Aver. ſ. 15. That diſtinction is now, however, exploded in *England*, and the cuſtom has become general of eſtimating the goods ſaved and loſt, at the price for which the goods ſaved were ſold; freight and all other charges being firſt deducted. Leg. Wiſb. art. 20. This rule is agreeable to the marine laws of *Wiſbuy*, which declare, that the goods thrown overboard ſhall be brought into a groſs average, and ſhall be rated at the ſame price for which other merchandize of the ſame ſort, preſerved from the ſea or enemy, was ſold. This cuſtom mentioned by Malyne Lex Merc. 1ſt part c. 26. *Molloy* was certainly new in *England* at the time he wrote; for it appears by *Malyne*, that in 1622, the diſtinction was obſerved of eſtimating the goods at prime coſt, if the jettiſon happened before half the voyage was performed: and if after, at the price the reſt of the goods ſold for, at the place of diſcharge. However, *Molloy* is a more modern authority; and *Magens* ſays, that the prevailing mode of ſettling averages

(*a*) It was lately held by the whole court of King's Bench that freight muſt contribute to a general average. *Da Coſta* v. *Newnham*, 2 Term R. 407.

rages now adopted in *England* is conformable to that rule, which has abolished the distinction. CHAP. VII.

Gold, silver, and jewels, at most places, contribute to a general average, according to their full value, and in the same manner as any other species of merchandize. It has been said, that an immemorial custom has prevailed at *Amsterdam*, that gold and silver shall only contribute for half their value: the reason for such a custom, one is at a loss to conjecture. In *England* no such custom prevails; but money and jewels must fall into the general average at their full price: and a modern writer assures us, that the practice was such in *London* when he wrote; and such, I believe it to be at this day.

1 Mag. 62.

[129]

Molloy, tit. Average, s. 4.

1 Mag. 62.

In a late case, the doctrine here advanced was mentioned and confirmed by Mr. Justice *Buller*, as clear law.

Peters v. Milligan, Sittings at Guildhall after Michaelmas, 1787.

The contribution is in general not made till the ship arrive at the place of delivery: but accidents may happen, which may cause a contribution before she reach her destined port. Thus when a vessel has been obliged to make a jettison, or, by the damages suffered, soon after sailing, is obliged to return to her port of discharge; the necessary charges of her repairs, and the replacing the goods thrown overboard, may then be settled by a general average.

Roccus de Navibus, Not. 96.

1 Mag. 60.

Thus I have endeavoured to lay before the reader an idea of what is meant by average; and, in order to do that more distinctly, I have defined what average is; I have shewn its origin; and what the necessary requisites are to render the act, whence average arises, legal. I then stated in general what accidents or expenses would authorize the sufferer to call for a contribution: the different kinds of property that were subject to such contribution; and lastly, the mode by which the value of this property was to be ascertained.

It only remains now to state, that the insurers are liable to pay the insured for all expenses arising from general average,

in

CHAP. VII.

Roccus de assecurationibus, Not. 62.

in proportion to the sums they have underwritten. *Roccus* says, "*Jactu facto, ob maris tempestatem, pro sublevanda navi, "an teneantur assecuratores ad solvendum æstimationem rerum "jactarum domino ipsarum? Dic eos non teneri, quia pro rebus "jactis fit contributio; inter omnes merces habentes in illa navi "pro solvendo pretio domino ipsarum, et ideo si assecuratus recu-"perat pretium rerum jactarum, non potest agere contra assecu-"ratores; tamen tenentur assecuratores ad reficiendum illam "ratam et portionem, quam solvit assecuratus in illam contribu-*

[130] "*tionem faciendo inter omnes, habentes merces in illa navi, quæ "portio cum non recuperetur ab aliis, habetur pro deperdita, et "proinde ad illam portionem tenentur assecuratores.*"

The opinion of this learned civilian is agreeable to the laws of all the trading powers on the continent of *Europe*, as well as to those of *England*, where the insurer, by his contract, engages to indemnify against all losses arising from a general average.

[130 *a*] In the former editions of this work, I had contented myself with stating the nature of general average, and that the sums paid on this account might be recovered against the underwriters. But I had omitted to state what remedy the person, whose goods were thrown overboard, or who had expended money for the general preservation of ship and cargo, had against those, whose goods or ship were preserved by such means. In the case of an expenditure of money, *probably* an action for money paid *might* be maintained against each of those, who were benefited by such expenditure. But as this would lead to a multiplicity of actions; and this species of action is not applicable to the case of goods thrown overboard, the better mode in all cases seems to be to apply for contribution to a court of equity, where effectual relief may be obtained against all the parties in one suit.

Com. Dig. tit. Chancery, (2 I) and Shower's Parl. Cas.

CHAPTER THE EIGHTH.

Of Salvage.

CHAP. VIII.

SALVAGE is ſo neceſſarily connected with the two former chapters, that it will be proper to take it into conſideration here, before we proceed to the other parts of this inquiry.

Salvage is an allowance made for ſaving a ſhip, or goods, or both from the dangers of the ſeas, fire, pirates, or enemies; and it is alſo ſometimes uſed to ſignify the thing itſelf which is ſaved; but it is in the former ſenſe only, in which we are at preſent to conſider it. Beawes Lex Merc. 146.

The propriety and juſtice of ſuch an allowance muſt be evident to every one; for nothing can be more reaſonable than that he, who has recovered the property of another from imminent danger by great labour, or perhaps at the hazard of his life, ſhould be rewarded by him, who has been ſo materially benefited by that labour. Accordingly, all maritime ſtates, from the *Rhodians* down to the preſent time, have made certain regulations, fixing the rate of ſalvage in ſome inſtances, and leaving it, in others, to depend upon the particular circumſtances. Kaim's Princ. of Eq. Introduct. p. 6. Leg. Rhod. ſ. 2. art. 45, 46, 47.

The law of *England*, the deciſions of which are not ſurpaſſ- by thoſe of any other nation, in juſtice and humanity, was not backward in adopting a doctrine ſo equitable in its nature, and ſo beneficial to thoſe whoſe property was endangered.

Thus in an action of trover, the defendants pleaded, that the goods, for which the action was brought, were in a ſhip, which took fire, and that they hazarded their lives to ſave them: but that they were ready to deliver the goods, if the pliantiff would pay 4*l.* for ſalvage. The court, upon a general demurrer to this plea, were obliged to give judgment for the plaintiff, becauſe the ſpecial plea did not confeſs a converſion. But upon the general point, for which this caſe is cited, Lord Chief Juſtice Hartford v. Jones, 1 Ld. Raym. 393. 2. Salk. 654.

Holt

CHAP. VIII. *Holt* held that the defendants might retain the goods till payment of the salvage, as well as a taylor, an ostler, or a common carrier: and salvage is allowed by all nations; it being reasonable, that a man should be rewarded, who hazards his life in the service of another. Therefore his lordship, in favour of so just a claim, allowed the defendant to waive his special plea, and plead the general issue.

As the propriety of such an allowance is admitted by all, the only difficulty that can arise upon the subject is, to ascertain in what proportions these gratuities and rewards must be allowed.

Vide the passages last cited. The laws of *Rhodes* fixing the rate of salvage in several instances, sometimes giving for salvage one-fifth of what was saved; at other times only a tenth; and at others, one half. Leg. Oler. art. 4. The regulations of *Oleron* left it more unsettled, and declared, that the courts of judicature should award to the salvers, such a proportion of the goods saved, as they should think a sufficient recompense for the service performed, and the expense incurred. Almost every state has regulations on this head peculiar to itself; and the legislature of this country has by various statutes expressed its ideas upon the subject. I shall first consider what rule it has established in cases of wreck, and then what the rate of salvage is in cases of recapture.

When a ship has been wrecked, the law of *England* has followed the laws of *Oleron* in declaring, that *reasonable* salvage only shall be allowed. But the statute will best shew the idea of the legislature.

12 Ann, stat. 2. c. 18. It appears from the preamble, that the infamous practices, which a former statute 27 *Edward* 3. *c.* 13. had endeavoured to suppress, of plundering those ships which were driven on shore, and seizing whatever could be laid hold of as lawful prize, still continued; or that if the property were restored to the owners, the demand for salvage was so exorbitant, that the inevitable Sect. 1. ruin of the trader was the immediate consequence. The statute, in order to prevent these mischiefs in future, enacted, that if a ship was in danger of being stranded or run ashore, the sheriffs, justices, mayors, constables, or officers of the customs, nearest the place of danger, should, upon application made to them, summon and call together as many men as should be thought neces-

sary

ſary to the aſſiſtance, and for the preſervation of ſuch ſhip in diſtreſs and her cargo; and that if any ſhip, man of war, or merchantman, ſhould be riding at anchor near the place of danger, the conſtables and officers of the cuſtoms might demand of the ſuperior officer of ſuch ſhip, aſſiſtance by his boats and ſuch hands as could be ſpared: and that if the ſuperior officer ſhould refuſe to grant ſuch aſſiſtance, he ſhould forfeit 100*l*.

Then follows the ſection reſpecting ſalvage. "And for the "encouragement of ſuch perſons as ſhall give their aſſiſtance "to ſuch ſhips or veſſels, ſo in diſtreſs as aforeſaid, be it enact-"ed, that the ſaid collectors of the cuſtoms, and the maſter "and commanding officer of any ſhips or veſſels, and all others, "who ſhall act or be employed in the preſerving of any ſuch "ſhip or veſſel in diſtreſs, or their cargoes, ſhall, within thirty "days after the ſervice is performed, be paid *a reaſonable re-"ward* for the ſame, by the commander, maſter, or other ſu-"perior officer, mariners, or owners of the ſhip or veſſel ſo "in diſtreſs as aforeſaid, or by the merchant whoſe veſſel or "goods ſhall be ſo ſaved; and in default thereof, the ſaid ſhip "or veſſel ſo ſaved ſhall remain in the cuſtody of the officers of "the cuſtoms until all charges are paid, and until the officers "of the cuſtoms, and the maſter or other officers of the ſhip "or veſſel, and all others employed in the preſervation of the "ſhip, ſhall be *reaſonably gratified* for their aſſiſtance and trou-"ble, or good ſecurity given for that purpoſe, to the ſatisfac-"tion of the parties that are to receive the ſame: and if any "diſagreement ſhall take place between the perſons, whoſe "ſhips or goods have been ſaved, and the officer of the cuſ-"toms, touching the monies deſerved by any of the perſons ſo "employed, it ſhall be lawful for the commander of the ſhip "or veſſel ſo ſaved, or the owner of the goods, or the mer-"chant intereſted therein, and alſo for the officer of the cuſ-"toms, or his deputy, to nominate three of the neighbouring "juſtices of the peace, who ſhall thereupon adjuſt the *quan-"tum* of the monies or gratuities to be paid to the ſeveral "perſons acting or being employed in the ſalvage of the ſaid "ſhip, veſſel, or goods; and ſuch adjuſtments ſhall be "binding upon all parties, and ſhall be recoverable in an ac-"tion at law: and in caſe it ſhall ſo happen, that no perſon Sect. 2.

"ſhall

CHAP. VIII. "shall appear to make his claim to all or any of the goods "that shall be saved, that then the chief officer of the customs "of the nearest port to the place where the said ship or vessel was so in distress, shall apply to three of the nearest "justices of the peace, who shall put him or some other responsible person in possession of the said goods, such justices taking an account in writing of the said goods, to be "signed by the said officer of the customs: and if the said "goods shall not be legally claimed within the space of "twelve months next ensuing, by the rightful owner thereof, then public sale shall be made thereof, and if perishable "goods, forthwith to be sold, and after all charges deducted, "the residue of the monies arising from such sale, with a fair "and just account of the whole, shall be transmitted to her "majesty's Exchequer, there to remain for the benefit of the "rightful owner, when appearing, who, upon an affidavit, "or other proof made of his or their right or property thereto, to the satisfaction of one of the barons of the coif of "the Exchequer, shall, upon his order, receive the same out "of the Exchequer."

Sect. 3. The statute then goes on to declare, that any other persons, than those mentioned in the preceding clause, endeavouring to enter such ship or vessel without the permission of the superior officer of the ship, or of the officer of the customs, *&c.* or molesting or hindering them in the preservation of the ship, or defacing the marks of the goods on board such ship, shall make double satisfaction to the party grieved, or on default thereof shall be sent to the house of correction for twelve calendar months: and that it shall be lawful for the officers of the ship to repel by force persons so endeavouring to enter without leave.

Sect. 4. It is also enacted, that if any goods, stolen from such ship shall be found on any person, they shall be delivered up to the true owner; or, in default, such person shall pay treble, the value.

[135] Sect. 5. The next section declares, that any person, boring holes in a ship in distress, or stealing a pump belonging thereto, shall be guilty of felony, without benefit of clergy.

This act was made perpetual by the 4 *Geo.* 1. *c.* 12; and as far as relates to our present subject, we can collect, that in cases of wreck, the rate of salvage is not fixed, but must be *reasonable*;

reasonable; that is, it muſt be a ſufficient recompenſe to thoſe who have encountered dangers for the preſervation of the ſhip and cargo, regard at the ſame time being had to the circumſtances of the owner of the property ſaved: and what ſhall be a ſufficient recompenſe is to be aſcertained by three juſtices of the peace. CHAP. VIII.

Notwithſtanding this ſalutary law had paſſed, the enormities complained of by the ſtatute of queen *Anne* ſtill continued, to the diſgrace of humanity and a civilized people; upon which the legiſlature were again obliged to interpoſe by a ſubſequent ſtatute, which I ſhould perhaps not have mentioned, had it not 26 Geo. II. c. 19. contained ſome additional regulations reſpecting ſalvage.

The ſtatute ordains, that perſons convicted of ſtealing goods Sect. 1.
from a ſhip wrecked, or in diſtreſs, or of obſtructing the eſcape of any perſon from a wreck, or of putting out falſe lights to lead ſuch ſhip into danger, ſhall ſuffer as felons without benefit of clergy. But where goods of ſmall value ſhall Sect. 2.
be ſtolen, without any circumſtances of cruelty, the offender may be indicted for petty larceny. Juſtices of the peace, upon Sect. 3.
information of ſhipwrecked goods being ſtolen or concealed, are empowered to iſſue ſearch warrants; and the perſons in whoſe cuſtody they may be found, refuſing to deliver them on demand, or to give a ſatisfactory account how they became poſſeſſed thereof, ſhall be committed to the common gaol for ſix months, or until payment of the treble value of ſuch goods. Goods offered to ſale, ſuſpected of being ſhipwrecked, are to Sect. 4.
be ſtopped; and notice ſhall be immediately given to a juſtice of the peace, and if the perſon offering the ſame to ſale cannot make out the property to be lawfully in him, the goods ſhall be returned to the owner, *upon a reaſonable reward for ſuch ſeizure (to be aſcertained by the juſtice)* and the offender ſhall be committed to the common gaol for ſix months, or until payment of the treble value of the ſaid goods.

And be it further enacted, "that in caſe any perſon or per- [136]
"ſons, not employed by the maſter, mariners or owners, or Sect. 5.
"other perſons lawfully authorized in the ſalvage of any ſhip "or veſſel, or the cargo or proviſion thereof, ſhall, in the ab-"ſence of the perſons ſo employed and authorized, ſave any "ſuch

CHAP. VIII. " ſuch ſhip, veſſel, goods, or effects, and cauſe the ſame to be " carried, for the benefit of the owners or proprietors, into " port, or to any near adjoining cuſtom-houſe, or other place " of ſafe cuſtody, immediately giving notice thereof to ſome " juſtice of the peace, magiſtrate, or cuſtom-houſe or exciſe " officer: or ſhall diſcover to ſuch magiſtrate, or officer, where " any ſuch goods or effects are wrongfully bought, ſold, or " concealed, then *ſuch perſon or perſons ſhall be entitled to a* " *reaſonable reward for ſuch ſervices*, to be paid by the maſ- " ters or owners of ſuch veſſels or goods, and to be adjuſted " in caſe of diſagreement about the *quantum*, in like manner " as the ſalvage is to be adjuſted and paid, by virtue of a " ſtatute made in the 12th of queen *Anne*."

Vide ſupra.

Sect. 6. " And be it further enacted, that for the better aſcertain- " ing the ſalvage to be paid in purſuance of the preſent act, " and the act before mentioned, and for the more effectual " putting the ſaid acts in execution, the juſtice of the peace, " mayor, bailiff, collector of the cuſtoms, or chief conſtable, " who ſhall be neareſt to the place where any ſhip, goods, " or effects, ſhall be ſtranded or caſt away, ſhall forthwith " give public notice for a meeting to be held as ſoon as poſ- " ſible of the ſheriff or his deputy, the juſtices of the peace, " mayors, or other chief magiſtrates of towns corporate, " coroners or commiſſioners of the land tax, or any five or " more of them, who are hereby empowered and required " to give aid in the execution of this and the ſaid former " act, and to employ proper perſons for the ſaving of ſhips " in diſtreſs, and ſuch ſhips, veſſels, and effects, as ſhall be " ſtranded, or caſt away; and alſo to examine perſons up- " on oath, touching or concerning the ſame, or the ſalvage " thereof, and to adjuſt the *quantum* of ſuch ſalvage, and " diſtribute the ſame among the perſons concerned in ſuch " ſalvage, in caſe of diſagreement among the parties, or the " ſaid perſons; and that every ſuch magiſtrate, &c. attend- " ing and acting at ſuch meeting, ſhall be paid four ſhillings [137] " a day for his expenſes in ſuch attendance out of the goods " and effects ſaved by their care or direction."

Sect. 7. " Provided always, that if the charges and rewards for ſal- " vage, directed to be paid by the former ſtatute, and by this

" act,

" act, ſhall not be fully paid, or ſufficient ſecurity given for " the ſame, within forty days next after the ſaid ſervices per- " formed, then it ſhall be lawful for the officer of the cuſtoms " concerned in ſuch ſalvage, to borrow or raiſe ſo much money " as ſhall be ſufficient to ſatisfy and pay ſuch charges and re- " wards, or any part thereof, then remaining unpaid, or not " ſecured as aforeſaid, by or upon one or more bill or bills of " ſale, under his hand and ſeal, of the ſhip or veſſel, or cargo " ſaved, or ſuch part thereof as ſhall be ſufficient, redeemable " upon payment of the principal ſum borrowed, and intereſt " for the ſame, at the rate of 4 *per cent. per annum.*"

The act alſo declares, that the commiſſioners of the land tax, the deputy-ſheriff, the coroner, and the officers of exciſe in each county, ſhall be the proper officers for putting theſe acts, in execution, together with thoſe perſons reſpectively named in the act of queen *Anne*. In the Cinque Ports however, the execution of theſe acts is entruſted to the lord warden of the Cinque Ports, the lieutenant of *Dover* Caſtle, the deputy warden of the Cinque Ports, the judge official and commiſſary of the court of Admiralty of the Cinque Ports, two ancient towns, and the members thereof, and to all and every other perſon and perſons appointed, or to be appointed by the lord warden of the Cinque Ports.

Sect. 9. Sect. 10.

The ſtatute proceeds to ſay, that perſons convicted of aſſaulting any magiſtrate or officer, when in the exerciſe of his duty reſpecting the preſervation of any ſhip, veſſel, goods, or effects, ſhall be tranſported for ſeven years; and the juſtices, in the abſence of the ſheriff, may take a ſufficient force with them to repreſs violence. It directs in the laſt place, that the officer of the cuſtoms who ſhall act in preſerving any ſhip or veſſel in diſtreſs, or the cargo thereof, ſhall cauſe all perſons belonging to the ſaid ſhip or veſſel, and others who can give any account thereof, or of the cargo thereof, to be examined upon oath before ſome juſtice of the peace, as to the name or deſcription of the ſaid ſhip or veſſel, and the names of the maſter, commander, or chief officer, and owners thereof, and of the owners of the ſaid cargo, and of the ports or places from or to which the ſaid ſhip or veſſel was bound, and the occaſion

Sect. 11. and 12. Sect. 15. [138]

CHAP. VIII. occasion of the said ship's distress; which examination the justices are to take down in writing, and they shall deliver a true copy thereof, together with a copy of the account of the goods to the officer of the customs, who shall transmit the same to the secretary of the Admiralty for the time being, that he may publish the same, or so much thereof, in the *London* Gazette, as shall be necessary for the information of persons interested therein. This act is not to extend to

Sect. 18. *Scotland.*

Thus anxiously has the legislature provided for the preservation of property wrecked, thereby diminishing those calamities which must unavoidably happen to all concerned in foreign commerce; and with no less anxiety and wisdom, it has appointed certain magistrates to ascertain what shall be a sufficient allowance for the salvage of a ship or goods in cases of wreck. The necessity of leaving the *quantum* to the arbitration of proper persons, to be decided according to the circumstances of each case, is obvious; because it is impossible to suppose two instances of such a calamity so similar to each other, that the trouble, danger, and expense of both shall be exactly equal. It would be contrary therefore, to the first principles of justice to decide, that the same sum should be the allowance, or recompense for every possible case of salvage. For instance, if a ship be found adrift at sea, having been abandoned by the master and crew, it seems reasonable, that the allowance for salvage should be greater than in a case where a man merely picks up goods cast upon the shore, and carries them to a place of security. Thus much for salvage in case of a wreck.

Vide ante, c. 4. p. 71.

We have formerly seen, that when the ships or goods of *British* subjects were retaken from an enemy, the original owner was entitled, by the marine law, to have them restored, upon paying to the recaptors a reasonable salvage, provided the recapture was before condemnation. It was also observed, that the statute law had extended the right of the original owner; so that he was entitled to have his ship and goods restored to him, whether they were retaken after [139] condemnation or before, however distant the time of recapture might be from that of the original taking. The statutes have also fixed the precise rate of salvage, which the recaptors shall be entitled to demand.

By

By the 13 *Geo.* II. ch. 4. and 29 *Geo.* II. ch. 34. Parliament fixed and afcertained the rate of falvage, in cafe of a recapture, proportioning the amount of the reward to the length of time the fhip or goods had been in the poffeffion of the enemy; becaufe the longer they remained in the hands of the enemy, fo much the lefs was the hope of recovery. At the fame time, however, thofe ftatutes fixed a boundary, beyond which the allowance fhould not pafs; namely, that in no cafe whatever, fhould the recaptors be entitled to more than a moiety of the property refcued from the enemy.

But the ftatute 33 *Geo.* III. ch. 66. f. 42. (which fection fee at length ante, p. 72.) has deftroyed that proportion, and has afcertained the rate in all cafes, however long the fhip has been in the enemy's poffeffion, to be one-eighth, if the recapture has been made by any of his majefty's fhips, and one-fixth, if made by a privateer or other fhip.

It is faid in the ftatute, that the falvage fhall be a proportion of the fhips and goods fo reftored: but a writer upon mercantile law obferves, that the wearing apparel of the mafter and feamen are always excepted from the allowance of falvage. Beawes Lex. Merc. 147.

The ftatute has alfo faid, it muft be an eighth, or a fixth, *&c.* of the *true value*. Now the valuation of a fhip, in order to afcertain the rate of falvage, may be determined by the policy of infurance, if there is no reafon to fufpect fhe is undervalued; and the fame rule may be obferved as to goods where there are policies upon them. If that, however, fhould not be the cafe, the falvers have a right to infift upon proof of the real value, which may be done by the merchant's invoices, and they muft be paid for accordingly. Beawes 147.

The only queftion then is, how far the infurers are affected by this allowance of falvage. By their own contract, they exprefsly agree to indemnify the infured againft fuch charges. "And in cafe of any lofs or misfortune, it fhall be lawful for "the affured, their factors, fervants, and affigns, to fue, la- "bour and travel for, in and about the defence, fafeguard, "and Vide the Appendix, No. 1.

CHAP. VIII.

"and recovery of the ſaid goods and merchandizes, and "ſhip, &c. or any part thereof, without prejudice to this in-"ſurance; to the charges whereof we the aſſurers will con-"tribute, each one according to the rate or quantity of his "ſum herein aſſured."

In the caſe of *Mitchell* v. *Edie* (1 Term Reports, 608.) Mr. Juſtice *Aſhhurſt* ſaid, it ſeemed to him, that the meaning of this clauſe was, that till the aſſured have been informed of what has happened, and have had an opportunity of exerciſing their own judgment, no act done by the maſter ſhall prejudice their right of abandonment.

In order to entitle the inſured to recover the expenſes of ſalvage, it is not neceſſary to ſtate them in the declaration, as a ſpecial breach of the policy; becauſe an inſurance is againſt all accidents, and ſalvage is an immediate and neceſſary conſequence of ſome of thoſe ſtated in a policy.

Carey v. King, Caſes in B. R. temp. Hardwicke, 304.

Thus in an action on a policy of inſurance, for inſuring goods on the ſhip A. the plaintiff declared, that the ſhip ſprung a leak, and ſunk in the river, whereby the goods were ſpoiled; the evidence was, that many of the goods were ſpoiled, but ſome were ſaved. The queſtion was, Whether the plaintiffs might give in evidence, the expenſes of ſalvage, that not being particularly ſtated in the declaration, as a breach of the policy?

Lord *Hardwicke*.—"I think they may give it in evidence, for the inſurance is againſt all accidents. The accident laid in this declaration is, that the ſhip ſunk in the river: it goes on and ſays, that by reaſon thereof the goods were ſpoiled. That is the only ſpecial damage laid; yet it is but the common caſe of a declaration that lays a ſpecial damage, where the plaintiff may give in evidence any damage that is within his cauſe of action. It was objected, that ſuch a breach of the policy ſhould be laid, that the inſurer may have notice to defend it. Now it is ſo in this caſe, for they have laid the accident, which is ſufficient notice, becauſe it muſt of courſe follow, that ſome damage did happen."

But

But although the insured may recover from the insurer the expenses of salvage; yet he shall only be entitled to an indemnity, and shall not receive a double satisfaction for the same loss. Thus if the insurer should have paid to the insured the expenses arising from salvage; and afterwards on account of some particular circumstances, the loss should be repaired by some unexpected means, the insurer shall stand in the place of the insured, and receive the sum thus paid to atone for the loss.

[142]

Randal v. Cockran. 1 Vez. 98.

It was so determined in a case before Lord *Hardwicke* in Chancery. The king having granted general letters of reprisal on the *Spaniards* for the benefit of his subjects, in consideration of the losses they sustained by unjust captures, the commissioners would not suffer the insurers to make claim to part of the prizes, but the owners only; although they were already satisfied for their loss by the insurers, who thereupon brought the present bill. The Lord Chancellor was of opinion, that the plaintiffs had the plainest equity that could be. The person originally sustaining the loss was the owner; but after satisfaction made to him, the insurer becomes the owner. No doubt, but from that time, as to the goods themselves, if restored in specie, or compensation made for them, the insured stands as a trustee for the insurer, in proportion for what he paid; although the commissioners did right in avoiding being entangled in accounts, and in adjusting the proportion between them. Their commission was limited in time; they see who was owner; nor was it material to them, to whom he assigned his interest, as it was in effect after satisfaction made.

Cases, however, may, and do frequently arise, where the salvage is so high, the other expenses are so great, and the object of the voyage is so far defeated, that the insured is allowed, by the laws of all trading nations, to abandon his interest in the property saved to the insurer, and to call upon him to contribute, as if a total loss had actually happened. What circumstances shall be deemed sufficient to justify the insured in making such an abandonment, will be the subject of the following chapter.

CHAPTER THE NINTH.

Of Abandonment.

CHAP. IX.

Chap. 4. p. 82. Pothier's Traité du contrat. d' Assurance 133.

WE have formerly seen, that the insured, before he can demand a recompense from the underwriter for a total loss, must cede or abandon to him his right to all the property that may chance to be recovered from shipwreck, capture, or any other peril, stated in the policy. It has also been observed, and from the preceding sentence it is obvious, that when we speak of a total loss, with respect to insurances, we do not always mean, that the thing insured is absolutely lost and destroyed: but that by some of the usual perils, it is become of so little value, as to entitle the insured to call upon the underwriter to accept of what is saved, and to pay the full amount of his insurance, as if a total loss had actually happened. Indeed, the word abandonment conveys the idea, that the whole property is not lost; for it is impossible to cede or abandon that which does not exist. When the underwriter has discharged his insurance, and the abandonment is made, he stands in the place of the insured, and is entitled to all the advantages resulting from that situation.

Vide c. 6. p. 98

See Randal v. Cockran, 1 Vez. 98. ante, c. 8.

From what has been said then, it appears that abandonment dates its origin from the period at which the contract of insurance was itself introduced; because insurance being a contract of indemnity, the insured can recover no more than the amount of the loss actually sustained: but if he were allowed to recover for a total loss, and might also retain the property saved, he would be a considerable gainer, which the law will not allow. Accordingly we find, that the doctrine of abandonment has obtained a place in the laws of all the maritime nations in the world, where insurance has been known: and in all those laws the definition of it is the same, namely, that when any goods or ships, that are insured, happen to be lost, taken, or spoiled, the insured is obliged to abandon such goods or ships for the benefit of the insurers, before he can demand any satisfaction from them. In this respect also, they seem to be agreed, that when an abandonment is made, it must be a total, not a partial

France, Rotterdam, Bilboa, Middleburgh.

[144]

Pothier 133. Ord of Lew. 14. art. 47. Ord. of Bilboa 32.

a partial one; that is, one part of the property insured shall not be retained, and the other part abandoned; a regulation certainly founded in justice. CHAP. IX.

The propriety and justice of abandoning in certain cases to the insurers being apparent, it will be proper to consider in what cases, and under what circumstances, the insured is entitled to exercise this power: for although in all cases the insured has a right to say, he will not abandon; yet he cannot at his pleasure harass the insurer, by saying he will abandon, and thereby turn that, which, in its own nature, was only a partial, into a total loss. 2 Burr. 697.

In questions of this nature, the opinion of learned foreigners must always have weight; because they are not questions of positive regulation, or municipal law, but of general and extensive import: not confined to any particular state, but founded on the great principle of reason, justice, and universal law. The learned *Roccus*, who has accurately examined the works of those writers that went before him, and who, after stating their various opinions, forms his own conclusions, has not been silent upon this occasion. He puts this question: "Assecurator, qui jam solvit æstimationem mercium deperditarum, si postea dictæ merces appareant et recuperatæ sint, an possit cogere dominum ad accipiendas illas, et ad reddendam sibi æstimationem, quam dedit?" He answers, "Distingue; aut merces, vel aliqua pars ipsarum appareant, et restitui possint, ante solutionem æstimationis, et tunc tenetur dominus mercium illas recipere, et pro illâ parte mercium apparentium, liberabitur assecurator, nam qui tenetur ad certam quantitatem respectu certæ speciei, dando illam, liberatur, et etiam, quia contractus assecurationis, est conditionalis, scilicet si merces deperdantur: non autem dicuntur deperditæ, si postea reperiantur. Verum si merces non appareant in illa pristinâ bonitate, aliter fit æstimatio, non in totum, sed prout tunc valent. Aut vero post solutam æstimationem ab assecuratore compareant merces, et tunc est in electione mercium assecurati vel recipere merces, vel retinere pretium." Roccus, No. 50.

CHAP. IX.

And although a subsequent passage in the same author may seem to contradict that just recited; yet when attended to, they are both perfectly consistent. He says, "sufficit "semel extitisse conditionem ad beneficium assecurati de "amissione navis, etiam quod postea sequeretur recuperatio; "nam per talem recuperationem non poterit præjudicari "assecurato."

Roccus, No. 66.

From this passage it may be inferred, that a total loss having once happened, it must always continue so. But it must be understood, with reference to the context, and other parts of the work, from which it appears, that in order to entitle the insured to recover as for a total loss, it must continue total, at the time when the offer of abandonment is made, at the time of the action brought, or at the time of the payment of the money.

Chap. 7. s. 1.

In a *French* treatise, called *Le Guidon*, it is said, that the insured may abandon to the underwriter, and call upon him for a total loss, if the damage exceed half the value of the thing; or if the voyage be lost, or so interrupted, that the pursuit of it is not worth the freight.

Ord. Lew. 14.
Ord. of Bilb.
Ord. of Rot.
2 Magens.

The same idea, with respect to the circumstances which will justify an abandonment, seems to prevail in almost all the foreign ordinances.

But in no country have the principles of abandonment been more accurately defined than in *England*: and it must be remembered, that the decisions, from which the following principles are selected, are of the greatest authority; that they are not merely the opinions of private speculative men, but the solemn and deliberate judgment of the grave and learned judges of the *English* courts; judgments formed after mature deliberation, and serious argument; established upon the solid and permanent *basis* of reason and good sense.

From those decisions we may collect, that the right to abandon must arise upon the object of the insured being so far defeated, that it is not worth his while to pursue it: such a loss as is equally inconvenient to him, as if it had been total. For instance, if the voyage be absolutely lost, or

2 Burr. 1209.

or not worth pursuing; if the salvage be very high *suppose a half*; if further expense be necessary; if the insurer will not engage at all events to bear that expense, though it should exceed the value, or fail of success: under these, and many other like circumstances, the insured may disentangle himself, and abandon, notwithstanding there has been a recapture.

Guidon, ch. 7. s. 1.

It is evident, that there may be circumstances, in which it would be contrary to every principle of justice, to suffer the insured to abandon; for a ship might be taken, and escape immediately, which would be no hindrance at all to the voyage: or she might be taken and instantly ransomed, which would amount only to a partial loss; in which cases the insured shall not be allowed to demand a recompense for a total loss.

2 Burr. 697, 1213.

It is also material to observe, that the right to abandon must depend upon the nature of the case at the time of the action brought, or at the time of the offer to abandon: a determination, founded, as I have said before, on the nature of the contract between the parties; because an insurer ought never to pay less upon a contract of indemnity, than the value of the loss; and the insured ought never to gain more.

Burr. 1214.

From what has been said, it will appear sufficiently evident, that the owner cannot abandon, unless at some period or other of the voyage there has been a total loss: and therefore, if neither the thing insured, nor the voyage be lost, and the damage sustained shall be found, upon computation, not to amount to a moiety of the value, the owner shall not be allowed to abandon.

1 Term Rep. p. 191.

These principles are fully illustrated and confirmed by the judgments given in the following cases.

The defendant had insured the ship *Success* from *London* to *Bermudas*, and so to *Carolina*; the ship was taken by a *Spanish* privateer, and afterwards retaken by an *English* privateer, and carried into *Boston* in *New England*, where, no person appearing to give security, or to answer the moiety, the recaptors were entitled to for salvage, she was condemned,

Pringle v. Hartley, in Chancery, 1744. 3 Atk. 195.

CHAP. IX.

demned, and sold in the court of Admiralty there; the recaptors had their moiety and the overplus money remained in the hands of the officers of that court. An action upon the policy was brought at law by the defendant here, who obtained a verdict against the now plaintiff.

The plaintiff brought a bill, suggesting the capture to be fraudulent, and done designedly by the captain; and now moved for an injunction to stay the proceedings at law.

It was contended for the plaintiff, that though the capture might not be fraudulent, yet the defendant ought not to recover more on the policy than a moiety of the loss, as the act of the 13 *Geo.* II. *c.* 4. *s.* 18. gives the thing saved to the owner, and he is entitled to receive it from the officers of the Admiralty: and that the plaintiff ought to be obliged to pay no more than the loss actually sustained, which cannot be ascertained till after the defendant shall have received the part, that might have come to him upon the salvage.

The defendant in his answer had sworn, that he had offered, and was now willing to relinquish his interest to the plaintiffs in the benefit of the salvage, and would give them a letter of attorney for that purpose to receive it.

Lord Chancellor *Hardwicke.*—"There is no ground for an injunction in this case; here there was an agreement to go to trial in one of these actions which had been brought, and to be bound by the event of that: at the time of the trial, they knew that the ship was retaken, and the manner of the capture.

"The *quantum* of the damage and loss sustained is the only thing now to be disputed; for it is impossible to carry on trade without insuring, especially in time of war. Therefore regard must be had to the insured, as well as to the insurer; and where there is no admission in the answer of any kind of fraud, though various pretences of that sort may be set up by the bill, they are not to be regarded. The question then arises on the statute of 13 *Geo.* II. with regard to the salvage.

"It

"It has been ſaid, there ought to be only half the loſs recovered on the policy; and as to that, the act has made great alteration in the law of nations, with reſpect to recaptures. CHAP. IX.

"The carrying a ſhip *infra præſidia hoſtium*, or *ſi pernoctaverit* with the enemy, makes it the prize of the perſon retaking it, as if it had been originally the ſhip of the enemy: but by the act the recaption is the reveſting of the property of the owner. If there is a ſalvage, that muſt be deducted out of the money recovered by the policy; but if none has come to the hands of the plaintiff in the action, the jury cannot take notice of it. The ſhip was condemned and ſold, becauſe the money was not paid, or ſecured to be paid by the owners. [148]

"It is uncertain whether the defendant will receive any thing or not: and if any thing be recovered, he muſt have an allowance for his expenſes in recovering.

"Therefore I take it, when he is willing to relinquiſh his intereſt in the ſalvage, he ought to recover the whole money inſured. It would be miſchievous, if it were otherwiſe, for then upon a recapture a man would be in a worſe ſituation, than if the ſhip were totally loſt." Injunction was denied.

But the firſt caſe to be found in our books, in which the doctrine of abandonment was fully gone into, in which its principles were ſettled, and applied to the particular circumſtances then before the court, was the caſe of *Goſs* and another againſt *Withers*.

It was a ſpecial caſe from the ſittings in *London*, upon two actions, on two diſtinct policies of inſurance; one upon a ſhip, and the other upon the loading. Goſs and another v. Withers, 2 Burr. 683.

The former was an inſurance on the *David* and *Rebecca*, at and from *Newfoundland* to her port of diſcharge in *Portugal* or *Spain*, without the *Streights*, or *England*, to commence from the time of her beginning to load at *Newfoundland*, for either of the above named places; and to continue till ſhe

ſhould

CHAP. IX. ſhould be arrived at her ſaid port of diſcharge, and there moored 24 hours at anchor in ſafety. The ſhip was, by agreement, to be valued at the ſum ſubſcribed, without further account. The inſurance was to be at ten guineas *per cent.* : and in caſe of loſs to abate two *per cent.* : and in caſe of average loſs not exceeding 5*l. per cent.* to allow nothing [149] towards ſuch loſs. And if the veſſel was diſcharged without the *Streights*, excepting the *Bay of Biſcay*, two guineas *per cent.* were to be returned : and if ſhe ſailed with convoy and arrived, two guineas more *per cent.* were to be returned. The plaintiffs declared upon a total loſs, by capture by the *French*.

The policy, declared upon in the other action, was an inſurance upon any kinds of lawful goods and merchandizes, loaden or to be loaden on board the aforeſaid ſhip ; and this policy for 7*l.* 7*s.* inſured 70*l.* The declaration alleged, that divers quantities of fiſh and other lawful merchandizes, to the value of the money inſured, were put on board, to be carried from *Newfoundland* to her port of deſtination, and ſo continued (except ſuch as were thrown overboard, as is after mentioned) till the loſs of the ſhip and goods. The declaration then avers, that a part of the ſaid goods were neceſſarily thrown overboard in a ſtorm, to preſerve the ſhip, and the reſt of the cargo ; after which jetſon, the ſhip, and the remainder of the goods, were taken by the *French*.

The caſe ſtates, that the ſhip departed from her proper port, and was taken by the *French*, on the 23d of *December*, 1756 : and that the maſter, mates, and all the ſailors, except an apprentice and landman, were taken out and carried to *France*. That the ſhip remained in the hands of the enemy *eight days*, and was then retaken by a *Britiſh* privateer, and brought in on the 18th of *January* to *Milford-Haven*, and that immediate notice was given by the inſured to the inſurer, with an offer to abandon the ſhip to their care. It was alſo proved at the trial, that before the taking by the enemy, a violent ſtorm aroſe at ſea, which firſt ſeparated the ſhip from her convoy, and afterwards diſabled her ſo far as to render her incapable of proceeding on her deſtined voyage, without going into port to refit. It was alſo proved, that part

part of the cargo was thrown overboard in the ſtorm: and the reſt of it was ſpoiled while the ſhip lay at *Milford-Haven*, after the offer to abandon, and before ſhe could be refitted: and the inſured proved their intereſt in the ſhip and cargo, to the value inſured.

Several queſtions ariſing upon the trial of the firſt of theſe cauſes it was agreed, that the jury ſhould bring in their verdict, in both cauſes, for the plaintiffs, as for a total loſs; ſubject, however, to the opinion of the court on the following queſtions, *viz.* [150]

1ſt. Whether this capture of the ſhip by the enemy, was or was not ſuch a loſs, as that the inſurers became liable thereby:

2dly. Whether, under the ſeveral circumſtances of this caſe, the inſured had or had not a right to abandon the ſhip to the inſurers, after ſhe was carried into *Milford-Haven*.

After two arguments, the court decided unanimouſly in favour of the plaintiffs; and in the opinion then delivered by Lord *Mansfield*, all the law upon this ſubject was fully diſcuſſed. It will not be neceſſary, however, to ſtate in this place what fell from his lordſhip upon the firſt of theſe queſtions, thus ſubmitted to the opinion of the court; becauſe that was very copiouſly treated of in a former chapter in which it was ſhewn, that whether property was or was not transferred to the enemy by a capture, and abſolutely loſt to the original owner, it could no way affect the contract entered into between an inſurer and inſured It will be ſufficient then to follow his lordſhip in the ſecond part of his argument. Vide ante, c. 4. p. 66. 69.

Lord *Mansfield*.—"The ſingle queſtion, therefore, upon which this caſe turns, is whether the inſured had, under all the circumſtances, an election to abandon, on the 8th of *January* 1757? The loſs and diſability were in their nature total, at the time they happened. During eight days the plaintiff was certainly entitled to be paid by the inſurer, as for a total loſs; and in caſe of a recapture, the inſurer would have ſtood in his place. The ſubſequent recapture is, a beſt, a ſaving only of a ſmall part: *half the value muſt be paid for*

ſalvage.

CHAP. IX. *salvage*. The disability to pursue the voyage still continued. The master and mariners were prisoners. The charter party was dissolved. The freight (except in proportion to the goods saved) was lost. The ship was necessarily brought into an *English* port. What could be saved might not be worth the expense necessarily attending it; which is proved by the plaintiff's offer to abandon. The subsequent title to restitution, arising from the recapture, at a great expense, the ship too [151] being disabled from pursuing her voyage, cannot take away a right vested in the insured at the time of the capture. But because he cannot recover more than he has suffered, he must abandon what may be saved. I cannot find a single book, ancient or modern, which does not say, that in case of a ship being taken, the insured may demand as for a total loss, and abandon. What proves the proposition most strongly is, that by the general law, he may abandon in the case merely of an arrest, or an embargo, by a prince not an enemy. Positive regulations in different countries have fixed a precise time before the insured should be at liberty to abandon in that case. The fixing a precise time proves the general principle. Every argument holds stronger in the case of the other policy with regard to the goods. The cargo was in its nature perishable, destined from *Newfoundland* to *Spain* or *Portugal*: and the voyage was as absolutely defeated, as if the ship had been wrecked, and a third or fourth of the goods saved.

Vide the stat. 13 Geo. II. c. 4. s. 18. now altered by 33 Geo. III. c. 66. s. 42.

Vide ante, c. 4. p. 78.

"No capture by the enemy can be so total a loss, as to leave no possibility of a recovery. If the owner himself should retake at any time, he will be entitled; and by the late act of parliament, if an *English* ship retake at any time, before condemnation or after, the owner is entitled to restitution upon stated salvage. This chance does not suspend the demand, for a total loss, upon the insurer: but justice is done, by putting him in the place of the insured, in case of a recapture. In questions upon policies, the nature of the contract, as an indemnity, and nothing else, is always liberally considered. There might be circumstances, under which a capture would be but a small temporary hindrance to the voyage; perhaps none at all: as if a ship were taken, and, in a day or two, escaped entire, and pursued her voyage. There are circumstances,

ſtances, under which it would be deemed an average loſs: if a ſhip taken be immediately ranſomed, and purſue her voyage, there the money paid is an average loſs. And in all caſes the inſured may chooſe not to abandon. In the ſecond part of the "Uſages and Cuſtoms of the Sea," (a *French* book tranſlated into *Engliſh*) a treatiſe is inſerted, called Le Guidon, in which, after mentioning the right to abandon upon a capture, he adds, "or any other ſuch diſturbance as defeats the voyage; or makes it not worth while, or worth the freight to purſue it; I know that in late times the privilege of abandoning has been reſtrained, for fear of letting in frauds; and the merchant cannot elect to turn that, which, at the time it happened, was in its nature but a partial, into a total loſs, by abandoning. But there is no danger of fraud in the preſent caſe. The loſs was total at the time it happened: it continued total, as to the deſtruction of the voyage. A recovery of any thing could only be had, by paying more than half the value, including the coſts. What could be ſaved of the goods, might not be worth the freight for ſo much of the voyage as they had gone, when they were taken. The cargo, from its nature, muſt have been ſold, where it was brought in. The loſs, as to the ſhip, could not be eſtimated; nor the ſalvage of half be fixed, by a better meaſure than a ſale. In ſuch a caſe, there is no colour to ſay, that the inſured might not diſentangle himſelf from unprofitable trouble and further expenſe, and leave the inſurer to ſave what he could. It might as reaſonably be argued, that if a ſhip ſunk were weighed up again at great expenſe, the crew having periſhed, the inſured could not abandon, nor the inſurer be liable, becauſe the body of the ſhip was ſaved. We are therefore of opinion, that the loſs was total by the capture, and the right which the owner had, after the voyage was defeated, to obtain reſtitution of the ſhip and cargo, paying great ſalvage to the recaptor, might be abandoned to the inſurers, after ſhe was brought into *Milford-Haven*."

Vide ante, p. 145.

[152]

The principles laid down in this caſe have been ſtrictly adhered to in all ſimilar caſes; and particularly in a modern one, which it will be proper to mention in this place, before we come to the great cauſe of *Hamilton* againſt *Mendes*,

CHAP. IX.

in which some other principles relative to this subject were established.

Milles v. Fletcher. Douglas 219.

It was an action on a policy of insurance, on the ship the *Hope* and her freight, from *Montserrat* to *London*. The plaintiff went for a total loss: the defendant insisted, that he was only entitled to recover for an average loss. The jury found a verdict for a total loss; and upon a motion for a new trial, the facts of the case appeared to be as follows: [153] the ship, when proceeding on her voyage, was captured on the 23d of *May*, by two *American* privateers, who took the captain and all the crew, and part of the cargo, which consisted of sugars, out of her. The rigging was also taken away. She was afterwards retaken, and carried into *New York*, where the captain arrived on the 23d of *June*, and, taking possession of her, found that part of what had been left of the cargo was washed overboard, that fifty-seven hogsheads of what remained were damaged, and that the ship was leaky, and in such a state, that she could not be repaired without unloading her entirely. The owners had no storehouses at *New York*, in which the sugars could have been put, while the ship was repairing, nor any agent there to advise or direct the captain. No sailors were to be had. The only method he had of paying the salvage, *which amounted to the value of forty hogsheads of sugar*, was by sale of part of the cargo, or the ship. The captain did not know of the insurance. If he had repaired the ship, his expenses would have exceeded the freight more than 100*l*. There was an embargo on all vessels at *New York* till the 27th of *December*; and by the destination of his ship, she was to have arrived at *London* in *July*. Under these circumstances, he consulted with his friends at *New York*, and resolved upon their opinion and his own, to sell the ship and cargo, as the most prudent step for the interest of his employers. The cargo was accordingly sold and paid for. The ship was also contracted for, but the person who had agreed to buy her, ran away, and the captain left her in a creek near *New York*, and returned to *England*, where he arrived in the *February* following, and gave the plaintiff notice of what had been done, which was the first information he received of it, and the plaintiff immediately claimed as for a total loss from the under-

writers,

writers, and offered to abandon. Lord *Mansfield* told the jury, that if they were satisfied the captain had done what was best for the benefit of all concerned, they must find as for a total loss, which they accordingly did. CHAP. IX.

Upon the motion for a new trial, the unanimous opinion of the court was delivered by

Lord *Mansfield*.—"The great object in every branch of the law, but especially in mercantile law, is certainty, and that the grounds of decision should be precisely known. I took great pains in delivering the opinion of the court in the cases of *Goss* v. *Withers*, and *Hamilton* v. *Mendes*. I read both those cases over last night, and I think that from them, the whole law between insurers and insured, as to the consequences of capture and recapture, may be collected. Wherever a question of law arises at *nisi prius*, I propose a case, or grant one, when asked for by the counsel, and I avoid as much as possible blending fact and law together, having seen the inconvenience of it in *Pole* v. *Fitzgerald*. But on the trial of this cause, it did not appear to me, that there was any question of law, and no case was asked for. It was impossible to ask for one, till the facts were ascertained; and when they were, it would have been impossible to state them in any way, which could have left a doubt on the law. It was not contended, that a capture *necessarily* amounts to a total loss between insurer and insured; nor, on the other hand, that on a capture and recapture, there may not be a total loss, though there remain some material tangible part of the ship and cargo. Neither was it contended, that the captain has an arbitrary power, by his act, to make the loss, either partial or total, as he pleases. A great deal has been said about what the Admiralty could, or would have done, in such a case, in order to pay the salvage. As to that, if no owner appeared, they would condemn the whole; but if they saw, from the ship's papers, that there was one, they would not. If there were different claimants of the ship and cargo, they would leave it to them to say, what part should be sold, and if they differed in opinion, would order the sale of such part as would be attended with the smallest loss. But all *that* is foreign to the present question, which is singly this, whether the consequences of the

[154]

Vide post.

CHAP. IX. the capture were ſuch as, notwithſtanding the recapture, occaſioned a total obſtruction of the voyage, or only a partial one, as in the caſe of *Hamilton* v. *Mendes*. In that caſe, and in *Goſs* v. *Withers*, great ſtreſs was laid on the ſituation of the ſhip and cargo, at the time when the inſured had notice, at the time of the offer to abandon, and at the time when the action was brought. No caſes ſay, that the bare [155] exiſtence of the hull of the ſhip prevents the loſs being total. The rule is laid down, "that if the voyage be loſt, or not "worth purſuing, if the ſalvage be high, if farther expenſe "be neceſſary, if the inſurer will not at all events undertake to pay that expenſe, &c. the inſured may abandon, "notwithſtanding a recapture." Here, at the time of the capture there were no hopes of a recovery; no friend's ſhip in ſight; no means of reſiſtance; all the crew were taken out, and part of the cargo; and the rigging alſo taken away. Afterwards the ſhip was retaken, and carried into *New York*. When ſhe was brought there, it ſtill continued a total loſs. Neither the inſurers, nor the inſured, had any agent in the place. The court of Admiralty muſt have proceeded *ſecundum æquum et bonum*, and might have ſold her for the benefit of thoſe concerned. When the inſured firſt had notice, and offered to abandon, (which was when the captain came to *England*) and when the action was brought, it was ſtill a total loſs. The voyage was abandoned, the cargo ſold, and the ſhip left to be ſold. The only anſwer the defendant makes, or can make to this, is, that the loſs was total indeed; but that the captain made it ſo, by his improper conduct; for that on his taking poſſeſſion of the ſhip, the loſs became partial, and that he ought to have purſued the voyage. But is this defence true in fact? The captain, when he came to *New York*, had no expreſs order; but he had an implied authority from both ſides, to do what was fit and right to be done, as none of them had agents in the place: and whatever it was right for him to have done, if it had been his own ſhip and cargo, the underwriter muſt anſwer for the conſequences of, becauſe this is within his contract of indemnity. Suppoſe there had been no inſurance, what ought the captain to have done? 1ſt. As to the cargo, according to the courſe of the voyage, the ſhip ſhould have arrived at *London* in *July*. On the capture, part had been taken out, ſome was waſhed overboard, 57 hogſheads

heads were damaged, and the whole, from the leaking of the veſſel, was in a periſhable ſtate. There were no ſtore-houſes; nor could the ſhip proceed in the ſtate ſhe was in. The crew were gone, and an embargo was laid on till *December*. What, ſhall a cargo, which was intended to arrive at *London* in *July*, be kept in a periſhable ſtate at *New York*, in a leaky veſſel, till *December?* 2dly, As to the ſhip, it was certainly better to ſell her, than to bring her to *London*. There was no crew belonging to her; and ſhe had no cargo. Even if [156] all the cargo had been left, the expenſes of repairs would have exceeded the freight. If ſhe had been brought home, the expenſe of bringing her might have been more than what ſhe would have ſold for in *London*. It has been ſaid, that the damage would not have fallen on the underwriters; but the argument drawn from thence is a fallacy; for that circumſtance goes to determine it to be the intereſt of the inſured to abandon the voyage. The point is, what did the owner ſuffer by the capture; and it appears that he ſuffered ſo much, that it was not worth while to purſue the voyage. The whole voyage was loſt. As the captain did not know of the inſurance, he had no temptation to give the turn of the ſcale to one ſide or the other. I left it to the jury to determine, whether what the captain had done was for the benefit of the concerned. If they had found "*that it was*" in words, where would have been the queſtion of law?"

The court therefore diſcharged the rule for a new trial.

It was neceſſary to be very particular in ſtating this caſe from the work of ſuch an accurate reporter as Mr. *Douglas*, for two reaſons: 1ſt, Becauſe it is a determination, exactly conformable to that of *Goſs* v. *Withers*, recognizing and confirming the principles there laid down; and 2dly, To relieve the court from the obſervations made, on account of the above deciſion. A caſe has appeared in print, under the name of *Milles* v. *Hayley*, upon the ſame policy, the ſame ſhip, and ſame voyage: but the author of the work, in which it appears, could not poſſibly have been preſent at the trial; and the facts muſt have been miſtated to him: or if preſent, he has not taken down the evidence with ſufficient accuracy. For he has not ſtated, that on the capture, part of the cargo, and alſo the rigging, were taken away: that part of what had

Weſkett on Inſurance, p. 4.

CHAP. IX. had been left of the cargo was washed overboard: that 57 hogsheads of the sugar that remained were damaged: that the ship was leaky, and in such a state, that she could not be repaired without unloading her entirely: that the salvage amounted to the value of 40 hogsheads of sugar: that the repairs would have exceeded the freight by more than 100*l.*: and that the embargo was to continue till the 27th of *December*: whereas [157] the ship ought to have arrived at *London* in the *July* preceding: all which circumstances are to be found in Mr. *Douglas*'s report: all of them are material to the decision of the cause, and upon all of them much stress is laid by Lord *Mansfield*, in delivering the judgment of the court. It was thought proper to note these differences; as nothing is so necessary in all cases, more especially in those of insurance, as the accurate and precise statement of circumstances.

But although the doctrine advanced in *Goss* against *Withers*, was so very general and comprehensive; yet it certainly is not to be considered, as precluding the possibility of an exception to the generality of the principle there established.

Indeed, from the whole tenor of the Chief Justice's very learned argument upon that occasion, it is apparent, that he had at that very time an exception in his view: and from some of the words he then used, it would almost induce one to suppose, that his lordship had foreseen the very case, which actually came to be decided within a few years afterwards.

Hamilton v. Mendes. 2 Burr. 1198. and 1 Black. 276.

It was a special case reserved at *Guildhall*, at the sittings there before Lord *Mansfield*, after *Michaelmas* term 1760, in an action brought against the defendant, as one of the insurers, upon a policy of insurance from *Virginia* or *Maryland* to *London*, of a ship called the *Selby*, and of goods and merchandize therein, until she shall have moored at anchor 24 hours, in good safety. The case stated for the opinion of the Court was as follows;

That the ship *Selby*, mentioned in the policy, being valued at 1,200*l.* and the plaintiff having interest therein, caused the policy

policy in queſtion to be made; and the ſame was accordingly made, in the name of *John Mackintoſh*, on behalf and for the uſe and benefit of the plaintiff, and was ſubſcribed by the defendant, as ſtated, for 100*l*. That the ſhip was in good ſafety at *Virginia*, where ſhe took on board 192 hogſheads of tobacco, to be delivered at *London*. That on the 28th day of *March*, ſhe departed, and ſet ſail from *Virginia* for *London*; and on the 6th day of *May* following, as ſhe was ſailing and proceeding in her ſaid voyage, was taken by a *French* privateer called the *Aurora* of *Bayonne*. [158] That at the time of the capture, the *Selby* had nine men on board; and the captain of the ſaid privateer took out ſix, beſides the captain, leaving only the mate and one man on board. That the *French* put a prize-maſter and ſeveral men on board the ſhip *Selby*, to carry her to *France*. That as the *French* were carrying her towards *France*, on the 23d day of the ſaid *May*, ſhe was retaken off *Bayonne*, by an *Engliſh* man of war; and accordingly ſent into *Plymouth*, where ſhe arrived the 6th day of *June* following. That the plaintiff, living at *Hull*, as ſoon as he was informed what had befallen his ſhip, the *Selby*, wrote a letter on the 23d of *June*, to his agent *John Mackintoſh*, living in *London*, to acquaint the defendant, "that the plaintiff did from thence abandon to him his intereſt in the ſaid ſhip, as to the ſaid 100*l*. by the defendant inſured." That the ſaid *I. M.* on the 26th of *June*, acquainted the defendant with the offer to abandon the ſhip; to which the defendant anſwered, "that he did not think himſelf bound to take to the ſhip; but was ready to pay the ſalvage, and all other loſſes and charges that the plaintiff ſuſtained by the capture." That upon the 19th day of *Auguſt*, the ſhip *Selby* was brought into the port of *London*, by the order of the owners of the cargo, and the recaptors: that the ſhip *Selby* ſuſtained no damage from the capture. That the whole cargo of the ſaid ſhip was delivered to the freighters, at the port of *London*, who paid the freight to *Benjamin Vaughan*, without prejudice. The queſtion, therefore, ſubmitted to the opinion of the court is, Whether the plaintiff, on the ſaid 26th day of *June*, had a right to abandon, and has a right to recover, as for a total loſs?

After

CHAP. IX. After two arguments at the bar upon this queſtion, and after the court had taken time to deliberate upon it, their unanimous reſolution was delivered by the Chief Juſtice.

Lord *Mansfield*.—" The plaintiff has averred in his declaration, as the baſis of his demand for a total loſs, " that by " the capture, the ſhip became wholly loſt to him." The general queſtion is, Whether the plaintiff, who, at the time of his action brought, at the time of his offer to abandon, and at the time of his being firſt apprized of any accident [159] having happened, had only, in truth, ſuſtained a partial loſs, ought to recover for a total one? In ſupport of the affirmative, the counſel for the plaintiff inſiſted on the four following points: 1ſt, That by this capture, the property was changed; and therefore, the loſs total for ever. 2dly, If the property were not changed, yet the capture was a total loſs. 3dly, That when the ſhip was brought into *Plymouth*, particularly on the 26th day of *June*, the recovery was not ſuch as, in truth, changed the totality of the loſs into an average. 4thly, Suppoſing it did, yet, the loſs having once been total, a right veſted in the inſured to recover the whole upon abandoning; of which right he could never be diveſted by any ſubſequent event.

As to the firſt point. If the change of property were at all material between the inſurer and inſured, it would not be applicable to this caſe; becauſe by the marine law of *England*, there is no change of property, in caſe of a capture, before 29 Geo. II. c. 34. ſ. 24. condemnation; and now by the act of parliament, the *jus poſtliminii* continues forever. I know many writers argue, between the inſurer and the inſured, from the diſtinction, whether the property was or was not changed by the capture, ſo as to transfer a complete right from the enemy to a recaptor, or neutral vendee, againſt the former owner. But arbitrary notions concerning the change of property by capture, as between the former owner and recaptor, or a vendee, ought never to be the rule of deciſion, as between the inſurer and inſured upon a contract of indemnity, contrary to the real truth of the fact. And therefore I agree with the counſel for the plaintiff, upon this ſecond point, that by this capture, while it continued, the ſhip was totally loſt, though it

be

be admitted, that the property, in the caſe of a recapture, never was changed, but returned to the former owner.

The third point depends, as every queſtion of this kind muſt, upon the particular circumſtances. It does not neceſſarily follow that, becauſe there is a recapture, therefore the loſs ceaſes to be total. If the voyage be ſo defeated, as not to be worth the further purſuit; if the ſalvage be high, and the other expenſes great; or if the underwriter refuſe to bear theſe expenſes; the inſured may abandon. But in the preſent caſe, the voyage was ſo far from being loſt, that it had only met with a ſhort temporary obſtruction; the ſhip and cargo [160] were both entirely ſafe; the expenſe incurred did not amount to near half the value; and upon the 26th of *June*, when the ſhip was at *Plymouth*, and the offer was made to abandon, the inſurer undertook to pay all charges and expenſes, to which the plaintiff might be put by the capture. The only argument to ſhew that the loſs had not then ceaſed to be total, was built upon a miſtaken ſuppoſition, that the recaptor had a right to demand a ſale, and to put a ſtop to any further proſecution of the voyage. But that is not ſo. The property returned to the plaintiff, pledged to the recaptors for one-eighth of the value, as ſalvage for retaking and bringing the ſhip into an *Engliſh* port. Upon paying this, the owner was entitled to reſtitution. The recaptor had no right to ſell the ſhip. If they differed about the value, the Court of Admiralty would have ordered a commiſſion of appraiſement. In this caſe, it was the intereſt of the owner of the ſhip, the owners of the cargo, and the recaptors, that ſhe ſhould forthwith proceed upon her voyage from *Plymouth* to *London*. But had the recaptor oppoſed it, or affected delay, the Court of Admiralty would have made an order for bringing her immediately to *London*, her port of delivery, upon reaſonable terms. Therefore it is moſt clear, that upon the 26th day of *June*, the ſhip had ſuſtained no other loſs, by reaſon of the capture, than a ſhort temporary obſtruction, and a charge which the defendant had offered to pay and ſatisfy. This brings the whole to the fourth and laſt point.

The plaintiff's demand is for an indemnity. This action then muſt be founded upon the nature of his damnification, as

CHAP. IX.

as it really is, at the time the action is brought. It is repugnant, upon a contract of indemnity, to recover as for a total loss, when the final event has decided, that the damnification, in truth, is an average, or perhaps no loss at all. Whatever undoes the damnification, in whole or in part, must operate upon the indemnity, in the same degree. It is a contradiction in terms, to bring an action for indemnity, when, upon the whole event, no damage has been sustained. This reason is so much founded in sense, and the nature of the thing, that the common law of *England* adopts it, though inclined to strictness. The tenant is obliged to indemnify his lord from waste; but if the tenant do, or suffer waste to be done [161] in houses, yet if he repair before any action brought, there lies no action of waste against him. (Co. Litt. 53. a.) He cannot, however, plead "*non fecit vastum*:" but the special matter. The special matter shews, that the injury being repaired before the action brought, the plaintiff had no cause of action: and, whatever takes away the cause, takes away the action. Suppose a surety sued to judgment; and afterwards, before an action is brought, the principal pays the debt and costs, and procures satisfaction to be acknowledged upon record: the surety can have no action for an indemnity, because he is indemnified before any action is brought. If the demand or cause of action does not subsist, at the time the action is brought, the having existed at any former time can be of no avail. But in the present case, the notion of a vested right in the plaintiff to sue as for a total loss, before the recapture, is fictitious only, and not founded in truth. For the insured is not obliged to abandon, in any case; he has an election. No right can vest as for a total loss, till he has made that election: he cannot elect, before advice is received of the loss; and if that advice shew the peril to be over, and the thing in safety, he cannot elect at all, because he has no right to abandon when the thing is safe. Writers upon maritime law are apt to embarrass general principles with the positive regulations of their own country: but they all seem to agree, that if the thing be recovered before the money is paid, the insured can only be entitled according to the final event." His lordship here cited the passage (Roccus Not. 50.) from *Roccus*, which we have already seen at the beginning of this chapter, and then proceeded thus:

"In

"In the case of *Spencer* v. *Franco*, though upon a wager policy, the loss was held not to be total, after the return of the ship *Prince Frederick* in safety; though she had been seized and long kept by the king of *Spain*, in a time of actual war. In the case of *Pole* v. *Fitzgerald*, though upon a wager policy, the majority of the judges and the house of lords held there was no total loss, the ship having been restored before the expiration of the four months, the time for which she was insured.

Vide ante, c. 4. p. 75.
Vide post, 170.

"The present attempt is the first that ever was made, to charge the insurer as for a total loss, upon an interest policy, after the thing was recovered: and it is said, the judgment in the case of *Goss* v. *Withers* gave rise to it. It is admitted, that that case was no way similar. Before that action was brought, the whole ship and cargo were literally lost; at the time of the offer to abandon, a fourth of the cargo had been thrown overboard; the voyage was entirely lost; the remainder of the cargo was fish perishing, and of no value at *Milford-Haven*, where the ship was brought in; the ship so shattered, as to want great and expensive repairs; the salvage was one half, and the insurer did not engage to be at any expense; it did not appear that it was worth while to try to save any thing: and the recaptor, though entitled to one half, as well as the owner of the ship and cargo, left the whole to perish, rather than be at any further trouble or expense. But it is said, though the case was entirely different, some part of the reasoning warranted the proposition now inferred by the plaintiff from it. The great principle relied upon was, "that as between the insurer and insured, the "contract being an indemnity, the truth of the fact ought "to be regarded; and therefore there might be a total loss "by a capture, which could not operate as a change of prop-"erty; and a recapture should not relate by fiction (like the "*Roman jus postliminii*) as if the capture had never happen-"ed, unless the loss was in truth recovered." This reasoning proved *è converso*, that if the thing in truth were safe, no artificial reasoning shall be allowed to set up a total loss. The words quoted at the bar were certainly used, "that there is "no book, ancient or modern, which does not say, that in "case of the ship being taken, the insured may demand for "a total loss, and abandon." But the proposition was applied to the subject matter, and is certainly true, provided the

CHAP. IX. the capture, or the total loss occasioned thereby, continue to the time of abandoning, and bringing the action. The case then before the court did not make it necessary to specify all the restrictions. But I will read to you *verbatim*, from my notes of the judgment then delivered, what was said, to prevent any inference being drawn, beyond the case then determined."

Vide ante, p. 150. His lordship, having read a great part of his former argument in that case, went on in this way.

From this mode of reasoning, it did by no means follow, that if the ship and cargo had, by the recapture, been brought safe to the port of delivery, without having sustained any damage at all, that the insured might abandon. But, without [163] dwelling longer upon principles or authorities, the consequences of the present question are decisive. It is impossible that any man should desire to abandon in a case circumstanced like the present, but for one of two reasons, namely, either because he has over-valued, or because the market has fallen below the original price. The only reasons, that can make it the interest of the party to desire, are conclusive against allowing it. It is unjust to turn the fall of the market upon the insurer, who has no concern in it, and could never gain by the rise. And an over-valuation is contrary to the general policy of the marine law; contrary to the spirit of the act of 19 *Geo.* II. a temptation to fraud, and a great abuse: therefore no man should be allowed to avail himself of having over-valued. If the valuation be true, the plaintiff is indemnified, by being paid the charge he was put to by the capture. If he has overvalued, he will be a gainer, if he be permitted to abandon: and he can only desire it, because he has over-valued. This was avowed upon the first argument: and that very reason is conclusive against its being allowed. The insurer, by the marine law, ought never to pay less, upon a contract of indemnity, than the value of the loss: and the insured ought never to gain more. Therefore, if there were occasion to resort to that argument, the consequence of the determination would alone be sufficient upon the present occasion. But upon principles, this action could not be maintained as for a total loss, if the question were to be judged by the

the ſtricteſt rules of common law: much leſs can it be ſupported for a total loſs, as the queſtion ought to be decided, by the large principles of the marine law, according to the ſubſtantial intent of the contract, and the real truth of the caſe. If the queſtion is to depend upon the fact, every man can judge of the nature of the loſs, before the money is paid. But if it is to depend upon ſpeculative refinements, from the law of nations, or the *Roman jus poſtliminii*, concerning the change or reveſting of property, no wonder that merchants are in the dark, when doctors have differed upon the ſubject, from the beginning, and are not yet agreed. To obviate too large an inference being drawn from this determination, I deſire it may be underſtood, that the point here determined is, "that the plaintiff, upon a policy, can only recover an in-"demnity, according to the nature of his caſe at the time "of the action brought, or (at moſt) at the time of his "offer to abandon." We give no opinion how it would be, [164] in caſe the ſhip or goods were reſtored in ſafety, between the offer to abandon, and the action brought; or between the commencement of the action, and the verdict. And particularly I deſire, that no inference may be drawn, "that "in caſe the ſhip or goods ſhould be reſtored after the money "paid as for a total loſs, the inſurer could compel the in-"ſured to refund the money, and to take the ſhip or goods;" that caſe is totally different from the preſent, and depends, throughout, upon different reaſons and principles. Here the event had fixed the loſs to be an average only, before the action brought; before the offer to abandon; and before the plaintiff had notice of any accident; conſequently before he could make an election. We are therefore of opinion, that he cannot recover for a total, but for a partial loſs only; the quantity of which has been eſtimated by the jury at ten pounds *per cent*.

But although the court did not chooſe unneceſſarily to decide, whether after payment as for a total loſs, the underwriter could oblige the inſured to refund, if it ſhould afterwards prove to be but partial: yet in the year 1766 this very queſtion came before them. It aroſe in the caſe of *Da Coſta* v. *Firth*, which was cited at large in the preceding chapter; and the court held, that as there was a ſolemn abandonment,

Da Coſta v. Firth. 4 Burr. 1966. Vide ante, c. 6. p. 118.

CHAP. IX. abandonment, and the money was paid, and as there was alſo an agreement that the inſurers ſhould be content with ſuch ſalvage as the ſum inſured bore to the whole intereſt, the inſured ſhould not be obliged to refund, but the inſurer ſhould ſtand in his place for the ſalvage.

It has been already ſaid, and from the preceding caſes it ſeems to be a neceſſary inference, that in order to entitle the owner to abandon, there muſt, at ſome period or other of the voyage, have been a total loſs; for he cannot be allowed to turn a partial into a total loſs. There was, however, a modern caſe, in which this was the ſingle point to be determined.

Cazalet and others v. Barbe, 1 Term Rep. p. 187.

It was an action on a policy of inſurance upon the ſhip *Friendſhip*, from *Wyburgh* to *Lynn*, ſubſcribed by the defendant for 100*l.* at two guineas *per cent.* The defendant pleaded a tender, and paid 48*l.* into court. The cauſe was [165] tried at *Guildhall*, before Mr. Juſtice *Buller*, when a caſe was reſerved for the opinion of the court, ſtating that the *damages ſuſtained by the ſhip in the voyage inſured, did not exceed* 48*l. per cent.* which ſum the defendant had paid into court, upon pleading in the action. That when the ſhip arrived at the port of *Lynn*, ſhe was not worth repairing. The queſtion for the opinion of the court was, whether the plaintiffs had a right to abandon.

This caſe came on to be argued when Lord *Mansfield* was abſent.

Mr. Juſtice *Willes*.—"The queſtion is, whether, under theſe circumſtances, the plaintiffs had a right to abandon; or, in other words, whether they can turn a partial into a total loſs. The finding of the jury in this caſe determines the queſtion, becauſe it is expreſsly found that the damage did not exceed 48*l. per cent.* The caſe then ſtates, that the ſhip was not worth repairing, but no mention is made of what was her real worth; ſo that the remaining materials of the ſhip, if ſold, may make up the difference between 48*l.* and 100*l. per cent.* There has been no loſs either of the ſhip or of the voyage; but, being an old ſhip, ſhe ſuffered ſo much, that ſhe was not worth repairing. I cannot now determine

termine that there was a total lofs, when the jury have already said, that there was only a lofs of 48*l*. *per cent*. As to the cafe cited of *Bond* v. *Hunter*, this queftion never occurred in it. The action was brought upon the homeward bound policy; and it was fufficient to fay, that that policy never attached, for the fhip had received her death's wound, in her outward-bound voyage. In the cafe of *Milles* v. *Fletcher*, a total end was put to the voyage. In the other cafes, the queftions arofe upon loffes which had happened during the feveral voyages; here the voyage has been performed, and the fhip is arrived; and after the jury have found that the damage fuftained did not amount to more than 48*l*. *per cent*. the court are precluded from faying it is a total lofs."

CHAP. IX.

Vide fupra, p. 152.

Mr. Juftice *Afhhurft*.—"The facts found in this cafe preclude any queftion, whether this can be conftrued to be a total lofs. If the infurers fhould be held liable here, it would be making them infure the goodnefs of the fhip; and if the owners can recover as for a total lofs in this cafe, they might equally have recovered on account of the bad condition of the veffel, though fhe had not received much damage at fea. It is not ftated that the fhip received her death's wound in the courfe of her voyage. When fhe came into port it was found fhe was not worth repairing; but *non conftat* if fhe had not received any damage during the voyage, fhe would have been worth repairing. And though the veffel was not in a found ftate, yet fhe had arrived in fafety twenty-four hours; and the jury having exactly defined what degree of damage fhe had fuftained, we cannot fay that the plaintiff ought to recover any more."

[166]

Mr. Juftice *Buller*.—"Nothing can be better eftablifhed than that the owner of a fhip can only abandon in cafe of a total lofs. The cafes which have been cited went upon that ground. In the cafe of *Jenkins* v. *Mackenzie*, though the fhip was brought into port, yet the capture, as between the affurer and affured, was a total lofs. But *there is no inftance where the owner can abandon, unlefs at fome period or other of the voyage there has been a total lofs*. No fuch event has happened here; for the jury have exprefsly found, that the lofs amounted only to 48*l*. *per cent*. Even allowing *total lofs* to

be

CHAP. IX. be a technical expreffion, yet the manner, in which the plaintiff's counfel has ftated it, is rather too broad. It has been faid, that the infurance muft be taken to be on the fhip as well as on the voyage; but the true way of confidering it is this: *it is an infurance on the fhip for the voyage.* If either the fhip, or the voyage be loft, that is a total lofs; but here neither is loft. The cafe of *Hamilton* v. *Mendes* is decifive." Judgment for defendant.

Vide fupra.

Furneaux v. Bradley. Eaft. 20 Geo. III.

In another cafe, an action was brought on a policy of infurance on the *Prince of Wales*, in port or at fea, for fix months, from the 18th *July*, 1777. The fhip in queftion was in government fervice, bound from *Cork* to *Quebec*. She arrived there, but the feafon being too far advanced before fhe was ready to return, fhe was removed into the bafon: but, on the 19th *November*, fhe was driven from thence by a field of ice, and damaged by running on the rocks. The condition of the fhip could not be examined till *April* following, after the expiration of the policy. She was then, however, found to be bulged and much injured, but not [167] thought irreparably fo. In the progrefs of the repair, difficulties arofe for want of materials; and the captain, after confulting the merchants and agents in the country, fold her. An account was made up, charging the infurers with the whole amount, and crediting them with the fums for which the fhip fold, as falvage.

Lord *Mansfield*, at the trial, faid—"The great point in the caufe is, whether this is a total lofs by this accident. It is a new queftion: upon which I fhall referve a cafe for the opinion of the court." After argument by counfel on both fides, his Lordfhip faid, the juftice of the cafe feemed to be, that the lofs in *November* fhould be taken as an *average*, not *a total* one; and that the whole court were of opinion, that the fhip fhould be confidered as damaged on the 19th of *November*, but not *totally loft*.

M'Mafters v. Shoolbred, Sittings at G. H. after Mich. 35 Geo. III. Efpinaffe's cafes at N. P. 237. S. C.

In a fubfequent cafe before Lord *Kenyon*, at *Nifi Prius*, it was held in an action on a policy for *fix months*, where the fhip had been captured and carried into *Charleftown*, fold by the captors, and purchafed by the captain for account of the

the original owners, that this was only to be confidered as a partial lofs, and that the owners could not abandon, Lord *Kenyon* being of opinion that the captain was agent for the owners, recovering the veffel upon their account, and paying a kind of falvage, the amount of which would be the lofs fuftained, and which only conftituted an average lofs. His lordfhip, however, admitted, that when the fhip had been captured and carried into port in the enemy's poffeffion, the affured at that period might have abandoned. But not having done fo till the veffel was recovered, they could now only go for an average lofs.

Thefe cafes, and the judgments upon them, have been cited at length, becaufe the principles of abandonment are fo clearly and accurately defined, and are fo aptly illuftrated by referring them to the particular circumftances arifing in thofe caufes, that it would be abfurd to infift more upon the fubject; as the reader muft from them be able to collect every thing relative to abandonment. Nor let it be objected, that thofe were almoft all cafes of abandonment after a capture; for many of the rules there laid down were general in their nature, comprehending cafes of wreck, and detention, *mutatis mutandis*, as well as thofe of capture. This will be beft explained, by putting two poffible cafes.

Suppofe a neutral fhip is arrefted, and detained by a foreign prince by an embargo, the owner immediately, upon hearing of this accident, would have a right to abandon; becaufe no man is bound to wait the event of an embargo. But if the fame fhip, that brings the account of the embargo, fhould alfo inform him that the embargo was taken off, that the fhip had only been detained two or three days, that very trifling or no damage had arifen, then it is impoffible to fay that the merchant may abandon; becaufe, as we have feen, it is a principle of good fenfe, that a man cannot make his election, whether he will abandon or not, till he receive advice of the lofs; and if by the fame conveyance, it appear that the peril is over, and the thing infured is in fafety, he has loft his election entirely; becaufe he has, and can have no right to abandon when his property is fafe.

2 Burr. 696.

2 Burr. 1211.

The

CHAP. IX.

4 Burr. 1966.

The ſame principle governs in the caſe of wreck; for let us ſuppoſe a trunk of bullion, as in the caſe of *Da Coſta* v. *Firth*, to be the property inſured; and that the ſhip being wrecked, this trunk of courſe goes to the bottom; the owner would inſtantly be entitled to abandon to the underwriter, and to call upon him to contribute, as in caſe of a total loſs. But if it ſhould ſo happen, that before the action was brought or before the offer was made to abandon, the bullion ſhould be recovered, and reſtored to the owner, at the place of deſtination, upon paying a moderate ſalvage; in that caſe, it would fall within the rule of *Hamilton* v. *Mendes*; and the aſſured would only be entitled to recover an indemnity, according to the nature of his caſe, at the time when the action was brought; conſequently he would not be allowed to abandon.

Manning v. Newnham, Trin. 22 Geo. III.

But it has been ſettled alſo by a ſolemn deciſion of the court of *King's Bench*, in what caſes a loſs ſhall be deemed to be total, after an accident by perils of the ſea. A policy was effected in *London* upon the ſhip *Grace*, her "*cargo* and "*freight*, at and from *Tortola* to *London*, warranted to depart "on or before the firſt of *Auguſt* 1781. The ſhip valued at "2,470 *l.* the freight at 2,250 *l.* and the cargo at 12,400 *l.* "At a premium of 25 guineas *per cent.* to return 10 *per cent.* "if ſhe depart the *Weſt Indies* with convoy for *England* and "arrives." At the head of the ſubſcriptions is the following declaration, *viz.* *on ſhip, freight, and goods, warranted free of particular average.* This ſhip, with her cargo, was a *Dutch* prize taken by a privateer of *Tortola*, and was there condemned; during the whole of her ſtay at *Tortola*, (four or five months) ſhe was never unloaded. On the firſt of *Auguſt* the whole fleet of merchantmen got under way, under the convoy of the *Cyclops*, &c. but not being able to get clear of the iſlands that day, they caſt anchor during the night, and the next day got clear of the iſlands. About 10 o'clock on the 2d of *Auguſt*, ſeveral ſqualls of wind aroſe, which occaſioned the ſhip to ſtrain and make water ſo faſt, that the crew were obliged to work both pumps; and, on the third, the captain made a ſignal of diſtreſs: in conſequence of which, ſhe was obliged to return to *Tortola*, under protection of of one of his majesty's ships. The captain made his protest, and a survey was had, by which the ship was declared unable to proceed to sea with her cargo, and that she could not be repaired in any of the *English* islands in the *West Indies*: and that many of the sugars in the bilge and lower tier were washed out, and several of the casks broke and in bad order. The ship and the whole of the cargo were sold accordingly at *Tortola*. The assured claim a total loss of ship, cargo, and freight, which the jury thought right, and found accordingly. A motion was made for a new trial, which upon full consideration was refused.

Lord *Mansfield*, after stating the evidence, and that his prejudices at the trial were in favour of the underwriters, proceeded thus: "but notwithstanding this inclination of my opinion, upon full consideration we think the jury have done right. If by a peril insured, the voyage is lost, it is a total loss; otherwise not. In this case the ship has an irreparable hurt within the policy; this drives her back to *Tortola*, and there is no ship to be had there, which could take the whole cargo on board. There were only two ships at *Tortola*, and both could not take in the cargo. To shew how completely the voyage was lost, and that no ship could be got, the assured have not been able to send that part of the goods, which they purchased, forward to *London*. It is admitted there was a total loss on the freight, because the ship could not perform the voyage. The same argument applies to the ship and cargo. It is a contract of indemnity; and the insurance is that the ship shall come to *London*. Upon turning it in every view, we are of opinion that the voyage was totally lost, and that is the ground of our determination." The rule was discharged.

From what was said in a former chapter, and from the cases just recited, it will appear, that in wager policies it was usual to set up a total loss between third persons, for the purpose of their wager, though in fact the ship was safe, and restored to the owner. But in some of these cases, the loss was held not to be total; and as in most of them general verdicts were given, and no report of the judge's direction Ch. 4. p. 69.

CHAP. IX.

tion is to be found, it is now impoſſible to determine upon what grounds the deciſions turned. As has been truly ſaid, however, theſe queſtions never can ariſe again, becauſe they originated from wager policies, which are now prohibited by law. But as the caſe of *Pole* v. *Fitzgerald* was one of thoſe, in which the majority of judges, and the Houſe of Lords held, that though the ſhip might be deemed loſt, for a time; yet as ſhe was afterwards recovered, the event of a total loſs had not finally happened, according to the conſtruction of the wager; and as it has frequently occurred in the courſe of our inquiries, it may be proper to give a ſhort account of it in this place.

Fitzgerald v. Pole, 5 Brown's Parl. Caſes, 131.

It was an action on a policy of inſurance on the ſhip *Goodfellow* privateer, at and from *Jamaica*, to any ports and places where and whatſoever, at ſea or ſhore, a cruiſing from place to place, for and during the term and ſpace of four calendar months; the ſhip was valued at 1,000*l.* *without further account*, and free from average. The defendant in 1744, had ſubſcribed 100*l.* and the plaintiff declared for a total loſs of the voyage by a mutiny of the men.

The cauſe came on to be tried at *Guildhall* before the Lord Chief Juſtice *Lee*, when a ſpecial verdict was found, ſtating, That the defendant had ſubſcribed the policy, ſtated in the declaration: that the *Goodfellow* was an *Engliſh* privateer, duly commiſſioned; was ſafe at *Jamaica* on the 14th of *June* 1744, and ſailed from thence the ſame day: that on the 10th of *July* 1744, ſhe took a *French* prize of the value of 4,200*l.* ſterling: that afterwards the ſaid ſhip was ſailing on her cruiſe, for a port or place called the *River of Dogs*, to fetch water; and while ſhe was ſo ſailing towards the *River of Dogs*, and within the four months mentioned in the policy, the crew mutinied againſt the captain and his officers; and by force carried the ſaid ſhip againſt the will of the captain and officers, who could not reſiſt, to *Jamaica*: and before her arrival there, cauſeleſsly, againſt the conſent of the ſaid captain, ſeized the boat, fire-arms, and cutlaſſes, carried off the ſame, and deſerted the privateer, by which the voyage and cruiſe were totally prevented and loſt for the remainder of the four months: that the ſhip arrived at *Jamaica*, and

and was there in good ſafety at and after the end of the four months; but was prevented by the mutiny and deſertion, from further purſuing her cruiſe: that the perſon inſured had intereſt in the ſhip to the amount of the ſum inſured.

This caſe was argued in the King's Bench, and judgment was given for the plaintiff. Upon a writ of error, the Court of Exchequer Chamber unanimouſly reverſed that judgment. The Houſe of Lords afterwards confirmed the judgment of reverſal, being of opinion, with the majority of the judges, that the inſurer, being, by the terms of the policy, free from all average, the plaintiff could not be enititled to recover, but in caſe of a total loſs; and the ſhip being found, by the ſpecial verdict, to be in good ſafety, at her proper port, at and after the end of the four months, for which the inſurance was made, there could be no loſs. The counſel for the plaintiff cited many caſes, in which the plaintiffs had judgment for a total loſs, although the ſhips remained in being; moſt of which have already been referred to in the chapter upon capture. But thoſe caſes were abſolutely denied by the other ſide; or, if admitted at all, it was inſiſted, that they made for the defendant. This circumſtance, among many others, ſtated in the introduction of this work, ſerves to evince the great ſuperiority which the modern practice of our courts, in matters of inſurance, has over the ancient.

Vidè ante, c. 4. p. 73. 2 Burr. 1200.

See the Introduction ſub fine.

In many of the maritime countries on the continent of *Europe*, the time, within which the abandonment muſt be made, is fixed by poſitive regulation. Thus in *France*, it is ordained, that all ceſſions or abandonments, as well as demands in virtue of the policy, ſhall be made as follows: In ſix weeks, for loſſes happening on the coaſts of the country, where the inſurance was made: in three months, in other provinces of our kingdom: in four months, on the coaſt of *Holland*, *Flanders*, and *England*: in a year, in *Spain*, *Italy*, *Portugal*, *Barbary*, *Muſcovy*, *Norway*: and in two years, for the coaſt of *America*, the *Braſils*, *Guinea*, and other diſtant countries. When theſe terms are elapſed, the demands of the aſſured ſhall not afterwards be admitted. In caſes of detention, the ſame ordinance provides, that the abandonment ſhall not be made before ſix months,

Ord. of Lew. 14. tit. Inſurance, art. 48.

CHAP. IX.

Art. 49. 2 Mag. 416.

months, if it happen in *Europe*, or *Barbary*. If in a more diſtant country, in a year; both to commence from the day of the notifying this detention to the inſurers. A ſimilar regulation to that laſt mentioned is to be found in the ordinances of *Bilboa*.

In the law of *England* till lately we had no limitation of time, with reſpect to abandonment, at leaſt that I was able to find: and I believe that none ſuch exiſted. But from what has been ſaid in the preceding part of this chapter, it would appear, that the inſured has a right to call upon the underwriter for a total loſs, and of courſe to abandon, as ſoon as he hears of ſuch a calamity having happened, his claim to an indemnity not being at all ſuſpended by the chance of a future recovery of part of the property loſt: becauſe, by the abandonment, that chance devolves upon the underwriter; by which means the intention of the contracting parties is fully anſwered, and complete juſtice is done.

Mitchell v. Edie, 1 Term Rep. 608.

In a modern deciſion it has been held by the court of *King's Bench*, that as ſoon as the inſured receive accounts of ſuch a loſs as entitles them to abandon, they muſt, in the firſt inſtance, make their election whether they will abandon or not: and if they abandon, they muſt give the underwriters notice in a reaſonable time, otherwiſe they waive their right to abandon, and can never afterwards recover for a total loſs. This determination was certainly equitable and juſt; for otherwiſe it was impoſſible to ſay, at what time the reſponſibility of the underwriter was to end, they would be liable to be called upon to contribute at any indefinite period, and a great deal of uncertainty would be introduced into this ſyſtem of law.

In a ſtill more recent caſe, the doctrine laid down by the court in *Mitchel* v. *Edie*, as to the obligation upon the aſſured to make his election, whether he will abandon or not, was adopted and confirmed.

Allwood v. Henckell, Guildhall Sittings in B. R. after Michaelmas, 1795.

Caſe on a policy of aſſurance on linen on board the *Amphitrite*, at and from *London* to *Jamaica*.

The *Amphitrite* was taken by a *French* privateer within a few leagues of *Jamaica*. Part of the property inſured was plundered

dered and taken out of the ſhip. The captain, boatſwain, and all but ſeven men, were taken out of her: a fortnight after ſhe was captured, as the captors were making their way to *America*; the ſhip with the remainder of her cargo was retaken by an *Engliſh* frigate, and taken under a prize maſter to *Antigua*. The ſhip and cargo were both ſold under a decree of the Vice Admiralty Court of *Antigua*, by a prize agent, who received the proceeds, and was to pay them over to the concerned, upon payment of one eighth ſalvage purſuant to the laſt prize act.

The capture and recapture were entered at *Lloyd's*, on the 15th of *February*, 1795; but it was not known where the ſhip was carried till the 30th of *March*, when a letter was received at *Lloyd's*, addreſſed to the owners and freighters and underwriters on ſhip *Amphitrite* and cargo, from the judge of the Vice Admiralty Court of *Antigua*, informing them of the arrival and ſale of ſhip and cargo under a decree of the court, and deſiring to have ſome agent appointed to remit the proceeds to *England*. Powers of attorney were ſent out in *April* by the aſſured for this purpoſe; and the proceeds were deſired to be remitted to the banking-houſe of *Smith*, *Payne*, and *Smith*, one of which gentlemen was agent to the aſſured. The defendant was acquainted in *April* of the loſs, but no abandonment was proved to have been made till *Auguſt*, near four months after Mr. *Payne*, who was the plaintiff's agent, had ſent out the power of attorney. On the part of the plaintiff, it was contended that, admitting there was no abandonment, in this caſe the property having been abſolutely ſold and converted into money, before the parties knew where the ſhip was taken to, the loſs was abſolutely total in its nature; and therefore there was no occaſion for an abandonment.

Lord *Kenyon*, though he did not give any decided opinion upon this point, inclined to think, "that an abandonment was neceſſary; and that the caſe was the ſame as if the property had remained in *ſpecie* at *Antigua*, and had not been ſold. That the aſſured is not bound to abandon in any caſe; and might, in caſe the ſales had been very advantageous, have taken the benefit of them in the ſame manner as they might have retained this property, if it had remained in ſpecie. *But*

CHAP. IX.

the aſſured muſt make his election ſpeedily, whether he will abandon or not, and put the underwriter into a ſituation to do all that is neceſſary for the preſervation of the property, whether ſold or unſold. He cannot lie by and treat the loſs as an average loſs, and take meaſures for the recovery of it, without communicating that fact to the underwriters, and letting them know that the property is abandoned to them."

Verdict for plaintiff, ſubject to an account as for an average loſs.

Da Coſta v. Newnham, 2 Term Rep. 407.

But if the inſured, hearing that his ſhip is much diſabled and has put into port to repair, expreſs his deſire to the underwriters to abandon, and be diſſuaded from it by them, and they order the repairs to be made; they are liable to the owner for all the ſubſequent damage occaſioned by that refuſal, though it ſhould amount to the whole ſum inſured. Becauſe the reaſon why notice of abandonment is deemed neceſſary, is to prevent ſurprize or fraud upon the underwriter: but in the caſe put, they have, by their own act, ſuperſeded the neceſſity of notice.

[173]

We have thus taken a view, in this and the eight preceding chapters, of the nature of that inſtrument by which the contract of inſurance is effected; and of the different modes, by which it may be conſtrued: we have treated of the various loſſes, to which the underwriter ſubjects himſelf by that contract; we have ſhewn, when the loſſes are to be conſidered as partial, when as total; and in what caſes, and under what circumſtances, the inſured ſhall be allowed to abandon to the underwriter. The courſe of our inquiry now naturally leads us to obſerve, in what inſtances the inſurer is diſcharged from any reſponſibility; either on account of the contract being void, from its commencement, by reaſon of ſome radical defect; or becauſe the inſured has failed to perform ſome of thoſe conditions, neceſſary to be fulfilled on his part, before he can call upon the inſurer for an indemnity.

CHAPTER THE TENTH.

Of Fraud in Policies.

CHAP. X.

IN treating of those causes, which make policies void from the beginning, or in other words, which absolutely annul the contract, it will be proper in the first place to consider, how far it will be affected by any degree of fraud. In every contract between man and man, openness and sincerity are indispensably necessary to give it its due operation; because, fraud and cunning once introduced, suspicion soon follows, and all confidence and good faith are at an end. No contract can be good, unless it be equal; that is, neither side must have an advantage by any means, of which the other is not aware. This being admitted of contracts in general, it holds with double force in those of insurance; because the underwriter computes his risk entirely from the account given by the person insured, and therefore it is absolutely necessary to the justice and validity of the contract, that this account be exact and complete. Accordingly the learned judges of our courts of law, feeling that the very essence of insurance consists in a rigid attention to the purest good faith, and the strictest integrity, have constantly held that it is vacated and annulled by any the least shadow of fraud or undue concealment.

2 Black. Com. 460. Grot. de jure belli, lib. 2. c. 12. s. 23. Pufendorff de jure nat. l. v. c. 9. s. 8. Bynkershoek, quest. jur. priv. l. 4. c. 26. Ord. de Lew. 14. s. 38. 1 Black. 594. 3 Burr. 1909.

After what has been said, it will hardly be necessary to mention, that both parties, the insurer and insured, are equally bound to disclose circumstances that are within their knowledge; and, therefore, if the insurer, at the time he underwrites, can be proved to have known that the ship was safe arrived, the contract will be equally void as if the insured had concealed from him some accident, which had befallen the ship.

In perusing the numerous cases and decisions, which, I am sorry to say, are to be found in our books under this head, it occurred to me, that they were liable to a threefold division:

CHAP. X. ſion: 1ſt, The allegation of any circumſtances, as facts, to the underwriter, which the perſon inſured knows to be falſe: 2dly, The ſuppreſſion of any circumſtances which the inſured knows to exiſt; and which, if known to the underwriter, might prevent him from undertaking the riſk at all, or if he did, might entitle him to demand a larger premium: and, laſtly, a miſrepreſentation. The laſt of theſe, a *miſrepreſentation*, ſeems to fall under the firſt head, the *allegatio falſi*; and ſo in ſome meaſure it does; becauſe Dougl. 247. wherever a perſon knowingly and wilfully miſrepreſents any thing he aſſerts a falſehood. But it was thought neceſſary to make a diviſion for itſelf; becauſe if a *material* fact be miſrepreſented, though by miſtake, the contract is void, as much as if there had been actual fraud: for the underwriter has computed his riſk upon information, which was falſe. Of each of theſe in order.

Nothing can be ſo clear a proof of fraud, as the aſſertion of the truth of ſome circumſtance, which the perſon aſſerting it muſt know to be falſe. In our reporters, we do not meet with ſo many caſes under this diviſion of the ſubject, as under the two following: and indeed, from the nature of the thing, it is impoſſible we ſhould; becauſe in ſuch a caſe, the only queſtion is, did the inſured aſſert this to be the truth. If he did, the inquiry is at an end; becauſe we are now preſuming it to be the aſſertion of a circumſtance within his own knowledge. This being a mere queſtion of fact, is not a ſubject for a reporter. But in the other caſes, there is greater room for inveſtigation; we may properly inquire, for inſtance, whether the inſured was bound to diſcloſe this fact; whether the miſrepreſentation was in a material part; and many other ſimilar queſtions of which we ſhall ſee the neceſſity hereafter.

The few following caſes will evidently ſhew, that our idea was right, when we ſuppoſed, that under the head of the *allegatio falſi*, the only inquiry would be, whether the perſon inſured, knowing the contrary, aſſerted a particular thing to be true.

Skinner 327. In a caſe before Lord Chief Juſtice *Holt*, in the reign of *William* and *Mary*, that learned judge held, that if the goods were

were insured as the goods of an *Hamburgher*, who was an ally, and the goods were, in fact, the goods of a *Frenchman*, who was an enemy; it was a fraud, and that the insurance was not good.

In another case, a letter being received, stating, that a ship failed from *Jamaica* for *London*, on the 24th of *November*, after which an insurance was made, and the agent told the insurer, that the ship failed the latter end of *December*; this was also held by Lord Chief Justice *Lee* to be a fraud, and the defendant had a verdict.

Roberts v. Fonnereau, Sitt. at Guildhall after Trin. Term, 1742.

Upon special case reserved for the opinion of the court, the following circumstances appeared.

It was an action on the case, brought for the recovery of a total loss, on a policy of insurance made on goods and merchandizes on board the ship *Bona Fortuna*, at and from *North Bergen* to any ports or places whatsoever, until her safe arrival in *London*. It was underwritten thus: "Warranted neutral ship and property." The defendant underwrote the policy for 150*l*. The defendant pleaded the general issue, and paid into court the premium received by him for the said insurance. This cause came on to be tried at *Guildhall* before Lord *Mansfield*; when it was admitted, that the plaintiff had interest on board the ship to a large value, to the amount of the sum insured. The ship, with the goods and merchandizes so loaden, and being on board her, after her departure from *North Bergen*, and before her arrival in *London*, proceeding on her voyage, was, by the force of winds and stormy weather, wrecked, cast away, and sunk in the seas; and the said goods and merchandizes were thereby wholly lost. It was expressly stated, "that the ship "or vessel, called the *Bona Fortuna*, and the property on "board, at and before the time she was lost, were not neu"tral property, as warranted by the said policy."

Woolmer v. Muilman, 3 Burr. 1419. 1 Black. 427.

Lord *Mansfield*, and the rest of the court, were of opinion, that it was too clear a case to bear an argument. This was *no contract*; for there was a falsehood, in respect of the condition of the thing insured: because the plaintiff insured neutral property, and this was not neutral property.

From

CHAP. X.

From the preceding caſe, we may collect this principle, that a falſe aſſertion in a policy will vitiate the contract; even though the loſs happen in a mode not affected by that falſity.

Another obſervation is ſuggeſted by the peruſal of the caſe of *Woolmer* and *Muilman*. It aroſe upon a warranty; and the learned judges declared, that the warranty being falſe, there was *no* contract. Now, as we ſhall ſee, when we come to the chapter on warranties, the general rule with reſpect to them is this, that the noncompliance with them does not vacate the contract from the beginning; but it amounts to much the ſame thing, namely, that the inſured, not having complied with thoſe conditions, which he had taken upon himſelf to perform, cannot recover againſt the underwriter.

But the following anſwer is ſubmitted, which, if allowed, will reconcile any ſeeming difference, that ariſes in the caſes upon the ſubject. Wherever a man warrants a thing to be true, which, at the time he does ſo, he muſt unavoidably know to be falſe, it comes under the *allegatio falſi*, and the contract is void, as in the caſe juſt reported. But if he warrant or undertake that a certain thing ſhall be done, for inſtance, that the ſhip ſhall ſail with convoy, or on a particular day; theſe being circumſtances materially varying the riſk, the underwriter ſhall not be reſponſible for a loſs, if they are not complied with: but the contract is not void from the beginning, nor does the inſured incur any moral guilt; becauſe they do not depend entirely for their performance upon the will of the perſon inſured, nor could they be within his knowledge, at the time he entered into the contract.

A ſhort time after the caſe of *Woolmer* againſt *Muilman* had been decided, another very ſimilar caſe came on at *Guildhall* before Lord *Manſfield*.

Fernandes v. De Coſta, Sittings after Hil. 4 G. 3.

It was an action on a policy of inſurance on goods laden on board ſuch a ſhip, warranted a *Portugueze*. The inſurance was made during the *French* war, when the premium would have been much higher on an *Engliſh* ſhip. The plaintiff gave partial evidence of her being a *Portugueze*; and that ſhe was obliged,

obliged, on account of perils of the sea, to put into a *French* port, by which the cargo was spoiled. This was admitted by the defendant, who contended that during her stay at the *French* port, she was libelled, and condemned as not being *Portugueze*: and that although the goods were lost by a different peril, yet in fact the ship was not *Portugueze*, (being insured as such) and that this vitiated the policy *ab initio*—and this was agreed to be law. In order to prove that she was not *Portugueze*, the defendant produced the sentence of condemnation, and the confirmation thereof in the courts of *France*; and an answer of the present plaintiff in the Court of Chancery here, by which it was admitted, that the ship was condemned as not being, or under pretence of not being, *Portugueze*.

Lord *Mansfield*.—"As the sentence is always general (without expressing the reason of the condemnation) attested copies of the libel ought in strictness to have been produced to shew upon what ground the ship was libelled against. But as the plaintiff has by his answer in Chancery admitted that she was condemned, as not being *Portugueze*; when added to the expression used in the sentence of confirmation, *that the ship was condemned in the court of prizes*, there is sufficient evidence for us to proceed upon." The defendant, the underwriter, had a verdict.

The second species of fraud, which affects insurances, is the concealment of circumstances, known only to one of the parties entering into the contract. Upon this head, the principles of law are perfectly clear, free from doubt or possibility of error. Concealment of circumstances vitiates all contracts, upon the principles of natural law. Insurance is a contract of speculation. The facts, upon which the risk is to be computed, lie, for the most part, within the knowledge of the insured only. The underwriter must therefore rely upon him for all necessary information; and must trust to him, that he will conceal nothing, so as to make him form a wrong estimate. If a mistake happen, without any fraudulent intention, still the contract is annulled, because the risk is not the same, which the underwriter intended. Good faith forbids either party, by concealing what he privately knows, to draw the other into a bargain, from his ignorance of that fact, and his belief of the contrary.

1 Black. Rep. 465.

1 Black. Rep. 594.

These

CHAP. X.

These principles have been uniformly supported by a variety of decisions.

De Costa v. Scandret, in Chancery, 2 P. Will. 170.

One having a doubtful account of his ship, that was at sea, namely, that a ship, described like his, was taken, insured her, without giving any notice to the insurers of what he had heard either as to the hazard, or the circumstances, which might induce him to believe that his ship was in great danger, if not actually lost. The insurers bring a bill for an injunction, and to be relieved against the insurance as fraudulent.

Lord Chancellor *Macclesfield*.—"The insured has not dealt fairly with the insurers in this case; he ought to have disclosed to them what intelligence he had of the ship's being in danger, and which might induce him, at least, to fear that it was lost, though he had no certain account of it. For if this circumstance had been discovered, it is impossible to think, that the insurers would have insured the ship at so small a premium as they have done; but either would not have insured at all, or would have insisted on a larger premium, so that the concealment of this intelligence is a fraud." Whereupon the policy was decreed to be delivered up with costs, but the premium to be paid back, and allowed out of the costs.

Seaman v. Fonnereau, 2 Stra. 1183.

In another case it appeared, that on the 25th of *August* 1740, the defendant underwrote a policy from *Carolina* to *Holland*. It came out in evidence, that the agent for the plaintiff had on the 23d of *August*, (two days before the policy was effected) received a letter from *Cowes*, dated the 21st of *August*, wherein it is said: "On the 12th of this month, "I was in company with the ship *Davy* (the ship in question;) at twelve at night lost sight of her all at once; "the captain spoke to me the day before that he was "leaky, and the next day we had a hard gale." The ship, however, continued her voyage till the 19th of *August*, when she was taken by the *Spaniards*; and there was no pretence of any knowledge of the actual loss at the time of the insurance, but it was made in consequence of a letter received that day from the plaintiff abroad, dated the 27th *June* before.

Lord

Lord Chief Justice *Lee* declared, "that as these are contracts upon chance, each party ought to know all the circumstances. And he thought it not material that the loss was not such an one as the letter imported; for those things are to be considered in the situation of them at the time of the contract, and not to be judged of by subsequent events. He therefore thought it a strong case for the defendant." The jury found accordingly. CHAP. X.

In an action on a policy of insurance, the case was, that the ship was insured *at and from Genoa*, liable to average; her loading consisting of pot-ash, verdigrease, cotton, and other perishable commodities. This loading was put on board *at Leghorn* the 10th of *August*, and the vessel had lain at *Genoa* above five months, being originally bound for *Dublin*; but losing her convoy, she put into *Genoa* the 13th of *August*, and lay there till the 5th of *January*, when she failed. And the insurance was made the 20th of *January*; at which time these circumstances were known to the assured, but not communicated to the underwriter. A few days after she put to sea, she was shattered by a storm, and the cargo considerably damaged. The jury found a verdict for the plaintiff; and a new trial was moved for, on this ground, that the policy was bad *ab initio*, for want of a due disclosure of the circumstances. Hodgson v. Richardson, 1 Blac. Rep. 463.

Lord *Mansfield*.—"The question is, whether here was a sufficient disclosure; that is, whether the fact concealed was material to the risk run. This is a matter of fact; and if material, the consequence is matter of law, that the policy is bad. Now who can say, that no risk was run, during the five months stay at *Genoa*, or no damage happened in that period? The policy is founded on misrepresentation: the ship is insured "at and from *Genoa* to *Dublin*; the adventure to begin "from the loading, to equip for this voyage." This plainly implies, that *Genoa* was the port of loading: and at the trial, all the witnesses said, that by usage, it was material to acquaint the underwriter, whether the insurance was to be at the commencement or in the middle of a voyage.

Mr. Justice *Wilmot*.—"The fact disclosed by this policy is not true, that *Genoa* is the loading port; for so it must be understood. In such cases I will not speculate upon the materiality,

CHAP. X. teriality, or immateriality of the fact. Not but that I think, the length of the stay at *Genoa* is very material, in case of such perishable commodities."

Mr. Justice *Yates*.—" The concealment of material circumstances vitiates all contracts, upon the principles of natural law. A man, if kept ignorant of any material ingredient, may safely say, it is not his contract. And I think this fact material, for the reasons before given." A new trial was accordingly granted.

The doctrine, so accurately laid down in the preceding cases, has since been the principle, on which several verdicts have been given, in causes of this nature; a few of which it will be proper to mention.

Ratcliffe and another v. Shoolbred, Sit. at Guild. after Trin. 1780.

An action was brought on a policy of assurance on goods, on board the *Matty* and *Betty*, at and from the coast of *Africa* to her last discharging port in the *British West Indies*. The objection made to paying the loss was, that there had been a material concealment, or misrepresentation of the true state or situation of the ship and voyage at the time of underwriting the policy. The ship had been sent out to trade on the coast of *Africa*, with directions to proceed from thence to the *British West Indies*, and to stop at *Barbadoes*, if she could get a *sale*; if not, to proceed to *Montego-Bay*. On the 2d of *October* she sailed from *St. Thomas's* on the coast of *Africa*, with a cargo of slaves, and was taken on the 6th of *December* following by an *American* privateer. A letter was received by a house at *Liverpool* on the 21st of *February*, mentioning, that the ship was well, and had sailed from *St. Thomas's* on the 2d of *October*. This information was communicated next day to the plaintiffs, who, in consequence of it, wrote the same evening to two different brokers, to get a *new* insurance on the ship, there having been one before, and another on the cargo, which last was the subject of the present action. In the instructions to the brokers, the plaintiffs say nothing of the ship from the time of her first sailing; but to one of the brokers, they wrote thus; " we should be " glad, if you would get us 600*l.* more on the ship, as she " is *rather long*; and we think it not prudent to run so large " a risk at so critical a time. We expect to hear soon " of "of her." It had afterwards occurred, that the policy might be affected, if intimation was not given of the letter, which had been received. The broker, therefore, by direction of the plaintiffs, added to the instructions: "the above ship "was on the coast the 2d of *October*;" but said nothing of her having sailed from *St. Thomas*. The policy was dated the 21st of *March*.

CHAP. X.

Lord *Mansfield*.—"The insured is bound to represent to the underwriter all the material circumstances of the ship and voyage. If he do not, though by accident only, or neglect, the underwriters are not liable: *à fortiori*, if he suppress or misrepresent from fraud. The question is, whether this be one of those cases, which is affected by misrepresentation or concealment? If the plaintiffs concealed any material part of the information they received, it is a fraud; and the insurers are not liable." The jury found for the defendant agreeably to his lordship's direction.

In another case, the policy was on the brig *Richard* at and from *Plymouth* to *Bristol*. Several letters passed between the plaintiff and the broker, who effected the policy, as to the premium at which the insurance could be made: at last, it was underwritten at four guineas *per cent*. The broker's instructions stated *the ship ready to sail on the* 24th *of December*. The broker represented to the underwriter, that the ship was in port, when in fact she had sailed the 23d of *December*.

Fillis v. Brutton, Sittings at Guildh. after Hil. 1782.

Lord *Mansfield* said, "that this was a material concealment and misrepresentation." The jury, however, hesitated: his lordship then laid down the following as general principles.—"In all insurances, it is essential to the contract, that the assured should represent the true state of the ship to the best of his knowledge. On that information the underwriters engage. If he state that as a fact, which he does not know to be true, but only believes it, it is the same as a warranty. He is bound to tell the underwriters truth. In the present insurance, the only material point is this: had the ship sailed, or was she in port?" Upon this, the jury found for the defendant.

But although the rule is laid down thus generally, that one of the contracting parties is bound to conceal nothing from the

CHAP. X. the other; yet it is by no means so general, as not to admit of an exception. *Aliud est celare, aliud tacere.* There are many matters, as to which the insured may be innocently silent. 1st, As to what the insurer knows, however he came by that knowledge. 2d, As to what he ought to know. 3d, As to what lessens the risk. An underwriter is bound to know political perils, as to the state of war or peace. If he insure a privateer, he needs not be told her destination. And, as men reason differently from the same facts, he needs not be told another's conclusions from known facts.

1 Black. Rep. 593.

These ideas were fully entered into, explained, and illustrated in the argument of Lord *Mansfield*, in delivering the opinion of the court in *Carter* v. *Boehm*.

Carter v. Boehm, 3 Burr. 1905. and 1 Black. R. 593. Vide ante, c. 1. p. 12.

This was an insurance cause upon a policy, interest or no interest, without benefit of salvage. The insurance was made by the plaintiff, for the benefit of his brother, governor *George Carter*. The jury found a verdict for the plaintiff; upon which a new trial mas moved for, on the ground, that circumstances had not been sufficiently disclosed. Lord *Mansfield* reported the evidence given at the trial; by which it appeared, that it was a policy of insurance for one year, namely, from the 16th of *October* 1759, to the 16th *October* 1760, for the benefit of the governor of *Fort Marlborough*, *George Carter*, against the loss of *Fort Marlborough*, in the island of *Sumatra*, in the *East Indies*, by its being taken by a foreign enemy. The event happened: the fort was taken by Count *D'Estaigne*, within the year. The first witness was *Cawthorne*, the broker, who produced the memorandum given by the governor's brother (the plaintiff) to him; and the use made of these instructions was to shew, that the insurance was made for the benefit of governor *Carter*, and to insure him against the taking of the fort by a foreign enemy. Both parties had been long in Chancery; and the depositions, there made on both sides, were read as evidence upon this trial. It was objected on behalf of the defendant, to be a fraud, by concealment of circumstances, which ought to have been disclosed; and particularly the weakness of the fort, and the probability of its being attacked by the *French*: which concealment was offered to be proved by two letters. The first was a letter from the governor

governor to his brother *Roger Carter*, his truſtee, and the plaintiff in this cauſe: the ſecond was from the governor to the *Eaſt India* Company.

The evidence in reply to this objection, conſiſted of three depoſitions in Chancery; ſetting forth, that the governor had 20,000*l.* in effects; and had only inſured 10,000*l.* and that he was guilty of no fault in defending the fort. The firſt of theſe depoſitions, was captain *Tryon*'s, which proved, that this was not a fort proper, or deſigned, to reſiſt *European* enemies; but only calculated for defence againſt the natives of the iſland of *Sumatra*: that the governor's office is not military, but only mercantile: and that *Fort Marlborough* is only a ſubordinate factory to *Fort St. George*. There was no evidence to the contrary; and a ſpecial jury found a verdict for the plaintiff.

After argument at the bar, upon the motion for a new trial, and time taken by the court to deliberate, their unanimous opinion was delivered by

Lord *Mansfield*.—"This is a motion for a new trial. In ſupport of it, the counſel for the defendant contend, that ſome circumſtances in the knowledge of governor *Carter*, not having been mentioned at the time the policy was underwritten, amount to a concealment, which ought, in law, to avoid the policy. The counſel for the plaintiff inſiſt, that the not mentioning theſe particulars does not amount to a concealment, which ought, in law, to avoid the policy; either as a fraud, or as varying the contract. 1ſt, It may be proper to ſay ſomething in general of concealments which avoid a policy. 2dly, To ſtate particularly the caſe now under conſideration. 3dly, To examine, whether the verdict, which finds this policy good, although the particulars objected were not mentioned, is well founded.

"Firſt, Inſurance is a contract upon ſpeculation. The ſpecial facts, upon which the riſk is to be computed, lie moſt commonly in the knowledge of the inſured only. The underwriter truſts to his ſtatement, and proceeds upon confidence, that he does not keep back any circumſtances within his knowledge, to miſlead the underwriter into a belief that the circumſtance does not exiſt, and to induce him to eſtimate the riſk, as if it did not exiſt. The keeping back ſuch circumſtance is a fraud; and therefore the policy is void.

CHAP. X.

Although the ſuppreſſion ſhould happen through miſtake, without any fraudulent intention; yet ſtill the underwriter is deceived, and the policy is void: becauſe the riſk run is really different from the riſk underſtood, and intended to be run at the time of the agreement. The policy would equally be void againſt the underwriter, if he concealed any thing; as if he inſured a ſhip on her voyage, which he privately knew to be arrived: and an action would lie to recover the premium. The governing principle is applicable to all contracts and dealings. Good faith forbids either party, by concealing what he privately knows, to draw the other into a bargain, from his ignorance of that fact and his believing the contrary. But either party may be innocently ſilent as to grounds open to both, to exerciſe their judgments upon. *Aliud eſt celare; aliud tacere: neque enim id eſt celare quicquid reticeas; ſed cum quod tu ſcias, id ignorare, emolumenti tui cauſâ, velis eos, quorum interſit id ſcire.* This definition of concealment, reſtrained to the efficient motives, and preciſe ſubject of any contract, will generally hold to make it void, in favour of the party miſled by his ignorance of the thing concealed. There are many matters, as to which the inſured may be innocently ſilent; he needs not mention what the underwriter knows, *ſcientia utrinque par pares contrahentes facit.* An underwriter cannot inſiſt that the policy is void, becauſe the inſured did not tell him what he actually knew, what way ſoever he came to the knowledge. The inſured needs not mention what the underwriter ought to know; what he takes upon himſelf the knowledge of; or what he waives being informed of. The underwriter needs not be told what leſſens the riſk agreed, and underſtood to be run by the expreſs terms of the policy. He needs not be told general topics of ſpeculation: as for inſtance, the underwriter is bound to know every cauſe, which may occaſion natural perils; as the difficulty of the voyage; the kind of ſeaſons; the probability of lightning, hurricanes, and earthquakes. He is bound to know every cauſe, which may occaſion political perils; from the rupture of ſtates; from war, and the various operations of war. He is bound to know the probability of ſafety, from the continuance and return of peace; from the imbecility of the enemy, through the weakneſs of their councils, or their want of ſtrength. If an underwriter inſure private ſhips of war, by ſea, and on ſhore from ports

Cicero de Officiis, lib. 3. c. 12, 13.

to

to ports, and from places to places, any where, he needs not be told the ſecret enterpriſes, upon which they are deſtined: becauſe he knows ſome expedition muſt be in view: and from the nature of his contract, he waives the information, without being told. If he inſure for three years, he needs not be told any circumſtance to ſhew it may be over in two: or, if he inſure a voyage with liberty of deviation, he needs not be told what tends to ſhew there will be no deviation. Men argue differently, from natural phænomena, and political appearances: they have different capacities, different degrees of knowledge, and different intelligence. But the means of information and judging, are open to both: each profeſſes to act from his own ſkill and ſagacity; and therefore, neither needs to communicate to the other. The reaſon of the rule, which obliges the parties to diſcloſe, is to prevent fraud, and encourage good faith; it is adapted to ſuch facts as vary the nature of the contract, which one privately knows, and the other is ignorant of, and has no reaſon to ſuſpect. The queſtion, therefore, muſt always be, "Whether there was, under all the circumſtances, at the time the policy was underwritten, a fair ſtatement, or a concealment: fraudulent, if deſigned; or, though not deſigned, varying materially the object of the policy, and changing the riſk underſtood to be run."

2dly. "This brings me in the ſecond place, to ſtate the caſe now under conſideration. The policy is againſt the loſs of *Fort Marlborough*, from being deſtroyed by, taken by, or ſurrendered unto any *European* enemy, between the 16th of *October* 1759, and the 16th of *October* 1760. The underwriter knew at the time, that the policy was to indemnify, to that amount, *George Carter* the *governor of Fort Marlborough*, in caſe the event inſured againſt ſhould happen. The governor's inſtructions for the inſurance bearing date at *Fort Marlborough*, the 22d of *September* 1759, were laid before the underwriter. Two actions upon this policy were tried before me in the year 1762. The defendants then knew of a letter written to the *Eaſt India* Company, which the Company offered to put into my hands; but would not deliver it to the parties, becauſe it contained ſome matters, which they did not think proper to be made public. An objection that occurred to me at the trial, whether a policy againſt the loſs of *Fort Marlborough*, for the benefit of the governor,

Vide ante, c. 1. p. 12.

CHAP. X.

governor, was good; upon the principle, which does not allow a sailor to insure his wages. But considering that this place, though called a fort, was really but a factory or settlement for trade; and that he, though called a governor, was really but a merchant: considering too, that the law allows a captain of a ship to insure goods which he has on board, or his share in the ship, if he be a part owner; and the captain of a privateer, if he be a part owner, to insure his share: considering also, that the objection could not, upon any ground of justice, be made by the underwriter who knew him to be governor, at the time he took the premium, and as with regard to principles of public convenience, the case so seldom happens (I never saw one before) any danger from the example is little to be apprehended: I did not think myself warranted, upon that point, to non-suit the plaintiff; especially as the objection did not come from the bar. Though this point was mentioned at the last trial, it was not insisted upon; nor has it been seriously argued, upon this motion, as sufficient alone to vacate the policy: and if it had, we are all of opinion, that we are not warranted to say, that it is void, upon this account. Upon the plaintiff's obtaining the two former verdicts, the underwriters went into a court of equity; where they have had an opportunity to sift every thing to the bottom, to get every discovery from the governor and his brother, and to examine any witnesses that were upon the spot. At last, after the fullest investigation of every kind, the present action came on to be tried at the sittings after last term. The plaintiff proved without contradiction, that the place called *Bencoolen* or *Fort Marlborough*, is a factory or settlement, but no military fort or fortress: that it was not established for a place of arms or defence against the attacks of an *European* enemy; but merely for the purpose of trade, and of defence against the natives: that the fort was only intended and built to keep off the country blacks: that the only security against *European* ships of war consisted in the difficulty of the entrance and navigation of the river, for want of proper pilots: that the general state and condition of the said fort, and of the strength thereof, were in general well known, by most persons conversant or acquainted with *Indian* affairs, or the state of the Company's factories or settlements; and could not keep secret or concealed from persons, who should endeavour, by proper inquiry, to inform themselves: that

there

there were no apprehensions or intelligence of any attack by the *French*, until they attacked *Nattal* in *February* 1760: that on the 8th of *February* 1760, there was no suspicion of any design by the *French*: that the governor at that time bought of the witness goods to the value of 4,000*l.* and had goods to the value of above 20,000*l.* and then dealt for 50,000*l.* and upwards: that on the first of *April* 1760, the fort was attacked by a *French* man of war of 64 guns, and a frigate of 20 guns, under the *Comte D'Estaigne*, brought in by *Dutch* pilots, was unavoidably taken, and afterwards delivered to the *Dutch*, the prisoners being sent to *Batavia*. On the part of the defendant, after all the opportunities of inquiry, no evidence was offered, that the *French* ever had any design upon *Fort Marlborough*, before the end of *March* 1760; or that there was the least intelligence or alarm, that they might make the attempt till the taking of *Nattal*, in the year 1760. They did not offer to disprove the evidence, that the governor had acted, as in full security, long after the month of *September* 1759; and had turned his money into goods, so late as the 8th of *February* 1760. There was no attempt to shew that he had not lost by the capture very considerably beyond the value of his insurance. But the defendant relied upon a letter, written to the *East India* Company, bearing date the 16th of *September* 1759, which was sent to *England* by the *Pitt*, captain *Wilson*, who arrived in *May* 1760, together with the instructions for insuring; and also a letter bearing date the 22d of *September* 1759, sent to the plaintiff by the same conveyance, and at the same time (which letters his lordship repeated.) They relied too upon the cross examination of the broker who negociated the policy, that *in his opinion*, these letters ought to have been produced, or the contents disclosed; and, that if they had, the policy would not have been underwritten. The defendant's counsel contended at the trial, as they have done upon this motion, that the policy was void: 1st, Because the state and condition of the fort, mentioned in the governor's letter to the *East India* Company was not disclosed. 2dly, Because he did not disclose, that the *French*, not being in a condition to relieve their friends upon the coast, were more likely to make an attack upon this settlement, rather than remain idle: 3dly, That he had not disclosed his having received a letter of the 4th of

February

CHAP. X. *February* 1759; from which it seemed, that the *French* had a design to take this settlement, by surprize, the year before. They also contended, that the opinion of the broker was almost decisive: the whole was laid before the jury, who found for the plaintiff.

"Thirdly, It remains to consider these objections; and to examine whether this verdict is well founded. To this purpose, it is necessary to consider the nature of the contract, at the time it was made. The policy was signed in *May* 1760. The contingency was, whether *Fort Marlborough* was or would be taken, by an *European* enemy, between *October* 1759 and *October* 1760. The computation of the risk depended upon the chance, whether any *European* power would attack the place by sea. If they did, it was incapable of resistance. The underwriter at *London*, in *May* 1760, could judge much better of the probability of the contingency, than governor *Carter* could at *Fort Marlborough* in *September* 1759. He knew the success of the operations of the war in *Europe*: he knew what naval force the *English* and *French* had sent to the *East Indies*. He knew, from a comparison of that force, whether the sea was open to any such attempt by the *French*. He knew, or might know, every thing which was known at *Fort Marlborough* in *September* 1759, of the general state of affairs in the *East Indies*, or the particular condition of *Fort Marlborough*, by the ship which brought the orders for the insurance. He knew that ship must have brought many letters to the *East India* Company, and particularly from the governor. He knew what probability there was of the *Dutch* committing, or having committed hostilities. Under these circumstances, and with this knowledge, he insures against the general contingency of the place being attacked by an *European* power. If there had been any design on foot, or enterprize begun, in *September* 1759, to the knowledge of the governor, it would have varied the risk understood by the underwriter; on account of his not being told of a particular design or attack *then subsisting*; and he estimated the risk upon the foot of an uncertain operation, which might or might not be attempted. But the governor had no notice of any design subsisting in *September* 1759. There was no such design in fact: the attempt was made without premeditation, from the sudden opportunity of a favourable occasion, by the connivance

nivance and aſſiſtance of the *Dutch*, which tempted *Comte D'Eſtaigne* to break his parole. Theſe being the circumſtances, under which the contract was entered into, we ſhall be better able to judge of the objections upon the foot of concealments. The firſt concealment is, that he did not diſcloſe the condition of the place. The underwriter knew the inſurance was for the governor. He knew the governor muſt be acquainted with the ſtate of the place. He knew the governor could not diſcloſe it, conſiſtently with his duty. He knew the governor, by inſuring, apprehended, at leaſt, the poſſibility of an attack. With this knowledge, without aſking a queſtion, he underwrote. By ſo doing, he took the knowledge of the ſtate of the place upon himſelf. It was a matter, as to which he might be informed various ways: it was not a matter, within the private knowledge of the governor only. But not to rely upon that, the utmoſt which can be contended is, that the underwriter truſted to the fort being in the condition in which it ought to be: in like manner, as it is taken for granted, that a ſhip inſured is ſea worthy. What is that condition? All the witneſſes agree, that it was only to reſiſt the natives, and not an *European* force. The policy inſures againſt a total loſs, taking for granted, that if the place was attacked, it would be loſt. The contingency, therefore, which the underwriter has inſured againſt is, whether the place would be attacked by an *European* force; and not whether it would be able to reſiſt ſuch an attack, if the ſhips could get up the river. It was particularly left to the jury to conſider whether this was the contingency in the contemplation of the parties: they have found that it was. And we are all of opinion, that in this reſpect, their concluſion is agreeable to the evidence. The ſtate and condition of the place were material in this view only, in caſe of a land attack by the natives.

"The ſecond concealment is, his not having diſcloſed, that, from the *French* not being able to relieve their friends upon the coaſt, they might make them a viſit. This is no part of the fact of the caſe: it is mere ſpeculation of the governor, from the general ſtate of the war. The conjecture was dictated to him from his fears. It is a bold attempt for the conquered to attack the conqueror in his own dominions.

CHAP. X.

dominions. The practicability of it, in this case, depended upon the *English* naval forces in those seas, of which the underwriter could better judge at *London*, in *May* 1760, than the governor could at *Fort Marlborough*, in *September* 1759. The third concealment is, that he did not disclose the letter from Mr. *Winch*, of the 4th of *February* 1759, mentioning the design of the *French* the year before. What that letter was, how he mentioned the design, or upon what authority he mentioned it; or by whom the design was supposed to be imagined, does not appear. The defendant has had every opportunity of discovery; and nothing has come out upon it, as to this letter, which he thinks makes for his purpose. The plaintiff offered to read the account *Winch* wrote to the *East India* Company, which was objected to; and therefore, it was not read. The nature of that intelligence, therefore, is very doubtful. But taking it in the strongest light, it is a report of a design to surprize the year before; but then dropt. This is a topic of mere general speculation, which made no part of the fact of the case upon which the insurance was to be made. It was said, if a man insured a ship, knowing that two privateers were lying in her way, without mentioning that circumstance, it would be a fraud. I agree to it. But if he knew that two privateers had been there the year before, it would be no fraud, not to mention that circumstance: because it does not follow that they will cruise this year, at the same time, in the same place; or that they are in a condition to do it. If the circumstance of this *design laid aside* had been mentioned, it would have tended rather to lessen the risk, than increase it: for the design of a surprize, which has transpired, and been laid aside, is less likely to be taken up again; especially by a vanquished enemy. The jury considered the nature of the governor's silence as to these particulars; they thought it innocent, and that the omission to mention them, did not vary the contract. And we are all of opinion, that, in this respect, they judged extremely right. There is a silence, not objected to at the trial, nor upon this motion; which might with as much reason, have been objected to, as the two last omissions; rather more. It appears by the governor's letter to the plaintiff, that he was principally apprehensive of a *Dutch* war. He certainly had, what he thought, good grounds for this apprehension. *Comte D'Estaigne* being piloted by the *Dutch*, delivering the fort

fort to the *Dutch*, and ſending the priſoners to *Batavia*, is a confirmation of thoſe grounds. Probably, the loſs of the place was owing to the *Dutch*. The *French* could not have got up the river without *Dutch* pilots: and it is plain, the whole was concerted with them. And yet, at the time of underwriting the policy, there was no intimation about the *Dutch*. The reaſon why the counſel have not objected to his not diſcloſing the grounds of this apprehenſion is, becauſe it muſt have ariſen from political ſpeculation, and general intelligence: therefore, they agree, it is not neceſſary to communicate ſuch things to an underwriter.

"Laſtly, Great ſtreſs was laid upon the opinion of the broker. But we all think, the jury ought not to pay the leaſt regard to it: it is mere opinion; which is not evidence: it is opinion after an event; it is opinion without the leaſt foundation from any previous precedent or uſage: it is an opinion, which, if rightly formed, could only be drawn from the ſame premiſes, from which the court and jury were to determine the cauſe: and therefore, it is improper and irrelevant in the mouth of a witneſs. There is no imputation upon the governor, as to any intention of fraud. By the ſame conveyance, which brought his orders to inſure, he wrote to the company every thing, which he knew or ſuſpected: he deſired nothing to be kept a ſecret, which he wrote either to them or his brother. His ſubſequent conduct, down to the 8th of *February* 1760, ſhewed that he thought the danger very improbable. The reaſon of the rule againſt concealments is, to prevent fraud and encourage good faith. If the defendant's objections were to prevail, in the preſent inſtance, the rule would be turned into an inſtrument of fraud. The underwriter here, knowing the governor to be acquainted with the ſtate of the place; knowing that he apprehended danger, and muſt have ſome ground for his apprehenſion; being told nothing of either, ſigned this policy, without aſking a queſtion. If the objection, "that he was not told," is ſufficient to vacate it, he took the premium, knowing the policy to be void, in order to gain if the alternative turned out one way; and to make no ſatisfaction, if it turned out the other: he drew the governor into a falſe confidence, that if the worſt ſhould happen, he had provided againſt total ruin; knowing, at the ſame time, that the indemnity, to which

CHAP. X.

which the governor trusted, was void. There was not a word said to him of the affairs of *India*, or the state of the war there, or the condition of *Fort Marlborough*. If he thought that omission an objection, at the time, he ought not to have signed the policy, with a secret reserve in his own mind to make it void: if he dispensed with the information, and did not think this silence an objection then; he cannot take it up now, after the event. What has been often said of the statute of frauds may, with more propriety, be applied to every rule of law, drawn from principles of natural equity, to prevent fraud: "that it should never be so turned, construed, or used, as to protect or be a means of fraud." After the fullest deliberation, we are all clear that the verdict is well founded; and that there ought not to be a new trial; consequently, that the rule obtained for that purpose ought to be discharged."

To have given this very elaborate and learned argument in the state in which it was delivered, certainly requires no apology; because from it may be collected all the general principles, upon which the doctrine of concealments, in matters of insurance, is founded, as well as all the exceptions, which can be made to the generality of those principles. To have abridged such an argument, would have very much lessened the pleasure of the reader, and would have been an injury to the venerable judge, who in that form delivered the opinion of the court. The rules, then advanced and illustrated, have since been confirmed by the opinion of the judges upon similar questions.

Planché and another v. Fletcher, Doug. 238.

The plaintiffs, *Planché* and *Jaquery*, merchants in *London*, insured goods, "on board the *Swedish* ship called the *Mary* "*Magdalena*, lost or not lost, at and from *London* and *Ramsgate* to *Nantz*, with liberty to call at *Ostend*, being a general ship in the port of *London* for *Nantz*." There was a declaration in the policy, "that the insurance was made on account of certain persons carrying on trade under the name "and firm of *Vallee* and *Duplessis*, Monsieur *Lassau le Jeune*, "*Guillaume Albert*, *et Poitier de la Gueule*." The defendant underwrote the policy for 300*l.* at three guineas *per cent.* The ship's clearances from the custom-house in *London* and her other papers, were all made out for *Ostend* only, but the ship and goods were intended to go directly from *London* to *Nantz*,

Nantz, without going to *Ostend*. Bills of lading in the *French* language, dated the 18th of *July* 1778, were signed by the captain in *London*, but purporting to be made at *Ostend*, and that the goods were shipped there to be delivered at *Nantz*. The policy was subscribed by the defendant on the 7th of *July*, and the lading was taken in between the 24th of *July* and the 17th of *August*. The proclamation for making reprisals on *French* ships, bore date the 29th, and appeared in the Gazette on the 31st of *July*. Two underwriters had signed the policy after the proclamation, at the same premium of three guineas; one on the 31st of *July*, and the other on the 7th of *August*. The ship sailed on the 24th of *August*, and was taken by a king's cutter, on her way to *Nantz*. After her departure from *Gravesend*, the captain threw overboard all the papers which he had received from the Customhouse at *London*. They had been obliterated by the Customhouse officers at *Gravesend*, and were no longer of any use. The ship was released by the Admiralty, but the goods were condemned. The plaintiffs had no connexion or share in the ship. Such were the material facts in this case as they were stated this day by Lord *Mansfield* in his report, upon a rule to shew cause why there should not be a new trial. The cause had been tried at the last sittings at *Guildhall*, and a verdict found for the plaintiff. The grounds for the application for a new trial were two: 1st, That there was a fraud on the underwriters, the ship having been cleared out for *Ostend*, and yet never having been designed for that place. 2dly, That as hostilities were declared after the policy was signed, and before the ship sailed, the defendant ought to have had notice, that he might have exercised his discretion, whether he would choose for a peace premium to run the risk of capture. Beside the facts abovementioned, his lordship stated, that the plaintiff had produced evidence to shew, that all ships, going with goods of *British* manufacture to *France*, clear out for *Ostend*, without meaning to go thither; and that this is universally understood by persons concerned in that branch of commerce. The reasons suggested for clearing out for *Ostend*, and afterwards making bills of lading as from that place, were, that the light-house duties are saved, which are payable when the voyage is known to be directly down the channel; and that the *French* duties are less upon goods from *Ostend*, than from *England*.

CHAP. X.

Sittings after Trin. 1779.

CHAP. X.

Lord *Mansfield.*—"This verdict is impeached upon two grounds. 1st. It is said there was a fraud on the underwriters, in clearing out the ship for *Ostend*, when she was never intended to go thither. But I think there was no fraud on them: perhaps, not on any body. What has been practised in this case was proved to be the constant course of the trade; and notoriously so to every body. The reason for clearing for *Ostend*, and signing bills of lading as from thence, did not fully appear. But it was guessed at. The *Fermiers Generaux* have the management of the taxes in *France*. As we have laid a large duty on *French* goods, the *French* may have done the same on ours; and it may be the interest of the farmers to connive at the importation of *English* commodities, and take *Ostend* duties, rather than stop the trade, by exacting a tax, which amounts to a prohibition. But, at any rate, this was no fraud in this country. One nation does not take notice of the revenue laws of another. With regard to the evasion of the light-house duties, the ship was not liable to confiscation on that account. 2d. The second objection is, that the policy was made before, and the ship sailed after, the proclamation for reprisals. But every man in *England* and *France*, on the 17th of *July*, expected the immediate commencement of a war. I will not say it was actually commenced; but the ambassadors of both countries were recalled; the *Pallas* and *Licorne* were taken; the fleets were at sea; and, as it appeared afterwards, were waiting for each other to fight. It does not appear that the goods were *French* property; an *Englishman* might be sending his goods to *France* in a neutral ship. But it is indifferent whether they were *English* or *French*. The risk insured extends to all captures; and as two other underwriters signed at the same premium, after the proclamation, it appears that the war risk was in view when the defendant signed. Shall he avail himself of an event, which increases the risk, but which he had in contemplation when he underwrote the policy? I am of opinion, that there should not be a new trial." The three other judges concurred; and the rule was discharged.

Mayne v. Walter B. R. East. 22 Geo. III.

A similar decision was made in the following case. It was an action on a policy of insurance on a *Portugueze* ship, at and from *Madeira* to her port of discharge in *Jamaica*, with liberty to touch at the *Leeward Islands*. The defendant underwrote

derwrote 150*l.* upon it: the ship was captured by a *French* privateer, and condemned in the court of Admiralty in *France*, on the ground of having an *English supercargo* on board. The action was brought to recover this loss from the underwriter, who refused to pay, alleging, that the plaintiff should have disclosed to him, that the supercargo was *English*. At the trial, a verdict was given for the plaintiff, upon a case reserved for the opinion of the court, and containing in substance the facts just stated. CHAP. X.

For the defendant it was insisted, upon the argument, that the agent for the insured ought to have disclosed this fact; and that it was the more material in this case, because during the present war, an ordinance passed in *France*, similar to one made in the last war in 1756, which declares, that no *Dutch* ship shall be allowed to take on board a supercargo, belonging to any nation at enmity with the court of *France*; and that if any ship, having such supercargo, be taken, it shall be condemned as lawful prize.

Lord *Mansfield*.—"It is an oppressive and arbitrary rule, and contrary to the law of nations. If both parties were ignorant of it, the underwriter must run all risks: and if the defendant knew of such an edict, it was his duty to inquire, if such a supercargo were on board. It must be a fraudulent concealment of circumstances, that will vitiate a policy. But it is remarkable, that neither party has said a word respecting the treaties between *France* and *Portugal*." Judgment was accordingly given for the plaintiff.

3d. We come now to the third great division of this chapter, namely, to cases in which policies are void by misrepresentation. Before we proceed to state the cases under this head, it will be proper to distinguish between a warranty and a representation. A warranty or condition is that, which makes a part of the written policy, and must be literally and strictly performed; and being a part of the agreement, nothing *tantamount* will do, or answer the purpose. A representation is a state of the case, not a part of the written instrument, but collateral to it, and entirely independent of it; and it is sufficient, that a representation be substantially performed. The consequence of a breach of a Vide post, c. 18.

warranty

CHAP. X.

warranty we ſhall take notice of hereafter. If there be a miſrepreſentation, it will avoid the policy, as a fraud, but not as a part of the agreement. Even written inſtructions, if they are not inſerted in the policy, are only to be conſidered as repreſentations; and in order to make them valid and binding as a warranty, it is abſolutely neceſſary to make them a part of the inſtrument, by which the contract of indemnity is effected. If a repreſentation be falſe in any material point, it will avoid the policy; and if the point be not material, the repreſentation can hardly ever be fraudulent. The principle upon which the policy is void in ſuch a caſe, we ſtated in the opening; that the underwriter has computed the riſk upon circumſtances, which were falſe, or which did not exiſt. Theſe doctrines are fully eſtabliſhed by a variety of judicial deciſions.

Pawſon v. Watſon, Cowper 785.

Upon a rule to ſhew cauſe why a new trial ſhould not be granted in this caſe, Lord *Mansfield* reported as follows: "This was an action upon a policy of inſurance. At the trial it appeared in evidence, that the firſt underwriter had the following inſtruction ſhewn to him: "Three thouſand "five hundred pounds upon the ſhip *Julius Cæſar*, for *Hal*-"*ifax*, to touch at *Plymouth*, and any port in *America*; *ſhe* "*mounts twelve guns and twenty men*." Theſe inſtructions were not aſked for, nor communicated to the defendant; but the ſhip was only repreſented *generally to him as a ſhip of force*: and a thouſand pounds had been done, before the defendant underwrote any thing upon her. The inſtructions were dated the 28th of *June* 1776, and the ſhip ſailed on the 23d of *July* 1776; and was taken by an *American* privateer. That at the time of her being taken, ſhe had on board 6 *four pounders*, 4 *three pounders*, 3 *one pounders*, 6 *half pounders*, which are called *ſwivels*, and 27 men and boys in all, for her crew; but of *them*, 16 only were *men*, (not 20, as the inſtructions mentioned) and the reſt boys. But the witneſs ſaid, he conſidered her as being ſtronger with this force, than if ſhe had 12 carriage guns, and 20 men: he alſo ſaid (which is a material circumſtance) that *there were neither men nor guns on board, at the time of the inſurance.* That he himſelf inſured at the ſame premium, without regard or inquiry into the force of the ſhip. Other underwriters alſo inſured at the ſame premium, without any other repreſentation than that ſhe was *a ſhip of force*. That to every four pounder,

pounder, there ſhould be five men and a boy. That in merchant ſhips, boys always go under the denomination of men. This was met by evidence on the part of the defendant, ſaying, that guns meant *carriage* guns, not *ſwivels*; and men meant *able men*, excluſive of *boys*. There were three cauſes of the ſame nature depending upon the ſame evidence. The defence in each was, that theſe inſtructions were to be conſidered as a warranty, the ſame as if they had been inſerted in the policy; though they were not proved to have been ſhewn to any but the firſt underwriter. In all the three caſes the queſtion for the court to determine, is, Whether the inſtructions, which were ſhewn to the firſt underwriter, are to be conſidered as a warranty inſerted in the policy; or as a repreſentation, which would avoid the policy, if fraudulent? If the court ſhould be of opinion, that the inſtructions amounted to a warranty, then a new trial is to be had in each without coſts; otherwiſe, the verdicts, which were all for the plaintiffs, are to ſtand. At the trial I was of opinion, that it would be of very dangerous conſequence, to add a converſation, that paſſed at that time, as part of the written agreement. It is a collateral repreſentation; and if the parties had conſidered it as a warranty, they would have had it inſerted in the policy. But ſecondly, if theſe inſtructions were to be conſidered in the light of a fraudulent miſrepreſentation; they muſt be both material and fraudulent: and in that light, I held, that a miſrepreſentation made to the firſt underwriter ought to be conſidered as a miſrepreſentation made to every one of them, and ſo would infect the whole policy. Otherwiſe, it would be a contrivance to deceive many: for where a good man ſtands firſt, the reſt underwrite without aſking a queſtion: and if he be impoſed upon, the reſt of the underwriters are taken in by the ſame fraud." The caſe was left to the jury under that direction.

After argument at the bar, Lord *Mansfield* aſked, Whether there was any caſe that made a difference between a written and a parol repreſentation? No anſwer being given, his lordſhip proceeded: "There is no diſtinction better known to thoſe, who are at all converſant in the law of inſurance, than that which exiſts between a *warranty* or condition,

W

CHAP. X.

tion, which makes part of a written policy, and a representation of the ſtate of the caſe. Where it is a part of the written policy, it muſt be performed. As if there be a warranty of convoy, there it muſt be a *convoy*; nothing elſe will anſwer the idea intended by the warranty: it muſt be ſtrictly performed, as being a part of the agreement; for in the caſe of convoy it might be ſaid, the party would not have inſured without convoy. But as, by the law of merchants, all dealings muſt be fair and honeſt, fraud infects and vitiates every mercantile contract. Therefore, if there be fraud in a repreſentation, it will avoid the policy, on account of the fraud, but not on account of the non-compliance with any part of the agreement. If in a life policy, a man warrant another to be in good health, when he knows at the ſame time he is ill of a fever, *that* will not avoid the policy on the ground of miſrepreſentation; (though it will be void for non-compliance with the warranty;) becauſe by the warranty, the inſured takes the riſk upon himſelf. But if there be no warranty, and he ſay, "the man is in good health," when in fact he knows him to be ill, it is *falſe*. So it is, if he do not know, whether he be well or ill; for it is equally falſe to undertake to ſay that, which he knows nothing at all of, as to ſay, *that* is true, which he knows is not true. But if he only ſay, "he believes the man to be in good health," knowing nothing about it, nor having any reaſon to believe the contrary; there, though the perſon is not in good health, it will not avoid the policy, becauſe the underwriter *then* takes the riſk upon himſelf. So that there cannot be a clearer diſtinction, than that which exiſts between a warranty, which makes part of the written policy, and a collateral repreſentation, which, if falſe in a point of materiality, makes the policy void: but if not material, it can hardly ever be fraudulent. So far from the uſage being to conſider inſtructions as a part of the policy, that parol inſtructions were never entered in a book, nor written inſtructions kept, till a few years ago, upon occaſion of ſeveral actions brought by the inſured upon policies, where the brokers had repreſented many things they ought not to have repreſented, in conſequence of which the plaintiffs were caſt. I adviſed the inſured to bring an action againſt the brokers, which they did,

and

and recovered in ſeveral inſtances: and I have repeatedly at *Guildhall*, cautioned and recommended it to the brokers, to enter all repreſentations made by them in a book. That advice has been followed in *London*; but it appeared lately, at the trial of a cauſe, that at *Briſtol*, to this hour, they make no entry in their books, or keep any inſtructions. The queſtion then is, whether in this policy the perſon inſuring has warranted that the ſhip ſhould poſitively and literally have 12 *carriage guns and* 20 *men*. That is, whether the inſtructions given in evidence are a part of the policy. Now I will take it by degrees. The two firſt underwriters before the court are *Watſon* and *Snell*. Says *Watſon*, "it is part of my agree- "ment, that the ſhip ſhall ſail with 12 guns, and 20 men; "and it is ſo ſtipulated, that nothing under that number will "do: ten guns with ſwivels will not do." The anſwer to this is, read your agreement; read your policy. There is no ſuch thing to be found there. It is replied, yes, but in fact there is, for the inſtructions, upon which the policy was made, contain that expreſs ſtipulation. The anſwer again is, there never were any inſtructions ſhewn to *Watſon*; nor were any aſked for by him. What colour then has he to ſay that thoſe inſtructions are any part of his agreement? It is ſaid, he inſured upon the credit of the firſt underwriter. A repreſentation to the firſt underwriter has nothing to do with that, which is the agreement, or terms of the policy. No man who underwrites a policy, ſubſcribes by the act of underwriting, to terms of which he knows nothing: but he reads the agreement, and is governed by that. Matters of intelligence, ſuch as that a ſhip is or is not miſſing, are things in which a man is guided by the name of a firſt underwriter, who is a good man, and to which another will therefore give faith and credit: but not to a collateral agreement, of which he can know nothing. The abſurdity is too glaring; it cannot be. By extenſion of an equitable relief in caſes of fraud, if a man is a knave with reſpect to a firſt underwriter, and makes a falſe repreſentation to him in a point that is material; as where having notice of a ſhip being loſt, he ſays ſhe was ſafe; that ſhall effect the policy with regard to all the ſubſequent underwriters, who are preſumed to follow the firſt. How then do *Watſon* and *Snell* underwrite the ſhip in queſtion? Without knowing whether ſhe had any force at all. *That* proves the riſk was equal to a ſhip of no force at all; and the premium

was

CHAP. X.

was a vast one; eight guineas. So much therefore for those two cases. The third case is that of *Ewer*, who saw the instructions, with the representation, which they contained. Did the number of guns induce him to underwrite the policy? If it did, he would have said, put them into the policy; warrant that the ship shall depart with 12 guns and 20 men. Whereas he does no such thing, but takes the same premium, which *Watson* and *Snell* did, who had *no* notice of her having any force. What does that prove? That he is paid and receives a premium, as if it were a ship of no force at all. The representation amounts to no more than this, I tell you what the force will be, because it is so much the better for you. There is no fraud in it, because it is a representation only of what, in the then state of the ship, they thought would be the truth. And in real truth the ship sailed with a larger force; for she had nine carriage guns and six swivels. The underwriters therefore had the advantage by the difference. There was no stipulation about what the weight of metal would be. All the witnesses say, that she had more force than if she had 12 carriage guns, in point of strength, of convenience, and for the purpose of resistance. The supercargo in particular says, "he insured the same ship and the same voyage, for the "same premium, without saying a syllable about the force." Why then it was a matter proper for the jury to say, whether the representation was false, or whether it was in fact an insurance as of a ship without force. They have determined, and I think very rightly, that it was an insurance without force. *Ewer* makes an objection, that the representation ought to be considered as inserted in the policy; but the answer to that is, he has determined whether it should be inserted in the policy or not, by not inserting it himself. There is a great difference, whether it shall be considered as a fraud. But it would be very dangerous to permit all collateral representations to be put into the policy. I am extremely glad to hear that a great many of the underwriters have paid. Mr. *Thornton* has paid, who was the first person that saw the instructions. Shall the rest refuse then? As to *Watson* and *Snell*, they have no pretence to refuse? for there is not a colour for the objection made by them. As to *Ewer*, we are

all

all ſatisfied with the determination of the jury againſt him. Therefore the rule for a new trial muſt be diſcharged."

N. B. On the *Monday* following, Mr. *Davenport* ſaid, he was deſired by the underwriters to aſk, whether it was the opinion of the court, that to make written inſtructions valid and binding as a warranty, they muſt be inſerted in the policy? Lord *Mansfield* anſwered, that moſt undoubtedly that was the opinion of the court: If a man warrant that a ſhip ſhall depart with 12 guns, and it depart with 10 only, it is contrary to the condition of the policy.

From the judgment pronounced in the cauſe juſt ſtated, we learn the difference between a warranty and a repreſentation: we learn alſo, that a performance in ſubſtance will ſatisfy a condition expreſſed in a repreſentation; but that nothing except a ſtrict and literal compliance will fulfil the terms of the former: and we alſo are inſtructed in the whole doctrine of repreſentation, as far as it affects the contract of inſurance. The poſitions advanced in the above caſe were ſo ſatiſfactory, that they have been adopted, as the ground of direction to juries, upon all queſtions of repreſentation; and have been followed by the court, whenever points of that nature have come before them for judgment.

Bize v. Fletcher, Sittings after Eaſter Term, 1779, Guildhall, Doug. Rep. 271.

This was an action on a policy of inſurance on the ſhip *Carnatic Eaſt Indiaman*, " at and from *Port L'Orient*, to the " iſles of *France* and *Bourbon*, and to all or any ports or places, " where, and whatſoever, in the *Eaſt Indies*, *China*, *Perſia*, " or elſewhere, beyond the *Cape of Good Hope*, from place to " place; and during the ſhip's ſtay and trade, backwards and " forwards, at all ports and places, and until her ſafe arrival " back at her laſt port of diſcharge in *France*." But at the ſame time that this policy was ſubſcribed, there was a ſlip of paper wafered to it, and ſhewn to the underwriters, on which was written the following repreſentation: " The ſhip has had " a complete repair, and is now a fine and good veſſel, three " decks. Intends to ſail in *September* or *October* next (1776.) " Is to go to *Madeira*, the iſles of *France*, *Pondicherry*, *China*, " the iſles of *France*, and *L'Orient*."

The ſhip did not ſail till the 6th of *December* 1776, and did not reach *Pondicherry* till the 23d of *July* 1777. She continued there till the 23d of *Auguſt* following, when, inſtead of proceeding to *China*, ſhe ſailed for *Bengal*, where having paſſed the winter and undergone conſiderable repairs, ſhe ſailed from thence early in the year 1778, (being the ſecond ſhip that left the *Ganges*;) returned to *Pondicherry*, and after taking in a homeward-bound cargo at that place, proceeded in her voyage back to *L'Orient*, but was taken in October in that year, by the *Mentor* privateer. The uſual time, in which the direct voyage between *Pondicherry* and *Bengal* is performed, is ſix or ſeven days; but the *Carnatic* was about ſix weeks in going to *Bengal*, and two months on the way back from thence to *Pondicherry*. Both going and returning, ſhe either touched at, or lay off *Madras*, *Maſulipatam*, *Viſigapatam*, and *Yanon*, and took in goods at all thoſe places.

It was contended in this cauſe, at the trial, that the repreſentation accompanying the policy reſtrained the voyage to the limits therein ſpecified. They produced ſome letters from the owners to their correſpondents, one of which was to the following effect: "We doubt not, but on account of "the ſtorm, the ſhip will be forced to go to *Bengal* to be "laid down, which cannot be done at *Pondicherry*; in which "caſe, our captain will have entered a proteſt, which we will "forward in time to you." In a ſubſequent letter, they ſay nothing of the ſtorm or leak; but mention a different cauſe for the ſhip's going to *Bengal*. Theſe letters, it was ſaid, raiſed a preſumption, that the neceſſity of going to *Bengal* was merely a pretence deviſed after the capture, and when the inſured began to apprehend that the words of the policy would not cover a voyage to that place.

Lord *Mansfield* told the jury, "that the firſt queſtion was, whether the policy was void, on account of miſrepreſentation. Now there is an eſſential difference between a warranty and a repreſentation. The warranty is a part of the contract: a riſk deſcribed in the policy is part of the contract. There can be no warranty by any collateral repreſentation. The ground, on which a repreſentation affects a policy, is fraud. The repreſentation muſt be fraudulent, that is, it

muſt

must be false and material in respect to the risk to be run. All risks are governed by the nature of them; and the premium is governed by the risk. Where a representation accompanies an instrument, it says, "I will have this understood as my present intention: but I will have it in my "power to vary it." The great question in this cause is, whether the representation was false, and that in a material instance. Fraud is found out by the materiality of the point it is charged in. It is to be considered then, whether they had really a view of going to *China*. A witness has proved that the difference of insurance is one *per cent.* on going to *Bengal*, and not to *China*. If you think that this was a misrepresentation to avoid paying the one *per cent.* you will find for the defendant. But if you are satisfied that the real intention, at the time of the representation, was to go to *China*, the plaintiff will be entitled to your verdict: for the insured may change his intention, go to *Bengal*, and yet be protected by the policy, which clearly admits of that voyage, and must be understood by both parties in a greater latitude than the representation, being expressed in different and much more comprehensive terms. If, upon the whole evidence, you shall be of opinion, that no fraud was intended, and that the variance between the intended voyage, as described in the slip of paper, and the actual voyage as performed, did not tend to increase the risk to the underwriters, *this slip of paper being only a representation*, you must find for the plaintiff." The jury found a verdict accordingly. And although in several causes upon the same slip, new trials were moved for, and granted; yet in this, which was the only cause in which there was a representation, the verdict was acquiesced in, and no motion respecting it ever was made.

CHAP. X.

Vide Doug. Rep. 271.

In the outset of this chapter, we took notice of a very material rule respecting misrepresentation; and which it now becomes necessary to repeat. If a representation be made to the underwriter of any circumstance which was false, this, if it be in a material point, shall vacate the policy, and annul the contract, *although it happen by mistake*, and without any fraudulent intention, or improper motive on the part of the insured. We also stated the principle, on which, in such a case, the contract is held to be void: because the insurer is

5 Burr. 1909.

CHAP. X. is led into error, and computes his risk upon circumstances not founded in fact; by which means, the risk actually run is different from that intended to be run, at the time the contract is made. On this ground it is, that the contract is as much at an end, as if there had been a wilful and false allegation, or an undue concealment of circumstances. The doctrine here meant to be advanced will be better understood, and more fully illustrated, by attention to the following case.

Macdowall v. Frafer, Doug. 247.

It was an action on a policy of insurance on the ship, "the "*Mary* and *Hannah*, from *New York* to *Philadelphia*." At the time when the insurance was made, which was in *London*, on the 30th of *January*, the broker represented the situation of the ship to the underwriter as follows: "The *Mary* and "*Hannah*, a tight vessel, sailed with several armed ships, and "was seen safe in the *Delaware on the 11th of December*, by "a ship which arrived at *New York*." In fact the ship was lost on *the 9th of December*, by running against a *cheveau de frise*, placed across the river. The cause came on to be tried before Lord *Mansfield* at *Guildhall*. The defence was founded on the misrepresentation as to the time when the ship was seen; and the representation and the day of the loss being proved, the jury found for the defendant. A rule was obtained on the part of the plaintiff, calling upon the defendant to shew cause why there should not be a new trial. After argument at the bar,

Lord *Mansfield* said: "The distinction between a warranty and a representation is perfectly well settled. A representation must be fair and true. It should be true as to all that the insured knows; and, if he represents facts to the underwriter, without knowing the truth, he takes the risk upon himself. But the difference between the fact as it turns out, and as represented, must be material. The case of the *Julius Cæsar* was very different from this. The ship there was only fitting out, when the insurance was made. No guns nor men were put on board. It was only said, what was meant to be done; and what was done, though different, was as advantageous, or more so, than what had been represented. There was no evidence of *actual fraud* in the present case, and no question of that sort seemed to be made. But there was a positive averment, that the ship was seen in the *Delaware*, on the 11th of *December*. The underwriter was deceived

Vide ante, the Case of Pawson v. Watson, p. 197.

deceived as to that fact, and entered into the contract under that deception. There was no evidence at the trial *when* she was seen in the *Delaware*, or in what condition: but suppose the fact had been explained in the manner now suggested, why did the insured take upon him to compute the day of the month, on which she had been seen? Why did he not mention exactly what his information was, and leave the underwriter to make the computation? In insurances on ships at a great distance, their being safe up to a certain day is always considered as a very important circumstance. I am of opinion, that the representation concerning the day was material."

Mr. Justice *Willes*.—"This is certainly only a representation; but, in an insurance on so short a voyage, it might have made a material difference whether the ship was known to be safe two days sooner or later. It ought to have been shewn, on the part of the plaintiff, that it was not material, but there was no evidence that the ship was met on the 9th, or any other day. The materiality was proper for the consideration of the jury."

Mr. Justice *Ashhurst*.—"The distinction, which the court has made in the cases on the *Julius Cæsar*, and some others, between a representation, and a warranty, is extremely just. There is *no imputation of fraud* in this case; but the insured should have been more cautious. In the former cases, the representation was of what was intended; here it was of a fact stated as having happened, within the knowledge of the insured. He should have made the representation in the same words, in which the intelligence is said to have been communicated to him."

Mr. Justice *Buller*.—"We cannot say the difference of the day was not material. The safety of the ship is the most material fact of any, in cases of insurance. The plaintiff admits that the place where she was met in safety, was material. Why was not the time equally so? There was no *intentional deceit*, and it is perhaps unfortunate that the insured made *the mistake*; but I think the verdict right."

The

CHAP. X.

The rule for a new trial was accordingly difcharged.

Shirley v. Wilkinfon, B. R. Mich. 22 Geo. III. Doug. Rep. 2d edit. 293.

A fimilar decifion was made by the fame learned judges at a period fubfequent to that of the cafe of *Macdowall* and *Frafer*.

Upon a motion for a new trial, Lord *Mansfield*, and the reft of the court, were clearly of opinion, that if the broker, at the time when the policy is effected, in reprefenting to the underwriter the ftate of the fhip, and the laft intelligence concerning her, does not difclofe the whole, and what he *conceals* fhall appear *material* to the jury, they ought to find for the underwriter, the contract in fuch cafe being void; although the concealment fhould have been *innocent*, the facts not mentioned having appeared *immaterial* to the broker, and having not been communicated merely on that account.

But as has been faid before, and as will appear from the cafes already cited, in order to vitiate the contract, the thing concealed muft be *material*, it muft be *fome fact*, and not merely a fuppofition or fpeculation of the infured: and the underwriter muft take advantage of any mifreprefentation, the firft opportunity, otherwife he will not be allowed to claim any benefit from it at a future period. If therefore the infured merely reprefent that he *expects* a thing to be done, the contract will not be void, although the event fhould turn out very different from his expectation.

Barber v. Fletcher, Doug. 292.

Thus upon a motion for a new trial, one of the grounds ftated to induce the court to grant it was, that fince the trial, a material reprefentation, which had been made to *Shulbred*, the firft underwriter upon the policy, and which turned out to be falfe, had been difcovered. *Shulbred* made an affidavit, by which it appeared, that when he figned the policy in *March* 1778, the broker was getting feveral others, on other fhips, fubfcribed at the fame time, all belonging to the fame owner, and faid, fpeaking of them all—" which veffels are " *expected* to leave the coaft of *Africa* in *November* or *December* 1777." In truth, the veffel in queftion had failed in *May* 1777, and *Shulbred* fwore, that, if he had known that circumftance, he would not have figned. There had been actions brought againft all the underwriters on the policy, except *Shulbred*.

Lord

Lord *Mansfield*.—"It has certainly been determined in a variety of cases, that a representation to the first underwriter extends to the others. But under what circumstances has the defendant gone to trial in this case? he certainly knew what had been represented to himself. He was acquainted with *Shulbred*, and had an opportunity of asking before the trial what had been represented to *him*. If therefore this evidence is *new*, it is owing to his own negligence. But the representation is not material; it was only an *expectation*, and the underwriters did not inquire into the ground of the expectation. This was lying by till after a trial, in order to make an objection if the verdict should be for the plaintiff." The rule was discharged.

There is another rule upon this subject, which it is material *particularly* to mention; although it may be collected from almost all the cases, that have already been quoted: and it is applicable to each of the three branches, into which this chapter has been divided. Wherever there has been an allegation of a falsehood, a concealment of circumstances, or a misrepresentation, it is immaterial, whether such allegation or concealment be the act of the person himself who is interested, or of his agent; for in either case, the contract is founded in deception, and the policy is consequently void. The reason of this rule is nothing more than that, which the law of *England* has for general convenience adopted, in treating of the relation between master and servant; declaring, that the master must always be responsible for the act of his servant, if done by his *express* or *implied* command. It would indeed be of very mischievous consequence, if a man might shelter himself from responsibility of any kind, by throwing the blame upon his agent: it would be to allow him to contradict a maxim of law, which says that no man shall be suffered to make any advantage of his own wrong: and would overturn that wise principle of equity, that when one or two innocent persons (for the master may without danger to the argument be supposed innocent) must suffer by the fraud or negligence of a third, he, who gave credit to that third person, shall bear the consequences arising from the confidence so reposed. If this be true, and it cannot be denied, of contracts in general, it must also be admitted in those of insurance, where, from the very nature of the case, the business is sel-

dom

CHAP. X.

dom transacted by the parties themselves; but is most commonly effected by the interposition of agents or brokers. The courts of justice have accordingly held, that any fraud in the agent of the insured vitiates and annuls the contract, as much as direct fraud in the insured himself: and this, although the act cannot be traced at all to the owner of the property; or even though he should be perfectly innocent.

Stewart and others v. Dunlop and others, H. Lords, det. Apr. 8, 1785.

In a case before the House of Lords, so late as the year 1785, this doctrine was confirmed. It came before the House on an appeal from the Court of Sessions in *Scotland*, which had determined in favour of the respondents, the underwriters. The case was shortly this: a man having arrived at *Greenock*, knowing of the loss of the ship insured, and meeting a friend and intimate acquaintance of the insured, and a partner with him in some other adventures, communicated the intelligence of the loss of the ship to him, *who desired it might be concealed*. The same day, as appeared by the evidence, the person, who had received this information, held a conversation with the plaintiff's clerk, who made this deposition "that neither at that time, nor at any other time of "the said day, had he any other conversation whatever with "the said Mr. *Boog*, or message from him, either in writing "or otherwise, relative to the *Peggy* (the ship insured,) nor "did he get *any hint* from him, or any other person, relative "to the making insurance upon her, further than the said "Mr. *Boog's asking the deponent if he knew whether there was "any insurance made upon her*, and if there was any account "of her." After this conversation, the plaintiff desired the clerk to write to get an insurance effected, which he did, without stating a word (at least it did not appear that he stated any) of this conversation to his master. Upon the whole of the evidence in this cause, although it did not appear by any deposition that the plaintiff knew of the loss of the ship, at the time he made the insurance, the Lords of Session decreed, "that the insurance made by the plaintiff would "not have been made, if the brigantine *Henrietta* had not "arrived in the road of *Greenock* the day preceding, and "brought intelligence that the ship *Peggy* was taken; and "therefore that the policy was void." The House of Lords confirmed this decree.

In

In the decisions of the House of Lords, the reasons of the judgment never appear; and even when the learned judges give their opinions upon any cause then depending in that house, authentic reports of them are not easily obtained: the consequence of this is, that one is frequently left to conjecture, upon what grounds the decree was pronounced. If we may be allowed to conjecture upon the case of *Stewart* v. *Dunlop*, it should seem, that as no direct or positive act of knowledge was brought home to the plaintiff himself, the conversation which the clerk had with Mr. *Boog*, was held to be a sufficient proof, that the loss was known to him, at the time he wrote the letter, at the desire of the plaintiff, ordering the insurance. If known to the clerk, the act of the agent, in such a case, becomes the act of the principal; because the law, upon general reasons of policy, will presume, that the principal must know whatever has come to the knowledge of the agent.

But in the end of the same year, a case was decided in the King's Bench, expressly upon the point of fraud in the agent; for it appeared that the insured was not guilty of any improper conduct in the transaction. In that case, the circumstances were numerous; and the judges gave their opinions *seriatim* upon the question.

It was an action on a policy of insurance for 110*l.* underwritten by the defendant on the 21st of *September*, 1782, at six guineas *per cent.* on a cargo of oats on board the ship *Joseph*, lost or not lost, at and from *Hartland* to *Portsmouth*, beginning the adventure from the loading thereof on board the said ship at *Hartland*. The defendant pleaded the general issue, and paid the premium into court. This cause came on to be tried before Mr. Justice *Buller* at *Guildhall*, when a verdict was found for the plaintiff, subject to the opinion of the court upon the following case.

Fitzherbert v. Mather, 1 Term Rep. p. 12.

That on the 27th of *July*, 1782, *William Bundock* of *Pool*, agent for the plaintiff, contracted with *Richard Thomas* of *Hartland*, a corn factor, for the purchase of 500 quarters of oats, to be consigned to *William Fuller*, at *Portsmouth*, on plaintiff's account; and desired *Thomas* to send him (*Bundock*) a bill

CHAP. X.

a bill of lading and invoice, and alſo a like bill of lading and invoice to the plaintiff at Mr. *Fiſher*'s at the *Tower*, *London*. That in purſuance thereof, *Thomas* ſhipped the oats on board the ſhip inſured, which ſailed from *Hartland on the 16th of September* 1782, and was loſt *the ſame day* off the pier of *Hartland*. That on *the 16th of September* 1782, *Thomas* wrote the two following letters to *William Bundock*, and to *Fiſher*.

To Mr. WILLIAM BUNDOCK.

SIR, *Hartland*, *Sept.* 16*th*, 1782.

This morning I loaded the *Joſeph* with 175 quarters of oats to the addreſs of *William Fuller*, *Portſmouth*, *and the ſloop ſailed immediately*; but I am afraid the wind is coming to the weſtward, and will force her back. I have ſent a bill of loading, and a letter, by the maſter, to Mr. *Fuller*; and alſo a bill of loading, and advice to Mr. *Fiſher*, that *he may inſure*, if he likes, as the equinox is near, &c.

R. THOMAS.

To CUTHBERT FISHER, Eſq.

SIR, *Hartland*, *Sept.* 16*th*, 1782.

By an order from Mr. *William Bundock* of *Pool*, I ſhipped this day on board the *Joſeph*, which immediately ſet ſail for *Portſmouth*, a cargo of oats as under; and by the ſame order, *as well as the order of Thomas Fitzherbert*, Eſq. I took the liberty of drawing on you at three days ſight, in favour of Meſſrs. *Scott* and *Willes*, or order, 106*l*. to be placed to the account of *Thomas Fitzherbert*, Eſq. *I wiſh the whole ſafe to hand*, and expect another veſſel to be loaded this week, weather permitting: this evening appears ſtormy.

R. THOMAS.

Then follows the bill of lading. The caſe further ſtates, that about *ſix* or *ſeven* o'clock of *the evening of the* 16*th of* September, Thomas *heard a report that the ſhip was on ſhore: and at ſix o'clock in the morning of the* 17*th*, *he knew the ſhip was loſt*. That the mode of ſending letters from *Hartland* to *London* is as follows: the letters are collected by a private hand, about

about one or two o'clock of the day, on which the post sets out from *Biddeford*, from which place it goes about nine o'clock in the evening. That the 16th of *September* was not a post day; *and the above letters did not leave* Hartland *till one o'clock in the afternoon of the* 17*th*, which was the post day from *Biddeford* to *London*: and the letters which went from *Biddeford* by the post of that evening, were received in *London* on the 20th of *September*. That on the 19th, the plaintiff wrote the following letter to *Fisher*.

Stubb-Lodge, Portsmouth, Sept. 19*th*, 1782.

Dear *Fisher*,

My correspondent, Mr. *Bundock*, having informed me, that he has sent two sloops to *Hartland* in *Devonshire*, to load oats on my account and risk, I beg the favour of you to insure my amount of the cargoes to *Portsmouth*, as soon as the bills are sent you. T. FITZHERBERT.

That the last mentioned letter, together with the former from *Thomas*, dated *September* 16th, we received by *Fisher* in *London*, on the 20th of *September*; and he thereupon directed the insurance in question to be effected: that on the 21st, the defendant subscribed the policy. Upon this case, after argument at the bar,

Lord *Mansfield* said: "this policy is effected by misrepresentation, and that misrepresentation arises *from the proper agent* of the plaintiff, who gives the intelligence. Now whether this happened by fraud or negligence, it makes no difference; for in either case the policy is void. As to the misrepresentation, the underwriter was warranted on the information of the agent to take for granted, that the ship was safe at 12 or 1 o'clock of the 17th of *September*; for the agent gives an account of the ship being loaded, and says, "I wish the whole "safe to hand." Then there was strong ground to believe on his letter, that she was safe when the post came away; and the post-mark shews the day when the letters were sent. How does this misrepresentation come? Why from *Thomas*, who writes to *Fisher*, and gives him notice of the ship's sailing, on purpose that he may insure; for so he says expressly in his letter to *Bundock*. He was honest at the time he wrote the

CHAP. X.

the letter; but on the 16th, at night, he hears that the ſhip is gone aſhore, and the next morning he knew that ſhe was abſolutely loſt. The poſt did not go out till the afternoon of that day; and he had full opportunity to ſend an account of the loſs. If *Thomas* were not guilty of fraud, at leaſt he was guilty of groſs negligence: but either way, if *Thomas* were perfectly innocent, this policy, being effected by miſrepreſentation, is void."

Mr. Juſtice *Willes*.—"*Thomas* is moſt clearly to be conſidered as the agent of the plaintiff. He ſhews by his letter to *Fiſher*, that he acts as well by the orders of *Fitzherbert* as of *Bundock*. If then *Thomas* be the agent of the plaintiff, he is moſt certainly liable for his miſrepreſentations: and in this caſe the miſrepreſentation is groſs."

Mr. Juſtice *Aſhhurſt*.—"On principles of policy, it is neceſſary that a man ſhould be anſwerable for the acts of his agent. It is often difficult to prove the privity of knowledge; and therefore the law will preſume, that facts known to the one, are alſo within the knowledge of the other. Nor is there any hardſhip on the plaintiff; for if this fact had been known, the policy could not have been effected."

Mr. Juſtice *Buller*.—"In order to ſhew, that *Thomas* was not the agent of the plaintiff, the counſel has aſſumed a fact, which is contrary to the caſe; for it is ſaid, that the inſurance was not made in conſequence of *Thomas*'s letter. But what is the fact? The plaintiff's letter to *Fiſher* deſires him to inſure, as ſoon as the bills of lading are ſent. By whom were they to be ſent? By *Thomas*; then he refers to *Thomas* for all the information, and as the foundation of the inſurance. The plaintiff, I dare ſay, is innocent; and ſo is the defendant. But if the plaintiff build his information on that of his agent, and his agent be guilty of a miſrepreſentation, the principal muſt ſuffer. It is the common queſtion every day at *Guildhall*, when one of two innocent perſons muſt ſuffer by the fraud or negligence of a third, which of the two gave credit. In this caſe, the plaintiff truſted; not the defendant: *Thomas* had very material information, which he did

did not communicate; the consequence of which is, that the policy is void, and the *postea* must be delivered to the defendant."

From these cases, the principle, which we sought to establish, is evident, *viz.* that whether the fraud or misrepresentation be the act of the insured, or of his agent, the policy is void, and the contract between the parties is vacated and annulled.

To have troubled the reader with all the cases that have come to trial upon the ground of fraud, would have swelled this chapter to the size of a volume; and at the same time would be wholly unnecessary, as every case of fraud must depend upon its own circumstances. It was thought sufficient to lay down the general principles, which the courts have adopted upon the subject, and which are applicable to each division of it as stated in the beginning of this chapter; and to cite two or three cases under each head, in order to confirm and illustrate the positions and principles advanced.

But as fraud is a charge of a very serious nature, materially affecting a man's credit, character and reputation, the law of *England* will never presume that any one is guilty of it; nor set aside a contract on that ground, unless it be *fully and satisfactorily* proved. The consequence of this favourable presumption is, that the burden of proof lies upon the person, who wishes to avail himself of the fraudulent conduct imputed. Thus if the insured is supposed to be guilty of fraud, the proof of it falls upon the underwriter; because he is the person, who is to derive a benefit from substantiating the charge. This is not only the law of *England*, but the law of common sense, founded on principles of equity and justice. Although it has been said, that fraud will not be presumed, unless it be *fully and satisfactorily proved*, it is not intended to convey an idea, that there must be a *positive* and *direct* proof of fraud, in order to annul the contract. The nature of the thing itself, which is generally carried on in a secret and clandestine manner, does not admit of such evidence; and therefore, if no proof but that of actual fraud were allowed in such cases, much mischief and villany would ensue, and pass with impunity. Circumstantial evidence is all that can be expected; and indeed, all that is

Roccus, Not. 51. 78.

 necessary

CHAP. X.

neceſſary to ſubſtantiate ſuch a charge. The prejudice entertained againſt receiving circumſtantial evidence, is carried to a pitch wholly inexcuſable. In the caſe before us, we have already ſhewn, it muſt be received; becauſe the nature of the inquiry for the moſt part admits of no other, and conſequently it is the beſt poſſible evidence that can be given. But taking it in a more general ſenſe, a concurrence of circumſtances (which we muſt always ſuppoſe to be properly authenticated, otherwiſe they weigh nothing) forms a ſtronger ground of belief, than poſitive and direct teſtimony generally affords; eſpecially when unconfirmed by circumſtances. The reaſon of this is obvious: a poſitive allegation may be founded in miſtake, or, what is too common, in the prejury of the witneſs: but circumſtances cannot lie; and a long chain of well connected fabricated circumſtances, requires an ingenuity and ſkill rarely to be met with; and ſuch a conſiſtency in thoſe who come to ſupport thoſe circumſtances, by their oaths, as the annals of our courts of juſtice can ſeldom produce. Beſides, circumſtantial evidence is much more eaſily diſcuſſed, and much more eaſily contradicted by teſtimony, if falſe, than the poſitive and direct allegation of a fact, which, being confined to the knowledge of an individual, cannot poſſibly be the ſubject of contradiction founded merely on preſumption and probability.

Another queſtion upon this ſubject remains to be diſcuſſed; and that is, whether the underwriter is bound to return the premium, or is liable to an action for it, in a caſe where fraud has been proved againſt the inſured; and conſequently where the contract is void, and no riſk has been run. The ordinances of *France* declare, that if fraud be proved againſt the inſured, he ſhall be obliged to reſtore to the inſurer that, which he has received from him, and alſo to pay him double the premium: and if fraud be proved againſt the inſurer, he ſhall in like manner be liable to reſtore the premium, and to pay double the ſum inſured to the owner of the property. A learned commentator upon theſe ordinances obſerves, that if this article ſuppoſe a full conviction of the crime, the puniſhment is too ſmall; and that here the puniſhment of the aſſurer and aſſured is nearly equal, although the crime of the aſſured is much greater, when the difference between the premium, and the value of the property is conſidered. Indeed, the idea of enriching one man by the puniſhment of another

Ord. of Lew. 14. tit. Inſ. art. 41.

2 Valin, 96.

CHAP. X.

other is itſelf a ſtrange one, and ſomewhat inconſiſtent with the preſent notions of criminal juſtice. The ground upon which it has been introduced into the edicts of *France* upon inſurances, muſt have been this, that as the inſurer in one caſe, and the inſured in the other, runs a conſiderable riſk by fraudulent allegations or concealments, they ſhall ſeverally be entitled to the ſums ſtated in the ordinance, as a recompenſe for the riſk they ſo incurred.

The law of *England* has hitherto been ſilent upon this ſubject, there being no poſitive declaration of the legiſlature reſpecting it: and our courts of juſtice had not till lately adopted any general rule, with reſpect to the return of premium in caſes of fraud. In two or three inſtances in the Court of Chancery where the underwriters have been relieved from the payment of the ſums inſured, on account of fraud, the decree has directed the premium to be returned.

Whittingham v. Thornborough, Precedents in Chancery, p. 20. and 2 Vern. 206.

Thus in a caſe in the year 1690, the defendant and others had come to the inſurance office and bought a policy for inſuring the life of one *Horwell*, (upon whoſe life they had no concern or intereſt depending) for a year; and the policy ran whether intereſted or not intereſted, at a premium of 5*l. per cent.* They took this way of drawing in ſubſcribers: they agreed with one *Marwood*, a known merchant upon the Exchange, and a leading man in ſuch caſes to ſubſcribe firſt; but in caſe *Horwell* died within the year, *Marwood* was to loſe nothing, but on the contrary was to ſhare what ſhould be gained from the other ſubſcribers. Upon the credit of *Marwood*'s ſubſcribing, ſeveral others (who had inquired of *Marwood* about *Horwell*, who was his neighbour) ſubſcribed likewiſe. *Horwell* lived about four months, and then died; and this bill was brought to be relieved againſt the policy: and this matter being all confeſſed by the anſwer, the court decreed the policy to be delivered up, *and the premium to be repaid.*

Da Coſta v. Scandret, 2 P. Wil. 170. Vide ante, p. 179.

So alſo in the caſe of *Da Coſta* v. *Scandret*, which has already been cited in a former part of this chapter, Lord *Macclesfield*, although he held the policy to be void, on the ground of fraud, decreed the premium to be returned to the inſured.

It is true, that during the argument in the caſe next to be quoted, the counſel cited a caſe of *Rucker* v. *Hollingbury*, in

 which

CHAP. X.

which the Master of the Rolls had been of a different opinion from that delivered in the two preceding cases. But Lord *Mansfield* said, that there must be some mistake in reciting the case before the Master of the Rolls; for the practice of the Court of Chancery was certainly agreeable to the two former cases.

Wilson v. Duckett, 3 Burr. 1361.

The case, in which this observation was made, was an action on a policy of insurance on a ship, with a count of a general *indebitatus assumpsit* for money had and received to the plaintiff's use: and damages were laid at 98*l*. The trial was had under a decree of the Court of Chancery, where the now defendant, the insurer, being there complainant, *had offered to pay back the premium, which was* 10*l*. No money was, in the present case, paid into court; though the usual course in these cases is for the defendant, the insurer, to bring the premium into court. The jury found a verdict for the plaintiff, for the ten pounds premium, on the count for money had and received to his use; although they were of opinion against the policy, upon the foot of fraud; and found against it, as being fraudulent. In fact, the first underwriter was only a decoy-duck, to induce other persons to underwrite the policy: and it had been previously agreed between the insured and him, that he should not be bound by signing the policy; which this court considered as a fraud, and therefore that the jury had given a right verdict in finding the policy fraudulent. With the concurrence of Lord *Mansfield*, (before whom this cause was tried) and of the counsel on both sides, it was agreed to bring this question before the court, Whether, upon a policy of insurance being found fraudulent, the premium should be returned to the plaintiff (the insured) or retained by the defendant (the insurer.) The cases abovementioned were quoted by the counsel for the plaintiff; but they, being all in Chancery, Lord *Mansfield* said, he wanted to know whether there was any common law determination to the same effect. As it did not appear that there was, his lordship said, It was plain what must be done in this case; for he looked upon *the offer made* by the complainant's bill in equity, to be the same thing as if the money had *actually been brought into court* in the present case.

But

CHAP. X.

But although the common law has been so silent upon the subject, as not to lay down any general rule; and although in all the cases stated, the premium was restored; yet if the fraud is notorious, palpable, and gross in its nature, the court may order, and has ordered the underwriter to retain the premium.

Thus where an action was brought by the insured to recover 150*l.* being the amount of the defendant's subscription; the ground of refusal was, that the insurance was fraudulent; and that the plaintiff knew of the loss of the ship at the time of effecting the policy. The counsel for the plaintiff were under the necessity of admitting that their client had made some fraudulent insurances upon this very ship, subsequent to the one now in dispute; but contended that news of the loss of the ship had not arrived, till after this particular one was effected. The evidence, however, was so strong as easily to convince the jury, that the plaintiff had received information of the loss before the order for making the insurance was given to the broker; and they found a verdict for the defendant. Tyler v. Horne, Sittings at Guildhall after Hil. T. 1785.

Lord *Mansfield* said, The fraud was so gross, that the premium should not be recovered from the underwriter.

At last this great question came to be expressly decided, where the agent of the assured only had been the guilty person; and the whole Court of King's Bench were of opinion, that in all cases of *actual* fraud on the part of the assured or his agent, the underwriter might retain the premium. Chapman and others, Assignees of Kennet, v. Fraser, B. R. Trin. 33 Geo. III.

It is proper also here to observe, that it has been laid down as clear law, that if the underwriter has been guilty of fraud, an action lies against him, at the suit of the insured, to recover the premium. Thus it was said by lord *Mansfield*, in the case of *Carter* v. *Boehm*, which has already been quoted at large in this chapter: "the policy would be void against the "underwriter, if he concealed any thing; as, if he insur- "ed a ship on her voyage, which he privately knew to be ar- "rived; and *an action would lie to recover the premium.*" 3 Burr. 1909.

By several of the foreign ordinances, the punishment of fraud, in matters of insurance, is exceedingly severe. By those Ord. of Amsterdam, art. 56. 2 Mag. 146.

CHAP. X.

those of *Amsterdam* it is declared, "that as contracts of insurance are contracts of good faith, wherein no fraud or deceit ought to take place, in case it be found, that the insured or insurers, captains, shippers, pilots, or others used fraud, deceit or craft, they shall not only forfeit by their deceit and craft, but shall also be liable to the loss and damage occasioned thereby, and be corporally punished for a terror and example to others; *even with death*, as pirates and manifest thieves, if it be found that they have used notorious malversation or craft." [219] The ordinances of *Middleburg* contain a provision exactly in the same words. At *Stockholm* also, it has been declared, that such an offender, besides restitution to the party injured, shall, according to the circumstances of every particular affair, be punished in his estate, honour, and life.

Art. 30. 2 Mag. 76. 2 Mag. 288.

Frauds in contracts of insurance have not as yet had any punishment affixed to them by the laws of *England*, that I have been able to learn: but there are one or two cases which have been declared to be felonies by positive statutes, where the act committed has been to the prejudice of the underwriters.

1 Ann. st. 2. c. 9. s. 4.

By a statute in the reign of queen *Anne*, it was enacted, that if any captain, master, mariner, or other officer, belonging to any ship, shall wilfully cast away, burn, or otherwise destroy, the ship, unto which he belongeth, or procure the same to be done, to the prejudice of the owner or owners thereof, or of any merchant or merchants that shall load goods thereon, (or by a subsequent statute, to the prejudice of any person or persons that shall underwrite any policy or policies of insurance thereon) shall suffer death as a felon; and the benefit of clergy is taken away from this offence by 11 *Geo.* I. *ch.* 29.

4 Geo. I. c. 12. s. 3.

These are the only provisions, which the legislature of this country has, as yet, thought proper to make for the prevention of crimes of this enormity: but as the records of our courts of justice evidently prove that frauds are too frequent in policies of insurance, greater severity than merely annulling the contract seems necessary, in order to put a stop to such offences.

CHAPTER the ELEVENTH.

Of Sea-Worthinefs.

HAVING, in the preceding chapter, treated very fully of the influence which fraud has upon the contract of infurance; we proceed to fhew, that other circumftances, in which no fraud whatever can be difcovered, or even fufpected, will alfo vitiate and annul the policy. Of this nature is the doctrine of Sea-Worthinefs. Upon this point it has been determined, that every fhip infured muft, at the time of the infurance, be able to perform the voyage, unlefs fome external accident fhould happen; and if fhe have a latent defect wholly unknown to the parties, that will vacate the contract, and the infurers are difcharged. This doctrine is founded upon that general principle of infurance law, that the infurers fhall not be refponfible for any lofs arifing from the infufficient or defective quality or condition of the thing infured.

There is in the contract of infurance a tacit and implied agreement that every thing fhall be in that ftate and condition, in which it ought to be: and therefore it is not fufficient for the infured to fay, that he did not know that the fhip was not fea-worthy; for he *ought* to know that fhe was fo, at the time he made the infurance. The fhip is the *fubftratum* of the contract between the parties; a fhip not capable of performing the voyage, is the fame as if there were no fhip at all; and although the defect may not be known to the perfon infured, yet the very foundation of the contract being gone, the law is clearly in favour of the underwriter; becaufe fuch a defect is not the confequence of any external misfortune, or any unavoidable accident, arifing from the perils of the fea, or any other rifk, againft which the underwriter engages to indemnify the perfon infured. To fupport a contrary doctrine would introduce a variety of frauds, as it would probably fubject the underwriter to account for the lofs, diminution, or wafte, which may happen from the

CHAP. XI.

the neceſſary and ordinary uſe of the thing inſured; or the wear and tear of the ſhip in the common courſe of the voyage: and all of theſe are riſks, to which the inſurer has never been conſidered as expoſed. From what has been ſaid, it appears, that the ground of deciſion in this caſe is perfectly diſtinct from any principle of fraud: that it depends merely upon this, that the inſured is preſumed to be better acquainted with the ſtate and condition of his ſhip than any other man; and that he has tacitly undertaken, that ſhe is in a condition to perform the deſtined voyage. But although the inſured ought to know whether his ſhip was ſea-worthy or not at the time ſhe ſet out upon her voyage; yet he may not be able to know the condition ſhe may be in, after ſhe is out a twelvemonth: and therefore, whenever it can be made appear, that the decay, to which the loſs is attributable, did not commence till a period ſubſequent to the inſurance, as ſhe was ſea-worthy at the time, the underwriter, it is preſumed, would be liable. Indeed, in a very late caſe upon another point, but where the ſame principle was much relied upon, Lord *Mansfield* ſaid, "By an implied warranty every "ſhip inſured muſt be tight, ſtaunch, and ſtrong; but it is "ſufficient if ſhe be ſo at the time of her ſailing. She may "ceaſe to be ſo in twenty-four hours after departure, and yet "the underwriter will continue liable."* Every caſe of this kind, it is true, muſt depend upon its own circumſtances; but when they are once aſcertained, the rule of law is clear and deciſive. The only material caſe upon this ſubject in the law of *England* is that of the *Mills Frigate*, which underwent a variety of diſcuſſion in ſeveral courts, and was finally determined in favour of the inſurers. I have uſed my utmoſt endeavours to procure a copy of the opinions of the judges upon that caſe, but they have been ineffectual: therefore the reader muſt be ſatisfied with a full ſtatement of the circumſtances, as they appeared upon the demurrer to the evidence,

5 Burr. 2804.

Eden v. Parkinſon, Doug. 708.

* But if a ſhip ſail upon a voyage, and in a day or two becomes leaky, and founders, or is obliged to return to port, without any ſtorm, or viſible or adequate cauſe to produce ſuch an effect, the preſumption is, that ſhe was not ſea-worthy when ſhe failed; and the jury, upon the plaintiff's own caſe, may draw ſuch a concluſion. *Munro and another* v. *Vandam*. Sittings at Guildhall before Lord Kenyon after Michaelmas Term, 1794.

CHAP. XI.

dence, and with the judgment given upon that demurrer, as it is recorded.

Before the proceedings in this caſe are ſtated, it will be neceſſary to mention, that an action had been brought in the court of Common Pleas on the ſame policy againſt one of the underwriters; and Lord *Camden*, who tried that cauſe, directed the jury to find a verdict for the plaintiff: but upon a motion for a new trial, his Lordſhip declared, that he had changed his opinion; and the whole court of Common Pleas laid down the principles above ſtated, and directed a new trial. Upon the ſecond trial, Lord *Camden* ſtated to the jury the opinion he had formed upon the ſubject, and a verdict was accordingly given for the defendant, which, upon a ſubſequent application, the court of Common Pleas refuſed to ſet aſide. The plaintiffs then commenced a new action in the court of Exchequer againſt another of the underwriters, and which is now the ſubject of our attention. [222]

Mills and another v. Roebuck. In the Excheq.

This was an action on a policy of inſurance, loſt or not loſt, at and from the *Leeward Iſlands* to *London*, warranted to ſail on or before the 26th of *July*, upon any kind of goods, wares, and merchandizes; and alſo upon the body, tackle, *&c.* of and in *the good ſhip or* veſſel called the *Mills Frigate*, beginning the adventure on the goods from the loading thereof on board the ſaid ſhip at *St. Kitts*, and upon the ſhip from her arrival at the *Leeward Iſlands*. The defendant undertakes to indemnify againſt the uſual riſks, for a premium of *2l. 10s. per cent.* The loſs was deſcribed in the firſt count of the declaration in theſe words: "That "the ſaid ſhip, after her departure from *Nevis* on her "voyage, and during her ſaid voyage, ſailing and proceed-"ing on the high ſeas by and through the force of winds and "tempeſtuous weather, and by and through the mere perils "and dangers of the ſeas, ſprung divers leaks, and became "very leaky, crippled, bulged, disjointed, ſplit, and wholly "loſt." In the ſecond count the loſs is alleged thus: "by and through the mere perils and dangers of the "ſeas, and by the ſtarting and looſening of one or more "plank or planks of the ſaid ſhip, and by accidentally "ſpringing one or more leak or leaks, the ſaid ſhip became "very leaky, crippled, *&c.* and totally unable to proceed on, "or perform the ſaid voyage." There were two other

counts

CHAP. XI. counts in the declaration upon a policy on freight to recover from the underwriter the amount of his insurance upon that also; and a fifth count for money had and received to the plaintiff's use. The defendant pleaded the general issue; with a notice of set off, having paid the premiums into court.

[223] This cause came on to be tried before Lord Chief Baron *Parker*; and the defendant demurred to the evidence produced on the part of the plaintiff. The demurrer follows in these words: Thereupon the said *John* and *Thomas Mills* (the plaintiffs) shew in evidence to the jury to prove and maintain the issue within mentioned on their part, to wit, that the defendant underwrote the policy of insurance, and that the plaintiffs were interested to the amount as in the declaration is mentioned: That the ship in question was a *French* built ship, and known to be so to the defendant at the time he underwrote the said policy: That the timbers of *French* ships are usually fastened with iron bolts or spikes, which are liable to grow rusty; and when the same are grown rusty, the timbers of such ships frequently become loose at once, and the ships are rendered incapable of bearing the sea, without any perceptible symptoms of decay: That the ship in question was purchased by the plaintiffs in the year 1757: that since that time she has been generally employed by the plaintiffs, who are *West India* merchants, in that trade; and large sums have constantly been insured on her and her cargoes: That in *February* 1764, being bound to the *Leeward Islands*, and back again to *London*, she sailed on her voyage: that before she sailed from *London* on that voyage, the plaintiffs ordered the captain to have every thing done to the ship, which he should think proper to repair her: That in pursuance of such orders, the ship was put into dock and repaired, where the ship carpenter did all such repairs to her as he was ordered, the expenses of which amounted to about 100*l.* of which about 30*l.* was for the sheathing and other repairs of her hull, and the residue in her upper works: that nothing more appeared to the ship carpenter, or the captain, to be wanting to make her fit and complete for the said voyage; but her iron bolts and spikes were not then examined, which could not be done without taking off her sheathing; an act never done where (as the case is here) the ship had been sheathed a little time before;

before: that *George Haley*, Esq. the firſt underwriter on this policy, and many other perſons by whom policies of inſurance are generally underwritten, keep a regiſter, in which the ſhips uſually inſured by them, are entered with an account of the age, conſtruction, and viſible goodneſs of the veſſels, and to whom they belong, and alſo employ a ſurveyor, whoſe buſineſs it is to ſurvey ſuch ſhips: that the ſhip in queſtion, at [224] the time of underwriting the policy, and long before, had been entered in ſuch regiſter; and previous to her laſt outward bound voyage, had been ſurveyed by one *Thomas Whitewood*, who was then employed by the ſaid *George Hayley*, and other underwriters, as ſuch ſurveyor; and, as far as appeared to the ſaid *Thomas Whitewood*, was in good condition, and perfectly fit to undertake a voyage to and from the *Leeward Iſlands*; but the ſurveyor did not, neither could he, examine the bolts and ſpikes for the reaſons aforeſaid; but did ſurvey as far as is ever practiſed in ſuch caſes: that the ſaid *George Hayley* had often before underwrote policies on the ſaid ſhip and her cargoes; and the witneſs, who was the inſurance broker, ſaid he believed Mr. *Hayley* knew as much of the condition of the ſhip as the plaintiffs did, and particularly on the outward bound voyage to the *Leeward Iſlands*, he underwrote 400*l.* on this ſhip: that in ſuch laſt outward bound voyage, the ſhip met with a great deal of bad weather; was very leaky, and could not get into *Madeira*, where ſhe was ordered to touch; but was obliged to bear away for the iſland of *Nevis*: that ſhe arrived at the iſland of *Nevis* on the firſt of *April* 1764, and from thence went to the iſland of *St. Chriſtopher*, where ſhe delivered her outward bound cargo, and had ſuch repairs done to her, as were then thought neceſſary, and to all appearance put into a proper condition for her voyage home; but her bolts and ſpikes were not, nor could be examined there: that about the end of the ſaid month of *April*, the ſhip failed from *St. Kitts* to *Nevis*, where the captain had been promiſed a loading for her home: that on her arrival at *Nevis*, the planters knowing that ſhe had been leaky in her outward bound voyage, were not willing to put ſugars on board her; and that in order to ſatisfy the planters there, that ſhe was in a proper condition to carry a cargo of ſugars to *London*, they propoſed to the captain, as a meaſure which would be fully ſatisfactory to them, that he ſhould ſubmit the ſhip to be ſurveyed by all the captains then in

CHAP. XI.

the harbour, being fix in number; and told him, that if they fhould report her to be fit for a voyage to *London*, they would then load her with fugars: that the captain did fubmit to fuch furvey, though it would have been for the intereft of the faid captains to report the fhip unfit for the voyage; as by that means they would have had an opportunity of gaining more freight and fooner: that on the [225] eighth day of *May* 1764, the faid captains, after having furveyed her carefully, but without examining her bolts and fpikes, which could not be done, there figned the following report: "*Nevis, May* 8th, 1764. At the requeft of captain *George Finch*, of the fhip *Mills Frigate*, we the fubfcribers did repair on board the faid fhip, and after due examination, it did appear to us, that the occafion of the fhip's making more water than ufual on her voyage from *London* to this place, was occafioned by fome neglect in caulking the faid fhip, which may very eafily be made tight, the faid fhip otherwife appearing to us to be ftrong and found; and when caulked, we are of opinion, will be fully fufficient to carry a cargo of fugars to *London*. *John Sheperd, &c.*" That afterwards the fhip was caulked according to the faid report, and that thereupon the planters fent their fugars on board, and the fhip was foon loaded with about three hundred and feventy hogfheads of fugar: that during the time of her loading, and until and at the time of her failing, which was about two months, the fhip continued tight, appeared to be in good condition, and made no more water than the beft fhips ufually do, and are expected to do: that the fhip failed from *Nevis* on the 26th day of *July* 1764, about eight o'clock in the evening, and the next day, about four o'clock in the afternoon, without any bad weather or extraordinary fwell of the fea, fhe fprang a leak, and the captain was obliged to bear away for *St. Chriftophers*, where he arrived on the 28th of *July*; that on his arrival there, he got the fhip unloaded to fee what was the matter with her, when it appeared that fhe had ftarted a plank: that he thereupon applied to the judge of the Court of Vice Admiralty for a warrant to furvey faid fhip; and a warrant was granted to four captains, and two fhip carpenters, or any three of them; four of whom did, according to fuch warrant, furvey the faid fhip, and did report, that fhe was unfit to proceed on her voyage without being thoroughly repaired; and that the expenfe of fo repairing her there, would

amount

amount to more than the value of the ſhip and freight; and ſhe was therefore condemned by the ſaid court as unfit for the ſaid voyage: that ſome of the iron bolts and ſpikes, with which the timbers of the ſhip in queſtion, like other *French* built ſhips, were faſtened, were broken in the plank that was ſo ſtarted, which the captain and the ſaid ſurveyors felt, by paſſing up their hands between the plank and the ſhip; and which appeared upon farther opening the ends of the plank; and that the ſaid plank was ſtarted from one end to the other: that it was owing to the ſaid bolts and ſpikes being grown ruſty and decayed, as then appeared to the captain and ſurveyors, that ſuch plank ſtarted: that he believed the ſurveyors, who condemned her, thought the ſame; wherefore, and ſuppoſing the other bolts and ſpikes in the ſhip were alſo grown ruſty and decayed, though that could not be known for certain, without ripping off her planks, and making a more ſtrict examination, the ſurveyors made their ſaid report of condemnation: that the ſaid plank was not taken off, nor could it be, without ſinking the ſhip, but continues at *St. Chriſtophers* as a hulk; that on the aforeſaid account, it was then concluded, and is now believed by the captain, *that the ſaid ſhip was not fit for the inſured voyage* home, at the time ſhe ſo ſailed from *Nevis* for *London, though to all outward appearance, ſhe was a very good ſhip, and,* as he then believed, *proper for the voyage;* and ſuch a ſhip as he, *from her outward appearance, ſhould have had no objection to ſail in again;* but had he known the decayed condition of her ſaid bolts and ſpikes before he ſet ſail on his homeward bound voyage, he would not have ventured his life in her: that there is no dock, nor ſcarce any materials for repairing ſhips at *St. Chriſtophers,* nor could ſhe ſail to any other place to be repaired; and that if this misfortune had happened in *North America,* or *England,* where there are proper docks and materials, ſhe might have been repaired for three or four hundred pounds: that while the ſaid ſhip was firſt at *St. Chriſtophers,* before ſhe had taken in her cargo, namely, on the 23d of *April* 1764, the captain wrote the following letter to the plaintiffs: [226]

"Gentlemen, *St. Chriſtophers, April* 23, 1764.

"I take the firſt opportunity of acquainting you, that I "arrived at *Nevis,* after a moſt diſmal paſſage, on the firſt "inſtant.

CHAP. XI.

"instant. On the sixth of *March*, at day-break, I made "the islands *Deserts*, distant about four leagues, ran down "for *Madeira*, with a fresh gale at E. S. E. till four in the "afternoon, when being within a mile off the shore, and "judging about five or six miles off *Fenchall Road, a very*

[227]

"*hard and dark squall took us suddenly with such violence, that* "*I was obliged to clear off the land under the courses.* It was "excessively hazy the whole evening after, that one could "hardly see the ship's length; so that it would have been "the greatest imprudence to have run the risk of overshoot-"ing our port, or running ashore. The gale increased, and, "in the night, came round to the N. E. and *the ship strained* "*so much by the pressure of sail we were obliged to carry on her in* "*that great sea, that it was with the utmost difficulty we could* "*keep her free.* On the eighth, at nine in the morning, reck-"oning myself nineteen leagues to leeward of *Madeira, our* "*ship so loosened,* that we could not carry sail upon a wind; "and seeing no probability of the wind shifting or abating "enough to give us a chance of beating up, bore away for "*Nevis*, judging it better for the preservation of the whole "than to run any hazard in endeavouring for the *Canaries* in "our weak, leaky, and distressed condition. I have consult-"ed with Mr. *Cottle*, the counsellor here, who advises me "to sell the flour and lime at public vendue, and to carry "the iron hoops, &c. back to *England. As the ship's com-*"*plaint has been chiefly in her upper works, I am obliged to have* "*her new nailed from the wail upwards;* and hope you will "find that what repairs are necessary to be made here, are "conducted with all the frugality circumstances will admit "of."

That the plaintiffs received this letter in *London* on the 13th day of *June* 1764, and, a day or two afterwards, gave it to *Matthew Towgood*, an insurance broker, to get 1,000*l.* insured on the freight home for the use of the owners, and 250*l.* on their fourth part of the said ship: that the said *Towgood* first shewed the policy in question, and the letter to the said *George Hayley*, on the 19th of *June* 1764, who, after reading over the letter, asked him what interest he had to insure; to which the broker answered, ship, freight, and cargo; and that he might write which he pleased: that thereupon the said *George Hayley* said he would underwrite the

ship,

ship, saying she would come home safe enough, notwithstanding the damage which the said letter imported she had received, as it was a summer voyage; but that she would very likely damage her cargo: that the said *George Hayley* was going to underwrite the said policy for 300*l.* on the said ship, and had wrote the figure 3; but on the said *Matthew Towgood*'s telling him, he was a bold man to write three hundred pounds after reading the said letter, the said *George Hayley* struck out the figure 3, and converted it into a 2, and accordingly underwrote the said policy for the sum of two hundred pounds on the said ship: that the said *Matthew Towgood* shewed the said letter to the said defendant *Roebuck*, and all the other underwriters on the said policy, before they underwrote the same; and the said defendant says, that the evidence aforesaid, in manner and form aforesaid, shewn by the plaintiffs to the jury, is not sufficient in law to maintain the issue within joined on the part of the said plaintiffs; and that he the defendant to the evidence aforesaid hath no necessity, nor by the law of the land is obliged to answer. Wherefore he prays judgment, and that the jury may be discharged from giving any verdict upon the issue. [228]

The plaintiffs join in demurrer.

Upon this demurrer, judgment was given in the Court of Exchequer for the underwriter. A writ of error was then brought in the Court of Exchequer Chamber, which was referred to Lord *Mansfield* and Lord Chief Justice *Wilmot*, who, after argument, also reported their opinions to be in favour of the defendants; agreeable to which report, judgment was accordingly pronounced. This is the only account, which can now be given of this case, as the report upon these occasions is generally made in private, and the reasons, upon which it is founded, are not publickly given. But from the above very accurate statement which has been procured from the record, it will appear, that the decision did not turn upon any fraud or concealment of circumstances; but, on the contrary, every thing was done in the most fair and honourable manner, and the underwriter was fully informed of every event, with which the insured was himself acquainted. The case was decided entirely upon the principle of sea-worthiness: that however innocent or unfortunate

CHAP. XI. fortunate the insured might be, yet if the ship was not sea-worthy, at the time of insuring, there was no contract at all between the parties; because the very foundation of the contract, the ship, was in the same condition as if it did not exist. That the conclusion thus drawn from the judgment given in the Exchequer Chamber, is not larger or more ex-[229]tensive than the decision will warrant, is evident from what was said by Lord *Mansfield*, when, upon a subsequent occasion the case of the *Mills Frigate* was relied upon in argument at the bar.

5 Bur. 2802.

In the case of the Earl of *March* v. *Pigot*, which came before the court of King's Bench in the year 1771, the case of the *Mills Frigate* having been mentioned, Lord *Mansfield* said, "The insured ought to know whether his ship was sea-worthy or not, at the time she set out upon her voyage; but how should he know the condition she was in after she had been out a twelvemonth? It is true the proposition laid down by the counsel in that case is merely, "that the case of the "*Mills Frigate* was an insurance upon a ship, which had a "latent defect totally unknown to the parties; and the in-"surers were holden not liable on account of the ship's not "being sea-worthy, though such defect was not known." Lord *Mansfield* is then reported to have said, "I differ totally in opinion from that doctrine;" and yet his Lordship is made to conclude with the sentence above stated, which is in effect the same with that which the reporter has put into the mouth of the counsel; and which in truth contains the whole doctrine of sea-worthiness, when the exception put by Lord *Mansfield* is added, namely, that the insured shall not answer for the sufficiency of the ship, after she has been out a considerable time. The probability is, that the counsel laid down the proposition in more extensive terms than the reporter states it, namely, that if the ship was not sea-worthy *at any time* during the voyage, the insurers would be discharged. By admitting this presumption, the whole will be easily reconciled; for then Lord *Mansfield*'s denial of such extensive doctrine is supported and illustrated by the distinction, which he afterwards takes in the conclusion of the sentence.

It

CHAP. XI.

It is ſingular, that the deciſion, which has occupied the whole of this chapter, ſhould have occaſioned ſo much diſcuſſion at the time it was determined, as that pamphlets were written upon both ſides of the queſtion; eſpecially when it is conſidered, that the doctrine there eſtabliſhed is by no means novel in itſelf, and is entirely conſonant to the laws of all the maritime and commercial nations in *Europe*.

[229 *a*]

The ſea-worthineſs of the ſhip being thus ſhewn to be an implied condition in this ſpecies of contract, it follows of courſe, that, in entering into the engagement, it is not neceſſary that there ſhould be any previous repreſentation of the condition of the ſhip; becauſe, unleſs it be fit for the performance of the voyage inſured, there is no binding contract; and any inſufficiency of the veſſel in a former voyage will not vacate the policy.

Shoolbred *v.* Nutt, Sittings at Guildhall after Hil. 1782.

Thus in an action upon a valued policy of inſurance upon the ſhip *Two Siſters*, and a cargo of wheat and wines, *from Madeira to Charleſtown*. The ſhip had ſailed *from London to Madeira*. The plaintiff, who was owner of the cargo, ordered his broker to procure an inſurance *from Madeira* for the voyage to *Charleſtown*, which was accordingly done; but he did not communicate to his broker or the underwriters two letters which he had received from his captain the day before he effected the inſurance, ſtating, that the ſhip had arrived at *Madeira*, but was very leaky, and that the pipes of wine had been half covered with water. But it was proved at the trial, that the leak had been completely ſtopped before ſhe ſailed from *Madeira*, and of courſe before the commencement of the riſk inſured. In her voyage to *Charleſtown* ſhe was taken, and the plaintiff abandoned.

Lord *Mansfield* told the jury, "that there ſhould be a repreſentation of every thing relating to the riſk, which the underwriter has to run, except it be covered by a warranty. It is a condition, or implied warranty, in every policy, that the ſhip is ſea-worthy; and therefore there need be no repreſentation of that. If ſhe ſail without being ſo, there is no valid policy. Here the leak was ſtopped before ſhe ſailed from *Madeira*, and ſhe ſailed in good condition from thence;

CHAP. XI.

and there is no occasion to ſtate the condition of a ſhip or cargo at the end of her former voyage." There was a verdict for the plaintiff.

Ord. of Lewis 14th, tit. Inſur. art. 12. 2 Val. 80.

In the ordinances of *Lewis* the fourteenth it is declared, that decay, waſte, or loſs, which happens from the internal defect of the thing inſured, ſhall not fall upon the underwriter. A commentator upon theſe ordinances has gone into the reaſon and principle of ſuch a regulation, and has ſhewn the propriety of it. He ſets out by obſerving, that this doctrine is of a date as ancient as the period when the *French* treatiſe called *Le Guidon* was publiſhed, which was about the year 1661, at which time, as appears by a reference to the book itſelf, it was conſidered as a ſettled principle, that loſſes, happening from cauſes of this nature, were not to be a charge upon the underwriter. The ſame author has alſo ſhewn, that ſuch a proviſion is adopted in favour of the inſurers by the ordinances of *Rotterdam* and *Amſterdam*. After ſtating theſe circumſtances, he proceeds to ſay, that when a ſhip is deemed incapable of finiſhing her voyage, the queſtion whether this event is a charge upon the underwriters or not, depends upon another; namely, whether it happened by the violence of the ſea, or other fortuitous circumſtance, or whether the diſability proceeds from age and rottenneſs. This will be determined by the inquiry which was made before the departure of the ſhip, in order to judge, whether it was in a condition to perform the voyage or not: if the latter was the caſe, the inſurers ought not to anſwer. In another part of this work, after laying down the ſame doctrine, he declares, that the indemnity will be void, even though the ſhip has been examined before her departure, and declared capable of performing the voyage; ſince the event has ſhewn clearly, that on account of latent defects it was no longer navigable; that is, if it were proved that parts of the ſhip were ſo rotten, weakened and deſtroyed, that ſhe was not in a proper ſtate to reſiſt the ordinary attacks of wind and ſea, inevitable in every voyage, then the underwriters are diſcharged. The reaſon is, that the examination of the ſhip before her departure extends only to the external parts, becauſe ſhe is not unripped; at leaſt not ſo as to diſcover the interior and latent defects, for which the owner or maſter of the ſhip continues always reſponſible, and that with the greater juſtice, becauſe they cannot be wholly ignorant of the bad ſtate

C. 5. art. 8.

2 Mag. 90. 140. 2 Val. 81.

1 Val. 654.

ſtate of the ſhip: but ſuppoſing them to be ſo, it is the ſame thing, being indiſpenſably bound to provide a good ſhip, able to perform the voyage. CHAP. XI.

The opinion of this learned foreigner is ſupported by two of his countrymen, *Pothier* and *Emerigon*.

Having thus ſhewn that the doctrine of ſea-worthineſs, as eſtabliſhed by the deciſions of our courts of juſtice, is confirmed by the declarations of foreign laws, and by the opinions of foreign writers; it is ſufficient now to ſay, that where the ſhip is not ſea-worthy the policy of inſurance is void, as well where the inſurance is upon the goods to be conveyed in the ſhip, as when it is upon the ſhip itſelf. For whenever a caſe ariſes with reſpect to damage done to goods through the inſufficiency of the ſhip, the queſtion, whether the maſter or owner is liable to make good the loſs, depends upon aſcertaining, whether the ſhip was in a condition to perform the voyage at the time of her departure, or became defective from bad weather, and the perils of the wind and ſea.

Pothier Tr. d'Aſſurance. n. 66. 1 Emerigon, p. 580.

2 Val. 164.

CHAPTER THE TWELFTH.

Of Illegal Voyages.

CHAP. XII.

WE proceed now to the consideration of another circumstance by which the contract of insurance is vacated and anulled *ab initio:* and it is this; that whenever an insurance is made on a voyage expresly prohibited by the common, statute, or maritime law of the country, the policy is of no effect. The principle, upon which such a regulation is founded, is not peculiar to this kind of contract; for it is nothing more than that which destroys all contracts whatsoever: that men can never be presumed to make an agreement forbidden by the laws; and if they should attempt such a thing, it is invalid, and will not receive the assistance of a court of justice to carry it into execution.

The most material case upon this point is that of *Johnson* and *Sutton*, which came on to be argued in the year 1779, and received the solemn opinion of the Court of King's Bench.

Johnson v. Sutton, Doug. 241.

It was an action on a policy of insurance on goods, on board the ship *Venus*, "lost or not lost, at and from *London* to *New York*, warranted to depart with convoy from the channel for the voyage." The cause was tried before Lord *Mansfield* at *Guildhall*, and a verdict was found for the plaintiff. The defendant obtained a rule to shew cause why there should not be a new trial. The facts, upon his Lordship's report, appeared to be these: the ship was cleared for *Halifax* and *New York*. She had provisions on board, which she had a license to carry to *New-York*, under a proviso in the prohibitory act of 16 *Geo.* III. *c.* 5. But *one half of the cargo, including the goods, which were the subject of this insurance, was not licensed*, and was not calculated for the *Halifax* market, but for *New York*. There had been a proclamation by Sir *William Howe* to allow the entry of unlicensed goods at *New York*; and though there were bonds usually given at the

the Cuſtom Houſe here, by which the captain engaged to carry the goods to *Halifax*, thoſe bonds were afterwards cancelled, on producing a certificate from an officer appointed for that purpoſe at *New York*, declaring, that they were landed there. *The commander in chief had no authority under the act of parliament to iſſue ſuch proclamation, or to permit the exportation of unlicenſed goods.* The *Venus* was taken in her paſſage to *New York* by an *American* privateer. The firſt ſection of the ſtatute prohibits all commerce with the province of *New York* (amongſt others) and confiſcates all ſhips and their cargoes, which ſhall be found trading, or going to, or coming from trading with them. In ſection the ſecond, there is a proviſo, excepting ſhips laden with proviſions for the uſe of his majeſty's garriſons or fleets, or for the inhabitants of any town poſſeſſed by his majeſty's troops, provided the maſter ſhall produce a licenſe ſpecifying the voyage, *&c.* and the quantity and ſpecies of proviſions; but by the ſame *proviſo*, it is declared, that goods not licenſed, found on board ſuch ſhip, ſhall be forfeited. After argument, upon the motion for a new trial,

CHAP. XII.

16 Geo. III. c. 5.

Lord *Mansfield* ſaid—"The whole of the plaintiff's caſe goes on an eſtabliſhed practice, directly againſt an act of parliament. If the defendant did not know that the goods were unlicenſed, the objection is fair as between the parties. If he did, he would not deſerve to be favoured. But, however that may be, it was illegal to ſend the goods to *New York*, and, *in pari delicto, potior eſt conditio defendentis*. It is impoſſible to bring this within the caſes cited (*a*), becauſe here there was a direct contravention of the law of the land." The rule for a new trial was made abſolute.

From this caſe much information is to be collected; for, 1ſt. the principle advanced at the beginning of the chapter is eſtabliſhed, that is, that an inſurance of a voyage, which is prohibited by ſtatute, is void. This caſe alſo ſerves to remove a diſtinction, which occurs in a very reſpectable writer. The learned *Roccus* obſerves, that if ſuch an inſurance, as

Roccus de Aſſecurat. n. 128.

(*a*) Theſe were caſes of inſurances on ſhips trading contrary to the revenue laws of foreign countries, of which more will be ſaid hereafter.

CHAP. XII.

as that of which we have been speaking, should be made, *ignorante assecuratore*, the insurer is discharged: from whence we are to infer, that in his opinion, if the insurer was acquainted with the nature of the voyage, he would continue liable. But the doctrine of the Court of King's Bench overturns such a distinction, because the very contract is a nullity, and a court of justice can never lend its authority to substantiate a claim, founded upon a contract which is absolutely repugnant to the known and established laws of the land. Of this opinion is *Bynkershoek*, who says, that even if it be told to the underwriter, that the voyage is illicit, he shall not be bound; because the contract is null and void, and where that is the case, the compliance with the terms of it depends upon the will of the contracting parties merely. But that which depends merely upon will is not a proper subject for a suit at law.

Bynk. Quæst. Jur. Pub. l. 1. c. 21. sub fine.

If a ship, though neutral, be insured on a voyage prohibited by an embargo, laid on in time of war, by the prince of the country, in whose ports the ship happens to be, such an insurance also is void. This depends upon the power of an embargo, the right of laying on which by the sovereign of this country in time of war is undoubted; although in time of peace it may be a different question. The right being admitted, it follows of course, that any act done in contravention of a proclamation of this nature, is illegal and criminal; because it is equally binding as an act of parliament, and a contract founded on such illicit proceedings is consequently void.

1 Black. Com. 270.

Vide ante, 79.

This was determined in a very modern case, upon a special verdict. It was an action on a policy of insurance on the *Bella Juditta*, a *Venetian* ship, *at and from London to the Grenades, with liberty to touch at Cork and Madeira to load.* The defendant pleaded the general issue; and the cause came on to trial before Mr. Justice *Buller*, when the jury found a special verdict, the material facts in which were these: That the ship was a *Venetian* vessel, and the plaintiff a subject of the state of *Venice*; that in *October* 1782, the ship sailed on her voyage from *London* to *Cork*, and there took in a loading

Delmada v. Motteux, B. R. Mich. 25 Geo. III.

of

of provisions, the property of *French* subjects, the enemies of the king of *Great Britain*. That the said ship, having taken in at *Cork* clearances and bills of lading for *Madeira*, an island belonging to the king of *Portugal*, sailed in *December* 1782, from *Cork* to that island, at which she was neither to unload any part of her cargo, nor to receive any goods on board, but where she took clearances and bills of lading for the island of *St. Thomas*, belonging to *Denmark*, whither she was not destined: that on her voyage from *Madeira* to *Grenada*, within 14 leagues of the latter, she was captured by an *English* man of war as prize, and carried to *St. Lucia*: that when the ship sailed from *London*, and from thence till after the capture, *Grenada* was in the possession of the *French* king. The special verdict further finds, that his majesty on the 18th day of *August* 1780, laid an embargo upon all ships and vessels laden or to be laden in the ports of the kingdom of *Ireland* with black cattle and hogs, beef, pork, butter, and cheese, or any sort of provisions. It is also found, that after the capture, a suit was commenced in the Vice Admiralty Court at *Barbadoes*, against the said ship and cargo, as belonging to the *French* king, or to some of his subjects; and the judge of that court did condemn the cargo as the property of the enemies of the king of *Great Britain*, which sentence was appealed from, and is now depending: that the judge of the said Court of Vice Admiralty was of opinion, that the said ship *Bella Juditta* was the property of *Abram Delmada* the plaintiff, and ordered that the ship should be restored; but he did not conceive the owner of the said ship to be entitled to any freight, or damages occasioned by the capture, because she was engaged in a wrong act, and the captor did no more than his duty; that the said ship was accordingly restored.

Upon this verdict, the question for the court to decide in point of law, was, whether the insurers upon the ship on this voyage were liable to pay for this loss of freight, and the damages occasioned by the capture.

Lord *Mansfield*.—" Is this voyage not a breach of the embargo? The king in time of war has an undoubted right to lay an embargo: in time of peace it is another question. Every power lays them on. If the ship had only been carry-
ing

CHAP. XII.

ing goods of an enemy on a voyage lawful for her to perform, ſhe might have been entitled to freight. But here the ſentence ſays, ſhe ſhall not. And why? becauſe ſhe has done a wrong thing. It is a fraud; for under colour of a neutral port, ſhe goes to an enemy's port. She breaks an embargo. What the conſequence of that is, has not as yet been ſettled: but to break an embargo is undoubtedly a criminal act; and wherever a man makes an illegal contract, this court will not lend him their aid." The defendant accordingly had judgment.

Though an inſurance upon a ſmuggling voyage, prohibited by the revenue laws of this country, would be void under the principle above ſtated; yet the rule has never been ſuppoſed to extend to thoſe caſes, where ſhips have traded, or intend to trade, contrary to the revenue laws of foreign countries, becauſe no country takes notice of the revenue laws of another: in ſuch caſes, therefore, the policy is good and valid; and if a loſs happen, the underwriter will be anſwerable.

Vide ante, c. 10. p. 193.

Thus in the caſe of *Planche* againſt *Fletcher*, which was ſtated at large in a preceding chapter, one of the objections taken to the inſurance was, that there was a fraud on the underwriters, the ſhip having been cleared out for *Oſtend*, although ſhe was never deſigned to go to that place. But Lord *Mansfield* declared for himſelf and his brethren, that it was no fraud on the underwriters, perhaps on nobody. The reaſon for clearing for *Oſtend*, and ſigning bills of lading, as from thence, did not fully appear: but it was gueſſed at. The *Fermiers Genereaux* have the management of the taxes in *France*. As we have laid a large duty on *French* goods, the *French* may have done the ſame on ours, and it may be the intereſt of the farmers to connive at the importation of *Engliſh* commodities, and take *Oſtend* duties rather than ſtop the trade, by exacting a tax, which amounts to a prohibition. But at any rate, this was no fraud in this country. One nation does not take notice of the revenue laws of another.

In another caſe, a ſhort time afterwards at *Guildhall*, Lord *Mansfield*, in his charge to the jury, advanced the ſame doctrine which had been eſtabliſhed by the whole court in the preceding caſe.

It

It was an action on a policy of insurance, at and from *London* to *Pensacola* and *Manshae* in the river *Missisippi*, with liberty to touch at *Portsmouth* and *Jamaica*. The ship insured, was employed in the usual trade in the river *Missisippi*, and traded at *Little Manshae*, on the island of *New Orleans*, part of the dominion of *Spain*. *Manshae*, the place mentioned in the policy, is part of the continent of *North America*, on that side of the river, which *France* and *Spain* by the treaty of *Paris* in 1763, surrendered to *Great Britain*, and is about 37 leagues higher up the river than *New Orleans*. The loss happened by a seizure of the ship at *Little Manshae* by the *Spanish* governor, as a reprisal for transgressions alleged to have been committed by a king's ship in the *Lakes*. The counsel for the defendant contended, that the policy in question was on a trading voyage, and that the trade itself was an illicit one. Lever v. Fletcher, Lond. Sitt. Hil. Vac. 1780.

Lord *Mansfield*.—"The first question is, whether this policy covers the trading on the *Missisippi* before the ship's arrival at *Manshae*. The trading at *Little Manshae* is a delay of the voyage, and an increase of the risk. If the policy do not cover this part of the trading, then it is a deviation, and there is an end of the contract, at least, so as to prevent the plaintiff from recovering. It is very clear what the trade is. Every trading with the subjects of *Spain* is illicit by the treaty of *Paris*. The navigation is free to both countries; and the municipal laws of both countries remain. *Though such trading be contrary to the laws of* Spain; *yet no country pays attention to the revenue laws of another. Therefore, if the defendant had, with full knowledge that it was a smuggling trade with* Spain, *made the insurance, then it might be a fair contract between the parties.* But the main question for consideration seems to be, whether this trading at *Little Manshae* was insured by the policy." The jury found for the defendant: and it may be presumed on the ground of deviation.

It cannot be improper, because it is nearly connected with the subject before us, to enter upon the inquiry, how far trading with an enemy, in time of actual war, is legal? The opinion of foreign writers upon this point, cannot fail to afford information upon the question. It has long been Guid. c. 2. s. 2, 3. 2 Val. 31.

settled

CHAP. XII.

settled in *France*, that all trading with enemies is illegal. This indeed is given as the reason for requiring to be inserted in the policy of insurance, the name and place of abode of the insured, the effects upon which the insurance is made, the name of the ship, and the place of loading and unloading. By complying with such a requisition, it is known in time of war, whether, notwithstanding the prohibition of commerce, which, according to these writers, a declaration of war always imports, the subjects of the king continue to trade with the enemies of the state, or with their friends and allies; by which means they would be able to convey warlike stores, provisions, and other prohibited goods to the enemy. But every thing of this kind being forbidden, as prejudicial to the state, would be liable to confiscation, and to be condemned as prize, whether found in ships of our country, or of friends and allies. The prohibition to insure the property of an enemy, which is almost generally established by the ordinances of foreign countries, proceeds upon the principle, that it is unlawful to trade with an enemy; because if commerce were allowed to be carried on between the hostile nations, there could not possibly be an objection to protect that commerce by means of the contract of insurance.

Bynk. Q. Jur. Pub. lib. 1. c. 3.

Ord. of Stockholm, &c. 2 Mag. 277.

The general law of *England* had not, till lately, laid down any express rule upon the subject; but we must take notice of what has passed in the courts of justice upon the question. The only ancient cases to be found in the books upon the subject are two; the one is in *Roll*'s Abridgment, and happened in the 13th year of the reign of *Edward* the Second. A license granted to certain merchants to buy and sell in *Scotland*, which was then at war with the king of *England*, was declared to be void; and consequently the trading held to be illegal. The other was a case put to the judges, in the time of Lord *Somers*, for their opinion upon the point, whether sending corn to the enemy, in time of war and famine, was a crime at the common law. The judges held it was a misdemesnor. It is to be observed, however, that the last was a case where provisions were supplied, which, as well as warlike stores, must be prohibited from the nature of the thing.

2 Roll. Abr. 173.

1 Term. Rep. p. 85.

The

CHAP. XII.

The first modern case, in which trading with an enemy came at all under consideration; although it did not then meet with any decision, was that of *Henkle* against the *Royal Exchange* Assurance Company, before Lord *Hardwicke* in the Court of Chancery, which upon a former occasion was cited much at length. His lordship there said; it might be going too far to say that all trading with enemies is unlawful: for that general doctri... would go a great way, even where only *English* goods a... exported, and none of the enemy's imported, which might be very beneficial. He was not satisfied with the answer given to the objection of an illicit trade, by citing the case of the *South Sea* Company; for that by no means determined the question. That was not a trading contrary to the law of this country; but contrary to the agreement of the company: which is different from a contract repugnant to the general law of the country, whether statute, common, or maritime law. The same answer might be given to Sir *Robert Nightingale*'s case, which was merely a plea in the Exchequer, upon the private right of the company, being contrary only to their statutes, and not to the general law of the land.

1 Vezey 317.

Vide ante, p. 1.

From this opinion, it is evident that the question was by no means settled in Lord *Hardwicke*'s mind: but in a subsequent case, Lord *Mansfield* strongly argues, that trading with an enemy is not forbidden by the general law of the country; for he says, that several acts of parliament have been *specially* passed, in order to make such trading illegal, which proves that the legislature did not think it was so before. The ship, indeed, in the last of these cases appeared to be neutral; and the court laid it down, that it had no where been held that an insurance upon a neutral ship trading to an enemy's port was void. But then Lord *Mansfield* went upon the doctrine of a subject's trading with enemies, and concluded thus: by the maritime law, trading with an enemy is cause of confiscation, provided you take him in the act; but this does not extend to neutral vessels.

Gist. v. Mason, 1 Term Rep. 84.

The next question which comes to be considered is, whether it be lawful to insure the property of an enemy. Whatever

CHAP. XII.

ever doubts might formerly obtain in *England*, either as to the legality or expediency of ſuch inſurances, the queſtion is now finally ſettled in the negative by two unanimous deciſions of the Court of King's Bench.

R. Brandon v. Neſbitt, 6 Term R. 23.

The firſt of thoſe caſes was an action on a policy of inſurance *on goods* on board the *Greyhound*, an *American* ſhip, at and from *London* to *Bayonne*; there was an averment in the declaration, that the policy was effected for the benefit, and on the account, of *David Brandon*, *Iſaac* and *David Valery*, and others who were intereſted in the goods; and another averment that the ſhip was captured as prize. The defendant pleaded that the perſons, in whom the intereſt was averred to be, were aliens born; and that before the ſhip failed, they were become alien enemies of our king.

The ſecond plea ſtated, that the perſons intereſted were living in *France*, and enemies, and that the goods were ſent from *London* after the commencement of the war, for the purpoſe of being landed and delivered in *France* to the king's enemies. The replication to the firſt plea ſtated, that the perſons intereſted were indebted to the preſent plaintiff in more than the value of the goods inſured. The replication to the ſecond, that the goods inſured were not prohibited at the time of the policy, and that they were ſhipped before the commencement of the war. To theſe replications there were demurrers.

Lord *Kenyon*, in giving the opinion of the court, ſaid, that they had conſidered this caſe, and unleſs any thing more could be urged at the bar to ſhake the opinion they had formed, they were of opinion, that judgment muſt be given for the defendant, on this ground, that an action will not lie either by or in favour of an alien enemy (*a*).

This

34 G. III. c. 79. ſ. 17.

(*a*) By a late act of parliament, which paſſed "for more effectually preſerving money or effects, in the hands of his majeſty's ſubjects, belonging "to, or diſpoſable by, perſons reſident in *France*, for the benefit of the in-"dividual owners thereof," commiſſioners were appointed for carrying the purpoſes of the act into effect: and by the 17th ſect. of the ſtatute, the commiſſioners were empowered to direct the money due on certain inſurances

This case, at first view, may appear to proceed merely upon the special plea; but in the same term another case was argued upon a special verdict, in which the only point discussed was the legality of insurances on enemy's property; and the principle of the decision in *Brandon* v. *Nesbitt* was held so clearly to control the other, that, on the authority of that decision, the counsel for the plaintiff abandoned the second argument, which the court had ordered. CHAP. XII.

The special verdict stated, that the plaintiff, on the 13th *March* 1793, being then resident in *Great Britain*, in pursuance of an order for that purpose, caused the insurance in question to be made on account of *Arrouet*, *Massot*, &c. and that *the goods* insured were by the policy warranted *French* property, and were so in fact: that the goods, which consisted of buttons, buckles, &c. of the manufacture of this kingdom, were shipped on board the *Nancy*, (an *American* ship,) on the 19th *March* 1793, by Messrs. *Humphreys* of *Birmingham*, in compliance with orders received in *January* 1793, from Messrs. *Arrouet*, *Massot*, &c. who were and still are subjects of *France*: that by two orders in council of 11th *February* 1793, general reprisals were granted against the ships, goods, and subjects of *France*; and a general embargo was laid on all vessels in *Great Britain*: but by another order of 26th *February* the said general embargo was declared not to extend to foreign vessels belonging to the subjects of any state in amity with his majesty, but that they might forthwith proceed on their respective voyages, provided the cargo did not consist of naval or military stores, or any other article, the exportation whereof was prohibited by any law or order of council then in force. The verdict then states the sailing of the ship on the voyage insured on the 21st *March* 1793, the subsequent capture of the vessel by some *English* subjects, and the condemnation of *the goods insured* as *French* property. Bristow v. Towers, 6 Term R. 35.

This special verdict was fully argued at the Bar, and a second argument was ordered: but after the decision of *Brandon*

ances to be paid; and, in case of refusal, actions might be brought with the approbation of the commissioners; and to such actions so brought under this authority, *alien enemy* is not pleadable.

CHAP. XII.

don v. *Nesbitt*, the counsel for the plaintiff said, that he declined the further argument of the case, as he had no hopes of convincing the court that this case could be distinguished from the principle on which the former had been so recently determined.

Lord *Kenyon*.—"It appears to the court in the same light, and there must be judgment for the defendant."

This important case has decided that the insurances of enemy's property are generally unlawful: but as the learned judges had not an opportunity of entering into the reasons of their judgment, it cannot be impertinent in a work, which professes to be a system of the law of marine insurances, to give a summary of the arguments on both sides of a question, which has been once or twice discussed in parliament, upon which very eminent men have entertained different opinions, although till lately it has never come fully and precisely in judgment in a court of common law.

Those who argue in favour of such insurances insist, that it would be of very dangerous consequence by a prohibition of the nature alluded to, to strip ourselves of a branch of trade, which we now enjoy almost without a rival, as more of this business is done in *England* than in all the rest of *Europe*. That not only the nations with whom we are at peace, but even those with whom we are at war, transact all this business in *London*; that the advantage thence derived to the kingdom is obvious, for the premiums produce a great balance in our favour, and where there is no capture, the trade of the enemy pays a tax to this country for its safety. On this ground, it has been also urged as a fact, that important intelligence has, by means of such insurances, been frequently obtained of the enemy's designs; and that in several wars, some of the richest prizes have fallen into our hands by information communicated by those employed to procure insurances upon them. With respect to the legality of such contracts, they contend, it never has been disputed, that they had been effected in all former wars without interruption, except when prohibited for about six months by the statute 21 *Geo.* II. *ch.* 4. and had not only been effected, but recov-

cered

ered upon in courts of justice, the objection of enemy's property never having been made. That the opinion of Lord *Hardwicke*, as delivered in *Henkle* v. *Royal Exchange Assurance*, and that of Lord *Mansfield*, frequently declared in parliament, and on the bench, was strongly in favour of such insurances. That the latter of these two illustrious judges, almost the last time he sat in court, adhered to that opinion; for in the course of his direction to a jury delivered so lately as 1786, he said, "It is for the benefit of this country to "permit these contracts upon two accounts; the one, be- "cause you hold the box, and are sure of getting the premi- "ums at least as a certain profit; the other, because it is a "certain mode of obtaining intelligence of the enemy's de- "signs, and I have known instances of intelligence procur- "ed by such methods." That the statutes, passed in the 21st *Geo.* II. and in the 33d of the present reign, to prohibit such insurances prove, by being partial in their operation, and limited in their duration, that in the opinion of the legislature these contracts were not prohibited by the general law of the land: Indeed, trading with an enemy does not itself seem to be contrary to law. For although some foreign writers condemn it, they do not advert to the method of carrying it on by the medium of neutral nations. Declaration of war does not necessarily import a prohibition of commerce; and wherever it may be conducted beneficially to a belligerent power, it is, as far as respects such power, perfectly justifiable. Even the writers on the law of nations enumerate instances of commerce being carried on between belligerent powers, by express stipulation, which is sufficient to shew that all commerce, by a declaration of war, is not of necessity interdicted. That this has been the opinion in *England*, the practice of the legislature in all former wars strongly proves, for they have passed statutes adapted to the exigency of the times, considering the subject in a light merely political; some of them imposing a general prohibition, though the restraint was frequently afterwards in part taken off; some which in the first instance imposed a partial restraint only; and some, which actually sanctioned a trade with an enemy, which in time of peace was illegal: the two first classes would have been wholly nugatory, if the doctrine,

1 Vez. 320.

Gist. v. Mason, 1 Term R. 84; and manuscript note of same case.

33 Geo. III. c. 27. s. 4.

that

CHAP. XII.

that insurances of this nature were illegal, had ever prevailed. Such statutes have been passed in every war from the reign of *Charles* the Second to the present time; which prove demonstrably, that parliament conceived a legislative prohibition was necessary to make the trading illegal, otherwise all or most of the acts alluded to would have been unnecessary and superfluous.

Bynk. Quæst. Jurif. Pub. lib. 1. cap. 3.

On the other hand it is contended by those who hold the insurance of enemy's property to be illegal and impolitic, that by the declaration of war, all commerce immediately and necessarily becomes prohibited between hostile nations; and if so, it follows that insurances must also be forbidden; for it cannot be lawful to do that indirectly, which is not permitted to be done directly. Instances of trading with enemies to be found in writers on general law, by express stipulation, only shew that governments occasionally make exceptions from the general rule to suit their own convenience; and to this source all the special statutes alluded to are referable; some of which too contain regulations of particular branches of commerce. Even where they extend to general prohibitions of trade with an enemy, it is for the purpose of superadding special penalties for checking bold offenders, who are not to be deterred by the ordinary prohibitions of the law, an observation which fully applies to the statute of 21 *Geo.* II. and to the Traiterous Correspondence Bill lately passed. But all the writers upon insurance concur in the illegality of such contracts. The author of *Le Guidon*, a work of great repute, published by Monf. *Cleirac* about the middle of the last century, is explicit upon the point; and the editor of the work observes, that this opinion is conformable to the ordinances of *Barcelona*, which passed so long ago as 1484. *Valin*, in his commentary, concurs in declaring the same law, and relates that by the *English* insuring *French* property in the then last war, one part of the nation rendered back to *France*, what had been taken by the other *jure belli*. *Bynkershoek*, to whose writings mankind are much indebted, dedicates a whole chapter of his work to this subject, and argues strongly both against the legality and expediency of such contracts. In the only two cases, in which the legality of trading with an enemy came in question in *England* (see ante, p. 238.)

Le Guidon, cap. 2. f. 5.

Valin, liv. 3. tit. 6. art. 3.

Bynk. Q. Jur. Pub. lib. 1. cap. 21.

p. 238.) it was held to be illegal. Even the expediency of ſuch contracts is greatly to be doubted. The *Engliſh* inſurers, who deal at a cheaper rate, and fulfil their engagements more punctually than thoſe of other nations, will, in time of peace, eaſily regain ſuch branches of that trade, as, by a prohibition during war, may be diverted into other channels. With regard to the ſuppoſed profit, that muſt ever be a matter of great uncertainty, for the premiums are not clear profit. In caſes of capture, there is no loſs to the enemy, and no gain to us: in loſſes by perils of the ſea, we bear the whole burthen, and there is actual gain to them, deducting indeed the premium in both caſes. In a national point of view, the detriment derived to us from the ſupport afforded to the commercial reſources of our enemies is beyond all computation. Our inſurers too are by this traffic rendered bad ſubjects of the country, by being intereſted againſt the ſucceſs of our own cruizers, in favour of the enemy's eſcape. The argument of procuring intelligence of the enemy's plans by theſe means is fallacious in the higheſt degree; for it never can be ſuppoſed, that underwriters would be the means of betraying the ſhips inſured into the power of our cruizers, by which they would be the greateſt ſufferers; on the other hand, the temptation muſt be very ſtrong to them to afford ſuch intelligence to the enemy of the ſailing of our armed veſſels, as may put them on their guard, and prevent them from falling into our hands. That ſuch intelligence had been given to the enemy was aſſerted as a fact in the debates in parliament in 1747; and the general law of the land will not tolerate a contract, which may lead the ſubject into ſo ſtrong a temptation to betray his duty. Even the opinions moſt favourable to this ſpecies of contract have never gone further than to contend, that inſurances upon enemy's property from a friendly or neutral port, or from one hoſtile country to another, were legal; but till the late caſes of *Brandon* v. *Neſbitt* and *Briſtow* v. *Towers*, it never was attempted to be argued, that an inſurance could legally be made on enemy's property, ſailing directly from this country to that of the enemy. Such is the ſum of the argument on both ſides of this great queſtion, which is probably now finally cloſed.

There is one ſpecies of inſurance which never could be made upon the ſhips or goods of an enemy, or even of a ſubject, and that is upon a voyage to a beſieged fort or garriſon, with a view of carrying aſſiſtance to them; or upon ammunition, other warlike ſtores, or proviſions; becauſe, from the nature of theſe commodities, they are abſolutely prohibited by the laws of all nations.

Having thus diſpoſed of theſe two important queſtions, it will be proper to conclude, by ſtating what the principle is, which is laid down in this chapter, and ſupported by authority. All inſurances upon a voyage generally prohibited by law, ſuch as to an enemy's garriſon, or upon a voyage directly contrary to an expreſs act of parliament, or to royal proclamation in time of war, are abſolutely null and void.

CHAPTER THE THIRTEENTH.

Of Prohibited Goods.

CHAP. XIII.

THE ſubject of the preſent chapter is materially connected with that of the foregoing; and indeed follows as a conſequence from the doctrine there advanced. We then ſaw that a contract founded upon that which was contrary to law, could never be carried into effect. Thus by the laws of almoſt all countries, the exportation and importation of certain commodities are declared to be illegal: to act contrary to that prohibition is clearly a contempt of legal authority; and conſequently a moral wrong. If the act itſelf be illegal, the inſurance to protect ſuch an act muſt alſo be contrary to law; and therefore void. Agreeably to this principle, it ſeems to have been laid down by the writers upon the ſubject, as a general and univerſal propoſition, that an inſurance being made, although in general terms, does not comprehend prohibited goods; and therefore when the inſured ſhall procure ſuch commodities to be ſhipped, *the underwriter being ignorant of it*, by means of which the ſhip and cargo are confiſcated, the inſurer is diſcharged. In this paſſage from *Roccus* it may be inferred, that if the underwriter *knew* that the goods were prohibited, the inſurance would be valid. But we truſt, it was ſufficiently ſhewn in the preceding chapter, that that will not alter the caſe: becauſe no conſent or agreement can render a contract good and valid, which, upon the face of it, is contrary to law. In *France* this rule was adopted ſo long ago as the year 1660; for in the work of a very reſpectable writer of that age we find this paſſage: *aſſeurances ſe peuvent faire ſur toute ſorte de merchandize, pourvu que le tranſport ne ſoit pas prohibé par les edicts et ordonnances du roy.* And from an authority no leſs reſpectable, it appears that the law of *France* has undergone no alteration ſince that period; for he ſays, "that thoſe effects, the importation or "exportation of which is prohibited in *France*, cannot be "the

Lord Kaim's Prin. of Eq. 66.

Roccus de Aſſecur. No. 21.

Le Guidon 2. art. 2.

Emerigon Traité des Aſſurance, tom. 1. c. 8. ſ. 5.

CHAP. XIII.

" the subject matter of the contract of insurance; and if " they should be confiscated, the insurers are not responsi- " ble, *even where the truth has been declared by a special clause* " *in the policy*. The assurance is void, and no premium is " due." This passage from the celebrated work just referred to, confirms the idea above started, with respect to the knowledge of the underwriter.

The law of *England*, whose commercial regulations have surpassed those of every other nation in the world, has also introduced such a rule into its system of mercantile jurisprudence: and the oldest writers upon the subject have taken notice of it. It is said, " if prohibited goods are laden aboard, " and the merchant insures upon the general policy, it is a " question whether if such goods be lawfully seized as pro- " hibited goods, the insurers out to answer. It is conceived " they ought not: for if the goods are at the time of the " lading unlawful, and the lader knew of the same, such " assurance will not oblige the insurer to answer the loss; for " the same is not such an assurance as the law supports, but " a fraudulent one."

Molloy, lib. 2. c. 7. s. 15.

But it is not upon the opinions of learned men merely, that this doctrine is founded in the *English* law; for the legislature have by positive statutes declared their ideas upon the subject. It appears from the preamble to that section of the statute about to be quoted, that a custom, highly prejudicial to the revenue of the country had prevailed, and was increasing to a very alarming degree, of importing great quantities of goods from foreign states in a fraudulent and clandestine manner, without paying the customs and duties payable to the crown: and that this evil had been encouraged and promoted by some ill designing men, who, in defiance of the laws, had undertaken as insurers, or otherwise to deliver such goods so clandestinely imported, at their charge and hazard, into the houses, warehouses, or possession, of the owners of such goods. In order to remedy this mischief, it was enacted, " that all and every person and persons, who, by way of " insurance or otherwise, should undertake or agree to deliv- " er any goods, wares, or merchandizes whatsoever, to be " imported from parts beyond the seas, at any port or place

4 and 5 W. and M. c. 15. s. 14, 15, 16. 500 l. penalty on persons insuring to import prohibited goods.

" whatsoever

" whatsoever within this kingdom of *England*, dominion of " *Wales*, or town of *Berwick upon Tweed*, without paying " the duties and customs that should be due and payable for " the same at such importation, *or any prohibited goods whatso-* " *ever*; or in pursuance of such insurance, undertaking or " agreement, should deliver, or cause or procure to be deliv- " ered, any prohibited goods, or should deliver, or cause " or procure to be delivered, any goods or merchandizes " whatsoever, without paying such duties and customs as " aforesaid, knowing thereof, and all and every their aiders, " abettors, and assistants, should for every such offence for- " feit and lose the sum of *five hundred pounds*, over and above " all other forfeitures and penalties, to which they are lia- " ble by any act already in force." It was also enacted, " that all and every person and persons, who should agree " to pay any sum or sums of money for the insuring or con- " veying any goods or merchandizes that should be so im- " ported, without paying the customs and duties due and " payable at the importation thereof, or of any prohibited " goods whatsoever, or should receive or take such prohibit- " ed goods into his or their house, or warehouse, or other " place on land, or such other goods, before such customs " or duties were paid, knowing thereof, should also for every " such offence forfeit and lose the like sum of five hundred " pounds; the one half of the said forfeitures to be to their " majesties, and the other half to the informer, or to such " persons as should sue for the same. And if the insurer, " conveyor, or manager of such fraud should be the discov- " erer of the same, he should not only keep the insurance " money or reward given him, and be discharged of the pen- " alties to which he was liable by reason of such offence, " but should also have to his own use one half of the for- " feitures hereby imposed upon the party or parties making " such insurance or agreement, or receiving the goods as " aforesaid: and in case no discovery should be made by the " insurer, conveyor, or manager as aforesaid, and the party " or parties insured or concerned in such agreement should " make discovery thereof, he should recover and receive back " such insurance money or premium as he had paid upon " such insurance or agreement, and should have to his own " use one moiety of the forfeitures imposed upon such insur- " er, conveyor, or manager as aforesaid, and should also be

Sect. 15. Like penalty on the insured.

CHAP. XIII. " discharged of the forfeitures hereby imposed upon him or " them."

A few years afterwards, lustrings, the manufacture of which till then was little known in *England*, having been worked to great perfection by the Royal Lustring Company, the legislature found it necessary to protect this branch of trade, by prohibiting the importation of such silks from foreign countries into this, without paying the duties, whether by direct means, or by the way of insurance. It was

8 and 9 W. 3. c. 36. f. 1. enacted, " that every person, who should import any foreign " alamodes or lustrings from parts beyond the seas, into any " port or place within the kingdom of *England*, dominion " of *Wales*, &c. without paying the rates, customs, impo- " sitions, and duties that should be due and payable for the " same at such importation, or should import any alamodes " or lustrings, prohibited by law to be imported, or should, " by way of insurance or otherwise, undertake or agree to " deliver, or in pursuance of any undertaking, agreement, " or insurance, should deliver, or cause to be delivered, any " such goods or merchandize, and every person who should " agree to pay any sum or sums of money, premium, or " reward for insuring or conveying any such goods or mer- " chandize, or should knowingly take or receive the same " into his, her, or their house, shop, or warehouse, custody " or possession, such person or persons should and might be " prosecuted for any of the offences or matters aforesaid, in " any action, suit, or information; and thereupon a *capias* " in the first process, specifying the sum of the penalties " sued for, should and might issue, and such person or per- " sons should be obliged to give sufficient bail and security " by natural born subjects, persons naturalized or denizens " to the officer executing the writ, to appear in court to an- " swer such suit, and at such appearance to give sufficient " bail to answer and pay all the forfeitures and penalties " incurred for such offence, or to yield his, her, or their " bodies to prison."

Sect. 2. The second section of this statute enables persons to sue for the penalties imposed by the former act of *William* and *Mary* by action of debt, bill, plaint, or information, in any of his majesty's courts of record at *Westminster*.

Wool

Mir. c. 1. ſ. 3. 11 Ed. 3. c. 1. 8 Eliz. c. 3. 12 Car. 2. c. 32. 7 and 8 W. 3. c. 28. 4 G. 1. c. 11.

Wool being the ſtaple manufacture of this kingdom, it was always deemed a heinous offence to tranſport it out of the realm: for we find it was forbidden at the common law; and afterwards more expreſsly in the reign of *Edward* the Third, ſince which period this branch of trade has been much attended to, and any offences againſt it have met with corporal and pecuniary puniſhments by ſeveral ſubſequent ſtatutes. This being the caſe, an inſurance upon wool ſo to be exported muſt have been void; becauſe the very foundation of the contract was contrary to law. But notwithſtanding theſe reſtrictions, the practice of exporting wool became ſo frequent, as well as the practice of inſuring ſuch cargoes, and undertaking to deliver them ſafely abroad, that it became neceſſary for the legiſlature to interpoſe, and by a new declaration of the law, and the impoſition of a heavy penalty, to endeavour to check the growing evil. Accordingly it was enacted, "that every perſon, who, by way of inſurance or "otherwiſe, ſhould undertake or agree, that any wool, wool-"fells, wool-flocks, mortlings, ſhortlings, worſted, *&c.* "ſhould be carried or conveyed to any parts beyond the "ſeas from any port or place whatſoever within this king-"dom or *Ireland*: or in purſuance of ſuch inſurance, un-"dertaking, or agreement, ſhould deliver, or cauſe to be "delivered, any of the ſaid goods in parts beyond the ſeas, "ſuch perſon, and all and every his aiders, *&c.* ſhould for "every ſuch offence forfeit and loſe the ſum of five hun-"dred pounds." The next ſection inflicts a like penalty on the inſured: and the following one, in order to encourage the parties to diſcloſe ſuch contracts, releaſes the party informing from all the penalties, to which he himſelf was ſubject, and alſo gives him the whole of the forfeiture, after deducting the charges of the proſecution.

12 Geo. 2. c. 21. ſ. 29.

500 l. penalty on the inſurer who inſures or procures wool to be landed in foreign parts.

Sect. 30.

Sect. 31.

But in order wholly to prevent this illicit exportation of wool, it was neceſſary for the legiſlature to go one ſtep further: becauſe as policies are frequently made on goods, as well as on ſhips, in which the inſurer undertakes, in conſideration of the premium, to bear all the riſks and hazards of the voyage; and as it is generally unknown to the inſurers what ſorts of goods are loaded on board any ſhip or veſſel, it happened that inſurances were made on wool or woollen yarn to be carried from *Great Britain* or *Ireland* to foreign ports, or on woollen manufactures to be carried from *Ireland*.

Therefore

CHAP. XIII.

Same act. f. 33. Infurances on woollen goods void.

Therefore it was declared, "that all policies of infurance, "which fhould be made on goods and merchandizes, loaden or to be loaden, on any fhip or veffel bound from *Great* "*Britain* or *Ireland* to foreign parts beyond the feas, which "fhould afterwards appear to be wool or woollen yarn, or "any other fpecies of wool or woollen manufactures from "*Ireland*; and all policies of infurance which fhould be made "on any fhip or veffel bound from *Great Britain* or *Ireland* "to foreign parts beyond the feas, which fhould have on "board any wool or woollen yarn, or any other fpecies of "wool or woollen manufactures from *Ireland*, fhould be "deemed and taken to be null and void, notwithftanding any "words or agreement whatfoever, which fhould be inferted in any fuch policy of infurance; and nothing fhould "be recovered by the affured in either cafe for lofs or damage, or for the premium which fhould have been given as "the confideration for infuring fuch goods and merchandizes, fhip or veffel."

This latter act, as far as relates to *Ireland*, has been repealed by a fubfequent ftatute of 20 *Geo.* III. *c.* 6.

28 Geo. 3. c. 38.

In a late feffion of parliament, an act paffed for reducing all the laws relative to the exportation of wool into one ftatute; and for the firft offence of that fort inflicts a penalty of 50*l.* with fix months folitary imprifonment for exporting wool, &c. The 45th fection of that ftatute declares that,

Sect. 45.

"every perfon or perfons who, by way of infurance or otherwife, fhall undertake or agree that any fheep, wool, or any "other of the enumerated articles in the ftatute, fhall be carried or conveyed to any parts beyond the feas, from any "port or place whatfoever within this kingdom, or in purfuance of fuch undertaking or agreement, fhall deliver, or "caufe or procure to be delivered any fheep, wool, &c. in "parts beyond the feas, fuch perfon or perfons, their aiders "and abettors, fhall upon conviction be liable to the fame "punifhment as the exporters."

Sect. 46.

The next fection inflicts a like penalty upon the perfons paying for fuch infurance.

Sect. 48.

But as infurances are frequently made on goods, the infurer not knowing what the goods are, it is declared that, "all

"policies

"policies of insurance which shall be made on goods and "merchandizes, laden or to be laden on any ship or vessel "bound from *Great Britain* to foreign parts, which shall "afterwards appear to be wool, woollen, or worsted yarn, "*&c.* shall be deemed and taken to be null and void, not-"withstanding any words or agreement whatsoever, which "shall be inserted in such policy of insurance, and nothing "shall be recovered by the assured from the insurer for loss "or damage, or for the premium which shall have been "given as the consideration for such insurance."

From an attentive review of these statutes, the idea of the *British* parliament may be clearly and decidedly collected: and the statutes just referred to, are the most general in their import that could be found upon the subject; and consequently the most proper to be mentioned here.

The question naturally occurs, what goods come under the description of prohibited goods, so as to render an insurance upon them void. To mention by name all the different kinds of merchandize, which fall under that description, would be tedious; and, as it should seem, wholly unnecessary. Thus much may be laid down as a general proposition, that all insurances upon goods, forbidden to be exported or imported, by positive statutes, by the general rules of our municipal law, or by the king's proclamation *in time of war;* or which from the nature of the commodity, and by the laws of nations, must necessarily be contraband, are absolutely null and void. Under the first division may be ranked all offences against the revenue laws of this country; and therefore if an insurance were made in order to protect smuggled goods, such insurance would doubtless be of no effect. To this head also may be referred any breach of navigation acts, which were established for the protection, encouragement, and advancement of our commercial and naval interests; and which have produced those effects to the wonderful extension of our commerce, and the aggrandizement of the nation. At a very early period of the history of this country, several wise provisions were made by parliament, solely with this view: but on account of the low state of commerce in those ages, which was the more depressed, by the warlike spirit of the nation, and the intestine commotions that agitated and disturbed the state, those provisions in

5 Rich. 2. c. 3.

CHAP. XIII. in some measure failed of their effect. But the most beneficial statute for the trade and commerce of *England* is the famous navigation act, which passed soon after the restoration of *Charles* the Second; the outlines of which were first framed, in the time of the commonwealth, by *Oliver Cromwell*. By the reports of historians, we do not find that he framed it with any view to those beneficial effects, which sprung from it, but with a partial and confined intention, being designed by him to mortify our own sugar islands, which were disaffected to the parliament, and held out for the king, by stopping the lucrative trade, which they then held with the *Dutch*. Another motive for his conduct was this, that as the *Dutch* were at that time rising into opulence and wealth, and had given him disgust; and as their commerce did not consist so much in the produce of their own country (which afforded but few commodities) as in being the general carriers and factors of *Europe*, he had it in his power to affect their trade in a considerable degree, by prohibiting all nations from importing into *England* in their own bottoms any commodity, which was not the growth and manufacture of their own country. At the restoration, however, those plans, the good effects of which had probably been experienced, were adopted by the legal and real constitution of the country, and were considerably improved by inserting clauses, which had been overlooked and omitted in the original design, or which time and experience had pointed out as necessary to the completion of that system, the beneficial effects of which are at this day most sensibly felt. It is not wholly impertinent in a work like the present to state briefly the outlines of a statute, so considerably affecting the commercial interests of the nation, and which has served as the ground-work of all subsequent laws for the good management of *British* navigation.

[Margin: Lobel, 132.]

[Margin: Hume's Hist. Eng. 211.]

[Margin: 12 Car. II. c. 18. s. 1.]

The first section of the act declares, "that no goods shall "be imported into, or exported out of, any plantations or "territories to his majesty belonging in *Asia*, *Africa* or *America*, but in such ships only as belong to the people of *England* or *Ireland*, *Wales* or *Berwick*, or are of the built of, "and belonging to, any of the said territories, as the proprietors thereof, and whereof the master, and three-fourths "of the mariners are *English*, (which word by the subsequent statute, 13 and 14 *Car*. II. ch. 11. s. 6. was explain-

"ed

"ed to mean his majesty's subjects of *England*, *Ireland*, and "his plantations generally) under penalty of the forfeiture "of all the goods and commodities which shall be imported "into, or exported out of, any of the said places, in any "other ship or vessel, as also of the ship and vessel." It is also declared, "that no goods of the growth, manufacture, or "production, of *Africa*, *Asia*, or *America*, be imported into "*England*, *Ireland*, *Wales*, *Guernsey*, *Jersey*, or *Berwick*, in "any other ships than such as belong to the people of *England*, *Ireland*, *Wales*, or *Berwick*, or of the plantations to "his majesty belonging, as the proprietors thereof, and "whereof the master and three-fourths of the mariners are "*English*, under the penalty of the forfeiture of all such "goods, and of the ship."

Sect. 3.

See an act of 2 W. and M. f. 1. c. 9. prohibiting the importation of thrown silk.

"No goods of foreign growth, production, or manufacture, which are to be brought into *England*, *Ireland*, *Wales*, "*Guernsey*, *Jersey*, or *Berwick*, in *English*-built shipping be-"longing to some of the aforesaid places, and navigated by "*English* mariners as aforesaid, shall be brought from any "other places but those of the growth or manufacture, or "from those ports where the goods are first usually shipped "for transportation, under the penalty of the forfeiture of "all such goods, as shall be imported from any other place, "as also of the said ship."

Sect. 4. This section was altered as to the importation of American drugs by 7 Anne, c. 8. f. 12.

"It shall not be lawful to load in any ships, whereof any "stranger or strangers born (unless such as be denizens, or "naturalized) be owners, part owners, or master, whereof "three-fourths of the mariners, at least, shall not be *English*, "any fish, victual, goods, and merchandizes, from one "port or creek of *England*, *Ireland*, *Wales*, *Guernsey*, *Jersey*, "or *Berwick*, to another port or creek of the same, under "penalty, and forfeiture of all such goods, together with "the ship or vessel."

Sect. 6.

"Where any privilege is given by the book of rates to "goods or commodities exported or imported in *English*-built "shipping, that is to say, shipping built in *England*, *Ireland*, "*Wales*, *Guernsey*, *Jersey*, *Berwick*, or in any of the lands, "dominions, and territories, belonging to his majesty, in "*Africa*, *Asia*, or *America*, that it always is to be under-"stood, that the master and three-fourths of the mariners "be *English*; and where it is required that the master and

Sect. 7.

"three-

CHAP. XIII. "three-fourths of the mariners be *English*, the true intent "thereof is, that they should continue such during the whole "voyage, unless in case of sickness, death, or being taken "prisoners in the voyage, to be proved by the oath of the "master or chief officer of the ship."

Sect. 8. The eighth section prohibits the importation of goods of the growth of *Muscovy*, *Russia*, or the *Ottoman* or *Turkish* empire into *England*, except in *English* built ships, whereof the master and three-fourths of the mariners must also be *English*, under the penalty of forfeiting both ship and goods.

Sect. 9. Upon this sect. see 13 and 14 Car. 2. c. 11. s. 23. 6 Geo. 1. c. 15. s. 1. And for preventing the practice of *colouring* aliens goods, the ninth section declares, that all wines of the growth of *France* or *Germany* imported in any other than *English* vessels, shall be deemed aliens goods, and pay all strangers customs and duties: which provision is extended to certain commodities, named in the act, of the growth of *Spain*, the *Canaries*, *Madeira*, *Portugal*, or the Western Islands, and of
Sect. 10. *Muscovy*, *Russia*, and *Turkey*. It was also ordained by the next subsequent section of the statute, in order to prevent the colouring or buying of foreign ships, that no foreign ship should pass as a ship to *England*, *Ireland*, *Wales*, or *Berwick*, until those claiming the said ship should make appear to the chief officer of the customs that they were not aliens, and should have taken an oath, that such ship was *bonâ fide*, and without fraud by them bought for a valuable consideration, expressing the sum, and also the time, place, and persons, from whom it was bought, and who were the part owners: upon which oath that they should receive a certificate, whereby such ship should in future pass, and be deemed a ship belonging to the said port, where the oath was so taken, and
Sect. 11. V. 6 Anne. c. 37. s. 21. receive the privileges of such ship. The officers of the customs are not to allow any privilege to any foreign built ship, until certificate granted, or proof of those things required by
Sect. 13. this act. By the 13th section it is provided, that this act is not intended to restrain the importation of any *East-India* commodities, loaden in *English* built shipping, whereof the master and three-fourths of the mariners are *English*, from the usual place of loading in those seas, to the southward and eastward of the *Cape of Good Hope*, although the said ports be not the very places of their growth. There is also a provision
Sect. 14 & 16. in favour of goods imported from *Spain*, *Portugal*, the *Azores*,

Madeira

Madeira or *Canary* iflands; and concerning goods and commodities from *Scotland*, and feal oil from *Ruffia*. The 17th fection impofes a duty upon every *French* fhip coming into *England*. And it was laftly enacted, that the fhips of *England*, *Ireland*, *Wales*, or *Berwick*, failing to any *Englifh* plantations in *Afia*, *Africa*, or *America*, fhould be bound in fufficient fureties, in proportion to the burthen of the fhip, to bring the goods loaded at fuch plantations into *England*.

CHAP. XIII.

Sect. 17.

Such were the provifions of this famous ftatute, framed by the wifdom of our anceftors for the promotion of our naval and maritime ftrength: upon this ftatute have all fubfequent commercial regulations been eftablifhed; and from this fource they have derived folidity and ftrength. But in vain have fuch rules been framed, if infurances upon the importation or exportation of the commodities mentioned in thefe ftatutes are to be tolerated. It would be to render void thefe good and wife plans, and to fet the acts of the legiflature at defiance. The conclufion is, that fuch infurances are abfolutely null, and of no effect.

t was faid, in a former part of this chapter, that an infurance upon any goods, the exportation or importation of which was forbidden by the royal proclamation in time of war, was equally void, as if prohibited by ftatute. The reafon of this is, that the king's proclamation in time of war has equal force with an act of parliament, and is no lefs binding upon his fubjects. The confequence of this doctrine is, that the breach of fuch a prohibition is equally criminal with the breach of a ftatute; and no contract can be founded upon fuch criminal act, or have any validity. Thefe principles were fully confidered in the preceding chapter; and the law upon the fubject was clearly fettled in the cafe of *Delmada* v. *Motteux*, there cited at length; in which it was held, that the king had an undoubted right to lay on an embargo in time of war: that the confequence of a breach of fuch a proclamation had not been fully afcertained, but it was certainly a criminal act; and wherever a man makes an illegal contract, the courts of juftice will not lend him their aid to compel a performance. The underwriter was accordingly difcharged from the demand fet up againft him.

1 Black. Com. 270.

Delmada v. Motteux, B. R. Mich. 25 Geo. 3. Vide ante, p. 234.

We

CHAP. XIII.

Grotius, lib. 3. c. 1. Bynk. lib. 1. c. 11.

We come now to consider those commodities which, from their nature, as well as by the laws of nations, are contraband. Upon this occasion *Grotius* and *Bynkershoek* are the best guides that can possibly be followed; and from them we may collect, that it is unlawful to carry any thing to besieged cities or fortresses: a rule which they declare to have been established by common consent, and the usage of all nations. *Grotius* divides goods into three kinds: such as can only be of use in time of war; and these are clearly contraband, such as arms and ammunition: 2dly, Such as answer no purpose in war, and are merely intended for pleasure; and these may be lawfully conveyed to an enemy. But the third kind are of a mixed nature, such as money, provisions, ships, and the materials of ships; in which case, before we can decide upon the propriety of exporting such commodities, the situation of the war between the contending parties is to be considered. Upon this point his reasoning is excellent: "If," says he, "I cannot defend myself "without intercepting the commodities intended for my en-"emies, necessity will give me the right, but still I shall be "liable to make restitution, unless some other cause of seiz-"ure appears. For if the conveyance of such commodities "to the enemy shall prevent the execution of my plans, and "he who carried them knew that I had besieged or blockad-"ed the town, and that peace or a surrender was expected, "he shall be answerable for the loss sustained by his mis-"conduct." With this opinion *Bynkershoek* for the most part coincides: because, as he observes, the siege alone is the cause why it is not lawful to carry any thing to the besieged, whether it be contraband or not: for a besieged city is never compelled to surrender by force, but by famine, and the want of other necessaries. If it were to be permitted to supply them with the things of which they stand in need, perhaps the assailants would be obliged to raise the siege. But as it is impossible to say of what things the besieged stand in need, or in what they abound, every species of commodity is forbidden to be carried into the garrison; for otherwise there would be no certain rule of settling disputes. This learned author, however, differs from *Grotius*, in that passage where he says, "the carrier of goods shall be answer-"able, if peace or a surrender was expected, and it was "frustrated by such means." *Bynkershoek* is of opinion, that

Lib. 3. c. 1. f. 5.

L. 1. c. 11.

such

CHAP. XIII.

such doctrine is neither consonant to reason, nor to the agreements entered into by the laws of nations. He reasons thus; "Quæ ratio me arbitrum constituit de futurâ deditione aut "pace? et si neutra expectetur, jam licet obsessis quælibet "advehere? imo nunquam licet, durante obsidione, et amici "non est causam amici perdere, vel quoquo modo deterio-"rem facere. Et qui advexit, non ultra tenebitur, quam de "damno culpâ dato? atquin in subditis id semper capitale "fuit, quin et in amicis, edicto ante monitis, sæpe et in non "monitis. Rursus, si quis nondum advexit, sed, dum adve-"here voluit, deprehendatur, sola rerum interceptarum re-"tentione erimus contenti, idque donec caveatur, nihil tale "in posterum commissum iri?" He concludes thus: "I "do not agree to that opinion, having learnt from the cus-"tom and usages of all nations, to sell all intercepted goods, "and often to inflict, if not a capital, at least a corporal "punishment."

Such are the opinions of these two very learned writers, who, although in some respects they differ, agree in establishing this as a settled, undisputed rule, that whoever conveys any necessaries to a besieged town, camp, or port, is guilty of a breach of the law of nations. This being the case, an insurance upon such commodities must necessarily be void and of no effect, agreeably to the principles which have already been advanced. Grot. Bynk. loc. cit.

One question only remains to be considered; how far insurances upon goods, the exportation and importation of which are forbidden by the laws of other countries, are valid? In *England*, the law is clear, as it has been laid down by two very great judges, that such insurances are good; because the foundation of the contract is not illicit. It has been expressly held by Lord *Mansfield* more than once, in which he has been confirmed by the whole Court of King's Bench, that one nation never takes notice of the revenue laws of another; and therefore such an insurance was certainly good and valid. A similar opinion seems to have been entertained by Lord *Hardwicke*; at least so much may be collected from his argument, in a case reported in *Vezey*.

Vide ante, p. 195. Doug. 238.

1 Vezey, 319.

But

CHAP. XIII.

1 Emerigon, p. 210.

But although this point is so clearly settled by the law of *England*, in which also the law of *France* coincides, it is certain that the expediency of it has been a question which has very much engaged the attention of some considerable *French* authors. Their opinions can in no way affect the law of *England*, which stands upon much higher authority than the sentiments of speculative men, however respectable; but it may be productive of some amusement, if not instruction, to see by what arguments the two different opinions are supported.

Pothier Tr. d'Assurances, c. 1. s. 2. art. 2. s. 2.

Those who contend that such insurances are illegal, argue in this manner: that they who carry on commerce in a country, are obliged, by the custom of nations, and natural law, to conform to the laws of that country, where they trade. Every sovereign has power and jurisdiction over every thing done in the country, where he has a right to command; he has consequently a right to make laws relative to commerce within his dominions, which bind all those who trade, as well strangers as subjects. No one can dispute with the sovereign the right he has to retain in his own country certain merchandizes which are there to be found, and to prohibit the exportation of them. To export them contrary to his orders, is to strike a blow at his undoubted authority; and consequently it is unjust. But admitting, say they, that a *Frenchman* would not himself be subject to the law of *Spain*, for the trade which he carries on in *Spain*, it cannot be denied that the *Spaniards*, whose assistance he requires, are subject to those laws; and that they offend extremely in assisting him to export that, the exportation of which is prohibited by law. This species of trade then is to be considered as illicit, and contrary to good faith; and consequently the contract of insurance, introduced in order to protect it, by charging the insurer with the risk of confiscation, is illicit, and cannot induce an obligation.

2 Val. Com. 129. 1 Emerigon, 212.

Those who support the opposite doctrine, contend, that the exportation or importation of commodities prohibited by foreign laws is no offence; and that the means employed to effect it are regarded by the law, as a laudable and ingenious exertion of skill. Thus the exportation of certain commodities is prohibited in *Spain*, which the government of that country has a right to do: but the laws of his Catholic

Majesty

Majeſty are not the rule of action for *Frenchmen*. It is allowed them to bring from *Spain* into *France* piaſtres, piſtoles, and ſilks, for the ſupport of the banks, the manufactures, and the commerce of that country. Theſe merchandizes are a lawful branch of trade; and there is no reaſon why they ſhould not be the ſubject matter of a contract of inſurance. But above all, they inſiſt, that they are juſtified by the conſtant cuſtom; and that the reaſoners on the other ſide ought to be leſs ſtrict, when it is conſidered, that this contraband trade is a vice common to all commercial nations. The *Spaniards* and *Engliſh*, in time of peace, practiſe it in *France*: it is therefore permitted to carry it on in their reſpective countries by way of repriſal.

Whatever difference there may be on the queſtion of expediency, it is univerſally admitted by the *French* writers, that inſurances upon ſuch goods are valid. We have already ſeen that the ſame ideas have been adopted by the law of *England*; and that every policy upon goods, the exportation and importation of which is not prohibited by the municipal laws of this country, or by the general laws of nations, is legal and binding upon the parties; and the underwriter muſt anſwer for every loſs ariſing by means of any of the uſual perils.

CHAPTER THE FOURTEENTH.

Of Wager-Policies.

CHAP. XIV.

HAVING in the four preceding chapters ftated the various cafes, in which the contract of infurance is void from its very commencement, on account of its repugnancy to thofe principles of juftice, equity, and good faith, which are the great foundation of all contracts between man and man; we proceed to treat of thofe policies, which by the pofitive ftatute law of the country are declared to be abfolutely null and void. Of thefe the largeft clafs are wager-policies, or policies as they are called, upon intereft or no intereft.

The nature of the contract of infurance, in its original ftate, was, that a fpecific voyage fhould be performed free from perils; and in cafe of accidents, during fuch voyage, the infurer, in confideration of the premium he received, was to bear the merchant harmlefs. It followed from thence, that the contract related to the fafety of the voyage thus particularly defcribed, in refpect either of fhip or cargo: and that the perfon infured could not recover beyond the amount of his real lofs.

In procefs of time, however, variations were made, by exprefs agreement, from the firft kind of policy; and in cafes where the trader did not think it proper to difclofe the nature of his intereft, the infurer difpenfed with the infured having any intereft either in the fhip or cargo. In this laft kind of policy (of which we are now to treat) "valued free from average," and "intereft or no intereft," it is manifeft, that the performance of the voyage or adventure, in a reafonable time and manner, and not the bare exiftence of the fhip or cargo, is the object of the infurance.

Such an object as that, from a reference to the real nature of an infurance, as ftated in the outfet of the chapter, namely, that it is a contract of indemnity from a real and manifeft, not

not from a supposed and ideal loss, must have been originally bad. Indeed it has been declared from the bench, in the reign of queen *Anne*, that such insurances were *formerly* bad; for it is said in that case, that in former times, if one had no interest, though the policy ran, *interest or no interest*, the insurance was void; because insurances were made for the benefit of trade, and not that persons unconcerned therein, or uninterested in the subject matter, should profit by them. Assievedo v. Cambridge, 10 Mod. 77.

The idea thus started is very much confirmed by what fell from the court in the case of *Depaiba* v. *Ludlow*: for the court there observed, that insurances upon interest or no interest were introduced *since* the revolution. Depaiba v. Ludlow, Comyns Rep. 360.

Taking it for granted then, that the law of *England* in this respect, previous to the revolution, was such, as these cases suppose it to be, it was perfectly consonant to the laws of most of the commercial states and countries in *Europe*. For we find that by positive regulations of *Middlebourg*, *Genoa*, *Konyngsburg*, *Rotterdam*, and *Stockholm*, all insurances upon wagers, or as interest or no interest, are declared to be absolutely void, and of no effect. 2 Mag. 70. 65. 88. 189. 257.

But though this mode of insuring thus gained a footing in *England*, yet when introduced, the courts of justice looked upon these contracts with a jealous eye; and by their determinations shewed the strong prejudices which they entertained against them. The Courts of Equity in particular manifested that their inclination would lead them as much as possible to suppress such a species of contract: nay, that they still considered them as void. This is evident from two cases in *Vernon*'s Reports.

In one of them, the defendant had lent money on a bottomry bond, but had no interest in the ship or cargo; the money lent was 300*l.* and he insured 450*l.* on the ship: the plaintiff's bill was to have the policy delivered up; because the defendant was not concerned in point of interest, as to the ship or cargo. Goddart v. Garrett, 2 Vern. 269. Trin. Term, 1692.

Per curiam. Take it that the law is settled, that if a man has no interest, and insures, the insurance is void, though it be expressed in the policy, *interested or not interested.* The

CHAP. XIV.

reason the law goes upon is, that insurances were made for the benefit of trade, and not that persons unconcerned therein, and who were not interested in the ship, should profit thereby; and *where one would have the benefit of the insurance, he must renounce all interest in the ship.* And the reason why the law allows that a man having some interest in the ship or cargo, may insure more, or five times as much, is, that a merchant cannot tell how much or how little his factor may have in readiness to lade on board his ship. *Per Cur.* Decree the policy to be delivered up to be cancelled.

From the spirit of this decision, it may likewise appear, that the Court of Chancery inclined to think, that an insurance made without the benefit of salvage to the insurer, was unconscientious, and a proper subject for relief in equity; for the Chancellor expressly says, where one would have the benefit of the insurance, he must renounce all interest in the ship.

Le Pypre v. Farr, 2 Vern. 716. In Chancery, Mich. Term, 1716.

In another case also, which was on a policy of insurance on goods, by agreement valued at 600*l.* and the insured not to be obliged to prove any interest: the Lord Chancellor ordered the defendant to discover what goods he put on board; for although the defendant offered to renounce all interest to the insurers, yet it must be referred to the Master to examine the value of the goods saved, and to deduct it out of the value or sum of 600*l.* at which the goods were valued by the agreement.

There was one very remarkable difference between policies upon interest, and such as were not, of which I believe notice has already been taken in a former part of this work; namely, that in policies upon interest, you recover for the loss actually sustained, whether it be total or partial: but upon a wager-policy, you can never recover but for a total loss. All the doctrine, which turns upon this distinction between interest and wager policies was considered at much length by Lord *Mansfield*, in the famous cause of *Goss* v. *Withers*, to which we have had occasion more than once to refer.

2 Burr. 683. Vide ante, p. 150.

Vide ante, c. 1. p. 8, 9.

It has already been observed, that the security given to the insured was very considerably increased by the erection of two Assurance Companies, which were incorporated by royal charter in the year 1720; for the legislature had taken care

care that thoſe corporations ſhould have ſufficient funds to anſwer any demands that might be made upon them, in the common courſe of buſineſs. But this additional ſecurity for the inſured ſoon produced many dangerous and alarming conſequences, which, if they had not been checked, would have proved very detrimental to the trade of this country. For inſtead of confining the buſineſs of inſurances to real riſks, and conſidering them merely as an indemnity to the fair dealer againſt any loſs, which he might ſuſtain in the courſe of a trading voyage, which, as we have ſeen, was the original deſign of them; that practice, which only prevailed ſince the revolution, of inſuring ideal riſks, under the names of *intereſt or no intereſt, or without further proof of intereſt than the policy, or without benefit of ſalvage to the underwriters*, was increaſing to an alarming degree, and by ſuch rapid ſtrides as to threaten the ſpeedy annihilation of that lucrative and moſt beneficial branch of trade. All theſe various kinds of inſurance juſt enumerated, (and many others, which the ingenuity of bad men found no difficulty in deviſing,) having no reference whatever to actual trade or commerce, were very juſtly conſidered as mere gaming or wager-policies; and therefore the legiſlature thought it neceſſary to give them an effectual check, and, by poſitive rules, to fix and aſcertain what property or intereſt a merchant ſhould be permitted to inſure.

Accordingly an act of parliament paſſed, in the 19th year of the reign of king *George* II, entitled "an act to regulate "inſurance on ſhips belonging to the ſubjects of *Great* "*Britain*, and on merchandizes or effects laden thereon." As this act is the moſt important and moſt extenſive in the whole code of ſtatute law, with regard to inſurances, I ſhall now cite as much of it at length, as relates to the preſent chapter, and afterwards the other clauſes of it under thoſe heads, to which they more immediately apply.

The cauſes, which co-operated to induce the legiſlative body to paſs ſuch an act, are fully ſtated in the preamble. "Whereas it hath been found by experience, that the mak-"ing aſſurances, intereſt or no intereſt, or without further "proof of intereſt than the policy, hath been productive of "many pernicious practices, whereby great numbers of "ſhips, with their cargoes, have either been fraudulently loſt 19 Geo. 2. c. 37.

"and

CHAP. XIV. "and destroyed, or taken by the enemy in time of war; and "such assurances have encouraged the exportation of wool, "and the carrying on many other prohibited and clandestine "trades, which by means of such assurances have been con- "cealed, and the parties concerned secured from loss, as "well to the dimunition of the public revenue, as to the "great detriment of fair traders; and by introducing a mis- "chievous kind of gaming or wagering, under the pretence "of assuring the risk on shipping, and fair trade, the insti- "tution and laudable design of making assurances, hath been "perverted; and that which was intended for the encour- "agement of trade and navigation, has, in many instances, "become hurtful of, and destructive to the same."

Sect. 1. "For remedy whereof be it enacted, that no assurance "or assurances shall be made by any person or persons, "bodies corporate or politic, on any ship or ships belonging "to his majesty, or any of his subjects, or on any goods, "merchandizes or effects, laden or to be laden on board of "any such ship or ships, *interest or no interest, or without fur- "ther proof of interest than the policy, or by way of gaming, or "wagering, or without benefit of salvage to the assurer*; and "that every such insurance shall be null and void to all in- "tents and purposes."

Sect. 2. "Provided always, that assurance on private ships of war, "fitted out by any of his majesty's subjects solely to cruize "against his majesty's enemies, may be made by or for the "owners thereof, interest or no interest, free of average and "without benefit of salvage to the insurer; any thing here- "in contained to the contrary thereof in any wise notwith- "standing."

Sect. 3. "Provided also, that any merchandizes or effects from "any ports or places in *Europe* or *America*, in the possession "of the crowns of *Spain* or *Portugal*, may be assured in such "way and manner, as if this act had not been made."

Sect. 4. The fourth section relates to re-insurances, which will be the subject of the following chapter.

Sect. 5. "And be it enacted, that all and every sum and sums of "money to be lent on bottomry, or at *respondentia*, upon any "ship or ships belonging to any of his majesty's subjects, "bound

" bound to or from the *East Indies*, shall be lent only on the " ship, or on the merchandize or effects, laden, or to be " laden, on board of such ship, and shall be so expressed in " the condition of the said bond: and the benefit of salvage " shall be allowed to the lender, his agents or assigns, *who* " *alone shall have a right to make assurance on the money so lent:* and " no borrower of money on bottomry or *respondentia*, as afore- " said, shall recover more on any assurance than the value of " his interest in the ship, or in the merchandizes or effects, " laden on board of such ship, exclusive of the money so " borrowed; and in case it shall appear, that the value of his " share in the ship, or in the merchandizes or effects laden " on board, doth not amount to the full sum or sums he hath " borrowed as aforesaid, such borrower shall be responsible " to the lender for so much of the money borrowed, as he " hath not laid out on the ship or merchandize laden thereon, " with lawful interest for the same, together with the assur- " ance, and all other charges thereon, in the proportion the " money not laid out, shall bear to the whole money lent, " notwithstanding the ship and merchandizes be totally lost."

Upon this last section, of which we shall treat more fully in the chapter on Bottomry, it may be sufficient in this place to observe, that none but the lender shall have a right to make insurance on the money lent. It is also to be remarked, that this regulation of insurance on bottomry or *respondentia* interest, extends only to *East India* ships: and therefore, an insurance of a *respondentia* interest upon any other ships may be made in the same manner as they used to be before this act. It has also been decided upon this clause of the act, that it never meant or intended to make any alteration in the manner of insurances: and it was declared by the whole court in the case of *Glover* v. *Black*, which was fully reported in a former chapter, to be the established law and usage of merchants, that *respondentia* and bottomry must be mentioned and specified in the policy of insurance.

Glover v. Black, 3 Burr. 1394. Vide ante, c. 1. p. 10.

By the first section of the act it is clear that at this day all insurances made contrary to it are absolutely void and of no effect; which, as has already been shewn, was also the case by the ancient law of this country. It may now be material

CHAP. XIV.

to consider first, what cases have, by the construction put by the learned judges upon this statute, been held not to fall within its description: and secondly, those which do, and in which the policies have consequently been holden to be void.

It was formerly a matter of doubt, whether the act was meant to extend to insurances of foreign property, and on foreign ships. The better opinion, however, was, that it did not; for it was clear, that such insurances did not fall within the words of the statute; and from an attentive consideration of the preamble, they do not seem to come under the description of the mischiefs, against which it was the intention of the legislature to provide. But these doubts are entirely at an end by several decisions of the courts; and particularly by a very modern case, in which it was expressly declared by the court, (and the reason for it stated) that the act was not designed to extend to foreign ships.

Thellusson v. Fletcher, Doug. 301.

The case was this: the policy was on goods, on board three *French* vessels, from *St. Domingo* to *Bourdeaux*. The material part of it, as to this case, was in the following words: "On all goods loaden or to be loaden on board the ships "*Le Soigneux*, *La Pucelle*, *Le Vainqueur*, all or any of them. "The said goods and merchandizes by agreement are, and "shall be valued at (*a*) on 25 casks of "clayed sugar, and 12 hogsheads of muscovadoes: *the policy* "*to be deemed sufficient proof of interest, in case of loss.*" The first count in the declaration stated, that goods to a great amount, being the property of certain foreigners, had been shipped on board *Le Soigneux*, and that she had been lost. The second averred, that the goods were shipped on board *the three ships, or some or one of them*, to the amount of the sum insured; and that two of them had been captured and the other lost.

This case came before the court upon a motion to set aside the writ of inquiry, which had been executed before the sheriff, after a judgment by default, on this ground: that the jury had assessed the damages to the amount of the defendant's subscription, without any proof of the amount or value, or any evidence whatever, except that of the defendant's handwriting

(*a*) This was blank, as here printed.

handwriting to the policy. In addition to this objection, an affidavit was produced, tending to shew, that in fact the insured had no interest. It was argued for the defendant, that by the express agreement of the parties, no other proof of interest but the policy was required; and this insurance on foreign ships and property was not within the statute prohibiting such policies; so that the plaintiff was entitled to recover the sum insured by the defendant, even if it could be proved that the insured had no property on board. The court said that this was not a policy within the statute, foreign ships not having been included in that act, on account of the difficulty of bringing witnesses from abroad to prove the interest. The only difficulty there could have been here, was from the circumstance of there having been three ships; but the second count was so framed, as to make the case the same as if there had been but one. By suffering judgment to go by default, the defendant has confessed the plaintiff's title to recover; and the amount was fixed by the stipulation in the policy.

It was formerly thought, that a *valued* policy was a wager-policy, like interest or no interest. But this idea is now exploded, as we shall presently shew by a solemn decision of the Court of King's Bench. Of the difference between open and valued and open policies much has been already said; and the origin of the latter was derived from this source, it being sometimes troublesome to the trader to prove the value of his interest, or to ascertain the quantity of his loss, he gave the insurer a higher premium to agree to estimate his interest at a precise sum. To recover upon this kind of policy, the insured need only prove that he had an interest, without shewing the value. If indeed it appeared, or could be made appear, that the interest proved was merely a cover to a wager, in order to evade the statute, there is no doubt such a policy would be void.

Vide ante, c. 1.

All this doctrine was very fully stated, and commented upon by Lord *Mansfield*, in giving judgment in a cause then depending in the Court of King's Bench. "A valued policy," said his Lordship, "is not to be considered as a wager "policy, or like *interest or no interest*. If it were, it would be "void by the act of 19 *Geo.* II. *c.* 37. The only effect of "the valuation is fixing the amount of the prime cost; just

Lewis v. Rucker. 2 Burr, 1167. Vide ante, c. 6. p. 104.

"as

CHAP. XIV.

"as if the parties had admitted it at the trial: but in every argument, and for every other purpose, it muft be taken that the value was fixed *in fuch a manner*, as that the infured meant only to have an indemnity. If it be undervalued, the merchant himfelf ftands infurer for the furplus. If it be *much overvalued*, it muft be done with a bad view; either to gain, contrary to the 19th of the late king; or with fome view to a fraudulent lofs: therefore an infured never can be allowed to plead in a court of juftice, that he has greatly overvalued, or that his intereft was a trifle only. It is fettled that upon valued policies, the merchant need only prove fome intereft, to take it out of 19 *Geo.* II. becaufe the adverfe party has admitted the value: and if more were required, the agreed valuation would fignify nothing. But if it fhould come out in proof, that a man had infured 2000*l.* and had intereft on board to the value of a cable only; there never has been, and I believe there never will be a determination, that by fuch an evafion the act of parliament may be defeated. There are many conveniencies from allowing valued policies: but where they are ufed merely as a cover to a wager, they would be confidered as an evafion. The effect of the valuation is only fixing conclufively the prime coft. If it be an open policy, the prime coft muft be proved; in a valued policy it is agreed." For thefe reafons Lord *Mansfield* held, that a valued policy is not void by the ftatute of the 19 *Geo.* II.

The paffage juft quoted at length was, in a fubfequent cafe referred to in the judgment of the court; and the doctrine there advanced was adopted and confirmed.

Grant v. Parkinfon, Michaelmas, 22 Geo. 3. in B. R.

It was an action on a policy of infurance on the fhip *Providence*, at and from *Surinam*, or whatfoever other ports in the *Weft Indies* at which the fhip might load, to *Quebec*. At the trial before Lord *Mansfield*, at the fittings after *Trinity* Term 1781, the principal queftion on the merits was, whether the plaintiff had an infurable intereft. It was an infurance on the profits expected to arife on a cargo of molaffes belonging to the plaintiff, who had a contract with government to fupply the army with fpruce beer. Lord *Mansfield* thought it an infurable intereft. But the part of the cafe, which calls for our attention at prefent, was a claufe declaring,

ing, "that in case of loss, it was agreed that the profits should "be valued at 1000 *l.* without any other voucher than the pol-"icy." This, it was insisted, rendered the policy void, as well within the letter, as within the spirit of the 19 *Geo.* II. *c.* 37.

Lord *Mansfield*, at the trial, inclined to think that the contract was a fair one; but still he could not get over the objection, the instrument being void on the face of it. His Lordship, however, saved the point for the opinion of the court, a verdict being entered for the plaintiff, subject to that reference.

In *Michaelmas* Term following, the matter came on to be heard; when, after full argument at the bar,

Lord *Mansfield*, C. J. said: "I have, since the sittings at "*Guildhall*, on further consideration, changed my opinion. I "then thought the present policy within the act of parlia-"ment: I now think otherwise. On the construction of "the act, it has uniformly been held, that a valued policy "is not void. It is incumbent on the plaintiff to prove some "interest; but it is not necessary to go into the whole value. "In the case of *Lewis* v. *Rucker*, this doctrine was much "considered."—[Here his Lordship read the words already reported; and then he proceeds thus] "This insurance is on "the profits of a cargo, belonging to a man, having a con-"tract to supply the army, and if it arrive, the profits are "pretty certain. The meaning of the policy is not to evade "the act of parliament, but to avoid the difficulty of going "into an exact account of the quantum. I cannot distin-"guish it from a valued policy; and there is no pretence "for saying it is a *wagering* one." The other judges concurred; and the *postea* was given to the plaintiff. (*a*)

Da Costa v. Firth, 4 Burr. 1966.

In another case also it appeared, that an insurance had been made upon any of the packet boats that should sail from *Lisbon* to *Falmouth*, or such other port in *England* as his majesty should direct, for one year from *October* 1763, to *October* 1764, upon any kinds of goods and merchandizes whatsoever. And it was agreed, that the goods and merchandizes *should be valued at the sum insured* on such packet-boat, *without*

Flint v. Le Mesurier, Sittings after Hilary Term, 1796, at Guildhall.

(*a*) In a very late case where the interest was declared by the policy to be "*on the commissions of the plaintiff as consignee of the cargo, valued at* 1500 *l.*" Lord *Kenyon* expressed a very strong opinion, that this was a good insurable interest, but the matter being compromised, it did not come to any decision.

CHAP. XIV. *without farther proof of interest than the policy;* and to make no return of premium for want of interest being on bullion or goods. The insured had an interest in bullion on board the *Hanover* packet, being one of the king's packets between *Lisbon* and *Falmouth:* and it was totally lost within the time mentioned in the policy.

Vide ante, p. 118. 164. This case has already been quoted for another purpose; but on this point, the court held, that this was a policy of a peculiar sort; and was an exception out of the statute of 19 *Geo.* II. *c.* 37. It is a mixed policy; partly a wager-policy, partly an open one: and it is a valued policy, and fairly so, without fraud or misrepresentation. Therefore the loss having happened, the insured is entitled as for a total loss.

It has also been solemnly settled, that upon a joint capture by the army and navy, the officers and crews of the ships, before condemnation, have an insurable interest, by virtue of the prize act, which usually passes at the commencement of a war.

Le Cras v. Hughes, B. R. East. 22 Geo. 3. This was so held in an action upon a policy of insurance on the ship *St. Domingo*, at and from *Omoa* to *London;* upon which a case was reserved for the opinion of the court. The facts of the case were these: Captain *Luttrell*, commanding five of his majesty's ships, and Captain *Dalrymple*, commanding a party of the land forces, captured two *Spanish* register ships, lying under the protection of Fort *Omoa:* that the ship *St. Domingo* (on which the insurance was made) was one of the prizes, and was coming home laden with the property then captured; upon which ship the defendant underwrote 500*l.*: and that the ship was lost by perils of the sea. The question was, whether, by virtue of the prize act of the 19 *Geo.* III. *c.* 67. the officers and crew of the ships under Captain *Luttrell* had such an insurable interest in the *St. Domingo*, as to entitle them to recover?

Lord *Mansfield*.—"There are two questions in this cause: 1st. Whether the sea officers had an insurable interest? This will depend on the prize act and proclamation. 2dly. Whether possession would entitle them to insure, upon the bare contingency of a future grant from the crown? As to the first, consider the act of parliament, which gives to all the people on board, that is, to the flag officers, commanders, and other officers; to the seamen, marines, and soldiers

on

on board every ſhip and veſſel of war, the ſole intereſt and property of and in all and every ſhip and veſſel, goods, and merchandizes, which they ſhall take during the war, after condemnation. Does the act ſay, that the ſeamen only ſhall take? does it leave a joint capture by the army and navy undefined? Certainly not. Suppoſe, for inſtance, a caſe which I remember to have happened: a *Dutch* and *Engliſh* fleet combined captured ſome ſhips; the *Engliſh* ſailors could not take ſolely; nor could the act mean that they ſhould have nothing. In the caſe in queſtion, ſuppoſe Captain *Dalrymple* had given no aſſiſtance, is there any doubt that Captain *Luttrell* would have taken the whole? The only difference is, that now he has not the merit of a ſole capture. The word "*ſoldiers*" in the proclamation, means ſoldiers on board the ſhip. Thus it ſtands on the act and proclamation. But ſuppoſing that doubtful, as far back as queen *Anne's* time down to the preſent, wherever a capture has been made by a king's ſhip or a privateer, the crown has always given a grant of it after condemnation. There is no inſtance to the contrary. Have not then the inſured ſuch an intereſt in the ſhip coming home, as to entitle them to an indemnity? Suppoſe a man is made agent of prizes; he has not the poſſeſſion of the property, and yet he has ſuch an intereſt in any ſhip coming home, that he may inſure. Here the inſured have the poſſeſſion, and a certain expectation of receiving the property captured for their own emolument from the crown."

Judgment for the plaintiff.

In the conſtruction of the act it has been holden, that all inſurances made by perſons having no intereſt in the event about which they inſure, or without reference to any property on board, are merely wagers, deſtructive of the true ends for which this contract was introduced into the mercantile world; and therefore are to be conſidered as abſolutely null and void.

Upon a motion for a new trial, Lord *Mansfield*, who had tried the cauſe, made the following report: This was an action brought by the plaintiff, who was a ſurgeon on board an *Eaſt Indiaman*, againſt the defendant, a paſſenger in the ſame ſhip, to recover a ſum of 1000 *l.* upon a ſpecial agreement, bearing date the 18th of *July* 1774; by which, after reciting, (Kent v. Bird, Cowp. 583.)

reciting, that "whereas the plaintiff had agreed to pay to "the defendant the sum of 20*l.* sterling at the next port the "ship should arrive at, it was witnessed that he the defend-"ant, in consideration thereof, did undertake that the said "ship should save her passage to *China* that season; and in "case she did not, that then he would pay to the plaintiff "the sum of 1000*l.* at the end of one month after the arri-"val of the said ship in the river *Thames*." At the trial it appeared, that the plaintiff duly paid the amount of the 20*l.* to the defendant at the next port, in pagodas: that the vessel being delayed below the Cape and *Madras* in consequence of a miscalculation of five days in the reckoning, and the monsoons setting in earlier than usual, she lost her passage. That the plaintiff had *some goods* on board, which were liable to suffer by the loss of the season; and that whilst it was still doubtful whether the ship would or would not save her passage, the captain had applied to each of the parties, to persuade them to rescind the agreement; representing that the sum to be paid in either event would be more than the loser could afford. That the plaintiff was willing to have cancelled the agreement; but the defendant positively refused. The jury found a verdict for the plaintiff, damages 980*l.* but I gave the defendant leave to move for a new trial upon the question, whether this were not an agreement within the statute 19 *Geo.* II. *c.* 37. and therefore void.

After this case had been fully argued at the bar,

Lord *Mansfield* said: "A policy of insurance is, in the nature of it, a contract of indemnity, and of great benefit to trade. But the use of it was perverted by its being turned into a wager. To remedy this evil, the statute of the 19 *Geo.* II. *c.* 37. was made: which, after enumerating in the preamble the various frauds and pernicious practices introduced by the perversion of this species of contract; and amongst others, that of gaming or wagering under pretence of insuring vessels, &c. proceeds, under general words, to prohibit *all* contracts of insurance by way of *gaming* or *wagering*. Here, the plaintiff gives so much to the defendant in consideration that the ship should save her passage to *China*; and if not, then, upon her returning safe to *England*, he is to receive 1000*l.* If the first of these events happened, the defendant won; but he could not lose, unless both happened.

pened. Is not this gaming? Is not this wagering? If this were allowed, all wagering policies would be turned into this form, and the act would be entirely defeated. If there is no interest in the case, it is gaming and wagering. Therefore there must be a new trial.

From this case we find, that the principle stated by Lord *Mansfield* in *Lewis* v. *Rucker* is confirmed: namely, that where a man insures 2000*l.* and it turns out in proof that he has an interest to the value of a cable only, such an interest will never be allowed to operate so as to evade the statute. For in this case, it appeared in evidence, that the plaintiff had *some goods* on board; but that was held not to be an interest sufficient to justify an insurance so evidently contrary to the act of parliament.

Indeed wherever the court can see upon the face of the policy, that it is merely a contract of gaming, where indemnity is not the object in view, they are bound to declare such policy void.

Lowry and another v. Bourdieu, Doug. 451.

The plaintiffs had lent to *Lawson*, captain of the *Lord Holland East Indiaman*, 26,000*l.* for which he had given them a common bond, in the penal sum of 52,000*l.* While he was with his ship at *China*, the plaintiffs got a policy of insurance underwritten by the defendant and others, which was in the following terms: "at and from *China* to *London*, beginning "the adventure upon the goods from the loading thereof on "board the said ship at *Canton*, in *China*, &c. and *upon the* "*said ship* from and immediately following her arrival at *Can*-"*ton* in *China*, valued at 26,000*l.* being the amount of cap-"tain *Patrick Lawson*'s common bond, payable to the parties, "as shall be described at the back of this policy; and it bears "date the 16th day of *December* 1775; and in case of loss, "*no other proof of interest to be required than the exhibition of the* "*said bond*: warranted free from average, and without bene-"fit of salvage to the insurer."

At the head of the subscription was written, "*On a bond as above expressed.*" Captain *Lawson* failed from *China*, and arrived safe with his privilege (as it is called) or adventure, in *London*,

CHAP. XIV. *London*, on the 1ſt of *July* 1777, none of the events inſured againſt having happened. The receipt of the premium was acknowledged on the back of the policy. This caſe came before the court upon an action for a return of premium, on the ground that, the policy being without intereſt, the contract was void. This caſe, as far as it relates to the queſtion of return of premium, will be conſidered in a future chapter; but in the courſe of the diſcuſſion, it became neceſſary to determine, whether the policy, juſt recited, was good within the ſtatute. At the trial which came on at the ſittings after *Trinity* term, 1780, the Chief Juſtice was of opinion, that this was a gaming policy prohibited by the ſtatute of 19 *Geo.* II. *c.* 37. and a verdict was given for the defendant. His lordſhip, however, having expreſſed a doubt upon the propriety of his opinion on other points of the cauſe, a motion for a new trial was afterwards made, and all the queſtions came to be debated before the court: when the majority of the judges confirmed Lord *Mansfield's* firſt direction upon all the points. It is true Mr. Juſtice *Willes* differed from his brethren upon that occaſion; the learned judge being of opinion, upon the queſtion relating to our preſent inquiry, that this was not a gaming policy: that it did not appear to him, that the parties had any idea they were entering into an illegal contract: that the whole was diſcloſed, and they *thought* there was an intereſt; this was a miſtake; but it is a new point of law.

The three other judges ſupported their opinions upon the following grounds.

Lord *Mansfield*.—" It is certainly true, in many inſtances, that firſt thoughts are beſt. I am now very much inclined to my firſt opinion. There are two ſorts of policies of inſurance; mercantile and gaming policies. The firſt ſort are contracts of indemnity, and of indemnity only; and from that principle a great variety of deciſions and conſequences have followed. The ſecond ſort may be the ſame in form; but in them there is no contract of indemnity, becauſe there is no intereſt upon which a loſs can accrue. They are mere games of hazard, like the caſt of a die. In the preſent caſe, the nature of the inſurance is known to both parties. The plaintiffs ſay, " We mean to game: but we give our reaſon

" for

"for it; Captain *Lawson* owes us a sum of money, and we "want to be secure in case he should not be in a situation to "pay us." It was a hedge. But they had no interest; for if the ship had been lost, and the underwriters had paid, still the plaintiffs would have been entitled to recover the amount of the bond from *Lawson*. This then is a gaming policy; and against an act of parliament."

Mr. Justice *Ashhurst*.—"A policy of insurance ought to be a mere contract of indemnity, and nothing more; but here the money might have been paid twice, which shews decisively that this was a gaming policy."

Mr. Justice *Buller*.—"It is very clear to me that the plaintiffs ought not to recover. There was no fraud on the part of the underwriters, nor any mistake in matter of fact. If the *law* was mistaken, the rule applies, that *ignorantia juris non excusat*. This was a mere gaming policy without interest." Agreeably to this opinion, the rule for a new trial was discharged.

The second section of the act in question, which allows of insurances being made on private ships of war, interest or no interest, seems sufficiently clear, and requires no explanation.

The third section, by which insurances upon any merchandizes or effects from any ports or places in *Europe* or *America*, in the possession of the crowns of *Spain* or *Portugal*, may be effected in the manner practised before this act was passed, seems to be obscurely worded. The learned commentator upon the law of *England*, observes, that the reason of this proviso is sufficiently obvious. Notwithstanding this authority, in order to comprehend the meaning of the legislature, we must observe, that the trade from *Spain* and *Portugal* to their respective colonies and establishments in *South America*, and the returns thereof, can only be carried on by their own subjects; and all other persons are prohibited from that trade by positive regulations of these respective States. The consequence of such a prohibition is, that all the goods and merchandizes which the subjects of this and other countries export from *Spain* and *Portugal*, must be in the names of *Spanish* subjects. So that it was absolutely necessary to make this exception (for no other proof but the policy itself can be brought) otherwise all insurances upon that branch of

Mr. Justice Blackstone, 2 Vol. Com. 460.

trade muſt have been entirely void. The words, however, ſeem to allow a greater latitude than was meant by the legiſlature in making ſuch a proviſion, for by adverting merely to the words, inſurances from any ports or places in *Europe* or *America*, belonging to *Spain* and *Portugal*, to *England* or other ports of *Europe* may be made, as if this act had never paſſed. Whereas by attending to the prohibition of trade juſt mentioned to any but the ſubjects of *Spain* and *Portugal*, as the commerce between theſe colonies and the parent countries can only be carried on by ſubjects, it is evident that the legiſlature intended rather to have ſaid, that inſurances on goods from ports belonging to *Spain* and *Portugal* in *Europe* to any ports in *America* belonging to thoſe courts; and from ſuch ports in *America* to ſuch ports or places in *Europe*, ſhall be valid and effectual contracts, than to authorize inſurances from the dominions of *Spain* and *Portugal* in *Europe* or *America*, to whatſoever place in the world the ſhip, in which theſe goods are to be carried, may happen to be deſtined. The words, however, certainly admit of that broad conſtruction; for the place of deſtination is not aſcertained.

Upon this ſection of the act, it may be obſerved, that the equitable conſtruction of ſuch contracts of inſurance as are protected by it, ſeems to be, that they may be made without intereſt, notwithſtanding the caſe of *Goddard* v. *Garrett*, above V. ante, p. 260. cited: ſince in ſuch inſtances it is impoſſible for the perſon inſured to bring any certain proof of intereſt on board.

Hitherto we have ſpoken merely of that part of this very ſalutary act which requires, that every perſon making ſuch a contract, ſhould have an intereſt in that which is the object of the inſurance. Another part of it ſtill claims our attention, that which prohibits re-aſſurances. What a re-aſſurance is; in what caſes it is prohibited; and when it is allowable, will form the ſubject of the following chapter.

CHAPTER THE FIFTEENTH.

Of Re-Aſſurance, and Double Inſurance.

CHAP. XV.

RE-ASSURANCE, as underſtood by the law of *England*, may be ſaid to be a contract, which the firſt inſurer enters into, in order to relieve himſelf from thoſe riſks which he has incautiouſly undertaken, by throwing them upon other underwriters, who are called re-aſſurers. This ſpecies of contract has obtained a place in moſt of the commercial ſyſtems of the trading powers of *Europe*; and it is allowed by them at this day to be politic and legal. The learned *Roccus* has decided expreſsly in favour of it; and has cited many reſpectable authorities in ſupport of his opinion. "Aſſecurator, poſt factum aſſecurationem, poteſt "ſe aſſecurari facere ab alio aſſecuratore, et iſte ſecundus "aſſecurator tenetur pro aſſecuratione factâ a primo, et ad "ſolvendum omne totum, quod primus aſſecurator ſolverit, "et iſta ſecunda aſſecuratio valet." By the ancient law of *France* ſuch aſſurances were reckoned valid, and perfectly conſiſtent with equity and good conſcience. The author of the Guidon obſerves, that if it ſo happen that the inſurers, after underwriting the policy, repent of their engagement, or are afraid to encounter the riſk, they are at liberty to re-inſure; but ſtill they cannot prevent the inſured from making his demand upon them in caſe of loſs, for having, by their ſignature, promiſed indemnity, they cannot, by any proteſtations to the contrary, diſcharge themſelves from their reſponſibility, without the conſent of the inſured. *Lewis* the Fourteenth, when, by the aſſiſtance of the famous *Colbert*, he promulgated thoſe ordinances, which will be a laſting honour to the French nation, adopted the idea that prevailed when the Guidon was written: for by an article in that celebrated code of laws, he expreſsly declared, "that it ſhould be lawful to the inſurers to make re-aſſurance with other men "of thoſe effects which they had themſelves previouſly inſured." It is not in *France* alone that this law prevails; for

Roccus de Aſſecur. Not. 12.

Le Guidon, c. 2. art. 19.

Ord. Lewis 14. tit. Aſſur. art. 20.

2 Mag. 190. 233. 419.

CHAP. XV.

for by the positive and express regulations and ordinances of *Koningsberg*, *Hamburgh*, and *Bilboa*, re-assurances are allowed to be effected, and consequently are lawful contracts.

1 Emerigon. p. 247.

Pothiér, tit. Assurance, No. 96.

By the passage cited from the Guidon it might be observed, that it was a distinguishing character of this species of contract, that notwithstanding a re-insurance, the first contract subsists as at first, without change or amendment. The re-insurer is wholly unconnected with the original owner of the property insured; and as there was no obligation between them originally, so none is raised by the subsequent act of the first underwriter. The risks of the insurer form the object of the re-insurance, which is a new independent contract, not at all concerning the insured; who consequently can exercise no power or authority with respect to it.

Agreeably to the laws of those countries just referred to, and consistently with the opinions of those respectable writers, whose works we have had such frequent occasion to mention, the law of *England* adopted their regulations, and permitted the underwriters upon policies to insure themselves against those risks for which they had inadvertently engaged to indemnify the insured: or where perhaps they had involved themselves to a greater amount, than their ability would enable them to discharge. Although such a contract seems perfectly fair and reasonable in itself, and might be productive of very beneficial consequences to those concerned in this important branch of trade; yet, like many other useful institutions, it was so much abused, and turned to purposes so pernicious to a commercial nation, and so destructive of those very benefits it was originally intended to promote and encourage, that the legislature was at last obliged to interpose, and by a positive law to cut off all opportunity of practising those frauds in future, which were become thus glaring and enormous.

19 Geo. II. c. 37. s. 4.

Accordingly by the fourth section of that statute, which formed the subject of the preceding chapter, it was enacted, "that it should not be lawful to make RE-ASSURANCE, unless "the assurer should be insolvent, become a bankrupt, or die; "in either of which cases, such assurer, his executors, ad- "ministrators,

" ministrators, or assigns, might make re-assurance, to the " amount before by him assured, provided it should be ex- " pressed in the policy to be a re-assurance."

From this act it is apparent, that all kinds of re-assurance are not prohibited; but wherever such a contract tends to the advancement of commerce, or to the real benefit of an individual, in such a case it shall be permitted. Thus in case of insolvency or bankruptcy, it is advantageous to the creditors in general, as well as to the individual, that a re-assurance should be made: for by these means the fund of the bankrupt's estate is not diminished in case of loss, and the insured has a better security for the payment of the amount of his damage, or at least a proportion of it. (*a*) If the insurer

(*a*) Formerly, if an underwriter became a bankrupt after he had subscribed the policy, and before a loss happened, the insured was not entitled to a dividend out of the bankrupt's estate. This being found a heavy inconvenience, and a discouragement to trade, parliament was obliged to interpose, and to alter the law in this respect. The statute recited, "that 19 Geo. II. c. 32. s. 2. " merchants and traders frequently lend money on bottomry, or at *respon-* " *dentia*, and in the course of their trade, frequently cause their ships or ves- " sels, and the goods and merchandizes loaded thereon, to be insured; and " that where commissions of bankruptcy have issued against the obligor " in such bottomry or *respondentia* bond, or the underwriter, or assurer in " such insurance, before the loss of the ship or goods, in such bond or pol- " icy of insurance mentioned, had happened, it had been made a question, " whether the obligee or obligees in such bond, or the assured in such poli- " cy of insurance, should be let in to prove their debts, or be admitted to " have any benefit or dividend under such commission, which might be a " discouragement to trade." It was therefore enacted, " that the obligee in " any bottomry, or *respondentia* bond, and the assured in any policy of insur- " ance, made and entered into, upon a good and valuable consideration, " *bona fide*, should be admitted to claim: and after the loss or contingency " should have happened, to prove his, her, or their debt and demands, in re- " spect of such bond or policy of insurance, in like manner as if the loss or " contingency had happened before the time of the issuing of such commis- " sion of bankruptcy against such obligor or insurer; and should be en- " titled unto, and should have and receive, a proportionable part, share, " and dividend of such bankrupt's estate in proportion to the other cred- " itors of such bankrupt, in like manner, as if such loss or contingency had " happened before such commission issued: and that all and every person " and persons, against whom any commission of bankruptcy should be award- " ed, should be discharged of and from the debt or debts, owing by him, " her, or them, on every such bond and policy of insurance as aforesaid, " and should have the benefit of the several statutes now in force against " bankrupts in like manner, to all intents and purposes, as if such loss or " contingency had happened, and the money due in respect thereof had " become payable, before the time of the issuing out the commission."

CHAP. XV. ſurer die, it is no leſs neceſſary and beneficial to his ſucceſſors, that there ſhould be a re-aſſurance, than it was in the former caſe of a bankruptcy: becauſe it will provide aſſets to ſatisfy the inſured in caſe a loſs ſhould happen, and thus ſecure the eſtate of the deceaſed for the benefit of his heirs. Indeed, in both caſes, the intention of the legiſlature ſeems to have been, to provide a fund for the payment of that proportion, which, in caſe of an inſolvency, the inſured will have a right to demand, in common with the other creditors; and for the payment of the whole, without prejudice to the heir, even in caſes where the anceſtor, at the time of his death, was in ſolvent circumſtances.

This act is worded in ſuch expreſs terms, excluding every ſpecies of re-aſſurance, except in the three inſtances of death, bankruptcy, or inſolvency, that a doubt, as it ſhould ſeem, could hardly be founded upon it. But as it was held, that the firſt clauſe of the ſtatute, prohibiting inſurances, *intereſt or no intereſt*, did not extend to foreign ſhips; ſo it was argued, that re-aſſurances made here on *the ſhips of foreigners* did not fall within the act. It might have occurred, however, that the firſt clauſe of the ſtatute is qualified, and only prohibits ſuch inſurances when made *on his majeſty's ſhips, or the ſhips belonging to his majeſty's ſubjects*: whereas the clauſe in queſtion is general and without reſtriction; the inference from which is, that the legiſlature had both objects in view, and meant wholly to prohibit the one, but not the other.

Vide ante, c. 14.

This point came on to be conſidered by the Court of King's Bench, in the year 1787, in the form of a ſpecial caſe, ſtating, that a re-aſſurance was made by the defendant on a *French veſſel*, firſt inſured by a *French underwriter* at *Marſeilles*, who was living, and who, at the time of ſubſcribing the ſecond policy, was ſolvent.

Andree v. Fletcher. 2 Term. Rep. 161.

The court (*Aſhhurſt*, *Buller*, and *Groſe*, juſtices) were unanimouſly of opinion, that this policy of re-aſſurance was void; and that every re-aſſurance in this country, either by *Britiſh* ſubjects or foreigners, on *Britiſh* or foreign ſhips, is void by the ſtatute; *unleſs the firſt aſſurer be inſolvent, become a bankrupt, or die.*

There

There is another ſpecies of re-aſſurance allowed by the laws of *France*, as eſtabliſhed by an ordinance of *Lewis* the Fourteenth, which was alſo taken from that ancient and excellent *French* treatiſe, that has been ſo frequently mentioned. By this regulation, it is declared lawful for the aſſured to inſure the ſolvency of the underwriter. By theſe means, the perſon inſured gets rid of thoſe fears, which he may have conceived concerning the ability of the inſurers to pay, and he gains a ſecond ſecurity to anſwer for the ſufficiency of the firſt. But it is not to *France* alone that this kind of contract is reſtrained; for by the poſitive laws of many other maritime States, ſuch re-aſſurances are valid and binding contracts. The *Engliſh* ſtatute, which has been the ſubject of this and the preceding chapter, takes no expreſs notice of this ſort of inſurance; becauſe, in truth, I believe it never was very much in practice in *England*: but, however, it ſeems clear that ſuch a circumſtance as the ſolvency of the underwriter, is not an inſurable intereſt; that a policy opened upon ſuch an event would be treated as a wager policy; and would conſequently fall within the ſtatute of *George* the Second, which declares all policies made by way of gaming or wagering, to be abſolutely null and void to all intents and purpoſes.

Le Guidon, c. 2. art. 20.

Ord. of Lew. 14. tit. Aſſur. art. 20.

2 Mag. 190. 419.

Having ſaid thus much of re-aſſurances, I ſhall proceed to conſider the nature of a double inſurance, and to ſtate the few caſes that have been determined upon the ſubject. I treat of it in this place, becauſe theſe two kinds of inſurance have been ſometimes confounded together, and ſuppoſed to mean the ſame thing: whereas no two ideas can be more diſtinct. We have already ſeen what is meant by a re-aſſurance. A double inſurance is where the ſame man is to receive two ſums inſtead of one, or the ſame ſum twice over, for the ſame loſs, by reaſon of his having made two inſurances upon the ſame goods or the ſame ſhip. The firſt diſtinction between theſe two contracts, is, that a re-aſſurance is a contract made by the firſt underwriter, his executors or aſſigns; to ſecure himſelf, or his eſtate: a double inſurance is entered into by the inſured. A re-aſſurance, except in the caſes provided for by the ſtatute, is abſolutely void: a double inſurance is not void; but ſtill the inſured ſhall recover only one ſatisfaction for his loſs. This requires explanation. Where a man has made a double inſurance, he may recover his

Double Inſurance.

1 Burr. 496.

19 Geo. II. c. 37. ſ. 4.

1 Black. Rep. 416.

CHAP. XV.

1 Burr. 492.

his loss, against which of the underwriters he pleases, but he can recover for no more than the amount of his loss. This depends upon the nature of an insurance, and the great principles of justice and good faith. An insurance is merely a contract of indemnity, in case of loss; it follows as a necessary consequence that a man shall not recover more than he has lost, or recover satisfaction greater than the injury he has sustained. This rule was wisely established, in order to prevent fraud, lest the desire of gain should occasion unfair and wilful losses. It being thus settled, that the insured shall recover but one satisfaction, and that in case of a double insurance, he may fix upon which of the underwriters he will for the payment of his loss, it is a principle of natural justice that the several insurers should all of them contribute in their several proportions, to satisfy that loss, against which they have all insured.

These principles have been fully declared to be law in several cases, which are now to be mentioned.

Newby v. Reed, Sit. in London in Easter Vacat. 1763. 1 Black. Rep. 416.

In the year 1763, it was ruled by Lord *Mansfield*, Chief Justice, and agreed to be the course of practice, that upon a double insurance, though the insured is not entitled to two satisfactions; yet, upon the first action he may recover the whole sum insured, and may leave the defendant therein to recover a rateable satisfaction from the other insurers.

Rogers v. Davis, Sittings in Mich. Vac. 17 Geo. III. before Lord Mansfield.

Thus also it was determined in a subsequent case at *Guildhall*. It was an action on a policy of insurance on a ship from *Newfoundland* to *Dominica*, and from thence to the port of discharge in the *West Indies*. It was a valued policy on the ship and freight; and on the goods as interest should appear. The ship sailed from *St. John*'s the 17th of *December* 1775, and the plaintiff declared as for a total loss. The defendant underwrote for 200*l.* and has paid into court 124*l.* This sum was paid on a supposition, that the underwriters on a former policy should bear a share of the loss. The plaintiff had originally insured at *Liverpool* on a voyage from *Newfoundland* to *Barbadoes* and the *Leeward Islands*, with an exception of *American* captures: but the plaintiff afterwards, for the purpose of securing himself against captures, and having altered the course of his voyage, made the present insurance. The plaintiff now insisted he

was

was entitled to receive the full amount of his insurance against the defendant, and not to any part from the *Liverpool* underwriters, because the voyage now insured was different from that insured at *Liverpool*. There was however a verdict for the plaintiff for his full demand, *with liberty for the defendant to bring an action against the Liverpool underwriters, if he thought fit.* CHAP. XV.

Accordingly in the *Easter* term following, an action was brought for money had and received to the use of the plaintiff, who was the defendant in the last cause, in order to recover a contribution for the loss which the plaintiff had been obliged to pay. It was agreed by both parties to admit, that on the *London* policy (which was the subject of the former action) 2200*l.* were insured; that on the two *Liverpool* policies 1700*l.* were insured: that the merchant was interested to the amount of 500*l.* on the ship; 300*l.* on the freight; and 1400*l.* on the cargo. That the plaintiff had paid 200*l.* loss, and 47*l.* for the costs. The question was, whether the defendant was liable to contribute any thing, and what. The whole interest was 2200*l.* and the whole insurance was 3900*l.* It was insisted by the counsel for the defendant, that the insurance in *London* was an illegal re-assurance; and therefore the plaintiff might have made a good defence in an action brought against him: and if so, he could not now recover over against the defendant. Davis v. Gildart, Sittings in East. Vac. 17 Geo. III. at Guildhall.

Lord *Mansfield*.—"The question seems to be whether the insured has not two securities for the loss that has happened. If so, can there be a doubt that he may bring his action against either? It is like the case of two securities; where, if all the money be recovered against one of them, he may recover a proportion from the other. Then this would bring it to the question, whether the second insurance is void as a *re-assurance*. But a re-assurance is a contract made by the insurer to secure himself; *and this is only a double insurance*." There was another ground taken in the cause, which is not material to be mentioned here: but upon this direction the plaintiff had a verdict.

Although a man, by making a double insurance, shall not be allowed to recover a double satisfaction for the same loss; yet various persons may insure various interests on the same thing, and each to the whole value (as the master for wages; 1 Burr. 496.
the

CHAP. XV.

the owner for freight; one person for goods, another for bottomry) and such a contract does not fall within the idea of a double insurance. There is a full case upon this subject, and a very elaborate argument of Lord *Mansfield*, in delivering the judgment of the whole Court of King's Bench, in which most of the questions relative to double insurances are clearly and decisively settled. In this cause the question was, whether the plaintiff ought to recover his whole loss, or only a half; it being objected that there was a double insurance. A verdict was found for the whole, subject to the opinion of the court upon Lord *Mansfield*'s report.

Godin and others v. The London Assur. Comp. 1 Burr. 489. 1 Black. Rep. 103.

Lord *Mansfield*, in delivering the opinion of the court, began, by stating the facts, as they appeared to him at the trial.

Mr. *Meybohm* of *St. Petersburg* had dealings with Mr. *Amyand* and Company of *London*, who often sent ships from *London* to Mr. *Meybohm* at *St. Petersburg*. *Meybohm*, as appeared by the evidence, was indebted, on the balance of their accounts, to *Amyand* and Company. *Amyand* and Company sent a ship, called *The Galloway*, *Stephen Barker*, master, to Mr. *Meybohm*, at *St. Petersburg*, to fetch certain goods. *Meybohm* sent the goods, and promised to send the bill of lading by the next post, but never did. Afterwards, in *August*, 1756, *Amyand* and Company got a policy of insurance from private underwriters, for 1100*l.* on the ship, tackle, and goods, at and from *London* to *St. Petersburg*, and at and from thence back again to *London*: which policy was signed by several private underwriters, quite different persons from the present defendants; and of this sum of 1100*l.* thus underwritten, 500*l.* was declared to be on $\frac{11}{60}$ parts of the ship, and the remaining 600*l.* to be on goods. Between the 26th of *August*, and the 28th of *September* 1756, (both included) Mr. *Amyand* insured 800*l.* more, with other private insurers: and this latter insurance was upon goods only: and was only at and from *St. Petersburg* to *London*. On the 28th, 29th, and 30th of *October* 1756, Mr. *Amyand* insured 900*l.* more with other private insurers: which last insurance was on goods only, at and from the *Sound* to *London*. So that the whole sum insured by *Amyand* and Company was 2800*l.* of which the sum of 2300*l.* was on goods, and the remaining 500*l.* was on the ship. Several letters being given in evidence,

evidence, it appeared that *Meybohm* wrote from *Petersburg* on the 7th of *September* 1756 (the date of his first letter on this subject) to *Amyand* and Company; and mentioned what goods he should send to them, referring to the invoice for particulars; and directed them to get insurance thereon, and to place the goods and the insurance to a particular account which he named in his letter; in which he also specified some iron, which was for Mr. *Amyand's* own account. This letter Mr. *Amyand* afterwards received (probably about the 27th of *October*) and in consequence of it made the insurance accordingly, upon the 28th, 29th, and 30th of the same *October*, as before-mentioned. *Meybohm*, having shipped the goods, endorsed the bills of lading to one Mr. *John Tamesz* in *Moscow* (the plaintiff in effect, in the present action) who, on the 7th of *October* 1756, wrote to his correspondent Mr. *Uhthoff* here in *London* to insure these goods. In this letter, he desires Mr. *Uhthoff* to insure the *whole*, that he (*Tamesz*) might be safe in all events; for he suspected that these goods were intended to be consigned by *Meybohm* to somebody else, and perhaps might be insured by some other persons. And he says they were transferred to him, in consideration of his being in advance to *Meybohm* more than their amount. This letter from Mr. *Tamesz*, with these directions to insure, was received by Mr. *Uhthoff*, on the 15th of *November* 1756. Mr. *Uhthoff* accordingly applied to the defendants, the *London* Assurance Company; and disclosed to them, at the same time, all these particulars: and they, upon the 16th of *November* 1756, after being thus apprised, *that there might be another insurance*, made the insurance now in question, for 2316*l.* on the goods at and from the *Sound* to *London*. The goods were lost in the voyage. Mr. *Uhthoff's* insurance was made by the plaintiffs *Godin, Guyon*, and Company, who are insurance brokers: and they declare that this insurance was made by order of *Henry Uhthoff*, Esq. This declaration is endorsed upon the policy, and is dated the 18th of *November* 1756. There is no doubt as to the value of the goods, or as to the loss of them. It is admitted by the defendants, that the plaintiffs ought to recover half the loss from them: but they say they ought to pay *only half*, not the *whole* of the loss. So that the only question is, whether the plaintiffs are entitled, upon the circumstances of this case, and upon the facts I have been stating, to recover the *whole loss* from the present defendants;

CHAP. XV. defendants; or only the *half* of his loss from *them*, and the remainder from the underwriters of Mr. *Amyand*'s policy. The verdict is found for the plaintiff, for the whole; but it is agreed to be subject to the opinion of this court, upon the question I have just mentioned.

First, to consider it as between the insurer and insured. As between them, and upon the foot of commutative justice merely, there is no colour why the insurers should not pay the insured the whole: for they have received a premium for the whole risk. Before the introduction of wagering policies, it was upon principles of convenience very wisely established, that a man should not recover more than he had lost. Insurance was considered as an indemnity only, in case of loss; and therefore the insurance ought not to exceed the loss. This rule was calculated to prevent fraud; lest the temptation of gain should occasion unfair and wilful losses. If the insured is to receive but one satisfaction, natural justice says that the several insurers shall all of them *contribute pro rata*, to satisfy that loss, against which they have all insured. No particular cases are to be found on this head: or, at least, none have been cited by the counsel on either side. Where a man makes a double insurance of the same thing, in such a manner that he can clearly recover against several insurers in distinct policies a double satisfaction, the law certainly says that he ought not to recover doubly for the same loss, but be content with one single satisfaction for it. And if the same man really and for his own proper account insures the same goods doubly, though both insurances be not made in his own name, but one or both of them in the name of another person, yet that is just the same thing; for the same person is to have the benefit of both policies. And if the whole should be recovered from one, he ought to stand in the place of the insured, to receive contribution from the other, who was equally liable to pay the whole. But in this case if *Tamesz* was not to have the benefit of both policies in all events, then it can never be considered as a double policy.

It has been said that the endorsement of the bills of lading transferred *Meybohm*'s interest in all policies, by which the cargo assigned was insured; therefore *Tamesz* has a right to Mr. *Amyand*'s policy; and that *Tamesz*, being the assignee of of *Meybohm*, is the *cestuy qui trust* of it, and may recover the money insured; and even that he may bring trover, or detinue, for the very policy itself: and it is urged from hence, that he either will, or may, have a double satisfaction for the same loss.

But allowing that by the endorsement of the bills of lading and assigning the cargo to *Tamesz*, he stands in the place of *Meybohm* in respect of his insurances; yet Mr. *Amyand* has an interest of his own, and had actually insured the ship and goods, to the amount of 1900*l.* (upon both together) prior to any directions or intimation received from Mr. *Meybohm*, to insure for him. Various people may insure various interests on the same bottom: (as one person for goods, another for bottomry, &c.) And here, Mr. *Amyand* had an interest of his own, distinct from that of Mr. *Meybohm*: he had a lien upon these very goods as a factor to whom a balance was due. And he had the sole interest in the ship; which was a part of the things insured by him. It is far from appearing, that even his last insurance (in *October*) was made on the account of *Meybohm*, or as agent for him. So far from it, Mr. *Amyand* insists upon it for his own benefit, (as he expressly declared at the trial) and absolutely refuses to give it up, or to suffer his name to be used by the plaintiff; though he was a witness for the defendants, and was produced by them, and inclined to serve them. So that the foundation of this argument, urged by the defendant's counsel, fails them; and there is, in reality, nothing to support it. But even supposing that Mr. *Amyand* had made his insurance, not upon his own account, but as agent or factor for Mr. *Meybohm*, and upon the account of *Meybohm*; yet even then *Tamesz* can never come against *Amyand*'s underwriters, or come at *Amyand*'s policy, to his own use. For *Amyand*, the factor of *Meybohm*, has possession of the policy, and appears to have been a creditor of *Meybohm* upon the balance of accounts between them, at the time when he made the insurance: and I take it to be now a settled point, "that a factor, "to whom a balance is due, has a lien upon all goods of his "principal, so long as they remain in his possession." *Kruzer* and others v. *Wilcox* and others, was a case in Chancery upon this point. It came on first before Sir *John Strange*, then Master of the Rolls, who decreed an account, and directed allowances to be made for what the factor had expended on account of the ship or cargo, and reserved all further direc-

tions

CHAP. XV. tions till after the master's report. It came on again, afterwards, for further directions, after the master's report, before the Lord Chancellor, who was attended by four eminent merchants, whom he interrogated publickly. After which he took time to consider of it; and on the first of *February*, 1755, decreed, "that the factor has a lien on goods consigned to him; not only for incident charges, but as an item "of mutual account for the general balance due to him so "long as he retains the possession. But if he part with the "possession of the goods, he parts with his lien, because it "cannot then be retained as an item for the general account." There was another case, in the same court, of *Gardiner* v. *Coleman*, a few months after; in which the former case, determined as I have mentioned, was considered as a point settled; and this latter case of *Gardiner* v. *Coleman* was decreed agreeably to it. So that Mr. *Amyand*, even considered as factor or agent to *Meybohm*, and as making the insurance upon *Meybohm*'s account, is yet entitled to retain the policy; *Meybohm* being indebted to him upon the balance of the account between them; and he has a lien upon the policy, whilst it continues in his possession. Therefore, even in this view of the case, Mr. *Tamesz*, must first have paid to *Amyand* the balance of his (*Amyand*'s) account, before he could have gotten that policy out of *Amyand*'s hands; and consequently, Mr. *Tamesz* was very far from being entitled to the benefit of it as a *cestuy qui trust*, absolutely and entirely.

But if the question, "whether *Tamesz* could take benefit of Mr. *Amyand*'s policy," were doubtful; yet here, *Tamesz* insured the goods with the defendants, expressly under the declaration of his suspicion, that there might have been a former consignation, and some former insurance made upon the goods by some other person: but he desired to insure the whole for his own security; and to this the defendants agreed, and took the whole premium. Mr. *Amyand* insisted upon his right to the whole benefit of his own policy, when he was examined as a witness; and is now litigating it in Chancery. It would neither be just nor reasonable, that *Tamesz* should only recover half of his loss from the defendants, and be turned round for the other half, to the uncertain event of a long and expensive litigation. I do not believe there ever will or can be a recovery by *Tamesz*, or those

those who shall stand in his place, against *Amyand*'s underwriters. However, if those underwriters are liable to contribute at all, the contribution ought to be among the several insurers themselves: but *Tamesz*, the insured, has a right to recover his whole loss from the defendants, upon the policy now in question, by which they are bound to pay the whole. For though here be two insurances, yet it is not a double insurance; to call it so is only confounding terms. If *Tamesz* could recover against both sets of insurers, yet he certainly could not recover against the underwriters of *Amyand*'s policy, without some expense; nor without also first paying and reimbursing to Mr. *Amyand* the premium he paid, and also his charges. This is by no means within the idea of a double insurance. Two persons may insure two different interests; each to the whole value; as the master, for wages; the owner, for freight, &c. But a double insurance is where the same man is to receive two sums instead of one, or the same sum twice over, for the same loss, by reason of his having made two insurances upon the same goods, or the same ship. Mr. *Tamesz* is entitled to receive the whole from the defendants, upon their policy; whatever shall become of Mr. *Amyand*'s policy: and they will have a right in case he can claim any thing under Mr. *Amyand*'s policy, to stand in his place, for a contribution to be paid by the other underwriters to them. But still they are certainly obliged to pay the whole to him. Therefore upon these grounds and principles, in every light in which the case can be put, we are all of us clearly of opinion, that the verdict is right, as it now stands for the whole; and that the *postea* must be delivered to the plaintiff.

In the course of what has been said upon double insurance, no notice has been taken of the laws of foreign states respecting this point: the reason of this silence is the great contrariety to be found in their laws upon the subject; it being almost impossible to mention two countries, whose regulations, as to this matter, are similar. In one, the contract is absolutely void, and a forfeiture ensues: in others, if the first policy amount to the value of the effects laden, the other insurers shall withdraw their insurance, retaining one half *per cent.*; and in some other countries, the double insurance is merely void, without any forfeiture being incurred. When there is such a diversity in the ordinances upon

Ord. of Middleb. 2 Mag. p. 77. Ord. of Frank. and Stockh. 2 Mag. 172. 267. Ord. of Bilboa, 2 Mag. p. 411.

CHAP. XV. upon the subject, it seemed needless to enter into them, especially as the law of *England* with respect to double insurance is so clear, and so well founded in reason and natural justice, as to require no illustration or confirmation from the laws of any other country.

Having, in this and the five preceding chapters, treated of those circumstances, by which the contract of insurance is rendered void from its commencement, on account of some radical defect, which prevents the policy from ever having any operation at all: and having, in the course of that inquiry, been led into a variety of discussion, involving in it a very material part of the law of insurance: we shall proceed to shew in what cases the policy, although not void *ab initio*, is rendered of no effect, because the insured has not himself fully complied with those conditions, which he has either *expressly* or *tacitly*, from the nature of his contract, undertaken to perform. Vide ante, p. 1. It was indeed observed in the first chapter of this work, that although the policy is not subscribed by the insured, yet there are certain conditions to be performed on his part, with as much good faith and integrity as if his name appeared at the foot of the policy: otherwise it is a dead letter, and he can never recover an indemnity for any loss, which he may happen to sustain.

CHAPTER THE SIXTEENTH.

Of Changing the Ship.

OF thoſe cauſes which will operate as a bar to the inſured's recovering upon a policy of inſurance, againſt the underwriter, the firſt to be mentioned is that of changing the ſhip; or, as it has commonly been called, changing the bottom. This will require but very little diſcuſſion. We formerly ſaid, that except in ſome ſpecial caſes of inſurances upon *ſhip or ſhips*, it was eſſentially requiſite to render a policy of inſurance effectual, that the name of the ſhip, on which the riſk was to be run, ſhould be inſerted. That being done, it follows as an implied condition that the inſured ſhould neither ſubſtitute another ſhip for that mentioned in the policy before the voyage commences, in which caſe there would be no contract at all: nor during the courſe of the voyage remove the property inſured to another ſhip, without the conſent of the underwriter, or without being impelled by a caſe of unavoidable neceſſity. If he do, the implied condition is broken, and he cannot recover a ſatisfaction, in caſe of a loſs, from the inſurer; becauſe the policy was upon goods, on board a particular ſhip, or upon the ſhip itſelf; and it becomes a material conſideration in a contract of inſurance, upon what veſſel the riſk is to be run; ſince the one may be much ſtronger, and more able to reſiſt the perils of the ſea; or by its ſwift ſailing, much better able to eſcape from the purſuit of an enemy than the other.

CHAP. XVI.

Vide ante, c. 1.

Malyne, it is true, in his *Lex Mercatoria*, appears to be of a different opinion; for he ſays, "It ſometimes happens, "that upon ſome ſpecial conſideration, this clauſe forbidding "the transferring of goods from one ſhip to another is in-"ſerted in policies of inſurance; becauſe in time of hoſtility "or war between princes, it might be unladen, in ſuch ſhips "of thoſe contending princes, by which the adventure would "be

Mal. Lex Merc. 113.

CHAP. XVI.

"be increased. But according to the usual insurances which "are made generally without an exception, the assurer is liable thereunto; for it is understood, that the master of a "ship, without some good and accidental cause, would not "put the goods from one ship to another, but would deliver "them, according to the charter-party, at the appointed "place." The reason given by *Malyne*, in support of his position, is by no means satisfactory, nor is it well founded in point of experience; neither has he adduced a single authority to corroborate the opinion advanced. Indeed, the whole current of authority turns the other way: at least, as far as I have been able to trace it.

Molloy, l. 2. c. 7. s. 11.

Molloy has said, that if goods are insured in such a ship, and afterwards in the voyage she becomes leaky and crazy, and the supercargo and master, by consent, become freighters of another vessel for the safe delivery of the goods; and then after she is loaded, the second vessel miscarries, the assurers are discharged. It is true, the sentence proceeds thus: "If these words be inserted, namely, *the goods laden to be trans-"ported and delivered at such place by the said ship, or by any other "ship, or vessel, until they be safely landed*, the insurers must an-"swer the misfortune." But this does not at all affect the general rule before laid down; for it only goes to shew that, which is not denied, that the parties may take a case out of the general rule of law, by a special agreement: and the exception proves the truth of the first proposition. Besides, in such a case, it should seem that the ship, in which the goods are laden, ought not to be changed, but upon necessity.

Roccus de Assecurat, Not. 28.

This opinion is confirmed by foreign writers. "Merces "si eâdem navigatione transferantur de unâ navi in aliam, "et si novissima navis, ubi merces transfusæ fuerunt, deper-"datur, tunc est inspicienda forma assecurationis, in quâ si "fuit dictum quod assecurentur merces, *quæ sunt in tali navi*, "tunc *assecurator non tenetur*, eo quod mentionem fecit in asse-"curatione de tali navi. Et ratio est, quia non par est ratio "assecurationis, *quando mercis devehuntur in una navi, et quan-"do in alterâ*; imo solet id principaliter considerari inter ip-"sos assecuratores, cum *una navis sit magis fortis quam alia*."

Santer. de Assecurat, p. 3. n. 35. Stracca glos. 8. n. 10.

Roccus

Roccus is corroborated by several learned writers upon this branch of jurisprudence.

In the law of *England*, there is only one case to be met with in print upon the subject; and that is not expressly in point to the present inquiry, although it seems to decide it. It was a case which came on at *Guildhall* before Lord Chief Justice *Lee*. The plaintiff had insured interest or no interest on *any ship* he should come in from *Virginia* to *London*, beginning the adventure *on his embarking* on board such ship; the money to be paid though his person should escape, or the ship be retaken. He embarked on the *Speedwell*; but she springing a leak at sea, he went on board the *Friendship*, and arrived safe at *London*: but the *Speedwell* was taken after he left her. And now, in an action against the underwriter, he was held liable; for the insurance is on the ship the plaintiff set out in: *and had that got safe home and the other been lost*, the plaintiff could not have recovered upon the ground of having removed his person into that ship in the middle of the voyage.

Dick v. Barrell, 2 Stra. 1248.

From this case it appears, that although no ship was named in the policy, yet the moment the ship was ascertained by the embarkation of the insured, the contract was at an end, provided the second ship had been lost; for so the words in *Italics* expressly import. *A fortiori*, therefore, the insured could not be entitled to recover, upon a change of the bottom, when the name of the vessel is expressly mentioned in the very instrument by which the contract is effected. And although the insured, notwithstanding the change of bottom, recovered in the case cited from *Strange*; it may be accounted for in two ways, consistent with the doctrine advanced in this chapter. In the first place, it was a gaming policy, interest or no interest; and the plaintiff was entitled to recover the moment the ship was taken, although perhaps he might not be interested at all; or perhaps the effects insured might be left in the first ship, although the plaintiff removed his person; in which case even at this day, upon a fair *bonâ fide* policy, he would be entitled to recover from the underwriters a satisfaction for the loss he had sustained.

CHAP. XVI.

The general doctrine relative to changing the bottom of the ſhip was alluded to by Lord *Mansfield*, when delivering the opinion of the court in the caſe of *Pelly* againſt the *Royal Exchange* Aſſurance Company, which has already been fully reported in a preceding chapter. "One objection," ſaid his Lordſhip, "was formed by comparing this caſe to "that of changing the ſhip or bottom, on board of which "goods are inſured: *which the inſured have no right to do.* (*a*) "For there the identical ſhip is eſſential; *that* is the thing "inſured. But that caſe is not like the preſent."

Vide ante, c. 2. p. 41. 1 Burr. 351.

From this paſſage it is evident, that Lord *Mansfield* intended to confirm the principle advanced in this chapter, namely, that when an inſurance is made on a ſpecific ſhip, and the inſured not being impelled by any neceſſity, without the conſent of the underwriter, changes the ſhip in the courſe of the voyage, he has not kept his part of the contract, and cannot recover againſt the underwriter.

(*a*) This is to be taken as a rule, ſubject to the exception of inevitable or urgent neceſſity: for it has been held, that the owners of goods inſured, by the act of ſhifting the goods from one ſhip to another, do not preclude themſelves from recovering an average loſs ariſing from the capture of the ſecond ſhip, if they act from neceſſity, and for the benefit of all concerned. See *Plantamour* v. *Staples*, 1 Term R. 611, note (a) and ante, chap. 1.

CHAPTER THE SEVENTEENTH.

Of Deviation.

DEVIATION, in marine infurances, is underftood to mean a voluntary departure, without neceffity or any reafonable caufe, from the regular and ufual courfe of the fpecific voyage infured. Whenever a deviation of this kind takes place, the voyage is determined; and the underwriters are difcharged from any refponfibility. It is neceffary, as we have feen, to infert in every policy of infurance, the place of the fhip's departure, and alfo of her deftination. Hence it is an implied condition to be performed on the part of the infured, that the fhip fhall purfue the moft direct courfe, of which the nature of things will admit, to arrive at the deftined port. If this be not done; if there be no fpecial agreement to allow the fhip to go to certain places out of the ufual track; or if there be no juft caufe affigned for fuch a deviation; it is but juft and reafonable, that the underwriter fhould no longer be bound by his contract, the infurer having failed to comply with the terms on which the policy was made. For if the voyage be changed after the departure of the fhip, it becomes a different voyage, and not that, againft which the infurer has undertaken to indemnify: (which is the true objection to a deviation) the rifk may be ten times greater, which probably the infurer would not have run at all, or at leaft would not, without a larger premium. Nor is it at all material, whether the lofs be or not be not an actual confequence of the deviation; for the infurers are in no cafe anfwerable, for a fubfequent lofs, in whatever place it happen, or to whatever caufe it may be attributed. Neither does it make any difference, whether the infured was, or was not confenting to the deviation.

CHAP. XVII.

Vide ante, c. 1.

Roccus, Not. 52.

Doug. Rep. 278.

Thefe principles have been eftablifhed by many decifions in the various courts of *Weftminfter Hall*, and alfo by a folemn determination in the Houfe of Lords.

The

CHAP. XVII.

Fox v. Black, Exeter assizes 1767, before Mr. Justice Yates.

The plaintiff was a shipper of goods in a vessel bound from *Dartmouth* to *Liverpool*: the ship sailed from *Dartmouth*, and put into *Loo*; a place *she must of necessity pass by*, in the course of the insured voyage. But as she had no liberty given her by the policy to go into *Loo*, and although no accident befel her in going into, or coming out of *Loo*, (for she was lost after she got out to sea again) yet Mr. Justice *Yates* held that this was a deviation, and a verdict was accordingly found for the underwriters.

Townson v. Guyon, before Lord Mansfield.

In another case an action was brought upon a policy on goods and other merchandizes, loaded on board the ship called the *Charming Nancy*, from *Dunkirk* to *Leghorn*. The ship came to *Dover*, in her way to procure a *Mediterranean* pass; and was afterwards lost.

Lord *Mansfield* was of opinion, that the calling at *Dover* was a deviation; and the plaintiff was nonsuited.

It was also held by Lord Chief Justice *Lee*, that if the master of a vessel put into a port not usual, or stay an unusual time, it is a deviation, and discharges the insurer.

The next case to be reported underwent a variety of discussion in the several courts in *Scotland*; and in all of them, judgment was given against the underwriters: but upon an appeal to the House of Lords, the various decrees of the courts below were reversed, agreeably to those principles adduced in the beginning of this chapter, and which have been uniformly admitted as found law.

Elliot and others v. Wilson and Co. 7 Brown's Parl. Cases, p. 459.

The harbour of *Carron*, situate near the head of the *Frith* of *Forth*, is chiefly resorted to by ships in the service of the *Carron* Company, who have a great iron work and considerable collieries in the neighbourhood. From thence vessels, intended principally to convey the manufactures of the company, their coals, and such goods as may be offered them on freight, sail periodically for *Hull*, and other places on the *Eastern* coast of *England*. This is a coasting or carrying trade, the vessels in going down the *Frith* touching at different places to take in additional loading, or to discharge part of what they have received at places higher in the river. Particularly it is usual for these vessels to call at *Borrowstowness*

rowstowness and *Leith*, and at *Morrison's Haven*, a port six miles farther down the *Frith*, and on the same side with *Leith* in the bay of *Prestonpans*. In *February* 1774, the respondents had occasion to ship fourteen hogsheads of tobacco on board one of these vessels for *Hull*; and desiring to insure them, gave the following instructions in writing to *Hamilton* and *Bogle* insurance brokers in *Glasgow*: "Please "to insure for our account by the *Kingston*, *George Finley*, "master, from *Carron* to *Hull*, *with liberty to call as usual*, "fourteen hogsheads of tobacco;" and these instructions were entered in the broker's books for the perusal of the underwriters, as is the practice at *Glasgow*. Upon the 9th of *February*, the appellants underwrote a policy of insurance in these terms; "beginning the adventure of the said tobacco, "at and from the loading thereof on board the said ship "*Kingston*, at *Carron* wharf, and to continue and endure "until said *Kingston* (*being allowed a liberty to call at Leith*) "shall arrive at *Hull*, and there be safely delivered." The respondents were not privy to the allowance to call at *Leith*, being thus substituted in the policy for the more general term, *as usual*, mentioned in the instructions to the broker. The premium agreed on was 1 *l.* 5 *s.* *per cent.* a rate equal at least, if not higher, than was usual to be given in the voyage, in cases where it was understood, or expressed in the policy, that the vessel might touch at the customary ports. And in particular, some of these appellants in *February* 1772, underwrote a policy upon this very vessel, and for the same voyage, with liberty to call at *Leith* and *Morrison's Haven*, at a premium of one *per cent.* only. The vessel thus insured had sailed from *Carron* five days before the date of the policy, that is, on the 4th of *February* 1774, it did not call or touch at *Leith*, *but put into Morrison's Haven*: set sail from thence on the 9th, got safe into the direct course from *Carron* to *Hull*, cleared the *Frith* of *Forth*, and proceeded with a fair wind, till on the evening of the 10th the vessel, being overtaken by a storm at *Holy Island*, on the coast of *Northumberland*, was wrecked, and the cargo totally lost. All these were facts admitted; nor was it alleged by the appellants, that the ship received the smallest damage, in going into, or coming out of *Morrison's Haven*. Intelligence of this misfortune reached *Glasgow* on the 14th of *February*, when the respondents for the first time saw the policy of insurance, or understood that it differed in terms

from

CHAP. XVII. from their instructions to the broker, in whose hands it remained. It did not, however, occur to them, that this slight variation would afford a pretext to the underwriters for refusing payment; nor does it seem to have then occurred to those gentlemen, who wrote immediately to the respondents, desiring they would request the *Carron* Company to give the necessary orders for preserving the tobacco, and forwarding it to *Hull*, promising to contribute towards the expense, so far as they were interested. Upon the 24th of *February*, however, the appellants, in an instrument drawn up by a public notary, protested against the ship's having gone into *Morrison's Haven*, as a deviation from the terms of the policy, which only contained a liberty to call at *Leith*; and absolutely refused payment of the loss. On this refusal, the respondents brought their action against the appellants in the court of admiralty in *Scotland*, the only competent court for determining questions about insurances, and other maritime affairs in that country, in the first instance. The appellants put in their defence, which was followed by other pleadings, in *January* 1775, the Judge Admiral pronounced the following interlocutor (or decree:) "Having "considered the whole circumstances of this case, and in "particular that it is not alleged by the defenders, that the "pursuers were in the knowledge of the ship the *Kingston* "being intended to put into *Morrison's Haven*, he repels "the defence pleaded by the defenders." The appellants reclaimed against this interlocutor, (petitioned for a review of the sentence) and answers being put in to their petition, the Judge Admiral, because they set forth, and seemed to found on conversations between them and the brokers, at the time of underwriting or settling the terms of the policy, allowed them to bring proof of what passed at and previous to making the insurance. But the appellants presented a second petition, declining to go into any proof, insisting that the cause turned singly upon the words of the policy, and demanding judgment on the abstract question, whether the vessel touching at *Morrison's Haven*, when not allowed by the policy, discharged the underwriters? whereupon the Judge again decreed in favour of the respondents. The appellants then sued out a writ of suspension from the Court of Session, of these sentences of the Judge Admiral; and after the usual preliminary step of procedure before the Lord Ordinary, the cause being reported to the whole bench of Lords, their

their Lordships having before them the opinions of several of the most eminent merchants both in *England* and *Scotland*, gave judgment for the respondents, in the month of *January* 1776, in the following terms: "Having advised informa-"tions, *hinc*, *inde*, and considered the policy of insurance "and the whole circumstances of the case, the Lords repel "the reasons of suspension, find the letters orderly proceeded," (that is, that the appellants were obliged to pay the sums underwritten, in terms of the Judge Admiral's decree) and their Lordships decree accordingly. The appellants having also reclaimed against this interlocutor, it was, in *March* 1776, finally confirmed. From these several decrees the present appeal was brought; and the House of Lords were of opinion, that a wilful deviation from the due course of the insured voyage, is in all cases a determination of the policy; that from that moment, the engagement between the insurers and insured is at an end; that it is immaterial from what cause, or at what place, a subsequent loss arises, the insurers being in no case answerable for it: that the going into *Morrison's Haven* was a wilful deviation from the due course of a voyage from *Carron* to *Hull*: that though it may be true, as contended on the part of the respondents, that ships sailing through the *Frith* of *Forth* have sometimes been permitted by the terms of a policy, underwritten at the same premium as the present, to go into that port, it could not avail in the present case, since the policy in question had given no such permission. It was therefore ORDERED AND ADJUDGED that the interlocutors complained of should be reversed.

Beatson v. Howard, B. R. Hil. 36 Geo. III. 6 Term R. 531.

In a late case upon a policy of insurance on a ship "*at and from Fisherow to Gottenburgh, and back to Leith and Cockenzie,*" it appeared that in the homeward voyage, she went *first* to *Cockenzie*, which lay nearer to *Gottenburgh* than *Leith*, and was stranded in the harbour of *Cockenzie*. There was a good deal of evidence given to shew that *Leith* harbour was the safer of the two; but the jury seemed to be of opinion, according to a note taken by Lord *Kenyon* at the time, that the construction of the policy was to be made by attending to the order in which the places were named in it. The jury, however, by consent of parties, to save the expense of going to trial again, found a verdict for the plaintiff, with permission to enter a verdict for the defendant, if the court should

CHAP. XVII. should agree that the above construction was the true one. The case came on to be discussed in court; and they were of opinion, that unless there be some usage proved, or some special facts to vary the general rule, the party insured must go to the several places mentioned in the policy, in the order in which they are named; and that to depart from that course is a deviation: and one of the judges added, that the parties by inserting the names contrary to the *natural* order of the places, shewed it to have been the intention of the parties to vary the natural course of the voyage. A verdict was entered for the defendant.

Clason v. Simmond, at Guildhall, Hil. sittings 1741.

In the argument of the preceding case, another was quoted by one of the learned judges, as having been decided before Lord Chief Justice *Lee*, where in an insurance on the *Gothic Lyon, at and from London to her ports of discharge in the Streights, as high as Messina*, his Lordship was of opinion, as she did not stop at *Marseilles* (for which place she had a cargo) in her way to the Streights, but meant to take it in her return, that this was acting contrary to the terms of the policy: for by her ports of discharge, must be understood such ports as it was intended goods should be delivered at, and the first of these was *Marseilles*.

These principles being once established, it follows, as a necessary consequence, that however short the time of deviation may be, if only for a single night, or even for an hour, the underwriter is equally discharged as if there had been a deviation for weeks or months: for the condition being once broken, no subsequent act can ever make it good.

Cock v. Townson, C. B. before Lord Camden Ch. Just.

The ship *George* was bound from *Cork* to *Jamaica* with a convoy in the course of a war: the captain, in concert with two other vessels, took advantage of the night, and being ships of force, cruised, and thereby deviated out of the direct course of their voyage, in hopes of meeting with a prize. Lord *Camden* clearly held, and a special jury of
[299] merchants, agreeably to his directions, determined, that from the moment the *George* deserted or deviated from the *direct voyage* to *Jamaica* the policy was discharged.

In a modern case, however, it seemed to be the general opinion of Lord *Mansfield* and a special jury, and was sworn to to be the usage by several witnesses, that if a merchant ship carry letters of marque, she may *chase* an enemy, though she may not *cruise*, without being deemed guilty of a deviation.

On an insurance of the *Mary* at and from *London* to *Cork* and the *West Indies*, the question was whether a ship, having letters of marque, could *chase* an enemy's ship, without being said to have deviated. The facts were, that in the night the *Mary* had descried a *Spanish* sail; and after chasing lost sight of her for six hours till the morning, when they engaged. The *Mary* did not make a prize of the *Spanish* sail, but she proceeded on her voyage, and was afterwards captured. It was agreed on all hands, that a ship, in such circumstances, might not cruise; and several witnesses spoke to the usage and practice of ships, which carried letters of marque, chasing an enemy. It was admitted on the part of the insurers, that if an enemy came in the way, the ship must defend or engage; but contended, that if the letter of marque lost sight of the enemy, that it was no longer chasing, but cruising. Lord *Mansfield* left it upon the evidence to the jury, who found for the plaintiffs; thereby deciding the question in the affirmative.

Jolly v. Walker, at Guildhall, East. Vac. 1781.

In a late case which came before the Court of King's Bench upon a motion for a new trial, the Judges were unanimously of opinion, that if the assured, without the knowledge of the underwriters, take out a letter of marque, (but without a certificate, which by the prize act of the 33 *Geo.* III. ch. 66. s. 15. is absolutely necessary to its validity) for the purpose of inducing the seamen to enter, and without any intention of cruising, this does not so essentially vary the risk as to avoid the policy.

Moss v. Byrom, 6 Term R. 379. ante, p. 91.

The doctrine that a voluntary deviation from the voyage insured vitiates the policy, has been held to be applicable to an insurance upon *freight* as well as to an insurance upon ship and goods.

Thus in a case upon a policy of assurance *on freight* of the ship *Bethiah at and from Bourdeaux to Virginia*, warranted *American* ship and property: the declaration alleged that the ship was an *American* ship and the property of *American* subjects. The plaintiff proved the ship to be *American*, and

Murdock v. Potts, sittings at Guildhall, after Trin. 1795.

it

CHAP. XVII.

it was to have been contended upon the part of the defendant, that the warranty extended to the goods on board as well as to the ship: but upon the evidence it appeared that the goods, whether *American* or not, *were to be carried in the ship from Bourdeaux to Saint Domingo*, and that she was only to call at *Norfolk* in *Virginia* for orders; this rendered it unnecessary to discuss or decide the question upon the construction of the warranty. Lord *Kenyon* being of opinion that the underwriters upon this policy had a right to expect that the goods, upon which the freight was payable, were consigned to *Virginia*, and that if the freight was payable for the carriage of them from *Bourdeaux* to *St. Domingo*, the underwriters were not liable for the loss, though the ship was to call at *Norfolk* for orders, the freight payable being in such case different from the freight insured: plaintiff was non-suited, and no application was made to set it aside.

Roccus n. 52.

But though the consequences of a voluntary deviation are fatal to the validity of the contract of insurance, yet wherever the deviation arises from necessity and a just cause, the underwriter still remains liable, although the course of the voyage is altered.

Elton v. Brogden, 2 Stra. 1264. Vide ante, p. 87.

This rule is illustrated by the following case. The ship *Mediterranean* went out in the merchants service with a letter of marque, and bound from *Bristol* to *Newfoundland*, insured by the defendant. In her voyage she took a prize, and returned with it to *Bristol*, and received back a proportionable part of the premium. Then another policy was made, and the ship set out, with express orders from the owners, that [300] if another prize was taken, the captain should put some hands on board such prize, and send her to *Bristol*; but that the ship in question should proceed with the merchants goods. Another prize was taken in the due course of the voyage, and the captain gave orders to some of the crew to carry her to *Bristol*, and designed to go on to *Newfoundland*: but the crew opposed him, and insisted he should go back, though he acquainted them with his orders; upon which he was forced to submit, and on his return his own ship was taken, but the prize got in safe. And now in an action against the underwriters, it was insisted, that this was such a deviation, as discharged them. But the court and jury held, that

this

this was excused by the force upon the master, which he could not resist; and therefore fell within the excuse of necessity, which had always been allowed. So the plaintiff had a verdict for the sum insured.

The general writers upon this subject have enumerated the various circumstances, which will operate as a justification to the insured, for leaving the direct track of the voyage, upon the ground of necessity and reasonable cause: such as to repair his vessel, to escape from an impending storm, or to avoid an enemy. In our reports of decisions in the *English* courts of justice, we find instances of all these various excuses being allowed as sufficient to justify a deviation; and also another species of excuse, namely, to meet a convoy, which, indeed, is nearly connected with that of avoiding an enemy. I shall rank all the cases, which apply to this branch of our inquiry, under these several divisions.

Roccus 52. Santer de Assecur. part 3. n. 52.

The first ground of necessity which justifies a deviation, is that of going into port to repair. If a ship is decayed, and goes to the nearest place to refit, it is no deviation; because it is for the general interest of all concerned, and consequently for that of the underwriters, that the ship should be put in a proper condition, capable of performing the voyage.

The ship *Eyles*, being at *Bengal* in the year 1732, the owner employed a Mr. *Halhead* to insure this ship in the *London* Insurance Office for 500*l.* the adventure thereon to commence from her arrival at *Fort St. George*, and thence to continue till the said ship should arrive at *London*; and that it should be lawful for the said ship, in the said voyage, to stay at any ports or places without prejudice. The *Eyles* came to *Fort St. George* in *February* 1733, in her way to *England*; but being leaky, and in very bad condition, upon the unamimous advice of the governor, council, commanders of ships, *&c. she sailed for Bengal to be refitted;* and after being sheathed, in her return upon her homeward-bound voyage, she struck upon the *Engilee Sands*, and was lost. Evidence was read on the part of the plaintiffs, to prove that *Bengal* was the proper place to refit, and that the ship went thither for that reason; that this was a voyage of necessity, and not a trading voyage, for she took nothing on board but water, provisions,

Motteux and others v. the London Assurance Company, 1 Atk. 545.

[301]

CHAP. XVII. provisions, and ballast. When this cause came on to be heard before Lord Chancellor *Hardwicke*, he refused to decide it but directed an issue at law. His Lordship, however, observed, that the general principles laid down by the plaintiff's counsel were right, as stress of weather, and the danger of proceeding on a voyage, when a ship is in a decayed condition: and in such a case, if she went to the nearest place, he should consider it equally the same, as if she had been repaired at the very place from whence the voyage was to commence, according to the terms of the policy, and no deviation. It is a very material circumstance, that the governor ordered the lading to be taken out, to shew the necessity of the ship's being repaired; but there is not a syllable of proof why she might not have been equally repaired at *Fort St. George*. His Lordship therefore directed an issue to try, whether the loss in *July* 1733, was a loss during the voyage, and according to the adventure which was agreed upon, or intended to be insured. On a trial at *Guildhall* in the court of Common Pleas, the jury found in favour of the plaintiff.

Guibert v. Readshaw, Sit. in Lond. Hil. Vac. 1781.

This was an action on a policy of insurance on the *Nancy*, at and from *La Rochelle* to the coast of *Africa*, during her stay and trade thereon, and at and from thence to her port of discharge in the island of *St. Domingo*. Three days after the ship sailed from *La Rochelle*, she met with a gale, which strained her seams, and split her mizen-yard and rigging. The crew came in a body to the captain, desiring for the preservation of their lives to make to some port to repair. The [302] vessel being a new one, and the captain finding that she had too little ballast, complied, and put into *Lisbon*, the nearest port; from whence, after taking in 500 rolls of tobacco as ballast, he proceeded to the coast of *Guinea*, traded there, and the ship was afterwards captured in the sight of *St. Domingo*, before she arrived. The defendant insisted, that going into *Lisbon* was a deviation, and called witnesses, who were of opinion, that in the latitude in which the storm happened, there could be no difficulty in repairing all the damage the vessel was described to have received, even in the worst weather, as she might have proceeded to the coast of *Africa*, and repaired there at a less expense; and that a ship, loaded like that in question, could not need additional ballast. On the cross crofs examination, it came out that the premium would not have varied, had the voyage been by the way of *Lifbon*.

Lord *Mansfield* left it to the jury, on the ground of neceffity to go to *Lifbon* for repairs. He faid, that much depended upon the circumftance, that no additional premium would have been required for liberty to touch there. If the jury believed the evidence of the witneffes, they muft find for the plaintiff, for that the whole of the defendant's cafe refted merely upon furmife and fufpicions alone. The plaintiff accordingly had a verdict.

The next excufe for leaving the direct courfe is ftrefs of weather. Upon this point the rule is this, that wherever a fhip, in order to efcape a ftorm, goes out of the direct courfe; or when, in the due courfe of the voyage, is driven out of it by ftrefs of weather, this is no deviation; becaufe it was occafioned by the act of God, which, by a maxim of law, is faid to work an injury to no man. It has alfo been held, that if a ftorm drive a fhip out of the courfe of her voyage, and fhe do the beft fhe can to get to her port of deftination, fhe is not obliged to return back to the point from whence fhe was driven. This rule is exemplified by the following cafe.

Harrington v. Halkeld, Sitt. in Lond. Mich. Vac. 1778.

In an action on a policy of infurance of the fhip *Atlantic*, warranted to fail with convoy from *England* to *St. Kitts* on or before the firft of *Auguft*; the queftion was, whether there had been a deviation. The fhip was feparated from her convoy by a ftorm. The captain being examined, faid, his object, after his feparation, invariably was to gain *St. Kitts*, [303] or to fall in with the convoy. That the fhip was taken by an *American* privateer in lat. 34. lon. 59. Several captains were examined, who fwore, that they would have taken the fame courfe to get to *St. Kitts*, or regain the fleet.

Lord *Mansfield*.—"The fingle queftion is, whether the captain was taken as he was going to *St. Kitts*. If he was not, he is perjured. The account he gives is, that on the 28th of *July* there was a ftorm, which feparated the fleet: that he did all he could to get to *St. Kitts*, and to direct his courfe fo as to meet the convoy croffing. The captain goes on the ground not to reafon, but to obey, be the confequence

CHAP. XVII.

what it might. He knows nothing of the insurance: he says to himself, If I obey, I am doing right. As to the protest, I do not see that it contradicts the captain's evidence. Other captains have looked at the log-book or journal; and they say they would have held the same course."

Verdict for the plaintiff.

Upon the subject of a departure from the course of the voyage, on account of stress of weather, another very important point has lately been determined, though the same principle runs through all the cases, that whatever happens by the act of God, shall not be imputed to man. On this ground it has been held, that if a ship be driven out of her port of loading by stress of weather into another, and then does the best she can to get to her port of destination, it shall not be deemed a deviation, though she do not return to the port from whence she was driven.

Delaney v. Stoddart, 1 Term Rep. p. 22.

The case here alluded to was an action upon the case against the defendant, for not having insured a ship and cargo, pursuant to the orders of the plaintiff, by means whereof he was damnified, the ship having been lost (*a*). It was tried before

Wilkinson v. Coverdale, Sittings in B. R. at Guildhall after Mich. Term, 34 Geo. III.

(*a*) It may be proper to explain the nature of this action. When a man undertakes, either by an implied or express promise, to do a thing for another, and he neglects to do it, or does it unskilfully, the law gives the person injured an action for the negligence. This is the case in question with respect to insurance; and the only difference between this action, and that on a policy against the underwriters, is in point of form; for the plaintiff in this action is entitled to recover the exact sum he ordered to be insured: and the defendant is entitled to every benefit, of which the underwriter could have taken advantage, such as fraud, deviation, non-compliance with warranty, &c.

Smith v. Lascelles 2 Term Rep. 187.

In a late case, the whole law upon this action was very fully and accurately stated by Mr. Justice *Buller*, and assented to by the whole Court; and upon this occasion that learned judge mentioned the three instances in which such an order to insure must be obeyed, otherwise this action will lie. First, where a merchant abroad has effects in the hands of his correspondent here, he has a right to expect that he will obey an order to insure, because he is entitled to call his money out of the other's hands when and in what manner he pleases. The second class of cases is, where the merchant abroad has no effects in the hands of his correspondent, yet if the course of dealing between them is such, that the one has been used to send orders for insurance, and the other to comply with them, the former has a right to expect that his orders for insurance will still be obeyed, unless the latter give him notice to discontinue that course of dealing. Thirdly, If the merchant abroad before Mr. Justice *Buller* at *Guildhall*, at the sittings after *Trinity* Term 1785; and a verdict was found for the plaintiff. CHAP. XVII.

Upon a motion for a new trial, the facts appeared to be these: The plaintiff, who lived at *St. Kitts*, wrote a letter to the defendant, dated the 30th of *April* 1781, informing him that he intended to purchase a ship, and offering the defendant a share. On the 4th of *May* 1781, he wrote a second letter to the defendant, acquainting him, that he had purchased the ship, but had only a share in it himself, the residue being divided into three or four more shares, one of which he had reserved for the defendant, in case he should wish to be concerned; and directing an insurance upon the ship *at and from St. Kitts to London*, warranted to sail with convoy. On the 28th of *June*, the defendant wrote to the plaintiff, that he had no objection to a fourth, or a share equal to the plaintiff's. [305] On the third of *July*, the plaintiff informed the defendant, that the ship had left the port to take in her cargo; that she let go an anchor at *Sandy Point*, but as the wind blew fresh, *she drove out, and could not come in again; that she was obliged to go to Eustatius*, and he therefore hoped that the defendant had not neglected to make the insurance, for fear of accidents. The defendant, on the 19th of *July*, wrote thus to the plaintiff: "The insurance you ordered shall be "done." Plaintiff again, on the 25th of *July*, wrote, *that the Friendship did all in her power to get up from St. Eustatius, but could not*, and therefore he sold her to Mr. *Ross* at *Eustatius*. I have already transcribed as much of the several letters

broad sends bills of lading to his correspondent here, he may engraft on them an order to insure, as the implied condition, on which the bills of lading shall be accepted, which the other must obey, if he accept them, for it is one entire transaction. For if the commission from abroad consist of two parts, the one to accept the bill of lading, the other to cause an insurance to be made, the correspondent cannot accept it in part, and reject it as to the rest.

So also if a merchant here accept an order for insurance, and limit the broker to too small a premium, in consequence of which no insurance can be procured, he is liable to make good the loss to his correspondent. Wallace v. Tellfair, Sittings after Trinity 1786 before Mr Justice Buller, 2 Term R. 188. note (*a*.)

But if a person, to whom such orders are sent, does what is usual to get the insurance made, that is sufficient; because he is no insurer and is not obliged to get insurance at all events. Thus if he send to Lloyd's and the underwriters refuse to take the risk at any premium; and he afterwards send to get insurance done at *Newcastle*, he has done his duty, and can never afterwards be charged in this action, more especially if the plaintiff adopt and approve his acts. Smith v. Cologan, 2 Term R. 188 note (*a*.) Nisi Prius before Mr. Justice Buller, Mich. 1787.

CHAP. XVII. ters as are material to the ſubject of this chapter; in addition to which, the following facts appeared in evidence: That the ſhip *Friendſhip* had ſailed from *St. Euſtatius*, on the 1ſt of *Auguſt* with the convoy, and that ſhe had afterwards foundered at ſea; that *St. Euſtatius* is in the direct road to *London* from *St. Kitts*, and the convoy from *St. Kitts* always looked into *St. Euſtatius*, to take up any ſhips that might be there; that if the *Friendſhip* had ſailed from *St. Kitts*, ſhe muſt have gone by *Euſtatius*; but would not have ſtopped there: that when ſhe was driven to *St. Euſtatius*, *after making ſeveral efforts to get back to St. Kitts* to finiſh her loading, and finding ſhe could not ſucceed, ſhe then took in the reſt of her loading at *St. Euſtatius*.

At the trial, ſeveral grounds of defence were made; but the only one, material for our conſideration was, that the remaining at *St. Euſtatius*, and not going back to *St. Kitts*, was a deviation. The learned judge, who tried the cauſe, was of opinion that it was not a deviation, being occaſioned by ſtreſs of weather. Upon this ground, amongſt others, the motion for a new trial was founded.

After argument at the bar,

Lord *Mansfield* ſaid, "The only material queſtion is, whether there is a deviation in this caſe: and that depends on the evidence. If a ſtorm drive a ſhip out of her voyage into any port, and being there, ſhe does the beſt ſhe can to get to her port of deſtination, ſhe is not obliged to return back to the point from whence ſhe was driven; but here the
[306] witneſſes ſay, ſhe tried to get back to *St. Kitts*, and could not: and it is a much eaſier navigation to go directly from *St. Euſtatius* to *London*, than to go back to *St. Kitts* firſt. And as to the taking in the cargo at *St. Euſtatius*, I do not find that the ſhip loſt any time by it. Every thing is the effect of the ſtorm, and occaſioned by it. This is the only point, on which I had any doubt, and it required ſome conſideration. It was a queſtion, which was proper to be left to a jury, whether this was the ſame voyage or not, and they have determined it."

Mr. Juſtice *Willes* inclined to a different opinion. "My only doubt is, whether it was the ſame voyage as that inſured. So far as the ſhip was driven by ſtreſs of weather,

so

so far there is an exception. When she is driven to *St. Eustatius*, she attempts to get back to *St. Kitts*; but I do not find that she made any attempt to get to *London* at that time. When she was at *St. Eustatius*, the owner of the ship sold her to *Ross*, who loaded her afresh with tobacco instead of sugar, which was to have been her original cargo; so that there is a new cargo, a new owner, and a new voyage. In these cases we lean very much to deviation. In a case lately determined in this court, it was held, that going to *Beaumaris*, though only a few leagues out of the way, was a deviation. It strikes me as a case of some difficulty: perhaps the jury had not evidence enough laid before them, on which to determine; for there is nothing said on the part of the defendant as to the usual course of the voyage. The risk was certainly increased by the ship's continuing at *St. Eustatius* so long; for the insurance, if good at all, was good all the time she lay by at *St. Eustatius*; and she might have continued there much longer. In my opinion, it is very well worth the re-consideration of a jury."

Mr. Justice *Ashhurst*.—"This ought to be considered as the same voyage insured. Wherever a ship is driven by stress of weather out of her own port into another, that shall not be considered as a deviation. Here the ship was forced by stress of weather to go to *St. Eustatius*; and being there, she endeavoured several times to get back to *St. Kitts*, but without effect. In fact it was better for the parties that the cargo should be completed at *St. Eustatius*; her continuing there, rather diminishes the risk than otherwise; because if she had gone back to *St. Kitts*, it would have taken up a longer time. If then every thing was done, that could be done, under such circumstances, for the benefit of the adventure, this shall not vacate the policy." [307]

Mr. Justice *Buller*.—"It has been much relied on in this case, that there was a change of property; but that, in my opinion, makes no difference. Then laying that out of the question, and supposing the ship as not being sold to *Ross*, I will first consider whether this is a different voyage. But that cannot be, as it would be contrary to the evidence: neither is it true, that the vessel afterwards pursued the same voyage by accident; for that part of the cargo, which

CHAP. XVII. ſhe took in at *St. Kitts*, continued on board of her the whole time, and the original intention of the ſhip's coming to *London* was likewiſe continued: the parties never thought of a different voyage. But it is ſaid, that ſhe took in another cargo at *St. Euſtatius*: what ſays the evidence? Where a captain has not taken in a full cargo, it is uſual to take in the reſt at *St. Euſtatius*; ſuch was proved to be the cuſtom of the voyage: and it was proved, that on a *voluntary* act of the captain's going to *St. Euſtatius*, the policy would have protected the ſhip's ſtay there; *à fortiori* it will, when the ſhip was driven there by ſtreſs of weather. As to the defendant's not being prepared at the trial to anſwer the uſage, he ought to have come prepared with that, which was the gift of his defence. Then was the riſk altered? had it been ſo, it was in the defendant's power to have proved it: but there was no proof that it was altered; part of the ſame cargo continues; nor does it appear that they meant to alter the cargo, for ſhe endeavoured to get back to *St. Kitts* to take in the reſt; but was prevented by ſtorms. I think the riſk would in reality have been much greater if ſhe had gone back; for ſhe muſt have come by the way of *St. Euſtatius* again in her paſſage home. The part of her cargo, which was taken in at the time the ſhip was driven from *St. Kitts*, has already been paid for by the defendant; even this would not have been paid for by the defendant, if he had conceived that the voyage had been at an end." The learned judges therefore, except Mr. Juſtice *Willes*, after giving their opinions upon the other points in the cauſe, ordered the rule for a new trial to be diſcharged.

[308] A deviation may alſo be juſtified, if done to avoid an enemy, or ſeek for convoy; becauſe it is in truth no deviation to go out of the courſe of a voyage, in order to avoid danger, or to obtain a protection againſt it.

Bond v. Gonſales, 2 Salk. 445.

In an action upon a policy, which was to inſure the *William Galley* in a voyage from *Bremen* to the port of *London*, warranted to depart with convoy; the caſe was this, the *Galley* ſet ſail from *Bremen*, under the convoy of a *Dutch* man of war to the *Elb*, where they were joined by two other *Dutch* men of war, and ſeveral *Dutch* and *Engliſh* merchant ſhips, whence they ſailed to the *Texel*, where they found a ſquadron of *Engliſh* men of war and an Admiral. After a ſtay of nine weeks, they ſet out from the

Texel, and the *Galley* was separated in a storm, and taken by a *French* privateer, taken again by a *Dutch* privateer, and paid 80*l.* salvage. CHAP. XVII.

It was ruled by Lord Chief Justice *Holt*, that the voyage ought to be according to usage, and that their going to the *Elb*, though in fact out of the way, was no deviation; for till after the year 1703, there was no convoy for ships directly from *Bremen* to *London*. And the plaintiff had a verdict.

On an insurance from *London* to *Gibraltar*, warranted to depart with convoy; it appeared there was a convoy appointed for that trade at *Spithead*; and the ship *Ranger*, having tried for convoy in the *Downs*, proceeded to *Spithead*, and was taken in her way thither. The insurers insisted that this being the time of a *French* war, the ship should not have ventured through the channel, but have waited in the *Downs* for an occasional convoy. And many merchants and office-keepers were examined to that purpose. Gordon v. Morley, Campbell v. Bordieu, 2 Stra. 1265.

But Lord Chief Justice *Lee* held that the ship was to be considered as under the defendant's insurance to a place of general rendezvous, according to the interpretation of the words *warranted to depart with convoy*. And if the parties meant to vary the insurance from what is commonly understood, they should have particularized her departure with convoy from the *Downs*. The juries were composed of merchants; and in both cases they found for the plaintiffs upon the strength of this direction.

In the case of *Bond* against *Nutt*, in which the material question was, whether a warranty had or had not been complied with, and which consequently will be fully stated in the following chapter, the point of deviation for the purpose of procuring convoy also came under the consideration of the court. Upon that occasion, Lord *Mansfield* and the whole court held, that if a ship go to the usual place of rendezvous, for the sake of joining convoy there ready, though such place be out of the direct course of the voyage, it is no deviation. [309] Cowp. Rep. 601.

And in a more modern case, the only question was, whether there was a deviation or not. Lord *Mansfield* there directed Enderby and another v. Fletcher, Sit.

CHAP. XVII. rected the jury to find for the plaintiffs, if they believed that the captain fairly and *bonâ fide* acted according to the best of his judgment: that he had no other view or motive but to come the safest way home, and to meet with convoy; for that it was no deviation to go out of the way to avoid danger.

tings in London, Trin. Vac. 1780.

In our law books we sometimes meet with cases, which say, that a deviation may be justified by the usage and custom of the trade. But that is not quite correct; for if by the usage of any particular trade, it is customary to stop at certain places, lying out of the direct course from *A.* to *B.* it is not a deviation to stop there; because it is a part of the voyage. There is no deception upon the insurer; because he is bound to take notice of the usages of trade; they are notorious to all the world; and when the usage has declared it lawful in a specific voyage to go to any place, though out of the immediate track, it is as much a part of the contract of insurance between the parties, as if it had been particularly mentioned. But in order to justify the captain of a ship in quitting the straight and direct line from the port of loading to that of delivery, there must be a precise, clear, and established usage upon the subject, not depending merely upon one or two loose and vague instances.

Salisbury *v.* Townson.

Where a ship was insured from *Liverpool* to *Jamaica*, and had put into the *Isle of Man*; it appeared that there were *some instances* of the *Liverpool* ships putting in there, but it was not the settled, common, established, and direct usage of the voyage and trade: it was therefore held a deviation, and the underwriters were discharged from any loss that happened subsequent to the deviation.

[310]

Having thus mentioned all the cases to be found in the books of reports, which operate as an excuse for a departure from the due course of the voyage, and which prevent those effects, which always follow a deviation, namely, the discharge of the insurer from his contract; it will be proper to observe, that it is not meant to insinuate that other circumstances may not frequently happen, which will have precisely the same consequences. For wherever a ship does that which is for the general benefit of all parties concerned, the act is as much within the intention and spirit of the policy, and consequently as much protected by it, as if expressed

Cowp. 601.

preſſed in terms. And therefore in all caſes, in order to determine whether a diverſion from the direct courſe of the voyage is ſuch a deviation as in law vacates the policy, it will be proper to attend to the motives, end, and conſequences of the act, as the true criterion of judgment.

If any of the circumſtances above ſtated do really and *bonâ fide* occur, ſo as to render a deviation abſolutely neceſſary, the ſhip muſt purſue ſuch *voyage of neceſſity* in the direct courſe, and in the ſhorteſt time poſſible, otherwiſe the underwriters will be diſcharged. Becauſe a voyage ſuperadded by neceſſity, ought to be ſubject to the ſame qualifications, and entitled only to the ſame ſort of latitude as the original voyage, it having become by operation of law, a part, as it were, of that original voyage.

This was laid down as law by the Court of King's Bench in a caſe, in which the voyage inſured was deſcribed in theſe words: "At and from *Port L'Orient* to *Pondicherry*, *Madras*, "and *China*, and at and from thence back to the ſhip's port, "or ports of diſcharge in *France*, with liberty to touch, in "the outward or homeward bound voyage, at the iſles of "*France* and *Bourbon*, and at all or any other ports or places, "what or whereſoever: and it ſhall be lawful for the ſaid "ſhip, *in this voyage* to proceed and ſail to, and touch and "ſtay at any ports or places whatſoever, as well on this ſide, "as on the other ſide, the *Cape of Good Hope*, without being "deemed a deviation." The ſhip did not ſail till the 6th of *December* 1776, and did not reach *Pondicherry* till the 23d of *July* 1777. She continued there till the 23d of *Auguſt* following, when, inſtead of proceeding to *China*, ſhe ſailed for *Bengal*, where having paſſed the winter, and undergone very conſiderable repairs, ſhe ſailed from thence early in the year 1778, (being the ſecond ſhip that left the *Ganges*) returned to *Pondicherry*; and, after taking in a homeward-bound cargo at that place, proceeded in her voyage back to *L'Orient*, but was taken in *October* in that year by the *Mentor* privateer. The uſual time, in which the direct voyage between *Pondicherry* and *Bengal* is performed, is ſix or ſeven days, but the *Carnatic* was about ſix weeks in going to *Bengal*, and two months on the way back from thence to *Pondicherry*. Both going and returning, ſhe either touched at, or lay off, *Madras*, *Maſulipatam*, *Viſigapatam*, and *Yanon*, and took in goods at

Lavabre v. Walter, Doug. 271.

[311]

CHAP. XVII. at all thoſe places. The plaintiffs reſted their caſe chiefly on this ground, that the voyage to *Bengal* was adopted by neceſſity for the ſafety of the ſhip, upon the *bonâ fide* opinion of the captain, and the reſt of the officers, and of one *Berard* the ſupercargo, who had the principal management. To prove this neceſſity it was ſworn by *Berard* and four mates, that the ſhip had been detained longer in *Europe* than at firſt was foreſeen, and that ſhe met with extremely bad weather on her outward paſſage; and at *Pondicherry* was ſo leaky, that it appeared to them that ſhe muſt be careened, which could only be done at *Bengal*, there being no other place ſo near, to which ſhe could proceed with ſafety, where that operation could be performed; for that no harbour between *Pondicherry* and the *Ganges* on the one ſide, and *Pondicherry* and *Bombay* on the other, would admit of ſo large a veſſel being hove down, her burthen being near 800 tons. Indeed it turned out when they got to *Bengal*, that ſhe could be repaired without careening: but this was only diſcovered, they ſaid, after ſhe was unloaded of much more of her contents than could have been done with ſafety in the open road of *Pondicherry*. All the witneſſes for the plaintiffs ſwore that they took the reſolution of going to *Bengal* much againſt their inclination; for that it would have been not only more for the advantage of the owners, but alſo more for their private intereſt as individuals, to go to *China*, they having prepared their own adventures for that market. Beſides the circumſtances of the leak, they aſſigned an additional reaſon for relinquiſhing the voyage to *China*, *viz.* that they had been ſo long detained at *Pondicherry*, from delays in unloading their outward-bound cargo, that they were not ready to leave that place, till it was too late to undertake the
[312] *China* voyage with any degree of prudence or ſafety; and they ſaid *Bengal* was the beſt place they could go to, in order to winter. The defence ſet up was; 1ſt, That the ſhip had never ſailed on the voyage inſured, her deſtination, *when ſhe left Europe*, having been for *Bengal*, and not for *China*. 2d, That ſuppoſing her to have ſailed on the voyage deſcribed in the policy, yet her going from *Pondicherry* to *Bengal*, inſtead of proceeding to *China*, was a deviation, and was not juſtified by neceſſity. In ſupport of the firſt ground of defence, certain ſecret inſtructions were relied upon which were found

found on board the ship, and were addressed by the owners at *L'Orient* to *Berard* the supercargo, and which though obscurely penned, gave great room to contend, either that, at her departure, it had been resolved to substitute the *Bengal* for the *China* voyage, or, at least, that the alternative was left with *Berard*, to be decided one way or the other, according to certain events in *India*, which events turned out in the sort of way that, according to the instructions, was to determine the voyage for *Bengal*. On the second ground, it was said, that from the plaintiff's own witnesses, there was no necessity for going to *Bengal*; and that instead of going directly thither, a trading voyage had been made from *Pondicherry*, which afforded a strong presumption that trading, and not the leak, or lateness of the season, was the object of going to *Bengal*. On the part of the defence also, several letters were read (written by the owners to their correspondents who had got their policy underwritten) to raise a presumption that the necessity of going to *Bengal* was merely a pretence devised after the capture; and when the insured began to apprehend that the words of the policy would not cover a voyage to that place. This is the substance of the evidence given in this and two other causes upon the same ship, though not on the same policy: in addition to which in the present case, the secret instructions given to *Berard* had been more attentively perused, and afforded stronger reasons than they at first seemed to do, that the voyage to *Bengal* was predetermined before the departure from *L'Orient*. The plaintiff's witnesses were much pressed, on this occasion, to say, whether the lateness of the season alone was such as, independent of the leak, would have determined them to abandon the *China* voyage; and on the other hand, whether the leak, independent of the other reason, would, in their opinion, have rendered it necessary so to do. [313] To this they said, they could not give a certain answer; for that, as neither of the cases had happened, they had not exercised their judgment upon them.

Vide ante, c. 2.

Lord *Mansfield* summed up very strongly against the plaintiffs, on the head of fraud. But, independent of that ground, he stated a new point against them, namely, that if necessity were admitted to have been the sole motive for substituting the voyage to *Bengal* in the place of that of *China*, *still it was*

incumbent

CHAP. XVII. *incumbent on the insured to have pursued that voyage of necessity directly, in the shortest and most expeditious manner; and that the delay in going from Pondicherry to Bengal, and the repeated steps by touching at different places, and trading there, were deviations, and not within the protection which the supposed necessity afforded to the direct voyage.*

Notwithstanding this direction, the jury found a verdict for the plaintiffs. Upon a motion for a new trial, after argument at the bar, the opinion of the Court of King's Bench was delivered by

Lord *Mansfield.*—"If this application were made upon the ground of impeaching the testimony of the plaintiff's witnesses, whatever my private sentiments might be, after two concurrent verdicts I should not be inclined to interpose. But, without impeaching the evidence, I think there ought to be a new trial, or rather, that the case has been ill decided. The question is, whether, without imputation on any body, circumstances have not happened to take the voyage out of the policy. A deviation from necessity must be justified, both as to substance and manner. *Nothing more must be done than what the necessity requires.* The true objection to a deviation is not the increase of the risk. If that were so, it would only be necessary to give an additional premium. It is, that the party contracting has voluntarily substituted another voyage for that which has been insured. If the voyage to *Bengal* was unavoidable, where was the necessity to trade? All the ports touched at were out of the direct course; and six weeks and two months were consumed, instead of six days. The justice of the case required a different decision." The rule for a new trial was accordingly made absolute.
[313 *a*] The cause was again set down for trial; but the plaintiffs, when they were ready to be called on, submitted to the opinion of the court, and abandoned their claim against the underwriters.

So also if a ship be insured upon a trading voyage, it is incumbent on the parties assured, to carry on that trade with usual and reasonable expedition, otherwise their conduct will amount to a deviation and discharge the policy.

Thus

Thus in an action by the assured against an underwriter on a policy of insurance on the ship *Blossom*, at and from the coast of *Africa* to the *West Indies*, with liberty to exchange goods and slaves; a verdict was given for the plaintiff. But upon a rule being obtained, to shew cause why there should not be a new trial, it appeared that there had been a great deal of contradictory evidence, and many points started at the trial; but the question now made, was, whether the plaintiff, by the use he made of the vessel on the coast of *Africa*, and the delay he there occasioned, was not the cause of the loss; that is, whether he did not make such use of her during her stay on the coast, contrary to the design of the policy, as amounted to a deviation. CHAP. XVII. Hartley v. Buggin, B. R. Mich. 22 Geo. III.

It appeared in evidence, that this ship stayed on the coast from *August* to *March*; that she was employed in receiving slaves on board, the produce of the cargoes of other ships, which were afterwards put on board other ships, and sent to the *West Indies*; that this is the employment of what they call a *factory ship*; but that a regular factory ship is thatched and covered, and receives the slaves till a sufficient number is collected to send away in the vessels; but it did not appear that any slaves, the produce of the *Blossom*'s own cargo were sent away in other vessels, but that her stay there was several months beyond the usual stay of ships in that trade. After argument at the bar,

Lord *Mansfield* said, "When different points are agitated at a trial, and a great deal of evidence applied to each, and the counsel go out of the cause, it is not to be wondered at if juries should lose their attention to the material point. The great advantage of a motion for a new trial, is, that after argument on the motion, the cause goes down again winnowed from the chaff of the first trial. The single point here is, whether there has not been what is equivalent to a deviation, whether the risk has not been varied? not material whether or not the risk has been greater. If a ship insured for a trade, is turned into a floating warehouse, or a factory ship, the risk is different, it varies the stay, for while she is used as a warehouse, no cargo is bought for her. The law being clear, how is the fact? The captain says she was not used

CHAP. XVII. used as a factory ship, his evidence is much impeached; but he says he was young in the trade; he never saw a factory ship but once, and was not in her; he might have a salvo, because this was not thatched; but was she used as a thatched ship is used? It is said that letters are not records; 'tis true they may be contradicted; but if they are from the parties, and are not contradicted, they are as strong as any records. The fact is clear, the risk is different in point of length, *&c.*"

Rule absolute for a new trial.

But though an actual deviation from the voyage insured is thus fatal to the contract of insurance; yet a deviation merely intended, but never carried into effect, is considered as no deviation, and the insurer continues liable. This has been frequently so decided. Thus in the case of an insurance from *Carolina* to *Lisbon*, and at and from thence to *Bristol*; it appeared, that the captain had taken in salt, which he was to deliver at *Falmouth*, before he went to *Bristol*; but the ship was taken in the direct road to both, and before she came to the point, where she would have turned off to *Falmouth*. It was held, that the insurer was liable; for it is but *an intention to deviate*, and that was held not sufficient to discharge the underwriter.

Foster v. Wilmer, 2 Stra. 1249.

Ld. Ch. Just. Lee.

2 Str. 1249.

In the case of *Carter* v. the *Royal Exchange* Assurance Company, where the insurance was from *Honduras* to *London*, and a consignment to *Amsterdam*: a loss happened before she came to the dividing point between the two voyages, for which the insurers were held liable to pay.

Dougl. 346.

The doctrine laid down in these cases has since been frequently recognized in subsequent decisions, and particularly by Lord *Mansfield* in the case of *Thellusson* v. *Fergusson*, which will be fully reported in the next chapter. The insurance was from *Guadaloupe* to *Havre*, and by the depositions it appeared that the ship sailed for *Havre*, and was always intended for *Havre*; but was directed to keep in the course of *Brest* for safety. One of the grounds of defence, was, that the ship never sailed from *Guadaloupe* to *Havre*, but on a voyage from *Guadaloupe* to *Brest*. Lord *Mansfield*, in answer, said, "the voyage to *Brest*, was, at most, but an *intended deviation*, not carried into effect."

If,

If, however, it can be made appear by evidence, that it never was intended nor came within the contemplation of the parties to sail upon the voyage insured; if all the ship's papers and documents be made out for a different place from that described in the policy, the insurer is discharged from all degree of responsibility, even though the loss should happen before the dividing point of the two voyages. This distinction was very properly taken by the Court of King's Bench, in a very modern case: and by that distinction they admitted the general doctrine, with respect to the intention to deviate, in its fullest extent. [315]

Wooldridge v. Boydell, Dougl. 16.

The ship *Molly* being insured "at and from *Maryland* to *Cadiz*," was taken in *Chesapeak Bay*, in the way to *Europe*. Upon this the insured brought this action against the defendant, one of the underwriters on the policy. The trial came on at *Guildhall* before Lord *Mansfield*, when a verdict was found for the defendant. A new trial being moved for, the material facts of the case appeared to be as follows: The ship was cleared from *Maryland* to *Falmouth*, and a bond given that all the *enumerated* goods should be landed in *Britain*, and all the other goods in the *British* dominions. An affidavit of the owner stated that the vessel was bound for *Falmouth*. The bills of lading were "To *Falmouth* and a market:" and there was no evidence whatever that she was destined for *Cadiz*. The place where she was taken, was in the course from *Maryland* both to *Cadiz* and *Falmouth*, before the dividing point. Many circumstances led to a suspicion that she was, in truth, neither designed for *Falmouth* nor *Cadiz*, but for the port of *Boston*, to supply the *American* army; but there was not sufficient direct evidence of that fact.—At the trial, Lord *Mansfield* told the jury, that if they thought the voyage intended was to *Cadiz*, they must find for the plaintiff. If, on the contrary, they should think there was no design of going to *Cadiz*, they must find for the defendant. It also appeared in evidence, that the premium to insure a voyage from *Maryland* to *Falmouth*, and from thence to *Cadiz*, would have greatly exceeded what was paid in this case. Upon the motion for a new trial being argued, the counsel for the plaintiff cited the two cases above stated from *Strange*'s Reports.

Lord

CHAP. XVII. Lord *Mansfield.*—"The policy, on the face of it, is from *Maryland* to *Cadiz*, and therefore purports to be a direct voyage to *Cadiz*. All contracts of insurance must be founded on truth, and the policies framed accordingly. When the insured intends a deviation from the direct voyage, it is always provided for, and the indemnification adapted to it. There never was a man so foolish as to intend a deviation from the voyage described, when the insurance is made, be- [316] cause that would be paying without an indemnification. Deviations from the voyage insured arise from after-thoughts, after-interest, after-temptation; and the party, who actually deviates from the voyage described, means to give up his policy. But a deviation merely intended, but never carried into effect, is as no deviation. In all the cases of that sort, the *terminus a quo*, and *ad quem*, were certain and the same. Here, was the voyage ever intended for *Cadiz?* There is not sufficient evidence of the design to go to *Boston*, for the court to go upon. But some of the papers say to *Falmouth* and a market: some to *Falmouth* only. None mention *Cadiz*, nor was there any person in the ship, who ever heard of any intention to go to that port. A *market* is not synonimous to *Cadiz*; that expression might have meant *Naples*, *Leghorn*, or *England*. No man, upon the instructions, would have thought of getting the policy filled up to *Cadiz*. In short, that was never the voyage intended, and consequently is not what the underwriters meant to insure."

Mr. Justice *Buller.*—"I am of the same opinion, I believe the law to be according to the authorities mentioned on the part of the plaintiff: but it does not apply here. This is a question of fact. There cannot be a deviation from that, which never existed. The weight of the evidence is, that the voyage was never designed for *Cadiz*."

Mr. Justice *Willes* and Mr. Justice *Ashhurst* concurring in the opinion delivered by Lord *Mansfield* and Mr. Justice *Buller*, the rule for a new trial was discharged.

Way v. Modigliani, 2 Term Rep. 30.

In a still later case the same doctrine was advanced, namely, that if a ship be insured from a day certain from *A*. to *B*. and

and before the day sail on a different voyage from that insured, the assured cannot recover; even though the ship afterwards fall into the course of the voyage insured, and be lost after the day on which the policy was to have attached.

[316 a]

Since the former edition of this work was published, the cases of *Wooldridge* v. *Boydell*, and *Way* v. *Modigliani*, have again come under discussion in the Court of Common Pleas; and it has been held by the four judges of that court, one of whom sat in the Court of King's Bench when the two cases just reported were decided, that where the *termini* of the intended voyage continue the same as those described in the policy, an intention to go to an intermediate port, though that intention should be formed previous to the ship's sailing, will not vitiate the insurance till actual deviation. The case has already been quoted for another purpose; and the facts as to this point are shortly these. The insurance was *at and from Grenada to Liverpool*; the ship sailed *from Grenada, bound for Liverpool*, but with a design *formed before the commencement of the voyage*, as appeared by the clearances, and was admitted on all sides, *to touch at Corke in her way to Liverpool*, but was totally lost before she arrived at the dividing point. In the course of the argument a case of *Stott* v. *Vaughan*, was mentioned, as having been tried before Lord *Kenyon*, at the sittings at *Guildhall*, after Hilary Term 1794, in which his Lordship nonsuited the plaintiff, in an action on a policy on this very ship, being of opinion that the case fell within those of *Wooldridge* v. *Boydell*, and *Way* v. *Modigliani*, and that there was no inception of the voyage insured. The Court of Common Pleas, however, having taken time to deliberate upon this case of *Kewly* v. *Ryan*, delivered their opinion as to the 3d question, that where the *termini* of the intended voyage were really the same as those described in the policy, it was to be considered as the same voyage, and a design to deviate, not effected, would not vitiate the policy. That, in *Wooldridge* v. *Boydell*, it appeared there was no intention that the ship should go to *Cadiz* at all, which was mentioned in the policy as her port of delivery; and in *Way* v. *Modigliani*, there was an actual deviation, by the ship going to fish on the banks of *Newfoundland*: those cases therefore were wholly

Kewley v. Ryan, 2 H. Black. Rep. p. 343. See ante, p. 19.

CHAP. XVII. wholly different from the present, for here the ſhip was really bound to *Liverpool*, though there were alſo clearances for *Corke*.

From the propoſition juſt eſtabliſhed, namely, that a mere intention to deviate will not vacate the policy, it follows as an immediate conſequence, that whatever damage is ſuſtained before actual deviation, will fall upon the underwriters.

[317] Green v. Young, 2 Ld. Raym. 840. 2 Salk. 444, S. C.

Thus it was held by Lord Chief Juſtice *Holt*, who ſaid, that if a policy of inſurance be made to begin from the departure of the ſhip from *England* until, &c. and after the departure a damage happens, &c. and then the ſhip *deviates*; though the policy is diſcharged from the time of the deviation, yet for the damages ſuſtained before the deviation, the inſurers ſhall make ſatisfaction to the inſured.

Doug. 758.

Subject to the rules already advanced, deviation or not is a queſtion of fact, to be decided according to the circumſtances of the caſe.

Vide poſt, c. 19.

In caſes of deviation, the premium is not to be returned; becauſe the riſk being commenced, the underwriter is entitled to retain it: but of this more will be ſaid in a ſubſequent chapter.

CHAPTER THE EIGHTEENTH.

Of Non-Compliance with Warranties.

IN the two preceding chapters we have seen the effect, which the non-observance of implied conditions has upon the contract of insurance; we shall now proceed to consider the nature of warranties; their various kinds; and how far they must be complied with on the part of the insured, in order to render the contract binding between the parties. A warranty in a policy of insurance is a condition or a contingency, that a certain thing shall be done, or happen, and unless that is performed, there is no valid contract. It is perfectly immaterial for what view the warranty is introduced; or whether the party had any view at all: but being once inserted, it becomes a binding condition on the insured: and unless he can shew that he has literally fulfilled it, or that it was performed, the contract is the same, as if it had never existed. We have already seen that the breach of an implied condition is sufficient to avoid the policy; *a fortiori*, therefore, the effect must be the same, where the condition is express, and not liable to misrepresentation or error, because it makes a part of the written contract. To say that the underwriter should answer for a loss, notwithstanding the other party has failed in his engagements, would be to make a different rule in this species of contract, from that which subsists in every other; although this of all other contracts depends most upon the strictest attention to the purest rules of equity and good faith. Indeed the obligation to a strict performance of all promises and conditions in every species of contract, may be deduced, as has been truly observed by an elegant moral writer, from the necessity of such a conduct to the well-being, or the existence of human society.

CHAP. XVIII.

1 Term Rep. p. 345.

Chap. 16, 17.

Paley's Mor. Phil.

We have said that a warranty must be strictly and *literally* performed; and therefore whether the thing, warranted to

 be

CHAP. XVIII.

be done, be or be not essential to the security of the ship; or whether the loss do or do not happen, on account of the breach of the warranty, still the insured has no remedy: because he himself has not performed his part of the contract, and if he did not mean to perform, he ought not to have bound himself by such a condition. And though the condition broken, be not, perhaps, a material one, yet the justice of the law is evident from this consideration; that it is absolutely necessary to have one rule of decision; and that it is much better to say, that warranties shall in all cases be strictly complied with, than to leave it in the breast of a judge or jury to say, that in one case it shall, and in another it shall not. The very meaning of a warranty is to preclude all inquiries into the materiality, or the *substantial* performance of it: and although sometimes partial inconveniences may arise from such a rule; yet upon the whole, it will certainly produce public salutary effects. The insured is bound not to draw the underwriter into error, by false declarations respecting those things about which the contract is made. *Debet præstare rem ita esse ut affirmavit.*

1 Term Rep. p. 346.

Pothiér Tr. du Contrat d'Assurance, p. 197.

But as a warranty must be strictly complied with in favour of the underwriter, and against the insured, equal justice demands, and the true meaning of the contract of insurance requires, that if a strict and literal compliance with the warranty will support the demand of the insured, the decision ought to be in his favour, especially when by such a decision all the words in the policy will have their full operation.

Blackhurst v. Cockell, 3 Term R. 360.

In an action on a policy on goods, dated 9th of *December* 1784, *lost or not lost, warranted well this 9th day of December* 1784: it appeared, that the warranty was at the foot of the policy; that the policy was underwritten between the hours of one and three in the afternoon of the 9th of *December*; that the ship was well at six o'clock in the morning, but was lost at eight o'clock in the same morning.

Upon a motion to set aside a nonsuit, which had been entered, Lord *Kenyon* Chief Justice, *Ashhurst*, *Buller* and *Grose*, Justices, were clearly of opinion, that the warranty was sufficiently complied with, if the ship were well at any time that day: that the nature of a warranty goes to determine the

the queſtion; for as it is a matter of indifference whether the thing warranted be, or be not material, and yet muſt be literally complied with; ſtill if it be complied with, that is enough: that there was good reaſon for inſerting theſe words, becauſe they protected the underwriter from loſſes before that day, to which he would otherwiſe have been liable, as the policy was on the goods from the lading: and thus too, the words *loſt or not loſt* have alſo their operation. CHAP. XVIII.

This being the caſe, it follows as a neceſſary conſequence, that it is very immaterial to what cauſe the non-compliance is to be attributed; for if the fact be, that the warranty was not complied with, though perhaps for the beſt reaſons, the policy has no effect. The contingency has not happened; and therefore the party intereſted has a right to ſay, that there is no contract between them. Upon this account it is, that if a ſhip be warranted to ſail on or before the 1ſt of *Auguſt*, and ſhe be prevented by any accident from ſailing till the 2d of *Auguſt*, as by the ſudden want of any neceſſary repair, or by the appearance of an enemy at the mouth of the port, the captain would do right not to ſail: but there would be an end of the policy. Cowp. 607.

In this ſtrict and literal compliance with the terms of a warranty conſiſts the difference between a warranty and a repreſentation.

Of this diſtinction ſomething was ſaid in a preceding chapter: it is ſufficient now to obſerve, that a warranty, as part of the agreement, and a condition on which it was made, muſt be *ſtrictly* complied with, whereas a repreſentation need only be performed *in ſubſtance*. In a warranty, the perſon making it takes the riſk of its truth or falſehood upon himſelf: in a repreſentation, if the inſured aſſert that to be true, which he either knows to be falſe, or about which he knows nothing, the policy is void on account of fraud. But a repreſentation, made without fraud, if not falſe in a *material* point, or if it be *ſubſtantially*, though not *literally* fulfilled, does not vitiate the policy. Vide ante, c. 10. Pawſon v. Watſon, Cowp. 787.

CHAP. XVIII.

But as reprefentations were very often made in writing, by way of inftructions for effecting a policy, it became neceffary to fpecify what written declarations fhould be deemed warranties, and what reprefentations. It was, therefore, by feveral decifions of the courts, held to be law, that in order to make written inftructions valid and binding as a warranty, they muft appear on the face of the inftrument itfelf, by which the contract of infurance is effected.

Pawfon v. Watfon, Cowper 790.

This was declared by Lord *Mansfield* in a very particular manner in anfwer to a queftion put to him by Mr. *Davenport* at the defire of the underwriters, after he had delivered the opinion of the court upon a queftion on a reprefentation.

Even though a written paper be *wrapt up in the policy*, when it is brought to the underwriters to fubfcribe, and fhewn to them at that time; or even though it be *wafered to the policy*, at the time of fubfcribing; *ftill it is not in either* cafe a warranty, or to be confidered as part of the policy itfelf, but only as a reprefentation. Both thefe inftances have occurred in caufes before Lord *Mansfield*.

Pawfon v. Barnevelt, at Guildh. Trin. Vac. 1779. Doug p. 12. in the notes.

In an action on a policy of infurance, the counfel for the defendant offered to produce witneffes to prove, that a written memorandum inclofed was always confidered as part of the policy. But Lord *Mansfield* faid, it was a mere queftion of law, and would not hear the evidence; but decided, that a written paper did not become a ftrict warranty, by being folded up in the policy.

Bize v. Fletcher, at Guildh. Eaft, Vac. 1979 Doug. p. 12 in the notes

In the other cafe it appeared, that at the time when the infurers underwrote the policy, a flip of paper was wafered to it, defcribing the ftate of the fhip as to repairs and ftrength, and alfo mentioning feveral particulars of her intended voyage, which particulars in the event had not been complied with. Lord *Mansfield* ruled, that this was only a reprefentation; and if the jury fhould think there was no fraud intended, and that the variance between the intended voyage, as defcribed in the flip of paper, and the actual voyage as performed, did not tend to increafe the rifk of the underwriters, he directed them to find for the plaintiff, which they accordingly did.

This

This verdict was afterwards set aside upon another ground. CHAP. XVIII.

It being thus settled, that a warranty must appear on the face of the instrument it still became a question, whether a warranty, written in the margin of the policy, was to be considered equally binding, and subject to the same strict rule of construction, as if inserted in the body of the policy itself. This point came under the consideration of the court in the case of *Bean* and *Stupart*, in which the material question was, whether, supposing it to be a warranty, *boys* were included under the word *seamen*. That case, as far it is material to our present inquiry, was as follows: Doug. 271.

The plaintiff insured the ship called the *Martha*, at and from *London* to *New-York*; the voyage to commence from a day specified; and in the *margin* of the policy were written these words, "Eight nine pounders with close quarters, six "six pounders on her upper decks; thirty seamen besides "passengers." Bean v. Stupart. Doug. 10.

Upon a motion for a new trial in this case, Lord *Mansfield* said, there is no doubt but this is a warranty. Its being written on the margin makes no difference. Being a warranty, there is no doubt but that the underwriters would not be liable if it were not complied with; because it is a condition on which the contract is founded.

In an action on a policy of insurance, it appeared that the following words were written transversely on the margin of the policy: "In port 20th *July* 1776." In fact, the ship had sailed the 18th of *July*. The question was, whether this marginal note was a warranty or a representation. Kenyon v. Berthon, Mich. Vac. 1779. Doug. p. 12. note (4)

Lord *Mansfield*.—"The question is, whether the ship's being in port on the 20th is part of the condition of the instrument. When it is on the face of the instrument, it is a part of the policy; so that here, if the ship was not in port, it is no contract. As to its being only in the margin, that makes no difference; it is all part of the contract when it is *once* signed. And though the difference of two days may not make any material difference in the risk, yet as the condition has not been complied with, the underwriter is not liable."

The

CHAP. XVIII.

The propriety of thefe decifions has never been queftioned, and the rule has been conftantly and tacitly acquiefced in from the time in which thefe cafes were determined till the year 1786, when, notwithftanding the uniformity of the determinations upon the fubject, it once more became an object of difcuffion.

De Hahn v. Hartley. 1 Term Rep. p. 343.

It came before the court upon a fpecial verdict: it was an action of affumpfit brought by the plaintiff (an underwriter) againft the defendant, to recover back the amount of a lofs which he had paid upon a policy of infurance. The defendant pleaded the general iffue. The caufe came on to be tried before Mr. Juftice *Buller*, at *Guildhall*, when the jury found a fpecial verdict, ftating:

That the defendant on the 14th of *June* 1779, gave to his infurance broker inftructions in writing, to caufe an infurance to be made on a certain veffel, called the *Juno*. (Then the inftructions are fet out in the verdict, figned by the defendant.) The verdict then ftates that the broker, in confequence of fuch inftructions, on the faid 14th of *June* 1779, did caufe a policy of infurance to be made on the *Juno*, upon goods and merchandizes laden on board, and alfo on the fhip, at and from *Africa*, to her port or ports of difcharge in the *Britifh Weft Indies*, at and after the rate of 15*l. per cent.* The verdict, after reciting two memorandums, not material, then proceeded to ftate, that *in the margin of the faid policy were written the words and figures following:* "Sailed from "*Liverpool* with 14 fix pounders, fwivels, fmall arms, and "50 *hands or upwards;* copper fheathed." That the plaintiff underwrote the policy for 200*l.* at a premium of 31*l.* 10*s.* That the *Juno* failed from *Liverpool* on the 13th of *October* 1778, having then only 46 *hands on board her*, and arrived at *Beaumaris*, in the Ifle of *Anglefea*, in fix hours after her failing from *Liverpool*, with the pilot from *Liverpool* on board her, who did pilot her to *Beaumaris*, on her faid voyage; and that at *Beaumaris* the *Juno* took in fix hands more, and then had, and during the faid voyage, until the capture thereof, continued to have 52 hands on board her. That the faid fhip in the voyage from *Liverpool* to *Beaumaris*, until and when fhe took in the faid fix additional hands, was equally fafe, as if fhe had had 50 hands on board her for that part of the voyage. The verdict then ftates, that the defendant

fendant was interested, and that the ship was captured: that on receiving an account of the loss of the vessel, the plaintiff paid to the defendant the sum of 200*l.* not having then had any notice that the said ship had only 46 hands on board her when she sailed from *Liverpool*.

For the defendant it was said, that this representation had no relation to the voyage insured; for that was *at and from Africa*, &c. whereas this is merely an account of the state of the ship at *Liverpool*.

Lord *Mansfield*.—"There is a material distinction between a warranty and a representation. A representation may be *equitably* and *substantially* answered: but a warranty must be *strictly* complied with. Supposing a warranty to sail on the 1st of *August*, and the ship did not sail till the 2d, the warranty would not be complied with. A warranty in a policy of insurance, is a condition or a contingency, and unless that is performed there is no contract. It is perfectly immaterial, for what purpose a warranty is introduced; but being inserted, the contract does not exist unless it is literally complied with. Now in the present case, the condition was, the sailing of the ship with a certain number of men, which not being complied with, the policy is of no effect."

Mr. Justice *Ashhurst*.—"The very meaning of a warranty is, to preclude all questions whether it has *been substantially* complied with: it must be *literally* so."

Mr. Justice *Buller*.—"It is impossible to divide the words written in the margin, in the manner which has been attempted at the bar; that that part which relates to the copper sheathing should be a warranty, and not the remaining part. But the whole forms one entire contract, and must be complied with throughout." Judgment for the plaintiff. A writ of error was brought in the Exchequer Chamber upon this judgment, which, after two arguments, was affirmed by the unanimous opinion of the eight Judges composing that Court. Michaelmas Term 1787. 28th Geo. III.

Having stated those rules, which apply to warranties in general, it will now be proper to consider the several kinds of warranties, and those principles which are peculiar to each species.

CHAP. XVIII.

ſpecies, confirmed by deciſions of the courts. It would be endleſs to enumerate the various warranties that are to be found in policies; becauſe they muſt frequently, and for the moſt part do depend upon the particular circumſtances of each caſe; ſuch as the number of men, of guns, being copper ſheathed, &c. But thoſe which moſt frequently occur in our books of reports, and upon which the greateſt queſtions have ariſen, may be reduced to three claſſes: Warranty as to the time of ſailing; warranty as to convoy; and warranty of neutrality. Of each of theſe we ſhall treat; obſerving in the firſt place, that thoſe rules which are applicable to warranty in general, muſt neceſſarily alſo apply to each of theſe individually.

Roccus, Not. 38.

1ſt. As to the time of ſailing. In moſt voyages, the time at which they are to commence is a material circumſtance; becauſe in every country there are ſome ſeaſons when navigation is much more dangerous than at others, owing to periodical winds, monſoons, and various other cauſes. Indeed, we have ſeen, that a man having once warranted to ſail on a particular day, whether the riſk be, in fact, materially altered or not by a breach of that warranty, the underwriter is no longer anſwerable. But this ſtrict adherence to the very day ſpecified, muſt have ariſen from the principles juſt ſtated: for if a latitude of one day were given, why not extend it farther? It has therefore been held, that when a ſhip has been warranted to ſail on a particular day, though the ſhip be delayed for the beſt and wiſeſt reaſons, or even though ſhe be detained by force; the warranty has not been complied with, and the inſurer is diſcharged from his contract.

Kenyon v. Berthon. Supra.

Hore v. Whitmore. Cowp. 784.

Thus, in an action on a policy of inſurance, upon a motion to ſet aſide the verdict which had been given for the plaintiff, the caſe appeared to be this. The declaration ſtated that a policy was made on the ſhip *New Weſtmoreland*, at and from *Jamaica* to *London*, *warranted to ſail on or before the 26th of July* 1776, free from capture, and free from all reſtraints and detainments of kings, princes, and people of what nation, condition, or quality ſoever. It further ſtated, that the ſaid ſhip was preparing and ready to ſail, and would have ſailed on the 25th of *July*, on her intended voyage, *if ſhe had not been reſtrained by the order and command of Sir Baſil Keith*,

Keith, the then governor of *Jamaica*, and *detained beyond the day*: that she afterwards failed and was captured. For the plaintiff it was said, that the usual clause against the detention of rulers and princes being inserted in this policy, the embargo, by which the ship was prevented from sailing on the day mentioned in the warranty, came expressly within the meaning of it, and therefore excused the delay.

On the other hand it was said, that the loss of the ship could in no possible respect be connected with the embargo. That the warranty was *positive and express*; that the ship should depart on or before the day appointed, and therefore must be complied with. Of this opinion was the court; and accordingly the rule to set aside the verdict for the plaintiff, and to enter a nonsuit was made absolute.

But the necessity of a punctual adherence to the day on which the ship is warranted to sail by the policy, is not peculiar to the law of *England*; for we find that foreign writers declare, that the same rule is universally adopted. If, say they, the owner of the ship or goods has said in the policy, that he will be ready to sail at a particular time, at which, perhaps, the navigation may be less dangerous; and on this account the insurer is more easily induced to underwrite the policy; and he afterwards delay the time of sailing, and the ship and goods perish, the underwriter is not bound, for he who neglects to depart at the appointed time, must, if he sail at a subsequent period, do it entirely at his own risk.(*a*)

Roccus, Not. 38.

If the warranty be to sail *after* a specific day, and the ship sail before, the policy is equally avoided as in the former case; because the terms of the warranty are as much departed from in the one case as in the other.

On the 8th of *December* 1777, a policy was underwritten by the defendant on goods in a *French* ship, *Le Comte de Trebon*, "at and from *Martinico* to *Havre de Grace*, with liberty to touch at *Guadaloupe*; *warranted to sail after the* 12th

Vezian v. Grant, bef. Mr. Just. Buller, Guildhall, East. Vac. 1779.

(*a*) Roccus, in this passage, quotes the work of Santerna, upon insurances, who, he observes, *exclamat contra magistros navium, et nautas, quando detinentur in portu a mulierculis, vel dulcedine vini.*

CHAP. XVIII.

"12*th of January*, and on or before the firſt of *Auguſt* 1778." The inſurance was made by the plaintiff on account of *Jacques Horteloupe* and *Louis Delamare*, of *Havre de Grace*, owners of the ſhip and cargo; at which time it was not known whether ſhe would load at *Martinico* or *Guadaloupe*, they having goods to come from both places; the policy was therefore intended to cover the riſk from both, or either of them. The ſhip, having finiſhed her outward voyage at *Martinico, ſailed from thence on the 6th of November* 1777, for *Guadaloupe*, where ſhe took in her whole loading, without returning to *Martinico*, which the captain intended to do, had he not got a complete cargo at *Guadaloupe*; from whence ſhe failed on the 26th of *June* 1778, and was taken on the 3d of *September*. The plaintiff demanded payment of the loſs from the underwriters, which being refuſed, he brought actions againſt them for the recovery thereof. This cauſe came on to be tried at *Guildhall*, before Mr. Juſtice *Buller*, when the defendant's objections were, that, according to the words of the policy, the voyage was to commence from *Martinico*, and not from *Guadaloupe*; and that the warranty of the time of failing was not complied with, *the ſhip having ſailed from Martinico before the* 12*th of January* 1778, to wit, on the 6th of *November* 1777. The jury, under the direction of the learned judge, were of that opinion, and accordingly found a verdict for the defendant.

But when a ſhip is warranted to ſail on or before a particular day, if ſhe failed from her port of loading, *with all her cargo and clearances on board*, to the uſual place of rendezvous at another part of the ſame iſland, merely for the ſake of joining convoy, it is a compliance with the warranty, though ſhe be afterwards detained there by an embargo beyond the day. The ground is, that when a ſhip leaves her port of loading, when ſhe has a full and complete cargo on board, and has no other object in view but the ſafeſt mode of failing to her port of delivery, her voyage muſt be ſaid to commence from her departure from that port. If, indeed, her cargo was not complete, it would not have been a commencement of the voyage. It is true, in the caſe about to be reported, Lord *Mansfield* was of a different opinion at the trial; and it certainly was a caſe of conſiderable difficulty: but when it came again before the court, it underwent a great deal of diſcuſſion, and after long and mature deliberation of

Cowp. 608.

all

all the judges, his Lordship candidly acknowledged that his former decision was wrong; and upon a subsequent occasion, he declared he was completely convinced, that the voyage commenced from the port of loading. As that is the leading case upon this subject, it is here reported at length.

This was an action on a policy of insurance upon the ship *Capel* in the *West India* trade, lost or not lost, *at and from* Jamaica *to* London; *warranted to have sailed on or before the 1st of* August 1776. The policy was effected on the 20th of *August* 1776, at a premium of 15 guineas *per cent.* to return 5 *per cent.* if the ship departed with convoy; and 8 *per cent.* if with convoy for the voyage, and arrived safe. At the trial there was no controversy about the facts; and they are shortly these: the ship was completely laden for her voyage to *England*, at *St. Anne's* in *Jamaica*; *and sailed from* St. Anne's Bay, *on the 26th of* July *for* Bluefields, *in order to join the convoy there*, *Bluefields* being the general place of rendezvous for convoy on the *Jamaica* station, like *Spithead* in *England*, and where a convoy then lay, which was expected to sail for *England* every day; but the greater part of the way from *St. Anne's* to *Bluefields*, is out of the direct course of the voyage from *St. Anne's* to *England*. That she arrived off *Bluefields* on the 28th or 29th of *July*, where she was immediately stopped by an embargo laid on all vessels being in any part of *Jamaica*, and was detained there till the 6th of *August*, when she sailed with the convoy for *England*; but afterwards, being separated in the passage, was taken by an *American* privateer. Upon these facts the jury found a verdict for the defendant. When this case was first argued at the bar, two points were relied upon for the defendant, in support of the verdict, which the jury had given in his favour: 1st. That the departure from *St. Anne's*, was not a departure from *Jamaica*, within the meaning of this policy. 2d. If it were, that the going to *Bluefields* was a deviation. Upon the first argument, Lord *Mansfield* said: One point now started is entirely new: that supposing the voyage to have begun from *St. Anne's*, the going to *Bluefields* (which, it is admitted on all hands, was out of the course of the voyage) though for the purpose of convoy only, shall be considered as a deviation. In answer, it has been said by the counsel for the plaintiff, that there are cases in which the contrary has been held: but they are not cited. I could

Bond v. Nutt. Cowp. 601.

Vide the preceding chapter.

CHAP. XVIII. could wish therefore that these cases might be particularly looked into, and this ground mentioned again. It is a very material point: but widely different from a warranty to depart on a particular day, which is a condition precedent that admits of no latitude.

The second point was again argued; and then the judges severally mentioned their ideas upon the subject, without coming at that time to any decision.

Lord *Mansfield*.—"I am extremely glad this motion has been made; the cause came on at *Guildhall*, by the candour of parties in the fairest manner. But I had no intimation of its being a cause of consequence till after the verdict; when I was informed 100,000*l.* depended upon it. The question was fairly tried, and the case has been very well argued on both sides. I have thought much of it since the trial. Some things are clear, and there are others which require consideration. The policy was made on the 20th of *August* 1776, upon the contingency of a fact, which must have existed one way or the other at the time the policy was underwritten. That contingency was, that the ship should have sailed on or before the 1st of *August*: consequently it must have taken place or not upon the 20th of that month. The port from whence the ship was to be insured, was, if I may use the expression, the whole island of *Jamaica*: but from which of the ports the ship would sail, neither party knew: therefore they have used the words, "at and from *Jamaica*:" by force of which she certainly was protected in going from port to port, and till she sailed. It follows that the word *sailed* in the warranty, must mean that she had sailed *on her homeward bound voyage*. The question then is a matter of fact; and one that admits of no latitude, no equity of construction, or excuse. Had she or had she not sailed on or before that day? That is the question. No matter what cause prevented her; if the fact is, that she had not sailed, though she staid behind for the best reasons, the policy was void: the contingency had not happened; and the party interested had a right to say, there was no contract between them. Therefore what was said in argument is very true: if she had been prevented by any accident from sailing till the second of *August*, as by the sudden want of any necessary repair, or if an enemy had been at the mouth of the port; the captain would have done very

very right not to sail, but there would have been an end of the policy. It is very different from the cases where a voyage has been begun: there the usage of the voyage may justify going a little out of the direct course. This also is clear; if the ship had broken ground, and been fairly under sail upon her voyage for *England* on the 1st of *August*, though she had gone ever so little a way, and had afterwards put back from the stress of weather, or apprehension from an enemy in sight, or had then been put under an embargo, and had been detained till *September*, it would still have been a *beginning* to sail; and the stoppage would have come too late: because the warranty was upon a fact antecedent. Such a case happened before me a day or two after the present action was tried. It was an insurance upon a ship from *Grenada* to *London*, *warranted to sail on or before the 1st of August*. She had barely begun to sail on the day, when she was stopped by an embargo, and detained beyond the time. I thought the voyage was begun: the jury were of that opinion; and there has been no motion for a new trial. I am giving no opinion, only breaking the case. Here the whole question turns upon this: did the voyage from *Jamaica* homeward begin from *St. Anne's*, or from *Bluefields*? Perhaps where a voyage is once begun, the going a little out of the way to join convoy may be very reasonable, and for the benefit of all parties: but still it does not vary the fact of sailing. Here it was very reasonable: but the question, whether the voyage began from *St. Anne's* or *Bluefields*, still remains. Another material circumstance arises, from the words, "at and from *Jamaica*." At the trial, I reasoned thus: "By the terms of the policy she was protected during her stay at *Jamaica*: by force of them, she had a right to go to any port, or all round the island; and she went to *Bluefields* for reasons best known to herself. Therefore the voyage began from *Bluefields*." Had the insurance been at and from the port of *St. Anne's*, it did strike me, that going round the island to *Bluefields*, would have been a deviation. But this is a question of so much value and consequence, that the court wishes to consider the case thoroughly, before they give a final decision upon it."

Thellusson v. Fergusson, at Guildhall, Hil. Vac. 1777.

Mr. Justice *Aston*.—"I shall be very glad to consider this case. As at present advised, it seems to me to depend upon a mere matter of fact: and therefore to be very different from

CHAP. XVIII. from the cases of deviation that have been put. In them, the change of voyage, being from necessity, is excused in point of law: but here, the whole question is, did the *Capel* sail from *Jamaica* on or before the 1st of *August*, according to the true sense and meaning of the policy. If she had fairly commenced her voyage, on her departure from *St. Anne's*, and the going to *Bluefields* is to be taken as the usage of the voyage, I should think the underwriters would be liable. So, if she had broken ground for the voyage, and had gone but a league, and been blown back again. But if she had found no convoy at *Bluefields*, she could not have staid there to wait for convoy: that would have vacated the policy. So, if her going to *Bluefields* is to be considered only as a continuation of her stay at *Jamaica*, the policy is at an end. She certainly was ready at *St. Anne's* to depart for the voyage: and she went to *Bluefields*, not to take in part of her cargo, (for then it would clearly not have been a commencement of the voyage) but from a most just motive. Whether that was or was not a commencement of the voyage, is clearly a matter of fact; and in this case a very material one; therefore ought to be very fully considered."

Mr. Justice *Willes*.—"This is clearly a matter of fact: I think if the ship upon her arrival at *Bluefields* had found no convoy, she could not have staid there; but must have sailed immediately: or if she had met with convoy, and had staid an unreasonable time for other ships, the insurers would not have been liable."

After these opinions, which evidently lean in support of the verdict, had been delivered, the court took further time to deliberate; and then their unanimous opinion was pronounced by

Lord *Mansfield*.—"We are all satisfied that the truth of the case is, that the voyage from *Jamaica* to *England* began from *St. Anne's*. That when the ship sailed from *St. Anne's*, she had no view or object whatsoever, but to make the best of her way to *England*. That the value of this question, admitted on both sides, shews, that every other ship under the same circumstances looked upon the touching at *Bluefields*, where the convoy then lay ready, to be the safest

safest course of navigation from *Jamaica* to *England*; and that it would have been unwise and imprudent for any ship not to have touched there. The great distinction is this: that she sailed from *St. Anne's* for *England by way of Bluefields*; and that it was not a voyage from *St. Anne's* to *Bluefields* with any object or view distinct from the voyage to *England*. If she had gone first to *Bluefields* for any purpose independent of her voyage to *England*, to have taken in water, or letters, or to have waited in hopes of convoy coming there, none being ready, that would have given it the condition of one voyage from *St. Anne's* to *Bluefields*; and another from *Bluefields* to *England*. But here, under all the circumstances, we think she had no other object than to come directly to *England* by the safest course." Therefore the rule for a new trial was made absolute.

A few years afterwards a similar decision was made; and the only difference between the cases was this, that in the case now to be mentioned, it was a condition inserted in one of her clearances, that she should pass *by the place* (at which she was detained by the governor beyond the day named in the warranty) to take the orders of government. But this was not thought sufficient to induce the court to depart from the decision in *Bond* and *Nutt*; especially as in this case, the place where the ship was detained was in the direct course of the voyage.

It was an action on a policy of insurance on the *French* ship *L'aimable Gertrude*, "at and from *Guadaloupe* to *Havre*, "*warranted to sail on or before the 31st of December*." It was tried before Lord *Mansfield*, when a verdict was found for the plaintiff. A motion having been made for a new trial, the case, from his Lordship's report, appeared to be as follows: *The ship took in her complete lading and provisions for France, and all her clearances and papers*, at a port, called *Pointe a Pitre*, in the island of *Guadaloupe*, and *sailed from thence on the 24th of October*, for *Basseterre*, where there is no port, but only an open road. The town of *Bassaterre* is the residence of the *French* governor. The ship arrived there at night, when the captain went on shore, and next day waited on the governor, who would not permit him to de- Thellusson v. Fergusson. Doug. 346.

part,

CHAP. XVIII. part, and to prevent it, took his ſhip's papers from him. At this place he was detained with his ſhip till the 10th of *January*, when he ſet ſail with a convoy, which had arrived ſome little time before, and being ſeparated after ſome days from the convoy, the ſhip was taken by an *Engliſh* veſſel. The captain, who was the only witneſs produced at the trial, ſwore, that notice had been given on the part of the governor, ſome days before he failed, to him and the other captains of ſhips at *Pointe a Pitre*, who were preparing to ſail for *Europe*, that a convoy was expected to be at *Baſſaterre* from *Martinico*, on the 25th of *October*; and that, in conſequence of this intimation, he had worked night and day to get ready, and had paid extraordinary gratifications to obtain the ſhip's papers and clearances as ſoon as poſſible; that the deſire of being in time for the convoy, was the only reaſon for this haſte; and that, although he was not able to ſail till the 24th, he was ſtill in hopes of being in time for the convoy, as he thought it might very probably have been detained at *Martinico* ſome days beyond its time. The laſt ſhip papers which he received at *Pointe a Pitre*, was *Le Role d'equipage*, or the muſter roll. This paper, which was much relied upon by the counſel for the defendant, was dated the 24th of *October*, and was in the following words: "Vu par nous, "chargé du detail des claſſes au department de La Grande "terre *Guadaloupe*, l'equipage denommé au role des autres "parts au nombre de vingt perſonnes, le capitaine compris. "Permis au Sieur *Jean Jacques Lethuillier* commandant le "navire *L'aimable Gertrude* du *Havre*, de s'en ſervir pour "faire ſon retour, au dit lieu, *paſſant a la Baſſaterre pour y* "*prendre les ordres du gouvernement* en obſervant les ordon- "nances et reglemens de la marine." Under this there was written, on the ſame paper, an account, dated the 30th of *October*, of ſome changes in the number of the crew, and under that, the following entry: "Vu par nous, ecrivain "de la marine chargé du detail des claſſes, les vingt cinq "perſonnes exiſtantes au preſent rôle, le capitaine compris. "Il eſt permis au Sieur *Lethuillier* commandant le navire "*L'amiable Gertrude*, du *Havre*, de faire ſon retour au dit "lieu en ſe conformant aux ordonnances et reglemens "royaux de la marine. A *Baſſeterre Guadaloupe*, le 2 *Janvier*, "1779." On another paper, called Le Congé, dated the 16th of *October*, which was read on the part of the plaintiff,

tiff, there was written, at the bottom, as follows: "Vu de "relache a la *Baſſeterre Guadaloupe*, pour y attendre un con- "voi pour *France*. Ce 28 *Octobre*, 1778, *Monentheil*." The captain ſwore that he underſtood the only reaſons for the condition in the muſter-roll, that he ſhould go to *Baſſe-terre*, were, the convoy was to be at that place, and that he might take ſuch diſpatches as were ready for *Europe*. He had not objected to it, becauſe in the regular courſe of his voyage to *France* from *Pointe a Pitre*, he muſt have gone that way, cloſe under the guns of *Baſſeterre*, in order to avoid *Montſerrat*, there being no other road, except they were to keep quite to the leeward, which is not the cuſtom. If he had arrived there in the day-time, he would not have caſt anchor, but would have ſent his boat for the diſpatches; but having arrived at night, his ſhip had been detained, contrary to his intention and expectation. The defendant's counſel to invalidate the captain's teſtimony, beſides the muſter-roll, and the entry under it, as above ſtated, read the proteſt made by the captain on his arrival at *Dover*; and alſo his depoſi-tion in anſwer to the 29th interrogatory in the proceedings in the Admiralty on the condemnation of the ſhip. The words of the proteſt, on which they relied, were as follows: "Whereupon he (the captain) waited on the proper officer "at *Pointe a Pitre* for his muſter-roll, and was by him in- "formed, it could not be granted, but on condition that he "ſhould firſt ſail to *Baſſeterre*, and *there wait* the directions "of the general of the iſland." And in a ſubſequent part, "Whereupon at his (the captain's) inſtance, the ſaid *John* "*Nicholas Lethuillier*, his father, came to *Baſſeterre*, and went "with Meſſrs. *Gobert* and *Boteul*, commiſſioners of commerce, "to the ſuperintendant, and alſo to the general of the iſland, "ſtating to them that the ſaid ſhip and cargo were inſured "upon condition that ſhe ſhould have departed from the iſland "of *Guadaloupe* before the 31ſt of *December*, the terms of which "inſurance they judged it eſſential to fulfil, notwithſtanding "which they were ſtill refuſed permiſſion to depart, and were "kept there until after the 31ſt of *December*." The depoſition relied on was as follows: "At the time the ſhip was firſt "purſued and taken, ſhe was ſteering her courſe towards "*Breſt*. Her courſe was not altered upon the appearance of

F F "the

CHAP. XVIII.

"the vessel, by which she was taken. Her course was at all "times, when the weather would permit, directed to *Brest*, "for which port she was directed to sail, although the destination was for *Havre de Grace*, by the ship's papers. She "was not, before nor at the time of the capture, *sailing beyond or wide of Havre de Grace*. She was then about eight "leagues west of *Ushant*, and her course was not altered to "any other port or place, but was obliged to be directed to "*Brest*, in consequence of the orders he had received, subsequent to the delivery of the ship's papers." In answer to the 27th interrogatory, his deposition was, "That all the "ship's papers found on board were true and fair, and none "of them false and colourable." At the trial, the captain swore, that he had received directions to keep in the course to *Brest* at *Basseterre* from his father, who had formerly commanded the ship; *but this was done as the safest way, in time of war, of getting to Havre, which still continued to be the place of the ship's destination.* Upon this evidence the defendant's counsel made two objections, as grounds for a new trial: 1st. That there had been no inception of the voyage on the 24th of *October*, nor till after the 31st of *December*: 2dly. That the ship never sailed on the voyage insured, *viz.* from *Guadaloupe* to *Havre*, but on a voyage from *Guadaloupe* to *Brest*. After both these points had been fully argued at the bar,

As to the 2d point vide ante, c. 17. p. 314.

Lord *Mansfield* said:—"In my apprehension, there is no contradiction between the parole evidence, and the protest and depositions. This captain had never heard of the case of *Bond* and *Nutt*. Under an insurance at such a place as *Guadaloupe* or *Jamaica*, the ship is protected in going from port to port in the island. But the question here is, whether the voyage was *bonâ fide* commenced; and stopt by accident. As to the condition about taking the orders of government, the ship could not sail from any part of the island without the governor's leave. But the captain when he left *Pointe a Pitre*, expected to meet convoy at *Basseterre*, and to proceed immediately without interruption. A convoy had been published, and he certainly would have gone to *Basseterre* at any rate, independent of the clause in the muster-roll. With regard to the second point, the voyage to *Brest* was, at most, but an intended deviation, not carried into effect."

Vide c. 17.

Mr.

Mr. Justice *Willes* and Mr. Justice *Ashhurst* concurred.

Mr. Justice *Buller*.—" The case in 1777 between the same parties is in point. There was no embargo there, nor in the present case, when the ship sailed. There must be a lawful *bonâ fide* sailing, which I think there was in this case. The ship was completely ready in all respects." The rule for a new trial was, therefore, discharged.

See Lord Mansfield's opinion in the cause of Bond v. Nutt, where he quotes the case alluded to.

Notwithstanding the uniformity of decision in all these cases, the judgment given in the last cause was not satisfactory to about twenty other underwriters upon the same policy, nineteen of whom obtained leave to consolidate their different causes, upon the usual terms, in order to bring the question once more into court. Accordingly, in the ensuing sittings, the cause was set down for trial.

See the Introduction for the History of the Consolidating Rule.

In this cause, the second point as to the deviation was abandoned; and on the first, the same evidence was given as upon the former occasion. The point was again fully argued for the defendant.

Thellusson v. Staples. Sittings at Guildhall. East. Vac. 1780.

Lord *Mansfield*.—" The single question on this policy is, whether the ship sailed on her voyage to *Havre* before the 31st of *December*. She certainly sailed from *Pointe a Pitre* completely loaded before that time. The doubt on the first question of this sort was this: the policy was " at and from " *Jamaica*;" now the word *at* certainly comprises the whole island, and, under that word, you may sail from one port to another every where along the coast of the island. The ship, therefore, in that sense, was still at *Jamaica*, after she had got to *Bluefields*. She did not leave *Bluefields* till after the day named in the warranty, and that place was quite out of the course of navigation from *St. Anne's* to *England*. I own, at the trial, I thought the voyage to *England* did not commence till the ship sailed from *Bluefields*, and, according to my opinion then, a verdict was found for the defendant. But there was a doubt. I therefore wished (as I always do in such cases) that the opinion of the court might be taken, in order to settle the point. The case, when it came on in court, was very ably argued; I was completely convinced, and the court were unanimously of opinion, that the voyage to *England* began when the ship sailed from *St.*

CHAP. XVIII.

Earle v. Harris, at Guildhall. Hil. Vac. 1780.

Anne's; and upon the fecond trial, the plaintiff had a verdict. *Earle* and *Harris* was ftill a ftronger cafe. *There* an embargo was actually publifhed before the fhip failed, and the Captain, immediately after croffing the bar, returned to make a proteft, and fent his fhip knowingly into the embargo: but he fwore that he expected the embargo was to be taken off, and that he fhould proceed immediately upon his voyage; and the jury believed him. In this cafe to go by fteps. There was public notification of a convoy to be at *Baffeterre* on the 25th of *October*. The captain thought that it might be ftopped a day or two at *Martinico*, and that he fhould get to *Baffeterre* in time. He worked night and day, paid double fees for his papers, and failed with full expectations of purfuing his voyage directly. He knew of no embargo, and *Baffeterre* was directly in his road. In that refpect, this cafe differs ftrongly from *Bond* v. *Nutt*. He was even in the regular voyage obliged to pafs under the cannon of *Baffeterre*. He had his mufter-roll, on condition of calling there; but he made no difficulty of taking it on that condition, becaufe he knew he muft pafs that way at all events. Did he not *bonâ fide* begin his voyage? He certainly had no idea, when he failed from *Pointe a Pitre*, of meeting with any ftop. So it was in the former cafe of *Thelluffon* v. *Ferguffon*. There was no idea of the embargo in that cafe, when the fhip failed. Here there is not the leaft fufpicion of fraud. This captain certainly did not know of the decifion in *Bond* v. *Nutt*. He thought, when he was detained at *Baffeterre* beyond the 31ft of *December*, that the policy was forfeited, which is a ftrong circumftance in the plaintiff's favour, for it fhews that the failing was not colourable. This queftion has undergone the confideration of a fpecial jury and of the court. Underwriters have a right to litigate queftions, which feem to them to be in their favour. But, at laft, there fhould be an end of litigation. If you fhould be of the fame opinion with the former jury and the court, you will find for the plaintiff:" which they did accordingly. The caufe of the twentieth underwriter, on the fame policy, who refufed to confolidate, ftood next in the paper for trial; but upon the above verdict being given, his counfel confented that a verdict fhould alfo be entered againft him.

The Grenada Cafe. Vide fupra.

From

From this long train of uniform and consistent determinations, it should seem that the question, what shall or shall not be a departure within the meaning of the warranty is now completely settled. In insurances *at and from London*, warranted to depart on or before a particular day, it has long been a question, what shall be a departure from the port of London; or rather what is the port of London: and it is singular, that this point has never yet been judicially determined. On the one hand it is said, that the moment a ship is cleared out at the custom-house and has all her cargo on board, if she quit her moorings in the river on or before the day warranted, that the warranty is complied with. On the other side it is contended, and with great appearance of reason, that a ship is not ready for sea, till she has got her custom-house cocket on board, which is the final clearance, and which she cannot have till she arrive at Gravesend: that till this cocket is received, the ship dare not proceed to sea under a penalty, and till then is not entitled to the drawbacks, and that Gravesend is always considered as the limits of the port of London, and unless the ship sail from thence on or before the day limited, there is no inception of the voyage, and the policy is forfeited.

In a late case, the Royal Exchange Assurance Company resisted a demand made upon them, in order to try this great question: but as it appeared from the evidence of the log-book that the ship did not in truth break ground till after the day named in the warranty, the plaintiff was nonsuited; and the question remains undecided.

Rogers v. Royal Exchange Assur. Comp. Sittings in C. P. after Mich. 1787, before Lord Loughborough.

The second species of warranty, which most frequently occurs in insurances, is that of sailing under the protection of convoy; that is, certain ships of force, appointed by government, in time of war, to sail with merchantmen from their port of discharge to the place of their destination. When the nature of a convoy is considered, it is highly reasonable, that the policy should be forfeited, if the insured fail to comply with so material a condition; because the risk, which the underwriter takes upon himself, is very considerably increased, in time of war, by the want of convoy. Accordingly, by the laws of this, and of all other maritime powers, if the insured warrant that the vessel shall depart with convoy, and it do not; the policy is defeated, and the underwriter is not responsible. We have already seen, that every

Postlethw. Dict. tit. Convoy.

1 Emerigon, Traité des Assurances, p. 16[illegible]

CHAP. XVIII. every warranty muſt be ſtrictly and literally complied with; and that a liberal and ſubſtantial performance merely will not be ſufficient. Hence in a warranty to ſail with *convoy* it becomes material to conſider, what ſhall be deemed *a convoy* within ſuch a condition. Upon this point, it has been ſolemnly ſettled by the Court of King's Bench, Mr. Juſtice *Willes* excepted, who differed from the other learned judges upon that occaſion, that it is not every ſingle man of war, which chooſes to take a merchant ſhip under its protection, that will conſtitute ſuch a convoy as a warranty means; but it muſt be a naval force under the command of a perſon appointed by the government of the country to which they belong. The reaſon of ſuch a deciſion is wiſe; becauſe government muſt be ſuppoſed to be better informed of the deſigns and ſtrength of the enemy, and what degree of force will be ſufficient to repel their attempts. In the caſe, in which theſe points were ſettled, it alſo became a queſtion, how far ſailing orders from the commander in chief to the particular ſhip or ſhips, were requiſite to the conſtitution of a convoy. But it was not thought neceſſary to decide that point, although it ſeemed to be the opinion of the majority of the judges, that they were not abſolutely eſſential.

Hibbert v. Pigou, B. R. Eaſter, 23 Geo. III. 1783.

This caſe came before the court upon a rule to ſhew cauſe why the verdict, which the defendant had obtained, ſhould not be ſet aſide, and a new trial had. It was an action upon a policy of inſurance on the ſhip *Arundel*, captain *Mann*, at and from *Jamaica* to *London*, *warranted to depart with convoy*. The inſurance was at 18 guineas *per cent.* to return 3 *per cent.* if the ſhip failed on or before the firſt of *Auguſt*. The facts appearing on the report of Lord *Mansfield*, who tried the cauſe, are theſe: On the 25th of *July* the *Arundel* failed from *Morant* harbour to *Kingſton*, where ſhe met the *Glorieux* man of war, Captain *Cadogan*, who was likewiſe on his way to join Admiral *Graves* at *Bluefields*. Lord *Rodney* had appointed Admiral *Graves* to rendezvous at *Bluefields*, in order to take the fleet of merchant ſhips, which were to ſail from thence upon the firſt of *Auguſt*, under his command, and to convoy them to *Great Britain*. Captain *Mann*, upon their meeting in *Kingſton* harbour, aſked for ſailing orders from Captain *Cadogan*, who ſaid, he had none, not having himſelf at that time joined the Admiral: but he was ſure that Admiral *Graves* would not ſail from *Bluefields* till the *Glorieux* joined him.

him. However, if he ſhould have failed, he, Captain *Cadogan*, would give Captain *Mann* failing orders, and take every care of the *Arundel* in his power. They proceeded together, and arrived at *Bluefields* on the 28th of *July*; but they found that Admiral *Graves* had failed two days before. The *Glorieux* and *Arundel* then failed from *Bluefields*, the former firing guns, giving ſignals, and behaving in every reſpect *like a convoy*. Upon the 5th of *Auguſt* a ſignal was made, that the fleet was in fight; and on the 7th they joined the fleet off *Cape Anthonio*. The *Arundel* was afterwards loſt in *September*, in a dreadful ſtorm, which diſperſed the whole fleet, and in which a vaſt number of the ſhips periſhed. Upon this evidence, the jury were of opinion, under the direction of the Chief Juſtice, that the terms of the warranty had not been performed, and they therefore found a verdict for the underwriters, the defendants. After this queſtion had been fully argued at the bar, the three judges, Mr. Juſtice *Aſhhurſt* being, at that time, one of the Lords Commiſſioners of the Great Seal, delivered their opinions ſeverally.

Lord *Mansfield*.—"Though the underwriters and inſured are equally innocent; yet I cannot help ſaying, that now, as well as at the trial, my inclination led me to wiſh, that the plaintiffs were in the right. But the more it is argued, it is the leſs liable to diſpute. There are hypothetical contracts and conditional contracts. In the former, the contract depends upon an event taking place; there is no latitude; no equity; the only queſtion is, has that event happened. But conditional contracts admit of a more liberal conſtruction. Now the only queſtion upon this contract is, whether this ſhip has departed with convoy. A great deal muſt be referred to the uſage of merchants. The government appoints a convoy for the trade, and alſo names a place of rendezvous. Then comes the reference to the uſage of merchants; the voyage is begun at *Kingſton*; but the riſk only commences at *Bluefields*. Now though Lord *Rodney* deſires the captain of the *Glorieux* to take any ſhips he may pick up in his way, and convoy them to *Bluefields*; yet the warranty in the policy by the uſage, does not require convoy to *Bluefields*. The ſecond reference to the uſage of merchants is, what is eſteemed a convoy by merchants. *A convoy is a naval*

force,

CHAP. XVIII.

force, under the command of that perſon, whom government has appointed. They truſt to the knowledge of government, which muſt be ſuppoſed to be better acquainted with the plans and force of the enemy, and with the ſtrength neceſſary to repel their attempts. Now this is the general uſage, to which matters of this kind are referred. Then let us ſee what the caſe is here.—Lord *Rodney* appoints Admiral *Graves* to go with ten ſail of the line to *Bluefields*; and from thence to convoy the *Jamaica* trade to *Great Britain*. When they come to the place of rendezvous, they take ſailing orders from the Admiral, *which are eſſential to convoy*, as by them they know the ſignals, for what places they are to ſteer, in caſe of diſperſion by ſtorm, or any other juſt cauſe (*a*). Admiral *Graves*, on the 26th of *July*, for reaſons beſt known to himſelf, thinks he has got all the ſhips, for which he ought to ſtay, and proceeds on his voyage. He leaves no order for the *Glorieux* to follow him to *Cape Anthonio*; and though it is very true, that it is in the power of the Commander in Chief to change the place of rendezvous, yet in this caſe it is not true, as was ſuppoſed in argument that *Cape Anthonio* was appointed. At the time of ſailing from *Bluefields*, the *Glorieux* was no part of the convoy; for ſhe did not come there till two days after the fleet was gone. Upon theſe facts it did appear to me, and to the jury at the trial, that the warranty was not complied with: I continue of the ſame opinion now; and that this rule ſhould be diſcharged."

Mr. Juſtice *Willes*.—"I cannot perfectly coincide with every thing which Lord *Mansfield* has laid down. The form of the contract is in general words, "*to depart with convoy*," without mentioning any particular day, or pointing out any ſpecific convoy. The terms of the policy ſeem to me to have been literally and ſubſtantially complied with; for there was no

(*a*) Since the former editions of this work, I have met with a caſe of *Veedon* v. *Wilmot*, at *Guildhall*, *July* 1744, in the time of Lord Chief Juſtice *Lee*, where the ſhip inſured had departed from *London*, and arrived at the *Downs* 22d *Auguſt*, where the *Grafton* and *Lenox* (the convoy) were under ſail, and the captain ſent one of his men on board for ſailing orders, which were refuſed; but the Commodore ſaid, "*keep on, and I will take care of you*;" and the ſhip being loſt that night by ſtriking on the ſhore, the queſtion was, if the ſhip was put under convoy, *having no ſailing orders*. And it was held ſhe was, and the plaintiff had a verdict.

no *laches* on the part of the *Arundel*; she came with all possible expedition, and was at *Bluefields* two days before the time appointed for sailing. When captain *Mann* found that the fleet was gone, he did every thing in his power for the security of the ship; for he put himself under the protection of the *Glorieux*, which was appointed by Lord *Rodney* to make a part of the convoy: and it appears in evidence, that in every respect Captain *Cadogan* behaved as a convoy. I have searched a good deal for cases; and I can only find one in *Strange* 1250, upon the subject of sailing orders; and I [342] do not think that case goes so far as to say, that sailing orders are essential to a convoy. The loss of the *Arundel* happened long subsequent to her joining the fleet; and I am therefore of opinion, that the warranty in this policy has been substantially performed."

Vide post, p. 348.

Mr. Justice *Buller*.—"In deciding this case, it is not necessary to say, whether sailing orders are essential or not: as at present advised, I do not say that they are absolutely necessary. The present question is simply this: did the *Arundel* sail with convoy. This is a condition which must be literally complied with, as all the cases agree. As to the question itself, it is undoubtedly a question of fact: and the facts of the case seem to me to prove, that the *Glorieux* was no part of the convoy. Admiral *Graves* had sailed before they arrived; and that circumstance, which my Lord stated, seems very material, that no orders were left behind for the *Glorieux*. I say that, on this evidence, she was not a part of the convoy: for in order to make her so, it must appear that she was under the orders of *Graves*. Did he leave her behind to take care of the ships that remained? If so, it would alter the case very materially. But there was no such idea; for if there had, the *Glorieux* would have remained at *Bluefields* for the rest of the ships, until the 1st of *August*: on the contrary, Captain *Cadogan*, finding that Admiral *Graves* was gone, immediately followed; for his sole object was to join Admiral *Graves*. *Ships must sail under the convoy appointed by the government of the country*, who proportion the strength of it to the necessity of the times. To what end would this care be taken, if merchantmen were to sail under the protection of single ships, with which they may happen to meet? I am therefore of opinion, that if a ship do not sail with the

CHAP. XVIII. convoy appointed by government, it is not a failing with convoy, within the terms of the policy." The rule for a new trial was therefore difcharged (*a*).

[343] Although the decifions of the Court of King's Bench require no additional authority to fupport them; yet it will be proper, merely by way of illuftration, to point out to the reader, in what cafes the opinions of foreign writers agree with the determinations of the *Englifh* courts of juftice. Monfieur *D'Emerigon*, a very diftinguifhed *French* writer upon this branch of jurifprudence, puts this cafe: "On avoit fait "des affurances fur un navire, de fortie de *Marfeille* jufq' "aux Detroits de *Gibraltar*, et dans la police il étoit dit que "le navire partiroit de *Marfeille fous l'efcorte d'un batiment de* "*roi*; *autrement, affurance nulle.* Une fregate, chargée de "munitions de guerre pour *Algefiras*, fe trouvoit à *l'Eftaque*. "Le navire affurè mit à la voile fous les aufpices de cette "fregate qui lui accorda protection, et qui partit en meme "temps. Confulté fur ce cas, je fus d'avis que fi le navire "ètoit pris par les ennemis, les affureurs feroient fondés a "refufer le payment de la perte: *car autre chofe eft d'etre fous* "*l'efcorte du'n batiment de roi, et autre chofe eft de naviguer fimplement fous fes aufpices.*"

1 Emerigon, p. 171.

See the Cafe.

From the cafe of *Hibbert* and *Pigou* we collect this; that a convoy appointed by the Admiral commanding in chief upon a ftation abroad, is a convoy appointed by government. And befides the inftruction it affords, applicable to the particular fubject, for which it was here inferted, it ferves to eftablifh fome principles laid down at the beginning of this chapter; that whether the lofs do or do not happen, on account of the breach of the warranty, ftill the policy is forfeited: for in this cafe, the fhip infured perifhed in a ftorm, long after fhe had joined the regular convoy; and confequently the lofs did not happen, on account of the breach of the condition.

Having

Sittings at Guildhall before Mr. Juftice Buller after Eafter Term 1784.

(*a*) Another action was brought upon the fame policy againft another of the underwriters; and altho' a verdict in that cafe was found for the plaintiffs; yet it feems to me to leave the doctrines above advanced unfhaken: for upon the fecond trial it was proved, beyond all doubt, that the Glorieux was in truth a part of the convoy, a fact, which was left doubtful on the firft; and it was upon that fact that Lord Mansfield and Mr. Juftice Buller chiefly relied.

Having seen what shall be deemed a convoy, let us proceed to consider what shall be a *departure* with convoy, within the meaning of a warranty *to depart with convoy*. The rule on this point is short and clear, that such a warranty implies, that the ship shall go with convoy from the usual place of rendezvous, at which the ships have been accustomed to assemble; as *Spithead*, or the *Downs*, for the port of *London*; and *Bluefields* for all the ports in *Jamaica*. And from the particular port to such usual place of convoy, the ship is protected by the policy.

[344]

Thus in an action on a policy of insurance by the defendant at *London*, insuring a ship from thence to the *East Indies*, *warranted to depart with convoy*; the declaration states, that the ship went from *London* to the *Downs*, *and from thence with convoy*, and was lost. After a frivolous plea and demurrer, the case stood upon the declaration, to which it was objected, That here was a departure without convoy. Lethulier's Case. 2 Salk. 443.

The clause, warranted to depart with convoy, must be construed according to the usage among merchants, that is, from such place, where convoys are to be had, as the *Downs*, &c. Per Curiam.

It is true, Lord Chief Justice *Holt*, upon that occasion, was of a different opinion; but the judgment of the other judges was relied upon, and confirmed in the following case by Lord Chief Justice *Lee*, and has also been recognized in several other cases, in which the question has come collaterally before the court. Indeed of late years, it has been tacitly acquiesced in; for there never is a convoy from the port of *London*.

On an insurance from *London* to *Gibraltar*, *warranted to depart with convoy*, it appeared that there was a convoy appointed for that trade at *Spithead*, and the ship *Ranger* having tried for convoy in the *Downs*, proceeded for *Spithead*, and was taken in her way thither. The insurers insisted, that this being the time of a *French* war, the ship should not have ventured through the *Channel*, but have waited in the *Downs* for an occasional convoy. And many merchants and office-keepers were examined to that purpose. But Lord Chief Justice *Lee* held, that the ship was to be considered as under Gordon v. Morley, 2 Stra. 1265.

CHAP. XVIII. under the defendant's insurance *to a place of general rendezvous*, according to the interpretation of the words, "warranted to "depart with convoy." *Salk.* 443. And if the parties meant to vary the insurance from what is commonly understood, they should have particularized her departure with convoy from the *Downs*. The jury was composed of merchants, who found for the plaintiff, upon the strength of this direction.

[345] Tom. 1. p. 166. A similar decision was made in the year 1781, by the Admiralty of *France*, which is reported in the work of *Emerigon*.

2 Salk. 443. Upon this kind of warranty, it is to be observed, that although the words commonly used are, "to *depart* with con-"voy," or, "to sail with convoy;" yet they extend to sailing with convoy throughout the whole of the voyage, as much as if those words were inserted. Indeed to suppose the contrary would introduce an infinite variety of frauds; as a ship would sail out of harbour with the convoy, continue with it for an hour or two, then leave it, and run every peril, at the risk of the underwriter. If, therefore, the convoy is only to go part of the way, that is not a compliance with the warranty; and the insurer is discharged from his engagements.

3 Levinz. 320. This was one of the points ruled in *Jeffreys* v. *Legendra*, that will be quoted at length presently, in which Lord Chief Justice *Holt* and the rest of the court held, that although the words of the policy only were "to depart with convoy," yet they extend to sail with convoy throughout the whole voyage.

In a more modern case, however, this doctrine came again in question; and after very full consideration, the opinion of Lord *Holt* was unanimously confirmed by the whole Court of King's Bench.

Lilly v. Ewer, Doug. 72. It was an action for money had and received, brought against an underwriter for a return of premium. The policy was on the ship the *Parker Galley*, "at and from *Venice* to the *Currant Islands*, and at and from thence to *London*," at a premium of five guineas *per cent.* "to return 2 *per cent.* "*if the ship sailed with convoy from* *Gibraltar*, and arrived."

The

The ſhip touched at *Gibraltar* on her way home, and failed from thence under convoy of the *Zephyr* ſloop of war, *but the convoy was deſtined only to go to a certain latitude, about as far as Cape Finiſterre,* being ordered on the *Liſbon* ſtation; and accordingly the ſhip and convoy ſeparated, and the ſhip arrived ſafe at *London*. The only queſtion in the cauſe was, whether, by the terms of the policy, the condition for the return of the premium was a *departure from Gibraltar with ſuch convoy as could be met with, for whatever part of the voyage that might happen to be, or a departure with convoy for the voyage.* [346] The trial came on before Lord *Mansfield* and a common jury, when a verdict was found for the plaintiffs.

A rule having been obtained to ſhew cauſe why there ſhould not be a new trial; the evidence from his Lordſhip's report appears to be thus: That the plaintiffs had called witneſſes (one of whom was Mr. *Gorman*, an eminent merchant) to prove that for ſome years paſt, when convoy *for the voyage*, or *the whole voyage* was intended, thoſe explanatory words had been added, and that, by this uſage, the expreſſions of "*ſailing with convoy,*" and "ſailing with convoy for the voyage," had received diſtinct technical meanings: "with convoy," ſignifying whatever convoy the ſhip ſhould depart with, whether for a greater or leſs part of the voyage. Several policies were alſo produced, which had been filled up at the office of the ſame broker, who had prepared that which had given occaſion to this cauſe, in which the words, "for "the voyage," or "for *England*," were added. The captain proved, that at the time when he left *Gibraltar*, no other convoy was to be had. The witneſſes for the defendant ſwore, that they underſtood the words "with convoy," to mean, *convoy for the voyage;* and the broker ſaid, that, at the time this policy was ſigned, he underſtood and apprehended it was ſo underſtood by all the parties, that the convoy was to be for the voyage, and that the return was ſuch as was uſual, when convoy for the voyage was meant. His Lordſhip, after ſtating the evidence, ſaid, that when the caſe was opened, he thought, on the face of the policy, that the words muſt mean for the voyage. He had not admitted the counſel to aſk the opinion of the witneſſes on the conſtruction; but to learn

CHAP. XVIII. learn whether there was any ufage in this cafe, which would give a fixed technical fenfe to the words. This was a queftion of fact to be afcertained by evidence, and proper for the confideration of a jury.

The cafe was fully argued at the bar.

Lord *Mansfield.*—"On the words I was ftrongly of opinion, that the policy meant a departure with convoy intended for the voyage. The parties could not mean a departure [347] with convoy, which might be defigned to feparate from the fhip in a minute or two; though when convoy for the whole of a voyage is clearly intended, an unforefeen feparation is an accident, to which the underwriter is liable; for the meaning of fuch a warranty is not that the fhip and convoy fhould continue and arrive together. But I ftill think that the evidence was properly admitted at the trial of this caufe; becaufe the fenfe contended for by the plaintiffs, was not inconfiftent with the words of the policy; and therefore it was material to fee what the ufage was. I laid great ftrefs on Mr. *Gorman*'s teftimony. I did not confider him as a common witnefs. However, it feems, from what I have heard fince, that people in the city are diffatisfied with the verdict, and think the evidence of the plaintiff's witneffes was founded on a miftake. Certainly critical niceties ought not to be encouraged in commercial concerns; and wherever you render additional words neceffary, and multiply them, you alfo multiply doubts and criticifms. It may be hard, becaufe words have been added in fome inftances, to force a conftruction in this cafe, from the omiffion of them. The queftion is of great importance." The rule was therefore made abfolute.

Doug. p. 74. note (7). The new trial came on before Lord *Mansfield* at the fittings after *Trinity* term, 19 *Geo.* III. when a verdict was found for the defendant, the infurer.

Doug. 73. But although it has been thus fettled, that a fhip muft depart with convoy for the whole of the voyage; yet in the laft cafe, it was truly faid by Lord *Mansfield*, that an un- 1 Emerigon, 166. forefeen feparation is an accident, to which the underwriter is liable. It is the law of reafon and common fenfe; for it would be the height of injuftice and cruelty to heap misfor-

tune

tune upon misfortune, and to say, that because a ship has been separated from her convoy by stress of weather, or the fury of the elements, that the insured shall suffer still greater misery, by being deprived of that indemnity which he had secured to himself by paying a sufficient and adequate premium. The law of *England* does not tolerate such principles; and the first decision upon the subject was such, that it never has been departed from in any instance.

[348]

Assumpsit on a policy of insurance made in the usual form, "from *London* to *Cadiz*, warranted to depart with convoy." Upon the general issue pleaded, the jury found a special verdict, stating, that the ship did depart from the port of *London*, in company of the convoy intended, and sailed together as far as the *Isle of Wight*, in pursuance of the voyage towards *Cadiz*; and there they were separated by stress of weather; that the convoy put into *Torbay*, and the insured ship into the port of *Fowey* in *Cornwall*. That three days afterwards, the wind setting right to bring the convoy down the channel, the master of the insured ship sailed out of *Fowey* on purpose to meet the convoy; but it did not come: and then the insured ship was seized with another storm, so that she could not return from whence she came, but was driven upon the *French* coast, and there taken by the enemy.

Jeffery v. Legendra, 3 Lev. 320. 2 Salk. 443. Carth. 216. 1 Shower, 320. 4 Mod. 58. S.C.

After several arguments of this special verdict, the plaintiff had judgment *per totam curiam*; and their principal reason was, because there was no manner of neglect, or other default found in the master of the ship; but it appeared he had done all in his power to keep in company of the convoy. It is found expressly, that he departed with convoy from his first port, which answers the words of the policy: but it would have been otherwise, if any fraud or neglect had been found in the master of the insured ship after his departure, notwithstanding he departed out of the first port with convoy; for the meaning of the words "*warranted to depart with convoy*" is, that the insured ship should keep company with the convoy, during the whole voyage, if possible.

Carthew, 216.

Even where the ship has by tempestuous weather been prevented from joining the convoy at all, at least, of receiving the

CHAP. XVIII. the orders of the commander of the ſhips of war, if ſhe do every thing in her power to effect it, it ſhall be deemed a ſailing with convoy, within the terms of the warranty.

Victoria v. Cleeve, 2 Stra. 1250.

The plaintiff had inſured on goods in the *John* and *Jane*, from *Gottenburgh* to *London*, with a warranty *to depart with convoy* from *Fleckery*. In *July* 1744, the ſhip ſailed from *Gottenburgh* to *Fleckery*, and there ſhe waited for convoy two [349] months. On the 21ſt of *September*, at nine in the morning, three men of war, who had one hundred merchant ſhips in convoy, ſtood off *Fleckery*, and made a ſignal for the ſhips there to come out, and likewiſe ſent in a yaul to order them out. There were fourteen ſhips waiting, and the *John* and *Jane* got out by twelve o'clock, and one of the firſt; the convoy having ſailed gently on, and being two leagues a-head. It was a hard gale, and by ſix in the afternoon, the ſhip came up with the fleet; but could not get to either of the men of war for ſailing orders, on account of the gale of wind. It was ſtormy all night, and at day-break the ſhip in queſtion was in the midſt of the fleet; but the weather was ſo bad, that no boat could be ſent for ſailing orders. A *French* privateer had ſailed among them all night; and it being foggy on the 22d, attacked the *John* and *Jane* about two, who kept a running fight till dark, which was renewed the next morning, when ſhe was taken. For the defendant it was inſiſted, that this ſhip was never under convoy, nor is ever conſidered ſo, till they have received ſailing orders; and if the weather would not permit the captain to get them, he ſhould have gone back.

Sir William Lee.

But the Chief Juſtice and the jury were both of opinion, that as the captain had done every thing in his power, it was a departing with convoy: and thoſe agreements are never confined to preciſe words; as in the caſe of departing with convoy from *London*, when the place of rendezvous is *Spithead*, a loſs in going thither is within the policy. So the plaintiff recovered.

But it is evident from all that has been ſaid, that if there be an opportunity of convoy; if the convoy throw out repeated ſignals to join; and by the negligence and delay of the captain of the inſured ſhip, the opportunity be loſt, the warranty to depart with convoy is not complied with, and the underwriter is diſcharged.

Thus

CHAP. XVIII.

Thus in an action on a policy of insurance tried before Lord *Mansfield*, the plaintiff was nonsuited, there being a warranty to depart with convoy; and it appearing from the evidence, that the commodore of the convoy had made signals for sailing from *Spithead* to *St. Helens* the night before, and had made repeated signals the next morning from seven o'clock till twelve, notwithstanding which, the ship insured had neglected to sail with him, and did not sail till two hours after, in consequence of which he was taken by a privateer. (*a*)

Taylor v. Woodness, Sittings at Guildhall, Hil. Vac. 4 Geo. 3.

Although we have thus seen, that a ship must not voluntarily depart from convoy during the voyage, yet this species of warranty must always be construed with reference to the usage of trade, and to the orders of government. For if the course upon a particular voyage has been to have a relay of convoy, protecting the trade from one port to another; or if government appoint a convoy to escort the trade of a place to a given latitude and no farther; and there be no other convoy on that station, a vessel, taking the advantage of such a convoy, has complied with the warranty to sail with convoy for the voyage.

Thus in an insurance on the ship William, "*at and from London to Jamaica*," *warranted to depart with convoy for the voyage*, Lord *Mansfield*, in the course of his summing up to the jury, said, "A warranty to sail with convoy means with "such a convoy as government pleases to appoint; and "whether it consists of separate ships at different stations or "not, it is a convoy for the voyage; therefore on that "point there is no doubt."

Smith v. Readshaw, London. Sittings after East. 1781.

The same doctrine was held by Lord *Kenyon*, in an action on a policy of insurance *at and from Cadiz to Amsterdam, warranted to sail with convoy for the voyage*. The ships insured had sailed from *Cadiz* under a *British* convoy; and were lost before they reached the *Downs*, where it was alleged they were to have taken a fresh convoy for *Amsterdam*. The underwriters insisted that the convoy should have been direct to *Amsterdam*. The assured, on the other hand,

De Garay v. Claggett. London, Sittings after Mich. 1795.

(*a*) As to the duty of the officers appointed for convoy to merchant ships, see it prescribed in the stat. of the 13 Cha. 2. stat. 1. c. 9. art. 17. which regulations were confirmed by the 22d of Geo. 2. c. 33. s. 2. art. 17.

hand, contended, that all convoy muſt be according to uſage, and that in many voyages there is no ſuch thing as a direct convoy, but that the veſſels proceed by relays of convoy from ſtage to ſtage. The ſpecial jury, with Lord *Kenyon*'s approbation, gave a verdict for the plaintiffs. And, although in that caſe, it is true, the underwriter had adjuſted the policy *with full knowledge* of all the circumſtances, which his lordſhip ſeemed to think concluſive, yet there were other cauſes on the ſame policy, where there was no adjuſtment; and upon Lord *Kenyon* and the jury declaring, that, without conſidering the adjuſtment, they thought the warranty had been complied with, the plaintiff had a verdict, and no motion was ever made for a new trial in any of theſe cauſes.

D'Eguino v. Bewicke. In C. B. Mich. 36 Geo. 3.

So alſo the Court of Common Pleas decided in an action on a policy on the ſhip *Little Betſey*, at and from *London* to *St. Sebaſtian*, *warranted to ſail with convoy*. The ſhip ſailed with other veſſels under convoy of ſeveral ſhips of war: and after a certain latitude, the *Weazel*, one of the men of war, was detached to convoy the *Spaniſh* ſhips; but the captain of that ſhip had orders to go with the *St. Sebaſtian* ſhips no further than *Bilboa*, and in fact he went no farther. A verdict paſſed for the plaintiff. When the caſe came on before the court on a motion for a new trial, it was argued for the underwriters, that warranties are to be ſtrictly complied with; and that however near the port of *St. Sebaſtian* might be to *Bilboa*, yet the principle was the ſame; and that a convoy to the latter place could no more be conſtrued to be a convoy to the former, than a convoy to the *Cape of Good Hope* could be a convoy to the *Eaſt Indies*, and for this was cited *Hibbert* v. *Pigou* (ſupra 339.)

Mr. Juſtice *Buller*.—" The caſe of *Hibbert* and *Pigou* is not applicable to this, for there a convoy was appointed and actually ſailed from *Jamaica* to *England*; as to the inſtance put at the bar of a convoy to the *Cape of Good Hope*, I entirely differ from the counſel on that point; for if government thought a convoy to the *Cape* was a ſufficient protection to the *Eaſt India* trade, and the uſage were for the *Eaſt India* ſhips to ſail with a convoy only to the Cape, and to conſider that as the *Eaſt India* convoy, and no other convoy was appointed to the *Eaſt Indies*, I ſhould hold that the warranty was complied with; though I agree if there was another

convoy

CHAP. XVIII.

convoy to the *East Indies*, it would be otherwise. The captain of a merchant ship has nothing to do with, nor can he know the instructions from the Admiralty to the king's officers, but must take such convoy as he finds. I am therefore of opinion that there is no ground at all for this motion."

Mr. Justice *Heath*.—"I am of the same opinion. The owner of a ship, when he makes an insurance, cannot know the orders of the Admiralty respecting convoys."

Mr. Justice *Rooke*.—"The ground stated at the bar seems to me to be more fit for the jury than the court, and the jury have found that the convoy was sufficient."

Lord Chief Justice *Eyre*.—"I am satisfied with the finding of the jury."

The rule for a new trial was therefore refused.

The third and last species of warranty, which falls under our consideration, is that of neutrality; or that the ship or goods insured are neutral property. This condition is very different from either of the two former; for if this warranty be not complied with, the contract is not merely avoided for a breach of the warranty, but it is absolutely void *ab initio*, on account of fraud. This ground was entered upon in the chapter of fraud; and the principle, on which the difference turns, is this. A man may warrant that his ship shall sail with convoy; and if that condition be not complied with, it is not his fault, because it depends upon the acts of other men: but still he is the sufferer, for he loses the benefit of his contract. So also if he warrant to sail on a particular day, and do not, he is guilty of no crime; for that was a circumstance, the performance of which depended on a thousand accidents, such as wind, weather, repair, &c. but as he had expressly undertaken, he loses the effect of his policy by non-compliance. But in neither of these cases, as I have said, is the insured, making such a warranty, guilty of any offence. Not so with him, who warrants property to be neutral. That is a fact, which at the time of insuring, must be within his own knowledge; and if he assert it to be neutral, knowing it to be otherwise, he is guilty of a wilful and deliberate falsehood, and incurs moral turpitude. In such a

[350]

Vide c. 10.

case,

CHAP. XVIII. case, therefore, the contract betwen the parties is absolutely null and void to all intents and purposes.

Woolmer v. Muilman. 4 Burr. 1419. 1 Blackst. Rep. 427. Vide ante p. 176.

Thus on a special case reserved for the opinion of the court, it appeared that an action was brought for the recovery of a total loss, on a policy of insurance made on goods, on board the ship *Bona Fortuna*, at and from *North Bergen* to any ports or places whatsoever, until her safe arrival in *London*, "*warranted neutral ship and property.*" The ship with the goods so being on board her, after her departure from [351] *North Bergen*, and before her arrival at *London*, proceeding on her voyage, was by force of the winds, and stormy weather, wrecked, cast away, and sunk in the seas; and the said goods were thereby wholly lost. The ship called *La Bona Fortuna*, at and before the time she was lost, *was not neutral property*, as warranted by the said policy. The question was, whether, under such circumstances, the plaintiff could recover. Lord *Mansfield*, after hearing counsel for the plaintiff, stopped those for the defendant, saying the point was too clear to be argued. There was a falsehood, with respect to the thing insured; for he insured neutral property, when it was not so: therefore there *is no contract*. We must give judgment for the defendant.

If, however, the ship and property are neutral at the time when the risk commences, this is a sufficient compliance with a warranty of neutral property: because it is impossible for the insured to be answerable for the consequences of a war breaking out during the voyage. The insurer takes upon himself the risk of peace or war; they are public events, equally known to both parties.

Eden and another v. Parkinson, Dougl. 705.

The plaintiffs insured the ship the *Yonge Herman Hiddinga*, and her cargo, "at and from *L'Orient* to *Rotterdam*, *warranted "a neutral ship and neutral property*." The ship being captured in the course of her voyage by some *English* men of war, the plaintiffs brought this action against the defendant, one of the underwriters on the policy, stating in their declaration, that the defendant subscribed the policy on the 28th of *November* 1780, and averring that the ship and cargo were, *at that time*, neutral property. The trial came on before Lord *Mansfield* at *Guildhall*, when a verdict was found for the plaintiffs, subject

subject to the opinion of the court upon a case stating, that the ship in question sailed from *L'Orient*, on the voyage insured, on the 11th of *December* 1780, having the insured cargo on board, *and both the ship and cargo were neutral property at the time of the ship's departure from L'Orient*, and so continued until the 20th of *December* 1780, on which day hostilities having commenced between the *English*, and the *Dutch*, the *Dutch* ceased to be a neutral power, and the ship and cargo ceased to be neutral property. They were taken on the 25th of *December* 1780, and condemned as lawful prize, in the Admiralty Court, on the 19th of *February* 1781.

[352]

Lord *Mansfield*.—" Many points have been gone into in the argument on both sides at the bar, which are not necessary for the decision of this case. For instance, there is no doubt but you may warrant a future event. But the single question here is, what is the meaning of this policy. I had not a particle of doubt at the trial, and I know the jury had none; but Mr. *Lee* pressed for a case, and I granted one out of respect to him. What is the case? It is an insurance upon a ship and her cargo, at and from *L'Orient* to *Rotterdam*. The insured warrant them neutral, and the defendant would have the court to add, by construction, " and so shall continue during the whole voyage." The contract is not so. The insured tell the state of the ship and goods *then*, and the insurers take upon themselves all future events and risks, from men of war, enemies, detentions of princes, &c. The parties themselves could not have changed the nature of the property; but they did not mean to run the risk of the war. If it made a difference what country the property belonged to, the underwriters should have inquired. The risk of future war is taken by the underwriter of every policy. By an implied warranty every ship must be tight, staunch, and strong; but it is sufficient if she be so at the time of her sailing. She may cease to be so in twenty-four hours after her departure, and yet the underwriter will continue liable. The case of *Lilly* v. *Ewer* turns quite the other way. The decision there was, that the ship must sail with convoy, according to the usage of the trade: that is, convoy destined to go as far as usual in that voyage. The present is the clearest case that can be. The warranty is, that things stand so at the time; not that they shall continue."

Vide ante c. 11.

Vide supra.

Mr.

Mr. Juſtice *Willes* and Mr. Juſtice *Aſhburſt* concurred.

Mr. Juſtice *Buller*.—"The caſe of *Lilly* v. *Ewer* is much againſt the defendant, for it was not contended there that the ſhip muſt *continue* with the convoy during the whole voyage. The *poſtea* was delivered to the plaintiffs."

[353]

Vide infra.

And afterwards in a ſubſequent caſe of *Saloucci* v. *Johnſon*, in the courſe of the argument, Mr. Juſtice *Buller* ſaid; I do not agree with the counſel, who contend, that the property muſt continue neutral during the whole voyage: if it be neutral at the time of ſailing, and a war break out the next day, the underwriter is liable.

Tyſon and another v. Gurney. 3 Term R. 477.

And in a ſtill later caſe, which came on for trial before Lord *Kenyon* at *Guildhall*, this point was one amongſt others ſaved for the opinion of the Court of King's Bench. But when the caſe came on to be argued, the counſel for the defendant abandoned the objection upon the authority of *Eden* v. *Parkinſon*; and *Saloucci* v. *Johnſon*: ſo that this point may now be conſidered as for ever cloſed.

Having ſeen what ſhall be deemed a compliance with a warranty, aſſerting that the property inſured is neutral; and having alſo conſidered what effect the breach of ſuch a warranty has upon the contract of inſurance; it may be proper to obſerve, before this chapter is cloſed, how far our courts of law hold the ſentences of foreign courts to be concluſive evidence, that the property was not neutral; ſo as to diſcharge the underwriters.

In the firſt caſe upon this point it was held, that the ſentence of condemnation by a foreign Court of Admiralty is not concluſive evidence, that the ſhip was not neutral; unleſs it appear that the condemnation went upon that ground: conſequently the underwriter remains liable. A ſentence of a Court of Admiralty binds all the world, as to every thing contained within it; but where the cauſe of condemnation does not appear to be on the ſpecific ground material to the point in iſſue, evidence muſt be admitted in order to explain it.

CHAP. XVIII.

Bernardi v. Motteux. Doug. 554.

Insurance of freight and goods was made upon the ship the *Jane* (or *Joanna*) at and from *Venice* to *London*, "*warranted neutral ship and neutral property*." The cause was tried before Lord *Mansfield*, at *Guildhall*, when a verdict was found for the plaintiff, subject to the opinion of the court, upon a case which stated as follows: That the defendant underwrote the policy; that the ship was taken by a *French* frigate, called *La Magicienne*, as she was sailing from *Venice* on her voyage to *London*; that the plaintiff offered to give evidence on the trial, that the property of the ship and the property of the cargo were *neutral*; and that the papers belonging to the ship *fell overboard by accident*, after she was brought to by the *French* frigate: but the defendant objected to such evidence being received; and he produced as the ground of his objection, the sentence of the condemnation of the ship in the *French* Admiralty Court, which was read, and is as follows: [354]

"Almeria. "The Joanna."

"*Louis Jean Marie de Bourbon, Duke de Penthievre*, Admiral of *France*. Seen by us, the *procés verbal*, made on board the snow *Joanna*, taken by the king's frigate *La Magicienne*, commanded by M. *De Boades*, dated the 2d of *December* last. Signed *Saint Owey*, steward, *Bouret*, *Dominico Zané*. Seen by the captain commander. Signed *Boades*;—purporting that the said 2d of *December* last, at five o'clock in the evening, his said majesty's frigate, *La Magicienne*, commanded by the said captain *De Boades*, being ten leagues east of *Cape de Moulines*, having discovered a snow steering south-south-west, the wind south-west, and having come up with her, and stopt her, *under Venetian colours*, after an hour's chase, the said M. *De Boades* ordered the captain to bring on board his muster-roll, passport, and bills of loading; with which order the captain did not readily comply, under a pretence that the sea was rough, and that his long boat was leaky; but, being at last obliged to comply, upon threats being made of firing on him, and being come on board, he declared, *that, in getting up the ship's side, the box containing his muster-roll, his patents, and passport, had fallen from his pocket into the sea*, and only shewed his bills of loading; by which they found the said snow, the *Joanna*, of 14 men, including officers, commanded by *Dominico Zané of Venice, sailed from Venice the*

"25th

CHAP. XVIII. "25*th of September, with a cargo of* 12 bales of ſilk, dried "raiſins, oil, &c. and other effects mentioned in the bills of "loading by him exhibited, for the *account of ſundry perſons* "*in Venice, conſigned to ſundry perſons in London, whither he was* "*bound.* Theſe *goods going into an enemy's country,* and the "loſs of his *papers,* which *had fallen into the ſea, raiſing ſuſ-*"*picions;* the ſaid ſnow had been ſtopped, and carried by "his majeſty's frigate, *La Magicienne,* to *Almeria,* where "ſhe had been put into the hands of the conſul, after the [355] "ſaid *Saint Owey,* lieutenant, acting as ſteward, and the ſaid "*Bouret,* enſign on board the ſaid frigate, had put their ſeal "on the ſaid ſnow, where they found no papers; and taken "on board the ſaid ſhip ten of the ſaid ſnow's crew, which "were replaced by ſix men from on board the *Magicienne,* "and three from the *Atalante,* with a coaſting pilot, who "have brought the ſaid ſnow into the port of *Almeria. The* "*premiſes conſidered,* We, by virtue of the power delegated to "us as aforeſaid, have declared, and declare, as good prize, "the ſhip the *Joanna,* her tackle, and apparel, together with "the goods of her cargo, and do adjudge them to the cap-"tors; that, in conſequence of this decree, the whole be "ſold (if not already done) in the uſual manner, and "the produce divided according to the deſire and or-"dinance of the king; made the 28th of *March,* 1778. "We order, by theſe preſents, the vice conſul of *France,* at "*Almeria,* to look to the execution of this our ordinance; "and hereby authorize and command the firſt tipſtaff, or "ſerjeant, to proceed in all forms requiſite thereto. Done "at *Paris* the 13th of *January* 1779, *Rigot.*" The queſtion ſtated for the opinion of the court, was, whether the ſaid ſentence was not concluſive evidence againſt the plaintiff's recovering in this action. In the courſe of the arguments, the third article of the regulations of the marine of *France,* bearing date the 26th of *July* 1778, and alſo the *procés verbal,* made at the time of the capture, though not ſtated in the caſe, nor given in evidence at the trial, were ſo much referred to, and ſeemed of ſuch weight to the court, that it will be neceſſary to inſert them in this place. Arret *for the regulation of the marine, &c.* 26th *July* 1778. Art. 3. "All veſſels "taken, of what nation ſoever, either neutral or allied, from "which it is known that *any papers* have been *thrown* into "the ſea, ſuppreſſed, or abſtracted, ſhall be declared good

"prize,

"prize, together with their cargoes, upon the mere proof "that *ſome papers* have been *thrown* into the ſea, without "any neceſſity of examining what thoſe papers were; by "whom they were thrown; and even though a ſufficient "quantity ſhould remain on board to *juſtify* that the ſhip "and the cargo belonged to friends or allies." The *procés verbal* need not be here repeated; for although it is not ſubſtantively ſet out in the caſe, yet it is copied almoſt *verbatim* in the ſentence of the *French* Admiralty. It was admitted at the bar, that the ſentence had been appealed from, and [356] had been affirmed; but nothing new or ſpecial appeared in the proceedings on the appeal. This caſe was twice argued at the bar; and after the ſecond argument, the court deſired that it might ſtand over, in order to give time to apply to the defendant for his conſent; that the above *arret* and the *procés verbal* ſhould be added to the caſe. To this propoſition the defendant would not conſent.

Lord *Mansfield*, upon the firſt argument, ſaid:—"The firſt principles are clear and admitted. All the world are parties to a ſentence of a Court of Admiralty. Here there is a monition publiſhed at the Exchange; and in other countries, at ſome place of general reſort; and any perſon intereſted may come in and appeal at any time, if there has been no *laches*. If there has, the time of appeal is limited. But the ſentence, as to that which is within it, is concluſive againſt all perſons, unleſs reverſed by the regular court of appeal. It cannot be controverted collaterally, in a civil ſuit. The difficulty here, is what the ground was, on which the *French* Admiralty went; whether the ground of enemy's property, or that of the papers having been thrown overboard. By the maritime laws of all countries, throwing papers overboard is conſidered as a ſtrong preſumption of enemy's property; and upon that principle the *arret* of 1778 is founded. But in all my experience, in *England* I have never known a condemnation on that circumſtance only. It is made uſe of as a ſtrong ground of ſuſpicion. The *arret* is very rigid. It is difficult to find out what the ground of this ſentence was. *I incline* to think the court went upon the ground of *enemy's property*, and conſidered the want of the papers as a ſtrong preſumption of that fact; but they did not examine the captain upon interrogatories, as to the contents of the papers;

pers; and, upon the whole, enough does not appear on this obscure sentence, to ascertain precisely on what it was founded, and some other method ought to be taken to inquire what the ground of it was. As to whatever it *meant* to decide, we must take it to be conclusive."

Willes and *Ashhurst*, Justices, concurred with his Lordship.

Mr. Justice *Buller* inclined to doubt, and said :—"To be sure, the sentence was obscure, but, taking it altogether, he
[357] did not think there was much difficulty in discovering the grounds of it. The two circumstances, of the cargo being consigned to the enemy, and the falling of the papers into the sea, are stated as the grounds of suspicion. The latter circumstance, papers falling into the sea, could not be a ground of condemnation. The other could raise no other suspicion, nor a presumption of any thing else, but the property being enemy's property. It follows, therefore, that the condemnation went upon that ground. If it had gone upon a *wilful throwing of papers overboard*, *that* would have been stated substantively as the ground. In the first place, lay the *arret* out of the case; and then wilful throwing papers overboard is only presumptive evidence of enemy's property. Then take the *arret*, still wilful throwing overboard might have been used as evidence of enemy's property, or it might have been a substantive ground under the *arret*: here it is not stated as a substantive ground."

Lord *Mansfield*, after the second argument, said, that if the *procés verbal* should be agreed to be made part of the case, it would clearly explain the ambiguity of the sentence; as it set forth the ground for taking the ship to have been the *arret* of *July* 1778. Without the *procés verbal*, he said, the sentence was equivocal; it took all in; and it was difficult to say what it went on. If the papers produced to the captor were fair, the property was neutral. But the *procés verbal* put the ground of the sentence out of all doubt.

Mr. Justice *Buller* also declared, that he thought the *procés verbal* must be taken as part of the proceedings, and, as that expressly referred to the *arret*, as the ground of the capture, and the sentence was consistent with it, the sentence must be taken to be founded on the *arret*. But he adhered to his former opinion,

opinion, *on the case as stated without the procés verbal*, namely, that the interpretation of the sentence, taken by itself, must be, that the condemnation went on the ground of enemy's property, and was, therefore, conclusive against the plaintiff.

The final refusal of the defendant was signified by Mr. *Lee*, who assigned as a reason for it, that the *procés verbal* was not a proceeding in the *French* Court of Admiralty, but merely an account of what passed on the capture, reduced into writing at the time. He also observed, that, in the sentence, all the *procés verbal*, *except* the concluding part, which refers to the *arret* of *July* 1778, was recited, and this afforded a strong argument for inferring, that the court had purposely omitted that part of it, to shew that they did not condemn the ship on the ground of the *arret*. [358]

Lord *Mansfield* disapproved much of the defendant's refusal, but he said he thought the justice of the case might still be got at, on the ground of the ambiguity of the sentence, which did not mention a word about the property *being enemy's property*; that it was clear the *French* Admiralty meant to proceed on the ground *of throwing the papers overboard*: and he agreed with the counsel for the plaintiff, that the *procés verbal* ought to be considered as part of the proceedings, and that the sentence ought not to have been read without it.

Mr. Justice *Buller* thought there was weight in what had been observed by Mr. *Lee*, on the reason for omitting the concluding part of the *procés verbal* in the sentence. Indeed it was not clear that what was now offered to be produced, was the same *procés verbal* which the sentence recites; and if it could be supposed that the captain had made another, omitting the reference to the *arret* as the ground of the capture, *that* could only be accounted for by his having found that the capture could not be supported on that ground.

Mr. Justice *Willes* thought it most manifest, that the *procés verbal* made at the time of the capture, was that on which the sentence proceeded. The sentence began with mentioning it, and recited it exactly, as to date, and every thing else, as far as it went. The word *purporting* did not require a recital of the whole; and it was not necessary for the Admiralty

CHAP. XVIII. ralty Court to ſet forth the captain's reaſons for detaining the ſhip. He had all along been of opinion that the ſentence was ſo ambiguous, that it did not appear that the cauſe of condemnation was that the property was neutral, and therefore had thought evidence neceſſary to explain it.

Mr. Juſtice *Aſhhurſt* concurred, as to the ambiguity of the ſentence, and that it was, therefore, not concluſive; and on that ground, Lord *Mansfield*, and *Willes* and *Aſhhurſt*, Juſtices, declared their opinion that the *poſtea* ought to be deliv- [359] ered to the plaintiff. *Lee* ſtill urged the danger of opening the ſentences of foreign Courts of Admiralty, which are generally informal; upon which Lord *Mansfield* ſaid, all the ſuppoſed inconvenience would be obviated, if the foreign courts would ſay in their ſentences, "*Condemned as enemy's property.*"

In the caſe juſt reported, it is admitted by all the Judges, that a ſentence of a Court of Admiralty abroad is binding upon all parties, as to what appears upon the face of it. And therefore if it appear evident, without a poſſibility of doubt or ambiguity, that the ſentence proceeded upon the ground of the property not being neutral, that is concluſive evidence againſt the inſured, that he has not complied with his warranty; and conſequently the underwriter is no longer reſponſible. This was fully ſettled in the caſe of *Barzillay* v. *Lewis*.

Barzillay v. Lewis, B. R. Trin. Term, 22 Geo. III.

It was an action on a policy of inſurance on a ſhip from *Liverpool* to *Amſterdam*, *warranted Dutch property*; and it was brought to recover for a total loſs, the ſhip having been captured by the *French*, and condemned by the Court of Admiralty there. The plaintiff (the inſured) was nonſuited in this action, from an idea, that the decree of the parliament of *Paris* was deciſive againſt him, that he had not complied with his warranty. Upon a motion to ſet aſide this nonſuit, the following facts appeared from the report of the judge who tried the cauſe: The ſhip in queſtion was originally a *French* privateer, called *L'Aimable Agathée*, which was taken by an *Engliſh* privateer, and carried into *Liverpool*; where ſhe got the name of *The Three Graces*. A merchant at *Liverpool* afterwards bought her for a houſe at *Amſterdam*, and a paſſport was ſent for her from thence. She was then inſured

ſured by a *Dutch* name, and warranted as in the policy; ſhe went to ſea, was captured by a *French* ſhip; and carried into *St. Maloes*, where ſhe was releaſed by the Vice Admiralty Court, as being *Dutch*. But upon an appeal to the parliament of *Paris*, the ſentence was reverſed, and ſhe was condemned as lawful prize, by the name of *The Three Graces of Liverpool*. It appeared in evidence, that there were certain *French* ordinances, which ordain, that where more than one third of the crew of a neutral ſhip are enemies to the king of *France*, the ſhip ſhall be confiſcated: that no ſhip ſhall be conſidered as transferred, till ſhe has been within the port of [360] the purchaſer: and that a paſſport ſhall be deemed fraudulent, unleſs the ſhip has been in the port from whence it has been obtained. The ſhip's crew in queſtion conſiſted of ſixteen, five of whom were *French*, four were *Danes*, two were *Swedes*, one was *Dutch*, one *Portugueze*, one *Hamburgher*, one *Norwegian*, and one *Iriſhman*. Some of the crew ſwore, that they were hired by *Engliſhmen*, and that both the ſhip and the cargo were *Engliſh*. They alſo ſwore, that when the ſhip which took them came in ſight, the captain ſailed back towards the *Engliſh* coaſt: but one of the crew having informed him, that the ſhip in ſight carried *Engliſh* colours, he reſumed his courſe.

Lord *Mansfield*.—"The ſentence of the Court of Appeal in *France* is concluſive. The queſtion is, what that ſentence means. She is condemned as not being a *Dutch* ſhip. The warranty is, that ſhe is *Dutch*, which is falſe. The law of nations is founded on eternal principles of juſtice; and in every war the belligerent powers make particular regulations for themſelves. But no nation is obliged to be bound by them, unleſs they are agreeable to the general laws of nations, but all third perſons and mercantile people are. In this caſe, the plaintiffs warrant this ſhip to be *Dutch*; and they know they muſt conform to the marine regulations of *France*. The inſurers took the riſk upon this warranty; but her paſs was not agreeable to the treaty. The parliament of *Paris* did not condemn her as the *Dutch* ſhip of *Amſterdam* by her *Dutch* name; but as "*The Three Graces of Liverpool*." Indeed ſhe had none of the requiſites of a *Dutch* ſhip; and the regulations require that ſhe ſhould have been into the port of the purchaſer, in order to transfer the property; the knowledge of all which circumſtances the inſured, by his

CHAP. XVIII. warranty, took upon himſelf. I am therefore of opinion, that the warranty was falſe."

Mr. Juſtice *Willes*, and Mr. Juſtice *Aſhhurſt* concurred.

Mr. Juſtice *Buller*.—" The ſtrongeſt ground ſeems to be, that ſhe was warranted to be *Dutch* property; and yet had none of the documents neceſſary to protect a neutral ſhip, conſiſtent with the regulations of the court of *France*." The rule to ſet aſide the nonſuit was accordingly diſcharged.

[361] De Souza v. Ewer, Sit. at Guildh. after Hilary 1789.

So alſo in another caſe, where an inſurance was made on the ſhip *Arainha de Portugal*, at and from *Liſbon* to *Bombay*, *warranted a Portugueſe ſhip*; the ſhip was captured in *December* 1782, by the *French*, under the command of Monſ. *de Suffrein*. The ſentence of *Suffrein* was in theſe words: We declare that the ſhip called the *Queen of Portugal*, carrying *Portugueſe* colours, was ſeized only in conſequence of the 7th article of the regulations concerning the navigation of neutrals, which ſays, that all ſhips of an enemy's conſtruction, which ſhall not carry a bill of ſale of a date prior to the hoſtilities, ſhall not be conſidered as neutral, and ſhall be declared good prize; and the ſaid ſhip having been built at *Bombay* under the name of *Arnable*, and navigated under *Engliſh* colours till 1781, when ſhe took *Portugueſe* colours, is abſolutely in the ſituation above-mentioned. The ſentence proceeded to declare, that the confiſcation did not proceed on the ground of want of papers, a *verbal procés* having proved, that they were deſtroyed by ſome ſeas ſhipped in the courſe of the voyage; and it alſo ſtated, that there were no contraband goods on board. From this ſentence *De Souza* appealed to the council of prizes at *Paris*; and, on the 4th of *January*, 1786, that board, after reciting the ſentence of *Suffrein*, proceeds thus: " We, by virtue of " the power given to us by our ſaid office of Admiral, adopt- " ing the declaration of the Bailiff *de Suffrein*, have declared, " and do declare the ſaid ſhip *Queen of Portugal*, *&c. good* " *prize*; and have, and do confiſcate the ſame for the bene- " fit of the king." *De Souza* ſtill further appealed to the King in council; and on the 8th of *May* 1787, the following ſentence was pronounced, after reciting all the former ſentences

ſentences and other documents in the cauſe: "His majeſty has "ordained, and does ordain, that the ſentence of the Coun-"cil of Prizes, of 4th *January* 1786, ſhall be executed, "agreeable to its form and tenure."

As ſoon as theſe ſentences were opened, Lord *Kenyon*, Chief Juſtice, was of opinion, that they were concluſive evidence againſt the warranty entered into by the plaintiff. The courts abroad, whoſe ſentences have been mentioned, were competent to the déciſion of the point; and we muſt ſuppoſe that they have done properly, and have acted according to the *jus inter gentes*. This ſhip was condemned becauſe ſhe had not thoſe documents to prove her neutrality, which are required by the ordinances of *France*. The courts which condemned this ſhip proceeded according to the laws of nations, as all courts of Admiralty do: but here it is ſufficient, that they had a juriſdiction over the ſubject matter. [362] See the opinion of Mr. Juſtice Buller in the preceding caſe, Acc.

The plaintiff was non-ſuited; and no application was ever made to ſet it aſide.

It has alſo been determined, that where no ſpecial ground at all is ſtated; but the ſhip is condemned generally as good and lawful prize, the court here muſt conſider it as concluſive evidence that the property was not neutral, and will not again open the proceedings of the court abroad in favour of the party, who has warranted his property to be neutral.

An action was brought upon a policy of inſurance on goods *warranted neutral* on board the *Thetis*, *a Tuſcan ſhip*, to recover the amount of the inſurance from the underwriters. The ſhip had been taken in the courſe of her voyage by a *Spaniſh* veſſel, carried into *Spain*, and her cargo was there condemned "*as good and lawful prize.*" There was an appeal to a ſuperior court, which reverſed the ſentence: but upon a further appeal, the latter deciſion was overturned, and the former confirmed. At the trial of this cauſe before Lord *Mansfield*, his lordſhip being of opinion that the ſentence of the *Spaniſh* Court of Admiralty was concluſive evidence of the falſehood of the plaintiff's warranty, the plaintiff was nonſuited. A motion was made, and fully argued

Saloucci v. Woodmaſs, B. R. Hill. 24 Geo. III.

CHAP. XVIII. gued to ſet aſide the nonſuit, which was unanimouſly refuſed by the whole Court of King's Bench.

Lord *Mansfield*.—"The policy here warrants that this cargo was neutral property. It appears from the policy itſelf, that the ſhip was neutral; becauſe it is called a *Tuſcan* ſhip; but the warranty is that the goods are neutral. It muſt be preſumed from the condemnation, as no other cauſe appears, that it proceeded on the ground of the property be-

Vide ſupra. longing to an enemy. In the caſe of *Bernardi* v. *Motteux*, the deciſion of the court turned upon the particular ground of the confiſcation appearing on the face of the ſentence; and that it did not appear to be on the ground of being enemy's property. This being ſo, the court gave the party an

[363] opportunity to ſhew by evidence, that the ſpecific ground was really the cauſe of the condemnation. In this caſe, at *Guildhall*, the counſel admitted the general rule; but they ſaid, if a copy of the proceedings could be had, a ſpecial cauſe would appear. The proceedings are now come; and from them it appears, that the queſtion turned entirely upon the property of the goods. For in the ſecond court, to which they appealed from the ſentence of the firſt, the queſtion was, whether the goods were free: the decree was, that they were. But the third court overturned the deciſion of the ſecond. It is ſufficient, however, that no ſpecial ground is ſtated; and therefore the rule muſt be diſcharged."

If the ground of deciſion appear to be not on the want of neutrality, but upon a foreign ordinance manifeſtly unjuſt, and contrary to the laws of nations, and the inſured has only infringed ſuch a partial law; as the condemnation did not proceed on the point of neutrality, it cannot apply to the warranty, ſo as to diſcharge the inſurer.

Mayne v. Walter, B. R. Eaſt. 22 Geo. III. In a policy of inſurance, *the ſhip was warranted to be Portugueſe*; and having been taken in her voyage by a *French* privateer, ſhe was carried into *France*. The Court of Admiralty condemned her becauſe ſhe had an *Engliſh* ſupercargo on board. It appeared that there was a *French* ordinance, prohibiting any *Dutch* ſhip from carrying a ſupercargo belonging to any nation at enmity with the court of *France*. In an action againſt the underwriter, theſe facts appeared; upon which, a verdict was found for the plaintiff,

ſubject

ſubject to the opinion of the court, upon this queſtion, whether the circumſtance of having an *Engliſh* ſupercargo, was a breach of neutrality; and whether ſuch a ſentence was concluſive. CHAP. XVIII.

Lord *Mansfield*.—"It is an arbitrary and oppreſſive regulation, contrary to the law of nations. If you were both ignorant of it, the underwriter muſt run all riſks; and if the defendant knew of the edict, it was his duty to inquire if there was ſuch a ſupercargo on board. It muſt be a fraudulent concealment to vitiate a policy. But it is remarkable that neither party has ſaid any thing of the treaties between *France* and *Portugal*." Judgment for the plaintiff.

[364]

One more rule is worthy of obſervation: which is, that though the veſſel be condemned as prize, yet if the grounds of the ſentence appear manifeſtly to contradict ſuch a concluſion, the court here will not diſcharge the underwriters by declaring that the inſured has forfeited his neutrality.

Saloucci v. Johnſon, B. R. Hill. 25 Geo. III.

An action was brought upon a policy of inſurance on the ſhip *Thetis*, a *Tuſcan* ſhip, *warranted neutral*. At the trial a verdict was found for the plaintiffs, ſubject to the opinion of the court, upon a caſe, ſtating, That the plaintiffs were *Tuſcan* ſubjects reſident at *Leghorn*: that the ſhip, having *neutral goods* on board conſigned to *London*, was captured off the coaſt of *Barbary* by a *Spaniſh* veſſel. That ſhe was carried into *Spain*, and there condemned as prize; which ſentence, upon appeal to a ſuperior court, was reverſed: but upon a further appeal, the laſt ſentence was reverſed, and the firſt confirmed. That the grounds of condemnation were two; 1ſt, That the ſhip *Thetis* refuſed to be ſearched, and reſiſted with force, having fired at the ſhip of the *Spaniard*: 2d, That the *Thetis* had no charter party on board. The Captain anſwers theſe two grounds thus; 1ſt, That he reſiſted and fired, the *Spaniard* having hailed him under falſe colours: 2d, That he had taken the goods on board by the piece, and had not freighted her to any individual; in which caſe a manifeſto was ſufficient, without a charter party. The ſentence of the laſt court admits the ſhip to

CHAP. XVIII. be neutral, for it ſtates it to be "the ſhip *Thetis*, a *Tuſcan* ſhip, &c."

Lord *Mansfield* was abſent at the argument of this caſe.

Mr. Juſtice *Willes*.—"This is clearly a neutral ſhip. Something was ſaid in argument about barratry; but I do not think the act of the Captain in this caſe amounts to that offence. The ſecond ground of condemnation is given up by the counſel: and the remaining queſtion, is, whether the Captain has been guilty of ſuch a breach of neutrality, as ſhould affect the owners. If a ſhip be neutral, and ſhe be ſtopped, thoſe who ſtop her muſt pay for the detention. But it is ſaid ſhe muſt ſtop to be ſearched. I find no authority for ſuch a poſition. Beſides, the circumſtances are very ſuſpicious. The Captain ſeems to have acted properly. Stoppage is always at the peril of the captors."

[365] Mr. Juſtice *Aſhhurſt*.—"I take the principle laid down at the bar to be true, that a ſhip warranted neutral, muſt conduct herſelf ſo as not to forfeit her neutrality. But the facts of this caſe do not admit of the application. I do not find, that a neutral ſhip muſt ſubmit to be ſearched. It is rather an act of ſuperior force, always reſiſted when the party is able; and the right falls within this poſition, that the ſearcher does it at his peril. If he find any thing contraband, or the property of an enemy, he is juſtified: if not, he pays coſts. Is there any thing to juſtify the ſearch in this caſe? certainly not, for the cargo was neutral."

Mr. Juſtice *Buller*.—"It is not neceſſary to give an opinion as to barratry; but I take it to mean a wilful act of the captain to the injury of the owners. This would have been barratry, if it had been an act, which forfeits the neutrality. Vide ſupra. I do not agree that the property muſt continue neutral during the whole voyage. If it be neutral at the time of ſailing, it is ſufficient; and if a war break out next day, the underwriter is liable. The anſwer given to the claim of ſearch is concluſive, that the party does it at his peril; juſt like the caſe of Cuſtom-Houſe officers. The practice of the Admiralty confirms it; for they give coſts in caſes of improper detention: which they would not do, if neutral ſhips were,

as

at all events, liable to be ſtopt. Detention by particular ordinances, which do not form a part of the law of nations, is a riſk within the policy. At firſt I compared this caſe in my own mind to that of an illegal voyage; but they are no way ſimilar; for a ſhip is only bound to take notice of the laws of the country ſhe ſails from, and of that to which ſhe ſails; but not the particular ordinances of other powers." Judgment was accordingly given for the plaintiff. CHAP. XVIII.

Theſe are the caſes which have been decided, relative to the judgments of foreign courts being concluſive, and the effects which they have upon the contract of inſurance; and from all of them it ſhould ſeem, that this general doctrine may be collected: That wherever the ground of the ſentence is manifeſt, and it appears to have proceeded expreſsly upon the point in iſſue between the parties; or wherever the ſentence is general, and no ſpecial ground is ſtated, there it ſhall be concluſive and binding, and the courts here will not take upon themſelves, in a collateral way, to [366] review the proceedings of a forum, having competent juriſdiction of the ſubject matter. But if the ſentence be ſo ambiguous and doubtful, that it is difficult to ſay on what ground the deciſion turned; or if there be colour to ſuppoſe, that the court abroad proceeded upon matter not relevant to the matter in iſſue; there evidence will be allowed in order to explain. And if the ſentence upon the face of it be manifeſtly againſt law and juſtice, or be contradictory, the inſured ſhall not be deprived of his indemnity; becauſe, to uſe the words of Mr. Juſtice *Buller*, any detention, by particular ordinances or decrees, which contravene or do not form a part of the law of nations, is a riſk within a policy of inſurance.

CHAPTER THE NINETEENTH.

Of Return of Premium.

CHAP. XIX.

HAVING in feveral chapters fpoken fully of the various cafes, in which policies of infurance are either abfolutely void, or are rendered of no effect by the failure of the infured in the performance of fome of thofe conditions, which he had taken upon himfelf: the next object of our inquiry will be, in what cafes, and under what circumftances, there fhall be a return of premium.

Loccenius de jure marit. l. 2. c. 5. f. 8.

1 Mag. 90.

Dougl. 255.

1 Vezey 319.

In all countries, in which infurances have been known, it has been a cuftom, coeval with the contract itfelf, that where property has been infured to a larger amount than the real value, the infurer fhall return the overplus premium: or if it happen that goods are infured to come in certain fhips from abroad, but are not in fact fhipped, the premium fhall be returned. If the fhip be arrived before the policy is made, and the underwriter is acquainted with the arrival, but the infured is not, it fhould feem the latter will be entitled to have his premium reftored, on the ground of fraud. But if both parties be ignorant of the arrival, and the policy be (as it ufually is) *loft or not loft*, I think in that cafe the underwriter fhould retain; becaufe under fuch a policy, if the fhip had been loft, at the time of fubfcribing, he would have been liable to pay the amount of his fubfcription. The parties themfelves frequently infert claufes in the policy, ftating, that upon the happening of a certain event, there fhall be a return of premium. Thefe claufes have a binding operation upon the parties; and the conftruction of them is a matter for the court, and not for the jury, to determine.— In fhort, if the fhip or property infured, was never brought within the terms of the written contract, fo that the infurer never has run any rifk, the premium muft be returned.

The principle, upon which the whole of this doctrine depends, is fimple and plain, admitting of no doubt or ambiguity.

ity. The riſk or peril is the conſideration for which the premium is to be paid: if the riſk be not run, the conſideration for the premium fails; and equity implies a condition, that the inſurer ſhall not receive the price of running a riſk, if, in fact, he runs none. It is juſt like the contract of bargain and ſale; for if the thing ſold be not delivered, the party who agreed to buy, is not liable to pay. Thus to whatever cauſe it be owing, that the riſk is not run, as the money was put into the hands of the inſurer, merely for the riſk of indemnifying the inſured, the purpoſe having failed, he cannot have a right to retain the ſum ſo depoſited for a ſpecial cauſe.

Pothier n. 179.

3 Burr. 1240.

Roccus, Not. 88.

Cowp. 668.

Accordingly in an action of *indebitatus aſſumpſit* brought by the plaintiff for 5*l.* received by the defendant to the plaintiff's uſe, where the general iſſue was pleaded; it appeared in evidence, that one *Barkdale* had made a policy of inſurance upon account for 5*l.* premium in the plaintiff's name, and that he had paid the ſaid premium to the defendant, and that *Barkdale* had no goods then on board, and ſo the policy was void. To this action two objections were taken: 1ſt, That it ſhould have been brought in *Barkdale*'s name, which was over-ruled: 2dly, That this ought to have been a ſpecial action on the cuſtom of merchants. Lord Chief Juſtice *Holt* cited a caſe of money depoſited upon a wager concerning a race, that the party winning might bring an action of *indebitatus aſſumpſit*, for money received to his uſe; for now, by the ſubſequent matter, it is become as ſuch. And, as to the caſe in queſtion, the money is not only to be returned by the cuſtom, but the policy is made originally void, the party, for whoſe uſe it was made, having no goods on board; ſo, that by this diſcovery, the money was received without any reaſon, occaſion, or conſideration, and conſequently it was received originally to the plaintiff's uſe. And ſo judgment was given for the plaintiff.

Martin v. Sitwell, 1 Shower, 156.

I cite this caſe for two purpoſes; becauſe it ſerves to ſhew in what form of action the plaintiff ought to demand a return of premium; and it alſo points out, that as early as the beginning of the reign of *William* and *Mary*, the true principle, on which the premium ought to be returned, was fully eſtabliſhed. It was ſaid in the introduction to this chapter, that clauſes are frequently inſerted in policies of inſurance, containing conditions, on the performance or non-perform-

ance

CHAP. XIX. ance of which, the premium is returnable; and that to decide upon the construction of such conditions is the province of the court, and not of the jury. Such a case occurs, which may properly be mentioned here.

Simond and another v. Boydell. Doug. 255.

This action was brought against an underwriter, for a return of premium. The material part of the policy was in these words: "At and from any port or ports in *Grenada* to "*London*, on any ship or ships that shall sail on or between "the first of *May* and the first of *August* 1778, at 18 guineas "*per cent.* to return 8*l. per cent. if she sails from any of the West* "*India islands, with convoy for the voyage, and arrives.*" At the bottom there was a written declaration that the policy was on sugars (the muscavado valued at 20*l.* per hogshead) for account of *L. Q.* being on the first sugars which shall be shipped for that account. The ship the *Hankey* sailed with convoy, within the time limited, having on board 51 hogsheads of muscavado sugar, belonging to *L. Q.* She arrived safe in the *Downs*, where the convoy left her; convoy never coming farther, and indeed seldom beyond *Portsmouth*. After she had parted with the convoy, she struck on a bank called the *Pan Sand*, at *Margate*, and 11 of the 51 casks of sugar were washed overboard, and the rest damaged. The ship was afterwards got off the bank, and proceeded up the river, arrived safe in the port of *London*, and was reported at the custom-house. The sugars saved were taken out at *Margate*, and, after undergoing a sort of cure, by a person sent from town for that purpose, they were carried to *London* in other vessels; and the 40 hogsheads being sold, produced 340*l.* instead of 800*l.* which was their valuation in the policy. The defendant had paid into court the value of the sugars lost, and and a return of 8*l. per cent.* on 340*l.* The plaintiffs insisted, that they were entitled to have 8*l. per cent.* also returned on the *valued* price of the eleven hogsheads of sugar, which were lost, and on the difference between what the remaining forty hogsheads produced, and their valued price. At the trial, before Lord *Mansfield*, the plaintiffs had a verdict to the full amount of their demand. The chief question, upon the motion for a new trial, was, to what the word "*arrives*" was intended to apply.

Lord

Lord *Mansfield*.—"The ancient form of a policy of insurance, which is still retained, is, in itself, very inaccurate; but length of time, and a variety of discussions and decisions, have reduced it to certainty. It is amazing, when additional clauses are introduced, that the merchants do not take some advice in framing them, or bestow more consideration upon them themselves. I do not recollect an addition made, which has not created doubts on the construction of it. Here a word or two more would have rendered the whole perfectly clear. However, I have no doubt how we must construe this policy. Dangers of the sea are the same in time of peace and of war; but war introduces hazards of another sort, depending on a variety of circumstances, some known, others not, for which an additional premium must be paid. Those hazards are diminished by the protection of convoy, and if the insured will warrant a departure with convoy, there is a diminution of the additional premium. If the insured will not warrant a departure with convoy, he pays the full premium, and in that case the underwriter says, "If "it turn out that the ship departs with convoy, I will return "part of the premium." [1] But a ship may sail with convoy, and be separated from it by a storm, or other accident, in a day or two, and lose its protection. On a warranty to sail with convoy, that would not be a breach of the condition; but, to guard against that risk, the insured adds, in policies of the present sort, "the ship must not only sail with convoy, "but she must *arrive*, to entitle me to the return." The words, *and arrives*, do not mean that the ship shall arrive in the company of the convoy, but only that she herself shall arrive. If she does, that shews, either that she had convoy the whole way, or did not want it. But, in the stipulation for the return of premium, no regard is had by the parties to the condition of the goods on the arrival of the ship. The construction, contended for by the defendant, is adding a comment longer than the text. If it had been meant that no return should be made, unless *all* the goods arrived *safe*, they would have said, "if the ship arrive *with all the goods*," or "*safely with all the goods*." The total or partial loss of the goods was the subject of the indemnity, and must be paid for by the underwriter. But, as to the return of the additional premium, whether the goods arrive safe or not, makes no part

[1] Vide ante, c. 18.

CHAP. XIX. part of the queſtion. The ſingle principle which muſt govern, is, that in the events which have happened, the war riſk has been rated too high.

Mr. Juſtice *Willes*, and Mr. Juſtice *Aſhhurſt*, were of the ſame opinion.

Mr. Juſtice *Buller*.—"I am of the ſame opinion. *The queſtion is for the deciſion of the court, not of a jury*, ſince it ariſes on the conſtruction of a written inſtrument. What gives riſe to an increaſe of the premium? The danger of capture. When that danger is diminiſhed, the conſtruction muſt be, that there ſhall be a proportional return of premium." The rule for a new trial was accordingly diſcharged.

Cowp. 668. By the law of *England*, it has been clearly ſettled, that, whether the cauſe of the riſk not being run, is attributable to the *fault*, *will*, *or pleaſure* of the inſured, ſtill the premium is to be returned. Foreign writers have in ſome meaſure differed in opinion upon this point; and it may not be improper to obſerve how far they vary or agree with our own. The *Italian* writers agree with us, that the contract in queſtion is conditional, and that the riſk is the very eſſence and main ſpring of the whole. But ſtill they inſiſt and contend, that it is not lawful for the aſſured, *by their own act*, to break the contract; and, that in ſuch a caſe, the inſurer is not obliged to return the premium. They hold, indeed, that if the voyage be put an end to by any accident, ſuch as the ſhip being burnt, or by public authority; or if more goods were *bonâ fide* inſured, than were actually on board: in the former caſes, the whole, and in the latter, a proportional part of the premium ſhould be returned. But if a man ſay he has goods on board, and inſure them, knowing that he has none, they aſk this queſtion: "An aſſecurator teneatur reſtituere pretium, "eo quod in navi non fuerunt merces? Videbatur aſſecurator teneri ad reſtitutionem pretii recepti: ſed in contrarium "eſt veritas, quod non ſolum non teneatur pretium reſtituere, imo poſſit patere illud; et ratio eſt, quia licet "emptio periculi non teneat in præjudicium promiſſoris, "tamen in ejus favorem, et in præjudicium aſſecurati falſa "aſſertio bene tenet."

(Roccus Not. 15. 82. 88.) (Roccus Not. 11.) (Santerna. part 3. n. 22.)

The

The *French* law-givers have, however, decided upon this point agreeably to our laws; and have accordingly, in the famous ordinances of *Lewis* the Fourteenth, inserted an article declaring, that if the voyage is entirely broken up before the departure of the ship, *even by the act of the insured*, the insurance shall be void, and the underwriter shall return the premium, reserving one half *per cent.* for his trouble. This article affords scope to *Valin*, the very learned commentator upon these ordinances, to point out the advantages which the insured enjoys above the insurer, in being thus able to put an end to the contract even after it is signed, which the underwriter can by no means effect. Indeed, when we consider that the premium is nothing more than the price of the perils, which the underwriters ought to run; and that the obligation to pay the premium contains this tacit condition, "*I will pay if the insurers run the risk*;" it is perfectly consistent with that principle, that when the risk is not run, whatever be the cause, the premium is not due to the insurers. Accordingly, in *England* it has always been the custom, when the policy is cancelled, to return the premium, deducting one half *per cent.*

2 Emerigon, 153. Ord. of Lew. 14. tit. Assur. art. 37.

2 Val. 93.

Pothiér Not. 179.

Molloy, l. 2. c. 7. s. 12.

The generality of the rule here established, would seem to extend it even to cases of fraud on the part of the insured. But the laws of *France*, upon this subject, have declared, that the insured shall be obliged to restore to the insurer, whatever he has received from him, and also to pay him double the premium. This question, relative to a return of premium, in cases of fraud, was very fully discussed in the chapter of fraud, and all the cases fully cited; to that chapter, therefore, I must now refer the reader.

Ord. of Lew. 14. tit. Insur. art. 41.

Vide ante, c. 10. p. 215.

Some of the statutes for preventing the exportation of wool, and other staple commodities of the kingdom, and which, in order more effectually to prevent such exportation, have declared policies of insurance on those articles, to be null and void, have enacted that the premium shall not be restored to the insured.

See ante, ch. 13. p. 249.

When a policy is void, being made without interest, contrary to the statute of the 19 *George* the Second, *if the ship has*

19 Geo. II. c. 37. Vide supra, c. 14.

arrived

CHAP. XIX. *arrived safe*, the court will not allow the insured to recover back the premium; according to the old rule of law, *in pari delicto potior est conditio possidentis*. But in the decision of the case, in which this doctrine was held, the court seemed to rely much upon the distinction of contracts executed and executory: that this was a contract *executed*, the ship having arrived before the demand was made; but when a contract *executory* is to be rescinded, it can only be done upon the equitable terms of putting all parties in their original situation. Mr. Justice *Willes* in this case differed in opinion from the rest of the court, for reasons delivered by the learned Judge, and which will appear in their proper place.

Doug. 454.

Lowry and another v. Bourdieu. Doug. 251. Vide ante, p. 272.

The plaintiffs had lent to *Lawson*, captain of the *Lord Holland East Indiaman*, 26,000 *l.* for which he had given them a common bond in the penal sum of 52,000 *l.* While he was with his ship at *China*, the plaintiffs got a policy of insurance, underwritten by the defendant and others, which was in the following terms: "At and from *China* to *London*, "beginning the adventure *upon the goods* from the loading "thereof on board the said ship at *Canton* in *China*, &c. and "*upon the said ship*, from, and immediately following her "arrival at *Canton*, valued at 26,000 *l.* being the amount of "Captain *Patrick Lawson*'s common bond, payable to the "parties as shall be described on the back of this policy: "and it bears date the 16th day of *December* 1775; and in "case of a loss, *no other proof of interest to be required than the* "*exhibition of the said bond: warranted free from average, and* "*without benefit of salvage to the insurer*." At the head of the subscriptions was written, "*On a bond as above expressed*." Captain *Lawson* sailed from *China*, and arrived safe with his privilege (as it is called) or adventure, in *London*, on the 1st of *July* 1777, none of the events insured against having happened. The receipt of the premium was acknowledged on the back of the policy. The insured brought this action for a return of the premium, on the ground that the policy being without interest, the contract was void. The cause came on before Lord *Mansfield*, at *Guildhall*, when his Lordship was of opinion, that the policy was a gaming policy, prohibited by the statute of 19 *Geo.* II. c. 37. and both parties equally guilty of a breach of the law; that the rule, therefore, of *melior est conditio possidentis*, was applicable to the case, and the

the plaintiffs could not recover the premium. A verdict was accordingly found for the defendant, agreeably to his Lordship's directions; but, the next morning, he expressed a doubt as to the propriety of his opinion, because the money had been paid upon an executory agreement, which could never have been completed. A new trial was then moved for and fully argued.

Lord *Mansfield.*—"It is certainly true, in many instances, that first thoughts are best. I am now very much inclined to my first opinion. There are two sorts of policies of insurance: mercantile and gaming policies. The first sort are contracts of indemnity, and of indemnity only; and from that principle a great variety of decisions and consequences have followed. The second sort may be the same in form; but in them there is no contract of indemnity, because there is no interest on which a loss can accrue. They are mere games of hazard; like the cast of a die. In the present case, the nature of the insurance is known to both parties. The plaintiffs say, "We mean to game; but we give our reason "for it; Captain *Lawson* owes us a sum of money, and we "want to be secure, in case he should not be in a situation "to pay us." It was a hedge. But they had no interest; for, if the ship had been lost, and the underwriters had paid, still the plaintiffs would have been entitled to recover the amount of the bond from *Lawson*. This then is a gaming policy, and against an act of parliament; and therefore it is clear that the court will not assist either party: according to the well known rule that *in pari delicto*, &c. Not that the defendant's right is better than that of the plaintiff's, but they must draw their remedy from pure fountains. I have returned to my old opinion; sometimes you miss the mark, by taking too long an aim."

Mr. Justice *Willes.*—"I shall make no apology for differing from the rest of the court in a case where such great abilities have entertained two different opinions. The premium has been paid, and yet no risk run; for the policy was void from the beginning, and the insured could not have recovered from the underwriters if the ship had been lost. But I cannot think it a gaming policy. It does not appear

to

CHAP. XIX.

to me that the parties had any idea they were entering into an illegal contract. The whole was disclosed, and they *thought* there was an interest. This was a mistake; but it is a new point of law. The case, cited from Precedents in Chancery, is not, perhaps, decisive, but it goes a great way; and it would be very hard that a party should lose that which he has paid under a mere mistake. I think, in conscience, the defendant ought to refund the premium."

Vide ante ch. 10. p. 216.

Mr. Justice *Ashhurst*.—"I am clear that there ought not to be a new trial. A policy of insurance ought to be a mere contract of indemnity, and nothing more; but here the money might have been paid twice; which shews decisively, that this was a gaming policy."

Mr. Justice *Buller*.—"It is very clear to me that the plaintiffs ought not to recover. There was no fraud on the part of the underwriters, nor any mistake in matter of *fact*. If the law was mistaken, the rule applies, that *ignorantia juris non excusat*. This was a mere gaming policy, without interest. There is a sound distinction between contracts executed and executory, and if an action is brought with a view to rescind a contract, you must do it while the contract continues executory, and then it can only be done on the terms of restoring the other party to his original situation. There was a case of *Walker* v. *Chapman*, some years ago in this court, where a sum of money had been paid in order to procure a place in the *Customs*. The place had not been procured, and the party who had paid the money, having brought his action to recover it back; it was held that he should recover, because the contract remained executory. So, if the plaintiffs in the present case had brought their action, before the risk was over, and the voyage finished, they might have had a ground for their demand; but they waited till the risk, such as it was, (not indeed, founded in law, but resting on the honour of the defendant) had been completely run. It makes no difference whether the premium was paid before the voyage or after it." The rule was discharged.

Andree v. Fletcher. 3 Term. R. 266. See ante p. 279.

And very lately it has been held upon the authority of *Lowry* v. *Bourdieu*, as not being distinguishable from it, that an an action for money had and received will not lie to recover back the premium of a re-assurance void by the statute of 19 *Geo.* II. *ch.* 37.

Lord *Mansfield*, after the rule was discharged in *Lowry* v. *Bourdieu*, said, he desired it might not be understood, that the court held, that, in all cases where money has been paid on an illegal consideration, it cannot be recovered back. That in cases of oppression, when paid, for instance, to a creditor to induce him to sign a bankrupt's certificate, or upon an usurious contract, it may be recovered, for, in such cases, the parties are not *in pari delicto*.

That the court, in the case of *Lowry* v. *Bourdieu*, proceeded upon the distinction between contracts executed and executory, is evident not only from Mr. Justice *Buller's* opinion, but is, in some measure, confirmed by what fell from Lord *Mansfield*, upon a subsequent occasion, when this case was cited; although it must be confessed, that the case about to be quoted, which was only decided suddenly at *nisi prius*, is a good deal shaken by the subsequent decision of *Andree* v. *Fletcher*.

Wharton v. De la Rive. Mich. vac. 1782, at Guildhall.

It was an action brought upon two wagers; one of 26*l.* 5*s.* to 100*l.* the other of 13*l.* 2*s.* 6*d.* to 30*l.* that the colonies of *North America* would be admitted or acknowledged independent states, by some public official act or instrument made or executed, on the part of the king or government of *France*, at some time on or between the 1st of *February* and the 1st of *April* 1778, both days inclusive. The defendant pleaded *non assumpsit*. Upon the opening of this case, Lord *Mansfield* directed the plaintiff to be nonsuited. But the counsel for the plaintiff insisted, that he was entitled to a verdict for the premium on the general count in the declaration, *for money had and received to his use*, which his Lordship permitted, on the ground of the contract being void, and of the defendant having money in his hands, which he ought not to retain. For the defendant it was said, that he was entitled to keep the premium; and the case of *Lowry* v. *Bourdieu* was cited; but Lord *Mansfield* thought it did not apply, as in that case the risk had been run. The point there decided was, that an insurance being made without interest,

and

CHAP. XIX. and the premium paid, the insured shall not recover back the premium, after the ship has arrived safe. And this upon the distinction, that the contract, though not a legal one, *was executed* before the relief was applied for, and no longer *executory*.

From the various cases upon the subject of return of premium, as well as from all that has already been said, it will appear, that in the *English* law there are two general rules established, which govern almost all cases. The first is, that where the risk has not been run, whether that circumstance was owing to the fault, the pleasure or will of the insured, or to any other cause, the premium shall be returned. This rule has already been pretty fully discussed. Another rule is, that if the risk has *once* commenced, there shall be *no* apportionment or return of premium afterwards. Hence in cases of deviation, though the underwriter is discharged from his engagement; yet the risk being once commenced, he is entitled to retain the premium. Though these rules are so plain and simple, that they seem to preclude all possibility of doubt or contention; yet there are few points in the law of insurance, which have given rise to a greater number of causes than those which relate to the subject of this chapter.

Cowp. 668.

It ought, however, to be acknowledged, that less litigation has taken place in those instances where the whole of the premium is either to be retained or restored, than in those, where, from the nature of the agreement between the parties, or the nature of the voyage, the contract becomes divisible, and the court can say, "a part of the premium "shall be retained for the risk run, and part shall be return-
3 Burr. 1240. "ed, as the risk has never commenced." This seems to be a refinement upon the rules just established; but it must, at the same time, be admitted, that *when it can be accomplished*, it is a refinement perfectly consistent with equity and good conscience. The one rule has provided, that if the risk be once begun, there shall be no return: but the other rule has said, and equity has also said, that a man shall not be paid for a risk which he has never incurred; from whence the deduction is easy and natural, that if there are two distinct points of time, or, in effect, two voyages either in the contemplation of the parties or by the usage of trade, and only one of the two voyages was made, the premium shall

be

be returned on the other, although both are contained in one policy.

The first time in which this doctrine was considered at any length, was in a case which came before the Court of King's Bench, in the year 1761.

It was a special case reserved at a trial at *nisi prius*, before Lord *Mansfield*, in *London*, upon an action for money had and received to the plaintiff's use, brought by the plaintiff, the insured, against the defendant, the insurer, for a return of part of the premium. It was an insurance upon a ship, at five guineas *per cent.* lost or not lost, *at and from London to Halifax in* Nova Scotia, *warranted to depart with convoy from Portsmouth*, for the voyage, that is to say, the *Halifax* or *Louisburgh* convoy. Before the ship arrived at *Portsmouth* the convoy was gone. Notice of this was immediately given by the insured to the underwriter; and at the same time he was also desired either to make the long insurance, or to return part of the premium. The jury find that the usual settled premium from *London* to *Portsmouth*, is one and a half *per cent.* They also find that it *is usual* for the underwriter, in such like cases, to return part of the premium; but the *quantum* is uncertain: (and the *quantum* must in its nature be uncertain, because it depends upon uncertain circumstances.) It is stated, that the plaintiff made an offer to the defendant of allowing him to retain one and a half *per cent.* for the risk he had run on such part of the voyage as was performed under the policy, viz. from *London* to *Portsmouth*.

Stevenson v. Snow. 3 Burr. 1237. and 1 Black. Rep. 318. S. C.

Lord *Mansfield*.—"I had not at the trial, nor have now, the least doubt about this question, myself. These contracts are to be taken with great latitude: the strict letter of the contract is not to be so much regarded as the object and intention of it. Equity implies a condition, "that the insurer shall not receive the price of running a risk if he run none." This is a contract without any consideration, as to the voyage from *Portsmouth* to *Halifax*; for he intended to insure that part of the voyage, as well as the former part of it, and has not. Consequently the insured received no consideration for this proportion of his premium; and then this case is within the general principle of actions for money had and received to the plaintiff's use. I do not go upon the usage: for the usage

CHAP. XIX. usage found is only that in like cases, it is usual to return a part of the premium, without ascertaining what part. If the risk is not run, though it is by the neglect or even the fault of the party insuring, yet the insurer shall not retain the premium. It has been objected, that the voyage being *begun*, and part of the risk being already run, the premium cannot be apportioned. But I can see no force in this objection. This is not a contract so entire, that there can be no apportionment: for there are two parts in this contract: and the premium may be divided into two distinct parts, relative, as it were, to two distinct voyages. The practice shews, that it has been usual, in such like cases, to return a part of the premium, though the *quantum* be not ascertained. And indeed, the *quantum* must vary as circumstances vary: so that it never can have been fixed with any precise exactness. But though the *quantum* has not been ascertained; yet the principle is agreeable to the general sense of mankind."

Mr. Justice *Denison*.—"It is most equitable that the defendant should only retain the premium for such part of the voyage, as he has run any risk: the insured has a right to have the other part restored to him. This is agreeable to the general principle of actions for money had and received to the use of the plaintiff: where the defendant has no right to retain, he must refund it."

Mr. Justice *Foster*.—"There is no consideration for the remainder of the premium; for in the voyage from *Portsmouth* to *Halifax*, no risk was run by the insurer, who only insured the voyage *with* convoy: therefore he has no right to retain the premium for this."

Mr. Justice *Wilmot* declared his concurrence most clearly and strongly. These kind of contracts, he observed, are, by the writers on this head, called *contractus innominati;* and the rule, which they lay down concerning them, is, that they are to be determined *secundum bonum et æquum*. The jury have here found an usage to return part of the premium in such cases; which is a strong proof of the equity of the thing: and nothing can be more just and reasonable. If the risk was once begun, the insured shall not deviate or return back, and then say, "I will go no further under this "contract,

"contract, but will have my premium returned." But upon this policy there are two distinct points of time, in effect two voyages, which were clearly in the contemplation of the parties; and only one of the two voyages was made; the other not at all entered upon. It was a conditional contract: and the second voyage was not begun; and therefore the premium must be returned, for upon this second part of the voyage, the risk never took place at all. This is agreeable to what the writers upon the subject lay down; and is the right and justice of the case. The *postea* was delivered to the plaintiff.

Some years afterwards, the principle established in the foregoing case was attempted to be applied to one, which it did not at all resemble. For the following case was an insurance for twelve months at 9*l. per cent.*; and because the ship was captured within two months after the contract was made, a return of premium was demanded, upon the principle of *Stevenson* v. *Snow*. But the contract in this case was entire; the premium was a gross sum stipulated and paid for twelve months; and the parties, when they made the contract, had no intention or thought of a subsequent division, or apportionment.

The case was thus:

Tyrie v. Fletcher. Cowp. 666.

It was an action, in the usual form, for money had and received to the plaintiff's use, for a return of part of the premium. The cause was tried at *Guildhall*, before Lord *Mansfield*, when, by consent, a verdict was found for the plaintiff, subject to the opinion of the court upon the question, Whether, under the circumstances of the case, a proportionable part of the premium ought to be returned or not. If the court should be of opinion that a proportionable part of the premium ought not to be returned, then a nonsuit was to be entered. It now came before the court upon a rule to shew cause, why a nonsuit should not be entered; and the case, as it appeared from the report, was shortly this. The policy was on the ship *Isabella*, at and from *London*, to any port or place, where or whatsoever, *for twelve months*, from the 19th of *August* 1776, to the 19th of *August* 1777, both days inclusive, at 9*l. per cent.* warranted free from captures and seizures by the *Americans*, and the consequences thereof. In all other respects, it was in the common form, against all

CHAP. XIX.

perils of the sea, *&c.* The ship sailed from the port of *London*, and was taken by an *American* privateer, about two months afterwards.

Lord *Mansfield*.—"It was very proper to save this case for the opinion of the court, because in all mercantile transactions, certainty is of much more consequence, than which way the point is decided; and more especially so, in the case of policies of insurance: because, if the parties do not choose to contract according to the established rule, they are at liberty as between themselves to vary it. This case is stript of every authority. There is no case or practice in point; and therefore we must argue from the general principles applicable to all policies of insurance. And I take it, there are two general rules established, applicable to this question: the first is, that where the risk has not been run, whether its not having been run was owing to the fault, pleasure, or will of the insured, or to any other cause, the premium shall be returned; because a policy of insurance is a contract of indemnity. The underwriter receives a premium for running the risk of indemnifying the insured, and to whatever cause it be owing, if he do not run the risk, the consideration, for which the premium or money was put into his hands, fails, and therefore he ought to return it. Another rule is, that if the risk has *once* commenced, there shall be no apportionment or return of premium afterwards. For though the premium is estimated, and the risk depends upon the nature and length of the voyage; yet, if it has commenced, though it be only for 24 hours or less, the risk is run; the contract is for the whole entire risk, and no part of the consideration shall be returned: and yet, it is as easy to apportion for the length of the voyage, as it is for the time. If a ship had been insured to the *East Indies* agreeably to the terms of the policy in this case, and had been taken 24 hours after the risk was begun, by an *American* captor, there is not a colour to say, that there should have been a return of premium. So much then is clear; and indeed, perfectly agreeable to the ground of determination in the case of *Stevenson* v. *Snow*. For in that case, the intention of the parties, the nature of the contract, and the consequences of it, *spoke* manifestly *two* insurances, and *a division* between them. The first object of the insurance was from *London* to *Halifax*: but if the ship did not depart from

from *Portſmouth*, with convoy, (particularly naming the ſhip appointed to be convoy,) then there was to be no contract from *Portſmouth* to *Halifax*: why then, the parties have ſaid, "we make a contract from *London* to *Halifax*, but on a certain contingency it ſhall only be a contract from *London* to "*Portſmouth*." That contingency not happening, reduced it in fact to a contract from *London* to *Portſmouth* only. The whole argument turned upon that diſtinction. Mr. *Yates*, who was counſel for the plaintiff, put it ſtrongly upon that head; and all the judges in delivering their opinions, lay the ſtreſs upon the contract compriſing two diſtinct conditions, and conſidering the voyage as being in fact two voyages: and it was the equitable way of conſidering it; for, though it was at firſt conſolidated by the parties, there was a defeazance afterwards, though not in words. I think Mr. Juſtice *Wilmot* put it particularly upon that ground; but it was the opinion of the whole court. There was an uſage alſo found by the jury in that caſe, that it was cuſtomary to return a proportionable part of the premium in ſuch like caſes, but they could not ſay *what* part. The court rejected this as a uſage for *uncertainty*; but they argued from it, that there being ſuch a cuſtom, plainly ſhewed the general ſenſe of merchants, as to the propriety of returning a part of the premium in ſuch caſes: and there can be no doubt of the reaſonableneſs of the thing. There has been an inſtance put of a policy where the meaſure is by time, which ſeems to me to be very ſtrong, and appoſite to the preſent caſe; and that is an inſurance upon a man's life for twelve months. There can be no doubt but the riſk there, is conſtituted by the meaſure of time, and depends entirely upon it: for the underwriter would demand double the premium for *two* years, that he would take to inſure the ſame life for *one* year only: in ſuch policies there is a general exception againſt ſuicide. If the perſon puts an end to his own life the next day, or a month after, or at any other period within the twelve months, there never was an idea in any man's breaſt, that part of the premium ſhould be returned. A caſe of general practice was put by Mr. *Dunning*, where the words of the policy are, "At and from, provided the ſhip ſhall ſail on or before the 1ſt of *Auguſt*:" and Mr. *Wallace* conſiders in that caſe, that the whole policy would depend upon the ſhip ſailing before the ſtated day. I do not think ſo. On the contrary, I think

Vide ſupra.

with

with Mr. *Dunning*, that cannot be. A loss in port *before* the day appointed for the ship's departure, can never be coupled with a contingency after the day: but if a question were to arise about it, as at present advised, I should incline to be of opinion, that it would fall within the reasoning of the determination of *Stevenson* v. *Snow*: and that there were two parts, or contracts of insurance with distinct conditions. The first is, I insure the ship in port, provided she is lost in port, before the 1st of *August*: and 2dly, if she be not lost in port, I insure her then during her voyage, from the 1st of *August* till she reaches the port specified in the policy. The loss in port must happen, before the risk upon the voyage could commence: and *vice versâ*; the risk in port must cease the moment the risk upon the voyage began. Let us see then, what the agreement of the parties is in the present case. They might have insured from two months to two months, or in any less or greater proportion, if they had thought proper so to do: but the fact is, that they have made *no division of time at all*; but the contract entered into is one entire contract from the 19th of *August* 1776, to the 19th of *August* 1777; which is the same as if it had been expressly said by the insured, "If you the underwriter will insure me for "twelve months, I will give you an *entire* sum; but I will not "have any apportionment." The ship sails, and the underwriter runs the risk for *two* months. No part of the premium then shall be returned. I cannot say, if there had been a recapture before the expiration of the twelve months, that the policy would not have revived."

Mr. Justice *Aston*.—"This case depends upon the words of the policy: and I am of opinion, it is one entire contract at a certain gross sum of 9*l*. *per cent*. for a certain period of time, *viz*. twelve months; and that no division is to be implied. The determination in *Stevenson* v. *Snow* went expressly upon this consideration, that there were *two distinct voyages*, and no consideration received by the insured for the premium upon the second voyage: and there certainly was not; for there never was any point of time, when any risk was run from *Portsmouth*. In *Bond* v. *Nutt*, the losses insured against were distinct, and unconnected with each other. 1st. A loss of the ship in port, if any should happen there. 2dly. A loss in the passage home, provided she sailed on a certain day. The risk in some policies may be distinct and divisible in

Vide ante, c. 18. p. 328.

in its nature. In the case of an insurance on a life, the sum is entire, and time is entire for the whole year. So in this case I think the contract is one entire contract: and therefore that there ought to be no return of premium."

Mr. Justice *Willes* and Mr. Justice *Ashhurst* were of the same opinion.

Per Curiam. Let a nonsuit be entered.

In a subsequent case, the Court of King's Bench adopted the same rule of decision, where the ship was insured for 12 months, and the risk ceased at the end of two. A distinction was attempted to be made, because in this case, the whole premium 18*l.* was acknowledged to be received from the insured *at the rate of* 15 *shillings per month*: and this, it was insisted, evidently shewed the parties intended the risk to continue only from month to month. This objection was, however, over-ruled; the court being of opinion, that the case last reported decided this; and that the 15*s.* per month was only a mode of computing the gross sum. The case was in substance as follows;

It was an action tried before Lord *Loughborough*, at the assizes for the county of *Northumberland*, in which the plaintiff declared,—That the defendant, in consideration that the plaintiff at his request, had underwritten several policies of insurance as to certain sums of money therein subscribed against his name, on the ships, merchandizes, and other things therein respectively specified, without receiving the full premiums therein mentioned, undertook and promised to pay the plaintiff so much money, as the premiums therein mentioned to be paid to him amounted to, with an averment that they amounted to 40*l.* There was another count for 40*l.* for money had and received by the defendant to the plaintiff's use. The defendant pleaded non assumpsit as to all except the sum of 3*l.* upon which plea issue was joined; and as to the 3*l.* he pleaded a tender, and paid that sum into court. Upon the plea of tender, issue was also joined. The jury found a verdict for the defendant upon the tender, and for the plaintiff upon the other issue, for the sum of 15*l.* subject to the opinion of the court, whether he was entitled

Loraine v. Thomlinson, Dougl. 564.

to

CHAP. XIX. to recover that ſum of 15*l.* or the ſum of 3*l.* only, upon a caſe, which ſtated, in effect, as follows: The plaintiff had underwritten 200*l.* on a policy effected at *Newcaſtle* (which was ſet forth *verbatim* in the caſe) whereby the ſhip the *Chollerford* was inſured, againſt capture by the enemy for *twelve months*, in the coaſting trade between *Leith* and the *Iſle of Wight*; beginning the 13th of *March* 1779, and ending the 13th of the ſame month, 1780. In the body of the policy it was ſtated, "That the aſſurers confeſſed themſelves paid "the conſideration due unto them by the aſſured, *at and after* "*the rate of* 15*s. per cent. per month*. At the bottom oppoſite "to the plaintiff's ſubſcription, was written, premium re-"ceived 16th of *March* 1779;" and on the back was endorſed, "*Newcaſtle* 15th of *March* 1779, Mr. *John Gaul Tomlinſon*, on his ſhip the *Chollerford*, himſelf maſter, *for twelve* "*months*, in the coaſting trade, at and between *Leith* and the "*Iſle of Wight*, beginning the 13th of *March* 1779, and end-"ing the 12th of *March* 1780. Enemy only. *At* 15*s. per* "*cent. per month*, 18*l.*" The premium was not paid, though expreſſed in the policy to have been paid, it being the uſage in *Newcaſtle* not to pay the premium at the time of making the inſurance; but at various times after the policies are effected, and ſometimes, not till twelve months after. The ſhip was loſt in a ſtorm, within the firſt two of the twelve months for which the inſurance was made, and the defendant tendered to the plaintiff 3*l.* as the premium for two months. The caſe then ſtates contradictory evidence given by witneſſes on both ſides, as to what had been done at *Newcaſtle* in ſimilar caſes; but which I forbear to ſet down; becauſe the Court of King's Bench was afterwards of opinion, that it ought not to have been received.

After the counſel for the defendant had been heard, the plaintiff's counſel was prevented by the court from proceeding.

Lord *Mansfield*.—"This is a mere queſtion of conſtruction, on the face of the inſtrument, and therefore parole evidence ſhould not have been admitted to explain it. It is an inſurance for twelve months, for one groſs ſum of 18*l.* They have calculated this ſum to be at the rate of 15*s.* per month. But what was to be paid down? Not 15*s.* for the firſt month, and ſo from month to month; but 18*l.* at once. Two caſes have

have been mentioned. *Stevenson* v. *Snow* was decided on the ground of there *being two voyages*. *Tyrie* v. *Fletcher* is directly in point against the defendant. There are two principles in these cases; 1st. If the risk has never begun, the whole premium is to be returned, because there was no consideration: 2d. When the risk has begun, there shall never be a return, although the ship should be taken in 24 hours."

Mr. Justice *Ashhurst*.—"The 15*s*. per month is only a mode of computing the gross sum."

Mr. Justice *Willes*, and Mr. Justice *Buller* concurring in opinion, the *postea* was delivered to the plaintiff.

The two last cases were insurances upon time; but from the principles laid down in them, and in the former case of *Stevenson* v. *Snow*, it seems perfectly clear, that when the contract is entire, whether it be for a specified time, *or for a voyage*, there shall be no apportionment or return, if the risk has once commenced. And therefore where the premium is entire in a policy on a voyage, where there is no contingency at any period, out or home, upon the happening or not happening of which, the risk is to end, nor any usage established upon such voyages; although there be several distinct ports, at which the ship is to stop, yet the voyage is one, and no part of the premium shall be recoverable.

A rule had been obtained to shew cause why there should not be a new trial in a case, which had come on before Lord *Mansfield* at *Guildhall*, when the jury found a verdict for the defendant. The case was this: It was an action on a policy of insurance, on the *French* ship *Le Pactole*, and her cargo, and the voyage was described in the policy in the following words: "At and from *Honfleur to the coast of Angola, during* "*her stay and trade there, at and from thence to her port or ports* "*of discharge in St. Domingo, and at and from St. Domingo* "*back to Honfleur*." The clause respecting the premium was as follows: "Slaves valued at 800 *livres Tournois per* head; "the ship at 1450*l*. sterling; other goods, &c. as interest "may appear; *at a premium of* 11 *per cent*." The ship sailed to *Angola*, and from thence, after staying some time there, to the *West Indies*. On her way to *Angola*, she put in at *Cayenne*, on the coast of *America*, and from *Cayenne* went

Bermon v. Woodbridge, Dougl. 751.

went to *Martinico*, confeſſedly out of the way to *St. Domingo*. In this cauſe, the firſt queſtion was a queſtion of fact, not material to our preſent inquiry, viz. whether the courſe taken was a deviation, or not, from the voyage inſured. After all the evidence had been heard, the jury thought it was, and accordingly found a verdict for the defendant. Upon their declaring this opinion, the counſel for the plaintiff inſiſted, that as there was a count in the declaration for money had and received, the voyage inſured ought to be conſidered as compoſed of three diſtinct parts or voyages; namely, from *Honfleur* to *Angola*; 2dly, from *Angola* to *St. Domingo*; and 3dly, from *St. Domingo* to *Honfleur*; and that, as the voyage from *St. Domingo* to *Honfleur* had never commenced, the premium ought to be apportioned, and a return made of that part which was paid to inſure the riſk from *St. Domingo* to *Honfleur*. Lord *Mansfield* took the opinion of the jury upon that point alſo; and they were clear there ought to be no return. Next day, however, his Lordſhip ſaid, he had turned that queſtion in his mind, and that he entertained ſome doubts upon it, and as it was a queſtion of law, deſired Mr. *Lee* to move for a new trial on that ground. It was, however, afterwards moved on both grounds; namely, on the queſtion of fact, whether the deviation was wilful: and 2dly, on the queſtion of law, whether, ſuppoſing it wilful, there ought to be a return of premium.—Theſe queſtions were fully diſcuſſed by three advocates on each ſide; and the court alſo took time to deliberate upon them: after which the Lord Chief Juſtice delivered the unanimous opinion of the whole court.

Lord *Mansfield*, after ſtating that, upon the queſtion of fact, they were perfectly ſatisfied with the verdict of the jury, proceeded thus: "If, however, the plaintiff ſhould ſucceed on the ſecond point, the determination would virtually allow him a new trial on the whole of the cauſe, becauſe no ſpecial caſe was reſerved. But, on the fulleſt conſideration, and after looking into all the caſes, (though my opinion has fluctuated) we are now all clearly of opinion, that there ought not to be any return. The queſtion depends upon this: Whether the policy contains one entire riſk on one voyage, or whether it is to be ſplit into ſix different riſks; for, by ſplitting the words, and taking "at" and "from" ſeparately,

separately, it will make six, viz. 1st, *At Honfleur*; 2d, *From Honfleur to Angola*; 3d, *At Angola*, &c. The principles are clear. Where the risk has never begun, there must be a return of premium; and if the voyages, in this case, are distinct, the risk from *St. Domingo* to *Honfleur* never began. On the other hand, if the risk has once begun, you cannot sever it, and apportion the premium. In an insurance upon a life, with the common exceptions of suicide, and the hands of justice, if the party commit suicide, or is executed in twenty-four hours, there shall be no return. The case is the same, if a voyage insured is once begun. Is this one entire risk? The insured and insurers consider the premium as an entire sum for the whole, without division: it is estimated on the whole at 11 *l. per cent.* And, which is extremely material, there is no where any contingency, at any period, out or home, mentioned in the policy, which happening, or not happening, is to put an end to the insurance. The argument must be, that, if the ship had been taken between *Honfleur* and *Angola*, there must have been a return. By an implied warranty every ship must be sea worthy when she first sails on the voyage insured, but she need not continue so throughout the voyage; so that, if this is one entire voyage, if the ship was sea worthy when she left *Honfleur*, the underwriters would have been liable, though she had not been so at *Angola*, &c.; but according to the construction contended for on behalf of the plaintiff, she must have been sea worthy, not only at her departure from *Honfleur*, but also when she sailed from *Angola*, and when she sailed from *St. Domingo*. The cases of *Stevenson* v. *Snow* and *Bond* v. *Nutt*, were quite different from this. They depended upon this, that there was a contingency specified in the policy, upon the not happening of which the insurance would cease. In *Stevenson* v. *Snow*, it depended on the contingency of the ship sailing with convoy from *Portsmouth*, whether there should be an insurance from that place. This necessarily divided the risk, and made two voyages. In *Bond* v. *Nutt*, it was held, that there were two risks, upon the same principle. "*At Jamaica*" was one; the other, viz. the risk "*from Jamaica*," depended on the contingency of the ship having sailed *on or before the first of August*: *that* was a condition precedent to the insurance on the voyage from *Jamaica* to *London*. The two cases of *Tyrie* v. *Fletcher*, and *Loraine* v. *Thomlinson*, are very strong, for if you

Vide ante, Ch. 12.

CHAP. XIX. you could apportion the premium in any case, it would be in insurances upon time. Therefore, on very full consideration, we think this one entire risk, one voyage, and that there can be no return of premium." The rule was discharged.

Meyer v. Gregson, B. R. East. 24 Geo. III.

Accordingly in another action for return of premium, tried before Mr. Justice *Willes*, on the Northern circuit, where a verdict had been given for the plaintiff, upon a motion to set aside the verdict, and to enter a nonsuit, a decision, similar to that of *Bermon* v. *Woodbridge*, was made. The insurance was "*At and from Jamaica to Liverpool, warranted to sail on or before the first of August, premium twenty guineas per cent. to return eight, if she sailed with convoy.*" The ship did not sail till *September*, and was lost. The jury apportioned the premium, and gave the plaintiff a verdict for eight guineas, the defendant having paid eight for the convoy into court, which was allowing four for the risk run by the defendant *at Jamaica*.

Lord *Mansfield*.—"It would be endless to go into inquiries about the risk at *Jamaica*. It appears on the evidence to be different on different sides of the island. Besides, the parties have divided the risk, with respect to convoy; for it is a premium of twenty guineas, to return eight if she sail with convoy: but there is an absolute warranty as to the sailing, and nothing said of the premium."

Mr. Justice *Willes* thought the premium should be apportioned.

Mr. Justice *Ashhurst* and Mr. Justice *Buller* agreed with Lord *Mansfield*, the latter observing, that as the parties have not considered it as two risks, nor estimated the risk at *Jamaica*, the court cannot do it for them. In all the insurances from *Jamaica*, the policy runs "at and from;" and though in many instances the voyage has not begun, yet there never was an idea of the premium being returned, and that no usage was found by the jury. The rule for entering the judgment of nonsuit was made absolute.

Vide supra.

I am aware that the decision in this case may seem to clash with what fell from Lord *Mansfield*, in delivering his opinion

in

in the case of *Tyrie* v. *Fletcher*; in which he put a supposed case of an insurance "at and from, *provided* the ship shall sail on or before the first of *August*." In such a case, his Lordship observed, *as then advised*, he should incline to think it a divisible risk. In this place, it would be sufficient to observe, in answer to such an objection, that the opinion then delivered by Lord *Mansfield*, was a mere *obiter dictum* upon a point, arising only in the course of argument; in which case, the greatest abilities are liable to mistake. But his Lordship delivered that opinion, with a wise and prudent reservation, that, *as at present advised*, he thought so and so; and it is no disgrace to any man, however renowned for knowledge, to alter an opinion, upon mature deliberation. There is, however, one very obvious distinction, upon which the court relied much, between *Meyer* v. *Gregson*, and the case put in *Tyrie* v. *Fletcher*: for in the latter, the insured has used a most significant word (*provided*) to mark the difference between the two parts of the risk; "*at and from*, "*provided she sail, &c.*" In the former, the insured as expressly provided for a return of premium, in case the ship sails with convoy; why did he not use the same precaution, lest she should not sail by the day limited? Having done it in the one case, it is to be presumed he did not mean to do it, or that the insurer would not consent that it should be done in the other: and as the parties had not divided the risk themselves, the court could not do it for them.

In another case upon an insurance "at and from any port "or ports in *Jamaica* to *London*, following and commencing "on her first arrival there, warranted to sail with convoy from "the place of rendezvous to *Great Britain*," the same questions were again agitated. But as the counsel differed upon the evidence given at the trial, the main question was not fully discussed by the court, but was sent back to a new trial. Gale v. Machell, B. R. East, 25 Geo. III.

The last case upon this subject, was also an action for a return of the premium. The policy was "at and from *Jamaica* to *London*, warranted to depart with convoy for the voyage, and to sail on or before the first of *August*, upon goods on board a ship called the *Jamaica*, at a premium of 12 guineas *per cent*." The ship sailed from *Jamaica* to *London*, on the 31st of *July* 1782, but without any convoy for the voyage. At the trial before Lord *Mansfield*, the jury found Long v. Allen, B. R. East. Term, 25 Geo. III.

CHAP. XIX. found a verdict for the plaintiff, subject to the opinion of the court upon a case, stating the facts already mentioned. In addition to which, they *expressly* find, "that it is the constant "and invariable usage in an insurance, at and from *Jamaica* "to *London*, warranted to depart with convoy, or to sail on "or before the first of *August*, when the ship does not de- "part with convoy, or sails after the first of *August*, to re- "turn the premium, deducting one half *per cent*."

Lord *Mansfield*.—"An insurance being on goods warranted to depart with convoy, the ship sails without convoy; and an action is brought to recover the premium. The law is clear, that if the risk be commenced, there shall be no return. Hence questions arise of distinct risks insured by one policy or instrument. My opinion has been to divide the risks. I am aware that there are great difficulties in the way of apportionments, and therefore the court has sometimes leaned against them. But where an express usage is found by the jury, the difficulty is cured. They offered to prove the same usage as to the *West Indies* in general; but I stopt them, and confined the evidence to *Jamaica*."

Vide Meyer v. Gregson.

Mr. Justice *Willes*, and Mr. Justice *Ashhurst*, concurred with his Lordship.

Mr. Justice *Buller*.—"The counsel for the defendant did right in his argument to make the chief question, Whether parole evidence of this usage ought to have been received. In mercantile cases from Lord *Holt*'s time, and in policies of insurance in particular, a great latitude of construction as to usage has been admitted. By usage, places come within the policy, which are not expressed in words; usage explains and even controls the policy. The usage here found by the jury is universal; and though in some cases one half *per cent*. may be a small premium for the risk *at*; yet the underwriters are aware that it is so. In *Meyer* v. *Gregson*, no usage was found. Besides in cases of this kind, where every thing is left to the whim and caprice of a jury, I lean much against them. Here a general and certain usage is found; and no inconvenience can result from it." The *postea* was delivered to the plaintiff.

From the tenor of all these cases it should seem, as my Lord *Mansfield* said in the case of *Long* v. *Allen*, that so many

many difficulties occur in apportioning the premium, that the courts are often obliged to decide againſt it, unleſs there be ſome uſage upon the ſubject. Even in the caſe of *Stevenſon* v. *Snow*, the jury found that it had been uſual to divide the riſk; and although the court rejected the uſage for uncertainty, becauſe it did not aſcertain what proportion of the premium ſhould be returned; yet they expreſsly ſay, that it ſerves to ſhew what the idea of the mercantile world is upon the ſubject. If, indeed, we look back to all the caſes reported in this chapter, we never find an apportionment take place, except in *Stevenſon* v. *Snow* and *Long* v. *Allen*, on account of the difficulty, unleſs there be ſome uſage, as in thoſe caſes, to guide and direct the judgment of the court.

Before this chapter is concluded, it will be proper to obſerve, that in the caſe of *Bond* v. *Nutt*, which was ſo often mentioned in the argument of the caſes upon apportionment, the queſtion never aroſe. In that caſe, the two material queſtions were, as may be ſeen by a reference to it in the two preceding chapters in this work, whether the ſhip had complied with a warranty of ſailing by a particular day: and whether in going to the place of rendezvous for convoy, ſhe was guilty of a wilful deviation. It was proper to mention this, to prevent miſconſtruction; and it was alſo taken notice of by Mr. Juſtice *Buller*, in the caſe of *Long* v. *Allen*. Vide ante, c. 18.

CHAPTER THE TWENTIETH.

Of the Proceedings upon Policies of Insurance.

CHAP. XX.

Vide the Introduction.

IN the present chapter, it is intended to point out in what manner, and by what form of legal proceeding, a man, who has insured property, and has sustained a loss, is to recover against the underwriters upon the policy. We have formerly seen, that the Court of Policies of Insurance fell into disuse, and the reasons why it did so: since which period all questions of this nature have been decided by the usual mode of trial, known to the laws and constitution of this country, namely, the trial by jury in the courts of common law. Cases of this nature are not the subject of inquiry even in a Court of Equity, because the demand is plainly a demand at law; and the loss and damage sustained are as much the object of proof by witnesses, as any other species of damage whatever. This was decided by a decree of Lord Chancellor *King*, whose opinion was afterwards confirmed by the House of Lords.

De Ghetoff and others v. the Governor and Company of the London Assurance. 3 Brown's Parliament Cases, 525.

In the year 1720, some merchants at *Ostend* set up a trade to the *East Indies*; and amongst others, one *James Maelcamp* equipped a ship, called the *Flandria*, for a voyage to *China*, wherein several persons were concerned. *Maelcamp* had the care and direction of the ship, and gave receipts to the several persons concerned, for the monies they paid, promising to be accountable to them for their respective proportions of the net profit of the voyage. These transactions being carried on mostly at *Ostend* or *Antwerp*, the several persons who had a mind to be concerned in the undertaking, gave directions to their correspondents at those places, to pay *Maelcamp* what sums they thought fit, and to take his receipts for the same. The appellants gave directions to one *Conninck* to pay several large sums to *Maelcamp*, on account of the said undertaking; and accordingly *Conninck* paid him divers sums, amounting to 35,000 guilders, and took distinct receipts for the same, according to the proportion for which the appellants were

were concerned therein: he also, by the order and direction of the appellants, and for their use or benefit, agreed with the respondents to insure on the said ship the *Flandria* 5000*l.* and by a policy, dated the 26th day of *December* 1720, this insurance was effected, at a premium of 12*l. per cent.* The ship sailed from *Ostend*, in order to proceed to *China*; but on her way was seized at *Bencoolen*, in the *East Indies*, by the governor, being an *English* settlement; and the ship and cargo were confiscated. The appellants, upon notice of this event, applied to the respondents for payment of the 5000*l.* insured; and produced to them the several receipts for their respective interests in the ship, and affidavits affirming the several sums therein mentioned, to have been really and *bonâ fide* paid. But the respondents refusing to pay, or make any satisfaction to the appellants, *they brought their bill in the Court of Chancery* against the respondents, and the said *Conninck*, praying, *that the respondents might be decreed to pay the appellants the said sum of* 5000*l. with interest*, according to their several and respective shares and proportions thereof. To this bill, the respondents put in a demurrer and answer, and to such part of the bill, as sought to compel them to pay the appellants the 5000*l.* or to make them any satisfaction for any loss, which had happened to the ship, they demurred; and for cause of demurrer shewed, that if the policy of insurance in the bill mentioned was forfeited, *a proper action at law lay to recover the money due thereupon*; and that the appellants, if they were entitled to such relief as they prayed by their bill, might have their complete and adequate remedy by an action at law, where such matters were properly cognizable, and where the appellants ought to prove their interest in, and the loss of the ship. The demurrer came on to be argued before Lord Chancellor *King*, when his lordship ordered it to stand over for two months till *Conninck*'s answer should come in; and if the appellants did not procure such answer in two months, the demurrer was to be allowed. *Conninck* accordingly put in his answer within two months, and thereby admitted, that he made the assurance in his own name, in trust and for the benefit of the appellants; but said, "*he did not care to permit the appellants to bring any action against the respondents in his name*; he being advised, that if any such action should be brought, and they should

CHAP. XX. ſhould not prevail therein, he would be perſonally liable to pay all the coſts and charges occaſioned in conſequence thereof. In ſupport of the demurrer it was urged, that the appellants' demand was plainly a demand at law, as they had nothing to prove but their intereſt, and the loſs of the ſhip, which were facts proper to be tried by a jury. That there was no equity ſuggeſted by the bill, but a pretended difficulty to produce witneſſes: and that their truſtee refuſed to permit them to bring an action in his name: that the former objection might with equal reaſon be ſuggeſted in almoſt every caſe of a policy of inſurance; and the latter appeared manifeſtly to be thrown into the bill merely to change the juriſdiction, and it was in a great meaſure falſified by the truſtee's anſwer, for he did not ſay that he ever refuſed, but only that *he did not care to permit his name to be made uſe of.* If bills of this kind were encouraged, it would be eaſy to bring all ſorts of property to be tried in a Court of Equity.

Upon theſe reaſons, Lord *King* allowed the demurrer; and upon an appeal to the Houſe of Lords, after hearing counſel upon it, it was ordered and adjudged, that the ſame ſhould be diſmiſſed; and the order complained of, affirmed.

There may, it is true, be caſes, where an application to a Court of Equity on the part of the inſured, is ſtrictly proper, and will be entertained. For inſtance, if the truſtee in a policy of inſurance do actually refuſe his name to the *ceſtui que truſt* in an action at law, there may be ſome pretence for going into a Court of Equity, as Lord *Hardwicke* has once obſerved. Or, if from a concurrence of circumſtances, the perſons, whoſe teſtimony is requiſite to the deciſion of ſome diſputed facts, reſide abroad, the Court of Chancery will grant a commiſſion to examine thoſe witneſſes. But it is not upon a mere general truſt, or the looſe ſuggeſtions of any of theſe facts, that this extraordinary interpoſition will take place.

1 Atk. 547. 2 Atk. 359.

There are alſo caſes in which the inſurers may go into equity to obtain injunctions to ſtay the proceedings againſt them at law: as in the laſt caſe mentioned, where the evidence of perſons abroad is requiſite for their defence; in which

Chitty v. Selwin and Martin. 2 Atk. 359.

which situation, they shall have a commission to examine witnesses abroad, and an injunction to stay proceedings at law in the mean time. Another ground for an application to a Court of Equity, is a suspicion of fraud on the part of the insured, and of which I fear the chapter on fraud produces too many instances: in such cases the court will compel the party charged to make a full disclosure upon oath of all the circumstances that are within his knowledge; and to deliver up all papers and documents that are at all material to the question. But except in these instances, all issues upon policies of insurance, must be tried in the courts of common law. Even if the parties, by a clause in the policy, agree that in case of a dispute, it shall be referred to arbitration, that will not be a sufficient bar to an action at law; provided no reference has been in fact made, nor is depending.

Vide c. 10.

Thus in an action upon a policy of insurance it appeared, that a clause was inserted, that in a case of any loss or dispute about the policy, it should be referred to arbitration: and the plaintiff averred in his declaration, that there had been no reference. Upon the trial at *Guildhall*, the point was reserved for the consideration of the court, whether this action would lie before a reference had been made; and it was held by the whole court, that if there had been a reference depending, or made and determined, it might have been a bar; but the agreement of the parties cannot oust this court; and as no reference has been, nor any is depending, the action is well brought, and the plaintiff must have judgment.

Kill v. Hollister. 1 Wils. 129.

Having thus seen in what courts the party injured in the contract of insurance is to seek for redress, let us now consider, by what form of action that redress is to be obtained. The act of parliament, by which the two Insurance Companies were erected, ordered, that they should have a common seal, by affixing which, all corporate bodies ratify and confirm their contracts. Hence a policy of insurance made by the *Royal Exchange* Assurance Company, or the *London* Assurance Company, is a contract under seal; and if the contract is broken, the proceedings against these Companies, must be by action of debt or covenant. From this circumstance a great inconvenience arose, for under the plea of the general issue to an action of debt or covenant, the true merits

6 Geo. I. c. 18.

CHAP. XX. of the cafe could feldom come in queftion: but in order to bring them forward, it became neceffary to plead fpecially. This was attended with fuch a heavy expenfe, fuch great delays, and frequent applications to Courts of Equity for relief, that the legiflature at laft interpofed, and enacted, "that

11 Geo. I. c. 30. f. 43. "*in all actions of debt*, to be fued or commenced againft either "of the faid corporations, upon any policies of infurance under the common feal of fuch corporations, for the affuring "of any fhip or fhips, goods or merchandizes, at fea, or going "to fea, it fhould and might be lawful to and for the faid corporations, in fuch action or fuit, to *plead generally that they* "*owed nothing* to the plaintiff or plaintiffs in fuch fuit or action; and that *in all actions of covenant*, which fhould be fued "or commenced againft either of the faid corporations upon "any fuch policy of affurance under the common feal of fuch "corporation for the affuring of any fhip or fhips, goods or "merchandizes, at fea or going to fea, it fhould and might be "lawful for the faid refpective corporations, in fuch action or "fuit, to plead generally, *that they had not broke the covenants* "in fuch policy contained, or any of them; and if thereupon "iffue fhould be joined, it fhould and might be lawful for the "jury, if they fhould fee caufe, upon the trial of fuch iffue, "to find a verdict for the plaintiff or plaintiffs in fuch fuit or "action, and to give fo much, or fuch part only of the fum "demanded, if it be an action of debt, or fo much in damages, if it be an action of covenant, as it fhould appear to "them, upon the evidence given upon fuch trial, fuch plaintiff or plaintiffs ought in juftice to have."

36 Geo. III. c. 26. In a fubfequent act of parliament the following claufe is inferted, "that if any action or fuit fhall be commenced, "brought, or profecuted againft the corporation of the *Royal* "*Exchange* affurance of houfes and goods from fire, by any "perfon or perfons, bodies politic or corporate, for or concerning any affurance or affurances by the faid recited "charter, or hereby authorized to be made, or relating to "the powers hereby granted, or concerning any other matter or thing herein or in the faid charter above recited "contained, the faid corporation and their fucceffors may in "fuch action or fuit plead the general iffue, and give the "fpecial matter in evidence."

The

The charter recited in the act is that, which enabled the company to make infurances for lives and againft fire; and therefore it fhould feem (a fimilar act having paffed refpecting the *London* Affurance Company) that in infurances on lives, and infurances againft fire, they may both plead the general iffue, as they might by virtue of the ftatute 11 Geo. I. in cafes of marine infurances. Thus it ftands with refpect to the corporations.

Wherever the contract of infurance is entered into with a private underwriter, it is done by the infurer merely fubfcribing his name to the inftrument, which is no more than what is called by the lawyers a fimple contract; the remedy for a breach of which is by an action of *affumpfit*, or an action upon the cafe founded upon the *promife* and undertaking of the infurer. There are, however, it is to be obferved, two kinds of actions of *affumpfit*: the one, what is denominated a general *indebitatus affumpfit*, in which the plaintiff ftates generally that the defendant, *being indebted* to him in fo much money for goods fold, &c. or for money lent to the defendant, or for money had and received to the ufe of the plaintiff, in confideration thereof, *undertook and promifed* to pay the amount; the other is called a *fpecial affumpfit*, which muft always be founded on fome particular or fpecial agreement. The former can never be ufed as the means to recover upon a policy of infurance. The only cafes, in which it can be at all ufed with refpect to this contract are, where money has been paid by miftake to the infured by the infurer, upon the fuppofition of a lofs, when in fact there was none; a rule which holds, whether the money was paid through the fraud or miftake of the receiver: or where the infured wifhes to recover back the premium which he has paid to the infurer. In thefe cafes, the proper mode is to bring an action of *indebitatus affumpfit* for money had and received to the plaintiff's ufe: and therefore in almoft all actions upon policies of infurance, it is ufual after the count for the fpecial *affumpfit*, to add one or two general counts; that if the policy fhould be fet afide, and the contract declared void, the infured may at leaft be enabled to recover the premium.

3 Blackft. Com. 157.

[398]

1 Salk. 22. Skinner 412.

It being thus evident, that the proper form of action, in order to recover upon a policy of infurance, is a fpecial *affumpfit*,

founded

CHAP. XX.

founded upon the exprefs contract of the perfon who figns it; it will follow as an immediate confequence, that the firft thing which is neceffary for the plaintiff to infert in his declaration, or ftate of the cafe, will be the policy itfelf, becaufe that is the foundation of the whole. He fhould alfo ftate, that it was figned by the defendant. The next averment will be, that in confideration of the premium being paid, the defendant had undertaken to indemnify againft the loffes fpecified in the policy. We faw in the firft chapter of this book, that the premium was the confideration upon which the whole contract refted; and that by the cuftom, the receipt of the premium was acknowledged in the body of the policy. It is then neceffary for the plaintiff to allege that goods and merchandizes were laden on board to the amount of the fum infured, and that the plaintiff was interefted therein; or if the infurance be upon the fhip, the infured's intereft muft, in the fame manner be averred. The next material averment is, that the property infured was loft, and by what means that lofs happened; in ftating which, the plaintiff muft bring it within one of the perils infured againft by the policy: but he muft always ftate it according to the truth. Thus he ought to fhew, that it was by perils of the fea, by capture, by fire, by detention, by barratry, or any of the other perils mentioned in the policy.

Vide ante, c. 1. p. 26.

[399]

Knight v. Cambridge. 2 Lord Raym. 1349. 1 Stra. 581.

Where the lofs had been by *barratry*, the breach was thus affigned, the proceedings being at that time in *Latin*, *per fraudem et negligentiam magiftri navis depreffa et fubmerfa fuit, et totaliter perdita et amiffa fuit;* and it was infifted, that this was not within the meaning of the word *barratry*, but the breach fhould have been exprefs, that the fhip was loft by the *barratry* of the mafter.

The court were unanimoufly of opinion, that there was no occafion to aver the fact in the very words of the policy; but if the fact alleged came within the meaning of the words in the policy, it was fufficient. Barratry imports fraud, and he that commits fraud, may properly be faid to be guilty of a neglect, namely, a breach of duty.

It is true that the practice at prefent, as I have reafon to believe from precedents which I have feen fettled by the ableft fpecial ſpécial pleaders, is to aver ſuch a loſs to have happened "by "the barratry of the maſter or mariners."

If the plaintiff in his declaration allege, that a total loſs has happened, and lay the damages as for a total loſs, it ſhall be no bar to his recovery, though he can only prove a partial loſs; for in an action for damages merely, a man may always recover *leſs*, but never *more* than the ſum he has laid in his declaration. A contrary doctrine was once attempted to be maintained; but was unanimouſly over-ruled.

Gardiner v. Croſedale. 2 Burr. 904. 1 Black. Rep. 198.

The caſe in which it was ſo determined, came before the court upon a queſtion reſerved by Lord *Mansfield* at *Niſi Prius* at *Guildhall*, upon an action on the caſe, on a policy of inſurance. The inſurance was made upon one fourth part of the ſhip *Encouragement*, and of its cargo, from *Greenland* to *London*, free from average under a certain value, from the ice. [400] The plaintiff *declared upon a total loſs* of the ſhip; the declaration expreſsly ſtated a *total loſs* of it; and the *damages* were laid for a *total loſs*. But the evidence only proved an *average or partial loſs*: it was not attempted to prove a total one; and it was only ſhewn that the ſhip had received *ſome* damage, which little more than 50*l.* would have repaired. The defendant's counſel objected at the trial, "that this evidence did not ſupport the plaintiff's declaration." They alſo repreſented the practice to have been on their ſide; namely, that proof of a partial loſs was not ſufficient to maintain a declaration for a total loſs. A verdict was taken for 20*l.* as for an average loſs: but it was agreed on both ſides that the verdict ſhould be ſubject to the opinion of the court, "Whether it was maintainable in point of law." If the court ſhould be of opinion that it was, the verdict was to ſtand; but if the court ſhould be of a contrary opinion, the plaintiff was to have a judgment of nonſuit againſt him.

Lord *Mansfield*.—"At the trial it appeared to me, and ſo the jury thought, that the preſent caſe could *not* be conſidered as a *total* loſs. The defendant's counſel objected, as they do now, that the jury could not take a partial loſs into their conſideration, upon an expreſs declaration for a total loſs: and I underſtood from them, that the practice ſupported their objection. Mr. *Norton*, who was counſel for the plaintiff at the

CHAP. XX. the trial, then argued to the contrary upon principles: and he alfo cited the cafe of *Walker* v. the *Royal Exchange Affurance Company*. But that cafe does not prove much; for that was a total lofs. I was fatisfied upon the principles, provided the practice did not interfere with them, which I was then told it did. I chofe to put it in fuch a fhape, that the opinion of the court might be had without delay or expenfe. No hardfhip was done to the defendant upon the *quantum* of the damages found: for the plaintiff took a great deal *lefs* than it clearly appeared on the evidence that the lofs amounted to. I cannot hear of any fuch determination as can fupport the objection that has been made by the defendant's counfel. Therefore it ftands fingly upon principles. And upon principles it is extremely clear, that the plaintiff may, upon this declaration, recover damages for a *partial* lofs. This is an action upon the cafe, which is a liberal action; [401] and a plaintiff may recover *lefs* than the grounds of his declaration fupport, though *not more*. This is agreeable to juftice, and confiftent with his demand. Here are two grounds of the plaintiff's declaration; namely, the policy, and the damage to the fhip. As to its being a total or a partial lofs, that is a queftion more applicable to the *quantum* of the damages, than to the ground of the action. The ground of the action is the fame, whether the lofs be partial or total: both are perils within the policy. As to the defendant's not coming prepared to defend a partial lofs; this indeed would be an objection if it were true. But the defendant does in truth come prepared to fhew, that either no damages had happened at all; or, at leaft, that damages have not happened to fuch a degree as the plaintiff has alleged in his declaration; or, that he did not fign the policy. As to the effects of a judgment by default, the defendant could not have been hurt by a judgment by default. For the plaintiff could not have recovered, even upon a writ of inquiry, any greater damages than he could prove to the jury fworn to affefs them, that he had actually fuffered. If the prefent objection were to prevail, it would introduce the addition of unneceffary counts in declarations, and an enormous fwelling of the records of the court. It is more convenient to lay the cafe fhort, than prolix. There is no proof of any practice contrary to the principles. It was the apprehenfion of fuch contrary practice, that was the only occafion of my having any doubt at the

the trial. I am now fully ſatisfied, that the plaintiff may recover either the *whole* or *leſs* than he has laid; and therefore this verdict ought, in my opinion, to ſtand. In an ejectment for more, the plaintiff may recover leſs: it is every day's practice."

Mr. Juſtice *Deniſon* concurred, and thought it a very plain caſe. It is an action for *damages* for the loſs of the ſhip. Now, in an action for damages, the plaintiff is to recover his damages according to his proof, *pro tanto*; but he is not, in an action for damages, obliged to prove all that he has alleged. If it had been an action of covenant for pulling down a houſe, would not the plaintiff be entitled to recover damages for pulling down *half* the houſe, provided he had proved that the defendant did it? This is no variance of the evidence from the declaration; the evidence tends, in a certain degree, to the proof of what is alleged in the declaration; it is not neceſſary to lay two counts in ſuch a declaration as this.

Mr. Juſtice *Foſter* was of the ſame opinion. [402]

Mr. Juſtice *Wilmot*.—"In actions for damages, the plaintiff may recover all, or for any part: the damages are ſeverable, and may be given PRO TANTO. Here damages are laid for a *total* loſs, which is only the meaſure of the damages: and the plaintiff proves a *partial* loſs; which only affects the meaſure of the damages, but is no variance from the allegations contained in the declaration. If this had been a judgment by default, yet the plaintiff could not, even in that caſe, have recovered damages for *any more* loſs than he was able to prove under the writ of inquiry of damages. And as to the defendant's not having ſufficient notice that he ſhould come prepared to defend againſt a partial loſs, I think he had ſufficient notice to come thus prepared: for he ought to come prepared to prove, "that no damage at all hap-"pened." If *any* at all happened, he will be liable *pro tanto*, if it be proved."

The *poſtea* was delivered to the plaintiff.

An attempt was alſo once made to nonſuit a plaintiff, becauſe the declaration alleged that he had a ſmaller intereſt than he appeared in proof to have. But this attempt alſo failed.

It

CHAP. XX.

Page v. Rogers. Sitt. at Guildhall, Hil. Vac. 1785.

It was an action on a policy of insurance, in which the declaration stated, that the plaintiff was possessed of one third of the ship on which the insurance was made. It was proved that the plaintiff had purchased the whole ship at one period; and as there was no evidence to shew that he had since parted with any share of it, the counsel for the defendant insisted, that the plaintiff had not proved his declation, which alleged him to have but one third.

Lord *Mansfield* over-ruled the objection, saying, that this was *primâ facie* sufficient evidence; for *omne majus continet in se minus*. (*a*)

[403]

3 Black. Com. 168.

We have seen that policies of insurance are seldom effected by the party himself really interested, but generally by the intervention of a broker employed by the insured, who transacts the business with the underwriters as attorney for his principal, from whom he receives his instructions, and from which, if he deviate, he is answerable to his employer in an action on the case; like any other person who undertakes any office, employment, trust, or duty, and who thereby impliedly undertakes to perform it with integrity, diligence, and skill. It is also common for the broker to open the policy in his own name, at the same time declaring for whose use, benefit, or interest, the same is made; how far such declaration is necessary we have formerly explained. As the policy may be made in the name of the broker, so also may the action be brought in his name, as was done in the case of *Godin* and the *Royal Exchange Assurance Company*, and a variety of other cases.

25 Geo. 3. c. 44. Vide ante, c. 1, p. 16, and see also 28 Geo. 3. c. 56, ante, p. 18. 1 Burr. 490. Vide ante, c. 15.

As this contract depends so much upon the purest good faith, and the most liberal communication of circumstances, relative to each particular case; when gaming insurances, without interest, were abolished by the legislature, in order effectually to answer the purpose intended, it became necessary to order that a disclosure of all insurances, effected on the same property, should be made even after an action brought.

Thus

(*a*) But if the plaintiff in this case had the whole ship, it seems that he could never bring another action for the other two thirds; because that would be a splitting of actions.

Thus it was declared, "That in all actions or suits brought "or commenced by the assured, upon any policy of assurance, the plaintiff in such action, or suit, or his attorney "or agent, should, within fifteen days after he or they "should be required so to do in writing by the defendant, or "his attorney or agent, declare what sum or sums he had assured, or caused to be assured in the whole, and what sums "he had borrowed at respondentia or bottomry, for the "voyage in question in such suit or action." CHAP. XX. 19 Geo. 2. c. 37. s. 6.

In addition to this very wise provision, it having appeared to the legislature, that some vexatious persons, notwithstanding the perfect willingness of the insurers to pay losses, to which they were liable, still persevered in bringing actions, by which the defendants were put to great and heavy charges, and had no means of paying the money into court; it was therefore enacted, "That it should and might be lawful for any person or persons, body or bodies corporate, "sued in any action or actions of debt, covenant, or any "other action or actions, on any policy or policies of insurance, *to bring into court any sum or sums of money*; and that "if any such plaintiff or plaintiffs should refuse to accept "such sum or sums of money so brought into court as aforesaid, with costs to be taxed, in full discharge of such action or actions, and should afterwards proceed to trial in "such action or actions; and the jury should not assess "damages to such plaintiff or plaintiffs, exceeding the sum or "sums of money so brought into court, such plaintiff or plaintiffs in every such case and cases, shall pay to such defendant "or defendants, in every such action or actions, costs to be "taxed; any law, custom, or usage, to the contrary notwithstanding." 19 Geo. 2. c. 37. s. 7. [404]

These preliminary steps being taken, the defendant is to put in his plea to the charge or declaration of the plaintiff; which by the act of parliament, is prescribed to the Assurance Companies, when they are defendants; namely, that they owe nothing, if the action be debt: or if it be covenant, that they have not broken the covenants, which they had undertaken to keep. But in the case of a private insurer, as the action is merely an *assumpsit*; so the answer to it is, *non assumpsit*; that is, the defendant has not promised as the plaintiff Vide supra.

CHAP. XX.

plaintiff has alleged. Under this plea, the defendant will have a right to take advantage of all thofe circumftances, which, as we have feen, will either render the policy void, or make it of no effect: fuch as fraud, want of intereft, not being fea-worthy, deviation, non-performance of warranties, and all other grounds ftated in former chapters.

Iffue being thus joined between the parties, the next object for our confideration is the proof, which it will be neceffary for the plaintiff to produce, in order to fupport his cafe. This inquiry will be rendered very eafy, by reflecting upon thofe allegations, which, as we have before fhewn, it is incumbent upon the plaintiff to infert in his declaration. We have feen, that the policy muft be fet out in the declaration; and confequently the firft evidence to be given, is, that the defendant's hand-writing is fubfcribed to the policy. This, in the liberality of modern practice, is feldom required to be done; as the fubfcription is ufually admitted; but in [405] ftrictnefs, it may be infifted on: and in a work of this nature, it is my bufinefs to point out every thing which either party is expected, or compellable to perform. When the fignature is once proved, the court and jury are in poffeffion of the extent of the contract (except as it may be further extended by *ufage*,) the conditions to be performed on either fide; and all the other circumftances relative to the rifk infured. And, although in the courfe of our inquiries, we have feen frequent inftances, where the ufage and practice of a particular trade, control and extend the written words of a policy, yet in no cafe fhall evidence of any agreement be allowed, which directly tends to contradict the policy: for to fuffer them to be defeated by agreements by parole, not appearing, would be greatly to diminifh their credit, and to render them of no value.

Vide ante, c. 2.

Thus in an action upon a policy of infurance "*from Archangel to Leghorn*," the defendant faid, that the agreement before the fubfcription was, that the adventure fhould begin, *but from the Downs*; but this agreement was not put into writing. Lord Chief Juftice *Pemberton* faid, that policies were facred things; and that a merchant fhould no more be allowed to go from what he had fubfcribed in them, than he that fubfcribes a bill of exchange, payable at fuch a day, fhall be allowed to go from it, and fay, it was agreed to be on

Kaines v. Knightly, Skinner, 54.

on a condition, when it may be that the bill had been negociated: for though neither of them are ſpecialties, yet they are of great credit, and much for the ſupport, conveniency, and advantage of trade. The jury, notwithſtanding this direction, found for the defendant: but afterwards there was a trial at bar, and a verdict was given for the plaintiff, according to the opinion of the court. CHAP. XX.

The policy not only proves the extent and nature of the contract; but it alſo eſtabliſhes another allegation in the plaintiff's declaration, namely, *that the premium was paid*: for it was formerly ſhewn, that every policy contains the following clauſe: "*confeſſing ourſelves paid the conſideration* "*due unto us for this aſſurance by the aſſured, at and after the* "*rate of* —— *per cent.*" Vide c. 1.

[406] The plaintiff having averred in his declaration, that he is *intereſted* to the amount of the property inſured, it is abſolutely neceſſary that this allegation ſhould be proved. This he muſt do by a production of all the uſual documents, ſuch as, *the bills of ſale*, bills of parcels, and the coſts of the outfit; *the bills of lading*, (*a*) ſigned by the maſter, ſpecifying the goods received on board, and for whom he is to carry them, cuſtom-houſe clearances, and every other paper which may be thought neceſſary to ſubſtantiate his right to the property. (*b*)

A man

(*a*) The firſt great cauſe, in which the law relative to bills of lading came much under diſcuſſion, was in a modern caſe of *Caldwell* and others v. *Ball*, reported very much at length, and with great accuracy in the 1ſt Term Reports, page 205. That caſe was fully argued at the bar, and very much debated on the bench. Amongſt other things the court held, that a bill of lading is an acknowledgment under the hand of the captain, that he has received ſuch goods, which he undertakes to deliver to the perſon named in the bill of lading: that it is aſſignable in its nature; and by indorſement the property is veſted in the aſſignee. That where ſeveral bills of lading of the ſame date, but of different imports, have been ſigned, no reference is to be had to time, when they were firſt ſigned by the captain: but the perſon who firſt gets one of them by a legal title from the owner or ſhipper, has a right to the conſignment. And where ſuch bills of lading, though different upon the face of them, are conſtructively the ſame, and the captain has acted *bonâ fide*, a delivery according to ſuch legal title will diſcharge him from them all. But if the intention of the parties appears to have been to bind the net proceeds only, in caſe of the arrival of the goods, an aſſurance, made on account of the indorſer, after ſuch indorſement, is good. Hibbert v. Carter, 1 Term Rep. 745.

(*b*) Two partners purchaſed a ſhip under a regular bill of ſale, conformable to the 26 Geo. III. ch. 60. (Lord *Hawkeſbury*'s act.) They afterwards took

CHAP. XX.

Russel v. Boheme. 2 Strange, 1127.

Sir William Lee.

A man having purchased goods beyond sea, in order to prove his property in the cargo, in an action upon a policy of insurance, produced a *bill of parcels* of one *Gardiner* at *Petersburgh*, with his receipt to it, and proved his hand. The defendant objected, that this was no evidence against the insurers; but the Lord Chief Justice allowed it.

Smith v. Lascelles, 2 Term R. 187.

Before the subject of interest is entirely closed, I will take the opportunity of mentioning what I omitted in a former chapter, that if a merchant abroad, who is interested in goods and the freight of a cargo, mortgage them to his creditor here for payment of money at a certain day, and by a letter, inclosing the bills of lading, direct an insurance, the mortgagor has still an insurable interest, although the mortgage was become absolute, before the letter directing the insurance was received: and therefore an action was held to lie against the agent for not insuring agreeably to the instructions contained in such letter.

[407]

It is in the last place, incumbent on the plaintiff to prove that a loss has happened, and that, by the very means, stated in the declaration. It is absolutely necessary, that this rule should be strictly adhered to; for otherwise the insurers would come into court prepared to defend themselves against one charge, and one species of loss; and they would then be obliged to resist a demand upon a quite different ground. This appeared clearly in a modern case.

Kulen Kemp v. Vigne, 1 Term R. 304.

It was an action on a policy of insurance, which came on to be tried before Mr. Justice *Buller*, who nonsuited the plaintiff. Upon a motion to set aside that nonsuit, the following report was made by the learned judge. The insurance was *upon goods* on board the ship *Emanuel*, at and from *Falmouth* to *Marseilles*, warranted a *Danish* ship; and on the policy was this memorandum: "The following insurance is "declared

took in two other partners, who paid their respective shares in the ship, but there was no transfer to them under the direction of the statute; and it was held that the four partners had not an insurable interest in *the freight*; for as the right to freight results from the right of ownership, these four partners had not shewn in themselves *jointly* (as laid in the declaration) either a legal or equitable title to the ship. *Camden and others* v. *Anderson*, 5 Term R. 709.

"declared to be on money expended for reclaiming the "ship and cargo, valued at the sum, which shall be declared "hereafter. The loss to be paid, *in case the ship does not ar-* "*rive at Marseilles*, and without further proof of interest "than this policy; warranted free from all average, and "without the benefit of salvage." It appeared that the plaintiffs were proprietors of the *cargo* but not of the *ship*. That the ship originally sailed with the cargo on board from *Riga* to *Marseilles*, and that an insurance had been effected at *Bremen* upon the cargo for that voyage; in the course of which she was taken, and brought into *Falmouth*, by an *English* privateer. That a sentence of condemnation had been there obtained, which was afterwards reversed upon the prize having been proved to be a neutral ship, but the expenses of procuring that reversal were ordered by the Admiralty Court to be *a charge upon the cargo*. The plaintiff's agents accordingly paid the sum of 1,031*l*. 14*s*. for the expenses of reclaiming the ship and cargo; and immediately procured the policy in question to be effected in *January* 1781, according to the purport of the memorandum. In the *February* following, the ship set sail from *Falmouth* with the original cargo on board, in the prosecution of her voyage to *Marseilles*; but on the 26th of the same month, *before her* [408] *arrival there*, was captured by a *Spanish* ship, and carried into *Ceuta* in *Spain*, where she was again condemned. An appeal was brought in the superior court of *Madrid*, which promising to be of long continuance, the cargo, which was of a perishable nature, was ordered to be sold, and the proceeds to be brought into court, to wait the event of the suit. In *May* 1783, the vessel was restored by sentence of the court, and the surplus of the proceeds, which arose from the sale of the cargo, was paid to the owners, deducting the expenses incurred in *Spain* in prosecuting the appeal. After all the charges paid, there only remained twenty-six rix dollars. As soon as the ship was liberated, she sailed from *Ceuta* to *Malaga*, in order to refit, and having there made the necessary repairs, set sail for *Bremen*, and in that voyage was lost. The insurance made upon the cargo at *Bremen* has been paid. The declaration averred, that "*whilst the ship was proceeding* "*in her said voyage from Falmouth to Marseilles, and before she* "*could arrive at Marseilles, she was captured by the Spaniards,* "*and thereby the said ship, and also the goods and merchandizes on* "*board her, were totally lost to the plaintiffs.*" At the trial it

was

CHAP. XX. was objected on the part of the defendant, 1ſt, That this was not an inſurable intereſt; and 2dly, That the plaintiffs could not recover upon the policy in this form of declaring, for they ſtated the loſs to have happened *by capture*; whereas, though the veſſel was captured, yet, having been afterwards reſtored, ſhe might have reached her deſtined port, notwithſtanding the capture, in which caſe the underwriters would have been diſcharged by the terms of the memorandum. I was of that opinion, and upon the laſt ground I nonſuited the plaintiffs."

This caſe was very fully argued both upon the merits, and the formal objection, after which all the Judges ſpoke upon the queſtion.

Lord *Mansfield*.—"A loſs accrued upon the cargo in the voyage: the underwriter is ſued and the loſs is averred in the declaration to be *by capture*. The fact of the caſe is, that the ſhip was taken by a *Spaniſh* privateer, but was afterwards reſtored, and in a condition to purſue the voyage, and was afterwards loſt in another voyage.

[409] Mr. Juſtice *Willes*.—"Upon this caſe, it is clear, that the plaintiffs cannot recover. In the firſt place there was certainly a deviation, for the ſhip ſet ſail for *Malaga* inſtead of proceeding to *Marſeilles*. Secondly, the plaintiff has declared for a loſs *by capture*: but, after the capture, the policy might ſtill have been complied with by the ſhip's going to *Marſeilles*; and therefore the loſs cannot be ſaid to have happened by that circumſtance."

Mr. Juſtice *Aſhhurſt* and Mr. Juſtice *Buller* alſo delivered their opinions, agreeing with Lord *Mansfield* and Mr. Juſtice *Willes* upon the formal objection; and both went much at large into the merits, upon which I forbear to follow them or the Chief Juſtice, as what paſſed upon that ſubject is not material to our preſent inquiry.

But where a loſs is averred to be by perils of the ſea, and ſome of the goods inſured are ſpoiled, and others ſaved, it is allowable to give the expenſe of the ſalvage in evidence upon ſuch

ſuch an averment, becauſe it is a conſequence of the accident laid in the declaration.

Cary v. King, Caſ. Temp. Hardwicke, B. R. 304.

In an action on a policy of inſurance, for inſuring goods on board the ſhip *A.* the plaintiff declares that the ſhip ſprung a leak, and ſunk in the river, whereby the goods were ſpoiled. The evidence was, that many of the goods were ſpoiled, but ſome were ſaved; and the queſtion was, Whether the plaintiff might give in evidence the expenſe of ſalvage, that not being particularly laid as a breach of the policy in the declaration.

Lord *Hardwicke* Chief Juſtice.—"I think they may give it in evidence; for the inſurance is againſt all accidents. The accident laid in this declaration, is, that the ſhip ſunk in the river; it goes on and ſays, that by reaſon thereof the goods were ſpoiled, that is the only ſpecial damage laid: yet it is but the common caſe of a declaration that lays ſpecial damage, where the plaintiff may give evidence of any damage that is within his cauſe of action as laid. And though it was objected, that ſuch a breach of the policy ſhould be laid, as the inſurer may have notice to defend it; it is ſo in this caſe, for they have laid the accident, which is ſufficient notice, becauſe it muſt neceſſarily follow that ſome damage did happen."

CHAPTER THE TWENTY-FIRST.

Of Bottomry and Refpondentia.

CHAP. XXI.

THE contract of bottomry is in the nature of a mortgage of a fhip, when the owner of it borrows money to enable him to carry on the voyage, and pledges the keel or *bottom* of the fhip, as a fecurity for the repayment: and it is underftood, that if the fhip be loft, the lender alfo lofes his whole money; but if it return in fafety, then he fhall receive back his principal, and alfo the premium or intereft ftipulated to be paid, however it may exceed the ufual, or legal rate of intereft. When the fhip and tackle are brought home, they are liable, as well as the perfon of the borrower, for the money lent. But when the loan is not made upon the veffel, but upon the goods and merchandizes laden thereon, which, from their nature, muft be fold or exchanged in the courfe of the voyage, then the borrower only is *perfonally* bound to anfwer the contract; who therefore in this cafe is faid to take up money at *refpondentia*. In this confifts the difference between *bottomry* and *refpondentia*; that the one is a loan upon the fhip, the other upon the goods: in the former the fhip and tackle are liable, as well as the perfon of the borrower; in the latter, for the moft part, recourfe muft be had to the *perfon* only of the borrower. Another obfervation is, that in a loan upon bottomry, the lender runs no rifk though the goods fhould be loft; and upon refpondentia, the lender muft be paid his principal and intereft, though the fhip perifh, provided the goods are fafe. But in all other refpects, the contract of bottomry and that of refpondentia are upon the fame footing; the rules and decifions applicable to one, are applicable to both; and, therefore, in the courfe of our inquiries, they fhall be treated as one and the fame thing, it being fufficient to have once marked the diftinction between them.

2 Blackf. Com. 457.

2 Blackf. Com. 458.

2 Valin Com. p. 4.

Thefe

These terms are alſo applied to another ſpecies of contract, which does not exactly fall within the deſcription of either; namely, to a contract for the repayment of money, not upon the ſhip and goods only, but upon the mere hazard of the voyage itſelf; as if a man lend 1000*l.* to a merchant to be employed in a beneficial trade, with a condition to be repaid with extraordinary intereſt, in caſe a ſpecific voyage named in the condition ſhall be ſafely performed: which agreement is ſometimes called *fœnus nauticum* or *uſura maritima*. But as this ſpecies of bottomry opened a door to gaming and uſurious contracts, eſpecially in long voyages, the legiſlature, at the time it ſuppreſſed inſurances upon wagering policies, introduced a clauſe, by which it was enacted, "That all ſums "of money lent on bottomry, or at reſpondentia upon any "ſhip or ſhips belonging to his Majeſty's ſubjects *bound to or* "*from the Eaſt Indies*, ſhould be lent only on the ſhip, or on "the merchandize or effects, laden or to be laden, on board "of ſuch ſhip, and ſhould be ſo expreſſed in the condition of "the ſaid bond; and the benefit of ſalvage ſhould be allow"ed to the lender, his agents or aſſigns, who alone ſhould "have a right to make aſſurance on the money ſo lent; and "in caſe it ſhould appear that the value of his ſhare in the "ſhip or in the merchandizes or effects laden on board of "ſuch ſhip, did not amount to the full ſum or ſums he had "borrowed as aforeſaid, ſuch borrower ſhould be reſponſible "to the lender for ſo much of the money borrowed, as he "had not laid out on the ſhip or merchandizes laden there"on, with lawful intereſt for the ſame, in the proportion "the money not laid out ſhould bear to the whole money "lent, notwithſtanding the ſhip and merchandizes ſhould be "totally loſt."

2 Blackſ. Com. 458. 1 Sidcrfin, 27.

Molloy, lib. 2. c. 11. ſ. 8.

19 Geo. 2. c. 37. ſ. 5.

This ſtatute has entirely put an end to that ſpecies of contract which was laſt mentioned, namely, a loan upon the mere voyage itſelf, as far, at leaſt, as relates to *India* voyages; but as none other are mentioned, and as *expreſſio unius eſt excluſio alterius*, theſe loans may be made in all other caſes, as at the Common Law, except in the following inſtance, which is another ſtatute prohibition. The ſtatute alluded to declares, that all contracts made or entered into by any of his Majeſty's ſubjects, or any perſons in truſt for them, for or upon the loan of any monies by way of bottomry, or any

7 Geo. 1. c. 21. ſ. 2.

CHAP. XXI. ship or ships in the service of foreigners, and bound or designed to trade in the *East Indies or parts aforesaid*, shall be null and void.

This act, it should seem, does not mean to prevent the king's subjects from lending money on bottomry on foreign ships trading from their own country to their settlements in the *East Indies*. The purpose of the statute was only to prevent the people of this country from trading to the *British* settlements in *India* under foreign commissions, and to encourage the lawful trade thereto.

Sumner v. Green, 1 H. Blacks. 301.

It lately became a question in the Court of Common Pleas, whether an *American* ship since the declaration of *American* independency, was *a foreign* ship, within the statute of the 7 *Geo.* 1. *ch.* 21. *s.* 2. It came before the court, upon a motion to discharge the defendant out of custody upon entering a common appearance. The defendant was held to bail upon a respondentia bond, which was executed by the defendant, who was an *American*, to secure the payment of a cargo shipped by the plaintiff on board an *American* ship in the *East Indies*, homeward bound from *Calcutta* to *Rhode-Island* in *America*. The ship had sailed from *England*, and landed a cargo of *European* goods in *Bengal*, previous to her taking in the cargo, on which the bond was given.

The court were much inclined to think the bond was void, the case being within the mischief designed to be remedied by the act. But as the question was of considerable consequence, they thought it not proper to be discussed on this summary application: but they ordered the defendant to be discharged on the ground, that where it appeared from the affidavit to hold to bail, that there was a probability of the contract being void, on which the action was founded, it would be wrong to detain the defendant in prison: more particularly as the plaintiff would by such means have an opportunity of tampering with the defendant in prison, and of escaping from the penalties of the act, by preventing the case from being brought before the court.

A loan upon the voyage, without a security on the ship or goods, is entirely prohibited by the laws of *France*; for in the

the marine ordinances of that country, there is a *general* regulation similar to that made here with respect to *India* ships: "Faisons defenses de prendre deniers a la grosse sur le corps "et quille du navire, ou sur les marchandises de son charge- "ment, *au delà de leur valeur*, au peine de'etre contraint, "*en cas de fraude*, au paiement des sommes entieres, non ob- "stant la perte ou prise du vasseau." And in another place it is said, that where a greater sum is borrowed than the ship or goods are worth, where there is no fraud, the contract is void, except as to the amount of the real value of the ship or goods. If then the contract be only binding as far as there is property to answer the loan, it follows that, by the laws of *France*, this contract cannot exist upon the hazard of the voyage merely, unless there be a security also upon the ship or goods.

CHAP. XXI.

Ord. of Lou. 14. tit. des Contrats à grosse Avant. art. 3.

Loc. cit. art. 15.

The contract of bottomry and respondentia seems to deduce its origin from the custom of permitting the master of a ship, when in a foreign country, to hypothecate the ship in order to raise money to refit. Such a permission is absolutely necessary, and is impliedly given him in the very act of constituting him master, not indeed by the Common Law, but by the Marine Law, which in this respect is reasonable; for if a ship happen to be at sea, and spring a leak, or the voyage is likely to be defeated for want of necessaries, it is better that the master should have it in his power to pledge the ship and goods (*a*) or either of them, than that the ship should be lost, or the voyage defeated. But he cannot do either for any debt of his own; but merely in cases of necessity, and for completing the voyage. Although the master of the vessel has this power while abroad, because it is absolutely necessary for purposes of commerce and navigation; yet the very same authority which gave that power in those cases, has denied it when he happens to be in the same place where the owners reside. Thus the laws of *Oleron*, in the place above cited, speak of the captain being in a foreign country, and first writing home to his owners for money, before he takes money on bottomry: and the laws of the *Hanse Towns*, which were founded on those of *Oleron*, speak

2 Blackst. Com. 457.

Barnard v. Bridgeman, Moor 918. fully reported in Hobart, p. 11.

Molloy, b. 2. c. 2. f. 14. Leg. Oler. art. 1 and 22.

Laws of the Hanse Towns, art. 60.

(*a*) That the master may hypothecate the goods as well as the ship, see Salk. 34. pl. 7.

CHAP. XXI.

speak the same language; for they say, "a master being in a "*strange country*, if necessity drive him to it, may take up "money on bottomry, if he cannot get it without, and the "owners shall bear the charge." In addition to this, all the cases, which have been determined at the Common Law upon the subject, seem to require that the ship should be abroad, as well as in a state of necessity, to justify the captain or master in taking money on bottomry. *Molloy* in express terms declares, that a master has no power to take up money on bottomry, in places where his owners dwell; otherwise he and his estate must be liable thereto.—If, indeed, the owners do not agree in sending the ship to sea, the majority shall carry it, and then money may be taken up by the master on bottomry for their proportion who refuse, although they reside upon the spot, and it shall bind them all. The two last rules are the same with the marine ordinances of *France* upon that point: for they also declare, that those who lend money to the master, in the place where the owners reside, without their consent, shall have no security or hypothecation, but on such part of the ship only as belongs to the master himself, even though the money was advanced for repairs, or for purchasing provisions. But that the shares of those owners, who refuse to send out the ship, shall be affected by the loan of money to the master for necessaries. The justice and propriety of such a regulation, are evident from considering that such a contract was only intended for the benefit of all parties in those places where the owners had neither a residence, nor any correspondents.

Hobart 11. Noy 95.

Molloy, l. 2. c. 11. s. 11.

Molloy, loc. cit.

Ord. of Lou. 14. tit. Av. a la grosse, art. 8 and 9.

2 Valin, Com. 10.

The contract of which we treat is of a different nature from almost all others: but that, which it most nearly resembles, is the contract of insurance: for the lender on bottomry or at respondentia, runs almost all the same risks, with respect to property on which the loan is made, that the insurer does with respect to the effects insured. There are, however, some considerable distinctions; for instance, the lender supplies the borrower with money to purchase those effects upon which he is to run the risk: not so with the insurer. There are also various other distinctions.

Pothiér, Tr. du pret. à la grosse Avant. not. 6.

But

But however similar they may be in other respects, they differ very much in point of antiquity. We have formerly endeavoured to shew, that the contract of insurance was certainly unknown to the traders of the ancient world: but it is equally clear that with the contract of bottomry and respondentia, or what was equivalent to it, they were perfectly acquainted. In those fragments of the famous sea laws of the *Rhodians*, which have been preserved and transmitted to our times, I think there are very evident traces of this species of contract. In one section it is said, "that when masters "of ships, who are proprietors of one third of the lading, "take up money for the voyage, whether for the outward or "homeward bound, or both; all transactions shall pass according to the writings drawn up between the master and "lender, and the latter shall put a man on board the ship to "take care of his loan." But in another place, these laws speak more explicitly, and with a direct reference to the distinction between naval interest, and that which is given for a land risk. "If masters or merchants borrow money for "their voyages, the goods, freight, ships, and money, being "free, they shall not make use of surety-ship, unless there be "some apparent danger either of the sea or of pirates. And "for the money so lent, the borrowers shall pay *naval interest*." From these two quotations, little doubt can be entertained, but that the *Rhodians* used to borrow and lend, upon the hazard of the voyage, for an increased premium. It was formerly seen, that the *Rhodian* laws in general were adopted by the *Romans*; and consequently that branch of them which relates to bottomry amongst the rest: for you can hardly open a book upon the *Roman* law, but you meet with chapters, *de nautico fœnore*, *de nauticis usuris*, which plainly shew that this contract was well known to the jurists of that distinguished nation. It was also called by them *pecunia trajectitia*: because it was given to the borrower to be employed by him in commerce upon and beyond the sea. It appears from *Valin*, that some writers of the *French* nation had supposed that this contract was wholly unknown to the ancients, and that it was peculiar to *France* alone. *Valin* very clearly exposes the absurdity of such an idea; and it seems to be sufficiently answered, if deserving of an answer, by what has been already said. In addition to this we may add, that so

Vide the Introduction.

Leg. Rhod. s. 1. art. 21.

Leg. Rhod. s. 2. art. 16.

Digest. lib. 22 tit. 2 Cod. lib. 4. tit. 33.

2 Valin, Com. 1.

far

CHAP. XXI.

far from being peculiar to *France*, it has obtained a place in the codes of all the maritime states, whose laws have been promulgated, or have been at all famous in the modern world. In this chapter we have already had occasion to cite two passages from the judgments, or laws of *Oleron* upon the subject, as well as the 60th article of the laws of the *Hanse* towns: and by a reference to the 45th article of the laws of *Wisbuy*, it will be found, the nature of bottomry, as well as its name, was perfectly known to the makers of those ordinances.

Art. 1 and 22. Laws of Wisb. art. 45.

In the *Guidon*, indeed, it is supposed that the contract of bottomry now in use, is not at all the same as that which was known to the ancients. This authority is respectable: but facts must speak for themselves; in addition to which, the celebrated *Emerigon* has observed, that the assertion of the author of the *Guidon* is only true with respect to the form which the modern regulations have given to this contract, the true origin of which is lost in its antiquity.

Le Guid. c. 18. art. 2.

2 Emerigon, p. 384.

In our definition of bottomry it was said, that if the ship arrive safe, the lender shall be paid his principal, and the stipulated interest due upon it, however much it exceed the legal rate. The true principle, upon which this is allowed, is not merely the great profit and convenience of trade, as has frequently been urged: but the risk which the lender runs of losing both principal and interest; for he runs the contingency of winds, seas, and enemies. It is therefore of the essence of a contract of bottomry, that the lender runs the risk of the voyage; and that both principal and interest be at hazard; for if the risk go only to the interest or premium, and not to the principal also, though a real and substantial risk be inserted, it is a contract against the statute of usury, and therefore void. This has been frequently so determined in our courts of law: and it is consonant to the ideas of foreign writers.

Molloy, lib. 2. c. 11. s. 8. 13.

2 Vezey, 148.

2 Vezey, 154.

12 Anne, stat. 2. c. 16.

Pothiér, Not. 16.

An action of debt was brought upon an obligation. The defendant pleaded the statute of usury, and shewed, that a ship went to fish in *Newfoundland*, (which voyage might be performed in eight months) and that the plaintiff delivered 50*l.* to the defendant, to pay 60*l.* upon the return of the ship

Sharpley, v. Hurrell Cro. Jac. 208.

ſhip off *Dartmouth*: and if the ſaid ſhip, by occaſion of leakage or tempeſt, ſhould not return from *Newfoundland* to *Dartmouth*, then the defendant ſhould pay the 50*l.* only; and if the ſhip never returned, he ſhould pay nothing. And it was held by all the court, not to be uſury within the ſtatute. For if the ſhip had ſtayed at *Newfoundland* two or three years, he ſhould have paid at the return of the ſhip but 60*l.* and if the ſhip never returned, then nothing; ſo that the plaintiff ran hazard of having leſs than the intereſt which the law allows; and poſſibly, neither principal nor intereſt.

This caſe was, upon another occaſion, mentioned in argument by one of the judges on the bench; the principle, on which it was decided, was recognized, and the caſe itſelf allowed to be law. Roberts v. Tremayne, Cro. Jac. 508.

So alſo in another caſe of debt upon an obligation, conditioned to pay ſo much money, if ſuch a ſhip returned within ſix months from *Oſtend* in *Flanders* to *London*, which was more by the third part than the legal intereſt of money; and if ſhe do not return, then the obligation to be void: the defendant pleaded, that there was a corrupt agreement betwixt himſelf and the plaintiff, and that at the time of making the obligation, it was agreed betwixt them, that he ſhould have no more for intereſt than the law permits, in caſe the ſhip ſhould ever return; and avers that the obligation was entered into by covin, to evade the ſtatute of uſury, and the penalty thereof: upon this averment the plaintiff took iſſue, and the defendant demurred. Joy v. Kent, Hard. Rep. 418.

Lord Chief Baron *Hale*.—"Clearly this bond is not within the ſtatute, for this is the common way of inſurance; and if this were void by the ſtatute of uſury, trade would be deſtroyed. It is not like to the caſe, where the condition of the bond is to give ſo much money, if ſuch or ſuch a perſon be then alive: for there is a certainty of that at the time. But it is uncertain and a caſualty whether ſuch a ſhip ſhall ever return or not."

In another caſe of debt upon an obligation for 300*l.* the condition was, that if ſuch a ſhip went to *Surat* in the *Eaſt Indies*, and returned ſafe; or if the owner, or the goods laden on board the ſhip returned ſafe, then the defendant was Soome v. Gleen. 1 Sid. 27. 1 Lev. 54. 1 C.

to

CHAP. XXI.

to pay the principal to the plaintiff, and 40*l.* for each 100*l.*; but that if the ship should perish by unavoidable casualties of sea, fire, or enemies, to be proved by sufficient testimony, then the plaintiff should have nothing. The doubt was, whether this was an usurious contract: and it was said to be so, because the payment depended upon so many things, one of which in all probability would happen. But the whole court held it not to be within the statute.

Lord Chief Justice *Bridgman* took a distinction between a bargain of this kind, and a loan; for where there is a bargain, as here, and the principal is hazarded, that cannot be within the statute of usury; but it is otherwise of a loan, where the principal is not in danger. Here there are apparent risks of the sea, fire and enemies, and the length of the voyage; all of which endanger the loss of the principal. These bottomry contracts are for the advancement of trade, and therefore judgment must be for the plaintiff.

These cases are all uniform in the principle which they go to establish, that, on account of the risk, the interest shall be larger than the common rate: but notwithstanding this, a case is to be found in the Equity Reports, which directly tends to destroy the rule of decision in all these cases.

Dandy *v.* Turner, 1 Equity Cases, Abr. 372.

A part owner of a ship borrowed money of the plaintiff upon a bottomry bond, payable on the return of the ship from the voyage she was then going in the service of the *East India Company*, who broke up the ship in the *East Indies*; and the owners brought their action against the Company, and recovered damages, which did not, however, amount to a full satisfaction. The plaintiff brought his bill to have his proportionable satisfaction out of the money recovered; but his bill was dismissed, and he was left to recover as well as he could at law; for a Court of Equity will never assist a bottomry bond, which carries *unreasonable interest*.

This case conveys a very unmerited censure upon bottomry bonds, not at all warranted by the long chain of uniform decisions in their favour. Indeed, from the very nature of the contract, they are to carry the naval interest, which is always greater than land interest, in proportion as the risks

run

run by the lender on bottomry are much greater than those which a lender upon common bonds incurs. (a) CHAP. XXI.

To be sure if a contract were made, by colour of bottomry, in order to evade the statute, it would be usurious and void, and highly deserving of all the censure and discouragement which the courts, either of law or equity, could possibly throw upon it. 4 Com. Dig. 193. 2 Vezey, 146.

In *England* then it is clear, from these cases, that there is nothing unlawful in the contract of bottomry: but some writers in foreign countries have endeavoured to hold it up to the world, as an illicit and an usurious bargain. *Straccha*, who has written upon insurances, has introduced a long dissertation to prove the truth of this position; and several other writers have either preceded or followed him in support of the same doctrines. If, indeed, the money so lent were given merely by way of a loan, and such excessive interest were demanded for the use of the money only; there might be force in the objection. But when it is considered as the price of the great risks incurred, it has not the least semblance of usury; it is a fair and conscientious contract highly beneficial to the commerce and general interests of society. Introd. de Assecur. Not. 26.

These authors have met with very able opposers in *Pothiér* and *Emerigon*, who have clearly shewn the fallacy of their doctrine; and they have proved to demonstration, that even the fathers of the church have acknowledged, that this contract has nothing in it offensive to religion or good morals. Almost all the writers of eminence agree with the two last named, as to the legality of loans on bottomry and at respondentia: and it is now universally admitted and practised in all the maritime and trading countries in *Europe*. Pothiér Avanture à la grosse, Not. 2. 2 Emer. 390. Loccenius, lib. 2. c. 6. Not. 3. Roccus de Navibus et Naulo, not. 50. 2 Black. Com. 457.

But as the hazard to be run is the very basis and foundation of this contract; it follows, that if the risk is not run, the lender cannot be entitled to the extraordinary premium; for that would be to open a door to means by which the statutes of usury might be evaded. This was so decided in the Court of Chancery.

The

(a) Mr. Fonblanque in his valuable edition of "A Treatise of Equity," has supposed that in the above passage I meant to complain of the interference of a Court of Equity in cases where *exorbitant naval interest* was demanded. But a little attention to the passage complained of, and also to what follows, will demonstrate, that I only alluded to general censures upon a species of contract so highly beneficial for commercial purposes. See Fonbl. vol. i. p. 243.

CHAP. XXI.

Deguilder v. Depeifter, 1 Vern. 263.

The cafe was upon a bottomry bond, whereby the plaintiff was bound in confideration of 400*l.* as well to perform the voyage within fix months, as at the fix months end to pay the 400*l.* and 40*l.* premium, in cafe the veffel arrived fafe, and was not loft in the voyage. It happened that the plaintiff never went the voyage, whereby the bond became forfeited, and he now preferred his bill to be relieved. Upon the former hearing, as the fhip lay all the time in the port of *London*, and there was no hazard of lofing the principal, the Lord Keeper thought fit to decree, that the defendant fhould lofe the premium of 40*l.* and be contented with his principal and *ordinary intereft*. And now, upon a rehearing, he confirmed his former decree.

Pothiér Traité a la Groffe Aventure, Not. 38. 2 Valin 10.

With this decree, which is equitable and juft, the *French* writers agree. They fay, that in fuch a cafe, "L'emprunteur fera bien obligé de rendre la fomme qui lui a été prêtée, "mais il ne fera pas obligé de payer en outre la fomme qu'il "a promis de payer pour le profit maritime; car le profit "maritime étant le prix des rifques que le prêteur devoit "courir des effects fur lefquels le prêt a été fait, il ne peut "lui être dû de profit maritime quan il n'a. couru aucuns "rifques, ne pouvant pas y avoir un prix des rifques, s'il n'y "a pas eu de rifques."

Vide the Appendix. No. 2.

Bottomry bonds generally exprefs from what time the rifk fhall commence, as that the fhip fhall fail from *London* to fuch a port abroad, &c. In fuch cafes, the contingency does not commence till the departure: and therefore if the fhip receive injury by ftorm, fire, &c. before the beginning of the voyage, the perfon borrowing alone runs the hazard. But if the condition be, "that if the fhip fhall not arrive at fuch a place by fuch a time, then, &c." in thefe inftances, the contract commences from the time of failing, and a different rule, as to the lofs, will neceffarily prevail.

Beawes Lex Merc. Red. 4th edit. p. 127.

2 Magens, 28. 166.

We have fhewn at the beginning of this chapter, that the amount of the loan on bottomry or refpondentia, in this country, is not reftrained by any regulation whatever; although it is in many maritime ftates by exprefs ordinances: that the only reftriction in the law of *England* is, with refpect to money lent on fhips and goods going to the *Eaft Indies*, which, by ftatute muft not exceed the value of the property on which

19 Geo. 2. c. 37, f. 5.

CHAP. XXI.

which the loan is made. It remains then to see what those risks are, to which the lender undertakes to expose himself. These are for the most part mentioned in the condition of the bond, and are nearly the same, against which the underwriter, in a policy of insurance, undertakes to indemnify, "*Limita hoc singulariter, ut creditor subeat periculum navigationis,* "*in casibus fortuitis tantum.*" These accidents are, tempests, pirates, fire, capture, and every other misfortune, except such as arise either from the defects of the thing itself, on which the loan is made, or from the misconduct of the borrower: for, says the *Italian* lawyer, last quoted, in continuation of the above sentence, "*Secus est si infortunium, vel naufragium* "*ex culpâ debitoris processerit, quia tunc creditor non tenetur de* "*periculo, et damno, in quod incurritur ex culpâ vehentis, prout* "*in simili deciditur in materiâ assecurationis, ut quantumcumque* "*assecuratio sit generalis non contineat periculum, aut damnum,* "*quod facto assecurati contingit.*"

Vide the Appendix. No. 2.

Roccus de Navibus. Not. 51.

2 Valin, 14 Roccus, loc. cit.

It seems to have been a doubt late in the last century, whether a loss by the attacks of pirates was a risk which the lender on bottomry had by his contract undertaken to bear; for it was argued in the King's Bench, in the reign of *James* the Second. But the court were of opinion, that piracy was one of the dangers of the seas; and the defendant had judgment.

Barton v. Wolliford, Comb. 56.

The lender is answerable likewise for losses by capture; or to speak more accurately, if a loss by capture happen, he cannot recover against the borrower; but in bottomry and respondentia bonds, capture does not mean a mere temporary taking, but it must be such a capture as to occasion a total loss. And therefore if a ship be taken and detained for a short time, and yet arrive at the port of destination within the time limited, (if time be mentioned in the condition,) the bond is not forfeited, and the obligee may recover.

This doctrine was laid down by the whole Court of King's Bench, in a case upon a bond of this nature; the proceedings on which were fully stated, when the unanimous opinion of the court was delivered by Lord *Mansfield*.—"This comes before the court upon a motion, on the part of the defendant, for a new trial. It was an action of debt upon a bottomry bond; the condition of which was, that upon the ship's safe arrival

Joyce v. Williamson, B. R. Mich. Term, 23 Geo. 3.

arrival at *New York*, a certain ſum of money ſhould be paid to the plaintiff; but that in caſe the ſhip ſhould miſcarry, be loſt, caſt away, or taken by the enemy, the plaintiff ſhould have nothing. The defendant pleaded three pleas: 1ſt, *Non eſt factum*; 2dly, That the ſhip did not arrive at *New York*, the port of deſtination; 3dly, That the ſhip was captured. Upon the two firſt pleas iſſue was joined: and to the laſt, there was a replication of recapture. The facts, which appeared in evidence on the trial, are theſe: *the ſhip was taken before her arrival at New York*, by two *American* privateers, which detained her for one month, and plundered her of her ſtores; at which time *ſhe was retaken* by an *Engliſh* privateer and carried into *Halifax*. The Admiralty Court adjudged her to be a good prize to the *Engliſh* privateer, and decreed that ſhe ſhould be reſtored to the original owners, on paying one eighth for ſalvage: that ſhe proceeded with the remainder of her cargo to *New York*, and earned her freight: that the value of the ſhip was not ſufficient to ſatisfy the bond. Theſe are the facts. Now it is clear, that, by the law of *England, there is neither average nor ſalvage upon a bottomry bond.* It was indeed contended at the bar on the part of the defendant, that this caſe was within the ſaving of the bond; for it is provided, that in caſe of loſs by *capture*, &c. the bond ſhould be void: and that here there was a capture, and a detention for one month. But upon conſideration, we think that a capture, within this condition, does not mean a *temporary capture*, but it *muſt be a total loſs*: now here it was not ſuch a capture as to occaſion a total loſs. The voyage was not loſt, for the defendant purſued it and earned his freight. Freight depends upon the ſafety of the ſhip; and as the freight was earned, the ſhip muſt have arrived ſafe at the port of deſtination. In whatever way we determine this caſe, there muſt be a hardſhip; but we are all of opinion, that the verdict is right, and that the rule for a new trial muſt be diſcharged."

From this caſe we not only learn what ſhall be deemed a capture, within the meaning of that word in a bottomry bond, but we derive from it a piece of very eſſential information, namely, that a lender on bottomry, or at reſpondentia, is neither entitled to the benefit of ſalvage, nor liable to contribute in caſe of a general average. This was expreſsly ſaid by by Lord *Mansfield* in delivering the judgment of the court. His Lordſhip's opinion is confirmed by the ſtatute of the 19th of Geo. the Second, c. 37. which allows the benefit of ſalvage to lenders upon ſhips or goods going to the *Eaſt-Indies*; clearly ſhewing that there was no ſuch thing at the Common Law, otherwiſe there was no occaſion to make ſuch a proviſion. 19 Geo. II. c. 37. ſ. 5.

In this reſpect our law differs from that of *France*, for the ordinances, and indeed it ſeems always to have been the caſe in that country, expreſsly declare, that the lenders on bottomry ſhall be ſubject to general or groſs average, in the ſame manner as inſurers are upon policies of inſurance; for that as theſe contracts depend upon the ſame principles, they are ſubject to the ſame regulations. Le Guidon, c. 19. Art. 5. 2 Valin, 19. 2 Emer. 504.

Our law in this reſpect is different alſo from that of *Denmark*. This lately appeared in a cauſe tried in the King's Bench before Lord *Kenyon* at *Guildhall*.

It was an action on a policy of inſurance upon a *reſpondentia* bond on ſhip and goods, at and from *B.* to *C.* The ſhip was *Daniſh*, and an average loſs was ſuſtained upon the goods to the amount of 6*l.* 15*s.* *per cent.* and the plaintiff, as holder of a *reſpondentia* bond, had been called upon to contribute; and now brought his action againſt the *Engliſh* underwriters for the amount of that contribution. Walpole *v.* Ewer. Sitt. after Trin. 1789.

Lord *Kenyon* Chief Juſtice.—" By the law of *England*, a lender upon *reſpondentia* is not liable to average loſſes; but is entitled to receive the whole ſum advanced, provided ſhip and cargo arrive at the port of deſtination. The plaintiff contends, that as by the law of *Denmark*, ſuch lenders upon reſpondentia are liable to average, and bound to contribute according to the amount of their intereſt, the inſurer muſt anſwer to them. The *Daniſh* Conſul has proved that he received a judgment of the Court of *Copenhagen*, the decretal part of which proves the law of *Denmark* to be as the plaintiff has ſtated it. The opinions of ſeveral men of eminence in that country have been offered on each ſide: but I reject them, becauſe the ſolemn deciſion of a court of competent juriſdiction is of much greater weight than the opinions of advocates, however eminent, or even than the extrajudicial opinions

CHAP. XXI. opinions of the most able judges. It seems as if in this case, the underwriters were bound by the law of the country, to which the contract relates." Verdict for the plaintiff. (*a*)

It has been said, that if the accident happen by the default of the borrower, or of the captain, the lender is not liable, and has a right to demand the payment of the bond. If, therefore, the ship be lost by a wilful deviation from the track of the voyage, the event has not happened, upon which the borrower was to be discharged from his obligation. This has been decided in several cases.

Western v. Wildy. Skinn. 152.

An action of debt was brought upon an obligation for performance of covenants in an indenture, wherein it was recited, that such a ship was in the service of the *East India Company*, and that it was to obey such orders as they or their factors

(*a*) This is not the only case, in which the insurers have been held liable to indemnify, the insured having been obliged by the law of a foreign country to pay a larger sum than by the laws of *England* could have been demanded: though to be sure, in the case about to be quoted, there seems to have been an usage proved; and upon that the learned Judge much relied.

Newman v. Cazalet. Sitt. at Guildh. after Hilary.

It was an action on a policy, upon a cargo of fish from *Newfoundland* to any port of *Spain*, *Portugal*, or *Italy*. The ship met with bad weather, and put into *Alicant* and *Leghorn* to repair. The captain being owner, presented a petition to the commercial court of *Pisa*, to adjust the general average, as he had put in for the general benefit of all concerned. The court, according to its usual course (which appears to be a very extraordinary one) adjusted the loss by charging the cargo at its full value, but the ship only at one half, and the freight at one third: and they also charged as a part of the general average, the seamen's wages and provisions, while in port. The defendant, as underwriter, had paid into court as much as would cover the average; if adjusted according to the memorandum in the policy, and the law and usage of *England*. The question was, whether the plaintiff having been compelled to pay beyond that sum according to the calculation of the sentence of the court of *Pisa*, it was conclusive upon the defendant, and the plaintiff was entitled to recover his average by the same standard. The plaintiff called several brokers, who said, that in repeated instances they had adjusted averages under similar sentences of the court of *Pisa*; and the underwriters, though with reluctance, had always paid them.

Mr. Justice *Buller*.—" On the general law, the plaintiff would fail; but in all matters of trade, usage is a sacred thing. I do not like these foreign settlements of average, which make underwriters liable for more than the standard of *English* law. But if you are satisfied it has been the usage, upon the evidence given, it ought not to be shaken." The plaintiff had a verdict accordingly.

factors should give; and that she was designed for a voyage from *London* to *Bantam*, and from thence to *China* or *Formosa*. The plaintiff lent 500 *l.* upon the hull of the ship, and the defendant covenanted to pay, if the ship went from *London* to *Bantam*, and returned from thence directly to *London*, 550 *l.* If from *London* to *Bantam*, and from thence to *China* or *Formosa*, and returned to *London* within 24 months, 650 *l.* If she returned not within 24 months, then to pay 5 *l.* per month above 650 *l.* till the 36 months; and if she returned not within 36 months, then to pay 710 *l.* unless it can be proved by *Wildy*, that the ship returned not, but was lost within 36 months. The ship, in fact, went from *London* to *Bantam*, and from *thence to Surat*, and other parts, and so returned to *Bantam*; and in her voyage from *Bantam* to *London*, was lost within 36 months: upon which the present action was brought.

The court inclined to be of opinion, that this ship having deviated from the voyage described, in going to *Surat*, the plaintiff was not to bear the loss, and was consequently entitled to recover. They, however, took time to deliberate; and after consideration, gave judgment for the plaintiff.

Williams v. Steadman. Holt's Reports, 126. Skin. 345. S. C.

In another case of debt upon a bottomry bond, the defendant pleaded, that the ship went from *London* to *Barbadoes*, *sine deviatione*, and afterwards she returned from *Barbadoes* towards *London*, and in her return was lost *in voyagio prædicto*; the plaintiff replied, that the ship in her return went from *Barbadoes* to *Jamaica*; and that after a stay there, she returned from *Jamaica* towards *London*, and was lost, and so shews a deviation. The defendant rejoined, that she was pressed into the king's service, and so was compelled to go to *Jamaica*, which is the deviation pleaded by the plaintiff; without this that she deviated after she was pressed. The plaintiff demurred, and judgment was given for the plaintiff. The plea of the defendant is not good; for he pleads that the ship went from *London* to *Barbadoes* without deviation, and that in the return she was lost in the voyage aforesaid: but it does not shew *without deviation*. Now the condition is so in express words, and he ought to shew expressly that he has performed the words of the condition.

The

CHAP. XXI.

The same rule of decision has been adopted in the Courts of Equity.

1 Equity Cases, Abr. 372. 2 Ch. Cases, 130.

The plaintiff entered into a penal bond to pay 40*s.* per month for 50*l.*: the ship was to go *from Holland to the Spanish islands, and to return to England:* but if she perished, the defendant was to lose his 50*l.* The ship went accordingly to the *Spanish* islands, took in *Moors* at *Africa*, then went to *Barbadoes*, and perished at sea. The plaintiff, being sued at law upon the bond, came into equity, suggesting that *the deviation was through necessity.* But this bill was dismissed, except as to the penalty.

C. 1. p. 14.

21 Geo. II. c. 4.

Lex. Merc. Red. 4th edit. p. 128.

There is no restriction by the law of *England* as to the persons, to whom money may be lent on bottomry, or at respondentia. (*a*) In a former part of this work, we gave the history of a statute introduced into our code of laws, to prevent insurances from being made on the ships or goods of *Frenchmen*, during the then existing war with *France*. The same statute also prohibited his majesty's subjects from lending money on bottomry or at respondentia on any ships or goods belonging to *France*, or to any of the *French* dominions or plantations, or the subjects thereof: and in case they should, such contracts were declared void; and the parties thereto, or the agent or broker interfering therein, were to forfeit 500*l.* That act was not of long continuance, on account of the peace, which almost immediately followed it: and these restraints upon this species of contract were never again revived by any subsequent positive law. (*b*)

It frequently happened, as appears by the preamble to the statute, that the borrowers on bottomry, or at respondentia, became bankrupts after the loan of the money, and before the event happened, which entitled the lender to repayment: by which means the debt could not be proved under the commission, and the lenders were left to such redress as they could obtain from the bankrupt, who had previously given up every thing

(*a*) See one exception as to loans on the ships of foreigners trading to the *East Indies*, ante page 411.

(*b*) See the arguments as to the legality of insuring the property of an enemy, *ante* p. 240, which necessarily tend also to prevent this species of contract from being entered into with an enemy.

thing to his other creditors. This being likely to prove a discouragement to trade, parliament was obliged to interpose; and it accordingly enacted, "That the obligee in any "bottomry or respondentia bond, made and entered into up-"on a good and valuable consideration, *bonâ fide*, should be "admitted to claim, and *after the contingency should have hap-"pened, to prove his or her debt or demands in respect of such "bond, in like manner as if the contingency had happened before "the time of the issuing of the commission of bankruptcy against such "obligor*, and should be entitled unto, and should have and "receive a proportionable part, share, and dividend of such "bankrupt's estate, in proportion to the other creditors of "such bankrupt, in like manner as if such contingency had "happened before such commission issued: and that all and "every person or persons, against whom any commission of "bankruptcy should be awarded, should be discharged of "and from the debt or debts owing by him, her, or them, "on every such bond as aforesaid, and should have the ben-"efit of the several statutes now in force against bankrupts, "in like manner, to all intents and purposes, as if such con-"tingency had happened, and the money due in respect "thereof had become payable before the time of the issuing "of such commission."

CHAP. XXI.

19 Geo. 2. c. 32. s. 2.

By the statute books it appears, that the masters and mariners of ships having taken upon bottomry greater sums of money than the value of their adventure, had been accustomed wilfully to cast away, burn, or otherwise destroy the ships under their charge, to the great loss of the merchants and owners: it was therefore enacted, "That if any captain, "master, mariner, or other officer belonging to any ship, "should wilfully cast away, burn, or otherwise destroy the "ship unto which he belonged, or procure the same to be "done, he should suffer death as a felon." The duration of this act having been limited to three years, it became extinct: but the necessity of such a provision was so great, that a similar law was made a few years afterwards, and is still in force.

16 Cha. 2. c. 6. s. 12.

22 & 23 Cha. 2. c. 11. s. 12.

As the commerce of the country increased to an amazing degree, so the custom of lending money on bottomry became also very prevalent: and as the lenders had subjected themselves to great risks, they began to think it necessary to pro-

 tect

CHAP. XXI. Vide ante c. 1. 3 Burr. 1394.

tect their property, by insuring to the amount of the money lent. In a former chapter, much was said of the mode by which insurances on such property were to be effected; and we then saw from the case of *Glover* v. *Black*, that it was necessary to insert in the policy that the interest insured was bottomry or respondentia, and that such was the law and practice of merchants. From this case too it is evident, that when a person has insured a bottomry or respondentia interest, and he recovers upon the bond, he cannot also recover upon the policy: because he has not sustained a loss within the meaning of his contract; and to suffer any man to receive a double satisfaction, would be contrary to the first principles of insurance law. As it is merely a contract of indemnity, a man shall never receive less; nor can he be entitled to recover more than the amount of the damage he has, in fact, sustained.

CHAPTER THE TWENTY-SECOND.

Of Insurance upon Lives.

AN Insurance upon Life is a contract, by which the underwriter for a certain sum, proportioned to the age, health, profession, and other circumstances of the person, whose life is the object of insurance, engages that that person shall not die within the time limited in the policy: or if he do, that he will pay a sum of money to him in whose favour the policy was granted. Thus if *A.* lend 100*l.* to *B.* who can give nothing but his personal security for repayment: in order to secure him, in case of his death, *B.* applies to *C.* an insurer, to insure his life in favour of *A.* by which means, if *B.* die within the time limited in the policy, *A.* will have a demand upon *C.* for the amount of his insurance.

CHAP. XXII.

1 Postlethw. Dict. of Tr. p. 150. Vide the Appendix. No. 3. 2 Blackst. Com. 459.

The advantages resulting from such insurances are many and obvious: and most of them may be reduced under the following classes. To persons possessed of places or employments for life; to masters of families and others, whose income is subject to be determined, or lessened, at their respective deaths; who, by insuring their lives, may secure a sum of money for the use of their families. To married persons, where a jointure, pension, or annuity, depends on both or either of their lives, by insuring the life of the persons entitled to such annuity, pension, or jointure. To dependents upon any other person, during whose life they are entitled to a salary or benefaction, and whose life being insured, will enable such dependents, at the death of their benefactor, to claim from the insurers a sum equal to the premium paid. To persons wanting to borrow money, who, by insuring their lives, are enabled to give a security for the money borrowed. These, and many other advantages, being so obvious, the Bishop of *Oxford*, Sir *Thomas Allen*, and some other gentlemen, were induced to apply to Queen *Anne* to obtain her

1 Postlethw. 150.

CHAP. XXII.

charter for incorporating them and their successors, whereby they might provide for their families, in an easy and beneficial manner. Accordingly, in the year 1706, her majesty granted her royal charter, incorporating them by the name of "The Amicable Society for a perpetual Assurance Office," giving them a power to purchase lands, an ability to sue and be sued in their corporate capacity, and a common seal for the more easy and expeditious management of the affairs of the Company.

The benefits, which accrued to the public from this species of contract, were found to be so extensive, that another office was established by deed enrolled in the Court of King's Bench at *Westminster*, for the insurance of lives only. The name of this office is, the "*society for equitable assurance on* "*lives and survivorships*." Besides this, the two Companies of the *Royal Exchange* and *London* Assurance, obtained his majesty's charter, to enable them also to make insurances on lives. The charter points out the advantages of such institutions; for it states, as the ground, on which such a permission is to be granted, "That it has been found by experience to be of benefit and advantage, for persons having "offices, employments, estates, or other incomes, determinable on the life or lives of themselves or others, to make "assurances on the life or lives, upon which such offices, "employments, estates, or incomes are determinable." Private underwriters also may enter into policies of this nature, as well as any other, provided the party, making the insurance, chooses to trust their single security.

The antiquity of this practice cannot be very easily ascertained; however we find traces of it in some very old authors. In the *French* book entitled *Le Guidon*, we find it mentioned, as a contract perfectly well known at that time in other countries. The author of that book, however, tells us in the same passage, that it was a species of contract wholly forbidden in *France*, as being repugnant to good morals, and as opening a door to a variety of frauds and abuses. Such, indeed, the law of *France* continues at this day: and insurances upon lives are prohibited in other countries of *Europe* by positive regulation. The same *French* author

Le Guidon, c. 16. art. 5, published in 1661.

2 Valin. 54.

2 Magens, 70.

LeGuid. loc.cit.

author has, however, gone a little too far in afferting, that the other countries, in which they had been till that time encouraged, were alfo obliged to forbid them. This had not certainly taken place at that time, as may be inferred from the 66th article of the laws of *Wifbuy*; and in *England* they never had been prohibited. The learned *Roccus* alfo takes notice of them as legal contracts, and quotes various authors in fupport of his opinion. Roccus de Affec. Not. 74.

Thefe infurances being thus fanctioned in *England* by royal authority, and the funds of the different focieties having very much increafed, and being fixed on a ftable and permanent foundation, contracts of this nature became fo much a mode of gambling (for people took the liberty of infuring any one's life, without hefitation, whether connected with him, or not, and the infurers feldom afked any queftion about the reafons, for which fuch infurances were made) that it at laft became a fubject of parliamentary difcuffion. The refult of that difcuffion was, that a ftatute paffed, by which it was enacted, "That no infurance fhould be made by any perfon or perfons, bodies politic or corporate, *on the life or lives* of any perfon or perfons, or on any other event or events whatfoever, wherein the perfon or perfons, for whofe ufe, benefit, or on whofe account, fuch policies fhould be made, *fhould have no intereft, or by way of gaming or wagering*; and every infurance made, contrary to the true intent and meaning thereof, fhould be null and void to all intents and purpofes." And in order more effectually to guard againft any impofition or fraud, and to be the better able to afcertain what the intereft of the perfon, entitled to the benefit of the infurance, really was, it was further enacted, by the fame ftatute, "that it fhould not be lawful to make any policy or policies on the life or lives of any perfon or perfons, or other event or events, without inferting in fuch policy or policies, the perfon's name interefted therein, or for whofe ufe, benefit, or on whofe account, fuch policy was fo made or underwrote. And that in all cafes where the infured had an intereft in fuch life or lives, event or events, no greater fum fhould be recovered, or received from the infurer or infurers, than the amount or value of the intereft of the infured in fuch life or lives, or other event or events."

1 Mag. 33. 14 Geo. 3. c. 48. f. 1. Sect. 2. Sect. 3.

It

CHAP. XXII.

It has been held that a perfon, holding a note given for money won at play, has not an infurable intereft in the life of the maker of the note.

Dwyer v. Edie. London Sittings after Hil. 1788.

An action was brought on a policy on the life of *James Ruffell* from the 1ft of *June* 1784 to the 1ft of *June* 1785. *Ruffell* was warranted in good health, and by a memorandum at the foot of the policy it was declared that it was intended to cover the fum of 5000*l.* due from *Ruffell* to the plaintiff, for which he had given his note payable in one year from the 14th of *May* 1784.—Two objections were made on the part of the defendant: 1ft, That part of the confideration for the note was money won at play: 2dly, That *Ruffell* at the time he gave the note was an infant.

Mr. Juftice *Buller* nonfuited the plaintiff upon the ground of part of the confideration of the note being for a gaming tranfaction; and therefore there was a want of intereft in the plaintiff. But as to the other objection on account of infancy, the intereft muft be contingent, for *Ruffell* might or might not avoid his note; and he doubted much whether till fo avoided, the note muft not be taken againft a third perfon to be the note of an adult, for the maker of the note only could take the objection. (*a*)

Anderfon v. Edie. B.R. London Sittings in Trinity Term 1795.

But a creditor has fuch an intereft in the life of his debtor, that he may infure it, and recover upon the policy.—Thus in an action on a policy of infurance on the life of Lord *Newhaven* from the 1ft of *December* 1792 to the 1ft of *December* 1793, the only queftion made by the defendant was as to the plaintiff's intereft, which it was contended was not fufficient to take this cafe out of the ftatute 14 Geo. III. c. 48. It appeared in evidence that Lord *Newhaven* was indebted to the

Cowper, 737.

(*a*) There is a cafe of *Roebuck* v. *Hammerton*, in which a policy made, in order to decide upon the fex of a particular perfon, was held to fall within the prohibition of this ftatute. In another cafe, a policy having been made, on the event of there being an open trade between *Great Britain* and the province of *Maryland*, on or before the 6th *July* 1778, Lord *Mansfield* faid, that it was clear the plaintiff could not recover. 1ft, Is this an intereft within the act? It was made to prevent gambling policies. Every man in the kingdom has an intereft in the events of war and peace; but I doubt whether that be an intereft within the act. But 2dly, The policy is void, by not having the name inferted according to the 2d fection of the ftatute.

Mollifon v. Staples. Sittings at Guildhall. Mic. Vac. 1778.

the plaintiff and a Mr. *Mitchell*, in a large ſum of money, part of which debt had been aſſigned by them to another perſon; the remainder, being more than the amount of the ſum inſured, was upon a ſettlement of accounts between the plaintiff and *Mitchell*, agreed by them to remain to the account of *Mitchell* only.

Lord *Kenyon* was of opinion, that this debt was a ſufficient intereſt: and ſaid that it was ſingular, that this queſtion had never been directly decided before. That a creditor had certainly an intereſt in the life of his debtor, the means by which he was to be ſatisfied may materially depend upon it, and at all events the death muſt in all caſes in ſome degree leſſen the ſecurity. Verdict for the plaintiff.

So alſo in a previous caſe, where an action was brought on a policy on the life of *William Holden* from the 17th *Auguſt* 1790 to *Auguſt* 1791, and during the life of the plaintiff; *Holden* had granted an annuity to the plaintiff's late brother, which annuity he had bequeathed to perſons not parties to this inſurance, having made the plaintiff executor of his will, and directed him to make aſſurance. Lord *Kenyon* thought this a ſufficient intereſt in the executor to ſupport the action. The cauſe proceeded, therefore: but the defendant had a verdict afterwards upon a different ground.

Tidſwell v. Angerſtein, Peak's N. P. Caſes, 151.

The remaining obſervations and rules upon this ſubject are very few and ſhort: becauſe thoſe general rules and maxims, upon which ſo much has been ſaid with regard to inſurances in general, are alſo applicable to this ſpecies of them: the ſame mode of conſtruction is to be adopted; fraud will equally affect the one as the other; the ſame attention muſt be paid to a rigid compliance with warranties; and the ſame rules of proceeding are to be followed.

[433]

With reſpect to the riſk, which the underwriter is to run, this is uſually inſerted in the policy; and he undertakes to anſwer for all thoſe accidents to which the life of man is expoſed unleſs the *ceſtuy que vie* put himſelf to death, or he die by the hand of juſtice. The policy, as to the riſk, generally runs in theſe words: "The ſaid inſurers, in conſideration of "the ſum paid, do aſſure, aſſume, and promiſe, that the ſaid "*A. B.*

Vide the Appendix, No. 3

CHAP. XXII. "*A. B.* ſhall, by the permiſſion of Almighty God, live and "continue in this natural life for and during the ſaid term, "or in caſe he the ſaid *A. B.* ſhall, during the ſaid term, or "before the full end and expiration thereof, happen to die "by any ways or means whatſoever, ſuicide or the hands of "juſtice excepted, then, *&c.*" We ſee, that this contract expreſsly ſays, the death muſt happen within the time limited, otherwiſe the inſurers are diſcharged. But ſuppoſe a *mortal wound* is received during the exiſtence of the policy, and the perſon languiſhes till after the term limited in the contract, what ſays the law? Agreeably to the deciſion of this point, in caſes of marine inſurances, not only the cauſe of the loſs, but the loſs itſelf, muſt actually happen, during the time named in the policy, otherwiſe the inſurers are not reſponſible. This very caſe was put by Mr. Juſtice *Willes*, in his argument, when delivering the opinion of the court, in the caſe of *Lockyer* v. *Offley*. Suppoſe, ſaid the learned judge, an inſurance upon a man's life for a year, and ſome ſhort time before the expiration of the term, he receive a mortal wound, of which he dies after the year, the inſurer would not be liable.

Vide ante c. 2. p. 31.

Vide ante p. 33.

But when an inſurance is made upon a man's life, who goes to ſea, and the ſhip in which he failed was never afterwards heard of, the queſtion, whether he did or did not die within the term inſured, is a fact for the jury to aſcertain from the circumſtances which ſhall be produced in evidence.

Patterſon v. Black. Sittings at Guildhall. Hil. vac. 1780.

Thus in an action on a policy of inſurance on the life of *L. Macleane*, Eſq. from the 30th of *January* 1772 to the 30th of *January* 1778, it appeared in evidence that about the 28th of *November* 1777, *Macleane* failed from the *Cape of Good Hope*, in the *Swallow* ſloop of war, which ſhip, not being afterwards heard of, was ſuppoſed to have been loſt in a ſtorm off the Weſtern Iſlands. The queſtion was, whether [434] *Macleane* died before the 30th of *January* 1778. In order to eſtabliſh the affirmative of that queſtion, the plaintiff called witneſſes to prove the ſhip's departure from the *Cape* with *Macleane*; and ſeveral captains ſwore that they failed the ſame day; that the *Swallow* muſt have been as forward in her courſe as they were on the 13th or 14th of *January*, the period

period of a moſt violent ſtorm, in which ſhe probably was loſt. That the *Swallow* was much ſmaller than their veſſels, which, with difficulty, weathered the ſtorm. CHAP. XXII.

Lord *Mansfield* left it to the jury, whether, under all the circumſtances, they thought the evidence ſufficient to convince them that *Macleane* died before the time limited in the policy; adding, that if they thought it ſo doubtful as not to be able to form an opinion, the defendant ought to have their verdict. The jury found for the plaintiff.

Theſe inſurances, when a loſs happens upon them, muſt be paid according to the tenor of the agreement, in the *full ſum* inſured, as this ſort of policy, from the nature of it, being on the life or death of man, does not admit of the diſtinction between total and partial loſſes. Lex Merc. Red. 4th edit. p. 294.

We have ſeen that private perſons, as well as the public companies, may be underwriters upon policies on lives; and as they frequently became bankrupts after the policy was underwritten, but before a loſs happened, it became a queſtion, whether the perſons intereſted in ſuch inſurances could claim the money, and prove the debt, under the commiſſion, as if the loſs had happened before it iſſued. In the chapter immediately preceding this, and in one prior to that, we took occaſion to obſerve, that in order to remedy an inconvenience of this nature, with reſpect to marine inſurances and bottomry bonds, a ſtatute had paſſed, allowing creditors, either on ſuch policies, or bottomry and reſpondentia bonds, to prove their debts under the commiſſion, as if the loſs or contingency had happened prior to that event. But as the words of the preamble to that ſection of the ſtatute were ſpecial, referring only to inſurances on ſhips, and goods, or contracts of bottomry, it was doubtful whether it extended to inſurances on lives, although the words of the enacting part were very general, namely, "the aſſured in *any policy of aſſurance, &c.*" In ſupport of this doubt it was urged, that great inconveniences would follow from extending the ſtatute to theſe policies, becauſe the riſk may remain unſettled for a long and indefinite number of years. The court, however, held, that the general words of the enacting part were not reſtrained by the preamble. Vide ch. 21. & chap. 14. 19 Geo. 2. ch. 37. ſ. 2. [435]

This

CHAP. XXII.

Cox v. Liotard, B. R. Hil. 24 Geo. 3. Dougl. Rep. p. 166. note.

This doctrine was laid down in an action on a policy of insurance on the life of *J. H. Boyd*, lately gone to the *East Indies*, on the event of his dying between the 5th of *April* 1780, and the 5th of *April* 1783. The defendant pleaded; 1st, Bankruptcy generally; and that the cause of action accrued before the bankruptcy: 2dly, That *the policy was made prior to the time of his becoming a bankrupt*, then the trading, petitioning creditor's debt, commission, proceedings, and certificate were specially set out, and that he was thereby discharged from the said policy, and all debts due at the time of the bankruptcy, without saying, that the cause of action accrued before the bankruptcy. To this last plea there was a general demurrer.

Lord *Mansfield*.—"The only question is, whether the *enacting words* of this statute, which are *general*, shall be restrained by the *preamble*, which is *particular*. I think they should not be restrained. The enacting clause comprehends *all* insurances, and consequently insurances *upon lives*. This is exactly the case of *Pattison* v. *Banks* (*a*); for there the preamble was *particular*, but the enacting clause was *general*."

Mr. Justice *Willes* and Mr. Justice *Ashhurst* concurred.

Mr. Justice *Buller*.—"In the case of *Mace* v. *Cadell*, it was held, that the enacting words of the statute of 21st of *Ja*. I. c. 19. were not restrained by the preamble (*b*). The incon- [436] veniences that have been urged, are not so great as are apprehended; for the creditors need not be delayed in their dividend. When a creditor has an insurance of this kind, he has nothing to do but to lay it before the commissioners, who will make a calculation, and lay aside as much as will give him a dividend equal to that of the other creditors. There must be judgment for the defendant."

It

(*a*) The question in *Pattison* v. *Banks* (*Cowper* Rep. 540.) arose upon the 7 *Geo*. 1. ch. 31. which allowed persons, who had given credit on bills, bonds, notes, and other securities, payable at a future day, and which were not payable at the bankruptcy of the debtor, to prove them under the commission. The preamble to the statute speaks of securities only for the sale of goods and merchandizes; but as the enacting words were general, the court held, that they extended to a bond for the payment of an annuity for a term of years.

(*b*) The statute of *James* enacts, "that if any person, at such time as he shall "become bankrupt, shall, *by the consent of the true owner, &c.* have in his pos-

"session,

It became a doubt in the reign of King *William*, when a policy on a life was to run from the day of the date thereof, till that day twelvemonth, and the person died on the day named, whether the insurer was liable. The court held that he was. The case was this: A policy of insurance was made to insure the life of Sir *Robert Howard* for one year, from the day of the date thereof; the policy was dated on the 3d day of *September* 1697. Sir *Robert* died on the 3d of *September* 1698, about one o'clock in the morning. Lord *Holt* held that from the day of the date excludes the day, but from the date includes it; (*a*) so that the day of the date must be excluded here, and the underwriter is liable.

Sir Robert Howard's Case, 2 Salkeld. 625. 1 Ld. Raymond, 480. S. C.

Although from a perusal of the note below, it will appear that no difficulty could occur on such a point at the present day; yet it is usual, in order to prevent disputes, to insert in the modern policies "*the first and last days included*."

Vide the Appendix, No. 3.

Policies on lives are equally vitiated by fraud or falsehood, as those on marine insurances; because they are equally contracts of good faith, in which the underwriter, from necessity, must rely upon the integrity of the insured for the statement of circumstances. Indeed, the case of *Wittingham* v. *Thornborough*, which we took occasion to cite in support of the

[437]

Vide ante, 216.

" session, &c. any goods, &c. whereof he shall be reputed owner, the commis- " sioners shall have power to sell the same in like manner as any other part " of the bankrupt's estate." The preamble says, " whereas it often happens " that many persons before they become bankrupts, *do convey their goods* to " other men, upon good consideration, and yet retain the possession, and " are reputed owners thereof, &c." The court in *Mace* v. *Cadell* (*Cowp.* 232.) held, that the statute extended to the goods of a *third person*, which he allowed the bankrupt to keep possession of, as well as to those which *originally* belonged to the bankrupt, although the preamble speaks only of the bankrupt's *original* property.

(*a*) In the law books, not perhaps much to the honour of the profession, this distinction taken by my Lord *Holt*, was at one time held to be law, at others not; sometimes, these expressions were held to mean the same thing; at others to be quite different. In the year 1777, however, this glaring absurdity was entirely done away, and the Court of King's Bench unanimously held, after much deliberation, that they mean the same thing; that they shall either be exclusive or inclusive, according to the context and subject matter, and shall be so construed as most effectually to support the deeds of the parties, and not to destroy them. See Lord *Mansfield*'s very elaborate argument upon this occasion, in which all the cases are fully stated and considered. *Pugh* v. the Duke of *Leeds*. *Cowper*'s Reports 714.

CHAP. XXII.

the doctrine laid down in the chapter upon Fraud in Marine Insurances, was a policy upon a life insurance.—In another case, the principles of fraud were considered as far as it affects this contract.

Stackpole v. Simon, Sittings at Guildhall. Hilary Vac. 1779.

It was an action on a policy of insurance for 150*l.* at four guineas *per cent.* in case *Drury Sheppey* should die at any time between the 1st of *April* 1777 and the 1st of *April* 1778, both days included, and during the life time of *John Sheppey*, the father of *Drury*: but in case the said *John* should die before the said *Drury*, the policy to be void; the question was, as to the representation of the life at the time of the insurance. The interest in the insurance was 900*l.* due from *Drury Sheppey* to the plaintiff. It was admitted, that the life expired within the time limited in the policy. *Drury Sheppy* had a place in the Custom-house of Ireland, and was in bad circumstances. He went to the South of *France* for the benefit of his health, or to avoid his creditors, and there died. The broker, who effected the policy, told the underwriters that the gentleman, for whom he acted, would not warrant, but from the account he (the broker) had received, *he believed it to be a good life.*

Lord *Mansfield.*—"As to the interest, this policy may be considered as a collateral security for the debt due to the plaintiff. Where there is no warranty, the underwriter runs the risk of its being a good life or not. If there be a concealment of the knowledge of the state of the life, it is a fraud. It is a rule that every subsequent underwriter gives credit to the representation made to the first; and it is allowed that any subsequent underwriter may give in evidence a misrepresentation to the first. The broker here does not pretend to any knowledge of his own, but speaks from *information*. There is no fraud in him." There was a verdict for the plaintiff.

Even where there is an express warranty, that the person is in good health, it is sufficient that he is in a reasonable [438] good state of health; for it never can mean, that the *cestuy que vie* is perfectly free from the seeds of disorder. Nay, even if the person, whose life was insured, laboured under a particular infirmity, if it can be proved by medical men that it did not at all, in their judgment, contribute to his death, the warranty of health has been fully complied with; and the insurer is liable.

Thus

Thus in an action on a policy made on the life of Sir *James Ross* for one year from *October* 1759 to *October* 1760, *warranted in good health at the time of making the policy*: the fact was, that Sir *James* had received a wound at the battle of *La Feldt* in the year 1747, in his loins, which had occasioned a partial relaxation or palsy, so that he could not retain his urine or *faeces*, and which was not mentioned to the insurer. Sir *James* died of a malignant fever within the time of the insurance. All the physicians and surgeons, who were examined for the plaintiff, swore, that the wound had no sort of connexion with the fever; and that the want of retention was not a disorder which shortened life, but he might, notwithstanding that, have lived to the common age of man: and the surgeons who opened him, said, that his intestines were all sound. There was one physician examined for the defendant, who said, the want of retention was paralytic; but being asked to explain, he said, it was only a local palsy, arising from the wound, but did not affect life: but, on the whole, he did not look upon him as a good life.

Ross v. Bradshaw, 1 Black. Rep. p. 312.

Lord *Mansfield*.—"The question of fraud cannot exist in this case. When a man makes insurance upon a life generally, without any representation of the state of the life insured, the insurers take all the risk, unless there was some fraud in the person insuring, either by his suppressing some circumstances which he knew, or by alleging what was false. But if the person insuring knew no more than the insurer, the latter takes the risk. In this case there is a warranty, and wherever that is the case, it must, at all events, be proved, that the party was a good life, which makes the question on a warranty much larger than that on fraud. Here it is proved that there was no representation at all as to the state of life, nor any question asked about it; nor was it necessary. Where an insurance is upon a representation, every material circumstance should be mentioned, such as age, way of life, &c. But, where there is a warranty, then nothing need be told; but it must in general [439] be proved, if litigated, *that the life was, in fact, a good one, and so it may be, though he have a particular infirmity.* The only question is, *whether he was in a reasonable good state of health, and such a life as ought to be insured on common terms.*" The jury, upon this direction, without going out of court, found a verdict for the plaintiff.

In

CHAP. XXII.

Willis v. Poole, Sittings at Guildhall, Easter Vac. 1780.

In a subsequent case, the same rule of decision was recommended and enforced. It was an action on a policy on the life of Sir *Simeon Stuart*, Bart. from the 1st of *April* 1779 to the 1st of *April* 1780, and during the life of *Eliza Edgley Ewer*. This policy contained a warranty that Sir *Simeon* was about 57 years of age, *and in good health on the 11th of May* 1779, and that Mrs. *Ewer* was about 78 years of age. The defendant, at the trial, admitted that Sir *Simeon* and Mrs. *Ewer* were of the respective ages mentioned in the warranty; that he died before the 1st of *April* 1780, and that she was living. Two questions were intended to have been made; 1st, As to the plaintiff's interest: 2d, On the warranty of health. The former was disposed of, by the plaintiff having proved a judgment debt. As to the latter, it appeared in evidence, that, although Sir *Simeon* was troubled with spasms and cramps from violent fits of the gout, he was in as good health, when the policy was underwritten, as he had been for a long time before. It was also proved by the broker, who effected the policy, that the underwriters were told, that Sir *Simeon* was subject to the gout. Dr. *Heberden*, and other gentlemen of the faculty, were examined, who proved that spasms and convulsions were symptoms incident to the gout.

Lord *Mansfield*.—"The imperfection of language is such, that we have not words for every different idea; and the real intention of parties must be found out by the subject matter. By the present policy, the life is warranted to some of the underwriters, *in health*, to others *in good health*; and yet there was no difference intended in point of fact. *Such a warranty can never mean that a man has not the seeds of a disorder*. We are all born with the seeds of mortality in us. A man, subject to the gout, is a life capable of being insur-
[440] ed, if he has no sickness at the time to make it an unequal contract." There was a verdict for the plaintiff.

Vide ante, ch. 19.

In a former chapter we saw, that when the risk is entire, and it is once begun, there shall be no apportionment or return of premium, though it should cease the very next day after it commenced. The same rule is applicable in every respect to the premium on life insurances; for the contract is entire, and if the person whose life is insured, should put an an end to it the next day after the risk commences, though the underwriter is discharged, there would be no return of premium. This has never been decided in any judicial determination expressly on the point, but it has frequently been declared to be the law upon the subject by the learned judges in the course of argument, when return of premium on marine insurances was the point under discussion. This was particularly done in the case of *Tyrie* v. *Fletcher*, by Lord *Mansfield*, when delivering the judgment of the court. Cowper, 669. "There has been an instance put," said his Lordship, "of a "policy where the measure is by time, which seems to me "to be very strong and apposite to the present case; and "that is an insurance upon a man's life for twelve months. "There can be no doubt but the risk there is constituted by "the measure of time, and depends entirely upon it: for the "underwriter would demand double the premium for *two* "years, that he would take to insure the same life for one "year only. In such policies, there is a general exception "against suicide. If the person puts an end to his own life "the next day, or a month after, or at any other period "within the twelve months, there never was an idea in any "man's breast, that part of the premium should be returned."

Afterwards in the case of *Bermon* v. *Woodbridge*, Lord *Mansfield* laid down the same doctrine. Douglas, 758. "In an insurance "upon a life, with the common exception of suicide, and "the hands of justice, if the party is executed, or commit "suicide, in twenty-four hours, there shall be no return."

From these opinions which have been frequently repeated in other cases, the law upon the subject of return of premium, as applicable to life insurances, seems perfectly ascertained; because except in the case of suicide or a public execution, the question can never arise.

CHAPTER THE TWENTY-THIRD.

Of Insurance against Fire.

CHAP. XXIII.

AN insurance of this sort is a contract, by which the insurer, in consideration of the premium which he receives, undertakes to indemnify the insured, against all losses, which he may sustain in his house, or goods, by means of fire, within the time limited in the policy. To enter upon a detail of the various advantages, which mankind have derived from this species of contract, would be a waste of time; because they are obvious to every understanding. As little does it fall within the compass of my plan to enumerate the various offices that have been instituted for the purpose of insuring property against fire; or the rules and regulations, by which they are severally governed. Some of them have been instituted by royal charter; others by deed enrolled; and others give security upon land for the payment of losses. The rules, by which these societies are governed, are established by their own managers, and a copy given to every person at the time he insures; so that, by his acquiescence, he submits to their proposals, and is fully apprized of those rules upon the compliance or non-compliance with which, he will or will not be entitled to an indemnity.

See 1 H. Black. 254.

The construction to be put upon those regulations, has but seldom become the subject of judicial inquiry; three instances only having occurred in our researches upon this occasion. In the proposals of the *London* Assurance Company, and some of the other offices, there is a clause by which it is provided, that they do not hold themselves liable for any loss or damage by fire, happening by any invasion, foreign enemy, *or any military or usurped power* whatsoever. It became a question, what species of insurrection should be deemed a military or usurped power within the meaning of this proviso. It was held by the Court of Common Pleas, against the opinion of Mr. Justice *Gould*, that it could only mean

mean to extend to houfes fet on fire by means of an invafion from abroad, or of an internal rebellion, when armies are employed to fupport it.

Drinkwater v. the Corporation of the London Affurance, 2 Wilfon 363.

The cafe in which this queftion arofe, was an action of covenant againft the defendants upon a Policy of Infurance of a malting office of the plaintiff's at *Norwich* from fire, in which policy there was a provifo that the corporation fhould not be liable in cafe the fame fhould be burnt by any invafion by foreign enemies, or any military or ufurped power whatfoever, and that the defendants had not kept their covenants, to the plaintiff's damage. The defendants plead firft the general iffue, that they have not broke their covenants, and thereupon iffue is joined. 2dly. They plead that it was burnt *by an ufurped power*; the plaintiff replies, that it was not burnt by *an ufurped power*, and thereupon iffue is alfo joined. This caufe was tried at *Norwich* affizes; a verdict was given for the plaintiff, and 469*l.* damages, fubject to the opinion of the court, upon the following cafe, viz. That upon *Saturday* the 27th of *November*, a mob arofe at *Norwich* upon account of the high price of provifions, and fpoiled and deftroyed divers quantities of flour; thereupon the proclamation was read, and the mob difperfed for that time. Afterwards another mob arofe, and burnt down the malting office in the policy mentioned. The queftion is, whether the plaintiff is entitled to recover in this action. This cafe was twice argued at the bar, and the court took time to deliberate; after which, as the judges differed in opinion, they delivered their opinions *feriatim*.

Mr. Juftice *Gould* was of opinion, that the malting office being burnt by the mob, who rofe to reduce the price of provifions, the fame was burnt by an *ufurped power*, within the true intent and meaning of the provifo in the policy: to fhew that it was an ufurped power for any perfons to affemble themfelves, to alter the laws, to fet a price upon victuals, &c. he cited *Popham* 122, where it is agreed by the juftices, that to attempt fuch a thing by force is felony, if not treafon; and therefore judgment ought to be for the defendant.

Mr. Juftice *Bathurft*.—" The words " *ufurped power*," in the provifo, according to the true import thereof, and the

 meaning

CHAP. XXIII.

meaning of the parties, can only mean an invasion of the kingdom by foreign enemies to give laws and usurp the government thereof, or an internal armed force in rebellion, assuming the power of government by making laws, and punishing, for not obeying those laws. The plea alleges that the malting office was burnt by *an usurped power* unlawfully exercised, but does not charge *that* usurped power as a rebellion, that a mob rose at *Norwich* on account of the price of victuals, and as soon as the proclamation was read, they dispersed; therefore judgment ought to be for the plaintiff."

Mr. Justice *Clive*.—"The words must mean such an usurped power as amounts to high treason, which is settled by the 25th of *Edward* Third. The offence of the mob in the present case was a felonious riot, for which the offenders might have suffered; but it cannot be said to be an usurped power; therefore I am of opinion that judgment should be given for the plaintiff."

Lord Chief Justice *Wilmot*.—"Upon the best consideration I am able to give this case, I am of opinion, that the burning of the malting office, was not a burning by *an usurped power* within the meaning of the proviso. Policies of insurance, like all other contracts, must be construed according to the true intention of the parties. Although the counsel on one side said, that policies ought to be construed liberally; on the other side, that they ought to be construed strictly; in a doubtful case I think the turn of the scale ought to be given against the speaker, because he has not fully and clearly explained himself. The imperfection of language to express our ideas is the occasion that words have equivocal meanings: and it is often very uncertain what the parties to a contract in writing mean. When the ideas are simple, words express them clearly; but when they are complex, difficulties often arise: and men differ much about the ideas intended to be conveyed by words: In the present case, what is the true idea conveyed to the mind by the words *usurped power?* The rule to find it out is to consider the words of the context, and to attend to the popular use of the words, according to *Horace*, *Arbitrium est, et jus, et norma loquendi*. My idea of the words, *burnt by an usurped power*, from the context

context is, that they mean burnt, or ſet on fire by an invaſion from abroad, or of an internal rebellion, when armies are employed to ſupport it, when the laws are dormant and ſilent, and firing of towns are unavoidable; theſe are the outlines of the picture drawn by the idea which theſe words convey to my mind. The time of the incorporation of this ſociety of the *London* Aſſurance Company, was ſoon after a rebellion in this kingdom, and it was not ſo romantic a thing to guard againſt fire by rebellion, as it might be now; the time, therefore, is an argument with me that this is the meaning of theſe words. Rebellious mobs may be alſo meant to be guarded againſt by the proviſo, becauſe this corporation commenced ſoon after the riot act; and if common mobs had been in their minds, they would have made uſe of the word *mob*. The words "*uſurped power*," may have a great variety of meanings according to the ſubject matter where they are uſed, and it would be pedantic to deſine the words in their various meanings; but in the preſent caſe, they cannot mean the power uſed by a common mob. It has not been ſaid, that if one or fifty perſons had wickedly ſet this houſe on fire, that it would be within the meaning of the words *uſurped power*. It has been objected, that here was an *uſurped power* to reduce the price of victuals, but this is part of the power of the crown; and therefore it was an *uſurped power*: but the king has no power to reduce the price of victuals. The difference between a rebellious mob and a common mob, is, that the firſt is high treaſon; the latter a riot or a felony. Whether was this a common or a rebellious mob? The firſt time the mob riſes, the magiſtrates read the proclamation, and the mob diſperſe; they hear the law and immediately obey it. The next day another mob riſes on the ſame account, and damages the houſes of two bakers; thirty people, in fifteen minutes, put this army to flight, they were diſperſed and heard of no more. Where are the *ſpecies belli* which Lord *Hale* deſcribes? This mob wants an univerſality of purpoſe to deſtroy, to make it a rebellious mob, or high treaſon. 1 *Hale*'s P. C. 135. There muſt be an univerſality, a purpoſe to deſtroy *all* houſes, *all* incloſures, *all* bawdy houſes, &c. Here they fell upon two bakers and a miller, and the mob chaſtized theſe particular perſons to abate the price of proviſions in a particular place:

 this

this does not amount to a rebellious mob. When the laws are executed with ſpirit, mobs are eaſily quelled; ſometimes a courageous act done by a ſingle perſon, will quell and diſperſe a mob. And ſometimes the wiſdom of an individual will do the ſame, as is thus beautifully deſcribed by *Virgil*;

Ac veluti magno in populo cum ſæpe coorta eſt
Seditio, ſævitque animis ignobile vulgus,
Jamque faces et ſaxa volant: furor arma miniſtrat.
Tum pietate gravem, ac meritis, ſi forte virum quem
Conſpexère, ſilent, arrectiſque auribus adſtant:
Ille regit dictis animos, et pectora mulcet.

But amongſt armies, the laws are ſilenced, and the wiſdom or courage of an individual will ſignify nothing. Upon the whole, I am of opinion, that there muſt be judgment for the plaintiff; and accordingly the *poſtea* was ordered to be delivered to the plaintiff, by three judges againſt one.

The Sun Fire Office has uſed words of a larger and more extenſive import than thoſe, which were the ſubject of diſcuſſion in the laſt caſe; for the proprietors of that company declare, that they will not pay any loſs or damage by fire, happening by any invaſion, foreign enemy, *civil commotion*, or any military or uſurped power whatever. A caſe has *unfortunately* ariſen, in which the meaning of theſe words, *civil commotion*, has been the ſubject of judicial inquiry.

Langdale v. Maſon and others, Sittings at Guildhall, Mich. Vac. 1780.

An action was brought on a policy of inſurance to recover from the Sun Fire Office a ſatisfaction for damage done to the plaintiff's houſes and goods by the rioters, who, it is very well known, and hiſtory will inform poſterity, in *June* 1780, to the terror and diſmay of the inhabitants of *London*, traverſed that city for ſeveral days, burning and deſtroying *Roman Catholic* chapels, public priſons, and the houſes of various individuals; the oſtenſible purpoſe of their aſſembling being to procure the repeal of a wiſe and humane law, (which had paſſed for ſome indulgences to *Roman Catholics*,) and who were at laſt only diſperſed by military force. As the circumſtances of theſe riots were very recent, they were not minutely gone into at the trial. It was, however, ſufficiently proved, that the plaintiff, on account of his religion, (being

(being a *Catholic*,) had been, amongſt others, ſelected as an object of the rage of the times, and that his houſes and effects were ſet on fire. The office defended this action, conſidering that they were protected by the article juſt recited, namely, "That they would not anſwer for any loſs, occaſioned by an invaſion, foreign enemy, *civil commotion*, or any military or uſurped power whatever." This point was argued much at length by the counſel on both ſides.

Lord *Mansfield*.—"Gentlemen of the jury, this is an action brought by the plaintiff againſt the defendants upon the policy of inſurance mentioned in the pleadings, for the value of property, which was conſumed by fire. Moſt undoubtedly every man's leaning muſt be to the ſide of the plaintiff, in order to divide the loſs in ſo great a calamity. But that leaning muſt be governed by rules of law and juſtice: and the only queſtion, that ariſes for your determination and that of the court, is ſingly upon the conſtruction of two words in the policy. It will be neceſſary, in order to inveſtigate this matter, to go into the hiſtory, which has been opened and explained to you, of other inſurance policies. In the year 1720, the *London* Aſſurance Company put into their policies all the words here uſed, except *civil commotion*. Whatever fire happens by a foreign enemy is clearly provided againſt: when they burn houſes, or ſet fire to a town, that is alſo provided for. What is meant by military or uſurped power? They are ambiguous; and they ſeem to have been the ſubject of a queſtion and determination. They muſt mean rebellion, where the fire is made by authority: as in the year 1745, the rebels came to *Derby*, and if they had ordered any part of the town, or a ſingle houſe to be ſet on fire, that would have been by authority of a rebellion. That is the only diſtinction in the caſe—it muſt be by rebellion got to ſuch a head, as to be under authority. In the year 1726, ſome years after the *London* Aſſurance Company had done it, the Sun Fire Office put in the exception; and in 1727, they put in other words: they do not keep to the form of the *London* Aſſurance: they do not ſay by invaſion from foreign enemies merely: they clearly provide againſt rebellion, determined rebellion, with generals who

Vide ſupra.

CHAP. XXIII. who could give orders. Though this be so guarded, the Sun Fire Office did not think it answered their purpose; and therefore they took the words *civil commotion*. Not only using those words, applicable to guard against a foreign enemy, against a rebellion, where there are officers and leaders, that can give authority and power; but they add other words as general and untechnical as can possibly be used; *civil commotion*, not civil commotion that amounts to *high treason*. They avoid saying civil commotions that amount to felony: they avoid saying civil commotions that amount to *misdemeanors*: but they use a general expression, "if the mis-"chief happens from a civil commotion," taking the largest and most general sense of the words that the language will allow: they do not even say a *riot*. It may be a question in point of law, whether an assembly or multitude be a riot. In that case, they do not say committing a felony, but speak of fire occasioned by civil commotion. The single question is, whether this has been a civil commotion. If there be a case, to which these words can be applicable, it is to a case of this sort. I cannot see any of the other words, to which it can be applied. Usurped power takes in rebellion, acting by usurped powers amongst themselves. From a foreign enemy the office is secured. But what is a civil commotion? it is something else. The present was an insurrection of the people resisting all law, setting the protection of the government at nought, taking from every man, who was the object of their resentment, that protection, as appears from the evidence given by the witnesses upon the facts, and which you all know as well as if no witnesses had been produced. What was the object and end of this violent insurrection? It took place in many parts of the town at the same time, and the very same night; the mob were in *Broad-street*, *St. Catherine's* in *Colman-street*, at *Blackfriar's Bridge*, and at the plaintiff's. What is the object? *General destruction, general confusion. It certainly was meant to aim at the very vitals of the constitution.* It was not a private matter, under the colour of *popery* only, to destroy all Papists under a pretence or a cry of *No popery*. But the general object was *destruction* and *confusion*. The Fleet Prison was burnt down: Newgate was burnt down the night before. The King's Bench Prison is burnt, and all the prisoners set at liberty. The new Bridewell is burnt; the Bank attacked: consider the consequences, if they had succeeded in destroying the Bank of *England*.

England. The Excise and Pay Offices in *Broad-street* were threatened. Military resistance, and an extraordinary stretch were made and justified by necessity. There was a great deal of firing, many men were killed; and the houses of a vast number of Papists were burnt and destroyed. What is this but a *civil commotion?* No definition has been attempted to be given of what it is. It is said, that this is a civil commotion distinct from usurped power and rebellion. It is admitted, that this kind of insurrection may amount to high treason: and, to be sure, it may. But the office do not put their expectation upon trying, whether they were guilty of high treason or not. There is no manner of doubt, that this was an insurrection for a grand purpose, to take from a set of men the protection of the law. That is levying war against the king; there is not any doubt of it. It is not put upon that, but on the ground of a civil commotion. It is not an occasional riot, that would be another question. I do not give any opinion what that might be. You will give your opinions, whether the facts of this case bring it within the idea of a civil commotion. I think a civil commotion is this: an insurrection of the people for general purposes, though it may not amount to a rebellion, where there is an usurped power. If you think it was such an insurrection of the people for the purposes of general mischief, though not amounting to a rebellion, but within the exception of the policy, you will find for the defendants. If not, you will find for the plaintiff." The jury, agreeably to the Chief Justice's direction, found for the defendants. (*a*)

CHAP. XXIII.

When

(*a*) In a policy of insurance against loss by fire from half a year to half a year, the assured agreed to pay the premium half yearly, "as long as the assurers should agree to accept the same, *within 15 days after the expiration of the former half year;*" and it was also stipulated that no insurance should take place, till the premium was actually paid; a loss happened within 15 days after the end of one half year, but before the premium for the next was paid; and it was held that the assurers were not liable, though the assured tendered the premium before the end of the 15 days, but after the loss.

Tarleton and others v. Staniforth, 5 Term Rep. 695.

The defendants in the above cause were members of a society at Liverpool, for the insurance of property from fire: but soon after the decision, the Royal Exchange Assurance Company, the Phœnix and some other Insurance Companies gave notice that they did not mean to take advantage of the judgment so pronounced, but would hold themselves liable for any loss during the 15 days that were allowed for the payment of the insurance upon annual policies, and all other policies for a longer period. But that policies for a shorter period than a year would cease at six o'clock in the evening of the day mentioned in the policy.

CHAP. XXIII.

See the printed proposals of the different Fire Offices.

When a fire happens, and the party sustains a loss in consequence of it, he is bound by the printed proposals of most of the societies, to give immediate notice thereof to the office in which he is insured; and as soon as possible afterwards, or within a limited time according to the regulations of some, to deliver in as particular an account of his loss, or damage, as the nature of the case will admit; and make proof of the same by his oath or affirmation, by books of accounts, or such other vouchers as shall be required, or as shall be in existence. It is also necessary that the insured should procure a certificate under the hands of the ministers and church-wardens, together with some other reputable inhabitants of the parish, not concerned in such loss, importing, that they are well acquainted with the character and circumstances of the sufferer or sufferers; and do know, or verily believe, that he, she, or they, have really, and by misfortune, sustained by such fire the loss and damage therein mentioned. When any loss is settled and adjusted, the sufferers are to receive immediate satisfaction, without any deduction.

See Worsley v. Wood, now depending in B. R. on this clause.

[449]

Beawes 4th edit. p. 294.

Vide p. 434.

In the *Lex Mercatoria* it is said, that policies on houses and lives admit of no *average*. That this is true of the latter cannot be denied, as we have already shewn in the preceding chapter; because the payment of the whole sum depends upon one single event, which must *wholly* happen, or not at all. But that it cannot be true of insurances against fire, either of houses or goods, is equally clear; for houses may be *partially* damaged, and goods may be *partially* destroyed. In which case, as insurance is a contract of indemnity, the end of the contract is answered by putting the party in the same situation in which he was before the accident happened. But if he were to recover the whole sum insured, he would be in a better situation, which the law will not allow. Indeed, from the above quotation from the printed proposals it is evident, that the offices consider themselves liable for partial losses. Nay, some of them, if not all, expresly undertake to allow all reasonable charges, attending the removal of goods, in cases of fire, and to pay the sufferer's loss, whether the goods are destroyed, lost, or damaged by such removal.

Royal Exchange Assurance Company. Sun Fire Office, Phœnix Fire Office, &c.

These policies of insurance are not in their nature assignable, for they are only contracts to make good the loss, which the

the contracting party himself shall sustain; nor can the interest in them be transferred from one person to another without the consent of the office.(a) There is a case in which, by the proposals, these policies are allowed to be transferred, and that is, when any person dies, the policy and interest therein shall continue to the heir, executor, or administrator, respectively, to whom the property insured shall belong; provided, before any new payment be made, such heir, executor, or administrator, do procure his or her right, to be indorsed on the policy at the said office, or the premium be paid in the name of the said heir, executor, or administrator. But in all other cases there can be no assignment; and the party claiming an indemnity must have an interest in the [450] thing insured at the time of the loss. These points were decided in two causes, one before Lord Chancellor *King*, and the other before Lord *Hardwicke*.

Lynch and another v. Dalzell and others. 3 Brown's Parl. Cases, 497.

On the 28th of *July* 1721, one *Richard Ireland*, took out from the Sun Fire Office, a policy of insurance, whereby it was witnessed, that whereas the said *Ireland* had agreed to pay, or cause to be paid to the said office, the sum of five shillings within fifteen days after every quarter-day, for the insurance of his house, being the *Angel* Inn at *Gravesend*, with his goods and merchandize as therein after expressed only, and not elsewhere, *viz.* the dwelling house, not exceeding 400*l.* and for the goods in the same only, not exceeding 500*l.*; and for the stable only, not exceeding 100*l.* all then occupied by *James Peck*, from loss and damage by fire: and so long as the said *Richard Ireland* should duly pay or cause to be paid five shillings a quarter, as therein mentioned, the said society did bind themselves, their heirs, executors, administrators, and assigns, to pay and satisfy the said *Ireland*, his executors, administrators, and assigns, within fifteen days after every quarter-day, in which he should suffer by fire, his loss not exceeding 1000*l.* according to the exact tenor of their printed proposals. The policy was subscribed the 28th of *July* 1721, by three of the trustees of the society. Some considerable time afterwards, *Richard Ireland* died, having made his will, and *Anthony* his son sole executor; who brought the policy to the office, and had an indorsement

(a) But in marine insurances, the policy may be transferred. Delaney v. Stoddart. 1 Term R. 26.

CHAP. XXIII. indorsement made thereon, that the same then belonged to him: and afterwards, namely, at or about *Christmas* 1726, he, the said *Anthony*, paid the office a premium of twenty shillings for one year's insurance, from *Christmas* 1726, to *Christmas* 1727, as by an article in the proposals, he was at liberty to do. On the 24th of *August* 1727, a fire happened at *Gravesend*, which, among others, destroyed the house mentioned in the policy; and some time afterwards the appellants applied to the office, and alleged, that they had purchased the house and goods of *Anthony Ireland*; that the same were their property at the time of the fire, and that they had an assignment of the policy made to them, at the same time [451] that the house and goods were assigned; and they produced an affidavit made by the appellant, *Roger Lynch*, in which he swore, that his loss and damage by burning the said house, amounted, at a moderate computation, to 500*l.* and upwards; and upon this affidavit was indorsed a certificate of the minister, churchwardens, and other inhabitants of *Gravesend*, that they verily believed, according to the best of their information, the appellants had sustained a loss of 500*l.* and upwards. But neither in the affidavit or certificate, was any mention made of any loss being sustained by the appellants by the burning of any goods in the said house; nor was any affidavit made by *Anthony Ireland*, in whom the property of the policy was, that he had suffered any loss. The appellants, however, insisted that the office should pay them 1000*l.* for their loss sustained by the burning of the house and goods: and they accordingly filed a bill in Chancery, setting forth, that *Anthony Ireland* agreed to sell and assign to the appellants the house, stables, and goods, and also, at the same time agreed to assign the policy; and that by indenture of the 24th of *June* 1727, for 250*l.* *Ireland* did assign to the appellants a lease he had of the house and stables for the residue of a term of 70 years, which commenced at *Midsummer*, 16 *Car.* II.; but the goods, for which the appellants, as they alleged, were to pay 500*l.* being intended for one *Thomas Church*, who was to hold the inn under the appellants, *Ireland*, by deed poll of the same date, sold the same to *Church* for his own use. The bill also stated, that by another writing of equal date, *Ireland* assigned the policy, and all money and benefit thereof, to the appellants. That although the bill of sale of the household goods was made to *Church*, yet, as the appellants paid the

the purchafe money for the fame, *Church* affigned his bill of fale to them, for fecuring the money they had paid for the goods ; and afterwards, by another writing, releafed to the appellants his benefit and intereft in the policy. The bill prayed fatisfaction.

The refpondents put in their anfwer, in which they fet forth the nature and method of the infurances made by the office, and admitted the policy in queftion, and the appellants' application for 1000*l.* lofs; but faid, that the affidavit produced, was not agreeable to the propofals; and that they had been informed and believed, that no affignment of the policy was made to the appellants, nor any affignment of goods made to them by *Church*, till after the fire. They infifted, that the policies, iffued by the office, were not, in their nature, affignable, the fame being only contracts to make good the lofs, which the contracting party himfelf fhould fuftain; and the policy in queftion was firft made to *Richard Ireland*, to pay *his* lofs, and was afterwards declared by indorfement to belong to *Anthony Ireland*; and that no other perfon was entitled to the benefit of it. The caufe proceeded to iffue, and witneffes were examined on both fides; and upon the appellants' own evidence it appeared, that the firft difcourfe between the appellants and Mr. *Ireland* about the policy, was after the execution of the affignment of the houfe, and that the agreement (if there was any) about the policy was not, at the time when the appellants agreed to purchafe *Ireland*'s term in the houfe. It appeared further, that the affignment of the policy, though bearing date *before*, was not made and executed till fome time *after* the fire; fo that the agreement for affigning the policy was a voluntary conceffion of *Ireland* without any confideration, and independent of the bargain for the houfe, and never made till after *Ireland*'s intereft in the policy, as to the houfe, was determined, by his felling his intereft in the thing infured, and not carried into execution till the thing was loft. As to the appellants' property in the goods, they proved an affignment from *Church* to them, as a fecurity for 300*l.* but omitted, in their interrogatories, the material queftion, *when this affignment was made:* though the refpondents by their anfwer, put the time plainly in iffue, by infifting, that it was after the fire; and it did not appear that the appellants ever had any property in the goods. The refpondents on their part proved, [452]

that

CHAP. XXIII. that the office did not infure any perfons longer than they continued their property in the thing infured: and that perfons dealing with them might not be miftaken, fuch notice was ufually given.

Lord Chancellor *King*.—" Thefe policies are not infurances of the fpecific things mentioned to be infured; nor do fuch infurances attach on the realty, or in any manner go with the fame as incident thereto, by any conveyance or [453] affignment: but they are only fpecial agreements with the perfons infuring, againft fuch lofs or damage as they may fuftain. The party infuring muft have a property at the time of the lofs, or he can fuftain no lofs; and confequently can be entitled to no fatisfaction. There was no contract ever made between the office and the appellants for any infurance on the premifes in queftion. Not only the exprefs words, but the end and defign of the contract with *Ireland* do, in cafe of any lofs, limit and reftrain the fatisfaction to fuch lofs as fhould be fuftained by *Richard Ireland* only; and the indorfement on the policy declared that right to his executor *Anthony Ireland* only. Thefe policies are not in their nature affignable; nor is the intereft in them ever intended to be transferable from one to another, without the exprefs confent of the office. The tranfactions in the prefent cafe, by changing their property backwards and forwards, and rendering it uncertain whofe the true property is, raife a fufpicion, and fully juftify the caution of the office, in preventing the affignment without confent of the managers, which method is purfued by all the infurance offices. Befides, the appellants' claim is at beft founded only on an affignment never agreed for till the perfon infured had determined his intereft in the policy, by parting with his whole property, and never executed till the lofs had actually happened." His lordfhip therefore difmiffed the bill.

Upon this decree there was an appeal to the Houfe of Lords; and after hearing counfel on both fides, it was ORDERED AND ADJUDGED, that the fame fhould be difmiffed, and the decree therein complained of affirmed.

A few

A few years afterwards this case was cited with approbation by Lord *Hardwicke*, and relied upon by him as the ground of his opinion.

Anne Strode having six years and a half to come in a lease of a house from the plaintiffs, on the 27th of *April* 1734, became a proprietor of the Hand-in-Hand Office, by insuring the sum of 400 *l.* on the house, for seven years; and on paying twelve shillings down, and three pounds some time after, the Company agreed "to raise and pay, out of the "effects of the contribution stock, the said sum of 400 *l.* to "her and her executors, administrators, and assigns, so often "as the house shall be burnt down within the said term, un-"less the directors should build the said house, and put it in "as good plight as before the fire; and on the back of the "policy it was indorsed, that if this policy should be assign-"ed, the assignment must be entered within twenty-one days "after the making thereof." Mrs. *Strode*'s lease expired at *Midsummer* 1740, the house was not burnt down till the *January* after 1740, and she made an assignment of the policy to the plaintiffs the 23d of *February* after 1740. The question is, whether the plaintiffs, the assignees of Mrs. *Strode*, are entitled to the 400 *l.* or to have the house built again; or whether the house being burnt down after Mrs. *Strode*'s property ceased in it, the Company are obliged to made good the loss to her assignee of the policy. The company made an order, subsequent in time to Mrs. *Strode*'s policy in 1738, "That, whereas policies expire upon the property of the in-"sured's ceasing, if there is no application of the insured to "assign, or to have the loss made up, then the person having "the property may insure the said house in the said office, "notwithstanding the term for which the house was origi-"nally insured, is expired." There was evidence read for the plaintiffs to shew that they tendered the assignment to the defendants, to enter in their books, but they refused to accept of it.

The Sadlers Company v. Badcock and others. 2 Atkyns 554.

[454]

Lord Chancellor *Hardwicke*.—"During the progress of this cause, while the defendants seemed to depend chiefly upon the subsequent order, I was of opinion against them. But,

CHAP. XXIII. But, upon hearing what was further offered, I think the plaintiffs are not entitled to be relieved. There may be three queſtions made in this cauſe: firſt, whether this accident, which has happened, is ſuch a loſs, as obliges the defendants to make ſatisfaction to the plaintiffs: ſecondly, whether upon the terms of the original policy, the office is obliged to do it: thirdly, which is rather conſequential of the former, whether the plaintiffs are properly aſſignees of Mrs. *Strode* under this policy. If this matter reſted ſingly upon the policy itſelf, I ſhould not think it ſuch a loſs as would oblige the defendants to make ſatisfaction. Under this policy the ſtate of the caſe is, Mrs. *Strode* was only a [455] leſſee, her time expired at *Midſummer* 1740, the houſe was burnt down in *January* after, *within the ſeven years;* the plaintiffs, the Sadlers Company, were ground landlords, and entitled to the reverſion of the term: upon the 23d of *February*, ſeven months after the expiration of the term, and one month after the fire, the aſſignment was made, and in conſideration of five ſhillings only; ſo that it muſt be taken as a voluntary aſſignment, as it ſtands before me. It has been inſiſted, on the part of the defendants, that the plaintiffs are not entitled to recover, as ſtanding in the place of Mrs. *Strode*, becauſe ſhe had no loſs or damage, her intereſt ceaſing before the fire happened. And this introduces the ſecond and third queſtions. I am of opinion it is neceſſary the party inſured ſhould have an intereſt or property at the time of inſuring, and at the time the fire happens. It has been ſaid for the plaintiffs, that it is in nature of a wager laid by the inſurance company, and that it does not ſignify to whom they pay, if loſt. Now theſe inſurances from fire have been introduced in later times, and therefore differ from inſurance of ſhips, becauſe there *intereſt or no intereſt* is almoſt conſtantly inſerted, and if not inſerted (*a*) you cannot recover unleſs you prove a property. By the firſt clauſe in the deed of contribution in 1696, the year this ſociety, called the *Hand-in-Hand Office*, incorporated themſelves, the ſociety are to make ſatisfaction in caſe of any loſs by fire. To whom, or for what loſs, are they to make ſatisfaction? Why, to the perſon inſured, and for the loſs he may have ſuſtained; for

(*a*) This caſe was decided in the year 1743, previous to the paſſing of the ſtatute of 19 *Geo.* II. ch. 37.

for it cannot properly be called insuring the thing, for there is no possibility of doing it, and therefore must mean insuring the person from damage. By the terms of the policy, the defendants might begin to build and repair within six days after the fire happens. It has been truly said, this gives the society an option to pay or rebuild, and shews most manifestly they meant to insure upon the property of the insured, because nobody else can give them leave to lay even a brick; for another person might fancy a house of a different kind. Thus it stands upon the original agreement. The next question will be, whether the subsequent order, made by the defendants in 1738, has made any alteration. I am of opinion it has not, for it was made only to explain a particular case in the policy: for it might have been a question, whether Mrs. *Strode* could have come, before the expiration of the term, to examine the books of the office, [456] and therefore this order was made to give her such a power. It has been strongly objected that the society could not make such an order. I am very tender of saying, whether they can or not. Because, on one hand, it might be hard to say, that as a society they cannot make any order for the good of the society: on the other hand, it would be a dangerous thing to give them a power to make an alteration that may materially vary the interest of the insured. The assignment is not at all within the terms of this order, because it is plain, it meant an assignment before the loss happened. Now with regard to the loss happening before the assignment made, Mrs. *Strode* was entitled to nothing but what was to be paid back upon the deposit. It is plain she thought so, for if she had imagined she had been entitled to 400 *l.* would any friend have advised her to make a present of it to the plaintiff? The case of *Lynch* v. *Dalzell*, in the House of Lords, shews how strict this Court and that House are, in the construction of policies, to avoid frauds." The bill here must be dismissed.

Vide supra.

In the body of the policy the company acknowledge the receipt of the premium at the time of making the insurance: and by the printed proposals of the different societies, it is expressly stipulated, that no insurance shall take place, till the

CHAP. XXIII.

premium be actually paid by the inſured, his, her, or their agent or agents. This premium or conſideration money is in all the offices at the rate of two ſhillings *per cent.* for any ſum not exceeding 1000*l.* and two ſhillings and ſixpence from 1000*l.* upwards. But this muſt be underſtood to mean the premium upon *common inſurances* only: for upon hazardous trades, and wooden buildings, &c. the premium is proportioned to the riſk. Beſides this, by a late act of parliament a duty of one ſhilling and ſixpence *per annum* is laid upon every hundred pounds of property inſured from fire. This duty, however, is not to extend to inſurances upon public hoſpitals.

22 Geo. 3. ch. 48. ſ. 1.
Sect. 2.

Ante ch. 19.

We have formerly ſeen, that whenever the riſk to be run was entire, there never was a return of premium, though the contract ſhould ceaſe and determine the next day after its commencement. This rule applies to inſurances againſt fire, which generally are made for one entire and connected [457] portion of time, which cannot be ſevered: and therefore if the property inſured ſhould be deſtroyed by fire, ariſing from the act of a foreign enemy, the very day after the commencement of the policy, though the underwriter would be diſcharged, yet there can be no apportionment or return of premium.

5 W. and M. c. 21. ſ. 3.
9 and 10 W. 3. ch. 25. ſ. 37.
10 Anne, ch. 26. ſ. 67.
12 Anne, ſt. 2. ch. 9. ſ. 21.
30 Geo. 2. ch. 19. ſ. 1.
5 Geo. 3. ch. 35. ſ. 4.
16 Geo. 3. ch. 34. ſ. 5.
17 Geo. 3. ch. 50.
17 Geo. 3. ch. 50. ſ. 24.

By reference to the ſeveral ſtatutes mentioned in the margin, it ſhould ſeem, that every policy of inſurance againſt fire, to the amount of 1000*l.* or under, muſt have various ſtamps which taken together are of the value of ſix ſhillings: and on all policies to the amount of *more* than 1000*l.* an additional duty of five ſhillings muſt be paid; to enforce which regulation, penalty of 10*l.* is impoſed (over and above the payment of the duties) upon any perſon, who ſhall ſign, ſeal, execute, or ſubſcribe any policy of inſurance, from fire, not being duly ſtamped, and ſhall alſo pay the additional ſum of 5*l.* before the ſame ſhall be ſtamped, ſo as to be available in law or equity, or be given or received in evidence in any court of juſtice.

Vide ante, ch. 9.

As the pureſt equity and good faith are eſſentially requiſite, as has been already ſhewn, to render the contract effectual when it relates to marine inſurances; ſo it need hardly

hardly be obſerved, that it is no leſs eſſential to the validity of the policy againſt fire: becauſe in the latter, as well as in the former, the inſurer, from the nature of the thing, is obliged, in a great meaſure, to rely upon the integrity and honeſty of the inſured, as to the repreſentation of the value and quantity of the property, which is the object of the inſurance.

APPENDIX, No. I.

Policy of Insurance on Ship or Goods.

In the Name of God, *Amen.*
as well in own Name, as for and in the Name and Names of all and every other Person or Persons to whom the same doth, may, or shall appertain, in Part or in All, doth make Assurance, and cause
and them and every of them to be insured, lost or not lost, at and from

Upon any Kind of Goods and Merchandizes, and also upon the Body, Tackle, Apparel, Ordnance, Munition, Artillery, Boat, and other Furniture, of and in the good Ship or Vessel called the

whereof is Master, under God, for this present Voyage,
or whosoever else shall go for Master in the said Ship, or by whatsoever other Name or Names the same Ship, or the Master thereof, is or shall be named or called; beginning the Adventure upon the said Goods and Merchandizes from the loading thereof aboard the said Ship,
the said Ship, &c. upon

and so shall continue and endure, during her Abode there, upon the said ship, &c. And farther, until the said Ship, with all her Ordnance, Tackle, Apparel, &c. and Goods and Merchandizes whatsoever, shall be arrived at
upon the said Ship, &c. until she hath moored at Anchor Twenty-four Hours in good Safety; and upon the Goods and Merchandizes, until the same be there discharged and safely landed. And it shall be lawful for the said ship, &c. in this Voyage, to proceed and sail to and touch and stay at any Ports and Places whatsoever
without Prejudice to this Insurance, the said Ship, &c. Goods and Merchandizes, &c. for so much as concerns the Assureds by Agreement between the Assureds and Assurers in this Policy are and shall be valued at

Touching the Adventures and Perils which we the Assurers are contented to bear, and do take upon us in this

 Voyage,

Voyage, they are of the Seas, Men of War, Fire, Enemies, Pirates, Rovers, Thieves, Jettifons, Letters of Mart and Counter-mart, Surprizals, Takings at Sea, Arrefts, Reftraints and Detainments of all Kings, Princes, and People, of what Nation, Condition, or Quality foever; Barratry of the Mafter and Mariners, and of all other Perils, Loffes and Misfortunes, that have or fhall come to the Hurt, Detriment, or Damage, of the faid Goods and Merchandizes and Ship, *&c.* or any Part thereof. And in cafe of any Lofs or Misfortune, it fhall be lawful to the Affureds, their Factors, Servants, and Affigns, to fue, labour and travel for, in and about the Defence, Safeguard, and Recovery of the faid Goods and Merchandizes and Ship, *&c.* or any Part thereof, without Prejudice to this Infurance; to the Charges whereof we the Affurers will contribute each one according to the Rate and Quantity of his Sum herein affured. And it is agreed by us the Infurers, that this Writing or Policy of Affurance fhall be of as much Force and Effect as the fureft Writing or Policy of Affurance heretofore made in *Lombard-ftreet*, or in the *Royal Exchange* or elfewhere in *London*. And fo we the Affurers are contented, and do hereby promife and bind ourfelves, each one for his own Part, our Heirs, Executors, and Goods, to the Affured, their Executors, Adminiftrators, and Affigns, for the true Performance of the Premifes, confeffing ourfelves paid the confideration due unto us for this Affurance by the Affured

at and after the Rate of
per Cent.

In Witnefs whereof we the Affurers have fubfcribed our Names and Sums affured in *London.*

N. B. Corn, Fifh, Salt, Fruit, Flour, and Seed, are warranted free from Average, unlefs general, or the Ship be ftranded; Sugar, Tobacco, Flax, Hemp, Hides, and Skins, are warranted free from Average, under Five Pounds *per Cent.* And all other Goods, alfo the Ship and Freight, are warranted free from Average under Three *per Cent.* unlefs general, or the Ship be ftranded.

APPENDIX,

APPENDIX, No. II.

Form of a Respondentia Bond.

Know all Men by these Presents, That
held and firmly bound to

in the Sum, or Penalty of
of good and lawful Mo. ey of
Great Britain, to be paid to the said
or to certain Attorney, Executors, Adminif-trators, or Affigns; to which Payment, well and truly to be made Heirs, Executors, and Ad-miniftrators, firmly by thefe Prefents, fealed with Seal. Dated this Day of in the Year of the Reign of our Sovereign Lord by the Grace of God of *Great Britain*, *France*, and *Ireland*, King, Defender of the Faith, and fo forth, and in the Year of our Lord One thoufand feven hundred and The Condition of the above-written Obligation is fuch, that whereas the above-named hath, on the Day of the Date above-written, lent unto the above-bound the Sum of upon the Merchandizes and Effects, to that Value laden, or to be laden, on board the good Ship or Veffel called the of the Burthen of Tons or thereabouts, now in the River *Thames*, whereof is Commander. If the faid Ship or Veffel do, and fhall with all convenient Speed, proceed and fail from and out of the faid River of *Thames*, on a Voyage to any Ports or Places in the *Eaft Indies*, *China*, *Perfia*, or elfe-where beyond the *Cape of Good Hope*, and from thence, do and fhall fail and return unto the faid River of *Thames* at or be-fore the End and Expiration of Thirty-fix Calendar Months, to be accounted from the Day of the Date above-written, and that without Deviation (the Dangers and Cafualties of the Seas ex-cepted.) And if the above-bound Heirs, Executors, or Adminiftrators, do and fhall, within Days next after the faid Ship or Veffel fhall be ar-rived in the faid River of *Thames*, from the faid Voyage, or at the End and Expiration of the faid Thirty-fix Calendar Months, to be accounted as aforefaid (which of the faid Times fhall firft and next happen) well and truly pay, or caufe to be paid, unto the above-named Executors, Adminiftrators, or Affigns, the Sum of of lawful Money of *Great-Britain*, together with of like Money, by the Calendar Month, and fo proportion-ably

ably for a greater or leſſer Time than a Calendar Month, for all ſuch Time, and ſo many Calendar Months, as ſhall be elapſed, and run out of the ſaid Thirty-ſix Calendar Months, over and above twenty Calendar Months, to be accounted from the Day of the Date above-written; or if in the ſaid Voyage, and within the ſaid Thirty-ſix Calendar Months, to be accounted as aforeſaid, an utter Loſs of the ſaid Ship, or Veſſel, by Fire, Enemies, Men, of War, or any other Caſualties ſhall unavoidably happen; and the above bound Heirs, Executors, or Adminiſtrators, do and ſhall, within Six Months next after the Loſs, pay and ſatisfy to the ſaid Executors or Adminiſtrators, or Aſſigns, a juſt and proportional Average on all Goods and Effects which the ſaid carried from *England* on board the ſaid Ship or Veſſel, and on all other the Goods and Effects of the ſaid which ſhall acquire during the ſaid Voyage, and which ſhall not be unavoidably loſt: then the above written Obligation to be void, and of no Effect; or elſe to ſtand in full Force and Virtue.

Sealed and delivered (being firſt duly ſtampt) in the Preſence of } *J. S.*

APPENDIX, No. III.

Form of a Policy of Inſurance upon a Life.

In the Name of God, *Amen.* do make Aſſurance, and cauſe , to be aſſured upon natural Life aged for and during the Term and Space of Calendar Months, to commence this Day of in the Year of our Lord One thouſand ſeven hundred and fully to be complete and ended. And it is declared, that this Aſſurance is made to and for the Uſe, Benefit, and Security, of the ſaid Executors, Adminiſtrators, and Aſſigns, in caſe of the Death of the ſaid within the Time aforeſaid, which the above Governor and Company do allow to be good and ſufficient Ground and Inducement for

for making this Aſſurance, and do agree that the Life of the ſaid is and ſhall be rated and valued at the Sum aſſured: The ſaid Governor and Company therefore, for and in Conſideration of *per Cent.* to them paid, do aſſure, aſſume, and promiſe, that the ſaid ſhall, by the Permiſſion of Almighty God, live, and continue in this natural Life, for and during the ſaid Term and Space of Calendar Months, to commence as aforeſaid; or in Default thereof, that is to ſay, in caſe the ſaid ſhall in or during the ſaid Time, and before the full End and Expiration thereof, happen to die, or deceaſe out of this World by any Way or Means whatſoever, that then the aboveſaid Governor and Company will well and truly ſatisfy, content, and pay unto the ſaid Executors, Adminiſtrators, or Aſſigns, the Sum or Sums of Money by them aſſured, and are here underwritten, hereby promiſing and binding themſelves and their Succeſſors to the Aſſured, Executors, Adminiſtrators, or Aſſigns, for the true Performance of the Premiſes, confeſſing themſelves paid the conſideration due unto them for this Aſſurance by the Aſſured. *Provided* always, and it is hereby declared to be the true Intent and Meaning of this Aſſurance, and this Policy is accepted by the ſaid upon Condition that the ſame ſhall be utterly void and of no Effect, in caſe the ſaid ſhall exceed the *Age* of or ſhall voluntarily go to *Sea* or into the *Wars*, by Sea or Land, without Licenſe in Writing firſt had or obtained for ſo doing, any Thing in theſe Preſents to the contrary hereof in any wiſe notwithſtanding. In witneſs whereof the ſaid Governor and Company have cauſed their common Seal to be hereunto affixed, and the Sum or Sums by them aſſured to be here underwritten, at their Office in *London*, this Day of in the Year of the Reign of our Sovereign Lord by the Grace of God of *Great Britain*, *France*, and *Ireland*, King, Defender of the Faith, *&c.* and in the Year of our Lord One thouſand ſeven hundred and The ſaid Governor and Company are content with this Aſſurance for £.

APPENDIX,

APPENDIX, No. IV.

Form of a Policy of Insurance against Fire.

BY the Corporation of the *Royal Exchange* Assurance of Houses and Goods from Fire

This present Instrument or Policy of Assurance witnesseth, That whereas agreed to pay into the Treasury of the Corporation of the *Royal Exchange* Assurance, at their Office on the *Royal Exchange, London,* for the Assurance of

from Loss or Damage by Fire. *Now know all Men by these Presents,* That the capital Stock, Estate, and Securities of the said Corporation, shall be subject and liable to pay, make good, and satisfy unto the said Assured Heirs, Executors, or Administrators, any Loss or Damage which shall or may happen by Fire to the said Goods aforesaid (except such Goods as Hemp, Flax, Tallow, Pitch, Tar, Turpentine, Glass, China, and Earthen Wares, Writings, Books of Accounts, Notes, Bills, Bonds, Tallies, ready Money, Jewels, Plate, Pictures, Gun-powder, Hay, Straw, and Corn unthreshed) within the Space of twelve Calendar Months from the Day of the Date of this Instrument or Policy of Assurance, not exceeding the Sum of

and shall so continue, remain, and be subject and liable, as aforesaid, from Year to Year, to be computed from the Day of in every Year, for so long Time as the said Assured shall well and truly pay, or cause to be paid the Sum of into the Treasury of the said Corporation, on or before the Day of which shall be in each succeeding Year, and the said Corporation shall agree thereto by accepting and receiving the same; which said Loss or Damage shall be paid in Money immediately after the same shall be settled and adjusted, or otherwise, if the said Loss or Damage shall not be adjusted, settled, and paid within sixty Days after Notice thereof shall be given to the said Corporation, by the said Assured, that then the said Corporation, their Officers, Workmen, or Assigns, shall, at the Charge of the said Corporation, at the End and Expiration of the said sixty Days, provide and supply the said Assured with the like Quantity of Goods of the same Sort and Kind, and of equal Value and Goodness with those burnt or damnified by Fire. *Provided always nevertheless,* and it is hereby declared to be the true Intent and Meaning

Meaning of this Deed or Policy, That the ſaid Stock, Eſtate, and Securities of the ſaid Corporation ſhall not be ſubject or liable to pay or make good to the Aſſured any Loſs or Damage by Fire, which ſhall happen by any Invaſion, Foreign Enemy, or any military or uſurped Power whatſoever. *Provided alſo*, That this Deed or Policy ſhall not take place or be binding to the ſaid Corporation until the Premium for one Year is paid, or in caſe the ſaid Aſſured ſhall have already made, or ſhall hereafter make any other Aſſurance upon the Goods aforeſaid, unleſs the ſame ſhall be allowed of and ſpecified upon the Back of this Policy: Or if the ſaid at the Time when any ſuch Fire ſhall happen, ſhall be in the Poſſeſſion of, or let to any Perſon who ſhall uſe or exerciſe therein the Trade of a Sugar-baker, Apothecary, Chymiſt, Colour-man, Diſtiller, Bread or Biſcuit-baker, Ship or Tallow-chandler, Stable-keeper, Inn-holder, or Maltſter, or ſhall be made uſe of for the ſtowing or keeping of Hemp, Flax, Tallow, Pitch, Tar, or Turpentine; but that in all or any of the ſaid Caſes theſe Preſents, and every Clauſe, Article, and Thing, herein contained, ſhall ceaſe, determine, and be utterly void and of none Effect, or otherwiſe ſhall remain in full Force and Virtue. In Witneſs whereof the ſaid Corporation have cauſed their common Seal to be hereunto affixed, the Day of in the Year of the Reign of our Sovereign Lord by the Grace of God of *Great Britain*, *France*, and *Ireland*, King, Defender of the Faith, &c. and in the Year of our Lord One thouſand ſeven hundred

N. B. This Policy to be of no Force, if aſſigned, unleſs ſuch Aſſignment be allowed by an Entry thereof in the Books of the Company.

TABLE

OF THE

PRINCIPAL MATTERS.

Admiralty.

Agent.

But

Bankruptcy.

Barratry.

If

If

So

will

Double Infurance.

Eaft India Voyages.

Election.

Embargo.

Enemy.

Where

This

A repreſentation

Inſurance.

Various

Lading (*Bill of.*)

Lighters.

Lives (*Inſurances upon.*)

Loss.

The

A ſhip

A policy

Registration.

But

Indeed,

Sailors.

Salt.

Salvage.

The

Trover.

Uſage.

Valuation.

Valuation.

Valued Policy.

Venice.

Void Policies.

See title *Fraud.*

Wager-Policies.

FINIS.